THE GREAT BRITISH BED AND BREAKFAST

KGP Publishing
Penrith, Cumbria, England

Published by: KGP Publishing, 54 Castlegate, Penrith, Cumbria CA11 7HY England

ACKNOWLEDGMENTS

Edited by: Ken Plant

Design and Layout by: Jennie Prior

Administration by: Joanne Cullen

Editorials & Foreword by: Karl Stedman

Maps and illustrations by: Jonathon Robinson

"Picture Stories by: Jenny Walter

Photographs with poetry by: Val Corbett

Cover Pictures
Front Cover "Summer Flowers" by: Stephen Darbishire
Back Cover "By the fire"by: Stephen Darbishire

ISBN Number 0-9522807-4-4

Distributed worldwide by: Portfolio

THE GREAT BRITISH BED & BREAKFAST
54 Castlegate
Penrith
Cumbria
CA11 7HY
England
Web Site: http://www.cumbria.com/gbbb/

CONTENTS

FOREWORD

Bed and Breakfasting' becomes more popular as the ever increasing size of our *Great British Bed & Breakfast* guide shows....and with good reason. Gone, thank goodness, are the days of the dragon-like landladies, with all their terrifying restrictions, the butt of every seaside comedian's jokes - to be replaced by proprietors who are able to offer an individual service, of a quality envied by many of the top hotels...comfort and cossetting in surroundings quite impossible to match by larger and as a consequence more impersonal establishments.

Of course, our hosts are opening their own homes to you the guests, so there is that certain pride of possession that is so important, and quite naturally the variation of style and ambience is vast. Whatever your holiday pleasure, you'll find it in our pages, from the smallest homely farmhouse to that splendid Georgian rectory. If your taste is to come 'home' to the crackle of a real live fire in some out of the way country cottage, or to be pampered amongst the antiques and period decor in some elegant town house, we have them awaiting your pleasure.

Food is of premier importance, particularly on holiday, and here our hosts really shine - in catering for relatively small groups, the cuisine is virtually to your individual taste - the ingredients personally selected, and much from local gardens, so freshness and quality is never in doubt. Little wonder our hosts report that their guests return over and over again.

What our hosts offer varies considerably, so if you have particular preferences it is advisable to check on booking....some offer vegetarian dishes...some, particularly in Scotland, offer high-tea instead of dinner. Some welcome dogs, some decidedly don't, some allow smoking only in designated rooms, some are licensed and others not....and it is well to ascertain if cheques or credit cards are acceptable.

Naturally we carefully select out hosts, and our correspondence tells us that we do a good job in this respect....we know what you like and we always endeavour to see that you get it. We like to feel that our hosts are situated in all parts of England, Scotland and Wales, so that wherever you plan your holiday, there is a welcome awaiting you. To help you in your choice 'The Great British Bed & Breakfast' has arranged accommodation by counties, with simple to read maps illustrated with line drawings to whet your appetite, and with an introduction to each section giving a very brief indication of the delights you may experience thereabouts....of course your hosts are invariably only too willing to extol the virtues of their particular neighbourhood, and their intimate knowledge of the district can only add to the pleasure of your stay.

There is simply no doubt about it, *The Great British Bed & Breakfast* aims to be excellent value for money, and if you haven't tried it yet - we think you'll enjoy it....our lists get longer each year, so we must be getting it right!

LONDON

The capital city of the United Kingdom was a Roman settlement in the first century AD. The medieval city developed around the first St. Paul's Cathedral, founded in the seventh century. Later William the Conqueror, recognising the strategic importance of London, chose this site to build his White Tower, the hub of the Tower of London. Over the following centuries the city guilds, now known as the Livery Companies, prospered and their successive elected leaders have become the Lord Mayors of London. Hit by the Black Death in 1348 and the Plague in 1665, four fifths of the city was then consumed by the Great Fire in 1666, cleansing the city of the pestilence and its appalling medieval slums, and making way for a period of planned building, much of it designed by Sir Christopher Wren. Wren rebuilt St. Paul's and a large number of city churches. During the Second World War much of central and suburban London was destroyed, leading to another period of rebuilding.

Most of London's very famous attractions are to be found in the West End, with Trafalgar Square and Nelson's Column at its centre. Here is the National Gallery, the church of St. Martin-in-the-Fields and the impressive Admiralty Arch leading into The Mall, that splendid avenue which leads to Buckingham Palace, the chief residence of the Queen. St. James's Park, arguably the most attractive of the royal parks, borders The Mall on one side and Birdcage Walk on the other. Birdcage Walk leads to Parliament

Square, the hub of Westminster, dominated by St. Stephen's Tower, housing Big Ben. The Houses of Parliament, one of the Capital's most photographed buildings, is a magnificent example of Gothic Revival architecture. Across the Square is Westminster Abbey where William I was crowned on Christmas Day 1066, and the site of every subsequent coronation. The Abbey contains memorials to many of the nation's most honoured dead. The other great city cathedral, St. Paul's, is the burial place of Nelson, Wellington and Sir Christopher Wren, the great architect of London whose epitaph 'If you seek his memorial, look about you' is singularly apt.

London is a great city of pageantry and ceremonial. Each day there is the Changing of the Guard at Buckingham Palace, Mounting the Guard at Horse Guards in Whitehall, and The Ceremony of the Keys at the Tower of London each evening at 9.53pm. Add to this the yearly and casual events such as the Lord Mayor's Show and the Gun Salutes, and there is scarcely an hour without some 'happening' somewhere. Most of the West End department stores are in Oxford Street or Regent Street; St. James' Street has its specialist shops, while Charing Cross Road is the place for books...Harrod's is in Knightsbridge, and Fortnum and Mason's in Piccadilly. There are numerous street markets: Brick Lane, Camden Lock, Portobello Road.....The list is virtually endless, but the Capital is extremely well served with helpful Information Centres, so no visitor should be short of advice on where to go and what to see.....and the best way of all to see the sights is still from the top of a London double-decker bus!

London Home-to-Home

19 Mount Park Crescent, London W5 2RN
Tel/Fax: 0181 566 7976

Anita Harrison and Rosemary Richardson of London Home-to-Home specialise in arranging good quality Bed & Breakfast accommodation in London homes. All offer something that is both unique and exceptional value for money.

They specialise in accommodation in lovely areas of West London such as Chiswick, Ealing, Parsons Green and Putney, all just a short walk from an underground station, shops and restaurants. In these areas the average cost for a twin or double room sharing bathroom is £23.00 per person per night; £28.00 with private bathroom. They also represent a select number of homes in more central areas, where prices are higher.

The accommodation has been chosen with great care, with hosts who take pleasure in welcoming guests to their homes. They provide up to 3 comfortable guest rooms of high standards of warmth and cleanliness. Television is provided in most rooms or in a guest sitting area. Hot drinks are freely available and included in the cost is a generous English breakfast.

Select from the list overleaf and be assured of comfort and reliability.

How to reserve your London B&B

Please telephone to discuss your requirements. We recommend that you book early for maximum choice.

Please note that the minimum booking period is 2 consecutive nights.

To secure your reservations we request a deposit of £6.00 per person for each night booked, payable by Visa, Mastercard or sterling cheque. We regret that the deposit is non refundable. The balance of payment is settled with your hosts during your stay, but we must point out that hosts cannot accept credit cards.

You will be sent an official confirmation, giving the name, address and telephone number of your hosts, together with a map and directions to your accommodation, if time allows.

Home 98/A (Nanette & Stylie)   **Just off Kensington High Street (Central London)**   A315, A3220

A beautifully preserved Victorian town house which is tastefully decorated and incorporates all modern facilities for guests' comfort, whilst retaining the authentic features of the period. TV's, hair dryers and hospitality trays are available in all rooms. Vivacious hosts offer high quality accommodation, serving breakfast in the elegant family dining room.
A welcoming atmosphere and friendly service is assured.

London Home-to-Home
Tel/Fax: 0181 566 7976

B&B from £42pp, Rooms: 4 en-suite double/twin, Non smoking,
Nearest underground: Earls Court - 10 minutes, Buses to sights,
A1 Airbus stops nearby at Earls Court

Home 98/B (Peter & Cristina)   **Camden Town area (Central London)**   Nearest Road A1,A4201

Stay in an elegant townhouse in fashionable Camden, close to Regent's Park! The owner architect has created three lovely guest rooms, two of them sharing a bathroom between them. Breakfast is served in a modern kitchen-diner, which is airy and beautiful. Trendy Camden Market nearby!
Prefers non-smokers. Parking: meters.

London Home-to-Home
Tel/Fax: 0181 566 7976

B&B from £35, Rooms: 1 double with private shower room, 1 double/twin
sharing bathroom, No smoking. Nearest underground: Camden Town, on
Northern line, 5 minutes, Buses to sights

Home 98/C   (Ann & James)   **Islington area**   Nearest Road A1, A1200

Comfortable, modern town-house situated in Canonbury Square, in fashionable Islington. One twin room overlooking a pretty public garden, and a smaller double room with washbasin, sharing a guest bathroom between them. Trendy, vibrant area, just ten minutes' from the centre of London. Numerous excellent restaurants nearby. Buses and tubes to the theatre district and all places of interest.
Will not accept smokers. Parking for one car available.

London Home-to-Home
Tel/Fax: 0181 566 7976

B&B from £30, Rooms: 1 double, 1 twin, sharing guest bathroom
Nearest underground: Highbury & Islington - 6 minutes
Buses to all parts

Home 98/D   (Hilary & Muffy)   **Parsons Green area**   Nearest Road A308/A3217

Enjoy your London stay in genteel surroundings with delightful hosts! Within easy reach of the smart shopping areas of the Kings Road and Chelsea, this lovely residence offers you the convenience of close proximity to the tube and buses, together with the charm of a traditional English home. Two double guest rooms available, and possibly an additional single for party bookings. Hosts, an author and her solicitor daughter, offer an interesting stay. One dog and one cat.
Smoking is not accepted in the home!

London Home-to-Home
Tel/Fax: 0181 566 7976

B&B from £30, Rooms 1 en-suite queen size double, 1 double & 1 single
sharing private bathroom. Nearest underground: Parsons Green
5 mins. Several buses to shops & sights! Limited parking available.

Home 98/E (Marilyn & Alan)   Swiss Cottage (Central London)   Nearest Road A41

A modern townhouse situated off the Finchley Road. Accommodation comprises a double/triple room with TV and en-suite bathroom and shower, a double/triple, twin, and dble/single, sharing a guest bathroom. Additional toilet and washbasin available also. Geared for visitors and offering a comfortable sitting area with TV, payphone, fax and word processing facilities. Between Hampstead Heath and Regents Park; 200 yds from Swiss Cottage underground. 6 minutes journey on the Jubilee Line to Baker Street for Madam Tussauds and Bond Street in the heart of Oxford Street shops.

B&B from £25pp, Rooms: 4 comfortable guest rooms,
Nearest underground: Swiss Cottage - 3 minutes,
Bus services to sights, A2 Airbus at Baker Street

London Home-to-Home
Tel/Fax: 0181 566 7976

Home 98/F (Martine & David)   Swiss Cottage area   Nearest Road A41,A5

Decorated with immense flair, this modern, elegant town-house provides super accommodation for visitors. Two double rooms are available, one with twin or king-size bed and en-suite facilities, the other providing twin beds and adjacent private bathroom. Hot drinks and TV's are available in both rooms. Guests are welcome to enjoy the lovely lounge. Breakfast is served in the light, airy kitchen/diner overlooking a pretty court-yard garden. 5 minute's walk from Swiss Cottage underground and buses, with Central London just 10 minutes away by tube.

B&B from £33, Room: 2 double/twin with bathrooms
Nearest underground: - Swiss Cottage - 5 minutes, Finchley Road - 10
minutes, Buses to sights, A2 Airbus to Baker Street. Parking available

London Home-to-Home
Tel/Fax: 0181 566 7976

Home 98/G (Dolores & Bert)   Parsons Green area   Nearest Road A308, A3217

Whether staying for 2 nights or a week you can be sure of a warm welcome with these cheerful and generous hosts. They offer a double room with queen sized bed, TV and hot drinks tray. Shower and wash basin are en-suite. There is also a pretty Laura Ashley single room with wash basin sharing a family bathroom. The atmosphere is friendly and informal. A popular choice! Some of London's trendiest restaurants in the area.

B&B from £28pp, Rooms: 1 en-suite double, 1 single,
Nearest underground: Parsons Green - 10 minutes,
Buses for Chelsea, Knightsbridge and Central sights

London Home-to-Home
Tel/Fax: 0181 566 7976

Home 98/H (Moira & Frank)   Parsons Green area   Nearest Road A217, A308

Self contained apartment for 2-4 guests on first floor of a family home. Comprises a twin bedroom with private bathroom, dining/living room with TV and comfortable sofa bed, additional bathroom and fully equipped kitchen. Lounge overlooks a pretty park. Frank & Moira are gracious and welcoming hosts who live on the ground floor in their elegant suite. Ideal for longer stays as guests can be totally self catering. However, hosts are delighted to provide breakfast food if guests prefer not to shop. A popular area for quality interior design/furniture and antiques. Excellent restaurants.

Self contained apartment from £33 per person,
Nearest underground: Parsons Green - 10 minutes,
Buses to various parts of London

London Home-to-Home
Tel/Fax: 0181 566 7976

Home 98/I (Felicity & Hugh)   Parsons Green area   **Nearest Road A308, A3217**

Ideally situated, within three minutes' walk of the tube station, and excellent restaurants and antique shops, this home offers three twin bedded rooms, two of them with wash basins. Shared bathroom, and additional toilet. TV and hot drinks in all rooms. Good quality accommodation in a much sought-after area!

London Home-to-Home
Tel/Fax: 0181 566 7976

**B&B from £23pp, Rooms: 3 twin sharing one bathroom,
Nearest underground: Parsons Green - 3 minutes, Many buses along
the New Kings Rd, to Chelsea, Knightsbridge and the Central sights.**

Home 98/J (Marjory & Christopher)   Hammersmith/Chiswick area   **Nearest Road A4, A315**

Wonderfully close to the tube, this family home offers a very beautiful and spacious twin guest room with wash basin, TV and hospitality tray. The room overlooks a tranquil garden. Private bathroom is adjacent. Christopher, a linguist, and Marjory, a teacher, are anxious to make their guests' stay as pleasant as possible. Enjoy an evening stroll along a lovely stretch of the river Thames, passing picturesque pubs and lovely gardens! Good restaurants and shops nearby.

London Home-to-Home
Tel/Fax: 0181 566 7976

**B&B from £26pp, Rooms: 1 twin/triple with private bathroom adjacent,
Nearest underground: Stamford Brook - 1 minute,
Buses to Trafalgar Square and Kew Gardens, Non smoking**

Home 98/K (Peter & Catriona)   Hammersmith/Chiswick area   **Nearest Road A4, A315**

This lively couple, an architect and PR consultant, offer 2 double and 1 twin guest rooms in their pretty restored Victorian house. A terraced home with a cottagey feel. Situated in the heart of historic Brackenbury Village and near the delightful Ravenscourt Park, their home makes a very comfortable base. Informal atmosphere. Imaginative breakfasts. Many good restaurants and pubs within an easy walk.

London Home-to-Home
Tel/Fax: 0181 566 7976

**B&B from £23pp, Rooms: 2 double, 1 twin/single, 2 guests' bathrooms,
Nearest underground: Ravenscourt Park - 8 minutes,
Hammersmith 15 minutes**

Home 98/L (Pat & Ralph)   Hammersmith/Chiswick area   **Nearest Road A315, A316**

These relaxed and adaptable hosts make guests very comfortable in their home. They offer 3 guest rooms: a spacious family room sleeping 4, as well as a double and a twin, all with wash basins and sharing a guest bathroom. Additional toilet. Lounge with TV available for guests. On summer evenings enjoys a walk beside the Thames nearby, or sample the numerous cafes along the High Road! Kew Gardens are a short bus ride away. Children welcome. Non smoking.

London Home-to-Home
Tel/Fax: 0181 566 7976

**B&B from £23pp, Rooms: 1 double/family, 1 double, 1 twin,
Nearest underground: Turnham Green - 8 minutes,
Easy access to Heathrow, Buses to the Central District**

Home 98/M (Peter & Valerie)   **Chiswick area**   **Nearest Road A315, B409**

Stay in villagey, unspoiled Chiswick, where writers and actors live! On the Bedford Park Garden Conservation Estate, this 1880's Norman Shaw home is just 3 minutes walk from the tube station, interesting boutiques and eating places. Valerie and Peter offer 3 guest rooms; a double and a twin (which can be triples) with guest bathroom, plus a beautiful double with queen-size bed and private bathroom. Sitting room for guests. A fine home, beautifully furnished by the owner who is a retired architect.

London Home-to-Home
Tel/Fax: 0181 566 7976

B&B from £23pp, Rooms: 1 double with bathroom, 1 double,
1 twin/triple, Nearest underground: Turnham - Green 3 minutes,
Easy access to Heathrow, Buses to Central London

Home 98/N (Janice & Jeremy)   **Acton Town area**   **Nearest Road A4, M4, A406**

Superb accommodation is offered in this home of grace and quality where the hosts delight in providing for guests' every comfort. Beautiful lounge available for guests. The mock-Tudor home is surrounded by beautiful gardens and is located on a lovely estate with a large park of historic interest close by. Kew Gardens and fascinating pubs along the river's edge within a 30 minute walk. There are 2 guest rooms available: a twin with en-suite bathroom, and a spacious and lovely double room with wash basin and private bathroom close by.

London Home-to-Home
Tel/Fax: 0181 566 7976

B&B from £28pp, Rooms: 1 double, 1 twin (with private facilities),
Nearest underground: Acton Town - 10 minutes,
Ideal for Heathrow arrivals.

Home 98/O (Anita & David)   **Ealing area**   **Nearest Road M4, A406, A40**

These friendly hosts offer superb hospitality in their restored Victorian family home. The pretty twin room with washbasin and large, comfortably furnished double or triple room overlook lovely gardens and lawns. A bathroom is reserved for guests. Enjoy the delights of village Ealing, just 5 minutes' walk away, where you find the tube station, a shopping mall and interesting pubs and restaurants!

London Home-to-Home
Tel/Fax: 0181 566 7976

B&B from £23, Rooms: 1 double/triple, 1 twin (share guest bathroom),
Nearest underground: Ealing Broadway - 5 minutes, Direct railway
lines to Paddington, Easy train link to Windsor, Bus to Kew Gardens

---

Home 98/P (John & Jane)   **Ealing area**   **Nearest Road M4, A40, A406**

A lovely family home of great character offering 1 twin room with private bathroom adjacent, overlooking landscaped patio and gardens. The home, built in the mid 1880's, has been tastefully furnished. Breakfast is served in the family kitchen/breakfast room which leads onto the garden. Hosts take every care to ensure their guests' comfort. Five minutes walk to a modern shopping mall and several first class restaurants. Open parkland nearby.

London Home-to-Home
Tel/Fax: 0181 566 7976

B&B from £28pp, Room: 1 twin with private bathroom adjacent,
Nearest underground: Ealing Broadway - 7 minutes,
Ealing Common - 6 minutes

Home 98/Q (Chantal & Benjamin) Ealing area   **Nearest Road A40, A406**

Three spacious guest rooms are offered in this imposing family residence. Two triples, one overlooking the tranquil garden of Ealing Abbey, share a lovely guest bathroom. Additionally, there is a charming double room with en-suite shower bathroom. Hostess teaches piano and speaks French. A quiet area of beautiful houses within 10 minutes walk of Ealing centre. Excellent selection of restaurants and pubs nearby. Ample room for off- street parking.

London Home-to-Home
Tel/Fax: 0181 566 7976

B&B from £23pp, Rooms: 2 triple sharing bathroom, 1 en-suite dbl,
Nearest underground: Ealing Broadway - 10 minutes,
Trains to Paddington and buses to Kew and Richmond

Home 98/R (Catherine & Janek) Ealing area   **Nearest Road A40, A406**

Polish host and his welcoming Scottish wife offer a suite of a double and a single room with guest bathroom on the second floor of their modern town house. Attractive, secluded estate. Guests are happy to return again and again, as the hostess's relaxed welcome encourages them to feel at home. Shops, malls and numerous restaurants and pubs lie 10 minutes walk away, at Ealing Broadway, the attractive local centre. Non smokers.

London Home-to-Home
Tel/Fax: 0181 566 7976

B&B from £23pp, Rooms: 1 double, 1 single, share guest bathroom,
Nearest underground: Ealing Broadway - 10 minutes,
British Rail to Paddington

Home 98/S (Muriel & Neville)   **Ealing area**   **Nearest Road M4, A406**

This gracious hostess offers 3 single rooms in a home of beauty and charm, decorated with a traditional English quality. A tranquil setting. Muriel, who is a piano teacher and keen gardener, does not accept smokers and is not available in August. At nearby Ealing Common tube station, with its choice of tube lines, is a comprehensive range of shops and restaurants. Easy commuting from Heathrow or Central London.

London Home-to-Home
Tel/Fax: 0181 566 7976

B&B £30pn, Rooms: 3 single rooms sharing bathroom,
Nearest underground: Ealing Common - 3 minutes,
Non smoking

Home 98/T (Rosemary & Ian)   **Ealing area**   **Nearest Road M4, A406**

Bed and Breakfast with a difference! Australian hosts offer a superb self-contained loft room in their beautiful home. Overlooking gardens and a pond. Double bed, en-suite shower bathroom, kitchenette with microwave, dining/sitting area with TV. Linen provided, also breakfast food. A warm and friendly welcome in a lovely home!

London Home-to-Home
Tel/Fax: 0181 566 7976

B&B from £26pp, Rooms: 1 double with en-suite shower bathroom,
Non smoking, Nearest underground: South Ealing - 10 minutes,
Buses to Kew and Richmond

Home 98/U (Jolanta & Peter)   Ealing Common area   Nearest Road A40, A406

Most attractive family home situated in a pretty street of Tudor-style houses. This lovely home offers a private area for guests on the second floor, comprising of two rooms and a private shower bathroom. One twin, one twin or triple, suiting a family or group of four or five. Very pleasing atmosphere!

London Home-to-Home
Tel/Fax: 0181 566 7976

B&B from £23pp, Rooms: 1 twin, 1 twin/triple sharing private bathroom
Nearest underground: South Ealing (Piccadilly line) 10-12 minutes,
Buses to Kew or Richmond, Very easy parking.

Home 98/V (Margaret & Colin)   Ealing area   Nearest Road M4, A40, A406

A good natured and adaptable Australian and her English husband offer a pleasant double room with washbasin and option of private bathroom in their comfortable family home. Non smokers. Easy access to Heathrow.

London Home-to-Home
Tel/Fax: 0181 566 7976

B&B from £23pp, Room: 1 double with washbasin,
Nearest underground: North Ealing - 2 minutes

Home 98/W (Maria & Damien)   Ealing Common area   Nearest Road M4, A406

Accommodation designed for a comfortable stay! Warm and friendly hosts offer a large loft room, providing triple accommodation with en-suite shower bathroom. Breakfast served in the conservatory overlooking the garden. Situated in a quiet, tree-lined street, a short stroll from shops, restaurants and two underground stations. Very handy for guests arriving from Heathrow. Maria speaks french. No pets. Free parking on street. Another triple room occasionally available also.

London Home-to-Home
Tel/Fax: 0181 566 7976

B&B from £28pp, Rooms: 2 triples with private bathroom
Nearest underground: Ealing Common - 10 minutes,

Home 98/X (Rita & Geoff)   Ealing Common area   Nearest Road A406, A/M4

These welcoming hosts offer a large, self-contained guest room on the top floor of their home. The room is thoughtfully planned, and comprises a sleeping area with double bed, and a sitting/dining area with facilities for self-catering. Generous supply of breakfast food provided. Short or longer term rates available. Private bathroom.

London Home-to-Home
Tel/Fax: 0181 566 7976

B&B from £26pp, Rooms: 1 double, self-catering, private bathroom
Nearest underground: Ealing Common - 5 minutes,
Unlimited parking available

Home 98/Y (Marian & Daniel)   **Ealing area**   **Nearest Road A406, A40**

In their comfortable Edwardian semi-detached home, Marian and Daniel offer a convenient base. The guest rooms comprise a double with private bathroom adjacent, plus a twin room with small shower bathroom en-suite. Situated on a quiet tree lined street just 5 minutes walk to a parade of shops and 2 tube stations. Easy parking. Ideal accommodation for families.

London Home-to-Home   **B&B from £23pp, Rooms: 1 double, sharing bathroom,**
Tel/Fax: 0181 566 7976   **1 twin with en-suite shower bathroom,**
Nearest underground: - North Ealing - 4 mins, West Acton - 7 mins.

Home 98/Z (Diana & Louis)   **Ealing area**   **Nearest Road A40, A406**

Relaxed, friendly hosts offer a loft conversion comprising a spacious and airy twin/triple room with private shower bathroom en-suite and an additional twin room. TV and hospitality tray. Modern three storey home, conveniently situated for 2 underground lines.

London Home-to-Home   **B&B from £28pp, Rooms: 1 twin/triple with en-suite facilities, plus 1 twin**
Tel/Fax: 0181 566 7976   **sharing bathroom,**
Nearest underground: West Acton - 7 minutes, North Ealing - 7 minutes

---

"Mrs Beezon! And Betty and Billy! so good to be back!"

BATH, BRISTOL &

The small county of Bath, Bristol & North East Somerset was formed in 1974 from the city and county of Bristol, part of South Gloucestershire and part of North Somerset. The Lower River Avon, which used to give the county its name, rises in the Cotswolds and flows south to Bradford-on-Avon, turns northwest to Bath and Bristol, and joins the Bristol Channel at Avonmouth after passing through the spectacular Clifton Gorge. The county is relatively flat with the exception of the Mendips, the limestone mass which stretches some thirty miles from the valley of the Frome virtually to the Bristol Channel and contains many dramatic caves. The views from the Mendips over Sedgemoor and to the Somerset Quantocks are quite breathtaking. This is a county of delights, catering for simply every taste, be it quiet walking, exploring fascinating old villages, wandering over open heath or enjoying traditional seaside pleasures.

At the centre and dominating the county lies Bristol, an ideal holiday venue. At one time the major port on the west coast, its prosperity was based upon trade with the colonies in sugar, tobacco and slaves, until the swift development during the late 1700s of Liverpool. Bristol took a dreadful battering during the Second World War, but there is much of the old Bristol to see and enjoy. The Cathedral, originally the church of the twelfth century abbey can boast one of the finest Norman interiors in Britain. Not to be missed is the large altarpiece commissioned in 1755 from William Hogarth for the Church of St. Mary Redcliffe, displayed in the Norman church of St. Nicholas - now a museum of ecclesiastical art. The famous Bristol Nails stand outside the Corn Exchange, four small bronze pillars set in the pavement, where city merchants completed their deals by paying on the nail'. The Theatre Royal, home since 1943 of the Bristol Old Vic, is the oldest theatre in the country in regular use.

This is a fascinating city, packed with interest, and Cabot Tower, the curious architectural folly, provides a wonderful view over its rooftops. The main seafaring activities are now mainly concentrated in Avonmouth, but Bristol dockland still retains its boating atmosphere, with a July regatta and its wealth of sailing dinghies, not forgetting its fine Industrial Museum.

Elegant Clifton is blessed with superb honey-coloured stone squares, crescents and terraces as well as that marvel of Victorian engineering, the Clifton Suspension Bridge; when it was built it was the longest and highest span ever attempted. Splendid as it is, Brunel had also planned for it to have supporting piers in the Egyptian style but he unfortunately died before his plans could be carried out.

North East Somerset

To the east of Bristol lies Bath, surely one of Britain's most magnificent cities. Although a spa since Roman times, its popularity blossomed during the Regency period. The Romans called the town Aquae Sulis - the waters of Sul (a local Celtic deity) and they built their baths connected with a temple. The delights of these hot springs became fashionable under the critical eye of that archetypal English dandy Beau Nash. Bath can lay claim to the best Roman ruins in England, as well as being the country's most perfect example of eighteenth century architecture. Built in the local golden coloured limestone against a setting of superbly proportioned and planned streets are fine individual features...The Royal Crescent and Lansdown Crescent, the lovely Pulteney Bridge with its Palladian houses by Robert Adam, and of course the spectacular Circus. Like Bristol, Bath is full of interesting places.....the oldest house in Bath, Sally Lunn's house is still baking Sally Lunns to a secret recipe, the Pump Room, Roman Baths, the Abbey, the Bath Industrial Heritage Centre, the Museum of Costume, and at Claverton Manor, the American Museum. The visitor could be excused for spending all their holiday in Bath....but that would be a shame, the county has even more to offer. Weston-super-Mare,

built by the Victorians around an old fishing village, has developed into one of the largest and most popular seaside resorts on the west coast with glorious sands, piers and all one would expect from a first class modern resort. North along the coast is Clevedon which once boasted the finest Victorian pier in England. Built around a small rocky bay with trees coming down to the water's edge, the town has interesting literary connections. Coleridge spent his honeymoon here and Thackeray wrote much of Vanity Fair when staying at Clevedon Court. The house, built about 1320 is one of the few surviving manor houses of this period. Chipping Sodbury, its prefix Chipping being the Old English word for market, is a lovely mixture of Georgian brick houses and golden Cotswold stone cottages, and nearby is magnificent Dodington House, built by James Wyatt for Christopher Codrington at the end of the eighteenth century. An ancestor of the owner was standard bearer to Henry V at Agincourt. The grounds laid out by Capability Brown contain two lakes joined by a picturesque Gothic cascade.

Bath, Bristol & North East Somerset is a compact county of only five hundred and seventeen square miles but within its boundaries is everything to tempt the most discriminating holidaymaker.

BATH, BRISTOL &

Places to Visit

Royal Crescent, *Bath* ~ built from 1767-1774, the elegant arc of houses was the masterpiece of John Wood the Younger.

Roman Baths, *Bath* ~ the Romans built this world famous bathing complex in the first century, yet the Great Bath was not discovered until the 1870's.

Bath Abbey, *Bath* ~ in 973 AD, Edgar was crowned the first king of England here. In the late 1490's the present abbey was begun with its fan vaulting and monuments.

St Catherines Court, *near Bath* ~ a small Tudor house with links to Henry VIII and Elizabeth I.

American Museum in Britain, *Claverton* ~ an 1820 manor house decorated in various Amercan styles with examples of Shaker furniture, quilts, Native American art and a replica of George Washington's Mount Vernon garden of 1785.

Dyrham Park, *near Bath & Bristol* ~ a beautiful William and Mary house now belonging to the National Trust, it was built 1691-1710 and has changed little over the years with fine panelled rooms, Dutch paintings and furniture.

Clifton Suspension Bridge, *Bristol* ~ opened in 1864, it was designed by Isambard Kingdom Brunel. The bridge spans the Avon Gorge at 702 feet (214m) long with the river some 245 feet (74.7m) below.

Bristol Cathedral, *Bristol* ~ a 'hall church' which took an exceptionally long time to build, the choir was built between 1298 and 1330, the transepts and tower were finished in 1515 but it was 350 years later when Victorian architect GE Street built the naive.

▶ *The Oldest House in Bath, built in 1480.*

▶ *On the Kennet and Avon Canal*

Clifton Zoological Gardens, *Bristol* ~ a landscaped zoo and gardens with some 300 species of wildlife and many endangered species.

ss. Great Britain, *Bristol* ~ by the same designer of the Clifton Suspension Bridge - Isambard Kingdom Brunel, it was the world's first large iron passenger ship. Launched in 1843, the ship is now being restored in the dock where it was originally built. The ship is next to the Maritime Heritage Centre.

City Museum and Art Gallery, *Bristol* ~ housing many different collections including Roman tableware, dinosaur fossils and the largest collection of Chinese glass outside China. There is also a collection of European paintings including works of Renoir and Bellini.

Blaise Castle House, **Henbury,** *near Bristol* ~ an 18th century house, now a folk museum with extensive woodlands.

Clevedon Court, *Clevedon* ~ a 14th century manor house with 13th century hall, 12th century tower and garden with rare trees. Thackeray wrote most of 'Vanity Fair' here.

Chew Magna ~ a pretty red sandstone village, with many of its buildings and church dating from the Middle Ages, when wool brought prosperity to the village. The High Street features small stone cottages along with fine 18th century mansions.

NORTH EAST SOMERSET

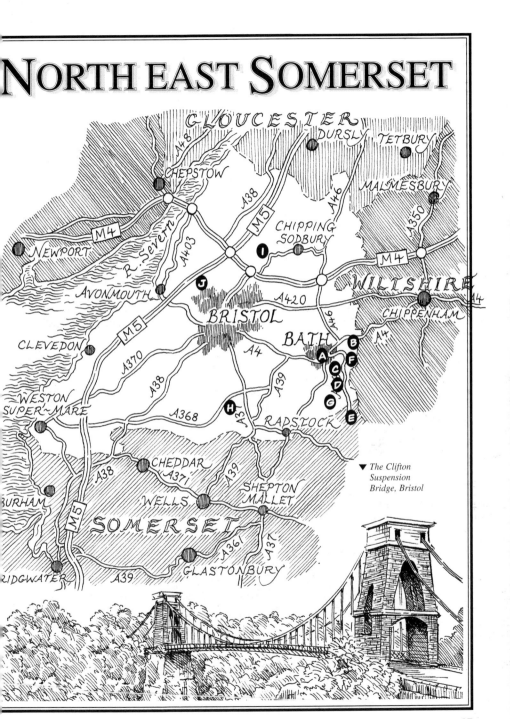

The Clifton Suspension Bridge, Bristol

The Old Red House, 37 Newbridge Road, Bath BA1 3HE Nearest Road A4

This charming Victorian Gingerbread House is colourful, comfortable and warm; full on unexpected touches and intriguing little curiosities. Its leaded and stained glass windows ae now double-glazed to ensure a peaceful stay. The extensive breakfast menu, a delight in it self includes waffles, pancakes, smoked salmon with scrambled eggs; and of course our English grills. We have well lit private parking and are on a frequent bus route. Dinner is available at a local riverside pub. Special rates for 3 or more nights. Brochure on request.

see PHOTO opposite

Chrissie Besley
Tel: 01225 330464
Fax: 01225 331661

B&B from £21pp, Rooms 1 twin, 3 double, 1 family, all en-suite,
No smoking, Children from 4, Pets restricted,
Open all year, Map Ref A

Sarnia, 19 Combe Park, Bath BA1 3NR Nearest Road A4/A431

Our large Victorian home has spacious bedrooms individually decorated with TV, tea/coffee, central heating and private facilities. Enjoy a 4-course breakfast in the sunny dining room. Choose from English, Continental or Vegetarian menu; sample our home-made jams. Off road parking and frequent bus service into Bath centre (2 km). Children are welcome, under 3's come free. We have a high chair, cot, playroom and secluded garden. Our aim is to make you welcome and help you enjoy Bath and its surroundings. AA Selected QQQQ.

Jill & Rob Fradley
Tel: 01225 424159

B&B from £22.50pp, Rooms 1 twin, 1 double, 1 family, all en-suite or
private bathroom, No smoking, Children welcome, No pets,
Open all year except Christmas & New Year, Map Ref A

Cranleigh, 159 Newbridge Hill, Bath BA1 3PX Nearest Road A431

Away from traffic and noise but just minutes from the heart of Bath. Cranleigh has lovely views, private parking and secluded sunny gardens. Guest bedrooms are all en-suite and exceptionally spacious. Imaginative breakfasts include fresh fruit salad and scrambled eggs with smoked salmon. The Webbers are a mine of information, always happy to help with routes, maps and suggestions. Ground floor bedrooms available. A no-smoking house. 'Short Break' reductions off season. AA QQQQ & RAC Highly Acclaimed. Recommended by the 'Which' Good Bed & Breakfast Guide. EMail: Cranleigh@btinternet.com

see PHOTO on page 21

Christine & Arthur Webber
Tel: 01225 310197
Fax: 01225 423143

B&B from £30pp, Rooms 2 twin, 2 double, 1 family, all en-suite,
No smoking, Children from 5 years, No pets,
Open all year, Map Ref A

Apsley House Hotel, Newbridge Hill, Bath BA1 3PT Nearest Road A431

David and Anne Lanz warmly welcome guests into their elegant Georgian house. Beautifully proportioned reception rooms overlook the pretty garden. Sumptuous decor, fine antiques and oil paintings create a gracious but relaxed atmosphere. Bedrooms are all en-suite, individually furnished and decorated and offer TV, direct dial telephones, hot drink facilities and hair dryers. Breakfast is a delight with full English and house specialities. Licensed bar. Local information available. Just over 1 mile west of centre. Private car park. AA 5Q, ETB Highly Commended.

David & Annie Lanz
Tel: 01225 336966
Fax: 01225 425462

B&B from £32.50pp, Rooms 3 twin, 5 double, 1 family, all en-suite,
Restricted smoking, Children from 5, No pets,
Open all year except Christmas, Map Ref A

---

left, **The Old Red House, Bath** *- see this page for details* **19**

see PHOTO on page 22

Gainsborough Hotel, Weston Lane, Bath BA1 4AB

Nearest Main Road A4

A large country house hotel in own attractive grounds near botanical gardens, municipal golf course and centre. Both spacious and very comfortable we provide a relaxing and informal atmosphere for our guests stay. The Abbey, Roman baths, and pump rooms are all within walking distance via the park. All 16 bedrooms are en-suite with colour and satellite TV, tea/coffee making facilities, direct dial telephones, hair dryer's, etc. The hotel has a friendly bar, 2 sun terraces, large car park and warm welcome.

Mrs R Warwick
Tel: 01225 311380
Fax: 01225 447411

B&B from £28pp,
Rooms 2 single, 12 twin/double, 2 family, all en-suite,
Open all year, Map Ref A

Grove Lodge, 11 Lambridge, London Road, Bath BA1 6BJ

Nearest Road A4 and A46

Grove Lodge is an elegant Georgian house built in 1788 and set in lovely gardens with views onto the wooded hills surrounding the city. Roy and Rosalie Burridge welcome you to their comfortable home which offers 6 excellent large rooms. Each has colour TV and tea/coffee making facilities are available. Continental or 4-course English breakfasts are offered and summer afternoon tea under the apple tree is not to be missed. Bath is an excellent centre for many beautiful and historic locations including the Cotswolds, Stonehenge, Wells and Glastonbury.

Roy & Rosalie Burridge
Tel: 01225 310860
Fax: 01225 429630

B&B from £22pp, Rooms 1 twin, 4 double, 1 family,
No smoking,
Open all year, Map Ref A

Cedar Lodge, 13 Lambridge, London Road, Bath BA1 6BJ

Nearest Road A4, A46

Within walking distance of historic city centre, this gracious detached Georgian house offers period elegance combined with modern comforts. Beautiful individually designed bedrooms, 1 with a 4 poster, 1 with a half-tester bed and 1 twin bedded. All with TV and en-suite/private facilities. Guests may relax in the lovely gardens or by the fire in the drawing room. Choice of breakfasts served with homemade preserves. Secure car parking. This is an ideal base for Bath, Stonehenge, Salisbury, Wells, Cotswolds and many other places of interest. Help given with planning your excursions.

Derek and Maria Beckett
Tel: 01225 423468

B&B from £25-£30pp, Rooms 1 twin, 2 double, all en-suite,
No smoking, Children welcome, No pets,
Open all year, Map Ref A

Wentworth House, 106 Bloomfield Road, Bath BA2 2AP

Nearest Road A367

see PHOTO on page 23

A highly recommended up-market bed and breakfast hotel built in 1887, standing in secluded gardens with stunning views of the valley. Situated in quiet area with free car park. Abbey and Roman Baths are within walking distance. High standard of accommodation. Small lounge/bar and outdoor pool. Horse riding and golf nearby. The tastefully decorated en-suite bedrooms offer colour TV, direct dial telephone, hair dryers and tea/coffee making facilities. Breakfast is a choice of full English and you can help your self to the buffet bar.

Mr & Mrs Kitching
Tel: 01225 339193
Fax: 01225 310460

B&B from £25-£35pp, Rooms 5 twin, 12 double, 1 family, all en-suite,
Restricted smoking, Children over 5, Pets by arrangement,
Open all year except Christmas & New Year, Map Ref A

right, Cranleigh, Bath - see page 19 for details

Gainsborough Hotel, Bath - see page 20

Wentworth House, Bath- see page 20

see PHOTO opposite

Haydon House, 9 Bloomfield Park, Bath BA2 2BY — Nearest Road A367

A true oasis of tranquillity, this secluded, elegantly furnished Edwardian town house is situated in a quiet residential area with easy parking, not far from the city centre. Every conceivable comfort is offered in the 5 tastefully decorated en-suite bedrooms including TV and a generous hospitality tray. Guests can enjoy a welcoming cup of tea in the beautifully appointed antique filled sitting room, with sunshine filtering through the vine clad pergola, and innovative breakfasts are stylishly served to a background of gentle classical music.

Gordon & Magdalene
Ashman-Marr
Tel/Fax: 01225 444919/427351

B&B from £30pp, Rooms 1 twin, 3 double, 1 family, all en-suite,
No smoking, No pets, Children welcome by arrangement,
Open all year, Map Ref A

see PHOTO on page 26

Oldfields, 102 Wells Road, Bath BA2 3AL — Nearest Road A367 (Exeter Road)

This elegant Victorian house hotel offers wholefood or traditional English breakfasts with Mozart in the background and morning newspapers. There is ample parking and a garden with views to the hills and crescents. All rooms, decorated with Laura Ashley and Liberty fabrics, have en-suite facilities, direct dial telephone, colour TV, hairdryers and tea/coffee making facilities. Two rooms are on the ground floor and are suitable for the less mobile. Only 10 minutes walk to city centre.

Berkeley & Moira Gaunt
Tel: 01225 317984
Fax: 01225 444471

B&B from £27.50pp, Rooms 8 double, 6 twin,
All rooms have private shower/wc,
Open all year except Christmas & January, Map Ref A

see PHOTO on page 28

Leighton House, 139 Wells Road, Bath BA2 3AL — Nearest Road A367

Marilyn and Colin Humphrey extend a friendly welcome to you at their delightful elegant Victorian home set in beautiful gardens, offering views over the city. With ample private parking, they are only 10 minutes walk from the city centre. The rooms offer every comfort, being tastefully decorated and furnished with en-suite facilities (bath, shower, wc and washbasin), direct dial telephone, hair dryer, colour TV, radio and beverage-making facilities. Superb breakfasts served to suit all tastes. Special breaks available.

Marilyn & Colin Humphrey
Tel: 01225 314769
Fax: 01225 443079

B&B from £31pp, Rooms 4 double, 3 twin, 1 family,
All rooms have full en-suite, No smoking,
Open all year, Map Ref A

see PHOTO on page 27

Highways House, 143 Wells Road, Bath BA2 3AL — Nearest Road A367

A warm and friendly welcome awaits you from the resident proprietors David & Davina James at this delightful and well appointed Victorian house. Guests who stay at Highways House will find a very relaxed and homely atmosphere. All bedrooms have private bath/shower rooms, TV and tea/coffee making facilities. A twin bedded room is on the ground floor. The large and very comfortable lounge and breakfast room are also on the ground floor. A full English breakfast. Only 10 minutes walk into Bath city centre. Car park. AA 4Q Selected, RAC Highly Acclaimed.

David & Davina James
Tel: 01225 421238
Fax: 01225 481169

B&B from £26pp, Rooms 1 single with private bathroom,
3 twin, 3 double, all en-suite, Restricted smoking, Minimum age 5,
No pets, Open all year except Christmas, Map Ref A

right, Haydon House, Bath - see this page for details

Oldfields, Bath – see page 24

Highways House, Bath - see page 24

Leighton House, Bath

see page 24

Holly Lodge, 8 Upper Oldfield Park, Bath BA2 3JZ **Nearest Road A367**

This charming Victorian town house commands panoramic views of the city and is delightfully furnished with individually designed bedrooms, some with 4 posters and superb bathrooms. Elegant and stylish, it is owned and operated with meticulous attention to details by George Hall. Superb breakfasts are enjoyed in the appealing breakfast room with the yellow and green decor and white wicker chairs. Furnished with antiques, this immaculate establishment, winner of an 'England of Excellence' award makes a pleasant base for touring Bath and the Cotswolds.

see PHOTO on page 31

George Hall
Tel: 01225 424042
Fax: 01225 481138

B&B from £37.50pp, Rooms 1 single, 2 twin, 4 double, all en-suite, No smoking, Children welcome, No pets, Open all year, Map Ref A

Cheriton House, 9 Upper Oldfield Park, Bath BA2 3JX **10 mins walk to City Centre**

Dating from the 1880's Cheriton House is located on Bath's southern slopes. Situated in a quiet street with splendid views, yet within easy walking distance of the city. The house has been carefully restored and redecorated and all rooms are attractively furnished. In the dining room a choice of breakfast is offered and in the sitting room there is a plentiful supply of books and brochures to help plan your day. Iris & John will be pleased to advise guests where to eat, visit, and what to see.

Iris & John
Tel: 01225 429862
Fax: 01225 428403

B&B from £29pp, Rooms: 6 double, 3 twin, all en-suite, Family room available on request, Open all year including Christmas, Map Ref A

Badminton Villa, 10 Upper Oldfield Park, Bath BA2 3JZ **Nearest Road A367**

A large Victorian family house located in a tree lined residential road on the southern slopes of Bath, with magnificient city views, yet only a 10 minute walk to the city centre. Sue and John Burton have established a quality bed and breakfast guest house with an international reputation. All rooms have first class en-suite facilities and are equipped with colour TV, hair dryer and tea/coffee making facilities. Lounge and gardens overlook city. A no smoking house. Car park. ETB Highly Commended. RAC Highly Acclaimed.

Sue & John Burton
Tel: 01225 426347
Fax: 01225 420393

B&B from £28pp, Rooms 1 twin, 3 double, all en-suite, No smoking, Children over 8, No pets, Open all year except Christmas & New Year, Map Ref A

Oakleigh House, 19 Upper Oldfield Park, Bath BA2 3JX **Nearest Rd 10 mins walk to City Centre**

Oakleigh House is situated in a peaceful location 10 minutes from the centre of Bath. Victorian elegance is combined with present day comforts and all bedrooms are en-suite and benefit from tea/coffee making facilities, colour TV, clock radio, hair dryer and tasteful furnishings. There is a car park for guests. A good base for touring Glastonbury, Stonehenge, Bristol, Wells, Salisbury and the Cotswolds.

David & Jenny King
Tel: 01225 315698
Fax: 01225 448223

B&B from £25pp, Rooms 3 double, 1 twin, all en-suite, Open all year, Map Ref A

Astor House, 14 Oldfield Road, Bath BA2 3ND   **Nearest Road A367, Wells Road**

Relax in comfort at Astor House. Enjoy varied delicious breakfasts and make the most of the World Heritage City of Bath. Ideally situated away from the traffic, yet only ¹/₂ mile from the Roman Baths in the centre. We offer a spacious and stylish Victorian home with a large, secluded, shady garden. All rooms have colour TV, tea/coffee making facilities and radio/alarm, a good outlook, some have splendid views. It is centrally located for touring with Stonehenge, Avebury, Bradford-on-Avon, Salisbury, Longleat and other delights a very easy drive away.

Rick & Kathie Beech
Tel: 01225 429134
Fax: 01225 429134

B&B from £17pp, Rooms 2 twin, 3 double, 1 family, some en-suite, No smoking, Children welcome, No pets, Open February - December, Not Christmas or New Year, Map Ref A

Paradise House, 88 Holloway, Bath BA2 4PX   **Nearest Road A367**

Paradise House is a Georgian (1735) Grade II listed building situated in a quiet cul-de-sac only 5 minutes walk from Bath city centre. Its ¹/₂ acre gardens at the rear command magnificent panoramic views over the entire city and surrounding hills. The comfortable bedrooms, all of which are en-suite, and equipped with tea/coffee making facilities and TV. A full English breakfast is served. Full details of all Bath's famous restaurants are available, including menus, maps and booking advice. The perfect touring base for Bath and the Cotswolds.

David & Janet Cutting
Tel: 01225 317723
Fax: 01225 482005

B&B from £32.50pp, Rooms 3 twin, 4 double, 1 family, all en-suite, Children welcome, No pets, Open all year except Christmas, Map Ref A

see PHOTO on page 32

Devonshire House, 143 Wellsway, Bath BA2 4RZ   **On the A367**

Lovely Victorian house built in 1880 incorporating an antique shop on the same premises.Individually decorated en-suite bedrooms and public rooms with many antiques. Full English or continental breakfast is served in our Victorian dining room. Three course home made candlelit evening meals are available on request at £15pp. Special diets are catered for. Parking is available in our secure courtyard, the city being only a short walk away. Special breaks available throughout the year. A non smoking house. AA and RAC Acclaimed.

Eileen Fermor & Albie Harris
Tel: 01225 312495
Fax: 01225 335534

B&B from £25pp, Dinner on request for £15, Rooms 1 twin, 1 double, 1 family, all en-suite, No smoking, Children welcome, No pets, Open all year, Map Ref A

---

9 Bathwick Hill, Bath BA2 6EW   **On Bathwick Hill**

Listed Georgian family home in much desirable part of Bath. Two twin bedrooms with baths. Full breakfast. Tea and Coffee making facilities in bedrooms. Use of drawing room with TV, Conservatory and large walled garden. Fine views over Bath. Short walk to city centre. Frequent bus services. Free car parking outside property. No license for alcohol. This is a private home with peaceful friendly atmosphere.

Mrs Elspeth Bowman
Tel: 01225 460812

B&B from £24pp, Rooms 2 twin with private bathrooms, No smoking, Minimum age 12, No pets, Open all year except Christmas, Map Ref A

above, **Villa Magdala, Bath see page 34**

left, **Paradise House, Bath - see page 30**

33

see PHOTO on page 33

Villa Magdala Hotel, Henrietta Road, Bath BA2 6LX　　　　　**5 minutes walk to City Centre**

A delightful Victorian town house hotel set in its own grounds, the Villa Magdala enjoys a peaceful location overlooking Henrietta Park only a few minutes level walk to the Roman Baths and Abbey. All 17 spacious rooms have private bathroom en-suite, telephone, television and tea/coffee making facilities. The hotel has its own private car park and is an ideal base for exploring Bath and the surrounding countryside.
E Mail: villa@BTinternet.com

Mrs Alison Williams
Tel: 01225 466329
Fax: 01225 483207

**B&B from £30pp, Rooms 5 twin, 12 double, all rooms are en-suite,
4-posters, triples and family rooms available,
Open all year, Map Ref A**

---

see PHOTO opposite

Brompton House, St John's Road, Bath BA2 6PT　　　　　**Nearest Road A46**

Built as a rectory in 1777 Brompton House is an elegant Georgian residence with its own car park and beautiful mature gardens. Only 5 minutes level walk from many of Bath's historic sights Brompton House is privately owned and run by the Selby family. The attractive residents' sitting room is furnished with antiques and the tastefully decorated en-suite bedrooms offer colour TV, radio alarm, direct dial telephone. hair dryers and tea/coffee. Full english, continental or wholefood breakfast.
EMail: BROMPTON_HOUSE@compuserve.com

David, Sue, Belinda & Tim Selby
Tel: 01225 420972
Fax: 01225 420505

**B&B from £30pp, Rooms 2 single, 7 twin, 7 double, 2 family,
No smoking, Minimum age 7 years, No pets,
Open all year except Christmas and New Year, Map Ref A**

---

see PHOTO on page 37

Eagle House, Church Street, Bathford BA1 7RS　　　　　**Nearest Road A4, A363**

Eagle House is a fine Georgian Mansion in 1 1/2 acres of garden in the lovely, peaceful village of Bathford 3 miles from the Heritage city of Bath. The house is elegant with a large drawing room with an open fire which is lit on chilly evenings. All bedrooms are en-suite and have TV and tea/coffee making facilities; they are spacious and some can accommodate parents with up to 3 children. (Children accompanying parents come free). A very warm welcome from resident owners, John & Rosamund Napier, and the atmosphere here is relaxed and informal. EMail: JONAP@PSIONWORLD.NET

John & Rosamund Napier
Tel: 01225 859946
Fax: 01225 859946

**B&B from £24pp, Rooms 1 single, 2 twin, 4 double, 1 family,
all en-suite, Children welcome, Pets welcome,
Open early January - late December, Map Ref B**

---

see PHOTO on page 39

Monkshill, Shaft Road, Monkton Combe, Bath BA2 7HL　　　　　**Nearest Road A3062**

This distinguished Edwardian house is set in its own beautiful gardens, on an English country hilltop commanding spectacular countryside views, and yet lies only 5 minutes from the centre of Bath. Stroll through the small medieval village of Monkton Combe, at the valley's base and return to tea amid the elegant antiques, fireplace and grand piano that complement the drawing room. The bedrooms are elegant, with colourful flowing drapes, charming brass beds, bath/shower & fine views over the gardens and valley below. Area of Outstanding Natural Beauty.

Michael & Catherine Westlake
Tel: 01225 833028
Fax: 01225 833028

**B&B from £28pp, Rooms 1 twin, 2 double, most en-suite,
No smoking, Children welcome, No pets, AA 5Q Premier Selected,
Open all year except Christmas & New Year, Map Ref C**

Pickford House, Bath Road, Beckington, Bath BA3 6SJ   Nearest Road A36

Pickford House is an elegant Regency style house built in honey coloured Bath stone. It stands on top of the hill overlooking the village of Beckington and surrounding countryside. Some bedrooms are en-suite and all have tea/coffee making facilities and TV; all are very comfortable and tastefully decorated. Angela is a talented and enthusiastic cook and offers an excellent 'pot luck' meal, or on request an extensive menu for special celebrations. The house is licensed with a large and varied wine list. In summer visitors may be offered an 'off-the-beaten-track pre dinner drive.

Ken & Angela Pritchard
Tel: 01373 8303292
Fax: 01373 830329

B&B from £15pp, Dinner from £12, Rooms 1 twin, 1 double, family, some en-suite, Restricted smoking, Children welcome, Pets by prior arrangement, Open all year, Map Ref A

Green Lane House, Hinton Charterhouse, Bath BA3 6BL   Nearest Road A36, B3110

Five miles south of Bath in undulating countryside on the borders of Somerset and Wiltshire lies the charming conservation village of Hinton Charterhouse. Green Lane House, originally 3 terraced 18th century stone cottages, has been tastefully renovated and attractively furnished. Traditional features such as exposed beams and open log fireplaces combine with modern comforts introduced throughout the 4 distinctively decorated guest bedrooms, homely residents lounge and breakfast room. Conveniently located within the village are 2 inns with restaurants.

Christopher & Juliet Davies
Tel: 01225 723631
Fax: 01225 723773

B&B from £20pp, Rooms 2 double, 1 en-suite, 2 twin, 1 en-suite, No smoking, Open all year, Map Ref D

The Plaine, North Street, Norton St Philip, near Bath BA3 6LE   Nearest Road B3110

The Plaine is a delightful listed building dating from the 16th century and situated in the heart of an historic conservation village. There are three beautiful en-suite rooms, all with 4 poster beds. Opposite is the famous George Inn, one of the oldest hosteleries in England. Breakfasts are prepared from local produce and served in the heavily beamed dining room with guests seated around one table. Colour TV and tea/coffee making facilities in all rooms. Lounge. Car parking. Central heating. Convenient for Bath, Wells, Stonehenge, Longleat and the Cotswolds.

Jon & Janet Whitwam
Tel: 01373 834723
Fax: 01373 834101

B&B from £25pp, Rooms 3 double en-suite, No smoking, Children over 5, No pets, Open all year except Christmas & New Year, Map RefE

Monmouth Lodge, Norton St Philip, near Bath BA3 6LH   Nearest Road B3110

Monmouth Lodge is a delightful house, tastefully remodelled with ground floor bedrooms en-suite, own patio doors, king size beds and quality furnishings, sumptuously furnished lounge and secluded garden for our guests. A short drive from Bath. Private parking. Excellent meals in 13th century pub nearby. AA 5Q. Winner of the West Country AA 'Best Newcomer' award, ETB Highly Commended.

Leslie & Traudle Graham
Tel: 01373 834367

B&B from £27pp, Rooms 2 twin, 1 double, 1 family, all en-suite, No smoking, No pets, Minimum age 4, Open all year except Christmas & New Year, Map Ref E

right, Eagle House, Bath - see page 34

Irondale House, 67 High Street, Rode, Bath BA3 6PB Nearest Road A36

A very warm welcome in our 18th century family house, set in lovely walled garden with wonderful views. Open fires, pretty bedrrooms with hair dryers and colour TV. Ideal for sightseeing Bath, Wells, Longleat and many other places of interest. An excellent full English breakfast to set you on your way. Jayne & Oliver have a lot of local knowledge and are very willing to help you plan your route. AA QQQQQ, Premier Selected.

Jayne & Oliver Holder
Tel/Fax: 01373 830730

B&B from £27pp, Rooms 1 twin, 2 double, most en-suite,
Restricted smoking, Children over 12, No pets,
Open all year except Christmas & New Year, Map Ref F

The Manor House, Wellow, Bath BA2 8QQ Nearest Road A367

This 17th century stone Manor House is set in the heart of an attractive farming village six miles from the Georgian city of Bath. Welcome to a comfortable family home with large bedrooms which have televisions and tea/coffee trays. The traditional breakfast includes home-baked bread. Cream teas are served in the courtyard and garden at weekends in the summer. The village pub serves meals. Wellow is within easy reach of Wells, Glastonbury and Cheddar and stately homes of Longleat, Stourhead and Dyrham.

Sarah Danny
Tel: 01225 832027

B&B from £17.50pp, Rooms 1 singe, 1 twin, 1 double, most en-suite,
No smoking, Children welcome, No pets,
Open all year except Christmas and New Year, Map Ref G

Overbrook, Stowey Bottom, Bishop Sutton, near Bristol BS18 4TN Nearest Road A368

Overbrook is a charming house, tastefully furnished with a lovely garden by a brook. Situated in a quiet and peaceful lane with a little ford by the gate. It offer one twin-bedded en-suite room and one double room with private shower and w.c. Each has TV, clock/radio, iron etc. A comfortable sunny sitting room with French windows leading into the garden for guests use. Bath Wells, Bristol and Cheddar Gorge within easy reach and superb trout fishing on Chew Valley Lake only 5 minutes away.

Mrs Ruth Shellard
Tel: 01275 332648
Fax: 01179 352052

B&B from £18pp, Rooms 1 single, 1 twin en-suite, 1 double, private
shower & wc, No smoking, Children welcome, No pets,
Open all year except Christmas & New Year, Map Ref H

Box Hedge Farm, Coalpit Heath, Bristol BS17 2UW Nearest Road Westerleigh Road

Box Hedge Farm is set in 200 acres of beautiful rural countryside. Local to M4/M5, central for Bristol and Bath. An ideal stopping point for the south west and Wales. We offer a warm family atmosphere with traditional farmhouse cooking. The large spacious bedrooms, one with a four-poster, have colour TV and tea/coffee making facilities.

Mrs Marilyn Collins
Tel: 01454 250786

B&B from £17.50 single, £30 double, Dinner from £7.50,
Rooms 1 single, 2 double, 1 family, Restricted smoking,
Open all year, Map Ref I

---

right, Monkshill, Bath - see page 34

Downs Edge, Saville Road, Stoke Bishop, Bristol BS9 1JD   **Nearest Road A4018**

Downs Edge is set in magnificent gardens on the very edge of Bristol's famous Downs, an open park of some 450 acres, and close to the spectacular Avon Gorge and it's breathtaking views. All rooms have televisions and hospitality trays with homemade biscuits. A residents lounge is available and there is generous car parking in the grounds. This uniquely peaceful location is convenient for the city centre, Clifton, the Universities, the many historic locations and places of interest in the city and the Cotswolds.

Mrs Philippa Tasker
Tel/Fax: 0117 9683264

B&B from £26pp, Rooms 2 single, 1 twin, 1 double, most en-suite,
No smoking, Children welcome, No pets,
Open all year except Christmas and New Year, Map Ref J

"There'll always be an England
While there's a country lane,"
Clarke Ross Parker

BEDFORDSHIRE, BERKSHIRE, BUCKINGHAMSHIRE & HERTFORDSHIRE

To see everything these lovely counties have to offer is an impossible task, to savour a taste is all the holiday maker can hope for - little wonder then that they return again and again. These are the Home Counties where seemingly every village has its own fascinating history. Being at the very heart of England and presumably considered safe from attack from 'outsiders' there are consequently few medieval castles, but examples of superb domestic architecture abound. This area has been populated since the very morning of time. The Ridge Way, that black and lonely path across the Berkshire Downs was a vital trade route during the Bronze Age. The Icknield Way, a prehistoric track, follows the high ground southwest from the Wash through East Anglia and the Chilterns to the Berkshire Downs, while the Roman Road Watling Street, running northwest from London, derives its name from the Anglo-Saxon word for St. Albans, which was the first place of importance on the journey from London.

The four counties are simply stippled with centres of interest - the list seems endless. Bedford, a town already well established in Anglo-Saxon times, is renowned for its association with John Bunyan, the author of Pilgrim's Progress who was imprisoned in Bedford gaol for his Nonconformist beliefs. Buckingham was established by Alfred the Great as a county town as far back as 888AD and remained such until the town was destroyed by fire in 1725 and the county government transferred to Aylesbury - renowned for its fine old inns, its links with the Parliamentary cause during the Civil War...and ducks. A statue of John Hampden, the Buckinghamshire MP who opposed Charles I, stands in the Market Square. Aylesbury of course, gave its name to the Vale which is one of England's richest dairy-farming regions. To the east is St. Albans, Two thousand years ago the largest Roman town in Britain then known as Verulamium. It was here that the Roman soldier Alban was executed for sheltering a Christian priest and was later canonised to become Britain's first Christian Martyr. In the eighth century the Saxons built an abbey on the site of St. Alban's shrine only to have it replaced by the Norman abbey in 1077. Only the abbey church remained following the Dissolution and is now the Cathedral Church of St. Alban, in length five hundred and fifty feet and one of the longest cathedrals in Britain. There is a wealth of interest in St. Albans...the area in front of the abbey's great gate was a medieval meeting place and the focus of rioting during the Peasant's Revolt of 1381, and the place in 1556 where a Protestant baker was burned at the stake as a heretic. In more pleasant vein, the Royal National Rose Society at Chiswell Green nearby, boasts over thirty thousand bushes...which are a glorious sight in July.

To the south is Windsor, dominated by its castle, the largest in Europe and of course one of the residences of the Royal Family. The castle is hugely popular attracting large crowds during the holiday season, but in addition to the castle there is the Great Park. This is all that is now left of the royal hunting forest that once stretched across southern Berkshire, but still comprises an impressive four thousand, eight hundred acres, and includes the three mile long Long Walk, a tree - lined avenue leading from the castle to the large artificial lake, Virginia Water. There is also a fascinating Royal and Empire Exhibition in Windsor railway station which is well worth a visit, and over the river is Eton with its college. The college chapel, a fine example of fifteenth century perpendicular architecture resembles King's College Chapel at Cambridge - and if the holiday visitor can possibly find the time, there are wonderful boat trips down the Thames. Just six miles southwest of Windsor is the village of Ascot where in 1711 Queen Anne established the Royal Ascot race meeting as a social as well as a sporting event. Newbury is an interesting old town and can boast the first factory to operate in England, when in the fifteenth century over a thousand wool weavers were employed by John Winchcombe - known as Jack of Newbury.

Could there I wonder be a more

charming place than Chalfont St. Giles with its picturesque cottages and church clustered round the village green. At one end of the main street of half-timbered cottages, is Milton's Cottage. It was here that the blind poet took refuge in 1665 to avoid the Great Plague raging in London, and it was here that he finished Paradise Lost and started Paradise Regained. First editions of his great works are on display here. In the Chess Valley is the intriguing nineteenth century village of Chenies, built for the estate workers of the medieval manor of the Dukes of Bedford.

If the towns and villages of this lovely area don't occupy the whole of the holiday maker's time there is interest enough in the glorious countryside, and who can resist the appeal of the great houses...Woburn Abbey, the home of the Dukes of Bedford, Hatfield House, seized from the Bishops of Ely by Henry VIII at the Dissolution....and then there is Chequers, the country home of British Prime Ministers, an Elizabethan mansion in the Chilterns near Princes Risborough, given to the nation by Lord Lee of Fareham.

There can really be no recommended centre for exploring this area, select where you will, and you will be surrounded with interest and spectacle that will fill your holiday with delight.

BEDFORDSHIRE, BERKSHIRE, BUCKINGHAMSHIRE & HERTFORDSHIRE

Places to Visit

Woburn Abbey, *Bedfordshire* ~ the abbey was built in the middle of the 18th century on the foundations of a large 12th century monastery. It now has a 350 acre safari park and deer park.

Whipsnade Wild Animal Park, *Bedfordshire* ~ this was one of the first zoos to reduce the use of cages. It is Europe's largest conservation park with over 600 acres containing more than 3000 species. It also has an adventure playground and sea lion display.

Luton Hoo, *Bedfordshire* ~ it was originally built in 1767, but in 1903 Sir Julius Wernher had it rebuilt in a French classical style, by the same architects as the Ritz Hotel. It is still the home of the Wernher family and includes paintings by Hoppner, Titian and Sargent.

Windsor Castle, *Berkshire* ~ the oldest continuously inhabited royal residence in Britain, the castle was orginally built from wood by William the Conqueror in 1070. In 1170, Henry II rebuilt it in stone and in the years to follow various additions have been made.

Hungerford, *Berkshire* ~ a town famous for its many antique shops.

Stowe, *Buckinghamshire* ~ the gardens were originally laid out in 1680 and in the following hundred years they were enlarged and transformed with monuments, Greek and Gothic temples, statues, bridges, lakes and trees. Many designers and architects including Sir John Vanburgh, James Gibbs and Capability Brown have contributed to the gardens.

Hughenden Manor, *Buckinghamshire* ~ Bejamin Disraeli, Prime Minister from 1874 - 1880, lived here for 33 years until his death. The Georgian villa is still furnished as it was in his day.

Knebworth House, *Hertfordshire* ~ a Tudor mansion and Jacobean banqueting hall, with a 19th century Gothic exterior by Lord Lytton, the statesman and novelist.

Gardens of the Rose, *Hertfordshire* ~ the twelve acre garden of the Royal National Rose Society with over 1700 varieties of plants.

Hatfield House, *Hertfordshire* ~ built between 1607 and 1611 for statesman Robert Cecil, it is still owned by his descendants. The palace was partly demolished in 1607 so that the new house could be built. Queen Elizabeth I spent much of her childhood here and she held her first Council of State here when she was crowned in 1558.

◀ *Tudor Cottages,*
Westmill,
Hertfordshire

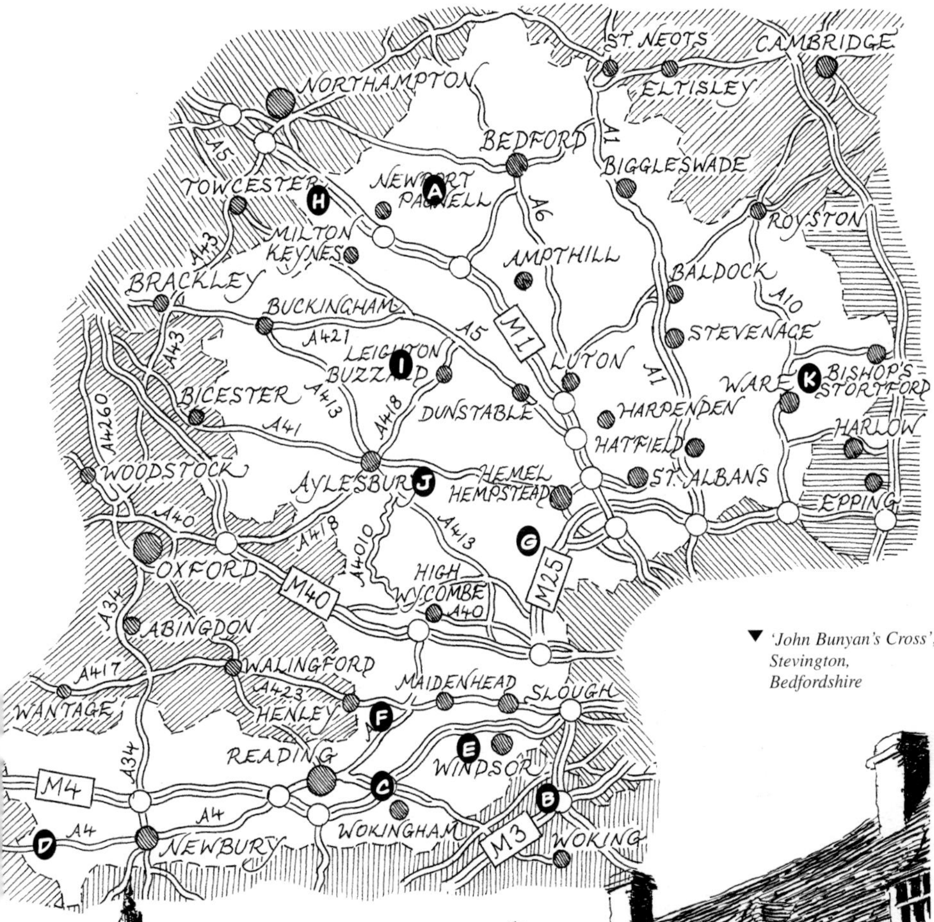
ST. NEOTS
CAMBRIDGE
ELTISLEY
NORTHAMPTON
BEDFORD
A1
BIGGLESWADE
A5
TOWCESTER
H
NEWPORT PAGNELL
A
A6
ROYSTON
MILTON KEYNES
AMPTHILL
A43
BALDOCK
BRACKLEY
A10
BUCKINGHAM
M1
STEVENAGE
A43
A421
A5
LEIGHTON BUZZARD
I
LUTON
A1
BISHOP'S STORTFORD
K
WARE
BICESTER
A413
A418
DUNSTABLE
HARPENDEN
A4260
A41
HARLOW
HATFIELD
WOODSTOCK
HEMEL HEMPSTEAD
J
AYLESBURY
ST. ALBANS
EPPING
A40
A418
A4010
A413
G
OXFORD
M25
M40
HIGH WYCOMBE
A40
A34
ABINGDON
A417
WALINGFORD
A423
MAIDENHEAD
SLOUGH
WANTAGE
HENLEY
F
E
A34
READING
WINDSOR
M4
C
B
A4
D
A4
NEWBURY
WOKINGHAM
M3
WOKING

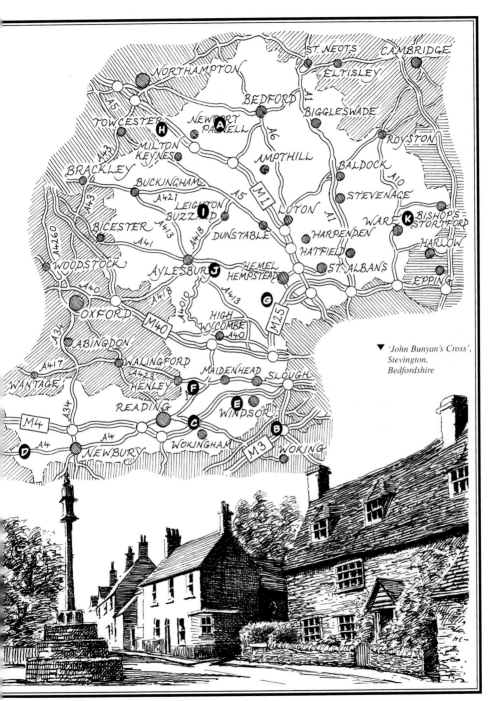

▼ *'John Bunyan's Cross', Stevington, Bedfordshire*

Firs Farm, Stagsden, Bedford MK43 8TB   Nearest Road A422

Firs Farm is a family run arable farm set in quiet surroundings ¹/₂ mile from the A422 midway between Bedford and Milton Keynes (M1 junction 14). The farmhouse is timber framed, set in a large secluded garden with swimming pool. The guest bedrooms are spacious and consist of 2 doubles (1 en-suite), and 1 twin, all with wash basin and tea/coffee making facilities. The guests' lounge has colour TV and open log fires. Breakfast is taken in the old bakehouse. A warm welcome awaits business and holiday guests.

Mrs Pam Hutcheon
Tel: 01234 822344
Fax: 01234 822344

B&B from £17pp, Rooms 1 twin, 2 double, 1 en-suite, Restricted smoking, Children welcome, Pets by arrangement, Open all year, Map Ref A

Ennis Lodge Guest House, Winkfield Road, Ascot, Berkshire SL5 7EX   Nearest Road A330, A329

Ennis Lodge is situated in the centre of Ascot within easy reach of Mainline Station, Waterloo 45 mins; M3, M4/M25 close by; Heathrow Airport 25 mins; Windsor Castle 10 mins; Ascot Racecourse 2 mins. Just a short drive to all major international golf courses. Ennis Lodge offers first class accommodation for the tourist and businessman alike. All rooms have en-suite/private facilities and colour TV, trouser press, hair dryer, radio alarm, tea/coffee making facilities, and more. Price includes full English breakfast. Off street parking is available. 10 minutes from Legoland theme park.

John & Siegi Miles
Tel: 01344 21009
Fax: 01344 21009

B&B/Rooms 1 single £35pn, 4 twin from £21pp,pn, 1 family, all with private or en-suite facilities, Restricted smoking, Children welcome, Small pets by arrangement, Open all year, Map Ref B

Lyndrick Guest House, The Avenue, North Ascot, Berkshire SL5 7ND   Nearest Road A30, M3, M4

Lyndrick offers good quality accommodation at less than hotel prices and is just 25 minutes from Heathrow. A warm welcome awaits guests and pride is taken in customer service. Full English breakfast is served in a pleasant conservatory and for early departees a continental breakfast can be supplied. London Waterloo is 40 minutes away on British Rail. Wentworth and surrounding golf courses are 10 minutes away. There is easy access to M3, M4 and M25. Bracknell and Windsor are 10 minutes and Reading 25 minutes. Ascot Racecourse is an easy walk.

Sue & Graham Chapman
Tel: 01344 883520
Fax:01344 891243

B&B from £24pp, Rooms 1 double, 2 twin, 1 single, We take Visa and Mastercard, Open all year, Map Ref C

Marshgate Cottage Hotel, Marsh Lane, Hungerford RG17 0QX   Nearest Road M4,A338

see PHOTO on page 47

Marshgate Cottage is tucked away at the end of a quiet country lane just ¹/₂ mile from Hungerford and four miles from M4. Guest rooms are in a traditionally designed addition to the original canalside 17th century thatched cottage. All rooms have en-suite shower and toilet, TV, phone and tea/coffee making facilities. Guests lounge and bar. Car park. The town has an abundance of antiques and speciality shops, canal trips, pubs and restaurants. Ideal base for touring southern England. Superb walking area.

Mike Walker
Tel: 01488 682307
Fax: 01488 685475

B&B from £24.25pp, Rooms 1 single, 2 twin, 3 double, 2 family, all en-suite, Restricted smoking, Children & pets welcome, Open all year, Map Ref D

Fishers Farm, Shefford Woodlands, Hungerford, Berkshire RG17 7AB　　　Nearest Road M4/J14

Charming period farmhouse with all modern comforts on a working sheep and arable farm. Surrounded by a large garden and farmland in a peaceful and secluded location yet only 1 mile from junction 14 of the M4. An ideal base for exploring the beautiful downland countryside and villages; also within easy reach of Bath, Oxford, Salisbury, Stonehenge, Windsor and Winchester. Heathrow is less than 1 hour away and Gatwick about 1¹/₂ hours. Heated indoor pool available all year. Excellent cooking using home grown produce.

Henry & Mary Wilson
Tel: 01488 648466
Fax: 01488 648706

B&B from £25pp, Dinner from £18.00, Rooms 1 twin en-suite, 1 double en-suite, 1 family, private bathroom, Restricted smoking, Children welcome, Pets by arrangement, Open all year, Map Ref D

---

3 Withey Close, off Gallys Road, Windsor, Berkshire SL4 5QX　　　Nearest Road A308

A modern detached house with large attractive garden and off street parking. Located in a quiet residential area 2 miles from Windsor Castle. The bedrooms are well decorated and equipped with firm beds, TV, tea/coffee making facilities and hand-washbasins. Apart from the local attractions of Windsor Castle and Legoland, central London is less than one hour away by car or public transport. Hampton Court, RHS Gardens, Wisley and Oxford are all within 1 hours drive. Heathrow 10 miles away.

Beryl & Arthur Bartram
Tel/Fax: 01753 860485

B&B from £18pp, Rooms 1 single, 1 twin, 1 double, No smoking, Open all year except Christmas & New Year, Map Ref E

Burchett's Place Country House, Burchetts Green, Maidenhead, Berkshire SL6 6QZ　　　Nearest Road A4

Burchett's Place is set in private grounds offering peace and tranquillity in picturesque unspoilt countryside. The house offers an enchanting combination of country house elegance with a warm homely atmosphere, perfect for relaxation. An ideal base for exploring beautiful Berkshire countryside. Close to Marlow, Henley, Windsor and conveniently situated (20 mins) from Heathrow and less than 1 hour from London. Bedrooms are spacious and delightfully furnished with beautiful antique furniture. The main drawing room has a magnificent open fire. Full English breakfast is served.

Hillier Family
Tel: 01628 825023
Fax: 01628 826672

B&B from £27.50 Rooms 1 single, 1 twin, 1 double, 1 family, all en-suite, No smoking, Children welcome, Pets by arrangement, Open all year, Map Ref F

Woodpecker Cottage, Warren Row, near Maidenhead, Berkshire RG10 8QS　　　Nearest Road A4

A tranquil woodland retreat away from crowds and traffic yet within ¹/₂ hour of Heathrow, Windsor, Henley and Oxford. Set in a delightful garden of about 1 acre and surrounded by woods where deer abound. The ground floor comprises en-suite double room with its own entrance, en-suite single, and a twin room with private bathroom. All have tea/coffee making facilities, and TV. There is a cosy sitting room with log fires in winter. A full English breakfast includes home made bread and jam made from fruit grown in the garden. Local pubs and restaurants are within easy reach. Barbecue area. E Mail: WOODCOT@MASTERKEY.CO.UK

Michael & Joanna Power
Tel: 01628 822772
Fax: 01628 822125

B&B from £20pp, Rooms 1 twin with private bathroom, 1 en-suite single, 1 en-suite double, No smoking, Minimum age 8, Open all year, Map Ref F

Windy Brow, 204 Victoria Road, Wargrave, Berkshire RG10 8AJ Nearest Road A4

Windy Brow is a large Victorian family home on the edge of this Thameside village. Heather Carver has done B&B for 10 years. All rooms are comfortable and traditionally furnished. Breakfast cooked in the Aga is served in the conservatory overlooking the garden and fields in the summer. Good food pubs and riverside restaurant within walking distance. All rooms have CTV, tea/coffee making facilities and hair dryer. Off road parking. Windsor 10 miles, Heathrow 1/2 hour, M4 5 miles, Henley 3 miles. One downstairs en-suite room.

Heather & Michael Carver
Tel: 01189 403336

B&B from £22.50-£27.50pp, Rooms 1 single, 2 twin/double, 1 family, some en-suite, No smoking, Children over 8, Pets by arrangement, Open all year excpet Christmas & Boxing Day, Map Ref F

Blackwell Farm, Latimer, Buckinghamshire HP5 1TN Nearest Road A404

Blackwell Farm is a 15th century farmhouse set in 200 acres of farm and woodland. The comfortable bedrooms all have tea/coffee making facilities and most are en-suite. One bedroom has a 4-poster. Guests may use the heated swimming pool and all weather tennis court. Conveniently situated for Heathrow, Windsor, Oxford and Cambridge which are between 20 minutes and 1 hour away by car. London is 30 minutes away by underground.

Annabel & David Briggs
Tel: 01494 762190
Fax: 01494 762190

B&B from £30pp, Rooms 1 single, 1 twin, 2 double, most en-suite, No smoking, Children welcome, No pets, Open all year except New Year, Map Ref G

Spinney Lodge Farm, Forest Road, Hanslope, Milton Keynes, Bucks MK19 7DE Nearest Road M1, J15, A508

Spinney Lodge is a arable beef and sheep farm. The lovely Victorian farm house with its large gardens has en-suite bedrooms with colour TV and tea making facilities. Evening meals by arrangement. Many historic houses and gardens to explore, and close to Woburn, Silverstone Stow, 12 minutes to Northampton, 15 minutes to Milton Keynes, 8 minutes to M1, Junction 15.

Mrs Christina Payne
Tel: 01908 510267

B&B from £18pp, Dinner by arrangement, Rooms 1 twin, 1 double, all en-suite, No smoking, Children over 12, No pets, Open all year except Christmas and New Year, Map Ref H

Richmond Lodge, Mursley, Milton Keynes, Buckinghamshire MK17 0LE Nearest Road A421

A country house set in three acres of gardens and orchard with a grass tennis court. Well situated for Woburn and Waddesdon Manor and other National Trust properties. Ideal access for central Milton Keynes and easy train journey to London (35 minutes) Leighton Buzzard to Euston. A warm comfortable house with a friendly welcome. Bedrooms are comfortable and have tea/coffee making facilities, and TV. A non-smoking home. Nearby activities include horse riding, golf and fishing.

Christine & Peter Abbey
Tel: 01296 720275

B&B from £19pp, Dinner from £12.50 by arrangement, Rooms 2 twin, 1 double, 1 en-suite, No smoking, Open all year, Map Ref I

Broadway Farm, Berkhamsted, Hertfordshire HP4 2RR　　　　　　　**Nearest Road A4251**

A warm welcome is guaranteed at Broadway, a working arable farm with own fishing lake. 3 comfortable en-suite rooms in converted buildings adjacent to farmhouse. Tea/coffee making facilities, colour TV, central heating, everything for the leisure or business guest - the relaxation of farm life in an attractive rural setting. Yet easy access to London, airports, motorways, and mainline rail services. So many places to visit, wherever your interests lie, walking, museums, historic houses, spectacular gardens, planes, canal boats and trains. EMail: a.knowles@broadway.nildram.co.uk

David & Alison Knowles
Tel/Fax: 01442 866541

B&B from £20pp, Rooms 2 twin, 1 double, all en-suite,
No smoking, Children welcome, No pets,
Open all year except Christmas & New Year, Map Ref J

Timber Hall, Cold Christmas, Ware, Hertfordshire SG12 7SN　　　　　　　**Nearest Road A10**

Timber Hall is a warm, welcoming house of great character in a quiet location in the Rib Valley and about half way between London and Cambridge. There are colour TV's and tea/coffee in all the bedrooms, and there is a large drawing room. There is a fine garden and good walks from the house. The varied eating places in the locality include an excellent pub restaurant at the end of the country lane to the house.

Mr & Mrs Shand
Tel: 01920 466086
Fax: 01920 462739

B&B from £20pp, Rooms 2/3 single, 1/2 twin, 1 double, some with private
bathroom, No smoking, Children over 8 years, Pets by arrangement,
Open all year except Christmas and New Year, Map Ref K

Please mention
THE GREAT BRITISH
BED & BREAKFAST
when booking your accommodation

"Enter these enchanted woods,
You who dare"
George Meredith

CAMBRIDGESHIRE &

There is a remarkable choice of venues in this area for the holiday-maker. In few other parts of the country would one find so much variation of scenery. In the south of Cambridgeshire are the gently rolling hills and chalk downs, beechwoods and lofty elms. This is a place rich in manor houses, churches and quaint villages, a place defended by the Anglo-Saxons who built their massive earthworks, Fleam Dyke, Devil's Dyke and Bran Ditch to keep out their covetous neighbours. In the north is the treeless bleak and lonely Fen with its wide vistas, strong winds...but fabulous sunsets.

Northamptonshire, the county of 'spires and squires', of wonderful churches and fine country houses, sits on its bed of glorious Cotswold limestone, which forms the Northamptonshire Uplands. This gently undulating country rises to about seven hundred feet above sea level in places.

The cities in this lovely area are naturally enough irresistible attractions. Cambridge, the home of arguably the greatest and certainly one of the oldest universities is a city of seemingly endless pleasures. It is a bustling market town and at the same time a place of cloistered peace. There are thirty colleges distributed over the city, many extremely old and each with a fascinating history. The town developed round the Anglo-Saxon bridge over the river, and William the Conqueror built his castle on the hill in 1068. The heart of the city is probably King's Parade, with grand old houses lining one side and King's College the other. Here too is glorious King's College Chapel begun in 1446 by Henry VI, the founder of the college. The delights of Cambridge are many but the city is also the centre for excellent excursions...to Anglesey Abbey, a National Trust property with impressive grounds...Wimpole Hall, also National Trust, a fantastic Georgian hall with restored Victorian stables and a large park containing rare breeds of domestic animals. Not to be missed is the spectacular Duxford Air Museum, a part of London's Imperial War Museum which houses Europe's largest collection of military aircraft.

Ely, an island in the fens until in the seventeenth century, when the fens were drained, infact takes its name from the old Saxon word Elig, which means 'eel island'. The small town is dwarfed by its magnificent cathedral. The west front and tower are Norman but in 1250 the east end was rebuilt in Purbeck marble to superb effect. The fine octagonal lantern based upon eight oak pillars is the work of Alan of Walsingham. To the south of Ely is Wicken Fen, the oldest nature reserve in Britain and a heaven for birdwatchers.

Peterborough until 1965 was administered as a separate county - the Soke of Peterborough, and flourished from the nineteenth century as a prosperous industrial town. Little remains of the old Peterborough...but the cathedral

NORTHAMPTONSHIRE

is a gem. The Norman nave has an impressive early thirteenth century painted roof contemporary with its equally impressive west front.

Northampton on the River Nene was described by Daniel Defoe as 'the handsomest and best built town in all this part of England' the reason very probably being that the town was destroyed by a great fire in 1675, and was rebuilt to a spacious and inspired plan. Northampton possesses one of only four round Norman churches in England, based upon the Crusader's reports of the Holy Sepulchre in Jerusalem. St. Matthew's church can boast some quite remarkable modern art, commissioned in the 1940s by its vicar, including a Madonna and Child by Henry Moore and a Crucifixion by Graham Sutherland. Not surprisingly for a town at the centre of the shoe industry, the town's museum contains the largest collection of boots and shoes in the world!

Huntingdon is an interesting town lying on the north bank of the Great Ouse and linked to Godmanchester by a fourteenth century bridge. The town is closely associated with the Cromwell family. Oliver Cromwell was born in Huntingdon in 1599, his great grandfather had a manor here and Oliver's grandfather even entertained Queen Elizabeth I here in 1564. Oliver attended the grammar school converted from the old Hospital of St. John the Baptist in 1565, as did the young Samuel Pepys some years later. Near Huntingdon is that other St. Ives....once called Slepe, but renamed strangely enough when the remains of a Persian Bishop St. Ivo were miraculously discovered in a field near the village.

There is now and has been great industrial achievement in this area - it was, after all at the Cavendish Laboratory in Cambridge that Rutherford split the atom....but within a few short miles of its industrial centres are wonderful areas of typically English countryside.

CAMBRIDGESHIRE &

Places to Visit

Fitzwilliam Museum, *Cambridge* ~ one of England's oldest museums with many antiquities, ceramics, illuminated manuscripts and paintings by Monet, Renoir, Picasso and Constable.

Kings College Chapel, *Cambridge* ~ built between 1446 and 1516, it is one of the most important examples of late medieval English architecture. The Chapel is 88 metres long, 12 metres wide and 29 metres high as instructed by Henry VI.

Ely Cathedral, *Cambridgeshire* ~ the cathedral took 268 years to complete, from when it was started in 1068. Itl dominates the small market town of Ely and the surrounding fens.

Anglesey Abbey, *Cambridgeshire* ~ the original abbey was built in 1135 but the only the crypt survived the Dissolution and was later incorporated into a manor house with furniture from various periods and a rare seascape by Gainsborough.

Imperial War Museum, *Duxford* ~ Duxford was a Spitfire base during the Battle of Britian, now it houses over 120 historic aircraft, midget submarines, military vehicles and a collection of civil aircraft including the prototype Concorde 001. In the summer major air displays are held.

Wicken Fen, *near Soham* ~ over 750 acres of undrained fenland owned by the National Trust, showing how East Anglia would have been before the 17th century.

Althorp, *near Northampton* ~ the family home of the Princess of Wales, with many fine pictures and porcelain.

Rockingham Castle, *near Market Harborough, Northamptonshire* ~ a Norman gateway and walls surrounding a mostly Elizabethan house with extensive gardens. Pictures and Rockingham china are also on display.

Holdenby House, *near Northampton* ~ with Elizabethan garden, original arched entrance, terraces, ponds and falconry and rare breeds centre.

Lamport Hall, *near Northampton* ~ a 17th and 18th century house with a programme of concerts and special events. The house also includes paintings, furniture and china.

▼ *The Bridge of Sighs, Cambridge*

Rushton Triangular Lodge, *near Kettering* ~ built by Sir Thomas Tresham in 1593. Everything about the building is triangular with three sides, three floors and trefoil windows.

Delapre Abbey, *Northampton* ~ orginally built as a Cluniac nunnery in 1145, most of its existing building dates from its rebuilding for the Tate family after the Dissolution of Monastries.

Kelmarsh Hall, *Northampton* ~ designed by James Gibbs, it was built in the 1720's and is one of two only surviving houses by this architect. The south lodge gates were designed in the late 18th century but were only made in the 1960's when the original plans where discovered.

54

NORTHAMPTONSHIRE

◀ Clipston,
Northamptonshire

▼ The 15th century
Bridge and Chapel,
St Ives, Cambridgeshire

Cathedral House, 17 St Mary's Street, Ely, Cambridgeshire CB7 4ER   **Nearest Road A10**

Cathedral House is situated in the centre of Ely within the shadow of its famous cathedral known as, 'the ship of the Fens' and within 2 minutes walk of Cromwell's House, the stained glass museum, shops and restaurants. A Grade II listed town house retaining many of its original features. Accommodation comprises 1 twin en-suite, a family suite and a luxurious double en-suite. All have TV and tea/coffee makers and views of the walled garden. A choice of full English or continental breakfast is served in the dining room overlooking the garden.

see PHOTO opposite

Jenny & Robin Farndale
Tel/Fax: 01353 662124

B&B from £25pp, Rooms 1 twin, 1 double, 1 family, all en-suite,
No smoking, No pets,
Open mid January - mid December, Map Ref A

Hill House Farm, 9 Main Street, Coveney, Ely, Cambridgeshire CB6 2DJ   **Nearest Road A10, A142**

A warm welcome awaits you at this spacious Victorian farmhouse, situated in the quiet village of Coveney, 3 miles west of the historic cathedral city of Ely. With open views of the surrounding countryside. Easy access to Cambridge, Newmarket and Huntingdon. Ideally placed for touring Cambridgeshire, Norfolk, and Suffolk. Wicken Fen and Welney Wildfowl Refuge are nearby. Bedrooms are tastefully furnished and decorated, have central heating, TV, clock radio, and tea/coffee making facilities. (1 on the ground floor). A comfortable lounge and garden available for guests' use. ETB 2 Crowns Highly Commended.

Mrs Hilary Nix
Tel: 01353 778369

B&B from £19pp, Rooms 1 twin, 2 double, all en-suite,
No smoking, Minimum age 12, No pets,
Open all year except Christmas, Map Ref B

Queensberry, 196 Carter Street, Fordham, Ely, Cambridgeshire CB7 5JU   **Nearest Road A14**

A warm welcome at this very English home a Georgian house set peacefully in large gardens on edge of village. 'Queensberry' is the ideal base from which to tour East Anglia: visit the University city of Cambridge; Historical Cathedral of Ely, "The Ship of the Fens", the famous market town of Bury St Edmunds and Newmarket the horseracing centre of the world. First village off A14 on Newmarket to Ely A142 road. Good restaurant within walking distance. Ample safe parking within the grounds.

see PHOTO on page 59

Jan & Malcolm Roper
Tel: 01638 720916
Fax: 01638 720233

B&B from £20-£25pp, Dinner by arrangement, Rooms 1 single, 1 twin,
1 double, 1 en-suite, No smoking, Children welcome,
Pets by arrangement, Open all year except Christmas, Map Ref C

Yardleys, Orchard Pightle, Hadstock, Cambridge CB1 6PQ   **Nearest Road A1307/A11/M11**

Yardleys is a very comfortably modern house in a quiet location in the pretty village of Hadstock, with thatched cottages, and Saxon church. Bedrooms, all with private facilities, have tea/coffee trays. Guest's lounge has TV. Gillian, a competent cook, enjoys welcoming visitors to her home. Evening meals by arrangement or try local pubs serving good food. Yardley's is convenient for Cambridge, Newmarket, Duxford, several stately homes, the pretty villages of Suffolk and Essex, or London one hour by train.

Gillian & John Ludgate
Tel/Fax: 01223 891822

B&B from £19.50pp, Dinner from £10.50, Rooms 2 twin, 1 double,
all en-suite, No smoking, Children welcome, No pets,
Open February - December, Map Ref D

---

left, Cathedral House, Ely - see this page for details   **57**

Model Farm, Little Gransden, Cambridgeshire SG19 3EA　　　　　Nearest Road B1046

A warm, friendly welcome awaits visitors to our farmhouse. Set in peaceful rural surroundings, the house offers lovely views over open countryside. The farmhouse was built in the 1870's of local bricks, and retains many of its original features while offering modern comforts. The former servant's rooms have been converted to provide a bedroom, with its own entrance via a spiral staircase. All the thoughtfully equipped bedrooms are en-suite with colour TV and tea/coffee facilities. Full cooked breakfast is available with home produced honey. EMail: modelfm@globalnet.co.uk

Mrs Sue Barlow
Tel/Fax: 01767 677361

B&B from £18pp, Rooms 1 double, 1 family, all en-suite, No smoking, Children welcome, Pets welcome, Open all year except Christmas and New Year, Map Ref E

Purlins, 12 High Street, Little Shelford, Cambridge CB2 5ES　　　　　Nearest Road M11/A10

An individually designed country house set in two acres of fields and woodland, in a quiet pretty village on the Cam four miles south of Cambridge. An ideal centre for visiting colleges, cathedrals, country-houses, the Imperial War Museum, and bird-watching. The comfortable en-suite bedrooms (two ground-floor) all have colour TV, radio and tea/coffee making facilities; a conservatory serves as the guests' sitting-room, and breakfast is provided to suit most tastes. Restaurants are nearby. On-drive parking for three cars.

Olga & David Hindley
Tel/Fax: 01223 842643

B&B from £21pp, Rooms 1 twin, 2 double, all en-suite, No smoking, Children over 8 years, No pets, Open mid February - December, Map Ref F

Chiswick House, Meldreth, Royston, Cambridgeshire SG8 6LZ　　　　　Nearest Road A10

see PHOTO on page 60

Chiswick House, 8 miles south of Cambridge, is an original timber-framed building dating from the late 1400's. Over the years it has been altered and extended but it remains fundamentally as it was built 500 years ago. Old beams, polished oak and flowers in every room combined with a warm welcome provide an atmosphere to relax in comfort. The royal crest of King James I is to be found above the fireplace in the drawing room. It is believed that the house was used by King James as a hunting lodge. The Jacobean panelling in the dining room dates from that period.

Mrs Bernice Elbourn
Tel: 01763 260242

B&B £21pp, Rooms 2 twin, 4 double, all en-suite, No smoking, Open all year, Map Ref G

Berry House, High Street, Waterbeach, Cambridgeshire CB5 9JU　　　　　Nearest Road A10

This lovely Georgian home is grade II listed building situated in a traditional English Village convenient for both the historic cities of Cambridge (3 miles) and Ely (8 miles). Ample private parking, a large garden in which to relax and two friendly dogs to provide a warm welcome. Both double en-suite bedrooms are situated in the beamed coach house which is always available to guests with large home cooked breakfasts and lively dinner parties held in the traditional dining room.

Phil & Sally Myburgh
Tel: 01223 860702
Fax: 01223 570588

B&B from £25-£30pp, Dinner from £20, Rooms 2 double, all en-suite, Children welcome, Pets by arrangement, Open all year except Christmas and New Year, Map Ref H

right, Queensberry, Fordham - see page 57

Threeways House, Everdon, Daventry, Northants NN11 6BL **Nearest Road M1/M40/A5/A45**

Threeways is a character stone house with delightful gardens, on the Green of this charming peaceful, conservation village. The guest rooms are separated from the family house by a large terrace. Come and indulge yourself! The very comfortably furnished bedrooms all have charming views, TV's, en-suite bathrooms, tea/coffee trays and central heating. We are proud of our delicious breakfasts which we serve in an elegant dining room. There are many nearby attractions to visit and idyllic local walks to enjoy. ETB 3 Crown Highly Commended.

Elizabeth Barwood
Tel: 01327 361631 or 0374 428242
Fax: 01327 361359

B&B from £22.50pp, Rooms 1 single, 1 twin, 1 double, 1 family, all en-suite, Restricted smoking, Children welcome, Pets restricted, Open all year, Map Ref I

The Maltings, Aldwincle, Oundle, Northamptonshire NN14 3EP **Nearest Road A605, A14, A1**

A lovely 16th century house and former agricultural maltings and granary. The main accommodation is in the granary which has been converted to 2 bedrooms 2 bathrooms and a sitting room. The remainder of the accommodation is in the beamed house which has Inglenook fireplaces. All bedrooms have private bathroom and tea/coffee making facilities. There is a very peaceful atmosphere, a lovely garden with unusual plants which is occasionally open under the National Garden Scheme. Many places of interest, and activities nearby. Visa/Mastercard accepted.

Margaret & Nigel Faulkner
Tel: 01832 720233
Fax: 01832 720326

B&B from £24.50pp, Rooms 3 en-suite twin, No smoking, Minimum age 10, No pets indoors, Open all year, Map Ref J

Rose Cottage, Tod Green, Woodend, Towcester NN12 8RZ **Nearest Road A5, A43**

Rose Cottage is situated on the edge of the picturesque village of Woodend. Each guest room is attractively furnished, comfortable beds, TV, tea/coffee making facilities. Log fires in winter and a flower filled sun terrace and garden for enjoyment on warmer days. Hospitality, comfort and tranquillity at its very best. AGA cooking, home grown vegetables and free range eggs (own). National Trust Canons Ashby and Stowe Gardens are within easy reach also Sulgrave Manor. Safe off road parking in driveway.

Mrs Ann Davey-Turner
Tel: 01327 860968
Fax: 01327 860968

B&B from £22.50pp, Dinner from £12, Rooms, 1 twin en-suite, 1 double with private bathroom, Children over 7, Dogs at our discretion, Open all year, Map Ref K

Please mention
THE GREAT BRITISH
BED & BREAKFAST
when booking your accommodation

left, Chiswick House, Meldreth - see page 58

CHESHIRE, MERSEYSIDE & GREATER MANCHESTER

To regard this area as the industrial centre of the northwest and dismiss it out of hand as a holiday venue would be extremely short sighted, as even the great commercial and industrial centres of Liverpool and Manchester have their 'other' side, and an extremely fascinating side it is. Manchester, the commercial centre for the Lancashire cotton industry, built impressive monuments to its prosperity, the enormous Gothic Town Hall designed by Alfred Waterhouse possesses a quite remarkable marble interior. In Deansgate, the flamboyant facade of Rylands Library expresses the Mancunian's pride in their success, as indeed does the Free Trade Hall, the Athenaeum and the Theatre Royal. Modern Manchester can offer the impressive G-Mex exhibition centre; the wonderful Museum of Science and Industry; and for television enthusiasts the Granada Studios offer a tour, which includes the set of the TV soap 'Coronation Street'; also there is the new MetroLink, the light rail tram system which crosses the city. The growth of the cotton industry saw Bolton (now a part of Greater Manchester) prosper, and here is a remarkable black and white half-timbered fifteenth century mansion known fancifully as Hall-i'-th'-Wood. Samuel Crompton, who was born in Bolton and lived in the mansion for a time is said to have invented his spinning mule here. The spinning mule, together with Hargreave's spinning jenny and Arkwright's water frame are to be seen in the Tonge Moor Textile Museum. Not to be outdone by its sister city, Liverpool, once England's second greatest port, is revamping many of the fine buildings that witnessed its proud maritime past. The Albert Dock, built in 1846 has been renovated to include shops, cafes and an offshoot of the London Tate Gallery and also 'The Beatles Story' a sight and sound experience of the music of the 1960s. The city provides a long list of modern galleries and museums, including an impressive Maritime museum tracing the history of the port. For the football enthusiast, Liverpool Football Club Visitor's Centre, Anfield Road, offers a fascinating display of trophies and memorabilia. Then there is the intriguing Planetarium as well as the traditional Walker Art Gallery, one of the countries finest provincial galleries.

The two Liverpool cathedrals, each masterpieces in their own right, face each other across the city. The Anglican cathedral a twentieth century Gothic structure designed by Sir Giles Gilbert Scott. The Roman Catholic cathedral designed by Sir Frederick Gibberd has in its modernist lantern tower some stained glass by John Piper and Patrick Reyntiens.

On the curve of the River Dee lies Chester, founded by the Romans during the first century AD as the main base for their legions in the northwest. The Roman name for the town was Deva, however Chester comes from the Latin term Castra Devana meaning 'camp on the Dee'. Chester can claim to be the only city in the country having a complete circuit of Medieval wall. During the Middle Ages the city was an extremely prosperous port, that is until the River Dee silted up. The red sandstone cathedral, restored during the nineteenth century, was originally the church of a Benedictine abbey and became a cathedral in 1541; the Medieval Mystery Plays have been revived and are performed outside the cathedral. The compact city is renowned for its picturesque central streets, a mixture of Tudor half-timbered buildings, Georgian red brick houses and nineteenth century 'fake' black and white buildings. Chester's pride is its wonderful old Rows, an upper tier of shops above those on street level forming a continuous covered shopping arcade. An elaborate wrought-iron clock presented to the city in 1897 to commemorate the Diamond Jubilee of Queen Victoria stands over the east gate of the city. Chester race meeting held since the sixteenth century on the Roodee, a meadow by the river, is the oldest meeting in England.

These three cities dominate this area, but there is a wealth of glorious scenery to explore a short drive from these centres. The lovely Cheshire Plain, the Delamere Forest north of Tarporley which comprises four hundred acres of dense woodland, including Hatch Mere and Oak Mere. The spectacular ruin of Beeston Castle perched on the summit of Peckforton Hills gives view of no less than eight counties, while from rugged Helsby Hill are superb views across Helsby Marsh to the Mersey. Knutsford is an attractive town of old black and white houses, said to have acquired its name from King Canute who it seems forded the local stream. Mrs. Gaskell by the way, used Knutsford as the model for 'Cranford' in her novel of that name. Two miles away is magnificent Tatton Park, fifty-four acres of formal gardens laid out in the eighteenth century by Humphrey Repton. The Hall is one of the National Trust's most visited properties.

If it's seaside that appeals, then Wallasey on the Wirral peninsular has wonderful sands, promenade, and all the amenities of a modern resort within a very short distance of the bright lights of Liverpool. The Wirral was once a great royal forest and game reserve...and also the haunt of footpads. The salt-marsh and tidal flats of the upper Dee estuary is now a great attraction for bird-watchers, the whole area being a wintering ground for waders and wildfowl.

CHESHIRE, MERSEYSIDE

Places to Visit

Quarry Bank Mill, *Styal, Cheshire* ~ one of the very first factories to use water to power its textile machines. Founded in 1784, it has now been fully restored as a working museum with England's largest working waterwheel, measuring over twenty four feet high and weighing over fifty tons.

Liverpool Cathedral, *Liverpool* ~ the world's largest Anglican cathedral, it was completed in 1978 after seventy six years of building work. Made from red sandstone, it was designed by Sir Giles Gilbert Scott and the foundation stone was laid by Edward VII in 1904.

Croxeth Hall and Country Park, *near Liverpool* ~ a historic mansion set in five hundred acres of parkland. The rooms have been recreated and furnished in Edwardian style. Other attractions include a Victorian walled garden, rare breeds of farm animals, miniature railway and adventure playground.

Speke Hall, *near Liverpool* ~ a half timbered manor house, parts date from 1490 with courtyard, dry moat and impressive Great Hall. There is also a 16th century priest hole, William Morris wallpaper and Mortlake tapestries.

Tatton Park, *Knutsford* ~ a Georgian house on a country estate with tree lined drive, Japanese gardens, orangery, sailing centre and adventure playground. The Old Hall has rooms showing various periods from the Middle Ages to the 1950's.

Albert Dock, *Liverpool* ~ Grade I listed warehouses, they have been restored to include television studios, museums, galleries, shops, restaurants and business premises.

Museum of Science and Industry, *Manchester* ~ part of the Castlefield Urban Heritage Park, the museum looks at Manchester's industrial past with collections of steam engines, display's on the Liverpool and Manchester Railway and the Electric Gallery about the history of domestic power. Across the road in the Air and Space Gallery, there are hot air balloons and space suits.

Granada Studio Tours, *Manchester* ~ at Granada Studios visit various television shows including the set of Coronation Street, Britains longest running soap opera.

Dunham Massey Hall, *near Altrincham* ~ a country house set in parkland. Thirty rooms in the house are on show with 18th century furniture and silverware. The National Trust have restored the gardens, which include an 18th century orangery and a well house which was used to supply the house with fresh water.

Jodrell Bank, *near Knutsford* ~ an award winning Science Centre standing at the foot of the Lovell telescope, one of the world's largest fully steerable radio telescopes. There are exhibitions on astronomy, satellites and space, as well as a thirty five acre arboretum with over two thousand species of plants.

▲ *The Rows, Chester*

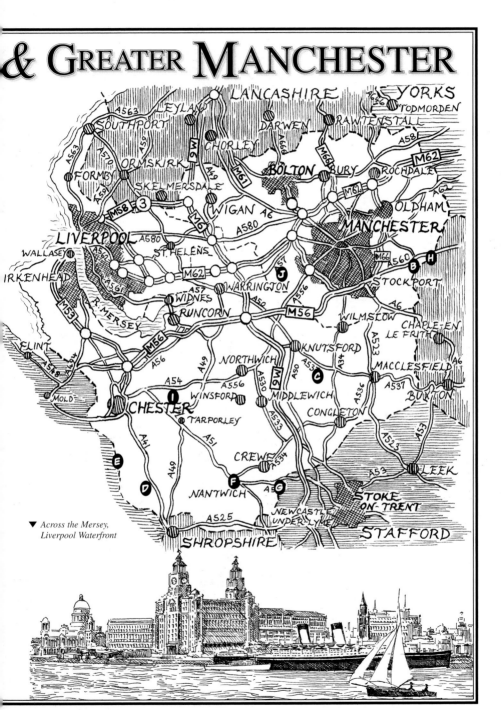

& GREATER MANCHESTER

▼ *Across the Mersey,*
Liverpool Waterfront

The Mount, Lesters Lane, Higher Kinnerton, Chester CH4 9BQ   **Nearest Road A55**

Victorian country house on the Chester/North Wales border set in an extensive 3 acre garden with tennis court, croquet lawn and large vegetable garden. Spacious bedrooms all with own bathrooms, TV and tea/coffee making facilities. Drawing room and conservatory for guest's use. An ideal place to relax and explore the North Wales coast and Cheshire. 45 minutes to Liverpool and Manchester. 1 hour to Anglesey, Bodnant Gardens, Port Sunlight, historic Chester, Erdigg, Offas Dyke and Llangollen. Excellent pubs in the village, half a mile away.

Jonathan & Rachel Major
Tel: 01244 660275
Fax: 01244 660275

B&B from £20pp, Dinner £15, Rooms 2 twin with private bath, 1 double en-suite, No smoking, Children over 12, Pets by arrangement, Open all year, Map Ref A

Needhams Farm, Uplands Road, Werneth Low, Gee Cross, near Hyde, Cheshire SK14 3AQ   **A560**

500 year old farmhouse, surrounded by scenic views. Residential licence. Views from all rooms. Log fires in winter. Warm welcome. Plenty of car parking. Needhams Farm is a working farm with cattle and sheep. Meals are served from 7pm to 9pm each evening. Special meals for children. Ideally situated for Manchester and surrounding areas including Manchester Airport. Nearest station is Romiley.

Mrs C Walsh
Tel: 0161 368 4610
Fax: 0161 367 9106

B&B from £16-£20pp, Evening Meals £7, Rooms 4 double, 1 family, 1 twin, 1 single, 6 en-suite, Open all year, Map Ref B

The Dog Inn, Wellbank Lane, Over Peover, near Knutsford, Cheshire WA16 8UP   **Nearest Road A50**

The Dog Inn nestles in the unspoilt countryside of Cheshire. This very popular pub is adorned with hanging baskets in the summer and offers the warmth of coal fires in the winter. Renowned for it's delicious food and large portions. The rooms are very well appointed with many extras. Guests are made to feel very welcome. The breakfasts are large. Good range of real ales, malt whiskey and fine wines. Tap room offers pools, darts, TV etc. Quiz Thursday and Sunday. Live music on Tuesday/Wednesday.

Frances & Jim Cunningham
Tel: 01625 861421

B&B from £47.50pp, Dinner from £7.95, Rooms 2 twin, 1 double, all en-suite, Children welcome, No pets, Open all year except Christmas night, Map Ref C

Laurel Farm, Chorlton Lane, Malpas, Cheshire SY14 7ES   **Nearest Road A41**

To one side of the drive is a large duck-pond, (cheeky ducks may well entertain you!). An outstanding peaceful situation in possibly some of the loveliest countryside in the county bordering North Wales and Shropshire. A beautiful farmhouse dating from 17th century. Matching the welcoming ambience is a house full or original character, old doors, beams etc, all with comfort in mind. Graciously furnished with antiques helps create a truly friendly, happy, relaxed atmosphere. A private 2 bedroom suite - ideal 4/5 guests. Great Breakfasts. Exceptional standard. AA QQQQQ Premier Selected.

see PHOTO opposite

Mrs Anthea Few
Tel/Fax: 01948 860291

B&B from £27pp, Dinner from £20.00, Rooms 1 single, 1 twin, 2 double, 1 twin/family, all en-suite, No smoking, Children over 12 years, No pets, Open all year, Map Ref D

---

left, **Laurel Farm, Malpas** *- see this page for details*   67

Broughton House, Threapwood, Malpas, Cheshire SY14 7AN Nearest Road A41

A peaceful and comfortable non-smoking home within the elegant Georgian stables built around the cobbled courtyard of a former 17th century mansion. An hour from Manchester. Ideal for visiting Chester and North Wales. Luxurious ground floor bedrooms, some with king-sized four-poster beds, all have en-suite bathrooms TV's, tea/coffee trays. Breakfasts usually served in the conservatory overlooking parkland with stunning views to the Welsh hills. Hard tennis court. Croquet lawn. Many charming pubs and restaurants nearby serve dinner. VISA, Mastercard, Switch accepted. Email: mcginn@broughtn.u-net.com

see PHOTO opposite

John & Valerie McGinn
Tel: 01948 770610
Fax: 01948 770472

B&B from £27pp, Rooms 1 twin, 2 double, all en-suite,
No smoking, Children from 10, No pets,
Open all year except Christmas and New Year, Map Ref E

Stoke Grange Farm, Chester Road, Nantwich, Cheshire CW5 6BT Nearest Road M6,A51

Attractive farmhouse in a picturesque canalside location. Hearty breakfast, vegetarians catered for. Individually styled en-suite rooms with colour TV. Four poster bedroom with balcony surveying Cheshire countryside also watch canal boats cruising the Shropshire Union. Relax in garden with lawns down to canal. Pets corner and peacocks. First class service at B&B and self-catering accommodation. Past Cheshire's Tourist Development Award Winners. Chester 20 mins, Crewe 10 mins. Near to Stapeley Water Gardens, Beeston and Cholmondeley castles, Jodrell Bank, Tatton Park and Chester Zoo.

Mrs Georgina West
Tel/Fax: 01270 625525

B&B from £20pp, Rooms 1 twin, 2 double, 1 family,
Restricted smoking, Children welcome, No pets,
Open all year, Map Ref F

Lea Farm, Wrinehill Road, Wybunbury, Nantwich, Cheshire CW5 7NS Nearest Road A500

Charming farmhouse set in landscaped gardens where peacocks roam on a dairy farm. Ample car parking. In beautiful rolling countryside. Spacious bedrooms. Luxury lounge. Pool, snooker, fishing available. From Nantwich take the A51 turning left at Stapeley Water Gardens. End of road turn right for village of Wybunbury, turn left down Wrinehill Road by church. 1 mile from village.

Mrs Jean Callwood
Tel: 01270 841429

B&B from £16pp (children half price if sharing with parents),
Dinner from £10, Rooms 1 double, 1 family, 1 twin, 2 en-suite,
Open all year, Map Ref G

Shire Cottage Farmhouse, Benches Lane, Marple Bridge, Stockport SK6 5RY Nearest Road A626

Real home from home accommodation in peaceful location. Magnificent views over Etherow Country Park and wooded valleys. All rooms have central heating, TV, tea/coffee making facilities, and shaver points. Some rooms are en-suite. Situated on the edge of the Peak District yet only 10 miles from airport and 15 miles from Manchester city centre. Many places of interest nearby, country homes, Derwent Dams, Quarry Bank Mill, Chatsworth House & Farm, Granada studio tours, Grand Metro Exhibition Centre, Jodrell Bank, etc. Early breakfasts can be catered for. Car parking.

Mrs Monica Sidebottom
Tel: 01457 866536

B&B from £19pp, Rooms 1 single, 1 twin, 1 double, 1 family, most en-suite,
also self catering cottage, Children welcome, Dogs by arrangement,
Open all year, Map Ref H

Roughlow Farm, Chapel Lane, Willington, Tarporley, Cheshire CW6 0PG   Nearest Road M6, A54

A delightful 18th century converted farmhouse in quiet situation with wonderful views to Shropshire and Wales. Attractive garden with cobbled courtyard and tennis court. Elegantly furnished to a high standard with en-suite facilities to 3 twin/double bedrooms. Roughlow Farm is well situated for easy access to Manchester, Chester, Wales, Liverpool and M6. From M6 (J19) take the A556 towards Chester. A54 Kelsall bypass turn left after passing Morreys Nurseries on right hand side, then left again at the pub in Waste Lane, continue bearing right at the next junction. (150 yds on left). ETB Highly Commended.

Mrs P F Sutcliffe
Tel/Fax: 01829 751199

B&B from £25pp, Dinner from £17.50 (Minimum 4 persons), Rooms 3 twin or double, all en-suite, 1 with own sitting room, Minimum age 6, No smoking, Open all year Christmas & New Year, Map Ref I

Old Packet House, Navigation Road, Broadheath, near Altrincham, Cheshire WA14 1LW   Nearest Road A556

The Old Packet House is a pretty black and white half-timbered pub. The rooms are very well-appointed with many extra touches. The atmosphere is homely, log fires in the winter, adorned with flowers in the summer. Food of a very good standard, hearty portions and can be served in smoking or non smoking areas. Pretty outside eating area to the rear of the property. Recommended by many guides. Close to M6, M62 and M56, 15 minutes to Airport. Centre of Manchester only 15 minutes away.

Frances & Jim Cunningham
Tel/Fax: 0161 929 1331

B&B from £45pp, Dinner from £10, Rooms 1 single, 1 twin, 2 double, all en-suite, Children welcome, No pets, Open all year except Christmas Day night, Map Ref J

"Blossom by blossom the spring begins"
Algernon Charles Swinburne

CORNWALL

You are seldom more than half an hour's drive from the coast in Cornwall - and what a coast! Granite cliffs withstanding the onslaught of white-crested Atlantic rollers, jagged rocks and treacherous reefs, romantic little fishing villages, wide unspoilt beaches and hidden coves, golden sands and sub-tropical flowers....a coastline that changes with amazing rapidity. This is without doubt a summer playground, with each village and town finely tuned to holiday pleasures. It is hard to believe that before the opening of the Saltash railway bridge in 1859, the River Tamar virtually isolated Cornwall from the rest of the country. Despite its holiday population there are still lonely places - Bodmin Moor, bleak, windswept and scattered with granite Tors, at its highest point, Brown Willy gives spectacular views across its barren waste. There are some fascinating ancient relics here, Hurlers Stone Circle and the Bronze Age burial chambers of Trethevy Quoit. Launceston, which once guarded the main route from Devon into Cornwall is perched on a hill with the remains of its Norman castle and quaint twisting streets. Just off the A30 is Jamaica Inn, the setting for Daphne du Maurier's novel of smugglers, tales of which abound hereabouts.....there are tales too of King Arthur and his knights. Tintagel claims to be King Arthur's Camelot, and the magnificently sited castle ruins on the impregnable headland with its steep-stepped approach certainly thrill the imagination, but the castle, built for the Earl of Cornwall in 1145, post-dates Arthur.

The tourist may find it hard to believe that up until the end of the nineteenth century Cornwall led the world in the production of tin and copper, but the hinterland is peppered with old workings, and many of today's resorts owe their development to the trade in tin, copper and lead. But it is to the coast that the holidaymakers flock. Bude, at one time notorious for shipwrecks, has a wonderful beach and is now a major surfing centre, while Padstow down the coast, though lacking a beach, can offer a glorious labyrinth of quaint streets and ancient houses - including Raleigh Court where Sir Walter Raleigh stayed when Warden of Cornwall. Newquay, the gem of this part of the coast has all the trappings of a first class resort including swimming, surfing, excellent beaches and a picturesque harbour...a far cry from its early days as a pilchard port. Further down the coast the views from St. Agnes Beacon are superb.

St. Ives needs little introduction, being a magnet to holiday makers and artists alike. Originally a fishing village of course, now what fishing is done is done by the holiday makers. The hotch-potch of cottages that line the narrow twisting streets make it a photographer's paradise. The sculptress Barbara Hepworth settled in St. Ives, as indeed did a number of twentieth century artists; her studio is now a museum. A branch of London's Tate Gallery features the St. Ives school of artists in a magnificent new gallery here. Sennen, the westernmost village in England is the spot so it is told, where King Arthur routed the Danes - against a backdrop of some of the most spectacular scenery in Cornwall. Penzance, a fine holiday centre with its Georgian houses, marks a change in climate from the harsh and rugged Atlantic coast to the lush, mild sheltered bays to the east.

Michael's Mount, a Benedictine church which became a fortress following the Dissolution, can be reached at low tide along a causeway across the sands. Lying some twenty-eight miles southwest of Land's End are the Scillies, a group of one hundred and forty or so rocky islands, although only five are inhabited. The extremely mild climate brought about by the Gulf Stream enables the Scillies to provide out of season flowers for the mainland markets. One of the Scilly Isles Tresco, is renowned for its magnificent gardens constructed around the ruins of a Benedictine Abbey by Augustus Smith and his family. Here is a graveyard of shipping wrecked on the treacherous granite reef, and the site of the first lighthouse constructed in 1858 on Bishop Rock, four miles southwest of St. Agnes. The so-called Cornish Riviera stretches from The Lizard to Looe, and Riviera is certainly no misnomer. The exceptionally mild climate brings holidaymakers in their droves to the golden sands, sub-tropical flowers and sparkling blue seas. Truro, the 'capital' of this glorious area boasts a cathedral with three spires. This is a coastline of charming and picturesque fishing villages...St. Mawes dominated by its castle is a fashionable yachting resort..

Mevagissey is a highly popular resort of narrow streets, there is breathtaking scenery and lovely beaches at Polstreath and Portmellon.... Polperro, is charming with its limewashed houses clustered round its small harbour...while Fowey is renowned for its regatta, and home of Sir Arthur Quiller-Couch who described Fowey as 'the town loved at first sight'.

Cornwall is rich in literary associations and little wonder with so much to inspire. Dame Agatha Christie was born in Torquay...Lord Tennyson called the town, 'the loveliest sea village in England'. Dylan Thomas honeymooned at Mousehole and called it 'really the loveliest village in England'. Thomas Hardy was fascinated by Tintagel. John Betjeman loved Cornwall, as did Virginia Woolf and Winston Graham, author of the Poldark books....But surely there could be no better recommendation for this quite remarkable county than that of Daphne du Maurier, who had no fewer than three Cornish homes.

Places to Visit

Antony House, *Torpoint* ~ an 18th century Queen Anne house faced with silver grey Pentewan stone and red brick, it is set in extensive grounds with a national collection of day lilies, magnolias and summer borders. Inside are excellent panelling and fine period furnishings.

Cotehele, *St Dominick, near Saltash* ~ set on the River Tamar in woodland, the medieval house was built between 1485 and 162.It has an open hall, kitchen, chapel and many private parlours and chambers. Outside are colourful terraced gardens and a valley garden with medieval dovecote. Cotehele Mill has been restored to working order with workshops. There are many woodland walks throughout the estate.

Glendurgan Gardens, *near Falmouth* ~ set in a wooded valley, a sub tropical garden with many rare and exotic plants. Other attractions are the recently restored 1833 laurel maze and the Giants Stride, a pole with ropes to swing from. The garden runs down to a beach and the tiny village of Durgan.

Jamaica Inn, *Bodmin Moor* ~ an 18th century inn with a small museum, it was made famous by Daphne du Maurier's well known tale of smuggling and romance.

Lanhydrock, *Bodmin* ~ a large house set in wooded and formal gardens above the River Fowey. It was rebuilt after a fire in 1881 but has kept many of its Jacobean features.

The Old Post Office, *Tintagel* ~ a 14th century long house with a large hall once used as a post office, now it has been restored in the fashion of the Post Office it was for nearly fifty years.

Pencarrow House & Gardens, *Bodmin* ~ an 18th century mansion set in woodlands and gardens. The house has a fine collection of paintings, china and furniture

St Michaels Mount, *near Penzance* ~ , approached by a causeway at low tide, this spectacular castle and church on top of a rocky island, dates from the 14th century. The castle has an armoury, Gothic drawing room and magnificient views towards Lands End.

Trelissick, *near Truro* ~ set in three hundred and seventy acres of parkland by the River Fal. Ornamental gardens with camellias, hydrangeas, magnolias and rhododendron. Art and craft gallery. The park has many walks and has views to the sea and Falmouth.

Trenice, *near Newquay* ~ built in 1571, this secluded Elizabethan manor house has an early gabled fagade. Inside are fireplaces, plaster ceilings, oak and walnut furniture and a collection of cloc ks. The garden has many different types of unusual plants and an orchard with many old varieties of fruit trees.

◀ *Granite Outcrop on Rough Tor*

CORNWALL

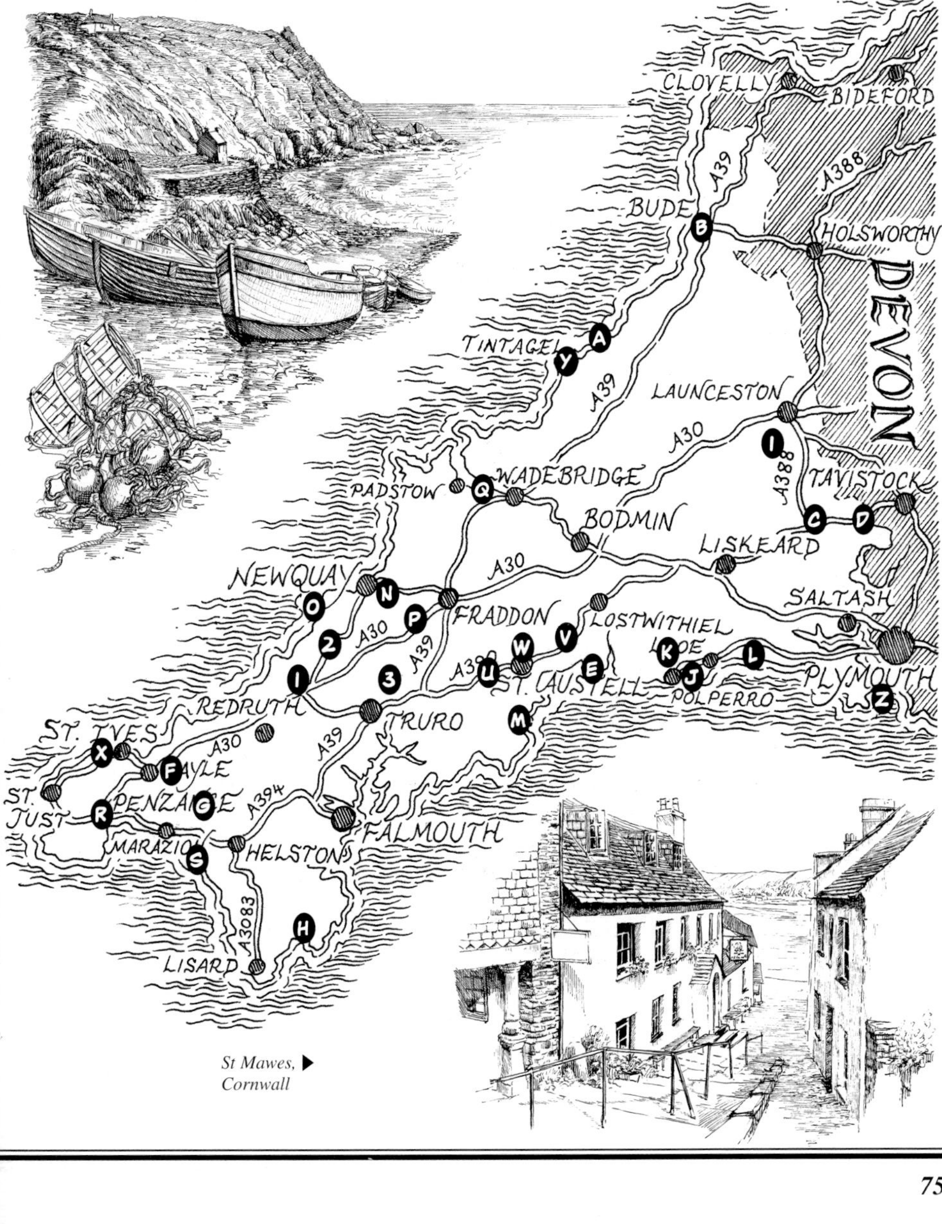

CLOVELLY
BIDEFORD
BUDE **B**
A39
A388
HOLSWORTHY
DEVON
TINTAGEL **Y A**
A39
LAUNCESTON
A30
I
A388
TAVISTOCK
PADSTOW **Q** WADEBRIDGE
BODMIN
C D
LISKEARD
SALTASH
NEWQUAY
A30
O N
P FRADDON
LOSTWITHIEL
PLYMOUTH
2 A30 **U W V** LOOE **K L**
I A39 **3** A30 **E** **J** POLPERRO **Z**
REDRUTH ST. AUSTELL
M
ST. IVES TRURO
X A30 **F**
HAYLE A39
ST. **R** PENZANCE A394
JUST **G** FALMOUTH
MARAZION **S** HELSTON
A3083
H
LISARD

St Mawes, ▶
Cornwall

75

Orchard Lodge, Gunpool Lane, Boscastle, Cornwall PL35 0AT   Nearest Road A39

Orchard Lodge, set in its own attractive gardens, is a large delightful base for a relaxing holiday. Offering 6 very pleasant guest rooms decorated and furnished to a high standard and all with modern facilities. A delicious full English or continental breakfast is served in the pretty dining room with pine furnishings and which overlooks the garden. Ample car parking. An ideal base for touring Cornwall. Overlooks the Jordan Valley. A warm and friendly welcome awaits you.

Bill & Eileen Purslow
Tel: 01840 250418

B&B from £18pp, Rooms 1 twin, 2 double, all en-suite, No smoking, No children, No pets, Open March - December, Closed Christmas & Open New Year, Map Ref A

Bottreaux House Hotel & Restaurant, Boscastle, Cornwall PL35 0BG   Nearest Road B3266

Bottreaux House stands in the old conservation area of this unspoilt beautiful harbour village. Our Three Crown Highly Commended rating offers superb accommodation for the discerning traveller. Bedrooms include all the refinments you may expect and direct dial phones, the restaurant offers a highly regarded comprehensive menu at affordable prices, and the warm relaxed atmosphere, together with the candlelit tables make this a place for romantics and lovers. The walking in the area is wonderful and we offer free use of mountain bikes. Http:/www.chycor.co.uk

Hazel & Graham Mee
Tel: 01840 250231
Fax: 01840 250170

B&B from £14-£19pp, Dinner from £12.00, Rooms 2 twin, 4 double, 1 family, all en-suite, Restricted smoking, Children from 9, Pets by arrangement, Open all year, Map Ref A

Cliff Hotel, Maer Down Road, Crooklets Beach, Bude, Cornwall EX23 8NG   Nearest Road A39

The Cliff has a wonderful location being 200 yards from Crooklets Beach and next to the National Trust cliff walk, "an area of outstanding natural beauty". Our facilities are first class with - Indoor Swimming pool, gym, all weather bowling green and tennis, all within 5 acres of lawns and with a wild flower mead. We feel our greatest attribute though is the home cooked fresh food and informal ambience.

see PHOTO opposite

Brian & Lin Sibley
Tel/Fax: 01288 353110

B&B from £22.50pp, Dinner available, Rooms 2 single, 2 twin, 4 double, 7 family, all en-suite, Children & pets welcome, Open April - end September, Map Ref B

Dozmary, Tors View Close, Tavistock Road, Callington PL17 7DY   Nearest Road A388, A390

Dozmary is a deceptively spacious dormer bungalow situated in a quiet cul-de-sac just a few minutes walk from the town centre. Ideal location for exploring south Devon, Cornwall, many National Trust properties and English Heritage monuments. Excellent views of Dartmoor, Bodmin Moor and the Tamar Valley from nearby Kit Hill Country Park. All rooms are en-suite and have colour TV, radio clock alarm, tea/coffee, central heating and hair dryer. ETB 1 crown commended. A reduction of £1 per person per night for 4 nights or more consecutive stay.

Thelma & Henry Wills
Tel: 01579 383677

B&B from £16pp, Rooms 1 twin, 1 double, 1 family, all en-suite, No smoking, No pets, Open all year except New Year, Map Ref C

---

left, Cliff Hotel, Bude - see this page for details

Tamar Valley B&B, Kelly Cottage, Lower Kelly, Calstock, Cornwall PL18 9RX   Nearest Road A390

Pat and Bill welcome you to share the tranquillity of their comfortable riverside home and garden. Rooms south facing each have a balcony where you can watch salmon leap and the activities of wildfowl. A short walk brings you to the National Trust Cothele House and gardens. St Mellion golf club, Dartmoor and the coast are within easy reach. Bus and train services to Plymouth and areas from our picturesque village. Evening meals by reservation. Open all year.

Pat & Bill Parnell
Tel: 01822 832380

B&B from £20pp, Dinner from £12.00, Rooms 2 twin, 2 double, 1 family, most en-suite, Restricted smoking, Children welcome, Pets by arrangement, Open all year, Map Ref D

Trevanion Guest House, 70 Lostwithiel Street, Fowey, Cornwall PL23 1BQ   Nearest Road A390/B3269

A warm and friendly welcome awaits you at this comfortable and spacious 16th Century Merchants House situated in the historic town of Fowey in the heart of Daphne Du Maurier country. An ideal base from which to walk the Coastal Path, visit the Lost Gardens of Heligan and National Trust Houses and Gardens, or explore the Cornish Riviera. All bedrooms are well furnished and have colour TV and tea/coffee making facilities. Large family room, most en-suite rooms. Non smoking. Car Parking.

Jill & Bob Bullock
Tel: 01726 832602

B&B from £16pp, Rooms, 1 single, 1 twin, 2 double, 1 family, most en-suite, No smoking, Children over 4 years, No pets, Open March - December, Map Ref E

Treglisson, Hayle, Cornwall TR27 5JT   Nearest Road A30

Situated in the quiet Cornish countryside Treglisson, a listed 18 century former mine captain's home, offers pretty en-suite rooms with comfortable beds, colour TV, tea/coffee making facilities, hair dryers and fresh flowers. Start the day with a swim in the indoor heated pool before tucking into a hearty breakfast which is served in the elegant dining room or conservatory. St Michael's Mount, St Ives, Lands End and many more places are within easy reach of Treglison.

Mrs C Runnalls
Tel: 01736 753141
Fax: 01736 753141

B&B from £19pp,
Rooms 2 double, 2 family, 1 twin,
Open all year except Christmas & New Year, Map Ref F

Little Pengwedna Farmhouse, Helston, Cornwall TR13 0AY   Nearest Road B3302

A friendly Cornish welcome and hearty home-cooked breakfast make a stay at this charming farmhouse a real treat. Renowned for cattle breeding, Little Pengwedna is ideally positioned for touring either coast, visiting beautiful Cornish gardens and many more places of interest. You'll find the 19th century granite farmhouse prettily and comfortably decorated with original paintings and an abundance of fresh flowers. Locally there are many excellent eating houses, including specialist fish resturants. We're easily reached on the B3302, just a few minutes from the A30.

Iris White
Tel/Fax: 01736 850649

B&B from £19pp, Rooms 1 twin, 2 double, most en-suite, Restricted smoking, Children welcome, No pets, Open all year, Map Ref G

Mellan House, Coverack, Helston, Cornwall TR12 6TH   **Nearest Road B3294**

Mellan House stands in a large garden and is 5 minutes from a safe sandy beach. Fishing, boating and windsurfing are available and a golf course is 6 miles away at Mullion. Coverack is a beautiful small fishing village in an area of outstanding natural beauty. Bedrooms have sea views and garden views and tea/coffee making facilities, and there is a comfortable lounge with colour television available for guests' use.

Mrs Muriel Fairhurst
Tel: 01326 280482

B&B from £18per person, Rooms 2 double, 1 single,
No smoking, Pets by arrangement,
Open all year except Christmas, Map Ref H

Hornacott, South Petherwin, Launceston, Cornwall PL15 7LH   **Nearest Road B3254**

Our 18th Century house nestles in a valley with sloping gardens and a stream, in part of Cornwall's unspoilt countryside. Our guests stay in a suite of twin bedroom with en-suite bathroom, and sitting room with TV, CD player and both bed and sitting rooms have French windows facing over our garden. There are a wealth of places to visit within easy reach from the National Trust properties of Lanhydrock and Cotehele, historic Launceston ancient capital of Cornwall, rugged Bodmin Moor and the spectacular coasts.

Mary-Anne Otway-Ruthven
Tel/Fax: 01566 782461

B&B from £25pp, Dinner by arrangement,
Open all year except Christmas & New Year, Map Ref I

Allhays Country House, Talland Bay, Looe, Cornwall PL13 2JB   **Nearest Road A387**

Set in extensive gardens just a few minutes walk from the sea. Allhays stands on a gently sloping hillside overlooking the beautiful Talland Bay. The emphasis is on comfort and the house is fully centrally heated and also has a log fire blazing in the lounge during colder weather. Most bedrooms have breathtaking views and are en-suite; all have tea/coffee making facilities, TV and telephone. Food is of a high standard and a new menu appears each day. Vegetarian and special diets can be catered for. An interesting selection of reasonably priced wines will complete your meal.

see PHOTO on page 80

Brian & Lynda Spring
Tel: 01503 272434
Fax: 01503 272929

B&B from £28pp, Dinner £15.50,
Restricted smoking, Minimum age 10, Pets welome,
Open all year except Christmas, Map Ref J

Harescombe Lodge, Watergate, near Looe, Cornwall PL13 2NE   **Nearest Road A387**

Harescombe Lodge overlooking the upper reaches of the West Looe River, originally built in 1760, was once the shooting lodge of the Trelawne Estate the home of the Trelawney family. Now tastefully restored and modernised it offers a high standard of comfort with all the bedrooms individually furnished and each having a private bath or shower and toilet en-suite. Situated in its own gardens with waterfalls and old stone bridges over the swiftly running stream in the secluded and picturesque wooded valley of Watergate.

Barry & Jane Wynn
Tel: 01503 263158

B&B from £17pp, Rooms 2 double, 1 twin all en-suite,
Minimum age 12,
Open all year, Map Ref K

Coombe Farm, Widegates, near Looe, Cornwall PL13 1QN   Nearest Road B3253

Relax in a lovely country house in a wonderful setting with superb views down a wooded valley to the sea. Enjoy delicious farmhouse cooking, candlelit dining, log fires, a heated outdoor pool and warm, friendly hospitality. Nearby golf, fishing, tennis, horse riding, glorious walks, beaches and National Trust houses and gardens. RAC Small Hotel of the Year, South West England 1996, ETB 3 Crowns Highly Commended, AA QQQQQ Premier Selected. Credit Cards: MasterCArd, Visa, Amex, Diners, Switch, Delta.

see PHOTO on page 82

Alex & Sally Low
Tel: 01503 240223
Fax: 01503 240895

**B&B from £26pp, Dinner from £15, Rooms 3 twin, 3 double, 4 family, all en-suite, No smoking, Minimum age 5,
Open March - November, Map Ref L**

Mevagissey House, Vicarage Hill, Mevagissey, Cornwall PL26 6SZ   Nearest Road B3273

Mevagissey House, built as a vicarage in 1847, is superbly situated above the village with panoramic views over the valley and the sea beyond. Each room is comfortably decorated and most have en-suite facilities. Tea/coffee makers and colour TV are provided in all rooms. A full English breakfast is served each morning. Licenced bar. The local gardens of Heligan are 2 miles away and several National Trust properties and lovely beaches are nearby.

John & Gill Westmacott
Tel: 01726 842427
Fax: 01726 844327

**B&B from £19pp, Rooms 1 twin, 1 double, 2 family,
Restricted smoking, Minimum age 7 years, No pets,
Open March - October, Map Ref M**

Manuels Farm, Quintrel Downs, Newquay, Cornwall TR8 4NY   Nearest Road A392

A delightful 17th century farmhouse, surrounded by charming gardens and set in a sheltered valley, just two miles from Newquay's magnificent beaches. There is a country atmosphere in the stylish bedrooms, which have brass beds, window seats overlooking the garden, and which are enhanced by antique and pine furniture. There is a lounge and a fascinating dining room with huge inglenook fireplace and an antique dining table around which guests gather for substantial farmhouse breakfasts. Jean provides local maps and books and can recommend places to visit.

Mrs Jean Wilson
Tel/Fax: 01637 873577

**B&B from £18.50pp, Rooms 1 single, 2 double, 1 family, most en-suite,
No smoking, Children welcome, Pets by arrangement,
Open all year except Christmas and New Year, Map Ref N**

Tregenna House, West Pentire Road, Crantock, near Newquay, Cornwall TR8 5RZ   Nearest Road A3075

Tregenna House is situated in the picturesque coastal village of Crantock with it's splendid sandy beach and through which runs the coastal path. An ideal centre for touring Cornwall with nearby facilities for coarse and sea fishing, riding, surfing and golf. Ample parking. Guests are made to feel 'at home' beside log fires in winter or around the heated swimming pool in summer. Bedrooms are centrally heated. with tea/coffee making facilities and TV, and most are en-suite. A warm welcome is provided with good home cooking and friendly atmosphere.

Sue & David Wrigley
Tel: 01637 830222

**B&B from £16-£17.50pp, Dinner from £9, Rooms 1 single, 1 twin, 1 double,
3 family, most en-suite, Restricted smoking, Children welcome, Pets by arrangement, Open all year, Christmas by arrangement, Map Ref O**

---

left, Allhays Country House, Talland Bay, Looe - see page 79   **81**

Degembris Farmhouse, St Newlyn East, Newquay, Cornwall TR8 5HY   Nearest Road A3058

The original manor house of Degembris was built in the 16th century and is now used as a barn. The present day house surrounded by attractive gardens, was built a mere two hundred years ago, and its slate hung exterior blends well with the rolling countryside over which many of the rooms have extensive views. Each bedroom is tastefuly decorated and well equipped. Hearty breakfasts and traditional evening meals are served in the cosy dining room. Take a stroll along the farm trail wandring through woodlands and fields of corn.

Kathy Woodley
Tel: 01872 510555
Fax: 01872 510230

B&B from £18-£20pp, Dinner from £10, Rooms 1 single, 1 twin en-suite, 1 double, 2 family en-suite, No smoking, Children welcome, No pets, Open all year except Christmas, Map Ref P

The Old Mill Country House, Little Petherick, near Padstow, Cornwall PL27 7QT   Nearest Road A389

The Old Mill Country House is a 16th century Grade II listed cornmill complete with waterwheel. Set in its own streamside gardens at the head of Little Petherick Creek just 2 miles from Padstow and in a designated area of outstanding natural beauty. The Old Mill is furnished throughout with antiques and collections of genuine artefacts to complement the exposed beams, original fireplaces and slate floors. This ensures that The Old Mill's original character and charm is retained.

Michael & Pat Walker
Tel: 01841 540388

B&B from £25.50, Rooms 2 twin, 5 double, all en-suite, Restricted smoking, Minimum age 14, Pets by arrangement, Open early March - end October, Map Ref Q

Woodstock House, 29 Morrab Road, Penzance, Cornwall TR18 4EZ   Nearest Road A30

Woodstock is a Victorian guest house situated in central Penzance just off the sea front and ideally placed for the Isles of Scilly ferry and heliport, and also the railway and bus stations. All rooms have TV, radios, hand basins and tea/coffee makers and many rooms have en-suite shower and toilet. A full English breakfast is served in the dining room and special diets can be catered for. To find us drive into the town past the railway stn and along the sea front. Turn right into Morrab Road as you approach the Queen's Hotel, 'Woodstock' is 200m on the right. ETB 2 Crown Commended, RAC listed, AA 3Q. EMail: WoodstocP@aol.com.

Cherry & John Hopkins
Tel: 01736 369049
Fax: 01736 369049

B&B from £12pp, Visa/Mastercard/Amex/JCB, Rooms 2 single, 3 twin, 2 double, 1 family, many en-suite, Children welcome, Open all year, Map Ref R

Con Amore Guest House, 38 Morrab Road, Penzance, Cornwall TR18 4EX   Nearest Road A30

Highly recommended and family run, we are ideally situated for just relaxing or for touring the Lands End Peninsula. We are situated opposite sub-tropical gardens and only 100 yards from the promenade and panoramic views over Mounts Bay and St Michaels Mount. All rooms have full central heating, colour TV's and tea/coffee making facilities all rooms are tastefully decorated with their own character we offer a varied menu with all tastes catered for. There is a reduction for children sharing. ETB 2 Crowns Commended.

Carol & Keith Richards
Tel/Fax: 01736 363423

B&B from £11pp, Rooms 1 single, 2 twin, 3 double, 2 family, most en-suite, Children & pets welcome, Open all year, Map Ref R

---

left, Coombe Farm, near Looe - see page 81

Ednovean House, Perranuthnoe, Penzance, Cornwall TR20 9LZ   **Nearest Road A394, A30**

Beautifully situated family run 160 year old Victorian house offering delightful, comfortable rooms, most having en-suite facilities and panoramic sea views. Situated in 1 acre of gardens and overlooking St Michael's Mount and Mount's Bay. It has one of the finest views in Cornwall. Relax in a comfortable lounge, library or informal bar and enjoy fine food and wines in the candlelit dining room, catering also for vegetarians. Pets welcome. Car park. Ideal for coastal walks and exploring from the Lizard to Lands End. ETB 3 Crowns, AA Recommended QQQ.

see PHOTO opposite

Arthur & Val Compton
Tel: 01736 711071

B&B from £20pp, Dinner from £15, Rooms 5 double, 2 twin, 2 single, most en-suite, Pets by arrangement,
Open all year except Christmas, Map Ref S

Boscean Country Hotel, Boswedden Rd, St Just-in-Penwith, Penzance, Cornwall TR19 7QP   Nearest Rd A3071

Beautiful country house in walled gardens overlooking sea and open countryside. Full central heating, log fires, home cooking of high standard. Tea/coffee facilities all bedrooms, Television lounge, bar with residents license. Ideal base for exploring far west of Cornwall, St Michaels Mount, St Ives etc. Just off Cliff Path. Ideal for walking holidays. Family run hotel with homey friendly atmosphere.

Joyce & Roy Lee
Tel/Fax: 01736 788748

B&B from £22pp, Dinner from £11.00, Rooms 4 twin, 4 double, 4 family, all en-suite, Restricted smoking, Children welcome, Pets by arrangement,
Open all year except Christmas and New Year, Map Ref T

The Wheal Lodge, 91 Sea Road, Carlyon Bay, St Austell, Cornwall PL25 3SH   **Nearest Road A38**

The Wheal Lodge has a superb position just above the sea in an area of outstanding beauty. The hotel, which adjoins the coastal path and is directly opposite the golf course, is a lovely character residence with an old fashioned homely atmosphere. There is an attractive residents' lounge and a spacious dining room with licenced bar. Bedrooms have en-suite facilities and courtesy trays, five bedrooms are on the ground floor. Breakfast is either continental or full English. Delicious Cornish food is served. Ample safe parking within the grounds. RAC Highly Acclaimed, AA QQQQ.

Jeanne & Don Martin
Tel: 01726 815543
Fax: 01726 815543

B&B from £30pp, Rooms 1 single, 2 treble or twin, 2 double, 1 family, all en-suite, Restricted smoking, Minimum age 8,
Open all year except Christmas, Map Ref M

Poltarrow Farm, St Mewan, St Austell, Cornwall PL26 7DR   **Nearest Road A390**

Our charming farmhouse is the ideal place for you to take time to relax and enjoy yourself. Tucked away in the countryside, yet so central for you to do as much or as little as you want. Gardens in the Spring, beaches in the Summer, the warm days of Autumn, but a log fire in the evenings. Everything you would expect from a Highly Commended Award.

Judith Nancarrow
Tel/Fax: 01726 67111

B&B from £20pp, Rooms 1 single, 1 twin, 2 double, 1 family, all en-suite, Restricted smoking, Children welcome, No pets,
Open all year except New Year, Map Ref U

---

left, Ednovean House, Perranuthnoe, Penzance - see top of this page

Anchorage House Guest Lodge, Nettles Corner, Tregrehan, St. Austell, Cornwall PL25 3RH   **A390**

Every attention has been paid to the smallest detail in this beautiful antique filled home. The richly furnished en-suite rooms are supremely comfortable with antique king size beds, satellite television and many thoughtful touches that anticipate every need, making your visit thoroughly special. Steven and Jane combine superb cooking, wonderful hospitality and pleasing informality for a stay to remember. Easy access to main roads and perfect for visiting historic treasures, NT gardens, Heligan, Carolyn Bay beach and golf. Private parking and a flower filled garden to enjoy.

Jane & Steven Epperson
Tel: 01726 814071

B&B from £25-£30pp, Dinner by arrangement £22.50 (5 courses),
Rooms 3 double, all en-suite, No smoking, No children, No pets,
Open all year, Map Ref V

Hembal Manor, Hembal Lane, Trewoon, St Austell, Cornwall PL25 5TD   **Nearest Road A3058**

Hembal Manor is a Grade II, 16th century, dwelling set in 6 acres of tranquil gardens. In 1569 Hembal was mentioned in the 'Feet of Fines'. Within the walled garden is a rare twin seater loo, reputed to be around 400 years old, well worth a visit! Tastefully decorated and furnished with period furniture to the highest standard. Bedrooms have TV, tea/coffee making facilities and central heating. A traditional or continental breakfast is served. A licensed bar to relax in after spending the day exploring the many places of interest. Easy access to the Lost Gardens of Heligan. ETB Highly Commended.

Sue & Mike Higgs
Tel: 01726 72144
Fax: 01726 72144

B&B from £25pp, Special rates available, Rooms 2 double, 1 twin,
all en-suite, No smoking, Minimum age 12, No pets,
Open all year except Christmas & New Year, Map Ref W

The Old Vicarage Hotel, Parc-an-Creet, St Ives, Cornwall TR26 2ET   **Nearest Road B3306**

The Old Vicarage. Secluded in wooded grounds in quiet residential area, is a lovingly restored Victorian rectory retaining the period ambience, but with every modern convenience, including full central heating. Lounge with extensive library and TV, well stocked Victorian bar with piano. Large choice of breakfast menu, including vegetarian, served in the elegant blue and gold dining room. Eight bedrooms most en-suite. All with colour TV, tea/coffee facilities, Victorian conservatory massed with plants. Large garden with putting green, badminton, swing and car park.

Jack & Irene Sykes
Tel/Fax: 01736 796124

B&B from £19pp, Rooms 1 twin, 4 double, 3 family, most en-suite,
Restricted smoking, Children and pets welcome,
Open Easter - October, Map Ref X

Rosebud Cottage, Bossiney, Tintagel, Cornwall PL34 0AX   **Nearest Road A39**

Rosebud Cottage is ¹/₂ mile from Tintagel in Bossiney. It is ideally located close by footpaths to Bossiney Cove and Rocky Valley, just 2 of the many coves to be found along the north Cornish coastline which justify the classification as an area of outstanding natural beauty. The cottage dates back 200 years. It overlooks farmland and has its own secluded garden with ample car parking. Tintagel is renowned for its castle ruins and the legend of King Arthur.

Mrs Rosemarie de Boyer
Tel: 01840 770861

B&B from £14pp, Dinner from £6.50,
Rooms 1 double, 1 family, 1 twin, Restricted smoking, Pets welcome,
Open all year, Map Ref Y

Trevigue, Crackington Haven, Bude, Cornwall EX23 0LQ   Nearest Road A3

16th Century farmhouse built around a cobbled courtyard close to spectacular cliffs and strangles beach. Work farm, 600 acres, awards for wildlife conservation. Guests sitting and dining rooms with log burning fires. All bedrooms en-suite two with TV's, all coffee/tea facilities. One room with romantic kingsize heavy carved oak bed. Licensed restaurant - gormet food. Licensed for civil wedding ceremonies.

Janet & Gayle Crocker
Tel/Fax: 01840 230 418

B&B from £30pp, Dinner from £18, Rooms 1 twin, 5 double, all en-suite, No smoking, Children from 12, No pets, Open all year except Christmas, Map Ref A

Cliff House, Devonport Hill, Kingsand, near Torpoint, Cornwall PL10 1NJ   Nearest Road B3247

Cliff House, a listed 17th Century building on the perimeter of Kingsand Mount Edgcumbe Country Park in the same conservation area spectacular views over Cawsand Bay, Plymouth Sound. 3 comfortable en-suite bedrooms all with tea/coffee making facilities. Large first floor sitting room with TV, video, CD player, Bleuthner grand piano, balcony overlooking village and sea. All freshly prepared wholefood cookery. Ideally situated for visiting Plymouth. Many National Trust properties in Cornwall and Devon. Walks along south Cornwall coastal footpath. Small car park. Local artists paintings for sale.

Ann Heasman
Tel: 01752 823110
Fax: 01752 822595

B&B from £18pp, Dinner from £9.00, Rooms 3 double, all en-suite, No smoking, Children welcome, No pets, Open all year, Map Ref Z

Rock Cottage, Blackwater, Truro, Cornwall TR4 8EU   Nearest Road A30

Our 18th century beamed cottage was formerly the village schoolmasters home. A haven for non smokers, we offer comfortable, attractive suite rooms with central heating, colour TV, radio, beverage tray. Charming stone-walled guest lounge always available. Breakfast is served in our cosy dining room with its antique Cornish range. Dinner by arrangement from A'La Carte menu. Situated in countryside village location 6 miles from Truro, 3 miles from the ocean. Ample parking - delightful gardens. ETB 3 Crown Highly Commended. AA QQQQ Selected, RAC Acclaimed.

Mrs Shirley Wakeling
Tel: 01872 560252

B&B from £22pp, Dinner by arrangement, Rooms 1 twin, 2 double, all en-suite, No smoking, children or pets, Open all year except Christmas and New Year, Map Ref 1

Ventongimps Mill Barn, Ventongimps, Callestick, Truro, Cornwall TR4 9LH   Nearest Road A3075

Ventongimps Mill Barn is a tastefully converted mill barn of traditional Cornish slate and stone situated in a quiet hamlet nestling in a sheltered valley. A stream runs through extensive gardens and lake on our estate of some 7 acres of fields and woods. Local coastal paths, offer breathtaking views, and the cathedral city of Truro is some 6 miles away. Evening meals served in our licensed bar with Portuguese cooking is a speciality. All rooms are en-suite and have TV. The coastal village of Perranporth with some 5 miles of sandy beaches is 2 miles distant.

Mr & Mrs Gibson
Tel: 01872 573275

B&B from £16pp, Dinner from £10.50, Rooms 1 single, 1 twin, 2 double, 4 family, all en-suite, Restricted smoking, Children welcome, Pets by arrangement, Open all year, Map Ref 2

Manor Cottage, Tresillian, Truro, Cornwall TR2 4BN   **Nearest Road A39**

Manor Cottage is a pretty regency period house situated in Tresillian, 5 minutes drive from Truro. Tastefully decorated bedrooms have TV's, courtesy trays and central heating. Our licensed restaurant is open Thursday, Friday and Saturday evenings, serving fresh local produce and homemade bread. Several of Cornwalls renowned garden and National Trust houses, lovely walks, golf, fishing, tennis and fine beaches are nearby. Breakfast is expertly cooked by the chef proprietor and served in our lovely conservatory. Member of the Food Inn Cornwall Association, A.A. 3Q

Carlton & Gillian
Tel: 01872 520212

B&B from £17pp, Dinner from £19.50, Rooms 1 single, 1 twin, 2 double, 1 twin, Restricted smoking, Children welcome, No pets, Open all year except Christmas, Map Ref 3

"I've just been getting some vegetables for our supper"

"I never saw daffodils so beautiful"
Dorothy Wordsworth

CUMBRIA

The dirt and grime of the Industrial Revolution at home, combined with revolution and the Napoleonic wars abroad, launched the Lake District into the limelight that it has been unable to avoid ever since. The Lake poets and artists eulogized, and the visitors came and went...and returned in ever increasing numbers...and little wonder. Cumbria, formed in 1974 from the ancient counties of Westmorland, Cumberland and the northern part of Lancashire, is of an ideal scale for the holiday maker. The characters of these three areas differ considerably, and the whole is a delight and offers the visitor an amazingly varied mixture of pleasures, and all within a relatively small locality. Despite its many attractions and the fact that Cumbria's popularity draws droves of holiday makers, there are still the quiet open spaces, the tranquil villages and lonely fells that so entranced Wordsworth.

The major attractions of this wonderful area are the mountains, four of them being over three thousand feet, which includes Scafell the highest peak in England; and the lakes, of which there are sixteen, ranging from Windermere the largest, being ten and a half miles in length, to Brotherswater only about half a mile long. Each mountain and lake has its own distinctive character and charm. Between the mountains are the spectacular passes, Kirkstone, Hard Knott and Wrynose. Negotiating them is an experience not to be missed, although preferably not in high season, and the resultant views are stunning. There are climbs in these mountains to tax the expert, but there is also plenty of scope for the amateur, scrambling over the fells to their heart's content. It is of course vital to note the advice given on correct clothing and weather conditions the weather here can change swiftly and dramatically. The lakes vary in character considerably, from the sombre Wastwater to bright and breezy Windermere, central to the main holiday activities. Windermere in summer is alive with pleasure craft of all shapes and sizes, water skiers and of course the lake steamers which ply between Lakeside, Bowness and Ambleside. Bowness, with its landing stage crowded with rowing boats, shingle shore and swans has all the brash sparkle of a lively seaside resort, while Ambleside at the northern end of the lake with its quaint old Bridge House is a fine centre for walking. Stockghyll Force is only a mile away and the 'Struggle', no misnomer, leads to the Kirkstone Pass and the glories of Ullswater. Martindale in the valley to the south of Ullswater is reached along an alarmingly twisting road and must be one of the loveliest parts of the district...a few miles from the holiday traffic and yet wild and deserted. By Gowbarrow Park is Aira Force, a picturesque waterfall close by the hill from which Wordsworth saw his 'host of golden daffodils'.

The spirit of William Wordsworth pervades this district and there are few places he has not written lovingly about, and with good reason. Grasmere is of course the mecca for Wordsworth enthusiasts. Here in the little churchyard are the graves of the poet and his family, simple plain stones under the trees. William, his wife and sister Dorothy lived at Dove Cottage, just outside the village, where they entertained the literary giants of the day including Charles Lamb, Samuel Taylor Coleridge and Sir Walter Scott. Keswick, to the north is a perfect centre for holiday walking. Situated on the edge of Derwentwater, the widest of the lakes, it is ideally placed for exploring glorious Borrowdale. Close by is the charming hamlet of Watendlath, the setting for Hugh Walpole's novel 'Judith Parish'. Here too is

Ashness Bridge, one of the most photographed subjects in the Lake District. A close contender for this honour must be Friar's Crag, the headland on the eastern shore of Derwentwater, and declared by John Ruskin to be one of Europe's finest scenic viewpoints. Castlehead, half a mile from Keswick, gives wonderful views across Derwentwater and Bassenthwaite Lake. It was around Bassenthwaite that John Peel, the subject of the English folk song, 'D'ye ken John Peel' hunted. He is buried in Caldbeck churchyard.

Hawkshead has Wordsworth connections, being the village in which he lodged when attending its tiny grammar school. Beatrix Potter lived and farmed in the district and her house, Hill Top Farm at Sawrey attracts huge numbers of visitors each year. Above Hawkshead is Tarn Hows, one of the prettiest sights and giving superb views of the Langdale Pikes, Fairfield, Helvellyn and Red Screes. It was on nearby Coniston Water in 1967 that Donald Campbell was killed attempting a new world water speed record. John Ruskin, who lived at Brantwood on the eastern shore of the lake is buried in Coniston churchyard.

There are four 'gateways' to this quite extraordinary district...Kendal in the south, the 'auld grey town' of limestone houses, home of Henry Vlll's sixth wife Catherine Parr; Appleby in the east, the ancient county town of Westmorland, renowned for its June horse fair and gypsy gathering; Cockermouth to the west, birthplace of Wordsworth, and Carlisle in the north, a fine cathedral city rich in the history of the border troubles.

The Cumbrian coastline suffers from the proximity of its glamorous neighbour over the mountains and its industrial degeneration...a great pity as there is glorious scenery here, wonderful sands and fascinating villages. The major towns are shaking off their old image and there is a vibrant spirit of rejuvenation.

As if this district was not sufficiently endowed, it stands sandwiched between the Yorkshire Dales National Park to the south and the Northumberland National Park to the north....whichever way the holiday makers choose to go they cannot be disappointed.

Places to Visit

Brantwood, *Coniston* ~ the former home of John Ruskin, a 19th century art critic, writer and philosopher. His paintings and memorabilia can still be seen.

Dalemain, *near Penrith* ~ a Georgian facade with a medieval and Elizabethan structure behind. Rooms open to the public include a Chinese drawing room with hand painted wallpaper, a drawing room with 17th century panelling. In the outbuildings there are several small museums and the gardens have a shrub rose collection.

Dove Cottage, *Grasmere* ~ this is the home of Willaim Wordsworth where he spent most of his creative years. There is a museum in the barn with many of Wordsworth's artefacts.

Grisedale Forest Park ~ created by the Forestry Commission, it provides the visitor with plenty to do, there is a visitor centre which tells the story of the forest and information on walks and wildlife. There are also many nature trails on which roe and red deer and red squirrels can be seen.

Hardknott Pass, *Eskdale* ~ this is a gruelling mountain road with many steep gradients and bends, at the summit are the Roman remains of Hardknott Fort and a spectacular viewof the valley below.

Hill Top, *Near Sawrey, Ambleside* ~ Beatrix Potter bought this little 17th century cottage in 1905, and it is where she wrote many of the Peter Rabbit books. She left the cottage to the National Trust in 1944 with instructions that the rooms should be kept.

Levens Hall, *near Kendal* ~ an Elizabethan mansion, built around a 13th century fortified tower. The famous topiary gardens where designed in 1694 by French horticulturist Guillaume Beaumont, the topiary trees are shaped into cones, spirals and pryamids, some are over six metres high.

Rydal Mount, *Rydal* ~ the Wordsworths moved here from Dove Cottage in 1813 and lived here until 1850. The gardens have a summerhouse where the poet often sat.

Talkin Tarn, *near Carlisle* ~ a sixty five acre lake in the Talkin Tarn Country Park. The lake has sandy bays and is ideal for boating and swimming, there are also many nature trails through woodland.

Ullswater, *near Penrith* ~ one of the Lake Dsitricts most beautiful lakes, stretching from the gentle farmland of Penrith to the dramatic hills and crags at the southern end. In summer, two restored Victorian steamers regularly sail between Pooley Bridge and Glenridding.

Wast Water ~ a mysterious black lake, it is edged on its eastern side by walls of scree over six hundred metres high. The eighty metre lake is England's deepest and whatever the weather it looks black. Boating on the lake is not allowed for conservation reasons but fishing is allowed with permits from the National Trust camp site.

▼ *Rydal Water*

CUMBRIA

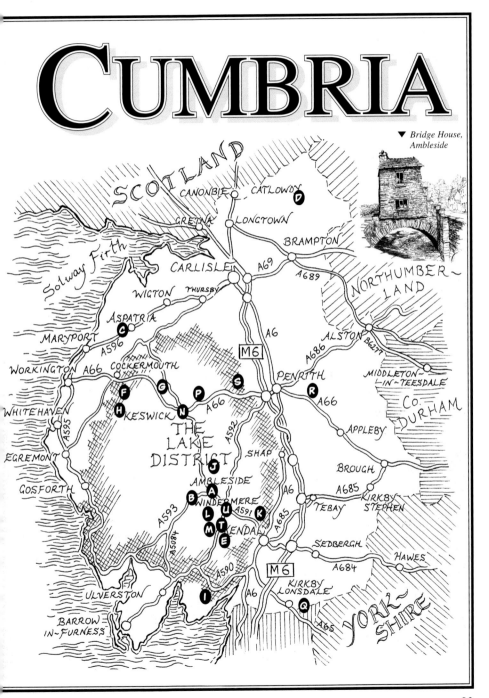

▼ Bridge House, Ambleside

SCOTLAND

Solway Firth

CANONBIE CATLOWDY **D**

GRETNA LONGTOWN

BRAMPTON

CARLISLE A69 A689

WIGTON THURSBY

NORTHUMBER~LAND

ASPATRIA **C**

MARYPORT A596

A6

ALSTON B6277

A686

MIDDLETON ~IN~TEESDALE

WORKINGTON A66 COCKERMOUTH

M6

PENRITH **R** A66

CO. DURHAM

WHITEHAVEN A595

F **G** **P** **S**

H KESWICK **N** A66 A592

APPLEBY

THE LAKE DISTRICT

SHAP

EGREMONT

A593

GOSFORTH

J

AMBLESIDE **A**

B WINDERMERE **L** **U** A591 **K**

M **T** KENDAL

E

BROUGH A685

KIRKBY~STEPHEN

TEBAY A685

SEDBERGH

A6

A684 HAWES

ULVERSTON **I**

A590

M6

A6

KIRKBY LONSDALE **Q**

A65

YORK~SHIRE

BARROW~IN~FURNESS

A5084 A593

A5092

Riverside Lodge, near Rothay Bridge, Ambleside - see opposite

Riverside Cottages, Riverside Lodge

2 Swiss Villas, Vicarage Road, Ambleside, Cumbria LA22 9AE · **Nearest Road A591**

A small Victorian terrace house set just off the main road in the centre of Ambleside, near the church, in a slightly elevated position overlooking Wansfell. There is immediate access to the cinema and shops and the wide variety of restaurants and cafes in the town. There are three double bedrooms (one with twin beds) recently refurbished in the traditional style. Each room has central heating, tea making facilities and colour TV. A full English or vegetarian breakfast available. We are open all year round and you are sure of a friendly welcome and good home cooking.

Mr D Sowerbutts
Tel: 015394 32691

B&B from £18pp,
Rooms 1 twin, 2 double,
Open all year, Map Ref A

Riverside Lodge, Rothay Road, near Rothay Bridge, Ambleside, Cumbria LA22 0EH · **Nearest Road A593**

A Georgian country house of immense charm and character offering superior 'B&B' accommodation in an idyllic riverside setting. All bedrooms have en-suite bathrooms and views of the river. Situated approximately 500 yards from the centre of Ambleside, midway between the centre and the head of Lake Windermere. Within the grounds there are also 5 self catering holiday cottages.

Alan & Gillian Rhone
Tel: 015394 34208

B&B from £23pp winter, £30pp summer, Rooms 1 twin, 3 double,
1 family, all en-suite, Restricted smoking,
Open all year except Christmas, Map Ref A

see PHOTO's opposite

Grey Friar Lodge Country Guest House, Clappersgate, Ambleside, Cumbria LA22 9NE · **Nearest Rd A593**

A warm personal welcome is extended to you by the Sutton family at their traditional Lakeland stone country house. An ideal countryside setting between Ambleside and the Langdales is enhanced by wonderful views and an established reputation for hospitality, comfort and imaginative home cooking. An RAC 'Small Hotel of the Year', AA Premier Selected QQQQQ, ETB 3 Crown Highly Commended. Recommended by other leading hotel guides. Fully illustrated brochure on request. EMail: gflodge@aol.com
England's Small Hotel of the Year 1997 - AA

Sheila & Tony Sutton
Tel: 015394 33158
Fax: 015394 33158

B&B from £23pp, Dinner from £16.50, Rooms 2 en-suite twin,
6 en-suite double, Restricted smoking, Children over 12, No pets,
Open March - October, Map Ref B

Castlemont, Aspatria, Cumbria CA5 2JU · **Situated on A596**

Castlemont is a large Victorian family residence in some 2 acres of gardens with unrestricted views of the northern Lakeland Fells and Solway Firth. Built of Lazonby stone, Castlemont combines the best of old world gracious living with the benefits of modern facilities. Start your day with a traditional English breakfast or a selected oak smoked kipper, perhaps a poached egg with haddock or ham? Loads of toast, butter and marmalade with pots of tea or coffee, all made on the ever willing Aga cooker.

David & Eleanor Lines
Tel: 016973 20205

B&B from £17pp, Dinner by arrangement, Rooms 1 en-suite double,
1 twin, 1 family, No smoking, Children welcome,
Open all year except Christmas & New Year, Map Ref C

Bessiestown Farm Country Guest House, Catlowdy, Longtown, Carlisle CA6 5QP   Nearest Road A7, B6318

AA, RAC & ETB Highly Commended. One of the nicest farm guest houses offering many of the delights of a small country hotel combined with the relaxed atmosphere of a comfortable family home. Peaceful and quiet. Delightfully decorated public rooms and warm pretty en-suite bedrooms with colour TV, radio and hostess tray. Delicious traditional home cooking using fresh produce whenever possible. Residential drinks licence. Touring base. Stop off for England, Scotland and N.Ireland. The indoor heated swimming pool is open from mid May to mid September. Family accommodation is in comfortable courtyard cottages.

Jack & Margaret Sisson
Tel: 01228 577219
Fax: 01228 577219

B&B from £21.50pp, Dinner from £11,
Rooms 2 double, 1 family, 1 twin, also 3 courtyard cottages,
No smoking, Open all year, Map Ref D

Lightwood Farmhouse Country Guest House, Cartmel Fell, Cumbria LA11 6NP   Nearest Road A592

Lightwood is a charming 17th century farmhouse retaining original oak beams and staircase. Standing in 2 acres of lovely gardens with unspoilt views of the countryside. 2 1/2 miles from the southern end of Lake Windermere. Excellent fell walking area. All rooms are en-suite, tastefully decorated and furnished with central heating, tea/coffee making facilities and some with colour TV. Cosy lounge with log fire and colour TV. We serve a good high standard of home cooking with seasonal home grown produce. ETB 3 Crown Commended. RAC listed.

Evelyn Cervetti
Tel: 015395 31454

B&B from £23pp, Dinner from £13, Rooms 2 twin, 3 double, 1 family,
all en-suite, Restricted smoking, Children welcome, No pets,
Open February - November, New Year B&B only, Map Ref E

Low Hall, Brandlingill, Cockermouth, Cumbria CA13 0RE   Nearest Road A66/A5086

Tea by the fire in winter, a cool drink in the garden in summer; whatever the season, a warm welcome awaits you at Low Hall. A friendly atmosphere fills every room in this 17th century farmhouse, commanding uninterrupted views of lake, stream, and fell. Breakfast is a feast, chosen from our extensive menu and specially prepared for you. Biscuits, hot drinks facilities, electric blankets, clock-radio and pretty bedrooms combine to make an idyllic, rural retreat offering excellent value for money.

Enid & Hugh Davies
Tel: 01900 826654

B&B from £25pp, Rooms 1 twin, 2 double, all en-suite,
No smoking, Children from 10, No pets,
Open all year except Christmas and New Year, Map Ref F

Lakeside, Bassenthwaite Lake, Cockermouth, Cumbria CA13 9YD   Nearest Road A66

An elegant family run Lakeland house offering friendly and relaxing hospitality, having oak floors and panelled entrance hall. Superb views across Bassenthwaite Lake to Skiddaw and surrounding fells. Keswick is only a short drive away, also the peaceful western fells and lakes of Buttermere and Crummock Water. The tastefully furnished bedrooms are all en-suite and have TV, radio alarm, hair dryer, and tea/coffee making facilities. A pleasant lounge in which to relax and delicious home cooking with a 4-course evening meal plus coffee and mints and wine if required.

Eric & Joan Murray
Tel: 017687 76358

B&B from £20pp, Dinner from £12.50, Rooms 1 single, 2 en-suite twin,
5 en-suite double, No smoking, Children welcome, No pets,
Open January - November, Map Ref G

Link House, Bassenthwaite Lake, Cockermouth, Cumbria CA13 9YD   **Nearest Road A66**

Surrounded by stunning scenery, Link House is a friendly, traditional, family run country house having been tastefully modernised to provide every comfort. Much period and antique furniture but more relaxing than formal. All bedrooms en-suite. Cumbria Crystal glasses and Wedgewood compliment moderately priced wine list and imaginative home cooking. Car park. Leisure Club facilities. Weekly terms. A warm welcome assured. ETB 3 Crowns Commended. AA QQQQ Selected.

Michael & Marilyn Tuppen
Tel: 017687 76291
Fax: 017687 76670

B&B from £26pp, Dinner from £13.00, Rooms 2 single, 2 twin, 3 double, 1 family, all en-suite, Restricted smoking, Children over 7 years, Guide dogs only, Open November - February, Map Ref G

Pickett Howe, Buttermere Valley, near Cockermouth, Cumbria CA13 9UY   **Nearest Road A66**

Winner of 2 National Awards. ETB's 1994 England for Excellence and Booker's 1997 Excellence in Independent Catering. Peacefully set amidst stunning mountain scenery, this 17th century longhouse offers caring, relaxing hospitality; an ideal touring/walking base. The cosy bedrooms have Victorian bedsteads, whirlpool baths, telephones and many extras. Slate floors and oak beams are enhanced by quality furnishings and antiques. Dani's 5-course dinners are a treat for both eyes and palate and the breakfast menu is outstanding - vegetarian choices always available.

see PHOTO opposite

David & Dani Edwards
Tel: 01900 85444
Fax: 01900 85209

B&B £37.50pp, Dinner £22.50, Rooms 1 twin, 3 double, all en-suite, No smoking, Minimum age 10, Pets welcome by arrangement, Open March - November, Map Ref H

Greenacres Country Guest House, Lindale, Grange-over-Sands LA11 6LP   **Nearest Road A590**

A friendly and relaxed atmosphere is assured at our lovely 19th century cottage at the foot of the beautiful Winster Valley in the National Park village of Lindale, 2 miles from Grange-over-Sands and 6 miles from the southern shores of Lake Windermere. 2 golf courses nearby. Our luxury bedrooms all have full en-suite facilities, TV, hair dryer, tea and coffee, and many thoughtful extras. Lovely conservatory and cosy lounge with log fire for the cold winter nights. Excellent home cooking. Licensed. ETB 3 Crowns Highly Commended, AA 5Q Premier Selected. No smoking.

Joe & Anne Danson
Tel: 015395 34578
Fax: 015395 34578

B&B from £25pp, Dinner from £13.50, Rooms 1 twin, 3 double, 1 family, all en-suite, No smoking, Children welcome, No pets, Open all year except Christmas & New Year, Map Ref I

Woodland Crag, How Head Lane, Grasmere, Cumbria LA22 9SG   **Nearest Road A591**

A warm welcome and an informal atmosphere are found in this delightful house, situated on the edge of Grasmere, near Dove Cottage. Secluded but with easy access to all facilities. The accommodation has five tastefully decorated bedrooms, all with individual character and wonderful views of the lake, fells or garden. Ideal for walking and centrally placed for the motorist. Enclosed parking. Tea/coffee making facilities. Guest lounge. TV in bedrooms. Totally non smoking.

John & Ann Taylor
Tel: 015394 35351

B&B from £25pp, Rooms, 2 single, 1 twin, 2 double, most en-suite, No smoking, Children over 12, No pets, Open all year, Map Ref J

Garnett House Farm, Burneside, Kendal, Cumbria LA9 5SF **Nearest Road A591**

Garnett House Farm is an AA listed RAC acclaimed 15th century farmhouse on a large dairy and sheep farm, just 1/2 mile from the A591 Kendal to Windermere road. All bedrooms have colour tv, radio, tea/coffee making facilities, and most are en-suite. The guests' lounge has 4ft thick walls and 16th century oak panelling. Old beams and an old oak spice cupboard in the dining room where you are served at separate tables. Good parking, close to village and public transport. Lovely views and many country walks from the farm. 6 miles to Windermere.

Mrs Sylvia Beaty
Tel: 01539 724542

B&B from £15pp, Dinner from £8, 3 night breaks during Nov - March from £48, Rooms 5 double and family, No pets, Open all year except Christmas, Map Ref K

Burrow Hall, Plantation Bridge, near Kendal, Cumbria LA8 9JR **Nearest Road A591**

Although built in 1648, this delightful guest house offers modern day comforts. It is situated amidst open countryside, mid-way between Kendal and Windermere on the A591, yet only 10 miles from junction 36 on M6. All 3 en-suite bedrooms which centrally heated, have colour TV, tea/coffee making facilities, radio alarm and hair dryer and are all tastefully decorated. There is a well furnished guests lounge. ETB 2 Crowns Highly Commended, AA QQQQ. A warm and friendly welcome is assured.

Maureen & Jack Craig
Tel: 01539 821711

B&B from £20.00pp, Rooms 2 double, 1 twin, No pets, No children, No smoking, Open all year, Map Ref K

Crook Hall, Crook, near Kendal, Cumbria LA8 8LF **Nearest Road B5284**

Tucked away up a private farm lane between Kendal and Windermere with beautiful scenery all around, Crook Hall is a working dairy/sheep farm of 250 acres. Several public footpaths abound with the Lake District hills beyond. Conveniently situated for Lakes and historic houses with golf course 1/2 mile away. Once belonging to a member of the English Royal family, this fine 17th century farmhouse is steeped in history. Tea/coffee making facilities provided in the residents' lounge which contains magnificent antique oak panelling.

Mrs Pat Metcalfe
Tel: 01539 821352

B&B from £16pp, Rooms 2 double/1 family, No smoking, No pets, Open March - December, Map Ref L

Tranthwaite Hall, Underbarrow, near Kendal, Cumbria LA8 8HG **Nearest Road M6, A6**

This magnificent farmhouse dates from the 11th century. Beautiful oak beams, doors and a rare antique black iron fire range. Tastefully modernised with full central heating. Pretty en-suite bedrooms with tea/coffee making facilities, hair dryer and radio. Attractive decor, fabrics and furnishings. This dairy sheep farm has an idyllic setting in a small picturesque village between Kendal and Windermere up an unspoilt country lane where wild flowers, deer and other wildlife can be seen. Many good country pubs and inns nearby. AA Selected. Cumbria Tourist Board Highly Commended.

Mrs D M Swindlehurst
Tel: 015395 68285

B&B from £19pp, Rooms 2 double, 1 twin, 1 family room, all en-suite, No smoking, Open all year, Map Ref M

---

right, Dale Head Hall, Lake Thirlmere - see page 102

Greystones, Ambleside Road, Keswick-on-Derwentwater CA12 4DP   **Nearest Road A66**

Greystones is a traditional stone built Lakeland house, situated in a quiet location, overlooking the grounds of Saint John's Church and with excellent views of the surrounding fells. Keswick town centre is a few minutes walk away as is Lake Derwentwater and the open fells. The spacious, individually designed bedrooms each have their own private facilities, television, radio and hot drinks tray. We have a private car park. Greystones is Three Crown Highly Commended by the Tourist Board, AA QQQQ Selected and RAC Highly Commended.

B&B from £23.50pp, Rooms 5 double, 2 twin, 1 single,

Janet & Robert Jones
Tel: 017687 73108

No smoking in bedrooms, No pets, Minimum age 10,
Open January - November, Map Ref N

The Ravensworth Hotel, 29 Station St, Keswick on Derwentwater, Cumbria CA12 5HH   **Nearest Road A591**

Ideally situated near the town centre and all it's amenities the lake and lower fells are just a short walk away. Tastefully furnished en-suite bedrooms have beverage tray, and colour television. Start your day with our hearty breakfast, enjoy the lakes by day and then while away the evening in the Herdwick Bar or relax in the spacious lounge. Personally run for twelve years we now rank among the top small hotels in Keswick. RAC Highly Acclaimed. AA Premier Selected. ETB Three Crowns Highly Commended.

B&B from £16pp, Rooms, 1 twin, 6 double, 1 family, all en-suite,

John & Linda Lowrey
Tel: 017687 72476

No smoking, Children over 6 years No pets,
Open February - November, Map Ref N

Thornleigh, 23 Bank Street, Keswick, Cumbria CA12 5JZ   **Nearest Road A591**

Thornleigh is a traditional Lakeland stone building situated in the town of Keswick. The attractive, en-suite, bedrooms have TV and tea/coffee making facilities and are situated at the rear of the building and generally free from the sound of traffic. All the rooms have magnificent views over the mountains and fells, thus making Thornleigh an idyllic base for walking or touring the Northern Lakes. The charming hosts, Ron and Pauline, offer a warm welcome, advice on enjoying the many aspects of the surrounding area and delicious full English breakfast for all guests, old and new.

B&B from £21pp, Rooms 6 double, all en-suite,

Ron & Pauline Graham
Tel: 017687 72863

Restricted smoking, Not suitable for children, No pets,
Open all year, Map Ref N

Dale Head Hall, Lakeside Hotel, Lake Thirlmere, near Keswick, Cumbria CA12 4TN   **Nearest Road A591**

see PHOTO on page 101

Alone on the shores of the Lake Thirlmere, in acres of mature gardens and woodlands, stands this historic Elizabethan Hall. Now lovingly restored by the resident owners, into one of Lakeland's finest country house hotels. Dale Head Hall offers you a warm welcome, elegant accommodation (including a 4-poster) and award winning cuisine. Just north of Wordsworth's, Grasmere and in the heart of the Lake District, Dale Head Hall is an idyllic starting point for exploring this most beautiful corner of England.

Alan & Shirley Lowe
Tel: 017687 72478
Fax: 017687 71070

B&B from £35pp, Dinner £27.50, Rooms 2 twin, 6 double, 1 family,
all en-suite, Restricted smoking, Children welcome, No pets,
Open all year expect New Year, Map Ref O

    right, Scales Farm Country Guest House, Threlkeld - see page 105

Blease Farm, Blease Road, Threlkeld, near Keswick, Cumbria CA12 4SF   Nearest Road A66

Come and be spoilt at our comfortably renovated 250 year old Cumbrian farmhouse. Set on the south facing slopes of the 2,800" Blencathra. All rooms in the house have stunning mountain views and all bedrooms are en-suite, with quality furnishings, TV and drinks tray. Log fires, sun room, smashing evening meals, garden, trout pond and hosts who offer a genuine friendly welcome come as standard. Over 200 local walks and drive sheets are available for guests use.

John & Ruth Knowles
Tel/Fax: 017687 79087

B&B from £25pp, Dinner from £16, Rooms, 1 twin, 2 double, all en-suite, No smoking, Minimum age 12, No pets, Open all year, Map Ref P

Scales Farm Country Guest House, Scales, Threlkeld, Keswick CA12 4SY   Nearest Road A66

Chris and Caroline welcome you to stay at Scales Farm, a 17th century farmhouse which has been beautifully renovated and converted. The farm is set on the lower slopes of Blencathra, just 10 minutes by car from Keswick and has wonderful open views to the south. All bedrooms are en-suite (2 ground floor) and have tea/coffee making facilities, fridge and TV. The guests' beamed sitting room has a woodburning stove and a full choice breakfast is served in the attractively decorated dining room. Ample parking space and pretty gardens. ETB 2 Crowns Highly Commended.

see PHOTO on page103

Chris & Caroline Briggs
Tel/Fax: 017687 79660

B&B from £23pp, Rooms 1 twin, 3 double, 1 family/double, all en-suite, No smoking, Dogs welcome by arrangement, Open all year except Christmas, Map Ref P

Cobwebs Country House, Leck, Cowan Bridge, Kirkby Lonsdale LA6 2HZ   Nearest Road M6,J36/A65

Set in four acres twixt for Dales Lakes. Victorian House of character. Full facility in all rooms. Log fires. Welcome trays. Conservatory restaurant overlooking fells. Cobwebs has been described as a restaurant with rooms we have gained an excellent reputation for our food. Modern English with a good splash of imagination country restaurant of the year. G.F.G. AA Red Star. Four course menu, changing daily. Three homemade breads. 200 wines. Arrive as guests, leave as our friends. A very warm welcome awaits. Self Catering available.

Paul Kelly & Yvonne Thompson
Tel/Fax: 015242 72141

B&B from £25pp, Dinner from £28, Rooms 5 single, 2 twin, 3 double, all en-suite, Restricted smoking, Children from 12, No pets, Open March - December, Map Ref Q

Hipping Hall, Cowan Bridge, Kirkby Lonsdale, Cumbria LA6 2JJ   Nearest Road A65

16th Century country house set in 3 acres of walled gardens on the Cumbria-Yorkshire borders, 2.5 miles East of pretty Kirkby Lonsdale, so an ideal base for touring both Lakes and Dales. Bedrooms are comfortably furnished (mostly antiques) with en-suite bathrooms, colour TV, radio, direct-dial phones, tea/coffee making facilities. Guests can help themselves to drinks from a sideboard in the conservatory before dining together very informally at one table in the Great Hall. All dishes are freshly prepared by Jos, accompanied by three wines (optional) selected by Ian. 8 $\frac{1}{2}$ miles from M6 Junction 36.

see PHOTO opposite

Ian & Jocelyn Bryant
Tel: 015242 71187
Fax: 015242 72452

B&B from £39pp, Dinner £23, Rooms 2 twin, 5 double, all en-suite, Restricted smoking, Children over 12 years, Pets welcome, Open March - November, Map Ref Q

---

*left, **Hipping Hall, Cowan Bridge** - see above for details*

Hornby Hall, Brougham, Penrith, Cumbria CA10 2AR   **Nearest Road M6/A66**

Hornby Hall was built about 1550 and is situated in tranquil countryside 1 mile off the A66, 3 miles south east of Penrith. It is a Grade II listed building with many interesting features, full of antique furniture. Al the bedrooms face south overlooking the garden. Guests have their own sitting room with log fire. The 16th century hall, now used as a dining room, has the original sandstone floor. Dinner must be booked in advance.Dry fly fishing on the River Eamont available. Ample car parking.

Mrs Ros Sanders
Tel/Fax: 01768 891114

B&B from £25pp, Dinner from £10.50, Rooms 1 single, 4 twin, 2 double, 1 family, some en-suite, Restricted smoking, Children welcome, Pets by arrangement, Open all year except Christmas & New Year, Map Ref R

Near Howe Farm Hotel, Mungrisdale, Penrith, Cumbria CA11 0SH   **Nearest Road A66**

see PHOTO opposite

A Cumbrian family home which is situated amidst 300 acres of moorland. 5 of the 7 bedrooms have private facilities and all have tea/coffee making facilities. Meals are served in the comfortable dining room and great care is taken to produce good home cooking with every meal freshly prepared. Comfortable residents lounge with colour TV, games room, smaller lounge with well stocked bar and for the cooler evenings an open log fire. The surrounding area can provide many activities and past-times including golf, fishing, pony trekking, boating and walking. Commended 3 Crowns.

Mrs Christine Weightman
Tel: 017687 79678
Fax: 017687 79678

B&B from £17pp, Dinner from £10, Rooms 3 double, 3 family, 1 twin, Also cottages to let sleep up to 7, Open March to November, Map Ref S

Fairfield Hotel, Brantfell Road, Bowness-on-Windermere, Cumbria LA23 3AE   **Nearest Road A591**

see PHOTO on page 108

Fairfield is a small friendly, family run, 200 year old Lakeland hotel found in a peaceful garden setting. 200 metres from Bowness village, 400 metres from the shores of Lake Windermere and at the end of the Dales Way (an 81 mile walk from Ilkley to Bowness). The Beatrix Potter exhibition is within easy walking distance. The well appointed and tastefully furnished bedrooms all have colour TV, hairdryer, a welcome tray and private shower/bathroom. Breakfasts are a speciality. Leisure facilities available. On site car parking Genuine hospitality and warm welcome. EMail Ray+barb@fairfield.dial.lakesnet.co.uk

Ray & Barbara Hood
Tel: 015394 46565
Fax: 015394 46565

B&B from £23pp, Dinner from £19.50 by arrangement, Rooms 1 single, 1 twin, 5 double, 2 family, all en-suite, No smoking, Children welcome, No pets, Open all year except November & December, Map Ref T

Parson Wyke Country House, Glebe Road, Bowness on Windermere LA23 3GZ   **Nearest Road A592**

Jean & David Cockburn would like to offer you a very warm welcome to their home, the former Rectory to St Martin's Church. Dating from 15th Century, it is the oldest inhabited house in the area, being listed Grade II. Situated in 2 acres over looking the lake at Parson Wyke, it is approached by a private drive off Glebe Road, and affords a quiet haven only a short stroll from the hustle and bustle of Bowness. Rooms are tastefully appointed with many period furnishings and en-suite facilities. All are equipped with colour TV. Private access to lake.

Jean & David Cockburn
Tel: 015394 42837

B&B from £25-£35pp, Rooms 1 twin, 1 double, 1 family, all en-suite, Restricted smoking, Children welcome, No pets, Open all year except Christmas & New Year, Map Ref T

Rockside, Ambleside Road, Windermere, Cumbria LA23 1AQ   Nearest Road A591

Rockside offers superb accommodation, and is situated 150 yards from Windermere village, train and bus station. All rooms have colour TV, tea/coffee making facilities, clock radios, telephone and hair dryer, most are en-suite. Large car park. RAC Acclaimed. ETB 2 Crowns. Help given to plan walks, car routes and activities. Choice of hearty English breakfasts.

Neville & Mavis Fowles
Tel: 015394 45343
Fax: 015394 45343

B&B from £17.50pp, Rooms 1 single, 2 twin, 4 double, 4 family, most en-suite, Restricted smoking, Children welcome, No pets, Open all year except Christmas, Map Ref U

The Archway, 13 College Road, Windermere, Cumbria LA23 1BU   Nearest Road A591

Impeccable Victorian Guest House. Beautifully restored and with a civilised and relaxing atmosphere. Antiques and country furniture, interesting paintings and prints, good books, fresh flowers, super mountain views. Renowned for gourmet home cooking emphasising fresh organic ingredients brought together in imaginative and nutritionally thoughtful menus. The breakfast fare offers everything from freshly squeezed fruit and vegetable juices and home made yogurts to spicy apple pancakes and the traditional English breakfast. Bread is wholemeal and home baked. We are a non smoking house.

Aurea Greenhalgh
Tel: 015394 45613

B&B from £22-£27pp, Dinner from £12.50, Rooms 2 twin, 2 double, all en-suite, No smoking, Children from 10, No pets, Open all year, Map Ref U

Orrest Head House, Kendal Road, Windermere, Cumbria LA23 1JG   Nearest Road A591

Orrest Head House, Windermere, is a charming country house dating back to the 16th century. All bedrooms are en-suite and have colour TV, and tea/coffee making facilities. It is set in 3 acres of garden and woodland and has distant views to mountains and lake. Close to the station and village with a very homely atmosphere.

Mrs Brenda Butterworth
Tel: 015394 44315

B&B from £19.50, Rooms 3 double, 2 twin, all en-suite, Rooms 3 double, 2 twin, Minimum age 6, No smoking, Open all year except Christmas Day, Map Ref U

see PHOTO on page 110

Oldfield House, Oldfield Road, Windermere, Cumbria LA23 2BY   Nearest Road M6, A6, A591

Oldfield House has a friendly informal atmosphere within a traditionally built lakeland residence. Ideally situated close to Windermere village, yet off the busy main road and also convenient to explore the Lake District. All rooms are en-suite, have colour TV, telephone and tea/coffee making facilities, two have 4-poster beds. The guest house is centrally heated throughout with a comfortable lounge. There are drying facilities and a private car park. Guests have free use of Parklands Country Club which includes a swimming pool and sports facilities. EMail: oldfield.house@virgin.net

Bob & Maureen Theobald
Tel: 015394 88445
Fax: 015394 43250

B&B from £19pp, Rooms 2 single, 2 twin, 3 double, 1 family, all en-suite, Non smoking, Children welcome, No pets, Open February - December, Map Ref U

Kirkwood Guest House, Prince's Road, Windermere, Cumbria LA23 2DD   Nearest Road A591

Kirkwood is a large Victorian stone house situated on a quiet corner between Windermere and Bowness ideally situated for exploring the Lake District. All rooms are en-suite with colour TV, tea/coffee making facilities and radio. Some rooms have 4-poster beds, ideal for honeymoons, anniversary, or just a special treat. There is a comfortable lounge in which to relax and for breakfast an extensive menu is offered including vegetarian and special diets (with prior notice). Help with planning walks and drives or choosing a mini bus tour is all part of the personal service.

Carol & Neil Cox
Tel: 015394 43907
Fax: 015394 43907

B&B from £19pp, Rooms 3 twin, 3 double, 4 family, all en suite, Restricted smoking, Children welcome, Pets by arrangement, Open all year, Map Ref U

Braemount House Hotel, Sunny Bank Road, Windermere, Cumbria LA23 2EN   Nearest Road A591

Braemount House is Victorian and built in the traditional style of Lakeland stone and green slate. Many of the original features are still present, adding period atmosphere. Being small you can rest assured of our personal attentive service. As Ian is a chef and Anne was born into the hotel profession, you see what a winning combination we are. All bedrooms are en-suite with bath/shower and are individually decorated having a lot of 'little' extras to make them guest friendly. Our dinner menu changes daily and we use fresh local produce including our own garden herbs.

Ian & Anne Hill
Tel: 015394 45967
Fax: 015394 45967

B&B from £22.50pp, Dinner from £17.50, Rooms 1 twin, 3 double, 1 family, all en-suite, No smoking, Minimum age 10, No pets, Open all year except Christmas & New Year, Map Ref U

Fir Trees, Lake Road, Windermere, Cumbria LA23 2EQ   Nearest Road A591

Ideally situated midway between Windermere and Bowness villages, Fir Trees offers luxurious bed and breakfast in a Victorian guest house of considerable charm. Antiques and beautiful prints abound in the public areas, while the bedrooms, all having private bath/shower rooms, are immaculately furnished and decorated. Breakfasts are simply scrumptious and the hospitality warm and friendly. Indicative of quality and value for money, Fir Trees has been given a "highly commended" award by the English Tourist Board and is enthusiastically recommended by leading guides.

see PHOTO on page 112

Mr & Mrs I Fishman
Tel: 015394 42272
Fax: 015394 42272

B&B from £21-£27pp, Rooms 2 twin, 4 double, 2 family, all en-suite, Children welcome, Non smoking, Open all year, Map Ref U

Rosemount, Lake Road, Windermere, Cumbria LA23 2EQ   Nearest Road A591

Rosemount is a quality family run guest house offering warm hospitality and value for money. It is ideally situated midway between the charming villages of Windermere and Bowness-on-Windermere within easy walking distance of both centres. Tastefully furnished and comfortable bedrooms, all with private facilities. Delicious breakfasts come highly recommended by their regular guests. Ample car parking. NON SMOKING

Steve & Helen Thomas
Tel: 015394 43739
Fax: 015394 48978

B&B from £18.50 - £26pp, Rooms 4 double, 2 single, 1 twin, 1 family, Children welcome, No smoking, Open February - December, Map Ref U

St John's Lodge, Lake Road, Windermere, Cumbria LA23 2EQ   **Nearest Road A5704**

St John's Lodge takes pride in personal recommendations received and the owner/managers, Doreen and Ray Gregory, are most anxious to meet your personal requirements. The hotel's residents' lounge is available at any time and a warm welcome awaits you at the friendly residents' bar where you can relax with your pre-dinner drink. A 4-course dinner is served each evening at 7pm. St John's Lodge is situated midway between the villages of Windermere and Bowness, just a 10 minutes walk from the lake pier.

Doreen & Ray Gregory
Tel: 015394 43078

B&B from £18.50pp, Dinner from £11.50, Rooms 9 double,
3 family, 1 twin, 1 single, Minimum age 3,
Open from February - November, Map Ref U

"We're taking the horses to the show tomorrow. Are you coming?"

*left, **Fir Trees, Windermere - see page 111***   ***113***

DERBYSHIRE & STAFFORDSHIRE

Important as these two midland counties were and still are industrially, they can also boast some of England's most picturesque countryside. The Peak District, designated in 1951 a National Park, was Britain's first National Park, covering an area of five hundred and forty two square miles, reaching as far north as the high ground between the industrial areas of Manchester and Sheffield. This is an exhilarating rolling landscape of rugged and wooded dales. Castleton, the nub of the Peak's caving district is superbly sited at the western entrance to the Hope Valley, with Peveril Castle towering over the village. Peak Cavern with its impressive entrance on the edge of Castleton is the largest cave in England. There are five caverns in all open to the public, one of them, Speedwell Cavern features an underground boat trip. Mam Tor, known as Shivering Mountain because of its frequent land-slips is a 1,700 ft. ridge topped by an Iron Age fort. This is magnificent walking, climbing and pot-holing country. Buxton is the undoubted capital of the district, an elegant former Spa town its spacious terraces, particularly the beautiful Palladian Crescent by John Carr was built in direct imitation of those in Bath. The town is renowned for its music festival held since 1979 in late July/early August. At Matlock Bath in the Derwent Gorge, another former spa town, there are superb views.....and a cable car to the Heights of Abraham. The impressive National Tramway Museum is nearby at Crich. This wonderful scenery provides a fitting background to two of the countries most magnificent stately homes. Chatsworth House, landscaped by Capability Brown and Joseph Paxton for the Dukes of Devonshire, has in its grounds the famous Cascade and the Emperor Fountain. The house itself contains a breathtaking

collection of furniture and art. Haddon Hall, the famous manor house, is in fact a twentieth century restoration. The oldest parts of the hall date from the thirteenth century with a fourteenth century banqueting hall and a remarkable chapel with fifteenth century murals. The fine oak and walnut panelled long gallery is early seventeenth century. Ashbourne, surrounded by lofty hills is an attractive market town with Henmore Brook, a tributary of the Dove running through it. Being on the fringe of the Peak District National Park it is an ideal centre for holiday makers wishing to explore this area. To the southwest is Derby, a modern city - created such by Queen Elizabeth in 1977 - but with a history stretching back to Roman times. Derby was the furthest point south reached by Bonnie Prince Charlie before his retreat in 1745 to his eventual defeat at Culloden. The city is renowned for Royal Crown Derby porcelain and in more recent days the manufacture of Rolls-Royce cars.

Much of the Peak District National Park lies in Staffordshire, and a couple of miles west of Biddulph on the lonely moors is a strange rock formation known as The Old Man of Mow. An eighteenth century folly was built on the summit, Mow Cop Castle, giving glorious views over the Cheshire Plains. At Biddulph Grange are rare shrubs planted amongst follies in an exotic Victorian garden. Stoke-on-Trent, the capital of North Staffordshire is in fact an amalgamation of six towns...Tunstall, Burslem, Hanley, Longton and Stoke, the 'five towns' made famous in the novels of Arnold Bennett, together with Fenton. Arnold Bennett was born near Hanley in 1867. Here in the 'Potteries' is created the wonderful fine pottery and porcelain of Wedgwood, Minton,

Copeland and Spode. For lovers of exquisite ceramics there is the Gladstone Pottery Museum, the Minton Museum, the Sir Henry Doulton Gallery, the Wedgwood Visitor Centre as well as the Etruria Industrial Museum and the City Museum and Art Gallery. For the more energetic and in lighter vein, just fifteen miles east is Alton Towers, the ruined home of the 15th Earl of Shrewsbury surrounded by probably Britain's most famous theme park. The lofty two hundred foot steeple of Cheadle's Roman Catholic church dominates this countryside, the church was designed by Pugin, one of the architects of the Houses of Parliament. Cheadle has some lovely half-timbered Elizabethan houses and is ideally situated for exploring the wooded Churnet Valley and the two hundred and fifty acres of moorland and marsh of the Hawksmoor Nature Reserve.

The Black Country is not a name one readily associates with holiday pleasures but on its very doorstep is Cannock Chase, thirty thousand acres of wild parkland, originally an oak forest and a royal hunting ground since the days of the kings of Mercia. Through the years the woodland has been largely cleared to provide fuel for industry, leaving a heathland plateau...nevertheless there are still fallow deer and some red deer left. Castle Ring, at eight hundred feet gives superb views across the Chase. Stafford, on the River Stow is an ancient town retaining some fine half-timbered houses. It was the birthplace of Izaak Walton the author of 'The Compleat Angler' and a perfect centre for visiting Cannock Chase. Abbots Bromley, renowned for its famous Tudor Horn Dance commemorating the granting of hunting rights to the folk of Needwood Forest, was the home of the Bagot family for four hundred years until they moved in the fifteenth century to nearby Blithfield Hall.

No visitor should leave this lovely area without visiting Lichfield. The beautiful cathedral with its three sandstone spires known as the 'Ladies of the Vale' was built in the thirteenth century. The Lady Chapel houses some magnificent sixteenth century stained glass from the Cistercian abbey of Herkenrode in Belgium. The city's most famous association is with Samuel Johnson whose statue faces that of his biographer James Boswell across Market Square. When Boswell rather disparagingly referred to Lichfield as a sleepy little place that seemed rather work-shy, Dr. Johnson retorted, 'it's a city of philosophers - we work with our heads!

The monuments to hard work are everywhere to be seen in these two counties, so too are sights to gladden the hearts of the most discerning visitors.

DERBYSHIRE &

Places to Visit

Arbow Low, *Derbyshire* ~ known as "the Stonehenge of the North', this stone circle dates from around 2000 BC and consists of 46 stones surrounded by a ditch.

Calke Abbey, *Derbyshire* ~ set in seven hundred and fifty acres of parkland with ponds and oak woods. The current house was built in 1701-1703 for Sir John Harpur, it has a stunning 18th century staircase. Attractive grounds with an 18th century orangery.

Chatsworth House & Gardens, *Derbyshire* ~ one of Britain's most impressive stately homes. Between 1687 and 1707 the old Tudor mansion was replaced with the Baroque palace. Capability Brown landscaped the gardens in the 1760's.

Kedleston Hall, *Derbyshire* ~ built between 1759 and 1765, the rooms feature many paintings. The park includes several original Adam buildings, a bridge, fishing pavillion and fine lakes with cascades.

Alton Towers, *Staffordshire* ~ the English equivalent to Disneyland with over one hundred rides of varying degrees. Entertainment for all ages, along with landscaped gardens by Capability Brown.

Cannock Chase, *Staffordshire* ~ over twenty thousand acres of heath and woodland. Once a Norman hunting ground, it still has fallow and red deer and has been designated as an Area of Outstanding Natural Beauty.

Shugborough Estate, *near Stafford* ~ a magnificient nine hundred acre estate of the Earls of Lichfield. The Park Farm, designed by Wyatt in 1805 houses a rare breeds centre and a working corn mill. There is also an eighteen acre garden with neo-classical monuments by James Stuart.

Wedgwood Visitor Centre, *near Stoke on Trent* ~ with displays of the works by Josiah Wedgwood from 1750 onwards. The skills of the potters are demonstrated and there is an opportunity to buy various pieces.

Dovedale ▼

STAFFORDSHIRE

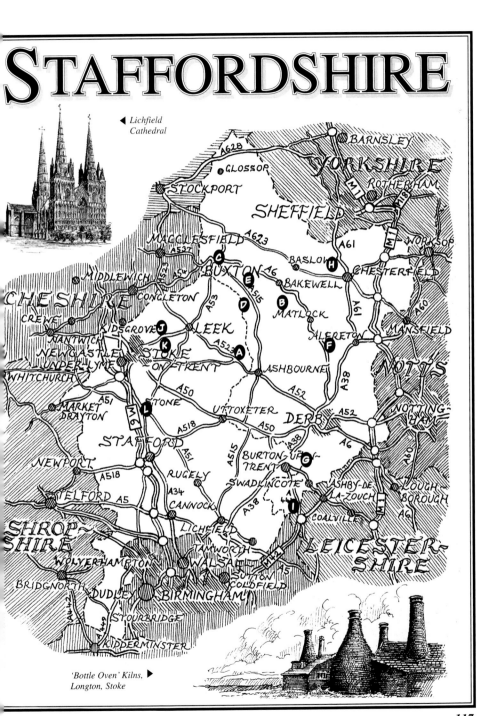

◀ Lichfield
Cathedral

'Bottle Oven' Kilns, ▶
Longton, Stoke

The Old Rectory, Blore, near Ashbourne, Derbyshire DE6 2BS   Nearest Road A52, A523

On the Staffordshire/Derbyshire border, in the scenic Peak District National Park, is the tiny, tranquil hamlet of Blore, with magnificent views of Dovedale and the Manifold Valley, four miles from the old market town of Ashbourne. Nearby are many stately homes including Chatsworth, Haddon, Hardwick, Kedleston and Calke Abbey. Stuart and Geraldine Worthington, both well travelled, entertain with style and flair in their attractive stone-built house with its gracious drawing room. Dinner is by candlelight with your hosts, in a formal house party atmosphere. Licensed.

Mr & Mrs Stuart Worthington
Tel: 01335 350287
Fax: 01335 350287

B&B from £38pp, Dinner from £21.50, Rooms 2 en-suite double, 1 twin with private facilities, All with TV and tea/coffee making facilities, No children, No pets, Open all year except Christmas, Map Ref A

Stanshope Hall, Stanshope, near Ashbourne, Derbyshire DE6 2AD   Nearest Road A515

Stanshope Hall, dating from the 16th century, stands on the brow of a hill between the Manifold and the Dove Rivers in the Peak District. The hall faces south across rolling landscape. Lovingly restored and retaining many of its original features. All bedrooms are en-suite with direct dial phone and tea/coffee making facilities. There is a guests' drawing room with piano and record player and local information table. Centrally heated throughout. Home cooked dinners with garden and local produce and a residents licence. Extensive breakfast menu. Brochure available.

Naomi Chambers & Nick Lourie
Tel: 01335 310278
Fax: 01335 310470

B&B from £25pp, Dinner £18, Rooms 1 twin with private facilities, 2 en-suite double, Restricted smoking, Open all year except Christmas, Map Ref A

Rock House, Alport, Bakewell, Derbyshire DE45 1LG   Nearest Road A6

Once part of the Duke of Rutland's "Haddon Estate", the Grade II listed property of "Rock House" gives bed and breakfast in a quiet and relaxed atmosphere in a hamlet little changed over 200 years. There is a small, cosy sitting room and bedrooms each have private facilities and country views. 80 yards away is the Lathkill River whose 'gin-clear' waters support lazing trout. The rural delights of the Peak National Park start at the door-step. A nourishing breakfast of your choice to commence the day. Car park.

Mrs Jan Statham
Tel: 01629 636736

B&B £20pp, Rooms 2 twin/single, 1 double, all private facilities, No smoking, No children, Pets only outside, Open all year, Map Ref B

Grosvenor House Hotel, 1 Broad Walk, Buxton, Derbyshire SK17 6JE   Nearest Road A6

Privately run, licensed hotel in quiet centre of historic spa town enjoying spectacular views overlooking 23 acres of landscaped gardens and Opera House. Bedrooms, both standard and de-luxe are tastefully decorated, en-suite and non-smoking with colour TV, radio/alarm and hospitality tray. Our charming lounge and dining room offer a home-from-home atmosphere with panoramic views. Excellent home-cooked cuisine. Comfort and hospitality assured. Scenic countryside, Chatsworth and Haddon Hall nearby. ETB 3 Crown Commended, AA 4Q's Selected and 'Which' Recommended.

Graham & Anne Fairbairn
Tel/Fax: 01298 72439

B&B from £25pp, Dinner £15, Rooms 1 twin, 5 double, 2 family, all en-suite, Restricted smoking, Children from 8, Guide dogs only, Open all year, Map Ref C

Biggin Hall, Biggin-by-Hartington, Buxton, Derbyshire SK17 0DH   Nearest Road A515

Beautifully restored, this stone built house dating from the 17th century, set 1,000 feet up in the Peak District National Park, is delightful in every way. Antiques, a log fire, a 4 poster bed give this home a wealth of charm. The food is outstanding with the owners priding themselves on the use of only the freshest and best produce available. The home baked bread is excellent! Perfect in every way. Easy access to the Spa town of Buxton, Chatsworth House, Haddon Hall, etc. Beautiful uncrowded footpaths from the grounds.

see PHOTO opposite

Mr J M Moffett
Tel: 01298 84451

B&B from £22.50pp, Dinner from £14.50, Rooms and Apartments, Minimum age 12, Open all year, Map Ref D

Staden Grange Country House, Staden Lane, Staden, Buxton, Derbyshire SK17 9RZ

A pleasant spacious country house enjoying views over open farmland. Attractive and comfortable en-suite rooms, some ground floor, 1 with 4 poster, each with satellite TV, radio, phone and tea/coffee makers. The "Foxlow Restaurant" offers excellent cuisine. Menus change daily. We provide a freshly cooked hearty English Breakfast. Lovely lounge and cocktail bar, also large garden. Riding, shooting, fishing, sauna and Jacuzzi. Ample parking. We have been established over 17 years. An ideal base to visit the wonderful Peak District. Come and enjoy.

Mrs MacKenzie
Tel: 01298 24965
Fax: 01298 72067

B&B from £27.50pp, Dinner available, Rooms 4 twin, 6 double, 1 family, all en-suite, Children & pets welcome, Open all year except Christmas & New Year, Map Ref E

Littlemoor Wood Farm, Littlemoor Lane, Riber, near Matlock, Derbyshire DE4 5JS   Nearest Road A615

A private lane leads to this peaceful and informal traditional Derbyshire stone farmhouse. Set among 20 acres of meadows and enjoying wonderful open views it is the perfect place to unwind. Many stately homes including Chatsworth House and other popular places of interest are nearby. Rooms are attractive and comfortable with TV and tea/coffee trays and guests may use the elegant dining room/study to relax. Bakewell, Ashbourne and M1 all within 20 minutes.

Simon & Gilly Groom
Tel/Fax: 01629 534302

B&B from £18pp, Dinner from £10.50, Rooms 1 single/twin, 1 double, 1 double/twin with private facilities, No smoking, Children from 9, No pets, Open all year except Christmas and New Year, Map Ref F

Bower Lodge, Well Lane, Repton, Derbyshire DE65 6EY   Nearest Road Repton High Street

Beautifully furnished Victorian house in quiet location near village centre. The comfortable bedrooms are equipped with tea/coffee making facilities and TV. There is a pleasant lounge where guests may relax. Ideally suited for visiting Chatsworth House, Kedleston Hall, Calke Abbey, Alton Towers, Donnington Park Race Track, Melbourne Hall and Sudbury Hall. East Midlands Airport and Birmingham Airport are within easy reach as is The National Exhibition Centre.

Elizabeth & Peter Plant
Tel: 01283 702245
Fax: 01283 704361

B&B from £25pp, Dinner from £17, Rooms 1 single, 2 twin/double with private facilities, 1 en-suite double, Children welcome, Pets by arrangement, Open all year except Christmas New Year and Easter, Map Ref G

Springwood House, Cowley Lane, Holmesfield, Sheffield, Derbyshire S18 5SD   **Nearest Road M1**

Situated in 5 acres with beautiful open views of the surroundings countryside in a peaceful location. On the edge of the Peak District National Park, yet within easy reach of Sheffield, Chesterfield - the M1. Golf, Horse riding, trout fishing and walking are easily accessible A wide variety of local hostelries. Serve excellent food. Springwood is furnished to a high standard. A warm welcome awaits each guest.

Mrs Avril Turner
Tel: 0114 289 0253
Fax: 0114 289 1365

B&B from £20pp, Rooms 1 twin en-suite, 1 double with private facilities,
Restricted smoking, Children welcome, Pets by arrangement,
Open all year except Christams & New Year, Map Ref H

The Old Hall, Netherseal, near Swadlincote, Derbyshire DE12 8DF   **Nearest Road A444**

The Old Hall is a Grade II* listed house dating from 1644 with an additional Edwardian wing. Originally a monastery, the house retains its unique character and original features whilst benefitting from all modern conveniences. The house is situated in 18 acres of beautiful mature gardens, woodland and open fields. Bedrooms are comfortable, spacious, attractively furnished, have private bathroom and are provided with tea/coffee making facilities. There is a lake for fishing, a croquet lawn and indoor table tennis. There are a variety of pubs and restaurants locally.

Mrs Clemency Wilkins
Tel: 01283 760258
Fax: 01283 762991

B&B from £22.50pp, Dinner from £12.50, Rooms 1 single, 1 twin,
1 double, all en-suite, No smoking, No children, No pets,
Open all year except Christmas & New Year, Map Ref I

The Old Vicarage, Leek Road, Endon, Stoke-on-Trent, Staffordshire ST9 9BH   **Nearest Road A53**

A traditional Victorian/Edwardian former vicarage, in a quiet setting, with good sized rooms. The comfortable bedrooms have TV, tea/coffee making facilities, wash basin and hair dryer. Guests have their own sitting room which overlooks the front garden. Breakfast is served at a large single table and there is a varied menu. Nearby is the Plough Inn which serves good luncheons and evening meals. Places of interest to visit include The Potteries, Alton Towers, Peak Park and Staffordshire Moorlands.

Mrs I Grey
Tel: 01782 503686

B&B from £17.50pp, Rooms 2 twin, 1 double,
No smoking,
Open all year, Map Ref J

The Hollies, Clay Lake, Endon, Stoke-on-Trent, Staffs ST9 9DD   **Nearest Road B5051, A53**

A warm welcome awaits you in this delightful Victorian house which has been sympathetically developed to its present comfortable standard. Situated in a quiet country setting in Endon and within easy reach of The Potteries, Staffordshire Moorlands and Alton Towers. Bedrooms are spacious, comfortable and have central heating, shaver points, colour TV and tea/coffee making facilities. The lounge and dining room overlook a secluded garden. There is a choice of breakfast and home made preserves. Private parking.

Mrs Anne Hodgson
Tel: 01782 503252

B&B from £17pp, Rooms 5 en-suite/private facilities, double, twin
or family, No smoking,
Open all year, Map Ref J

Micklea Farm, Micklea Lane, Longsdon, near Leek, Stoke on Trent, Staffs ST9 9QA   Nearest Road A53

A lovely 18th century cottage set in pleasant gardens complete with a swing for children. Micklea Farm is ideally situated for visits to Alton Towers, the Peak District and the Potteries. The food is excellent, much of which is home grown garden produce. There is a cosy sitting room with an open fire and the house is traditionally furnished and decorated. Whether relaxing or sightseeing this is an ideal base and a warm welcome is guaranteed.

Mrs Barbara White
Tel: 01538 385006
Fax: 01538 382882

B&B from £16pp, Dinner from £11, Rooms 2 single, 2 twin/double,
No smoking, No pets,
Open all year except Christmas, Map Ref K

The Boat House, 71 Newcastle Road, Stone, Staffordshire ST15 8LD   Nearest Road A34

Easily accessible from the M6 and A34, the historic town of Stone, in the beautiful Trent Valley is centrally located for visiting Wedgwood, The Potteries, Peak District, Shrewsbury, Chester etc. A former 18th century inn set in delightful gardens alongside the Trent and Mersey Canal,. The Boat House provides comfortable accommodation in a double and a twin room, with private bathroom, TV and hospitality tray. Guest lounge and ample safe parking. Wide choice of local restaurants and pubs offering good food.

Mrs G. Adams
Tel: 01785 815389

B&B from £18.50pp, Rooms 1 twin, 1 double, private bathroom,
No smoking, Children from 10, No pets,
Open all year except Christmas & New Year, Map Ref L

Please mention
THE GREAT BRITISH
BED & BREAKFAST
when booking your accommodation

DEVONSHIRE

Devon has many faces and its great variety of scenery and indeed climate makes it an ideal holiday county. The rugged northern coast, boasting England's highest cliffs, is a spectacular display of dark grey rocks moulded by the crashing beakers whipped up by Atlantic gales. In contrast the southern coast, the so-called Devon Riviera is noted for its extremely mild climate, its lush vegetation and its sweep of golden sands. Between the two lies the stark desolate beauty of Dartmoor...a large part of which is designated National Park. There are so many diverse attractions in this glorious county, that the holiday maker is spoilt for choice no matter where they might be.

Bideford, once the most important port in North Devon, the great Elizabethan seafarer Sir Richard Grenville secured the town's first charter from Queen Elizabeth I, is now a busy holiday town with steep narrow streets and a quite spectacular bridge over the River Torridge. Nearby is Westward Ho, named after the novel by Charles Kingsley, while adjacent is Appledore where the River Torridge meats the Taw, a delightful picturesque seaside village. Clovelly to the west needs little introduction, being one of the most photographed villages in the country, and further westward at Hartland Quay is some of the most dramatic coastal scenery with rock strata contorted into fantastic shapes, leading south to Welcome, a pretty village and home of the Rev. R.S.Walker who in the late nineteenth century wrote 'The Song of the Western Men'. Barnstaple was an important port for the wool trade until the River Taw silted up. Still a prosperous market town it has some lovely old houses and an impressive Long Bridge. Ilfracombe which developed around an ancient fishing port during the nineteenth century, is the largest resort on the North Devon coast. Its beach of shingle with its many caves is overlooked by the town rising steeply in terraces. This lovely holiday centre is close to Exmoor with its two hudred and sixty five square miles of National Park. Great Torrington from its high vantage point above the River Torridge gives spectacular views over the countryside.

There is no denying that Dartmoor is a bleak place...this great expanse of windswept moor, the highest part of England south of the Pennines, is daunting with its granite outcrop known as Tors, its Bronze Age hut circles and its strange burial mounds, but it is wonderful walking, and of course riding country. Close by is a fascinating abandoned Medieval village and another viewpoint, Hound

Tor. Close-by Widecombe-in-the-Moor is renowned for its large granite fourteenth century church known as 'the Cathedral of the Moor' and of course for 'Widecombe Fair' which is held each September....made famous by the folk song 'Uncle Tom Cobleigh'. The northern terminus of the delightful Dart Valley Railway is at Buckfastleigh. Benedictine monks took thirty years to build Buckfast Abbey a mile to the north of the village. Completed in 1938, the monks sell their tonic wine and honey in theirshop. Tavistock, the western capital of the moor, developed as a town around the tenth century Benedictine abbey. Crowndale Farm, a mile from Tavistock was the birthplace of Sir Francis Drake. Dawlish down to Brixham is regarded as the Devon Riviera. Here are bright blue seas, palm trees and resorts which attract visitors by the thousand and naturally such popularity ensures all the most modern amenities. Here is yachting and sailing to match any Mediterranean resort. Torquay is the largest and most famous of the Devon seaside resorts, ideally sited overlooking Tor Bay. Its extremely mild climate makes Torquay an all the year round resort. There is a lot to see in and around the town, including twelfth century Torre Abbey and the famous Kent's Cavern, one of the oldest known human dwellings in the country. Nearby Paignton,

somewhat overshadowed by its big sister, is nevertheless a popular resort with a zoo, shingle and sand beaches and glorious views from Roundham Head, It was south at Brixham in 1688 that William of Orange landed. Dawlish is an elegant, part Regency, part Victorian town much like its neighbour Teignmouth. Both have lovely gardens and are excellent holiday centres.

Despite its horrendous destruction in one of the World War II Baedeker raids, Exeter retains many interesting features. The Cathedral miraculously escaped the bombing almost unscathed and is a treasure house of Gothic detail, its nave being the longest span of Gothic vaulting in the world. The magnificent west front is covered with carved figures...the intricate detailed carving is continued inside on the remarkable misericordes. The Guildhall in the High Street, its floor resting on granite columns, is claimed to be the oldest municipal building in England. Exeter is an excellent base for touring this corner of Devon. The city has a modern University and all the amenities you would expect to find, but like all the Devon resorts, just a few miles away are secluded villages, quiet lanes and the glories of the Devon countryside.

Places to Visit

Arlington Court, *near Barnstaple* ~ a house covered in lots of lichens and mosses because of the pure air around it. The house contains many collections and the gardens have several walks throughout the grounds.

Burgh Island ~ a short walk across the sands at low tide from Bigbury-on-Sea takes you back to the 1920's and 30's. It was here Archibald Nettlefold built the luxury art deco style Burgh Island Hotel in 1929. The hotel was a famous retreat for Agatha Christie, Noel Coward and the Duke of Windsor.

Castle Drogo, *Drewsteignton* ~ situated on a Dartmoor Crag with views into the wooded gorge of the River Teign, it was the last castle to be built in Britain. It combines 20th century conveniences with a medieval atmosphere. Visitors may play croquet on the large circular lawn.

Coleton Fishacre Garden, *near Dartmouth* ~ a twenty acre garden developed by Lady Dorothy D'Oyly Carte. The garden contains a large collection of tender and exotic plants.

Killerton, *near Exeter* ~ a hillside garden surrounded by parkland and woods. The house was built in 1778 and includes a music room where visitors may play the piano or organ. There is a collection of Paulise de Bush costumes from the 18th century to the present day which are displayed in a series of period rooms.

Lundy Island ~ an unspoilt island with rocky headlands and amazing animal and bird life. Cars are not permitted on the island. so there is a steep walk to the village from the landing beach. In the village there is a church, tavern and castle.

Lydford Gorge, *near Okehampton* ~ best known for the spectacular White Lady Waterfall which falls through the rocks and trees to the river below. A walk through the gorge takes you to the Devil's Cauldron, a whirlpool where the river rushes through a series of potholes.

Morwellham Quay, *near Gunnislake* ~ a neglected and overgrown industrial site until 1970, it has now been restored into a thriving industrial museum. The museum is brought to life by characters in costume who give various demonstrations, or you can ride a tramway deep into a copper mine.

▼ *Brixham Harbour*

DEVONSHIRE

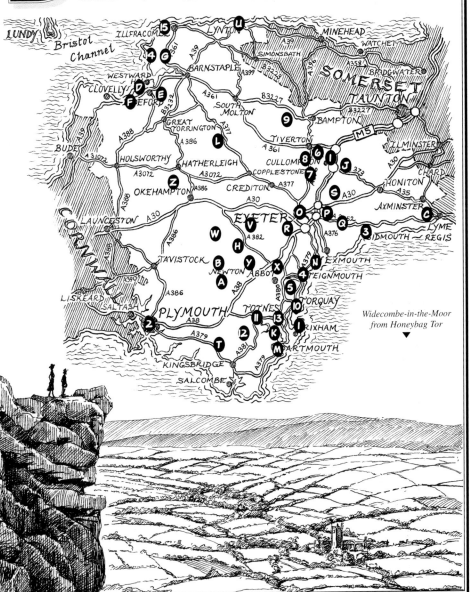

Widecombe-in-the-Moor
from Honeybag Tor
▼

Wellpritton Farm, Holne, Ashburton, Devon TQ13 7RX   **Nearest Road A38**

A warm welcome, personal attention, mouthwatering farm produced food, and Devonshire cream every day awaits you at Wellpritton a beautiful farmhouse on the edge of Dartmoor, where there are goats, lambs, horses, dogs and chickens. Set in the heart of the countryside and yet only 3 miles from the A38 and 1/2 hour from Exeter, Plymouth and Torbay. Riding, fishing, walking sailing and golf are all nearby. The farmhouse is modernised to a high standard with a wood burner and exposed beams in the residents lounge, most rooms are en-suite and all have tea/ coffee facilities. There is a games room also an outdoor swimming pool.

Mrs Susan Gifford
Tel: 01364 631273

B&B from £18pp, Dinner from £9, Half Board £175 weekly, Rooms 2 twin, 2 double, most en-suite, Restricted smoking, Open all year, Map Ref A

New Cott Farm, Poundsgate, near Ashburton, Devon TQ13 7PD   **Nearest Road A38/B3357**

A friendly welcome, beautiful views, pleasing accommodation awaits you at New Cott Farm. A working farm in Dartmoor National Park. Relax in our conservatory after you have enjoyed the freedom and tranquillity of open moorland and Dart Valley or the many attractions of Devon. Lots of lovely homemade food. Tea/coffee and hot chocolate in your en-suite bedrooms. Ideal for lessable guests. TB category 3. B&B. Dinner by prior arrangement. Telephone for a brochure.

Mrs Margaret Phipps
Tel/Fax: 01364 631421

B&B from £18pp, Dinner from £10.50, Rooms 1 twin, 2 double, 1 family, No smoking, Children from 5, No pets, Open all year except Christmas, Map Ref B

The Manor House, Combpyne, near Lyme Regis, Axminster, Devon EX13 6SX   **Nearest Road A3052**

The Manor House was once a nunnery and has a history dating to before the 13th century. Set in spectacular 3 acre grounds and gardens, it offers an ideal centre for exploring beautiful East Devon. One mile from the sea, the tiny village of Combpyne is perfect for those who enjoy peace and country relaxation. Lyme Regis, 5 miles, was the setting for filming Jane Austen's 'Persuasion' and the 'French Lieutenants Woman'. Good pubs and restaurants locally. We look forward to welcoming you. Prebooking only December, January and February.

Nicky & Donald Campbell
Tel: 01297 445084
Fax: 01297 445084

B&B from £23pp, Rooms 1 twin, 2 double, all en-suite or private bathroom, Children welcome, Open all year except Christmas & New Year, Map Ref C

see PHOTO opposite

Lower Winsford, Abbotsham Road, Bideford, Devon EX39 3QP   **Nearest Road A39**

Visitors are welcome at Lower Winsford, to share our comfortable family home. Enjoy the relaxing atmosphere with caring attention at all times. Explore the beautiful countryside around here with many coastal walks. Dartmoor and Exmoor are easily accessible. Unique Clovelly is close by. Rosemoor gardens are always worth a visit. Come and see for yourself.

Mrs Margaret Ogle
Tel: 01237 475083
Fax: 01237 425802

B&B from £19pp, Rooms 1 double en-suite, 1 twin with private bathroom, No smoking, Open Easter - September, Map Ref D

---

left, The Manor House, near Lyme Regis - see details above

The Pines at Eastleigh, Bideford, Devon EX39 4PA **Nearest Road A386**

A warm and friendly welcome awaits you at The Pines at Eastleigh. Relax and enjoy the Grade II listed Georgian former farmhouse, set in 7 rural acres high above Bideford. Freshly cooked traditional English food, featuring local produce is complemented by an imaginative wine list. Ground floor rooms overlook the quiet courtyard. Colour TV, welcome tray, hairdryers, central heating, telephones are standard. Large selection of books and maps to borrow. Licensed. Log fires in winter. Mastercard/VISA. RAC Highly Acclaimed. AA 4Q's. ETB 3 Crowns Highly Commended. EMail: barry@barpines.demon.co.uk

Barry & Jenny Jones
Tel: 01271 860561
Fax: 01271 861248

B&B from £29pp, Dinner from £14, Rooms 2 single, 1 twin, 4 double, all en-suite, cots available, No smoking, Children & pets welcome, Open all year, Map Ref E

Lower Waytown, Horns Cross, near Clovelly, Bideford, Devon EX39 5DN **Nearest Road A39**

This beautifully converted barn and roundhouse has been transformed into a delightful, spacious home offering superb accommodation. Tastefully furnished with antiques the unique round, beamed guests' sitting room adjoins the attractive dining room where delicious breakfasts are served. Bedrooms are en-suite and equipped for every comfort. Relax in extensive grounds with ponds, waterfowl and black swans. Situated in unspoilt countryside with spectacular coastal scenery, pretty coves and coastal footpaths nearby, picturesque Clovelly lies 5 miles westward. AA QQQQQ, Premier Selected.

Chris & Caroline May
Tel/Fax:01237 451787

B&B from £22.50pp, Rooms, 1 twin, 2 double, all en-suite, No smoking, Children over 12 years, No pets, Open all year except Christmas & New Year, Map Ref F

Denham Farm & Country House, North Buckland, Braunton, Devon EX33 1HY **Nearest Road A361**

Off the beaten track this 1700's farmhouse is situated in the centre of a totally unspoilt hamlet only 2 ¹/₂ miles from the superb coast line and sandy beaches of Putsborough and Woolacombe. All en-suite rooms are warmly inviting. The delicious home cooking is definitely tempting. Close by are many attractions including market towns, and Exmoor. Denham has its own games room and play area. RAC Acclaimed, AA QQQ, ETB 3 Crowns Commended. Short break special offers and self catering available.

Mrs Jean Barnes
Tel: 01271 890297
Fax: 01271 890297

B&B from £25pp, Dinner from £12, Rooms 6 double, 2 family, 2 twin, Restricted smoking, Open all year except Christmas, Map Ref G

see PHOTO opposite

Chapple Farm, Chapple Road, Bovey Tracey, Devon TQ13 9JX **Nearest Road B3387**

Chapple is a 14th century farmhouse set in its own farmland 1 ¹/₂ miles from Bovey Tracey on the east side of Dartmoor. Stylishly decorated accommodation in three spacious bedrooms. A full English breakfast is served in the dining room and guests can relax in their own drawing room with TV. A country house in the traditional English manner with cottage style gardens, Chapple is perfect for exploring the Devon countryside, walking, riding or simply relaxing. A warm friendly welcome awaits you at this lovely family home. Reduced rates for children.

Mrs Raphaela Allerfeldt
Tel: 01626 832284

B&B from £19pp, Rooms 1 twin with private bathroom, 1 double, 1 family, Restricted smoking, Children welcome, No pets, Open February - November, Map Ref H

---

left, Denham Farm & Country House, North Buckland - see details above **131**

Rullands, Rull Lane, Cullompton, Devon EX15 1NQ   Nearest Road M5 (Junction 28)

A comfortable 16th century house set amidst beautiful, peaceful, rolling countryside and yet only a few minutes from M5 and historic Tiverton and the market town of Cullompton. Within easy reach of all country pursuits - golf, shooting, fishing, riding, etc. Hard tennis court in grounds. There is an elegant dining room where delicious home cooked meals are served and an interesting wine list is available. All bedrooms are en-suite, have colour TV and courtesy trays.

Georgina Charteris   **B&B from £25pp, Dinner from £15,**
Tel: 01884 33356   **Rooms 2 double, 1 twin, 2 single, Restricted smoking,**
Fax: 01884 35890   **Open all year, Map Ref I**

Millhayes, Kentisbeare, near Cullompton, Devon EX15 2AF   Nearest Road M5,J28

Millhayes is situated in the picturesque village of Kentisbeare, which is only 3 miles from the M5 (junction 28). It is approximately halfway between Taunton and Exeter and within easy reach of the North and South coasts. It also provides a good base for touring Devon villages, Dartmoor and Exmoor. A well stocked 2 acre coarse fishing lake and tennis court are available for guests' use.

Jacki Howe   **B&B from £22.50pp, Rooms 2 single, 1 twin, 1 double, most en-suite,**
Tel: 01884 266412 **No smoking, Children over 12 years, No pets,**
Fax: 01884 266412 **Open all years except Christmas and New Year, Map Ref J**

The White House, Manor Street, Dittisham, Devon TQ6 0EX   Nearest Road A3122/A38

An 18th century traditional stone built house in this picturesque village overlooking the beautiful River Dart. Friendly atmosphere. Full English breakfast. Guest sitting room. Terrace. Parking. Only a few hundred yards from the River, both village pubs, shops and Church. Lovely walks, sailing, fishing, golf, swimming, steam trains and the coast nearby. Easy access to lovely Totnes and the Port of Dartmouth. Plenty of good places to eat a short drive away. Peace and quiet. Dartmoor is also easily reached for riding, driving and walking.

                        B&B from £25pp, Rooms 1 twin, 1 double, all en-suite or private facilities,
Hugh & Jill Treseder **No smoking, Children welcome, No pets,**
Tel/Fax: 01803 722355 **Open all year, Map Ref K**

Eggesford Barton, Eggesford, Chulmleigh, Devon EX18 7QU   Nearest Road A377

Eggesford Barton sits in 100 acres of woodland and meadows in the Taw Valley. This historic courtyard setting, approached through an archway, offers guests a chance to relax; there is a TV lounge, two separate drawing rooms, piano, log fires and classic cars collection. All rooms have tea/coffee making facilities and most of Devon's tourist attractions are within one hour drive. Eggesford Barton also suits businessmen with its modern communication systems.

Jean & Peter Heyes **B&B from £20pp, Dinner from £10.00, Rooms 1 single, 5 twin, 2 double,**
Tel: 01769 580255   **most en-suite, No smoking, Children over 12 years, No pets,**
Fax: 01769 580256   **Open all year, Map Ref L**

Ford House, 44 Victoria Road, Dartmouth, Devon TA6 9DX　　　　　　　Nearest Road A3122

Ford House is a listed Regency House with three comfortable en-suite bedrooms with king or queen size double beds or twin beds, fridges, telephones, colour TVs, radio clock alarms, tea/coffee. Breakfast is served 8am to 12 noon. The traditional full English using free range eggs and dry cured bacon, kippers, smoked haddock, scrambled eggs with smoked salmon or devilled kidneys. Our coffee is freshly ground and orange juice freshly squeezed. We have private parking and are within easy walking distance of the centre of Dartmouth.

Richard & Jayne Turner
Tel/Fax: 01803 834047

B&B from £25pp, Dinner from £25.00, Rooms 2 twin, 2 double, all en-suite, Children welcome, Pets welcome, Open October - March, Map Ref M

Broome Court, Broomhill, Dartmouth, Devon TQ6 0LD　　　　　　　Nearest Road A3122

Broome Court is tucked into a south facing hill, overlooking 3 copses and surrounded by green, undulating south Devon countryside rich in wildlife. The old farm buildings surround a paved courtyard abounding with flowers and shrubs and in the centre a goldfish pond with fountain playing. Breakfast is served in the old farmhouse kitchen - the sort of hearty breakfast dreams are made of. No noise or smell of traffic at Broomhill - nor the hub-hub of everyday life - but the peace and tranquillity of the rolling Devon countryside awaiting you.

Tom Boughton & Jan Bird
Tel: 01803 834275

B&B from £27.50pp, Rooms 1 twin, 2 double, all en-suite, also family unit, Restricted smoking, Children over 12 welcome, Pets by arrangement, Open all year, Map Ref M

West Hatch Hotel, 34 West Cliff, Dawlish, Devon EX7 9DN　　　　　　　Nearest Road A379

West Hatch is your guarantee of a warm welcome and a relaxed stay in our small friendly hotel. A detached house of character with stained glass windows, antiques and oak panelled staircase. We're centrally situated, overlooking the sea. All bedrooms are well-equipped, en-suite and are on ground or first floor. Luxurious four poster room, bar and separate lounge, invigorating spa bath and private parking. Choose from extensive English or continental menu. Awarded AA 4 Q's, RAC Highly Acclaimed and ETB Highly Commended. Major credit cards accepted.

Pat & Dave Badcock
Tel/Fax: 01626 864211

B&B from £21pp, Rooms 1 twin, 7 double, 2 family, all en-suite, Restricted smoking, Children welcome, No pets, Open all year except Christmas & New Year, Map Ref

---

The Edwardian, 30 & 32 Heavitree Road, Exeter, Devon EX1 2LQ　　　　　　　Nearest Road M5, A30 & A38

Two elegant Edwardian townhouses, one a former rectory. Tasteful period decor and furnishings throughout. Near Roman Walls, Cathedral & city centre. Large choice of rooms - single, twins, doubles (including 3 romantic 4-posters: one on ground floor) and rooms for 3 or 4 persons. All en-suite with antique bedsteads. Spa bath. English & vegetarian freshly prepared breakfasts. Hosts' families have lived in Devonshire for generations. They have a thorough knowledge of the west country. Large car park opposite. Discounts for stays of three nights or more.

Michael & Kay Rattensbury
Tel: 01392 276102 & 254699
Fax: 01392 276102

B&B from £22pp, Rooms 2 single, 3 twin, 7 double, 1 family, all en-suite, Children & pets welcome, Open all year except Christmas & Boxing Day, Map Ref O

Raffles, 11 Blackall Road, Exeter, Devon EX4 4HD　　　　　**Nearest Road Exeter Central**

Raffles is a spacious Victorian house furnished in keeping with that period. All rooms are provided with private bathroom, central heating, TV, and tea/coffee making facilities. A traditional English breakfast is served between 7.30 and 9.30 am, an alternative lighter breakfast is also available. A 3 course evening meal can be provided on request and there is a residential table licence. Only 5 minutes walk from the centre of this historic city with all its amenities including the beautiful Norman Cathedral, 14th century Guildhall, shops, gardens, etc. Lock up garages available.

Sue & Richard Hyde　　　　**B&B from £23pp, Dinner from £12, Rooms 2 single, 1 twin, 2 double,**
Tel: 01392 270200　　　　**2 family, all en-suite, Pets by arrangement,**
Fax: 01392 270200　　　　**Open all year, Map Ref O**

Holbrook Farm, Clyst Honiton, Exeter, Devon EX5 2HR　　　　　**Nearest Road A3052**

Enjoy the warm welcome, spectacular views and peaceful surrounding of our dairy farm. Spacious en-suite rooms furnished to a high standard. All with colour TV and hot drinks facilities, off road parking. Excellent local eating places. Situated just off the A3052 Sidmouth Road at Clyst St. Mary 2¹/₂ miles Junction 30 (M5). The cathedral city of Exeter is only a short drive away as are the coast and moors making this an ideal base for any holiday. AA QQQQ Selected. Ground floor room available.

　　　　B&B from £19pp, Rooms 1 twin, 1 double, 1 family, all en-suite,
Heather Glanvill　　　　**No smoking, Children welcome, No pets,**
Tel: 01392 367000　　　　**Open all year, Map Ref P**

Wood Barton, Farringdon, Exeter, Devon EX5 2HY　　　　　**Nearest Road A3052**

Wood Barton is a 17th century farmhouse in quiet countryside, yet only 3 miles from the M5 junction 30. An excellent traditional English breakfast is served cooked on an Aga. Spacious en-suite bedrooms with central heating and hospitality trays. Within 6 miles are the city of Exeter, sandy beaches, National Trust houses, bird reserve, fishing lake, golf course and children's farm and adventure park.

　　　　B&B from £18pp, Rooms 1 twin, 1 double, 1 family, all en-suite,
Mrs Jackie Bolt　　　　**No smoking, Children welcome, No pets,**
Tel: 01395 233407　　　　**Open all year except Christmas & New Year, Map Ref Q**

Drakes Farm House, Drakes Farm, Ide, near Exeter, Devon EX2 9RQ　　　　　**Nearest Road A30/M5**

Drakes Farm House is a listed old oak beamed house with full central heating, set in a large garden in centre of quiet village, with a listed public house and one of the longest road fords in the country. Situated just 2 miles from M5 and cathedral city of Exeter. Convenient for coast and moors. Two restaurants within 5 minutes easy walking distance. Separate TV lounge for guests. Laundry facilities. Tea/coffee making in all rooms. Ample off street private parking.

Mrs Nova Easterbrook　　　　**B&B from £15-£17.50pp, Rooms 1 twin en-suite, 2 double, 1 en-suite,**
Tel: 01392 256814 & 495564　　　　**1 family en-suite, No smoking, Children welcome, No pets,**
Fax: 01392 256814　　　　**Open all year, Map Ref R**

---

　　　　*right, **Court Barton, Aveton Gifford** - see page 136*

Down House, Woodhayes Lane, Whimple, Exeter, Devon EX5 2QR   Nearest Road M5, A30

Edwardian elegance with 20th century comfort. Down House is a peaceful and secluded country house set in 6 acres of gardens, paddocks and orchard. There are splendid views across Whimple Village to cider country, the Tiverton Hills and on a clear day Dartmoor. Easy access from the A30 and M5. Exeter, Honiton and Sidmouth all within 9 miles. The spacious and tastefully appointed rooms have colour TV, tea/coffee making facilities, hair dryer and trouser press. There is a large comfortable south facing guest lounge. Garden games: Croquet, 18 Hole Putting, Boules, Quoits, Skittles and Badminton.

Mike & Joanne Sanders
Tel: 01404 822860

B&B £18-£23pp, Rooms 1 single, 2 twin, 2 double, 1 family, all en-suite, No smoking, Children welcome, Pets by arrangement, Open all year, Map Ref S

Court Barton, Aveton Gifford, Kingsbridge, Devon TQ7 4LE   Nearest Road A379

Court Barton is a 16th century Grade II listed manor house. The farm dates from before Domesday times and is now a small mixed farm. There is a cosy lounge with lots of holiday reading. Many of the pleasant bedrooms are en-suite and all have colour TV. Central heating throughout with log fires in colder weather. English breakfast, or special diets can be catered for by arrangement. Walking, bird watching, sailing, swimming, golf, tennis and horse riding all close by. EMail: jill@devfarms.avel.co.uk

Jill Balkwill
Tel: 01548 550312
Fax: 01548 550312

B&B from £18pp, Rooms 2 double, 2 family, 2 twin, 1 single, most are en-suite, Open all year except Christmas, Map Ref T

Helliers Farm, Ashford, Aveton Gifford, Kingsbridge, Devon TQ7 4ND   Nearest Road A379

Helliers Farm is a small working sheep farm on a hillside. Dating from 1749 Helliers, set in the heart of Devon's unspoilt countryside, 1 mile from the village of Aveton Gifford and 4 miles from Kingsbridge. Recently modernised the farmhouse offers spacious accommodation, traditional dining room, comfortable lounge with TV, and a games room. Adjoining the paved courtyard, spring water feeds a water garden and down the hill there is an extensive fish pool. The charming bedrooms all have tea/coffee trays, and one of the doubles is en-suite. ETB 2 crowns highly commended

Mrs C Lancaster
Tel: 01548 550689
Fax: 01548 550689

B&B from £17.50pp, Rooms 2 double/twin, 1 family, 1 en-suite, No smoking, Open all year except Christmas, Map Ref T

see PHOTO on page 135

right, Wooston Farm, Moretonhampstead - see page 138

Rockvale Hotel, Lee Road, Lynton, Devon EX35 6HW **Nearest Road A39**

In the centre of Lynton yet quietly and peacefully situated on the sunny southern slopes of Hollerday Hill away from the traffic with glorious views and ample level private parking. Our eight pretty bedrooms all have tea/coffee making facilities, colour TV, central heating and telephones. Award winning cuisine and an extensive wine list will enable you to relax and unwind in the informal atmosphere of our guest lounge and bar. The perfect spot for walking or touring Exmoor and the surrounding villages.

David & Judith Woodland
Tel: 01598 752279
or 01598 753343

B&B from £22-24pp, Dinner £14.00, Rooms 1 single, 1 twin,
5 double, 1 family, all en-suite, No smoking, Children from 4, No pets,
Open March - October, Map Ref U

St. Vincent House, Castle Hill, Lynton, Devon EX35 6JA **Nearest Road A39**

Come and relax in our elegant Grade II listed guest house. We are quietly situated with a secluded, sunny garden, just a short walk from the coastal footpath with its spectacular scenery. Enjoy excellent home cooking, dinner by candlelight, good wines and a comfortable lounge with log fire for cooler spring and autumn evenings. Our pretty bedrooms have colour TV and tea/coffee facilities, some are en-suite. We are ideally situated for walking or touring the beautiful Exmoor area. A warm friendly welcome awaits you.

Dave & Mandy Peak
Tel: 01598 752244

B&B from £17pp, Dinner £12.50, Rooms 1 single, 2 twin, 2 double,
1 family, 3 en-suite, No smoking, Children over 8 years, No pets,
Open February - November, Map Ref U

Wooston Farm, Moretonhampstead, Devon TQ13 8QA **Nearest Road A30/B3212**

Wooston, once part of the manor house estate owned by Lord Hambledon, is situated high above Teign Valley in the Dartmoor National Park. Views over open moorland and plenty of walks, golf, fishing and riding nearby. The farmhouse is surrounded by a delightful and well managed garden of half an acre. There are 3 warm and pleasant bedrooms, 2 en-suite, 1 with 4 poster, 1 with private bathroom with every facility included. Excellent breakfast are served to start your day. ETB 2 Crowns Highly Commended. AA 4Q Selected.

Mary Cuming
Tel/Fax: 01647 440367

B&B from £19pp, Rooms 1 twin, 2 double, all en-suite,
No smoking, Children over 8 years, No pets,
Open all year except Christmas, Map Ref V

Great Sloncombe Farm, Moretonhampstead, Devon TQ13 8QF **Nearest Road A382**

Share the magic of Dartmoor all year round while staying in our lovely 13th century farmhouse full of interesting historical features. A working dairy farm set amongst peaceful meadows and woodland abundant in wild flowers and animals including badgers, foxes, deer and buzzards. A welcoming and informal place to relax and explore the moors and Devon countryside. Comfortable, en-suite rooms, central heating, TV's and coffee/tea making. Delicious Devonshire suppers and breakfasts with new baked bread. ETB 3 Crowns Highly Commended. AA 4Q Selected.

Trudie, Robert, & Helen
Merchant
Tel: 01647 440595

B&B from £10-£21pp, Dinner from £11, Rooms 2 double, 1 twin,
Minimum age 8, No smoking,
Open all year, Map Ref V

see PHOTO on page 137

Gate House, North Bovey - see page 141

Gate House, North Bovey, near Moretonhampstead, Devon TQ13 8RB   **Nearest Road A30/A38**

Gate House, in the Dartmoor National Park is a 15th century thatched home in a medieval village amidst breathtaking scenery. Rooms are charmingly furnished offering classical country style elegance with all modern facilities. Most rooms have beamed ceilings and there is a massure granite fireplace with bread oven and log fires in the sitting room. There is a large secluded garden with swimming pool and spectacular views. There are many opportunities for bird watching, walks on Dartmoor and the coast, or visiting National Trust properties.

John & Sheila Williams
Tel/Fax: 01647 440479

B&B from £23pp, Dinner from £14.00, Rooms 1 twin, 2 double, all en-suite, No smoking, Children over 15 years, Pets by arrangement, Open all year, Map Ref W

see PHOTO on page 139

The Thatched Cottage, 9 Crossley Moor Road, Kingsteignton, Newton Abbot TQ12 3LE   **Nearest Road A380**

The Thatched Cottage Restaurant a Grade II listed 16th century thatched longhouse of great character. A licensed restaurant with cosy cocktail bar featuring a large open fireplace. Serving only fresh food prepared to the highest standards at value for money prices. All rooms have central heating, colour TV and tea/coffee making facilities and are well furnished and decorated.

Klaus & Janice Wiemeyer
Tel: 01626 65650

B&B from £20pp, Dinner a la carte or £12 Table D'hote menu, Rooms 1 single, 2 double/twin, 1 family suite (2 rooms), all en-suite, No smoking, Open all year, Map Ref X

see PHOTO opposite

Brookside, Lustleigh, Newton Abbot, Devon TQ13 9TJ   **Nearest Road A382**

Brookside, with a history dating back to the 15th century, is situated in the picturesque village of Lustleigh, within the Dartmoor National Park. Its landscaped garden contains an old granite bridge and is raised up on what was once a railway embankment. The comfortably furnished bedrooms and balconied guest lounge have superb views across the garden, river, village cricket field and open countryside. All bedrooms have washbasin, central heating and tea/coffee making facilities. Glorious countryside for walking and touring with many places of interest to visit.

Judy & John Halsey
Tel: 01647 277310

B&B from £19pp, Light suppers from £4, Rooms 1 twin, 2 double, No smoking, Children welcome, Pets by arrangement, Open all year, Map Ref Y

Sampsons Farm, Preston, Newton Abbot, Devon TQ12 3PP   **Nearest Roads A38, A380, B3195, B3193**

Thatched 14th century longhouse with oak beams, panelling and inglenook fireplaces. Sampsons is a Grade II listed building, low beams, creaky floors and hidden away in the hamlet of Preston with lovely walks along River Teign. Always a warm welcome and a cheerful atmosphere. All rooms have tea/coffee making facilities, and colour TV. The restaurant has an excellent reputation with only the finest produce being used. House speciality $1/2$ duckling, homemade sweets. Licensed bar and cellar with wines from around the world. Stable barn conversion 3 luxury en-suite rooms, one with bath.

Nigel Bell
Tel: 01626 354913
Fax: 01626 354913

B&B from £18.50-£30pp, Dinner from £12.50-£25, Rooms 5 double en-suite, 3 double non en-suite, Cottage with 2 bedrooms, (doubles), Open all year, Map Ref Y

---

left, The Thatched Cottage, Kingsteignton - see details above   **141**

Fairway Lodge, Thorndon Cross, Okehampton, Devon EX20 4NE   **Nearest Road A3079**

All rooms are comfortably appointed and lockable. Your receive a front door key on arrival, guests may stroll over our ten acres of organic pasture which accommodate miniature Shetland Ponies and Aberdeen Angus Cattle. Approx 3/4 acre of gently sloping garden with disabled access to ground floor accommodation. Organic fruit, vegetables and preserves which are served at table. Beverage facilities in all rooms. Ample off road parking. Ideal central base for rural pursuits. Guest TV lounge. Quiet relaxing happy home. Come and enjoy the peace. Top 20 Finalist of AA Landlady of the Year 1996/97.

Daphne & Andy Burgoine
Tel/Fax: 01837 52827

B&B from £18pp, Dinner from £9.50, Rooms 1 twin, 1 double, 1 family, all en-suite, Restricted smoking, Children welcome, Pets welcome, Open all year, Map Ref Z

Elberry Farm, Broadsands, Paignton, Devon TQ4 6HJ   **Nearest Road A3022**

Elberry Farm is a working farm with beef, poultry and arable production. The farmhouse is between 2 beaches both within a 2 minute walk. Broadsands being a safe bathing beach has been awarded the European Blue Flag 1994. As an alternative there is a 9 hole pitch and putt golf course opposite; and a short drive away there is the zoo, town centre and the National Park. The comfortable bedrooms all have tea/coffee making facilities. Guests are welcome to relax in the lounge; and stroll around the secluded garden. Baby sitting service available by arrangement.

Mrs Mandy Tooze
Tel: 01803 842939

B&B from £13pp, Dinner from £5.50, Rooms 1 twin, 3 double/family, Restricted smoking, Pets by arrangement, Open January - November, Map Ref 1

Irvines Bed & Breakfast, 50 Grand Parade, West Hoe, Plymouth, Devon PL1 3DJ   **Nearest Road A374**

Irvine's Bed & Breakfast is a well appointed small guest house offering very comfortable accommodation. We offer traditional English Breakfast, attractive bedrooms have TV, tea/coffee making facilities. Some parking at rear. Overlooking Drake's Island and Plymouth Sound it is well within walking distance of the city centre, barbican and other local amenities. Ideally situated for passengers using the ferries. Plymouth is also in ideal centre for touring both Devon and Cornwall.

Pat & Alex Irvine
Tel: 01752 227739

B&B from £15pp, Rooms 1 twin, 1 double, Restricted smoking, No pets, Open February - December Map Ref 2

Netton Farmhouse, Noss Mayo, near Plymouth, Devon PL8 1HB   **Nearest Road A379**

The hamlet of Netton is located about 1/2 mile from the beautiful Yealm Estuary and picturesque village of Noss Mayo. The stunning views of the South Devon Coastal path are but a few minutes walk from the house. We offer 3 beautiful bedrooms with en-suite or private facilities - one rooom is located on the ground floor - a seperate guest lounge/breakfast room is also offered. Within the grounds we have a heated indoor swimming pool, tennis court and 'fun' croquet lawn. Homemade muesli, preserves and bread are freshly baked and complememnt the traditional farmhouse fayre. ETB Highly Commended. AA QQQQ Selected.

Mrs Lesley-Ann Brunning
Tel: 01752 873080
Fax: 01752 873080 - call first

B&B from £23pp, Dinner from £14, Rooms 1 twin, 2 double, all en-suite, No smoking, Children welcome, Pets by arrangement, Open all year except Christmas, Map Ref 2

---

     right, Fonthill, Shaldon- see page 144

Cheriton Guest House, Vicarage Road, Sidmouth, Devon EX10 8UQ Nearest Road A3052

Cheriton Guest House is a large town house which backs on to the River Sid, with the 'Byes' parkland beyond. There are private parking spaces at the rear. The half mile walk to the seafront, via the town centre, is all on level ground. Cheriton is notorious for its fine cooking and varied menus. There is a comfortable lounge with colour TV. Beautiful secluded rear garden for the exclusive use of guests. All bedrooms have central heating, colour TV and tea/coffee making facilities and all rooms are en-suite.

Diana & John Lee
Tel: 01395 513810

B&B from £18pp, Dinner from £7, Rooms 3 single, 5 double/twin, 2 family, all en-suite, Restricted smoking, Children welcome, Pets by arrangement, Open all year, Map Ref 3

Thomas Luny House, Teign Street, Teignmouth, Devon TQ14 8EG Nearest Road A381

Thomas Luny House, the home of Alison and John Allan and their family was built by the marine artist Thomas Luny, tucked away in a conservation area. The house, surrounded by a beautiful secluded walled garden, is tastefully furnished with antiques and has 4 themed en-suite bedrooms, two with views of the River Teign. Each bedroom has remote controlled TV and direct dial telephone. There is ample car parking in the front courtyard. Teignmouth is an excellent centre for exploring South Devon and Dartmoor.

Alison & John Allan
Tel: 01626 772976

B&B from £25pp, Rooms 2 twin, 2 double, Children from 12, No pets, Open February - December, Map Ref 4

Fonthill, Torquay Road, Shaldon, Teignmouth, Devon TQ14 0AX Nearest Road A379

Fonthill is peacefully situated in its own beautiful grounds of 25 acres, close to the pretty coastal village of Shaldon. The 3 delightful bedrooms have views of the gardens and the River Teign, and the village pubs and restaurants are within easy walking distance. There is a hard tennis court and the coastal path to Torquay is nearby. Dartmoor National Park is within easy reach, also Plymouth, Exeter and several fine National Trust properties. Fonthill is an AA 'Selected' guest house and ETB 'Highly Commended'.

Mrs Jennifer Graeme
Tel: 01626 872344
Fax: 01626 872344

B&B from £25pp, Rooms 3 twin with private or en-suite bathroom, No smoking, No pets, Open March - November, Map Ref 5

Virginia Cottage, Brook Lane, Shaldon, Teignmouth, Devon TQ14 0HL Nearest Road B3199

Virginia Cottage is a Grade II listed 17th century house set within a peaceful, partly walled, garden offering a delightful and relaxing place to stay. The pretty bedrooms with en-suite/private facilities, and tea/coffee makers, overlook the gardens and there is an attractive sitting room with large inglenook fireplace. A short walk to the coastal village of Shaldon where good pubs and restaurants are to be found. This is an ideal location for walking or exploring the Dartmoor National Park, Cathedral city of Exeter and delights of Devon. Car parking in grounds.

Jennifer & Michael Britton
Tel: 01626 872634
Fax: 01626 872634

B&B from £23pp, Rooms 2 twin, 1 double, all en-suite, No smoking, Minimum age 12, No pets, Open March - December, Map Ref 5

see PHOTO on page 143

Poole Farm, Ash Thomas, Tiverton, Devon EX16 4NS   **Nearest Road A361, M5**

Poole Farm is an attractive old farmhouse, which has recently been renovated. It is set in 18 acres of pasture with a pretty garden and lovely views. Bedrooms are en-suite with colour television and tea/coffee making facilities. It is in a quiet hamlet but only 15 minutes from the M5 and Tiverton Parkway railway station. An ideal touring centre for Dartmoor, Exmoor and the coast, there are several National Trust properties nearby and places of interest as well as many gardens.

Mrs Jenny Shaw
Tel: 01884 820201

B&B £20pp, Dinner from £15 by prior arrangement,
Rooms 1 twin, 1 double, both en-suite, No smoking, Children welcome,
Pets by arrangement, Open all year, Map Ref 6

Bickleigh Cottage Hotel, Bickleigh, near Tiverton, Devon EX16 8RJ   **Nearest Road A396**

see PHOTO on page 145

Situated on the bank of the River Exe near Bickleigh Bridge, a landmark famous for its scenic beauty, Bickleigh Cottage Country Hotel has been privately owned by the Cochrane family since 1933. The original cottage was built circa 1640 with additions in the 1970's. All bedrooms are en-suite and have tea/coffee making facilities. The location of Bickleigh makes it a perfect centre for touring Devon. Exeter with its cathedral and maritime museum, Tiverton Castle, Knightshayes Court and Killerton House are all nearby.

R S H & P M Cochrane
Tel: 01884 855230

B&B from £23.50pp, Dinner from £11.40, Rooms 1 single, 3 twin,
4 double, all en-suite, Restricted smoking, Minimum age 14,
Open April to October, Map Ref 7

Little Holwell, Collipriest, Tiverton, Devon EX16 4PT   **Nearest Road M5/A361/A396**

Little Holwell is a traditional Devon Longhouse believed to be 13th Century with beamed ceilings, spiral staircase and an inglenook fireplace. The house is centrally heated, with log fires in the winter. You are assured of a warm welcome with a refreshing cup of tea. An optional evening meal is available, cooked on our traditional Aga using the best local produce. From the garden you can enjoy pleasant views over the surroundings countryside, or set off on one of the many interesting walks in the area. Ideal touring centre.

Mrs Ruth Hill-King
Tel/Fax: 01884 257590

B&B from £16pp, Dinner from £8.50, Rooms 2 double, 1 family,
most en-suite, No smoking or pets,
Open all year except Christmas, Map Ref 8

Newhouse Farm, Oakford, Tiverton, Devon EX16 9JE   **Nearest Road A396/B3227**

Enjoy a real taste of country living on our sheep farm on the edge of Exmoor. The farmhouse, built in 1600 is down a stone lane and has pretty bedrooms with en-suite, colour TV and tea/coffee trays. There's a beamed dining room, lounge with inglenook and a quiet garden for relaxing. We serve traditional breakfasts with home-made bread and preserves; also delicious four-course dinners if you wish. We're ideal for visiting National Trust houses, gardens and touring coasts and moors. Recommended by Which? B&B Guide, AA 4Q Selected.

Anne Boldry
Tel: 01398 351347

B&B from £18pp, Dinner from £11.00, Rooms 1 twin, 2 double,
all en-suite, Restricted smoking, Children from 10, No pets,
Open March - December, Map Ref 9

right, The Old Forge at Totnes- see page 149

Kingston House, 75 Avenue Road, Torquay, Devon TQ2 5LL   Nearest Road A3022

Everyone is assured of our West Country welcome, not optional but guaranteed, with Brian & Anita. Combine Victorian elegance with modern amenities, ensuring a relaxing, enjoyable visit. Tastefully decorated en-suite bedrooms with tea/coffee facilities and television. Comfortable guests lounge and extensive breakfast menu. RAC "Highly Acclaimed" award in recognition of high standards and facilities. AA QQQQ "Selected" award for quality, constantly providing high levels of service and comfort. Level walk seafront, harbour/town via beautiful Torre Abbey Gardens, English Riviera Centre. Private car parking.

Brian & Anita Sexon
Tel: 01803 212760

B&B from £14.50pp, Rooms 2 single, 1 twin, 2 double, 1 family, all en-suite, Children over 8, No pets, Open all year except Christmas and New Year, Map Ref 10

The Old Forge at Totnes, Seymour Place, Totnes, Devon TQ9 5AY   Nearest Road A381, A384, A38

Find a warm welcome in relaxing surroundings all year round in this historic 600 year old stone building with cobbled drive and coach arch leading into the delightful walled garden. It is a rural haven, 4 minutes walk from Totnes town centre and riverside. Luxurious and cosy cottage style rooms are all en-suite with CTV, radio-alarms, hair dryer and beverage tray. Licensed. Own parking. Huge breakfast menu, (traditional, vegetarian, continental and special diets). Conservatory leisure lounge with whirlpool spa. Speciality golf breaks. AA Selected Award. ETB Highly Commended.

Mrs Jeannie Allnutt
Tel: 01803 862174
Fax: 01803 865385

B&B from £25pp en-suite dble/£35 single, Rooms 1 sgle, 2 twin, 2 dble, 5 family, all en-suite, ground floor rooms available, No smoking indoors, Children welcome, Pets only in cars, Open all year, Map Ref 11

see PHOTO on page 147

Orchard House, Horner, Halwell, Totnes, Devon TQ9 7LB   Nearest Road A381

Tucked away in the countryside of the South Hams, between Totnes and Kingsbridge, Orchard House, with its peaceful setting nestles within an old cider orchard. It offers superb accommodation: all bedrooms are en-suite with colour TV, tea/coffee making facilities and beautiful furnishings. Breakfasts are ample, with cereals, juic,e yoghurts and grapefruit, followed by a cooked platter with toast and croissants. Also, guests' own sitting and dining room with antique furnishings and a log fire. Large garden and private parking.

Mrs Helen Worth
Tel: 01548 821448

B&B from £20pp, Rooms 1 twin, 1 double, 1 family, all en-suite, No smoking, Children over 3 years, No pets, Open March - November, Map Ref 12

see PHOTO opposite

The Red Slipper, Stoke Gabriel, Totnes, Devon TQ9 6RU   Nearest Road A385

A small, friendly, licenced establishment appointed to a high standard, located in the centre of a picturesque and peaceful village on the River Dart. Launching facilities are available. The attractive, en-suite, bedrooms have remote control colour television, clock/radio, hair dryer, tea/coffee making facilities, fresh flowers, fruit and sweets. A sheltered courtyard garden is available all day. A la Carte dinner is served by arrangement Monday to Staurday using mainly local produce together with traditional Sunday lunch. Parking available. AA 4 Q's.

John & Elizabeth Watts
Tel: 01803 782315
Fax: 01803 782315

B&B from £22.50pp, Dinner from £13.50, Rooms 3 twin, 1 double, 1 family, all en-suite, Restricted smoking, Children welcome, Pets by arrangement, Open mid March - end October, Map Ref 13

---

left, Orchard House, Halwell, Totnes - see above for details

Sandunes, Beach Road, Woolacombe, Devon EX34 7BT   Nearest Road A361

Sandunes is a very pleasant, most comfortable, modern, non smoking guest house. All rooms are en-suite with tea/coffee trays and most rooms have television. There is also a guest television lounge, garden and sun patio with stunning views out to sea. Ample car parking facilities are available. This is an ideal base for touring or for enjoying our 'Blue Flag' award beach. Ilfracombe, Lynton, Lymouth and Exmoor are within easy reach also the gardens of Marwood and Rosemoor. Regret no children or pets.

Jean & Charles Boorman
Tel: 01271 870661

B&B from £18pp, Dinner £10, Rooms 1 single, 1 twin, 5 double, all en-suite, No smoking, No children, No pets, Open March - October, Map Ref 14

Sunnycliffe Hotel, Chapel Hill, Mortehoe, Woolacombe, Devon EX34 7EB   Nearest Road A361

Small award winning quality hotel set above picturesque Devon Cove on heritage coast.   All bedrooms have magnificent sea views, colour TV, tea/coffee making facilities, and are en-suite. Five course dinner with varied menu prepared from fresh local produce. Plenty of walks through hidden valleys, coastal paths where countryside greets the sea in breathtaking scenic beauty. Regret no children or pets. Brochure available.

Mr & Mrs G. Oakes
& Mr & Mrs D. Budden
Tel/Fax: 01271 870597

B&B from £25pp, Dinner from £15, Rooms 6 double, 2 twin, Minimum age 12, Restricted smoking to bar area only, Open February - November, Map Ref 15

Please mention
THE GREAT BRITISH
BED & BREAKFAST
when booking your accommodation

"Trees old, and young, sprouting a shady boon
For simple sheep"
John Keats

DORSET

The many lovers of the novels of Thomas Hardy know that his fictional county of Wessex is in fact Dorset, and there are few parts of Dorset he doesn't include under a pseudonym in his novels. Dorset is a perfect holiday venue as its scenery varies so considerably, and being such a small county - only fifty miles from east to west and twenty-five from north to south, the visitor is able to move conveniently from one attraction to another. Not only does the county offer delightful rural scenery, it also boasts a fascinating coastline and in the east of the county there is wonderful walking country, wild heath-land and lonely hills. In direct contrast is the valley of the Stour, Shaftsbury is a fine centre for exploring this valley and the Blackmoor Vale. Hardy calls the town by its ancient name 'Shaston' in his novels. Built seven hundred feet above the Blackmoor Vale, the town developed around a nunnery endowed by King Alfred the Great.

The picturesque cobbled Gold Hill with its eighteenth century stepped houses is one of the most photographed subjects in a county of glorious sights. Dorchester is the administrative centre of Dorset, and a market town of great antiquity and charm, today little changed I fancy from Thomas Hardy's 'Casterbridge'. Hardy's birthplace at nearby Bockhampton affords a view of the heathland which so inspired him.

Overlooking Chesil Beach and the Isle of Portland is the Hardy Monument - commemorating another Thomas Hardy, Nelson's flag-captain at the Battle of Trafalgar. North-east of Dorchester is Tolpuddle, the village made famous by six farm labourers who formed their own trade union in 1834 and are known as the Tolpuddle Martyrs, as for their efforts they were sentenced to seven years transportation to Australia. Maiden Castle, south-west of Dorchester is the most impressive Iron Age fort in Britain, believed to have been occupied first around 2,000 BC.

For anyone who is interested in fossils, the coast of Dorset is renowned. Lyme Regis in a National Nature Reserve is a lovely resort much enjoyed by Jane Austen and its Regency houses are much the same as they were in her days. The winding sea wall known as the Cobb is of Medieval origin and was made famous through the film of John Fowle's novel The French Lieutenant's Woman. At Weymouth whose popularity was ensured when George III took to sea-bathing, are elegant houses in Classical style reflecting the taste of those who flocked to emulate their monarch. But long before these times the town was a notable port appreciated by Romans, Saxons and Normans before eventually Henry VIII developed it as his naval base. The harbour is protected by the Isle of Portland, a plateau of rock connected to the mainland by a shingle causeway, which is in turn a part of the ten miles of Chesil Beach. The enclosed lagoon, known as Fleet is a haven for birds.

Poole, one of the largest shallow-water anchorages in the country, was developed as a major port in the thirteenth century and was the haunt of pirates and smugglers. The town is a marvellous holiday centre with fine sandy beaches and wonderful historical buildings. In the middle of the bay is Brownsea Island, the birthplace of the Boy Scout movement and a Nature Reserve owned by the National Trust. Across the bay is impressive Corfe Castle, its ruined Norman keep towering over the quaint village of grey stone houses. It was here in 978AD that King Edward the Martyr was murdered. North of Poole stands Wimborne Minster, home for some years of Thomas Hardy, who wrote in one of his poems of the twin-towered chequered Minster Church of St. Cuthberga. To the north is Cranborne, an attractive village with a grand main street lined with brick and timber houses. Here the Chase Court controlled the hunting rights in Cranborne Chase, a royal forest and now an area of beautiful rolling, wooded countryside. The highest village in Dorset is Ashmore, surrounded by fine beech and sycamore trees. From its lofty perch

there are magnificent views over Cranborne Chase and across the Solent to the Isle of Wight. Sherborne is a perfect base for exploring west Dorset, and is rich in historical associations. Sir Walter Raleigh lived in Sherborne Old Castle for fifteen years. Its Medieval abbey church was built in the eighth century as a cathedral, and is constructed of golden Ham Hill stone. The famous Sherborne School was rebuilt in 1550 replacing a cathedral school reputedly attended by King Alfred the Great. To the south, and cut into the turf of the chalk hillside is the monstrous one hundred and eighty feet tall naked figure of the Cerne Abbas Giant. Probably one thousand, five hundred years old, it is believed to be associated with pagan fertility rites.

Whether it is fossils, ancient monuments, impressive manor houses, seaside pleasures, lazy days in wonderful countryside or the sampling of Dorset's Blue Vinny cheese, there is more than enough in this glorious county to keep the holiday maker occupied....and anxious to return for more.

Places to Visit

Abbotsbury Swanary, *Abbotsbury* ~ a unique colony of swans established by monks in the 14th century.

Brownsea Island, *Poole* ~ a five hundred acre nature reserve with deer, red squirrel and water fowl. It was used in 1907 by Baden Powell to launch the Boy Scout movement, today it is owned by the National Trust.

Chesil Beach, *Dorset* ~ a strange phenomenon, it is made up of a seventeen mile bank of peebles up to thirty five feet high and up to two hundred yards wide enclosing the Fleet Lagoon. The stones are naturally graded by the currents.

Compton Acres, *Dorset* ~ over nine acres of beautiful gardens with views over Poole Harbour and the Purbeck Hills. Italian and Japanese gardens have been reproduced in detail and there are water gardens and woodland walks.

Corfe Castle, *Wareham* ~ the ruins of a one thousand year old castle dominating the Isle of Purbeck. The ruins have many medieval defensive features and with some of the best early Gothic architecture in England.

Guildhall Museum, *Poole* ~ an insight into the civic and social life of Poole during the 18th and 19th centuries, displayed in a Georgian market house.

Kingston Lacey, *Dorset* ~ a 17th century mansion restored with ornate interiors. The Spanish Room in gilded leather with a guilded ceiling from a Venetian palace. It also houses an amazing art collection with work by Van Dyck, Rubens, Lely, Lawerence and Jan Brueghel the Elder and a collection of Eygptian artefacts.

Maiden Castle, *near Dorchester* ~ this is not castle but is the finest earthworks in Britain. Built in the 1st century BC, it was fortified with ramparts and complex entrances. In 43 AD, the Romans slaughtered its inhabitants and today all its structures have gone but its series of concentric rings covering one hundred and fifteen acres are still impressive.

Parnham House, *Beaminster* ~ a Tudor manor house with some later work by architect John Nash. The house has leaded windows, some spectacular plasterwork, gardens and workshops.

Wimborne Minster, *Dorset* ~ founded in 705 AD and rebuilt in 1120, the Minster Church of St Cuthburga dominates this small market town. On the outside of the Minster is a colourful Quarter Jack figure which strikes the church bell every ▼ *Corfe* fifteen minutes.   *Castle*

DORSET

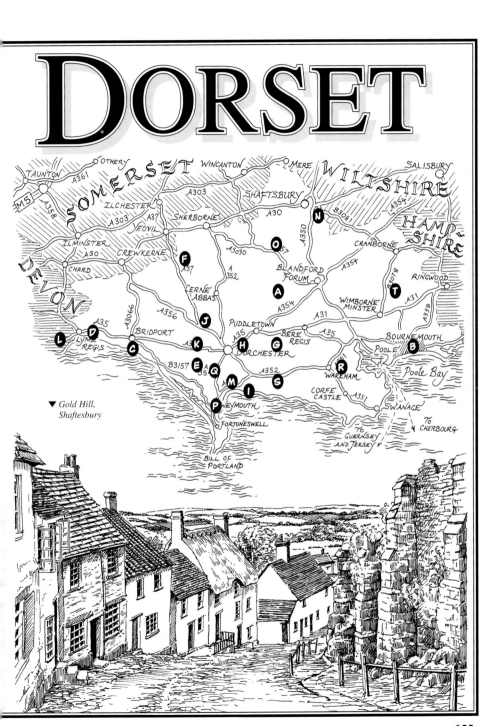

▼ Gold Hill,
Shaftesbury

Stocklands House, Hilton, Blandford, Dorset DT11 0DE   **Nearest Road A354**

A peaceful, comfortable and sunny house in 12 acres yet well situated for sightseeing and only 30 minutes from the coast. The delightfully appointed ground floor bedrooms offer every comfort. Heated outdoor pool (June/September), clay shooting, table tennis, wonderful walks or bring your horse and enjoy some lovely riding. Relax by the log fire, play the piano or Trivial Pursuit! Yours hostess is an excellent cook and will tempt you with delicious dinners, breakfasts, picnics or a Dorset cream tea. Special diets catered for.

Mrs Sumner-Fergusson
Tel: 01258 880580
Fax: 01258 881188

B&B from £18.50pp, Dinner from £10, Rooms 2 twin, 1 double, all en-suite, Restricted smoking, Children & pets by arrangement, Open all year except Christmas and New Year, Map Ref A

Gervis Court Hotel, 38 Gervis Road, East Cliff, Bournemouth BH1 3DH   **Nearest Road A338**

Gervis Court Hotel is a Victorian house of character set in its own grounds nestling amongst the pine trees. It is a pleasant surprise to find the beautiful sandy beach, conference centre, shops and theatres only a few minutes walk away. We have ample parking, some ground floor bedrooms all with bathrooms, TV and tea/coffee facilities. Gervis Court Hotel is in an ideal spot for exploring the delights of Bournemouth, New Forest and the unspoilt Dorset countryside and coastline.

Alan & Jackie Edwards
Tel: 01202 556871
Fax: 01202 556871

B&B from £18pp, Rooms 1 single, 2 twin, 6 double, 3 family, all en-suite, No smoking, Children welcome, No pets, Open all year, Map Ref B

The Boltons Hotel, 9 Durley Chine Road South, West Cliff, Bournemouth BH2 5JT   **Nearest Road A338**

This comfortable Victorian House in the heart of the West Cliff. Twelve En-suite bedroomed family hotel situated in its own secluded grounds yet within a few minutes walk of main beaches, shops and The Bournemouth International Centre. Colour TV, tea/coffee making facilities. Bargain breaks available. Seasonally heated outdoor pool. Open all year, Christmas programme. Ample parking. VISA. AA QQQQ. RAC Highly Acclaimed.

Mary Messham
Tel: 01202 751517
Fax: 01202 751629

B&B from £27.50pp, Dinner from £12.00, Rooms 1 single, 2 twin, 7 double, 2 family, Restricted smoking, Children from 5, Pets by arrangement, Open March - December, Map Ref B

Britmead House, West Bay Road, Bridport, Dorset DT6 4EG   **Nearest Road A35**

A recently refurbished, licensed hotel with a reputation for friendliness and high standards. Pleasantly located a short walk from West Bay Harbour, Chesil Beach and the Dorset Coastal Path. Bedrooms are well equipped with many extras. The south west facing lounge and dining room overlook the garden beyond which is open countryside. Private car parking. Food is renowned for its excellence using local fish and fresh produce when possible. Swimming, golf, fossil hunting, seafishing, walking all nearby. AA 4QQQQ Selected, RAC Acclaimed, Les Routiers, ETB 3 Crown Highly Commended.

Ann & Dan Walker
Tel: 01308 422941
Fax: 01308 422516

B&B from £20pp, Dinner £13.50, Rooms 4 double, 3 twin, all en-suite, 1 room is on the ground floor, Minimum age 5, Restricted smoking, Pets by arrangement, Open all year, Map Ref C

right, Brambles, Melbury Bubb - see page 158

Newlands House, Stonebarrow Lane, Charmouth, Dorset DT6 6RA   Nearest Road A35

A house of character offering you a comfortable place to stay, delicious food and wine. Accommodation includes guest sitting room and bar lounge. No smoking except in bar lounge. We are quietly situated in about 2 acres of garden, in an area of outstanding natural beauty, adjacent to Lyme Regis, the heritage coastal path and the famous fossil cliffs. All rooms have central heating. colour TV and tea/coffee making facilities. There is ample car parking within our grounds. ETB 3 Crowns Commended. AA 4Q Selected. RAC Acclaimed.

Anne & Vernon Vear
Tel: 01297 560212

B&B from £23.75pp, Dinner £14.50, Rooms 3 single, 2 en-suite, 3 en-suite twin, 4 en-suite double, 2 en-suite family, Restricted smoking, Children from 6 years, Special breaks, Open March - October, Map Ref D

The Old Post Office, Martinstown, Dorchester, Dorset DT2 9LF   Nearest Road B3159

Situated in the Winterbourne Valley, The Old Post Office, is a stone and slate Georgian cottage used as the village post office until 1950. It is part of a row of cottages that are all listed buildings. Winterbourne St Martin (Martinstown) is in the heart of Hardy country, 2 miles from the Neolithic Hill Fort of Maiden Castle, Hardy's monument and the town of Dorchester. The coast and beach are 5 miles away and it is an ideal walking and touring base. The bedrooms all have washbasins, tea/coffee making facilities, and some have TV.

Mrs Jane Rootham
Tel: 01305 889254

B&B £15- £17.50pp, Dinner from £10, Rooms 2 twin, 1 double, Children welcome, Pets by arrangement, Open all year, Map Ref E

Brambles, Woolcombe, Melbury Bubb, near Dorchester, Dorset DT2 0NJ   Nearest Road A37

A delightful thatched cottage set in peaceful countryside near the historic towns of Dorchester and Sherborne, and a short drive to the coast. Beautifully appointed and well equipped, it offers every comfort, and a friendly welcome. The pretty bedrooms always have fresh flowers, also colour TV and tea/coffee making facilities. There is a wide choice of breakfast, including traditional, continental, vegetarian or fruit platter. There are many places of interest to visit and walks to explore. Parking within grounds. Special rates for longer stays.

Anita & Andre Millorit
Tel: 01935 83672
Fax: 01935 83003

B&B from £20pp, Rooms 2 single, 1 twin en-suite, 1 double en-suite, No smoking, Children welcome, No pets, Open all year except Christmas & New Year, Map Ref F

see PHOTO on page 157

Vartrees House, Moreton, Dorchester, Dorset DT2 8BE   Nearest Road B3390, off A35

A peaceful, secluded, country house built by Hermann Lea, a friend of Thomas Hardy, set in 3 acres of picturesque woodland gardens which attract wildlife. Accommodation throughout is spacious and comfortable. Tea/coffee making facilities in all rooms. TV lounge. Situated near the pretty village of Moreton with its renowned church containing engraved windows by Laurence Whistler and the burial place of Lawrence of Arabia. Coast 4 miles. Station $^1/_4$ mile. Excellent local pubs. A delightful base for a peaceful and relaxing holiday.

Mrs D M Haggett
Tel: 01305 852704

B&B from £18pp, Rooms 2 double, 1 twin, Children - minimum age 10, Pets by arrangement, Open all year, Map Ref G

right, Magiston Farm, Sydling St Nicholas - see page 161

Muston Manor, Piddlehinton, Dorchester, Dorset DT2 7SY Nearest Road B3143

Originally built in 1609 by the Churchill family, it remained in their ownership until bought by the present owners in 1975. Situated in the peaceful Piddle Valley with its many good pubs, the house is set in five acres, surrounded by farmland. Large comfortable, well-furnished rooms with tea/coffee making facilities and central heating. Heated swimming pool in season.

Mr & Mrs O B N Paine
Tel: 01305 848242

**B&B from £19pp, Rooms 2 double, 1 en-suite,
No smoking, Children welcome over 10, Pets by arrangement,
Open April - October, Map Ref H**

The Creek, Ringstead, Dorchester, Dorset DT2 8NG Nearest Road A353

Ringstead is situated on the Heritage Coastal path approximately 7 miles from both Weymouth and Dorchester. It is within easy reach of many important National Trust properties and is ideally situated for artists, bird watchers, walkers and watersport enthusiasts. The house has a large garden overlooking the seashore and surrounded by farmland. There is full central heating and showers in all bedrooms and a spacious sitting room and comfortable dining room. Gourmet evening meals available by arrangement. A heated swimming pool during summer months.

Mrs Fisher
Tel: 01305 852251

**B&B from £18.50pp, Dinner from £10.50, Rooms 2 double,
Minimum age 8, No smoking, No pets,
Open all year, Map Ref I**

Magiston Farm, Sydling St Nicholas, Dorchester, Dorset DT2 9NR Nearest Road A37

Magiston Farm is a 16th century farmhouse with inglenook fireplaces and antique furniture. A river runs through the large well kept garden. The 400 acre farm is set in a peaceful Dorset valley in the centre of Thomas Hardy country. Tea and coffee facilities and armchairs in each bedroom. Delicious evening meals are available on request. An ideal touring spot for discovering beautiful Dorset.

Mrs T Barraclough
Tel: 01300 320295

**B&B from £17.50pp, Dinner by arrangement £9.50, Rooms 2 single,
2 twin, 1 en-suite, 1 double, Smoking allowed, Minimum age 10,
Pets welcome, Open all year except Christmas, Map Ref J**

see PHOTO on page 159

Lamperts Cottage, Sydling St Nicholas, near Cerne Abbas, Dorset DT2 9NU Nearest Road A37

16th century thatched listed cottage with stream running in front. Situated in a peaceful village in the beautiful Sydling Valley. Bedrooms are prettily decorated with dormer windows. Breakfast is served in the dining room which has an Inglenook fireplace, bread oven and beams. Central heating and tea/coffee makers. West Dorset is an ideal touring centre with beaches. The countryside is excellent for walking with footpaths over chalk hills and through hidden valleys. Guidebooks and maps available to borrow.

Nicky Willis
Tel: 01300 341659
Fax: 01300 341699

**B&B from £19pp,
Rooms 1 double, 1 twin, 1 family,
Open all year including Christmas, Map Ref J**

see PHOTO opposite

---

left, Lamperts Cottage, Sydling St Nicholas - see details above

Lower Lewell Farmhouse, West Stafford, Dorchester, Dorset DT2 8AP Nearest Road A35, A352

A 17th century farmhouse authentically improved and situated among a patchwork of fields in rolling Dorset countryside. Reputed to be Talbothays Dairy from Thomas Hardy's 'Tess of the D'Urbervilles'. Built in Portland stone under a red tiled roof with a Victorian brick and slate extension, this is a homely farmhouse with beams, log fires and plenty of space. Hearty breakfasts from the farmhouse kitchen are served at separate tables in the dining room with Inglenook fireplace. There are good local pubs offering snacks and restaurant meals.

Mrs Marian Tomblin
Tel: 01305 267169

**B&B from £18pp, Rooms 1 twin, 1 double, 1 family all with tea/coffee making facilities, TV lounge,
Open all year, Map Ref H**

Churchview Guest House, Winterbourne Abbas, Dorchester, Dorset DT2 9LS Nearest Road A35

Our 17th century Guest House noted for warm, friendly hospitality, traditional breakfasts and delicious evening meals, makes an ideal base for exploring beautiful West Dorset. Our character bedrooms are comfortable, well appointed and include televisions and hospitality trays. Meals taken in our period dining room feature local produce, cream and cheeses. Relaxation is provided by two attractive lounges and licenced bar. Your hosts will give every assistance with local information on attractions, walks and touring to ensure you of a memorable stay. ETB 3 Crown Commended. AA QQQ.

Michael & Jane Deller
Tel: 01305 889296

**B&B from £19.50pp, Dinner from £12, Rooms 1 single, 3 twin, 4 double, 1 family, most en-suite, Pets welcome, No smoking,
Open all year, Map Ref K**

see PHOTO opposite

Willow Cottage, Ware Lane, Lyme Regis, Dorset DT7 3EL Nearest Road A3052

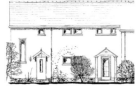

Willow Cottage enjoys tranquillity and unrivalled views over National Trust pastureland and coastline. Within 200 yards is the South West Coastal Path and the Cobb, Lyme's harbour is a short cliff top walk away. The cottage annexe offers privacy to a party of up to three guests. Both bedrooms command splendid seaviews and the double bedded room opens onto a sun balcony. Colour TV and tea/coffee making facilities in private breakfast room.

Geoffrey & Elizabeth Griffin
Tel: 01297 443199

**B&B from £20pp, Rooms 1 single, 1 double en-suite,
Minimum age 8, Pets by prior arrangement,
Open March - November otherwise by special arrangement, Map Ref L**

Rashwood Lodge, Clappentail Lane, Lyme Regis, Dorset DT7 3LZ Nearest Road A3052

Rashwood Lodge is an unusual octagonal house located on the Western hillside with views over Lyme Bay. Just a short walk away is the coastal footpath and Ware Cliff famed for its part in "The French Lieutenants Woman". The bedrooms have their own private facilities. There is an additional twin room for extra family members. The rooms have colour TV and tea/coffee making facilities and benefit from their south facing aspect overlooking a large and colourful garden set in peaceful surroundings. Golf course 1 mile away.

Mrs Diana Lake
Tel: 01297 445700

**B&B from £20pp, Rooms 1 twin, 2 double, most en-suite,
No smoking, Children from 5, Pets by arrangement,
Open February - November, Map Ref L**

---

left, Churchview Guest House, Winterbourne Abbas - see details above   **163**

The Beehive, Church Lane, Osmington, Weymouth, Dorset DT3 6EL   Nearest Road A353

The quaint village of Osmington, with its enchanting array of pretty stone and thatched cottages like 'The Beehive' is probably one of Dorset's best kept secrets. This is an area of great natural beauty with scenic coastal and inland walks. Mary is a most convivial host having led an interesting life working in Africa for some years. She can provide light suppers of imaginative soups with local cheese, bread and fruit. In winter Dorset dinners are offered using local recipes of tipsy rabbit or long piddle lamb followed by Tyneham pears or buttered oranges, served around the cosy kitchen table.

Mary Kempe
Tel: 01305 834095

B&B from £16pp, Light suppers from £4.50, Dinner from £9.50,
Rooms 1 twin/double, 1 double en-suite, 1 sgle all with tea/coffee makers,
No smoking, Min age 6, Pets by request, Open Mar-Dec, Map Ref M

Rookery Nook, Chapel Lane, Osmington, Dorset DT3 6ET   Nearest Road A353

Take a well earned break in our modern home, situated in the picturesque conservation village of Osmington. Just four miles from Weymouth. Surrounded by beautiful Hardy countryside. Close to NT houses and gardens. Your pretty twin en-suite bedroom has colour TV, radio and tea/coffee making facilities. Relax in our attractive secluded garden and conservatory. Guide books and maps to borrow. Carol offers a generous cooked vegetarian breakfast with free range eggs and home made preserves. Special diets with notice. Short walk to pub. Parking. Brochure available.

Carol Sutton
Tel: 01305 835933

B&B from £18pp, Rooms 1 en-suite twin,
No smoking, children or pets,
Open March - November, Map Ref M

Dingle Dell, Osmington, Weymouth, Dorset DT3 6EW   Nearest Road A353

Dingle Dell lies down a quiet lane at the edge of this charming village, a mile from the coast. Set back among old apple trees in its own lovely garden, with roses covering the mellow stone walls, it provides a peaceful spot to relax, and a pleasant base from which to explore the many local attractions. Large, attractive rooms overlook gardens and countryside, providing comfort, colour TV, and tea/coffee facilities. Generous English breakfasts, or special diets by request. A warm personal welcome guaranteed. ETB listed Highly Commended.

Joyce & Bill Norman
Tel/Fax: 01305 832378

B&B from £19.50pp, Rooms 1 twin, 1 double en-suite,
No smoking, children or pets,
Open March - October, Map Ref M

Melbury Mill, Melbury Abbas, Shaftesbury, Dorset SP7 0DB   Nearest Road A350, B3081

Down a few hundred yards of country lane you will find peace and tranquillity in the form of Melbury Mill. A charming Georgian stone farmhouse with its mill alongside. Set in 9 acres of meadows and over-looking a pond abounding with waterfowl. Bedrooms (all en-suite) are large and centrally heated. Dinners are provided using fresh local produce (please book in advance). Located 2 miles south of Shaftesbury famous for its 'Gold Hill' and Abbey ruins. Ideal base for walking and visiting National Trust properties. Brochure available.

Richard & Tavy
    Bradley-Watson
Tel: 01747 852163

B&B from £22.50pp, Dinner from £15 by prior arrangement,
Rooms 2 twin, 2 double, all en-suite and with tea/coffee making
facilities, Restricted smoking, Open all year, Map Ref N

Stourcastle Lodge, Gough's Close, Sturminster Newton, Dorset DT10 1BU   Nearest Road B3092

Built in 1732 this residence offers very high standards and quality throughout. The bedrooms have impressive Victorian bedsteads, stencilled borders, antique furniture and modern well equipped bathrooms some with whirlpool baths. Peacefully situated down a lane yet moments from the town centre or fields and riverside walks. Oak beams, log fires and view of the lovely garden from every room. Jill is a gold medallist chef so with dishes like baked poussin with creamy curry sauce followed by boozy bread and butter pudding this is an excellent place to both stay and eat.

Ken & Jill Hookham-Bassett
Tel: 01258 472320
Fax: 01258 473381

B&B from £25.50pp, Dinner from £16, Rooms 2 twin, 2 double, 1 family, all en-suite, all have tea/coffee making facilities, Restricted smoking, Open all year, Map Ref O

Fiddleford Millhouse, Fiddleford, Sturminster Newton, Dorset DT10 2BX   Nearest Road A357

A peaceful magical grade I listed farm/manor house of great architectural interest with lovely garden running down to the river Stour in totally secluded quiet location. Beautifully furnished and decorated home. 3 large bedrooms one with half tester bed and 16th century moulded plaster ceiling and own bathroom, one large bedroom with king size 4 poster and one other very pretty double bedroom. Central heating, TV and tea/coffee in all bedrooms. Pub in easy walking distance. Ideally situated for beautiful walks.

Jennifer & Anthony Ingleton
Tel: 01258 472786

B&B from £18pp, Rooms 3 double, 1 en-suite, No smoking, Children over 12 years, Pets by arrangement, Open all year, Map Ref O

Lovells Court, Marnhull, Sturminster Newton, Dorset DT10 1JJ   Nearest Road A303, A30

Lovells Court is a rambling country house of character furnished with antique pine and offering spacious en-suite accommodation. It is situated in the peaceful village of Marnhull, commanding fine views across the Blackmore Vale. There are many villages and towns of interest nearby offering good food. This makes an excellent base for discovering Dorset and Somerset. Nearby places of interest include the market town of Sturminster Newton. Abbeys of Sherborne and Milton Abbas, Salisbury and Wells Cathedrals. National Trust properties, Bath etc.

Mrs Mary Ann Newson-Smith
Tel: 01258 820652
Fax: 01258 820487

B&B from £22pp, Rooms 2 double, 1 twin, No smoking, No pets, Open all year, Map Ref O

Yew House Farm, Husseys, Marnhull, Dorset DT10 1PD   Nearest Road B3092

Spacious family home recently built in traditional style. All rooms en-suite, tea/coffee making, TV in all rooms. Guest sitting room. Located away from road. Safe parking and very quiet. Superb views over the Blackmore Vale. An excellent base to explore most of Dorset and neighbouring Somerset and Wiltshire. Many National Trust Properties within easy distance. Tourist Information in each room. Maps and recommended walks. We look forward to welcoming you to our home. For further info please telephone or fax.

Mrs Gill Espley
Tel: 01268 820412
Fax: 01268 821044

B&B from £22pp, Dinner from £15, Rooms 1 twin, 2 double, all en-suite, No smoking, Children from 12, No pets, Open all year except Christmas & New Year, Map Ref O

Cumberland Hotel, 95 Esplanade, Weymouth, Dorset DT4 7BA   Nearest Road M27/A35

We are a small friendly hotel personally run by resident proprietors for over twenty years. Central sea front position, 12 bedrooms all with colour TV, tea tray, central heating, hair dryers, all bedrooms en-suite. We are open all year. Short break holidays all year. We are members of ETB 3Crown AA 4Q Selected. Close to town centre Railway Station and Bus. All meals are freshly cooked by our qualified chef patron. For colour brochure please telephone or fax. Plenty of parking. Close to the Cumberland Hotel.

Mrs Hampshire
Tel/Fax: 01305 785644

B&B from £21pp, Dinner from £12.00, 2 twin, 7 double, 3 family, all en-suite, Restricted smoking, Children from 8, No pets, Open all year, Map Ref P

Friars Way, Church Street, Upwey, Weymouth, Dorset DT3 5QE   Nearest Road B3159

Escape from the usual Dorset tourist routes into this magical wooded valley. A labour of love has created something special, where guests are treated to the very best hospitality. Taste Christina's home made jams and bread and enjoy a peaceful retreat in our 17th Century thatched cottage and adjoining converted stables. All bedrooms have TV facilities/selection of hot drinks. Guest's lounge available in both properties. The beautiful gardens have been featured on TV. Ideally situated for visiting the coast and Dorset's quaint villages. Lovely walks.

see PHOTO opposite

Les & Christina Scott
Tel/Fax: 01305 813243

B&B from £20pp, Rooms 1 twin, 3 double, 2 en-suite, 2 private facilities, No smoking, Children over 12 years, No pets, Open all year except Christmas and New Year, Map Ref Q

Old Granary, The Quay, Wareham, Dorset BH20 4LP   Nearest Road A351

This 250 year old former grain store nestles beside the River Frome and the Quay in this interesting old town. On the restaurant menu fresh grilled sea bass is a popular choice. The bedrooms are beamed on the three upper floors and have bathrooms. Scenic water colours by a local artist cover the walls. The restaurant, with swagged curtains and riverside bar make, a delightful setting to enjoy drinks and cream teas with food served all day. Staff are friendly and efficient. Mooring, boat hire and trips arranged locally.

Mr & Mrs D Sturton
Tel: 01929 552010
Fax: 01929 552482

B&B from £20pp, Dinner from £15.95, Rooms 3 double, 2 twin, 1 private bathroom, 4 en-suite, all have tea/coffee making facilities, No smoking, Open all year, Map Ref R

Long Coppice, Bindon Lane, East Stoke, Wareham, Dorset BH20 6AS   Nearest Road A352

Long Coppice is situated in a peaceful country lane 1 1/2 miles from the A352 at Wool and is ideal for those who wish to get away from it all and relax in rural surroundings. We have 8 acres of our own gardens, woodlands and meadows. Guest accommodation is seperate and the rooms are spacious and comfortably furnished, the family room ha its own garden which guests can relax and is ideal for young children. Centrally situated for local attractions, Lulworth Cove is 4 miles away as well as many good pubs nearby for evening meals.

Sarah Lowman
Tel: 01929 463123

B&B from £19pp, Rooms 1 twin, 1 family, both en-suite, No smoking, Children welcome, Pets by arrangement, Open all year except Christmas, Map Ref S

Thornhill, Holt, Wimborne, Dorset BH21 7DJ　　　　　　　　　　Nearest Road A31

You are sure of a warm welcome in this charming thatched family home which is set in peaceful, rural surroundings. There is a large garden and hard tennis court which guests may use. The house is situated 3½ miles from Wimborne, near the centre of a village, but well away from the road and the location is ideal for exploring the coast, New Forest and Salisbury area. There are plenty of local pubs offering good food.

John & Sara Turnbull
Tel: 01202 889434

B&B from £20pp, Rooms 1 single, 1 twin, 1 double,
No smoking, No children, No pets,
Open all year including Christmas & New Year, Map Ref T

"Who's a beautiful boy, then?"

ESSEX

Few counties in Britain can match Essex for varied scenery. Epping Forest fringing London, now covering something in the region of five and a half thousand acres is all that is left of an enormous sixty thousand acre royal hunting ground. Here is glorious heath, forest and rolling countryside ideal for rambling. In stark contrast the southern coastline is highly industrialised but contains Southend, London's own seaside resort, boasting seven miles of uninterrupted seafront, and the world's longest pier along which a railway runs. It has changed considerably since the Prince Regent sent his Princess Caroline here. Georgian elegance has given way to the brash seaside resort offering all the fun of the fair. Southend is the daytripper's delight, and if its bright lights and loud music- and mud-you're after, then Southend is the place for you. But to the north from Shoeburyness up to the Blackwater Estuary is a wild, lonely windswept expanse of land. This is the place of wildfowlers and marshfarmers. This great area was reclaimed from the sea during the seventeenth century by Dutch engineers, resulting in many miles of dyke and walls, outside of which the remote islands, creeks and waterways are enjoyed by small boat sailors. Further north, the glorious water meadows are dominated by Colchester, the capital city before the Roman invasion, standing on a ridge above the River Colne. Colchester was in fact the earliest Roman town in Britain. The great Norman keep, built on the ruins of the Roman temple of Claudius is the largest in Europe. Colchester owed its later prosperity to the cloth trade, being a

centre of the Flemish weavers who settled here in the sixteenth and seventeenth centuries. It is claimed that Old King Cole of the nursery rhyme gave the town its name. Colchester is a perfect holiday centre with its one hundred and eighty acres of public parks and gardens. To the south are the Layers...Layer-de-la-Haye offering superb views over the one thousand two hundred acre Abberton reservoir, haunt in season of innumerable wildfowl, Layer Breton and Layer Marney having some fine old houses. To the south of Colchester is the lovely valley of the Stour leading to Manningtree, famous for its swans and sailing barges. Jutting out to sea south of the busy port of Harwich is the Naze with its tower built to warn mariners of the treacherous West Rocks. Walton on the Naze offers safe bathing and excellent fishing while the salt marshes behind the town are a paradise for bird-watchers. Further along the coast is Clacton-on-Sea, a Victorian seaside resort with fine tree-lined streets, attractive gardens and a sandy beach. Chelmsford, the county town of Essex, was once an agricultural centre with a livestock market dating back to 1,200 AD, but with the construction of the Chelmer and Blackwater Navigation in 1797, and the development of the railway in 1843, the town swiftly grew as and industrial centre. It is nevertheless an excellent holiday venue. Nearby Danbury gives glorious views across sweeping gorse common and over the Blackwater Estuary. Danbury's six hundred year old church and timber-framed Griffin Inn are well worth a visit, as is Danbury Place set in a large park. Ingatestone to the south is a fascinating village possessing some grand Georgian brick and mock-Tudor houses. Ingatestone Hall. It was built in 1540 for the Tudor Secretary of State, Sir William Petre. The Elizabethan composer William Byrd was a frequent visitor to the Hall. To the east of Chelmsford is Maldon, the site of 'The Battle of Maeldune' celebrated in the tenth century epic poem, where in 991 AD the Anglo-Danish army of Brythnoth was routed by Viking invaders. The estuary of the Blackwater is packed with pleasure boats and barges. The rolling countryside north to Saffron Walden has a liberal scattering of lovely villages. The east is pleasantly wooded, the west to the borders of Cambridgeshire windswept low chalk hills. The ancient woolen town of Saffron Walden is one of the most attractive in the county. From the Middle Ages until the eighteenth century this was the centre of the saffron crocus industry reflected in its name. Nearby is spectacular Audley End, originally the Benedictine Abbey of Walden given to Lord Audley by Henry VIII following the

Dissolution. In 1603 the Earl of Suffolk laid the foundations there of one of the largest Jacobean houses in England. Although now only a fraction of its original size, it is a wonderful sight in its Capability Brown landscaped park. To the south are the quaint villages known collectively as The Rodings. Immortalised in the paintings of George Morland and the writings of Anthony Trollope, these villages are a delight that no visitor to Essex should miss.

Places to Visit

Audley End House, *Saffron Walden* ~ when it was built in 1614, this was the largest house in England. A Jacobean mansion with original hall and many fine plaster ceilings. The gardens the 18th century park, which has many temples and monuments.

Coggeshall Grange Barn, *near Colchester* ~ the oldest surviving timber framed barn in Europe, it was originally part of a monastery. It was restored in the 1980's and houses a small collection of farm carts and wagons.

Colchester Castle, *Colchester* ~ built by the Normans on the site of a Roman temple. Only the keep remains and is now a museum housing some the country's best archaeological collections.

Dedham Church, *Dedham* ~ this tall church tower appears in many of landscape painter John Constable's pictures including the 'View on the Stour near Dedham' painted in 1822.

Epping Forest ~ over six thousand acres of forest, in the past it was a favourite hunting ground for kings; now it is popular with walkers. A variety of wildlife live in the forest and its open land and lakes, including deer.

▼ *Wendens Ambo*

Layer Tarney Tower, *near Tiptree* ~ an eight storey Tudor gatehouse built in the 16th century, it was supposed to be part of a mansion which never got built. The Tower offers panoramic views over the Essex countryside.

Mistley Towers, *near Manningtree* ~ Richard Rigby, Paymaster General, poured his money into a spa at Mistley, and employed Robert Adam to deisgn a church, but it was discovered that he had embezzled money and work stooped. Today, a green waterside with maltings buildings, Georgian facades and swans are the only reminder of what it was. The twin towers of a demolished Mistley church have been kept as a landmark.

St Osyth's Priory, *St Osyth* ~ a former Augustinian Abbey, it still has a 13th century chapel and various other buildings dating from the 13th to the 18th century. The gatehouse contains many works of art including ceramics and Chinese Jade.

St Peter's-on-the-Wall, *Bradwell-on-Sea* ~ a simple stone building standing isolated on the shore. It was built in 654 from the remains of a Roman fort by St Cedd, who used it as his cathedral. It was restored in the 1920's after being used as a shed since the 17th century.

The Church, Stock, near Chelmsford

ESSEX

The Bauble, Higham, near Colchester CO7 6LA   Nearest Road B1068 off A12

Welcome to our home, a comfortable period property carefully modernised on the edge of the picturesque hamlet of Higham. In quiet location between the River Brett and Stour. In the Heart of Dedham Vale made famous by John Constables paintings. Guest are invited to relax and enjoy 1 1/2 acres of garden, play tennis or swim in the heated pool. Ideal for touring East Anglia. All rooms have TV, tea/coffee facilities there is also a comfortable sitting room. ETB 2 Crowns Highly Commended. AA 4Q Selected.

Nowell & Penny Watkins
Tel: 01206 337254
Fax: 01206 337263

**B&B from £20pp, Rooms, 1 single, 2 twin, all en-suite,
No smoking, Children over 12 years, No pets,
Open all year, Map Ref A**

Mill House, The Causeway, Halstead, Essex CO9 1ET   Nearest Road A131

Halstead is a Market Town which boosts plenty of pubs, restaurant including traditional Indian, Italian and excellent Chinese restaurants. Mill House is an 18th Century listed town house with a delightful garden sloping down to the river Colne. Adjoing the house and straddling the river is Townsford Mill Antique Centre with three floors of antiques and collectables, recently used for filming the Love Joy series. All rooms are decorated in Period Style with tea making facilities and TV. All major credit cards accepted. No smoking.

Malcolm & Geraldine Stuckey
Tel: 01787 474451

**B&B from £22.50pp, Rooms 1 twin, 2 double, all en-suite,
No smoking, Children over 12 years, No pets,
Open all year except Christmas & New Year, Map Ref B**

see PHOTO opposite

Aldhams, Bromley Road, Lawford, Manningtree, Essex CO11 2NE   Nearest Road A120, A137

Aldhams offers a peaceful stay for guests who enjoy countryside and a lovely garden. A rose garden gives colour all summer and in the spring the drive is yellow with daffodils. Tea is offered in the afternoon and a wide choice is available for breakfast. There are many excellent places to eat nearby, and for those wishing to explore, Constable country and Beth Chatto's garden are only a few minutes drive. Ideal too for the Port of Harwich, walking, bird watching and sailing. A popular base for a break all year round.

Mr & Mrs C McEwen
Tel/Fax: 01206 393210

**B&B from £20pp, Rooms 1 twin, 2 double, en-suite available,
No smoking, Children welcome, No pets,
Open all year except Christmas & New Year, Map Ref C**

Dairy House Farm, Bradfield Road, Wix, near Manningtree, Essex CO11 2SR   Nearest Road A120

We love welcoming visitors to our spacious farmhouse set in 700 arable acres. Peace and beautifully furnished en-suite accommodation are offered with tea and homemade cakes on arrival. The guests' lounge and bedrooms have drinks trays and colour TV. There is a large garden for relaxation and a games room for the energetic. Suffolk villages, constable country, Beth Chatto's garden, seaside towns and historic Colchester are all within easy reach as are the ports of Harwich and Felixstowe. AA "QQQQ". English Tourist Board Highly Commended.

Bridget & Alan Whitworth
Tel: 01255 870322
Fax: 01255 870186

**B&B from £18pp, Rooms 1 single, 1 twin, 1 double, all private/en-suite,
Restricted smoking, Children from 11, No pets,
Open all year except Christmas and New Year, Map Ref D**

The Wick, Hatfield, Peverel, Essex CM3 2EZ　　　　　　　　　　**Nearest Road A12**

The Wick is a Grade II listed 16th century farmhouse in a pleasant rural setting with a large garden, duck ponds and stream. The drawing room is nicely furnished as is the pretty dining room. Bedrooms are pleasantly decorated and have tea/coffee making facilities. Delicious home cooked evening meals are available on request. Well situated for London, Suffolk and East Coast ports.

Mrs Linda Tritton　　　　**B&B from £20pp, Dinner from £10, Rooms 2 twin,**
Tel: 01245 380705　　　**Minimum age 10,**
Mobile: 0976 246082　　**Open all year, Map Ref E**

Duddenhoe End Farm, Duddenhoe End, near Saffron Walden CB11 4UU　　**Nearest Road B1039-B1383**

Duddenhoe End Farm is a 17th century house with beams and inglenook fireplaces. There are 3 delightful bedrooms all with en-suite or private bathroom and tea/coffee making facilities and TV. Guests lounge. A warm welcome is assured. Excellent restaurant and pubs within 3 miles for dinner. Ideally situated for Cambridge, Audley End House, Saffron Walden, Newmarket, Duxford Air Museum, Wimpole Hall. London 1 hour away by train. A no smoking house.

Mrs Peggy Foster　　　**B&B from £19pp Rooms 1 twin, 2 double, all en-suite,**
Tel: 01763 838258　　**No smoking, Minimum age 10, No pets,**
　　　　　　　　　　　　Open all year, Map Ref F

Rowley Hill Lodge, Little Walden, Saffron Walden, Essex CB10 1UZ　　　**Nearest Road B1052**

Rowley Hill Lodge was built in 1830 and has been extended over the years. It now has two guest bedrooms, each with its own bathroom. The twin room looks out over the secluded garden with dovecote, and the double room faces Saffron Walden. Both rooms have colour TV and tea/coffee trays and the bathrooms have powerful showers as well as baths. Saffron Walden (1 1/2 miles, B1052) is a delightful market town with good shops and many eating places. Also close to Cambridge and Duxford Aircraft Museum.

Edward & Kate Haslam　　**B&B from £19.50pp, Single occupancy £25, Rooms 1 twin, 1 double, both**
Tel: 01799 525975　　　**en-suite, Restricted smoking, Children welcome, Pets by arrangement,**
Fax: 01799 516622　　　**Open all year except Christmas & New Year, Map Ref G**

Please mention
THE GREAT BRITISH
BED & BREAKFAST
when booking your accommodation

"Where the thistle lifts a purple crown
Six foot out of the turf,
And the harebell shakes on the windy hill -
O the breath of the distant surf!"
Francis Thompson

GLOUCESTERSHIRE

There is so much choice in this fair county. If the Vale of Gloucester, the Forest of Dean, the Vale of Berkeley and the Cotswolds are not enough, then there is the City of Gloucester, Cheltenham and Cirencester together with a clutch of some of the most attractive villages in England to explore.

The honey-yellow stone towns and villages of the Cotswolds have enchanted visitors for generations. The range of gently rolling limestone hills intersected by small deep valleys stretching north-east from Bath provides the glorious stone which adds so much to the picturesque charm of the region, a region rich since Medieval times from the wool of Cotswold sheep. This is a perfect holiday county, with its meandering roads and quaint villages. Stow-on-the-Wold, its ancient houses clustered round a large market square, was once a busy wool centre which held one of the largest livestock markets in Britain.

Northleach to the south, also in the past an important centre of the wool trade, retains much of its Medieval past in its narrow winding streets including some fascinating Tudor houses and a magnificent fifteenth century woolmerchants' church. Cirencester is a wonderful centre for touring the whole area. Named Corinium by the Romans, three great Roman highways originate here, Akeman Street, Foss Way and Ermine Street. The three thousand acre Cirencester Park in the grounds of Lord Bathurst's stately home is at the far end of Cecily Hill, one of Cirencester's finest streets. At nearby Bibury, described by William Morris as the most beautiful village in England are some delightful former weaver's cottages, and in Arlington Mill is the impressive Cotswold Museum. North Cerney, Nailsworth, Bisley and Tetbury each have their own particular charm and features. Two miles west of Tetbury at Beverstone are the ruins of the castle which in 1051 sheltered King Harold. At Sapperton on the River Frome just west of Cirencester are lovely views over Golden Valley. North is Cheltenham, an elegant Regency Spa - a market town until the discovery of mineral springs in 1718,

and patronised by George III under whose approval the handsome terraces and tree-lined avenues were developed. The house in which the composer Gustav Holst was born is now a museum. Cheltenham has two festivals, the Music Festival in June or July and the Festival of Literature held in the Autumn.

Gloucester, on the River Severn is the administrative centre of the county and was the Roman settlement of Glevum, an important fort established to defend the river crossing west into Wales. Renowned for its magnificent cathedral which houses a stained glass window endowed in 1352 to commemorate the victory at Crecy, and the superb fan vaulting of the cloisters which is the earliest in the country. Gloucester is one of the locations of The Three Choirs Festival.

At the head of the Vale of Gloucester stands the ancient town of Tewkesbury. Steeped in history, it was here in 1471 that Edward IV confirmed his claim to the throne. The town has some splendid timbered black and white houses and old inns, but Tewkesbury's pride is the abbey church of St. Mary the Virgin, saved by the people of the town from destruction at the Dissolution. They collected £453 in 1539 to buy the church from Henry VIII. The high altar is a thirteen and a half feet long slab of Purbeck marble consecrated in 1239. Amongst Tewkesbury's

many interesting inns is the Royal Hop Pole Inn mentioned in the Pickwick Papers. south of Gloucester is Stroud at the junction of five valleys, and famous for its West of England cloth. Below the town is Minchinhampton Common, a National Trust property of six hundred acres giving wonderful views over the Golden Valley and the Stroudwater Hills. To the north is the interestingly named Paradise, where Charles I stayed while laying siege to Gloucester. So delightful did he find the spot that he named it Paradise. The birdwatcher's paradise is Slimbridge, the Wildfowl Trust founded by the artist Peter Scott, boasting the world's largest and most varied collection of wildfowl. For the nature lover the Forest of Dean is an irresistible attraction. St. Briavels situated above the River Wye is the ideal walking centre. Its medieval castle used by early English Kings when they came to hunt in the forest, gives glorious views across twenty seven thousand acres.

The Valley of Berkeley, thousands of acres of low-lying land on the eastern bank of the Severn, criss-crossed by lanes with hump-backed bridges over gently flowing waterways is dominated by Berkeley Castle, in the dungeons of which Edward II was murdered in 1327. No visitor to this lovely town should leave without seeing the fine east window of the parish church, a memorial to Edward Jenner who was born in Bereley and who invented vaccination.

Places to Visit

Berkeley Castle, *Berkeley* ~ a compact fortress with circular Norman keep and inner bailey. It has been the home of the Berkeley family for eight hundred and fifty years. King Edward II was murdered in the dungeon in the keep. Magnificient collections of paintings, tapestries and carvings are on display and outside there is a deer park and terraced gardens.

Cirencester Park, *Cirencester* ~ it was laid out in 1714 by the 1st Earl of Bathurst with the assistance of poet Alexander Pope. The mansion is surrounded by a yew hedge, which is supposedly the tallest in the world.

Gloucester Cathedral, *Gloucester* ~ built in the 14th century. The ceiling has fan vaulting and the east windows commemorate the Battle of Crecy.

Hidcote Manor Garden, *near Chipping Campden* ~ a ten acre arts and crafts garden on a hilltop created by horticulturist Major Lawerence Johnstone. Consisting of a series of small gardens separated by walls and hedges.

Painswick, *Gloucestershire* ~ a picturesque Cotswold village with a collection of old stone cottages. The churchyard has ninety nine yew trees, trimmed into giant lollipops and tunnels.

Pitville Pump Room, *Cheltenham* ~ built 1825 to 1830 the domed Pump Room is modelled on the Greek Temple of Ilissos in Athens. The salty alkaline water can still be tasted and Cheltenham's Gallery of Fashion can be visited.

Slimbridge Wildfowl and Wetlands Trust, *Slimbridge* ~ founded in 1946 by naturalist Sir Peter Scott, its the world's largest collection of wildfowl with over one hundred and eighty different types of ducks, geese and swans. The Tropical House has a pink flamingo colony and other exotic varieities of bird.

Sudeley Castle, *near Winchcombe* ~ set in the Cotswolds and originally built in the 15th century, it became ruins after the Civil War and was rebuilt in the 19th century. Sudeley was favoured by Tudor royalty and became the home of Katherine Parr, the only of Henry VIII's wives to outlive him.

Tintern Abbey ~ founded in 1131 and set in the wooded valley of the Wye, it is one of Britain's most beautiful abbey ruins.

▼*Arlington Row, Bibury*

GLOUCESTERSHIRE

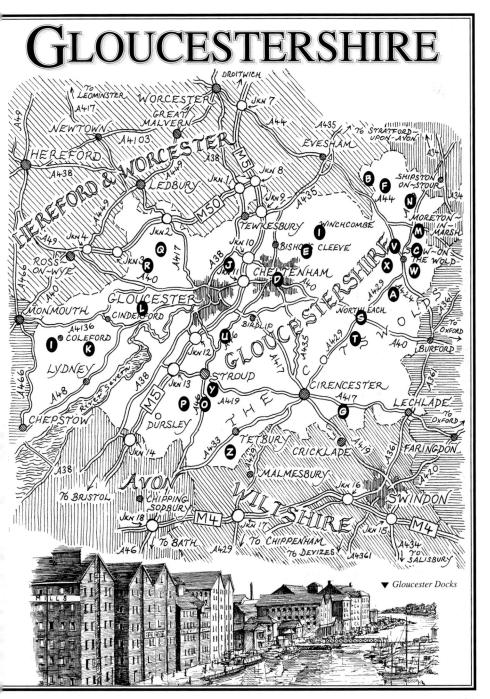

TO LEOMINSTER A417
DROITWICH
WORCESTER JKN 7
GREAT MALVERN
NEWTOWN A4103
HEREFORD A449
A44 A435
A438 **EVESHAM**
TO STRATFORD-UPON-AVON
A34
LEDBURY M5 JKN 8
JKN 1 JKN 9 A435
B
F **SHIPSTON ON-STOUR**
A44 A134
N
TEWKESBURY **WINCHCOMBE** **MORETON-IN-MARSH**
JKN 2 A417 JKN 10 **I** **M**
Q **BISHOPS CLEEVE** **E** **V** **COW-ON THE WOLD**
R A38 **J** **CHELTENHAM** **X** **C** **W**
ROSS-ON-WYE JKN 3 A40 **J** **D** A40 **A**
A466 **GLOUCESTER** **NORTHLEACH** **S** A424
MONMOUTH **CINDERFORD** **L** **BIRDLIP** A429 **T** A40 **BURFORD** **TO OXFORD**
A4136 **U** A435 A429
COLEFORD JKN 12 A417
I **K** **STROUD** **CIRENCESTER** **LECHLADE**
LYDNEY JKN 13 **Y** A419 A417 **TO OXFORD**
A466 A48 **P** **O** **G**
CHEPSTOW **DURSLEY** **FARINGDON**
JKN 14 **TETBURY** A419 A36
Z **CRICKLADE** **SWINDON**
A38 **MALMESBURY** A4361 JKN 16
TO BRISTOL **CHIPPING SODBURY** JKN 15 M4
JKN 18 M4 JKN 17 A434
TO BATH A429 **TO CHIPPENHAM** **TO DEVIZES** A4361 **TO SALISBURY**
A46 A38

▼ *Gloucester Docks*

MILLS

The Old Rectory, Willersey, Broadway - see opposite for details

Coombe House, Rissington Road, Bourton-on-the-Water GL54 2DT   **Nearest Road A429, A424**

Coombe House is a quiet, non smoking haven. Ideal for guests who appreciate high levels of cleanliness and gentle elegance. Serene small drawing room. Pretty, thoughtfully equipped en-suite bedrooms with tea/coffee making facilities and TV. Talking to plants encouraged in a garden planted with the unusual! This beautiful village is set in the heart of the picturesque Cotswolds, an area of outstanding beauty. London 75 miles (M40). Oxford/Warwick 26 miles. Liquor licence. Visa/MC/Amex.

Graham & Diana Ellis   **B&B from £29.50pp, Rooms 2 twin, 5 double, family on request,**
Tel: 01451 821966   **all en-suite, No smoking, No pets, Open all year except Christmas Eve**
Fax: 01451 810477   **and Day & New Year's Eve, Map Ref A**

Upper Farm, Clapton on the Hill, Bourton on the Water, Gloucestershire GL54 2LG   **Nearest Road A429**

A working family farm of 140 acres in a peaceful undiscovered Cotswold village 2 miles from the famous Bourton-on-the-Water. The listed 17th century stone farmhouse has been tastefully restored and offers a warm and friendly welcome with exceptional accommodation and hearty farmhouse fayre. The heated bedrooms are of individual character some are en-suite with TV and one is ground floor. From its hill position Upper Farm enjoys panoramic views of the surrounding countryside and being centrally located makes it an ideal base for touring, walking or merely relaxing.

Helen Adams   **B&B from £17pp, ETB 2 Crown Highly Commended,**
Tel: 01451 820453   **Rooms 3 double, 1 family, 1 twin, some en-suite, No smoking,**
Fax: 01451 810185   **Minimum age 8, Open March - November, Map Ref A**

Lansdowne Villa Guest House, Lansdowne, Bourton-on-the-Water, Glos GL54 2AT   **Nearest Road A429**

Situated at the quiet end of this lovely village and within easy reach of the many attractions of the beautiful Cotswolds. Tony and Maire-Anne Baker extend a warm welcome to their guests and invite them to enjoy the relaxed atmosphere of their tastefully modernised home, bedrooms have been well equipped and comfortably furnished with coordinated fabrics, there is a cosy lounge for guests a choice is offered from the table evening menu. A wide choice of beers, wines and spirits are also available.
EMail: lansdowne@star.co.uk   http://www.star.co.uk/lansdowne/

Tony & Marie-Anne Baker   **B&B from £21pp, Dinner from £12.50, Rooms 2 single, 1 twin, 8 double,**
Tel: 01451 820673   **1 family, all en-suite, Restricted smoking, Children welcome, No pets,**
Fax: 01451 822099   **Open February - December, Map Ref A**

The Old Rectory, Church Street, Willersey, Broadway, Gloucestershire WR12 7PN   **Nearest Road A44**

The Cotswold stone 17th century Rectory is quietly tucked away opposite the Church. With hills behind and a dry stone wall surrounding the delightful garden, this is an idyllic spot. Superb breakfasts in the elegant dining room, log fires in winter. Many places for eating close by. The Bell Inn - one minute walk. Specialist paint finishes used to great effect in en-suite bedrooms. Four poster beds, TV and all facilities. Crabtree and Evelyn toiletries. Non smoking. Special winter rates including supper tray. Car parking - good base for walking and touring. EMail: beauvoisin@btinternet.com

Chris & Liz Beauvoisin   **B&B from £30-£47.50pp, Rooms 1 twin, 5 double, 2 family, 6 en-suite,**
Tel: 01386 853729   **2 private, No smoking, Children over 8, Guide dogs only,**
Fax: 01386 858061   **Open all year except Christmas, Map Ref B**

see PHOTO's opposite

College House, Chapel Street, Broadwell, Gloucestershire GL56 0TW   **Nearest Road A429**

College House is a 17th century house located in a quiet and enchanting Cotswold village. It has delightful accommodation with luxurious bedrooms and bathrooms two of which are en-suite. Exposed beams, shutters, flagstone floors and mullioned windows abound. Sitting room with large stone fireplace for exclusive guest use. Breakfast and, if desired, 3 course dinners are served in the beamed dining room. The popular villages of Bourton-on-the-Water and Chipping Camden are close by and Cheltenham, Oxford and Stratford are easily accessible.

B&B from £23, Dinner from £17.50,

Sybil Gisby
Tel: 01451 832351

Minimum age 16, No pets,
Open all year except Christmas, Map Ref C

Clarence Court Hotel, Clarence Square, Cheltenham, Gloucestershire GL50 4JR   **M5,J9 & J10**

This privately owned B&B Hotel was once the townhouse of the Duke of Wellington. He came to Cheltenham to take the waters in-between fighting all those battles against Napoleon! The house overlooks gardens in a peaceful, tree-lined regency square yet is only a short stroll from the amenities and shops of Cheltenham. It is an ideal touring centre for the Cotswolds with its numerous stately homes and gardens. There is a lovely lounge, ample free parking, a licensed bar, and TV and tea/coffee making facilities in all the individually decorated rooms.

Brian & Susan Howe
Tel: 01242 580411
Fax: 01242 224609

B&B from £25-£33.50pp, Rooms 6 single, 9 twin/double, 3 family,
all en-suite, Children welcome, Pets by arrangement,
Open all year, Map Ref D

Cleeve Hill Hotel, Cleeve Hill, Cheltenham, Gloucestershire GL52 3PR   **Nearest Road B4632**

see PHOTO's opposite

This award winning no smoking Hotel offers the ultimate in Bed & Breakfast. Positioned near the summit of Cleeve Hill, the bedrooms offer some of the most spectacular views in the Cotswolds. All bedrooms are elegantly furnished to the highest standards with en-suite bathrooms, TV with Movie Channel, direct dial, telephone, hairdryers and hospitality tray. The generous breakfasts have been described as the best ever, excellent pub and restaurants abound in the area. ETB Deluxe, AA Premier Selected, Which Hotel Guide, County Hotel of Year 95.

John & Marian Enstone
Tel: 01242 672052
Fax: 01242 679969

B&B from £30pp, Rooms 1 single, 2 twin, 5 double, 1 family, all en-suite,
No smoking, Children from 8, No pets,
Open all year except Christmas & New Year, Map Ref E

Orchard Hill House, Broad Campden, Chipping Campden, Glos GL55 6UU   **Nearest Road A44, B4081**

see PHOTO on page 186

Orchard Hill House is beautifully restored from an original 17th century farmhouse. Breakfast is served around a 10 ft elm farmhouse table in our flagstone-floored dining hall with inglenook fireplace. The bedrooms, 2 of which are in the main house and 2 in a lovely converted barn in the courtyard, are gloriously appointed and overlook pretty gardens and countryside. All are en-suite and have tea/coffee making facilities and TV. Plenty of car packing space.

Mrs C Ashmore
Tel: 01386 841473
Fax: 01386 841030

B&B from £22.50 - £28.50, Rooms 1 twin, 2 double, 1 family, all en-suite,
No smoking, Children welcome, No pets,
Open all year except Christmas, Map Ref F

Cleeve Hill Hotel,
Cheltenham

- see opposite for details

The Pond House, Lower Fields, Weston Rd, Bretforton, nr Chipping Campden WR11 5QA Nearest Rd B4035

Superb country home, peaceful position in farmland, without passing traffic. Friendly, relaxed atmosphere with high standard of comfort and service. Wonderful breakfasts in our conservatory with panoramic views of the Cotswolds Hills. The perfect base to explore many famous gardens, historical sites, castles, 3 miles from Broadway, Chapping Campden, near to Stratford-upon-Avon, Cheltenham and Evesham. All bedrooms are en-suite, with colour TV, radio, hair dryer and tea/coffee facilities. Ample parking. AA 4Q Selected, ETB 2 Crown Highly Commended. Phone for a detailed brochure.

Anne & Ray Payne
Tel: 01386 831687

**B&B from £20-£26pp, Rooms 2 twin, 2 double, all en-suite,
No smoking, Children over 5, No pets,
Open all year, Map Ref F**

The Masons Arms, Meysey Hampton, Cirencester, Gloucestershire GL7 5JT   **Nearest Road A417**

Set beside the village green this Cotswold 17th century coaching inn provides you with modern amenities and comfort in a beautiful rural setting. Individually decorated en-suite rooms have tea/coffee making facilities and colour TV; some with beams and open stonework. They offer an ideal base to explore the Cotswolds and surrounding countryside. The traditional bar, with log fires and cosy pews, is also an ideal haven for residents and local customers alike with a warm welcome assured. Home-made fayre and wines available daily in the bar and separate restaurant.

Andrew & Jane O'Dell
Tel: 01285 850164
Fax: 01285 850164

**B&B from £32pp, Dinner from £5, Rooms 1 twin, 6 double, 1 family,
all en-suite, Children welcome, Dogs by arrangement,
Open all year, Map Ref G**

Woodlands, Upper Swell, near Stow-on-the-Wold, Gloucestershire GL534 1EW   **Nearest Road B4077**

Luxurious small guest house in 1/4 acre of gardens. In quaint Cotswold village with breathtaking views over lake and hills. All bedrooms are deluxe ensuites with colour TV and tea/coffee facilities. There is a lounge for guests where light snacks are served. Ample car parking is available. We are situated in the village of Upper Swell just 1 mile from the tourist town of Stow-on-the-Wold. ETB 2 Crown Commended, AA 4Q's Selected.

Brian & Kathryn Sykes
Tel: 01451 832346

**B&B from £25pp, Rooms 1 single, 3 double, all en-suite,
Children & Pets welcome,
Open all year, Map Ref V**

Tudor Farmhouse Hotel & Restaurant, Clearwell, near Coleford, Glos GL16 8JS   **Nearest Rd A466**

Set in a gentle valley between the Forest of Dean and the Wye Valley, this peaceful and welcoming old farmhouse has stood since the 13th century and features oak beams and original wall panelling. The bedrooms are tastefully furnished in traditional style, some have 4 poster beds and all have colour TV, tea/coffee facilities, central heating and en-suite bath or shower and wc. In the lounge is an inglenook fireplace. The dining room has open stonework, oak beams and is the ideal way to enjoy the imaginative freshly prepared cuisine. AA Restaurant Red Rosette & 5Q, ETB 3 Crown Highly Commended.

see PHOTO on page 188

Deborah & Richard Fletcher
Tel: 01594 833046
Fax: 01594 837093

**B&B from £28.50pp, Dinner from £18.25,
Rooms 7 double, 4 family, 2 twin, all en-suite,
Open all year, Map Ref I**

---

left, Orchard Hill House, Broad Campden - see page 184

Frogfurlong Cottage, Frogfurlong Lane, Down Hatherley, Gloucestershire GL2 9QE   **Nearest Road A38**

Frogfurlong Cottage is situated on the green belt area within the triangle formed by Gloucester, Cheltenham and Tewkesbury. Originally 2 cottages, built in 1812 but recently modernised and extended. It stands on its own, back from the road and surrounded by fields. There is an indoor heated swimming pool which guests may use mornings and evenings. The accommodation, which is totally self contained, consists of a double bedded room equipped with tea/coffee tray, TV, luxury bathroom and jacuzzi. Garden and ample parking. A real 'get away on our own' break.

Clive & Anna Rooke
Tel: 01452 730430

B&B from £18pp, Dinner from £9.50 by arrangement,
Rooms 1 en-suite double, No smoking, No pets, No children,
Open all year except Christmas & New Year, Map Ref J

Edale House, Folly Road, Parkend, near Lydney, Royal Forest of Dean GL15 4JF   **Nrst Rd A48, B4234**

Edale House is a fine Georgian residence facing the cricket green in the village of Parkend at the heart of the Royal Forest of Dean. Once the home of local GP, Bill Tandy, author of "A Doctor in the Forest". The house has been tastefully restored to provide comfortable en-suite accommodation with every facility including tea/coffee equipment, TV, and hair dryer, etc. Enjoy delicious, imaginative cuisine prepared by chef/proprietors and served in the attractive dining room. Within easy reach of Wye Valley. Riding, cycling, canoeing, walking, etc., are all close at hand.

Sheila & James Reid
Tel: 01594 562835
Fax: 01594 564488

B&B from £20pp, Dinner from £15.50, Rooms 1 twin, 4 double,
all en-suite, Children and pets by arrangement,
Open all year, Map Ref K

Gunn Mill House, Lower Spout Lane, Mitcheldean, Gloucestershire GL17 0EA   **Nearest Road A40, A48**

Nestling in Flaxley Valley in the Forest of Dean, Gunn Mill House stands in 5 acres of gardens and paddocks, bounded by its mill stream which flows to a 17th century mill. The Andersons have refurbished their Georgian home to a high standard, filling it with collectables from their travels around the world. By day enjoy the beauty of the Royal Forest, between restful nights in this peaceful spot. Large outdoor swimming pool, a couple of bikes may be borrowed. So also can the family dog! A roaring log fire and great hospitality add to the dinner party atmosphere. Website: http:/www.visit-glos.org.uk/

David & Caroline Anderson
Tel: 01594 827577
Fax: 01594 827577

B&B from £20pp, Dinner on request £18, Liquor Licence, Suites
1 double, 1 twin, 1 family; 2 double rooms en-suite, No smoking,
Children & Pets welcome by arrangement, Open all year, Map Ref L

see PHOTO on page 190

Townend Cottage, High Street, Morton-in-Marsh, Gloucestershire GL56 0AD   **Nearest Road A429**

A warm welcome awaits you in our 17th century cottage and coach house in the heart of the Cotswold. Each room is unique with TV and tea/coffee. We welcome all families to the comfort of our family home. Why not relax in our superb garden after a day touring the lovely Cotswold country. We have a separate guest lounge plus TV. A full English breakfast is part of the holiday treat. We are near Stratford, Cheltenham, Bath and Oxford and we can meet you at the local station.

Chris & Jenny Gant
Tel: 01608 650846

B&B from £36 per room, Rooms 1 twin, 2 double, 1 family, most en-suite,
Restricted smoking, Children welcome, No pets,
Open all year except Christmas and New Year, Map Ref M

---

left, Tudor Farmhouse Hotel & Restaurant, near Coleford - see page 187

The Cottage, Oxford Street, Moreton in Marsh, Gloucestershire GL56 0LA   **Nearest Road A44**

A friendly greeting awaits you in this grade II listed Cotswold Cottage with exposed beams and inglenook fireplace. Ideal touring centre for the Cotswolds, Stratford-upon-Avon and Cheltenham. Many delightful pubs and restaurants within easy walking distance. Accommodation comprises one twin and one double room with shared bathroom and one double room in the Peter Rabbit Cottage in the garden. Colour TV in all rooms, also tea/coffee making facilities. Pretty garden available for guests use. No smoking. Ample parking. Walking distance to Railway Station.

Lorraine & Richard Carter
Tel/Fax: 01608 651740

B&B from £18pp, Rooms, 1 twin, 1 double, 1 double en-suite,
No smoking, Children over 8, No pets,
Open February - December, Map Ref M

Newlands Farmhouse, Aston Magna, Moreton-in-Marsh, Gloucestershire GL56 9QQ   **Nearest Road A429**

If you would like to "Stay off the beaten track" this 16th century Tudor House offers a high standard of accommodation. The house sympathetically restored is attractive having beams, stone floors and furnished with antiques. Bedrooms are large and comfortable having their own vanitory units, tea/coffee facilities and central heating. Everywhere are fresh flowers and pot plants. Guests have their own lounge with television. Nearby are lovely gardens, Hidcote, Kiftsgate plus many more. Centrally situated for touring Stratford, Broadway The Slaughters, Campden and Bibury.

Mr & Mrs Hessel
Tel: 01608 650964

B&B from £18.50pp, Rooms 1 twin, 1 double, 1 en-suite,
No smoking, children or pets,
Open February - November, Map Ref N

The Vicarage, Nailsworth, Gloucestershire GL6 0BS   **Nearest Road A46 - Avening Road**

The Vicarage is a large Victorian family house. The bedrooms are spacious and comfortable with antique furniture, and equipped with tea/coffee making facilities, the twin with TV. The house is warm and quiet and centrally heated throughout. The town centre is 2 minutes walk with several very good restaurants. Nailsworth is convenient for visits to Bath, Cirencester, Cheltenham and an excellent base for lovely country walks.

Mrs P Strong
Tel: 01453 832181

B&B from £20pp, Rooms 2 single, 1 twin,
No smoking, Pets welcome,
Open all year except Christmas, Map Ref O

The Laurels, Inchbrook, Nailsworth, Gloucestershire GL5 5HA   **Nearest Road A46**

The Laurels is a rambling old house with a warm atmosphere. Relax beside an open fire in the panelled study, play snooker or board games in the beamed lounge or take advantage of the licensed dining room where excellent home cooked meals are served. Enjoy the wildlife in the garden - many types of birds, also badgers, foxes and deer visit the feeding station by the stream. All bedrooms are en-suite and with TV and tea/coffee making facilities. There is an outdoor heated swimming pool for guests' use in the summer. Self catering cottage also available.

Mrs Lesley Williams-Allen
Tel: 01453 834021
Fax: 01453 834004

B&B from £19pp, Dinner from £12, Snacks from £1.75,
Rooms 2 double, 2 twin, 2 family, all en-suite, No smoking, Children &
pets welcome, Open all year including Christmas, Map Ref P

---

left, Gunn Mill House, Mitcheldean - see page 189

Old Court Hotel, Church Street, Newent, Gloucestershire GL18 1AB   **Nearest Road M50**

Once the family home of the Lord of the Manor this magnificent house is set in a delightful one acre walled garden. Thoughtful modernisation has ensured many period features remain creating a relaxing and elegant atmosphere. The Georgian panelled dining room offers superb cuisine, resulting in an enviable reputation for both quality and imagination. All bedrooms are individually styled with private facilities, tea/coffee, direct dial telephone, radio and colour TV. The 4-poster bedroom is particularly spacious and is perfect for special occasions. ETB 3 Crowns.

Ron & Sue Wood
Tel: 01531 820522

B&B from £22.50pp, Dinner £13.75,
Rooms 1 family, 1 4-poster, 2 double, 2 twin, all en-suite,
Open all year, Map Ref Q

Orchard House, Aston Ingham Road, Kilcot, near Newent, Glos GL18 1NP   **Nearest Road M50, B4222**

see PHOTO opposite

Orchard House is a delightful Tudor style country house completely surrounded by 5 acres of peaceful gardens. A beautifully appointed home with a relaxed and friendly atmosphere, every modern comfort and delicious food. A very high standard of accommodation, including a Regency style dining room, luxurious double and en-suite bedrooms, original oak beams, TV lounge and winter log fires, a conservatory, fountain courtyard and croquet lawn. Residential licence.

Mrs Anne Thompson
Tel: 01989 720417
Fax: 01989 720770

B&B from £24.50pp, Dinner from £17.50,
Minimum age 12, No pets, No smoking,
Open all year, Map Ref R

Cotteswold House, Market Place, Northleach, Gloucestershire GL54 3EG   **Nearest Road A40/A429**

Relax in our 350 year old Cotswold stone wool merchants home with beamed ceilings, 13th century panelling and Tudor archway. We have the choice of a double suite or two double/twin bedrooms each with their own bathroom - all large, elegant and well-equipped. Enjoy traditional English food and a friendly welcome. Find us in the centre of this ancient market town of Northleach in the centre of the Cotswolds - an ideal touring base. AA QQQQ Selected.

Elaine & Graham Whent
Tel/Fax: 01451 860493

B&B from £22.50pp, Dinner from £14.00, Rooms 1 twin, 2 double,
all en-suite, No smoking, children or pets,
Open all year except Christmas and New Year, Map Ref S

Market House, The Square, Northleach, Gloucestershire GL54 3EJ   **Nearest Road A429, A40**

A 400 year old Cotswold stone house of 'olde worlde' charm yet with modern facilities. This enchanting and pretty Grade II listed house features an inglenook fireplace and many exposed beams. The very comfortable, well appointed and centrally heated, bedrooms (1 en-suite), all have wash hand basins, tea/coffee makers, and touring guides. Northleach is a tiny, tiny town with a wonderful selection of restaurants and inns. A delicious English breakfast completes your stay. Packed lunches on request. Ideal base for touring locally and Stratford, Bath, Oxford and Woodstock. AA recommended.

Theresa & Mike Eastman
Tel: 01451 860557

B&B from £18pp, Rooms 1 double en-suite, 1 twin/double, 2 single,
No smoking, No pets, Minimum age 12,
Open all year, Map Ref S

---

     right, Orchard House, near Newent - see above for details

Northfield, Cirencester Road, Northleach, Gloucestershire GL54 3JL   **Nearest Road A429, A40**

Detached family house in the country close to all local services in the small market town of Northleach with its magnificent church, musical and countryside museums - sure to please. Excellent centre for visiting lovely Cotswolds villages. Easily reached by car are Cheltenham, Oxford, Cirencester, Stratford, Burford Wildlife Park, local golf course, fishing, Cotswold walks and horse riding. All rooms are en-suite with central heating, TV, and tea/coffee trays, log fire in lounge. Large gardens to relax in or to enjoy a selection of freshly prepared evening meals. Brochure.

Pauline Loving
Tel: 01451 860427

B&B from £19pp, Dinner from £6, Rooms 1 twin, 1 double, 1 family, all en-suite, No smoking, Children welcome, No pets, Open all year except New Year, Map Ref T

Painswick Mill, Kingsmill Lane, Painswick, Gloucestershire GL6 6SA   **Nearest Road A46**

A beautiful Grade II listed Cotswold stone mill house dating from 1634 is set in 4 acres of lawn and trees traversed by 2 streams featuring a water garden. The property has rare old fireplaces, beamed ceilings and oak panelling. Two of the bedrooms are beamed and have tea/coffee making facilities with TV. A lounge, garden and hard tennis court available for guests Painswick, Queen of the Cotswold is a good base for touring and walking. Superb local pubs and restaurant serve delicious meals.

Mrs J M Wells
Tel: 01452 812245

B&B from £25pp, Rooms 1 twin with private bathroom, 2 double en-suite, Restricted smoking, Children over 10 years, No pets, Open all year except Christmas, Map Ref U

The Limes, Evesham Road, Stow-on-the-Wold, Gloucestershire GL54 1EJ   **Nearest Road A424**

The Limes is a large Victorian, family house, established as bed and breakfast accommodation for over 20 years. Pleasantly situated over-looking fields and the attractive garden with ornamental pool. The comfortable bedrooms are spacious and are equipped with radio/alarms, tea/coffee making facilities and Satellite TV. A short walk of about 4 minutes to the town centre. Car parking available. Choice of breakfast including vegetarian catered for. Many guests, from home and abroad, return each year. Recommended by the AA and RAC.

Helen & Graham Keyte
Tel: 01451 830034/831056

B&B from £17pp, Rooms 3 en-suite double - £19pp, 1 family, 1 twin, Children welcome, Pets by arrangement, Open all year except Christmas, Map Ref V

Bretton House, Fosseway, Stow-on-the-Wold, Gloucestershire GL54 1JU   **Nearest Road A429, Fosseway**

Bretton House is an elegant Edwardian Rectory personally run to combine high standards with comfort and friendly, homely atmosphere. Set in 2 acres of garden/woodland in the heart of the Cotswolds, we enjoy glorious views, yet are only minutes walk from Stow. Our 2 double bedrooms (with 4-poster beds) and 1 twin, are all tastefully decorated, having en-suite bathroom, colour TV and tea/coffee tray. Stow is very central for exploring the beautiful villages and countryside and we hope Bretton House makes an ideal and memorable setting for restful breaks.

Barry & Julia Allen
Tel: 01451 830388

B&B from £21pp, Dinner from £12.50, Rooms 1 twin, 2 double, all en-suite, Restricted smoking, Minimum age 10, Pets by arrangement, Open all year except Christmas, Map Ref W

*The Dial Cottatge,
near Stroud*

- see page 197 for details

The Old Grain House, Rectory Barns, Lower Swell, Stow on the Wold, Glos GL54 1LH   Nearest Rd A429/B4068

Beautifully decorated barn, ideally situated for both walking or driving through the Cotswolds. Lower Swell is situated just 1 mile from Stow-on-the-Wold with Oxford, Cheltenham, Stratford on Avon all within easy reach. The typical Cotswold village of Burford Bourton on the Water and the Slaughters are close by. God pub food also close by.

Mrs Elizabeth Campbell-Winton
Tel: 01451 832348

B&B from £22.50pp, Rooms 1 single/double, 1 double, private bathroom,
No smoking, children or pets,
Open all year except Christmas and New Year, Map Ref X

The Dial Cottage, Amberley, Minchinhampton Common, near Stroud, Gloucestershire GL5 5AL

With its origins dating back to 1600 The Dial Cottage is situated on Minchinhampton Common, National Trust Land, with its ancient golf course, quaint pubs, famous five valley walks. Well positioned for the Cotswolds, Wales, Bath, Badmington, Slimbridge, Berkley & Sudley Castles. Accommodation is en-suite with antique beds, exposed beams, uneven floors, nooks and crannies, complemented by modern amenities. Besides peace and tranquillity, guests can anticipate a personal service and a breakfast menu that reflects country cooking. Non-smoking. Licensed. Car park. ETB Highly Commended.

see PHOTO's on page 195

Pamela & David Veen
Tel: 01453 872563
Fax: 01453 873057

B&B from £25-£38.50pp, Rooms 1 twin, 3 double, 1 family, all en-suite,
No smoking, Children over 11, No pets,
Open March - end November, Map Ref Y

Tavern House, Willesley, near Tetbury, Gloucestershire GL8 8QU   Nearest Road A433

Delightfully situated 17th century former Cotswold coaching inn, only 1 mile from Westonbirt Arboretum. Superb luxury bed and breakfast. All rooms en-suite with direct dial phone, colour TV, tea maker, hair dryer, trouser press, etc. Guests lounge. Charming secluded walled garden, Ample parking. Convenient for visiting Bath, Bristol, Gloucester, Cheltenham, Bourton-on-the-Water. AA, RAC, ETB Highly Commended. English Tourist Board Silver award winner for excellence. Bed & Breakfast of the Year 1993. Colour brochure with pleasure. EMail: Tavern House Hotel@uk business.com

see PHOTO opposite

Janet & Tim Tremellen
Tel: 01666 880444
Fax: 01666 880254

B&B from £28.50pp, Rooms 1 twin, 3 double, all en-suite,
Restricted smoking, Minimum age 10, No pets,
Open all year, special rates for Christmas and New Year, Map Ref Z

Almsbury Farm, Vineyard Street, Winchcombe, Glos GL54 5LP   Nearest Road B4632

This four hundred year old Grade II listed Cotswold stone house offers a high standard of comfortable accommodation and a very warm welcome. Set in lovely countryside on the edge of the village. Almsbury Farm offers the best of both worlds. Leave your car and explore the Cotswold Way and local walks and visit Sudeley Castle on foot or travel to Stratford, Broadway, Cotswold villages or Oxford which are all within easy reach.

Annie Hitch
Tel: 01242 602403

B&B from £22pp, Rooms 1 double, 1 family, both en-suite,
Restricted smoking, Children over 10 years, Pets by arrangement,
Open January - November, Christmas by arrangement, Map Ref 1

left, Tavern House, near Tetbury - see above for details

Gower House, 16 North Street, Winchcombe, Gloucestershire GL54 5LH   **Nearest Road B4632**

Gower House, a 17th century town house, is situated close to the centre of Winchcombe, a small picturesque country town on the 'Cotswold Way', and is an ideal base for exploring the Cotswolds. Ramblers, cyclists and motorists are all equally welcome and there is ample parking to the rear. The three comfortable bedrooms all have colour TV, radio, tea/coffee making facilities, washbasins, full central heating and are served by 2 bathrooms each with shower and bath. In addition a TV lounge and a large secluded garden are available for guests' use.

Sally & Mick Simmonds
Tel: 01242 602616

B&B from £18pp, Rooms 2 twin, 1 double,
Restricted smoking, No pets,
Open all year except Christmas, Map Ref 1

"Both Beauty and Brandy with rosettes, Well done!"

"Buttercups and daisies,
Oh, the pretty flowers;
Coming ere the springtime,
To tell of sunny hours"
Mary Howitt

HAMPSHIRE
& the ISLE of WIGHT

From north to south this lovely county unrolls to reveal a staggering variety of holiday pleasures. Probably the most diverse of the counties of southern England, the chalk North Downs and the sandy heathland of the north-east change into a charming landscape of wooded wold cut by streams and scattered with delightful villages. The most attractive scenery is probably around Selborne in the east and the woodlands of the New Forest in the west. Selborne is the birthplace of Gilbert White, the pioneer of natural history who in 1789 published The Natural History and Antiquities of Selborne, one of the finest records of the English countryside written.

The north of the county is cut by the Roman Road known as Portway which ran from the Roman camp of Calleva Atrebatum at Silchester to Salisbury. Andover is well placed from which to visit this section of Hampshire...the Andover Downs, the valley of the River Anton, Hurstbourne Tarrant on the Bourne Rivulet in the pretty valley of Uphusband, and Wherwell, an ancient and attractive village of thatched cottages giving magnificent views across the Test valley. Further north is Highclere Castle, the seat of the Earls of Carnarvon, and on the summit of nearby Beacon Hill is the grave of the Fifth Earl, who in 1922 opened a tomb to reveal the spectacular treasures of Tutankhamen. In the extreme east of the county is Farnborough, the home of the Royal Aircraft Establishment and the impressive Air Show held every other year in the first week of September. Close by is Aldershot, the 'home of the British Army'. The Heroes Shrine in Manor Park is dedicated to the dead of World War II.

Filtered clear by the chalk downs is the River Test, one of England's finest trout rivers. To travel the length of this river is a delight, as the valley contains some picturesque villages. It was around the source of the river at Steventon that Jane Austen was born in 1775, and lived for the first twenty-three years of her life. At Longstock, a village of fascinating old houses the Danes had a shipyard where their longships were serviced. And speaking of fascinating old houses, the three Wallop villages, Over, Middle and Nether are renowned for their thatched cottages and fine churches. Romsey's development followed that of its abbey founded by the son of Alfred the Great. Regrettably all that now remains is the Norman abbey church, which incidentally contains the remarkable Ramsey Psalter, a fifteenth century illuminated manuscript. Broadlands House, a mile from the town was the home of Lord Palmerston whose statue stands in Romsey Market Place. The house later became the home of the Mountbatten family.

At the centre of Hampshire lies Winchester, a major religious and commercial centre in medieval times, and the capital city of Saxon England.The city is rich in every period of architecture after the thirteenth century. Its cathedral, the longest medieval cathedral in Europe, is a magnet to visitors, and contains monuments to Jane Austen and Isaak Walton, the 'Compleat Angler' who lived for some time in the cathedral close. During the Middle Ages St. Swithin's Shrine here was an important centre for pilgrims from Europe on their way to Becket's Shrine at Canterbury. The Tourist Information Centre is housed in the impressive Gothic revival guildhall built in 1871. Near the west gate is the Great Hall containing "King Arthur's Round Table".... interesting, but unfortunately a medieval fake! A statue of King Alfred, King of Wessex stands in Broadway. Winchester College, founded in 1382 by Bishop William of

Wykeham is one of the country's leading and oldest public schools and was very probably used as a model for Eton College. The great natural amphitheatre just three miles from Winchester at Cheesefoot Head was used by General Eisenhower when he addressed the allied troops before the D Day landings in 1944. There is a great deal to attract the visitor around the city...Avington House for instance, where Nell Gwynne lived when Charles II was in Winchester, Twyford, where Alexander Pope spent his school years and Crawley, immortalised by Thackeray in his novel 'Vanity Fair'.

The New Forest, a royal hunting ground established in 1079 for the Norman kings, strangely enough in so populated an area, still retains its remoteness. It is a splendid place for walking, picnics and camping. Near Minstead is the Rufus Stone, marking the supposed spot where William II was killed by an arrow fired by Walter Tyrrell, while hunting in 1100. Beaulieu Abbey, built by King John, destroyed by Henry VIII and rebuilt in part in 1872 as Palace House, is the home of Lord Montagu,whose National Motor Museum holds the finest collection of its kind. To the south is Buckler's Hard, which in the eighteenth centuy employed no fewer than four thousand men building the ships for Nelson's navy, of oak from the New Forest.

The Isle of Wight is extremely popular with the holidaymaker, having a scenic beauty all of its own. The walks over Tennyson Downs from Freshwater Bay provide memorable views of The Needles. Godshill, Mottistone, Shorwell, Sandown and Calbourne offer the visitor special delight. At Carisbrooke, the old capital of the Island, there is the great Norman Castle in which Charles I was imprisoned, while Osborne House, designed by Prince Albert and Thomas Cubitt, was a great favourite of Queen Victoria. Newport, capital of this busy holiday island is of course the ideal centre for the visitor who has the difficult if pleasant task of choosing priorities. There are picturesque villages in profusion, breathtaking coastal walks, seaside towns with golden sands and excellent bathing, and for the sailor, Cowes, which is the home of the Royal Yacht Squadron.

HAMPSHIRE &

Places to Visit

Carisbrooke Castle, *Isle of Wight* ~ a medieval castle which for centuries was the home of the islands governor. Donkeys still raise water from the well in the middle courtyard.

Danebury Hillfort, *near Nether Wallop* ~ an impressive oval shaped, thirteen acre Iron Age fortress with three lines of ditches and ramparts increasing in strength and height towards the centre. Built in the 6th century BC until around 100 BC, when improved defences and fortified entrance still did not prevent it being overrun.

Hillier Gardens and Arboretum, *Ampfield* ~ founded by Sir Harold Hillier, the famous nurseryman in 1953. One hundred and sixty six acres of gardens with over forty two thousand plants and trees.

Mottisfont Abbey, *Mottisfont* ~ founded in 1201, this Augustinian priory was given to Lord Sandys after the Dissolution, he turned it into a house. It was remodelled and extended in Georgian times.

Historic Dockyard, *Portsmouth* ~ now partly opened to the public, it houses a collection of historic ships including the hull of the Mary Rose, Henry VIII's flagship which sank on its maiden voyage to fight the French in 1545. HMS Victory, the English flagship on which Nelson was killed at Trafalgar, has now been fully restored, also on display is HMS Warrior, the 1860 ironclad warship.

The New Forest, *Hampshire* ~ one hundred and forty five square miles of heath and woodland. William the Conqueror's 'new' forest, despite its name, is one of the few primeval oak woods in England.

Nunwell House, *Brading, Isle of Wight* ~ a part Georgian, part Jacobean house house with fine gardens and channel views. Charles I spent his last night of freedom here.

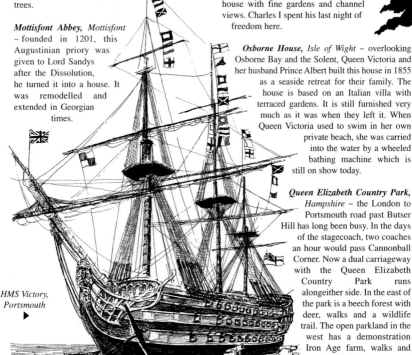

Osborne House, *Isle of Wight* ~ overlooking Osborne Bay and the Solent, Queen Victoria and her husband Prince Albert built this house in 1855 as a seaside retreat for their family. The house is based on an Italian villa with terraced gardens. It is still furnished very much as it was when they left it. When Queen Victoria used to swim in her own private beach, she was carried into the water by a wheeled bathing machine which is still on show today.

Queen Elizabeth Country Park, *Hampshire* ~ the London to Portsmouth road past Butser Hill has long been busy. In the days of the stagecoach, two coaches an hour would pass Cannonball Corner. Now a dual carriageway with the Queen Elizabeth Country Park runs alongeither side. In the east of the park is a beech forest with deer, walks and a wildlife trail. The open parkland in the west has a demonstration Iron Age farm, walks and wonderful views.

HMS Victory, Portsmouth ▶

the ISLE of WIGHT

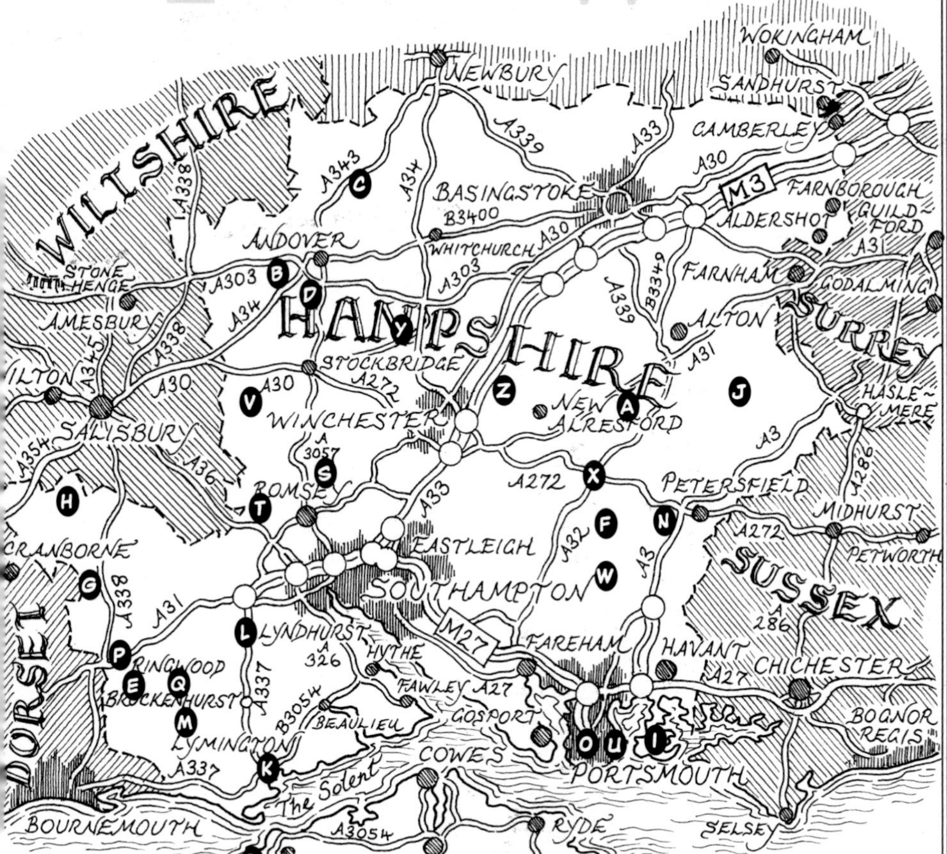

WOKINGHAM
NEWBURY
SANDHURST
WILTSHIRE
A339
A33
CAMBERLEY
A343
A34
A30
M3
A338
BASINGSTOKE
FARNBOROUGH
GUILDFORD
B3400
ALDERSHOT
ANDOVER
A30
WHITCHURCH
A31
STONE HENGE
A303
A303
B3349
FARNHAM
GODALMING
A34
A339
AMESBURY
HAMPSHIRE
ALTON
SURREY
A338
A345
STOCKBRIDGE
A31
WILTON
A30
A272
A30
HASLEMERE
WINCHESTER
NEW ALRESFORD
SALISBURY
A3057
A3
A354
A36
A272
PETERSFIELD
A286
ROMSEY
MIDHURST
A33
A272
CRANBORNE
EASTLEIGH
A32
PETWORTH
A3
SUSSEX
A338
SOUTHAMPTON
A286
DORSET
A31
LYNDHURST
M27
FAREHAM
HAVANT
A326
HYTHE
RINGWOOD
CHICHESTER
A27
BROCKENHURST
A337
FAWLEY
A27
B3054
BEAULIEU
GOSPORT
BOGNOR REGIS
LYMINGTON
COWES
A337
PORTSMOUTH
The Solent
BOURNEMOUTH
A3054
RYDE
SELSEY
FRESHWATER
NEWPORT
SANDOWN
ISLE OF WIGHT
SHANKLIN
VENTNOR

Medieval Architecture, Romsey ▶

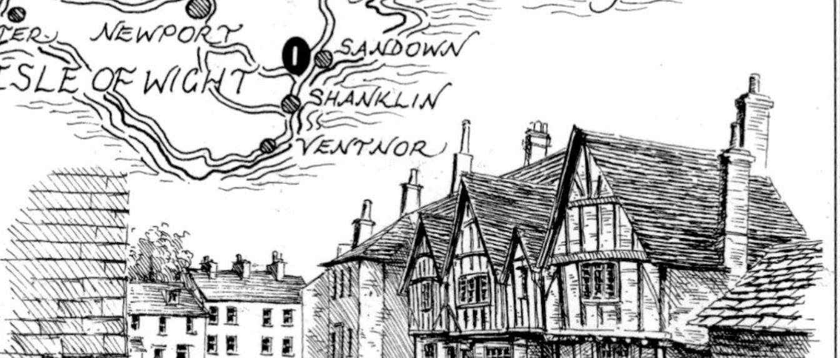

Thickets, Swelling Hill, Ropley, Alresford, Hampshire SO24 0DA   Nearest Road A31

This spacious country house surrounded by a two acre garden has fine view across the Hampshire countryside. There are two comfortable twin bedded rooms with private bath or shower room. Tea/coffee making facilities available. Guests sitting room with TV. Full English breakfast. Local attractions are Jane Austen's House ten minutes by car. Winchester with its fine cathedral twenty minutes away. Salisbury, Chichester and The New Forest within easy reach. Heathrow Airport one hour.

David & Sue Lloyd-Evans
Tel: 01962 772467

**B&B from £20pp, Rooms 2 twin, both with private facilities,
Restricted smoking, Children from 10, No pets,
Open all year except Christmas and New Year, Map Ref A**

Broadwater, Amport near Andover, Hampshire SP11 8AY   Nearest Road A303

A 17th century listed thatched cottage with old oak beams, offering quiet and cosy accommodation in a relaxed and friendly atmosphere, set in a secluded cottage garden, in a peaceful village near Stonehenge. Within minutes of the A303 and having easy access to airports and ferries. A private sitting room with traditional fireplace and colour TV. ETB 2 Crown Commended, AA QQQ.

Mrs Carolyn Mallam
Tel: 01264 772240
Fax: 01264 772240

**B&B from £22.50pp, Rooms 2 en-suite twin,
Restricted smoking, Children welcome, No pets,
Open all year, Map Ref B**

Frenches Lodge, Little London, Andover, Hampshire SP11 6JG   Nearest Road A343, A303

Frenches Lodge is a Grade II listed 300 year old thatched farm house with old oak beams and open fire, offering quiet accommodation in a friendly atmosphere. It has a secluded garden with country walks into the surrounding woods. Breakfast times are flexible and served in the sunny conservatory overlooking the garden. It is within half an hour of Winchester, Salisbury and Newbury Racecourse. Golf courses are close by. Dinner is served in the dining room by arrangement.

Charles & Gilly Radford
Tel: 01264 365358

**B&B from £20, Dinner from £15, Rooms 1 single, 1 twin, 1 double,
adjacent facilities, Children welcome, Pets by arrangement,
Open all year except Christmas & New Year, Map Ref C**

Malt Cottage, Upper Clatford, Andover, Hampshire SP11 7QL   Nearest Road A303

Walk around the beautiful six acre garden with chalk stream and lakes, or sit by the fire in the beamed sitting room. Malt Cottage, an ideal stop from London/Heathrow to the West Country, is situated in a picturesque village with many thatched cottages. There are 3 attractive bedrooms with private or en-suite facilities. This is an ideal, central position for exploring locally, Stonehenge, Salisbury and Winchester or within an hour Bath, Oxford, andPortsmouth. You will receive a warm welcome in a delightful home.

see PHOTO opposite

Patricia & Richard Mason
Tel: 01264 323469
Fax: 01264 334100

**B&B from £20pp, Rooms 1 twin, 2 double, all en-suite,
Restricted smoking, Children welcome, No pets,
Open all year except Christmas & New Year, Map Ref D**

left, Malt Cottage, Andover- see details above

Tothill House, Black Lane, off Forest Road, Burley, Christchurch BH23 8DZ   Nearest Road A35

Tothill House is in an idyllic woodland setting on the southern fringe of the New Forest adjoining Poors Common, an area designated for outstanding natural beauty and noted for its flora and fauna. All bedrooms are en-suite, have colour TV, and tea/coffee making facilities. A wide variety of local sporting and recreational activities available with fine sailing waters on the Solent, bathing beaches and excellent selection of golf courses. Private fishing lakes nearby. AA QQQQ Selected.

Mrs Wendy Buckley
Tel: 01425 674414
Fax: 01425 672235

**B&B from £25pp, Rooms 2 double, 1 twin, all en-suite,
Minimum age 15, No pets, No smoking,
Open all year except Christmas & New Year, Map Ref E**

Drayton Cottage, East Meon, Hampshire GU32 1PW   Nearest Road A32/A272

Drayton Cottage is an immaculately maintained 200 years old flint and chalk country cottage, with superb views, surrounded by pasture land. Antiques and oak beams in the guest lounge and breakfast room, and a conservatory overlooking the attractive garden, provide a luxurious yet cosy atmosphere in which to relax. Bedrooms have TV, and tea/coffee making facilities. Parking is easy and guests have their own entrance and stairs. Portsmouth, Chichester, Winchester, Selbourne and Petworth are all within easy reach. ETB Highly Commended.

Mrs Joan Rockett
Tel: 01730 823472

**B&B from £20pp, Rooms 1 twin/double en-suite, 1 double with private
shower room, Restricted smoking, No children or pets,
Open all year except Christmas, Map Ref F**

Cottage Crest, Woodgreen, Fordingbridge, Hampshire SP6 2AX   Nearest Road A338

Cottage Crest is situated in a delightful spot on the edge of the New Forest, set in its own 4 1/2 acres of garden surrounded by ancient and ornamental forest with superb views of the River Avon in the valley. The en-suite bedrooms are spacious, decorated to very high standard and have TV and tea/coffee making facilities. A short walk takes one into the village with its local pub which serves excellent meals. Within easy reach of the coast and Isle of Wight. It is the ideal place to either relax, in the peaceful surroundings, or visit the many interesting places in the area.

Mrs Lupita Cadman
Tel: 01725 512009

**B&B from £20pp, Rooms 1 twin, 2 double, all en-suite,
Children welcome, No pets,
Open all year except Christmas, Map Ref G**

Hendley House, Rockbourne, Fordingbridge, Hampshire SP6 3NA   Nearest Road A338, A354

Beautiful, south facing, 16th century grade II listed house, with later additions, situated on the edge of the village and overlooking water meadows and farmland. Elegantly decorated with a wealth of beams and a relaxed family atmosphere. Log fires in winter and heated swimming pool in spacious garden in summer. You will be assured of a warm welcome as Nick and Pat love entertaining (Nick is a wine merchant). An ideal base for exploring the New Forest and visiting National Trust and other houses and gardens. Within easy reach of the south coast.

Mrs Pat Ratcliffe
Tel: 01725 518303
Fax: 01725 518546

**B&B from £24pp, Rooms 1 twin with en-suite shower,
1 double with private bathroom, Minimum age 10, No pets
Open early February - end November, Map Ref H**

Cockle Warren Cottage Hotel, 36 Seafront, Hayling Island, Portsmouth PO11 9HL   **Nearest Road A27**

Cockle Warren is a delightful seaside cottage hotel with large gardens and heated swimming pool. All rooms are en-suite with colour TV, phones etc, some have 4 poster beds and overlook the sea. French and English country cooking, homemeade bread and French wines can be enjoyed in the pretty conservatory. Restful lounge with log fire, antiques and memorabilia. Conveniently situated between the Roman city of Chichester and historic city of Portsmouth, with its HMS Victory and the Mary Rose. Hayling Island is renowned for its mild climate, clean air and beach. National winners with the RAC and AA.

Diane & David Skelton
Tel: 01705 464961
Fax: 01705 464838

B&B from £26pp, Dinner £24.50, Rooms 4 double, 1 single, 1 triple,
Older children welcome, Pets by arrangement,
Open all year, Map Ref I

see PHOTO on page 207

Land of Nod, Headley, Hampshire GU35 8SJ   **Nearest Road A3/B3002**

A large neo Georgian house set in 7 acres of mature garden in the centre of 100 acres of private woodland estate. All rooms have TV and tea/coffee making facilities. Situated 1 hour from Heathrow, Gatwick, London, Portsmouth. 10 Historic houses within 1 hour. Some of the finest gardens within easy reach. Golf, tennis, fishing, riding available locally. A wonderful place in which to relax or from which to tour. Unlimited parking. A car is essential which can be hired locally.

Jeremy & Philippa Whitaker
Tel: 01428 713609
Fax: 01428 717698

B&B from £25pp, Dinner by prior arrangement £20pp, Rooms 3 twin,
2 en-suite, No smoking, No pets or children under 12,
Open all year except Christmas, Map Ref J

see PHOTO opposite

Albany House, Highfield, Lymington, Hampshire SO41 9GB   **Nearest Road A337**

Built about 1830, this elegant Regency residence has large, well proportioned rooms with quality furnishings and sumptuous bathrooms. Situated in a quiet position overlooking a green yet only moments from Lymington's thriving shopping centre with interesting boutiques, narrow cobbled streets and ancient Saturday market. A ferry to the Isle of Wight operates all year. A comfortable lounge with books and log fire. An excellent dinner is served in the elegant dining room. Bedrooms have tea/coffee making facilities, TV and are en-suite.

Mrs Wendy Gallagher
Tel: 01590 671900

B&B from £26pp, Dinner from £12.50, Rooms 1 twin, 1 double,
1 family, all en-suite,
Open all year except Christmas. Map Ref K

Jevington, 47 Waterford Lane, Lymington, Hants SO41   **Nearest Road A337**

Comfortable family home situated in quiet lane midway between High Street/Marinas. Ideal base for New Forest, Solent coastline walks. 10 minutes drive to Isle of Wight ferry, 10 minutes walk to ancient market town. Good selection of pubs and restaurants. Tea/coffee making facilities, TV, off street parking. Children welcome. No smoking. Places of interest to visit include Beaulieu, Winchester, Stonehenge, Portsmouth, Bournemouth and Southampton. Bike hire, riding, sailing and nature walks in the New Forest can all be arranged.

Ian & June Carruthers
Tel: 01590 672148

B&B from £18pp, Rooms 1 twin, 1 double, 1 family, all en-suite,
No smoking, Children and pets welcome,
Open all year, Map Ref K

---

left, **Land of Nod, Headley- see details above**

St Mary's Lodge, Captains Row, Lymington, Hampshire SO41 9RR — Nearest Road M27

An elegant Georgian interior designed house situated in the old area of Lymington close to the town quay. Quaint with fishing boats and visiting yachts. Boutiques, shops, pubs and first class restaurants minutes away. Well known Saturday antiques market. Two marinas and ferry to the Isle of Wight. Wonderful walks in the New Forest and Beaulieu. Convivial hosts providing a memorable stay.

Mrs P A Thomson
Tel: 01590 678576

B&B from £25pp, Rooms 2 double, 1 twin, 2 single,
Minimum age 8, No smoking, Pets by arrangement,
Open all year, Map Ref K

The Penny Farthing Hotel, Romsey Road, Lyndhurst, Hampshire SO43 7AA — Nearest Road A337

Ideally situated in Lyndhurst village centre, The Penny Farthing Hotel, offers smart en-suite rooms with remote control colour TV and tea/coffee making facilities. We also have a residents lounge with bar and a large private car park to the rear. The Hotel was completely refurbished in 1993 and all rooms named after bicycles. We have bicycles to hire and secure lock up store if you would like to bring your own. Lyndhurst village has a good selection of pubs, restaurants, cafes, shops and the New Forest Visitor Centre and Museum.

Mike & Jane Saqui
Tel: 01703 284422
Fax: 01703 284488

B&B from £22.50pp, Rooms 1 single, 2 twin, 6 double, 2 family,
Restricted smoking, Children welcome, Pets by arrangement,
Open all year except Christmas, Map Ref L

Yew Tree Farm, Bashley Common Road, New Milton, Hampshire BH25 5SH — Nearest Road A35

Two lovely spacious bed sitting rooms marvellously comfortable, with double or twin beds and both with own bathroom, in a traditional, cosy, thatched farmhouse on the edge of the New Forest. Extensive breakfasts (taken in bedroom), Homemade dinners (if ordered in advance), using top quality produce. Private entrance and ample private parking. Very easily located. Turn off the A35 between Lyndhurst and Christchurch onto the B3058. Yew Tree Farm is a small holding with 9 acres of grassland and is home to a charming home bred house cow named Holly.

Mrs Daphne Matthews
Tel/Fax: 01425 611041

B&B from £27.50-£35pp, Dinner from £15-£18.50, Rooms 1 twin with
private bathroom, 1 en-suite double, No smoking, No children, Pets if
kept in car, Open all year except Xmas & New Year, Map Ref M

Twentyways Farm, Ramsdean, Petersfield, Hampshire GU32 1RX — Nearest Road Ramsdean Road

Twentyways Farm is a converted 17th century barn nestling in 20 acres of paddocks and gardens tucked beneath the brow of ancient Butser Hill in the picturesque Meon Valley. Maureen and David Farmer offer you a warm welcome in either of the 2 comfortable bedrooms with en-suite facilities and TV. Tea or coffee can be enjoyed in the spacious galleried drawing room or relaxing in the flint walled courtyard by the pool with Italian fountain playing and an abundance of gaily coloured flowers. A generous English breakfast, all needs catered for, to be enjoyed in the oak dining room.

Maureen & David Farmer
Tel: 01730 823606

B&B from £25pp, Rooms 2 en-suite twin,
No smoking, No children,
Open all year, Map Ref N

Fortitude Cottage, 51 Broad Street, Old Portsmouth, Hampshire PO1 2JD   Southern end of A3

A charming unusual town house overlooking the quayside in the heart of Old Portsmouth. Built on the site of a 16th century cottage destroyed during the 2nd war and named after an 18th century warship. The immaculately maintained bedrooms and bathrooms are decorated in delicate pastel shades and needlepoint pictures and flowers abound. Breakfast is served on pine tables in a beamed room with views over the water. Carol has won 'Britain in Bloom' awards for her window boxes and hanging baskets; and 'Heartbeat' for healthy food choices. Most major credit cards accepted.

see PHOTO on page 217

Mrs C A Harbeck
Tel: 01705 823748
Fax: 01705 823748

B&B from £21pp, Rooms 3 rooms all en-suite with tea/coffee making facilities, No smoking, No children, Open all year, Map Ref O

The Nest, 10 Middle Lane off School Lane, Ringwood, Hants BH24 1LE   Nearest Road A31, B3347

A lovely Victorian family house. Situated in a quiet residential lane within 5 minutes walk of Ringwood town centre, an ancient market town with many restaurants and inns. Ample parking. Beautifully decorated, very clean and well maintained. Breakfast times are flexible and served in the delightful sunny conservatory overlooking the gardens. Pretty colour co-ordinated 'Laura Ashley' style bedrooms with pine furnishings. Local activities include fishing, golf, riding and forest walks. An excellent base to explore the New Forest. 30 mins drive Bournemouth, Salisbury & Southampton. AA Selected. Highly recommended.

Mrs Yvonne Nixon
Tel/Fax: 01425 476724
Mobile: 0589 854505

B&B from £16pp, Rooms 2 double, 1 twin, 1 single, No smoking, Open all year, Map Ref P

Plantation Cottage, Mockbeggar, near Ringwood, Hampshire BH24 3NL   Nearest Road A338

A charming 200 year old grade II listed cottage set in three acres in the beautiful New Forest between Ringwood and Fordingbridge. Mockbeggar is a peaceful hamlet where wild ponies graze by the roadside, and is also within easy reach of Bournemouth, Poole and Salisbury. There are many excellent pubs and restaurant in the area, which is ideal for walking, cycling and riding at stables close by. Guest lounge and garden available all day. Holiday cottage also available. All rooms en-suite. Sorry no smoking and no children.

Jane Yates
Tel: 01425 477443

B&B from £22.50pp, Rooms 1 twin, 1 double, all en-suite, No smoking, children or pets, Open all year, Map Ref P

Holmans, Bisterne Close, Burley, Ringwood, Hampshire BH24 4AZ   Nearest Road A31/A35

Holmans is a charming country house in the heart of the New Forest, set in four acres with stabling available for guests' own horses. Superb walking, horse riding and carriage driving with golf course nearby. A warm friendly welcome is assured. All bedrooms are en-suite and tastefully furnished with tea/coffee making facilities, radio and hairdryer. Colour TV in guest lounge with adjoining orangery and log fires in winter.

Robin & Mary Ford
Tel/Fax: 01425 402307

B&B from £20pp, Rooms 1 twin, 2 double, all en-suite, No smoking, Children welcome, Open all year except Christmas and New Year, Map Ref Q

Michelmersh House, Michelmersh, Romsey, Hampshire SO51 0NS   Nearest Road A3047, A31

Michelmersh House is a late Georgian farmhouse set in 4 acres of grounds in the pretty village of Michelmersh. It stands on high ground overlooking the famous river Test Valley in a quiet position. The rooms are beautifully furnished and spacious with large beds. Coffee/tea facilities. The sitting room. Available at all times, is a lovely sunny room with comfortable sofas and television. A delightful home. Ideal for exploring Hampshire and south Wiltshire and with many good pubs and restaurant nearby.

Mrs Jennifer Lalonde
Tel: 01794 368644

B&B from £20pp, Dinner from £17.00, Rooms 1 single, 1 twin, 1 double, 2 private bathrooms, 1 en-suite, No smoking, Children over 12, No pets, Open mid January - mid December, Map Ref S

Wellow Mead, Wellow Drove, Sherfield English, Romsey, Hampshire SO51 6DU Nearest Road M27, A27, A36

Wellow Mead is a beautiful, thatched house standing in 7 acres, on Florence Nightingale's old estate, minutes from the New Forest. The Grain Store is romantic and rustic, hung with soft muslins. The beamed snug suite (1690) has an inglenook, old oak staircase and bath on clawfeet. A tented ceiling adorns the Onion Store. The last 2 suites have wood burners. All have their own private sitting rooms. Heated indoor pool in plant filled conservatory (May-Oct) for candlelit swims. Stonehenge, historic Portsmouth, Salisbury and Winchester within easy reach. Charming market town of Romsey is packed with pubs and restaurants.

Julia Montgomery
Tel: 01794 323227
Fax: 01794 323202

B&B from £35pp, Rooms 3 suite, all en-suite, No smoking, Children welcome, Pets by arrangement, Open all year except Christmas and New Year, Map Ref T

see PHOTO opposite

Glencoe Guest House, 64 Whitwell Road, Southsea PO4 0QS   Nearest Road M27, M275

Glencoe is a Victorian town house ideally situated in a quiet residential road, yet convenient to all amenities. Only 2 minutes from the sea front and a short drive to the Continental Ferry Port. Places of historic interest are within walking distance, also the Hovercraft which will get you to the Isle of Wight in 10 minutes. Glencoe offers high standards of comfort with attractive rooms. For added comfort bedrooms are all equipped with tea/coffee making facilities and TV.

Mrs June Gwilliam
Tel/Fax: 01705 737413

B&B from £17.50pp, Rooms 2 single, 2 twin, 2 double, 1 family, most en-suite, Restricted smoking, Children welcome, No pets, Open all year, Map Ref U

---

11 Clarence Parade, Southsea, Hampshire PO5 3NU   Nearest Road M27, A3M, A27, M275

This elegant Georgian style house has magnificent direct sea views across the sea and the Isle of Wight. 3 large, beautifully decorated and tastefully furnished bedrooms all with en-suite or private facilities, TV and tea/coffee makers. Easy for parking. Convenient for historic ships and ferries to France, Spain and Isle of Wight. Large choice of pubs, restaurants and shops within 2 minutes walk. The historic Cathedral cities of Winchester and Chichester are within easy reach. Gatwick and Heathrow Airports 1 hour 20 minutes drive away. Christine and Adrian enjoy helping to plan your day. German is spoken.

Adrian & Christine Taylor
Tel: 01705 736510 Fax: 01705 874844
Mobile: 0402 986145

B&B from £20pp, Dinner by arrangement, Rooms 3 twin/double, 2 family, all en-suite, Smoking allowed, Children welcome minimum age 12, No pets, Open all year, Map Ref U

---

left, Wellow Mead, Sherfield English - see details above   **213**

Yew Tree House, High Street, Broughton, Stockbridge, Hampshire SO20 8AA   Nearest Road A30

This delightful Grade II listed early Georgian house is set in the heart of the peaceful award-winning village of Broughton. It is furnished with many antiques, guests may use the sitting room and their bedrooms are a good size with comfortably firm beds. The beautiful walled garden always provides flowers for every room. Many guests comment upon the special atmosphere of this home and the exceptional warm welcome they receive. The place to stay awhile and visit Winchester, Salisbury and Jane Austen country.

Philip & Janet Mutton
Tel: 01794 301227

B&B from £21pp, Dinner from £15, Rooms 1 single, 1 twin, 1 double, all private/en-suite, No smoking, Children welcome, No pets, Open all year, Map Ref V

Forest Gate, Hambledon Road, Denmead, Waterlooville, Hampshire PO7 6EX   Nearest Road B2150

This is a fine Grade II listed Georgian residence, built around 1790, and is situated on the outskirts of the village overlooking farmland. Set in approximately 2 acres of garden with lawns, rose beds, pond and tennis court. The elegant drawing and dining rooms have mahogany floors with French doors opening onto a paved garden terrace. The comfortable bedrooms are en-suite have tea/coffee making facilities and TV. Nestling in the South Downs, Denmead is on the Wayfarers Way, a scenic 70 mile walk from Emsworth to Newbury. Dinner is available by arrangement.

Torfrida & David Cox
Tel: 01705 255901

B&B from 18pp, Dinner from £10, Rooms 2 twin (en-suite), No smoking, Minimum age 10, Open all year except Christmas & New Year, Map Ref W

Home Paddocks, West Meon, Hampshire GU32 1NA   Nearest Road A32, A272

Home Paddocks, is the much cherished home of the Ward family. It is on the outskirts of West Meon set in a large garden with tennis court and croquet lawn. Part of the house dates back to the 1560's with Victorian conservatory. The comfortable bedrooms, with private facilities, are equipped with tea/coffee makers. A drawing room, dining room, sitting room, conservatory and 'live-in' kitchen are also available to guests. Ideally situated for visiting Portsmouth, Southampton, New Forest, Isle of Wight and much more. There are many pubs, restaurants and theatres in the area.

The Ward Family
Tel: 01730 829241
Fax: 01730 829577

B&B from £22pp, Dinner from £12, Rooms 2 en-suite twin, Restricted smoking, Minimum age 7, Pets by arrangement, Open all year except Christmas, New Year and Easter, Map Ref X

Church Farm, Barton Stacey, Winchester, Hampshire SO21 3RR   Nearest Road A30, A303

A 15th century scheduled (Grade II*) tithe barn with Georgian additions, the attractive furnished living rooms leading out of Tudor Hall with its original flagstone floor, face south over the croquet lawn. There is an adjacent, recently converted coach house, centrally-heated like the main house. Here a family of up to five may be totally self-contained and would be most welcome to dine with the Talbots in the candlelit dining room.. Church Farm is in th heart of Wessex; within easy reach of famous cathedral cities of Winchester and Salisbury, Stonehenge, Oxford, Heathrow and Gatwick, Newbury and Goodwood.

see PHOTO opposite

James & Jean Talbot
Tel/Fax: 01962 760268

B&B from £30pp, Supper £15, Dinner £25, Rooms 2 single, 3 double/twin, all private bathroom, Children welcome, Pets by prior arrangement, Open all year, Map Ref Y

The Trout Inn, Itchen Abbas, near Winchester, Hampshire SO21 1BQ   **Nearest Road B3047**

The Trout Inn lies in the lovely Itchen Valley on the B3047 between Winchester and Alresford. Traditional British cooking and non-smoking dining room. Bar meals and snacks available. Children's play area. Six comfortable en-suite rooms with colour television and tea/coffee making facilities. AA Listed 4Qs.

David Lee Smith
Tel: 01962 779537
Fax: 01962 860652

B&B from £35 single, £60 double, Rooms 2 twin, 4 double, 2 family, all en-suite, No smoking, Children welcome, No pets, Open all year except Christmas, Map Ref Z

The Grange Country House, Alverstone, near Sandown, Isle of Wight   **Nearest Road A3055, A3056**

The Grange is in the centre of the hamlet of Alverstone. Built in 1877 this was the island home of Lord Alverstone. Peaceful gardens of $^3/_4$ acre surround the house. An excellent menu is served in the dining room prepared by your hostess. After dinner coffee is taken in the comfortable lounge. The en-suite bedrooms with tea/coffee making facilities, are bright and airy with views overlooking the the rolling downs. The Grange is situated for all aspects of the Island and is ideal for walking, the E Yar nature walk and Nunwell trail pass through the village.

Geraldine & David Watling
Tel: 01983 403729

B&B from £19pp, Dinner from £13.50, Rooms 1 single, 2 twin, 3 double, 1 family, all en-suite, Children welcome, No pets, No smoking, Open February - November, Map Ref 1

Strang Hall, Uplands, Totland Bay, Isle of Wight PO39 0DZ   **Nearest Road B3322**

Strang Hall is an Edwardian family home decorated in the arts and craft style with splendid views over the Downs and Solent, set peacefully in the hills above Totland Bay. The large garden leads onto a short walk to the beach. Yarmouth and Freshwater are within 2 miles with golf, tennis etc. The West Wight is famous for its good country walks.

Vera F. McMullan
Tel/Fax: 01983 753189

B&B from £20pp, Dinner from £10.00, Rooms 1 single, 1 twin, 1 double, 1 family, some en-suite, Restricted smoking, Children welcome, No pets, Open all year except Christmas & New Year, Map Ref 2

Please mention
THE GREAT BRITISH
BED & BREAKFAST
when booking your accommodation

right, Fortitude Cottage, Portsmouth - see page 211

HEREFORDSHIRE
& WORCESTERSHIRE

The glorious Malvern Hills stand between the low plains of Herefordshire and the Worcestershire Vale of Evesham. Used extensively by ancient man as defensive positions, the well preserved hillforts of the Hereforshire Beacon and the Worcestershire Beacon, remain witness to their prowess as military builders. Today, these lovely hills offer the holidaymaker wonderful walking country and superb views ranging from the Welsh Marches in the west to the Cotswolds in the east. The Malverns inspired much of the music of Sir Edward Elgar who, until his death in 1934 directed his own music at the Three Choirs Festival - the major music festival which takes place in August each year rotating between Worcester, Hereford and Gloucester cathedrals. Not only do Herefordshire and Worcestershire offer the visitor two quite remarkable 'capital' cities, they offer also some of the most spectacular river scenery in the country.

Hereford, once the Saxon capital of West Mercia, is delightfully situated by the River Wye in an area renowned for its cattle and its cider making. A perfect centre for touring, the city has some excellent medieval architecture, but its pride and joy is undoubtedly its sandstone cathedral begun in 1107, with its impressive library of over one thousand, four hundred chained books, the largest of its kind in the world, and its priceless thirteenth century map of the world, the famous Mappa Mundi. Of lesser importance but of interest is the plaque marking the birthplace of Nell Gwynne in nearby Gwynne Street. A short distance away at Abbey Dore are the remains of a huge Cistercian abbey, while to the east is Kilpeck, whose fine Norman church is lavishly carved with mythical beasts. West from Hereford is an excellent Black and White Village Trail,

taking the visitor through Weobley, Pembridge whose six hundred year old fortified church tower was used by villagers as a defence against Welsh raiders, Eardisland with its fourteenth century Staick House and lovely Lyonshall.

The River Wye, famous for its salmon, enters a spectacular wooded sandstone gorge as it nears its end. It's hard to visualise this beautiful place at one time being a centre of industry, but during the fifteenth and sixteenth centuries these woodlands supplied charcoal for a flourishing iron-smelting industry...in fact brass was actually invented here in 1568. Symonds Yat, a popular visitors attraction overlooks the meander of the Wye. Ross-on-Wye is the main tourist centre of the district with its Georgian houses and arcaded market house. To the north is Ledbury with another impressive market house, built in the sixteenth century, half-timbered and standing on pillars of chestnut. The Feathers Inn is one of the finest examples of seventeenth century half-timbering in Britain. John Masefield, a former Poet Laureate, was born here and the town was a favourite of the Brownings and Wordsworth...and little wonder, the place is picturesque in the extreme. Malvern Wells and Great Malvern, sheltering under the Malvern Hills, were brought to prominence in the eighteenth century when a Dr.Wall advertised the medicinal efficacy of its spa water.

Leominster is wonderfully situated at the junction of Pinsley Brook and the River Lugg, amongst cider-apple orchards and hopfields, although its prosperity is based upon its fine-spun wool from local sheep, which long ago were exported to establish the great Australian and South American flocks.

Like Herefordshire, Worcestershire is blessed with lovely rivers, and none more attractive than the Teme which, when the river is in flood can flow a rich red from the underlying red sandstone. The countryside here is lush, the banks of the River Teme bordered by hop fields, orchards and market gardens. A mile from where the Teme and the Severn join stands glorious Worcester, the administrative centre of Worcester and Hereford, dominated by its eleventh century cathedral. Worcester became an Anglo Saxon town after becoming a diocese in 680AD. Wool was the source of the city's medieval wealth, but since 1751 the manufacture of Worcester porcelain has become its best known activity. The city is rich in ancient and interesting houses....the Guildhall, designed in 1722 by a pupil of Sir Christopher Wren, incorporates a carving of the head of Oliver Cromwell nailed by the ears over the doorway. Worcester was an important centre during the Civil War, and Charles II's headquarters during the Battle of Worcester was the Commandery, founded in 1085 as a hospital by St. Wulstan. The cathedral houses the tomb of King John who died in 1216.

Above the tomb is the oldest royal effigy in England. The County Cricket Club founded in 1865 must have one of the finest locations in the country.

And could there be a finer sight than the Vale of Evesham in Spring when the fruit trees are in blossom. Evesham, the centre of this fruit growing area is an elegant town built around a now-ruined Benedictine abbey, whose one hundred and ten feet high Bell Tower stands in the centre of the town. The obelisk on Green Hill is in memory of Simon de Montfort, the father of the House of Commons who died in battle in 1265. On the edge of the Vale of Evesham under the Cotswold Hills stands arguably the prettiest of the many lovely villages hereabouts, Broadway, a riot of colourful cottage gardens and honey-coloured stone.

The southern area of the county is undeniably lovely, but despite its proximity to the industries of Birminham there is fine walking country in the hills of Clent and Lickey.

HEREFORDSHIRE &

Places to Visit

Berrington Hall, *near Leominster, Herefordshire* ~ an elegant, compact house designed by Henry Holland and built between 1778 and 1783 for the Rt. Hon. Thomas Harley. The Digby Collection of French Regency furniture is on display. The gardens contain many exotic and interesting plants.

Croft Castle, *Leominster, Herefordshire* ~ set in beautiful countryside with superb views towards the Brecon Beacons. The house retains its ancient walls and corner towers although it has been modified over the centuries when the fine ceilings and staircase were added.

Goodrich Castle, *Goodrich, Herefordshire* ~ situated five miles south of Ross-on-Wye, this 12th century red sandstone fort sits on the top of a rock high above the river.

Hereford Cathedral, *Hereford* ~ a small Norman cathedral with pink sandstone columns lining the nave. The central tower was built around 1325, the building underwent an extensive restoration after the 14th century west tower collapsed in 1786. The cathedral houses the Mappi Mundi, a map of the world drawn in 1290 by clergyman Richard of Haldingham and a chained library with over one thousand, four hundred books.

The Fleece Inn, near Evesham, Worcestershire ~ a medieval farmhouse in the centre of the village, containinga collection of family furniture. It became a licensed house in 1848 and remainly almost unaltered.

Hanbury Hall, *Droitwich, Worcestershire* ~ set in four hundred acres of parkland, it has been the Vernon family home for more than three centuries and was remodelled in 1701. Showrooms are open to the public, they include paintings by Sir James Thornhill and Dutch flower paintings and there is also a collection of fine porcelain.

Lower Brockhampton, *Bringsty, Worcestershire* ~ a late 14th century moated manor house with a detached half timbered 15th century gatehouse and there are also ruins of a 12th century chapel in the grounds.

Snowshill Manor, *near Broadway, Worcestershire* ~ a Cotswold manor house with the Charles Paget Wade's 'Collection of Craftmanship' with English, European and Oriental furniture, musical instruments, clocks, model ships and other collections in nearly twenty one rooms.

Worcester Cathedral, *Worcester* ~ the tower collapsed in 1175 then it suffered a terrible fire in 1203 before the prsent structure was started in the 13th century. The nave and central tower were completed in the 1370's. In 1874, Sir George Gilbert Scott designed the High Gothic choir with 14th century carved misericordes. Henry VIII's brother is buried in the chantry chapel.

◀ *Goodrich Castle, Hereford*

▶ *The Vale of Evesham*

WORCESTERSHIRE

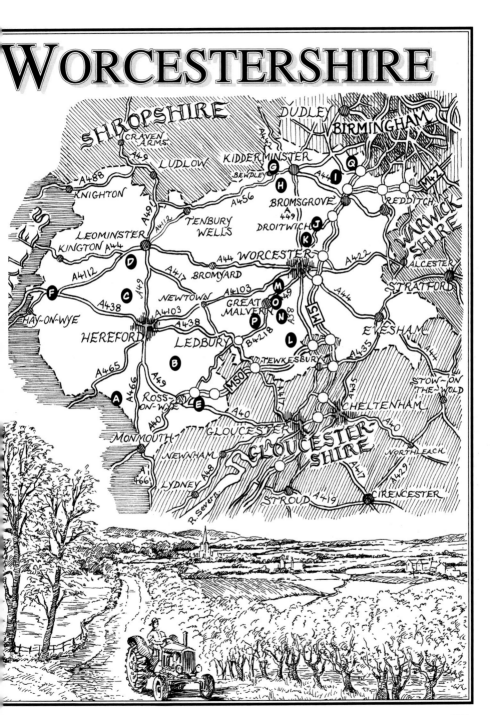

The Old Rectory, Garway, Herefordshire HR2 8RH **Nearest Road A466, B4521**

Our home has a very welcoming atmosphere, smell of log fires, a grandfather clock, arrangements of flowers and Aga cooking make you feel at home. The Blue room has a double four poster, the Pink room has twin beds. They both have TV, tea/coffee making facilities and hand basins. They share a bathroom, plus separate loos and shower room. The acre of peaceful garden has wonderful views to Black Mountains and Brecon Beacons. Hereford 15 miles, Ross 11 miles, Monmouth 8 miles. ETB Highly Commended.

Caroline Ailesbury
Tel: 01600 750363
Fax: 01600 750364

B&B from £18pp, Dinner from £15, Rooms 1 twin, 1 double,
No smoking, Children over 8 years, No pets,
Open March - October, Map Ref A

The Bowens Country House, Fownhope, Hereford HR1 4PS **Nearest Road B4224**

Peacefully situated opposite the church on the edge of the village on the B4224 in the Wye Valley AONB, midway between Hereford and Ross-on-Wye. Ideal for touring, walking and exploring Welsh Borders, Malverns, Cotswolds, Brecon Beacons and the wooded countryside of Herefordshire. Tastefully restored 17th century country house set in 2 acres of gardens. Comfortable, well appointed bedrooms, each with TV, telephone, central heating and tea/coffee facilities. Oak beamed lounge with inglenook fireplace. Superb home-cooked meals, including vegetarian dishes, using local/home produce. ETB 3 Crowns Commended.

Mrs Carol Hunt
Tel: 01432 860430
Fax: 01432 860430

B&B from £25pp, Dinner available, Table D'Hote £12,
Rooms 1 single, 6 twin/double, 3 family, all en-suite,
Children welcome, Pets by arrangement, Open all year, Map Ref B

Appletree Cottage, Mansell Lacy, Hereford, Herefordshire HR4 7HH **Nearest Road A480**

Appletree Cottage was originally one cottage and then a cider house and eventually 2 converted farm cottages. One cottage was built in 1450 and the more modern one around the late 16th century. The house is fully centrally heated. There is an open plan sitting room with wood burning stove and dining room. English country breakfasts are served. We are surrounded by many places of historical interest.

Mrs Monica Barker
Tel: 01981 590688

B&B from £15pp, Rooms 1 single/double, 2 twin, 1 en-suite,
All rooms have tea/coffee making facilities,
No smoking, Open all year, Map Ref C

Highfield, Newtown, Ivington Road, Leominster, Herefordshire HR6 8QD **Nearest Road A44**

Highfield stands in a large garden with unspoilt views of open farmland and distant mountains and enjoys a pleasant rural situation just 1 1/2 miles from the old market town of Leominster. The house was built around the turn of the century and accommodation is elegant, comfortable and friendly being well proportioned and attractively decorated. Meals are carefully prepared from good fresh ingredients and delightfully served in the charming dining room. All gastronomic needs and desires are catered for and a modest wine list is available. Groups and house parties welcome. ETB 2 Crowns Commended.

Catherine and Marguerite
Fothergill
Tel: 01568 613216

B&B from £18.50pp, Dinner from £12 by arrangement,
Rooms 1 double, 2 twin en-suite/private facilities,
Open all year, Map Ref D

---

right, Rudhall Farm, Ross on Wye - see details on page 224

see PHOTO on page 223

Rudhall Farm, Ross-on-Wye, Herefordshire HR9 7TL **Nearest Road B4221**

Set in rolling countryside with millstream and lake, yet central for exploring the picturesque Wye Valley and beyond. Elegant early-georgian farmhouse offering accommodation of character and charm with that touch of luxury, bedrooms having co-ordinated fabrics and every 20th century facility. Friendly hospitality where guests' comfort is of prime importance. AGA cooked breakfasts (diets catered for). Welcoming teatray on arrival servedeither in the sitting room or terraced garden. Excellent eating houses nearby. Non smokers preferred. Also self catering Mill cottage for 4 nearby.

Mrs Heather Gammond
Tel: 01989 780240
Mobile: 0585 871379

B&B from £19.50pp, Rooms 2 double, guests bathroom,
No smoking, No pets,
Open all year except Christmas and New Year, Map Ref E

Winforton Court, Winforton, Herefordshire HR3 6EA **Nearest Road A438**

A warm welcome and country hospitality awaits you at 16th century Winforton Court in the beautiful Wye Valley. Furnished with antiques, and collections of old china and samplers, yet offering 20th century comforts. Spacious drawing room, log fires, library and old world gardens. Delightful bedrooms - one with 4-poster bed. Hearty breakfasts (vegetarian available) served in magnificent former court room. Explore nearby Hay-on-Wye, Black Mountains, Golden Valley and Welsh Marches. Horse riding, golf and flying available. We also have a luxury self-catering cottage which sleeps 4.

Mrs Jackie Kingdon
Tel: 01544 328498

B&B from £22pp, Rooms 3 double, all with private bathrooms,
tea/coffee making facilities & hair dryers, Restricted smoking,
Pets by arrangement, Open all year except Christmas, Map Ref F

Lightmarsh Farm, Crundalls Lane, Bewdley, Worcestershire DY12 1NE **Nearest Road B4190**

Lightmarsh Farm is a small pasture farm which lies a little over 1 mile north of the picturesque and historic settlement of Bewdley. The 18th century farmhouse enjoys an elevated position with fine views southwards towards Worcester. Inside there is a cosy lounge with inglenook fireplace where a log fire burns on chilly evenings and the bedrooms which enjoy delightful views, have tea/coffee making facilities. The pleasant garden offers an opportunity to relax and watch the wildlife. ETB Highly Commended 2 Crowns.

Mrs P A Grainger
Tel: 01299 404027

B&B from £20pp, Rooms 1 double, 1 twin, both with private facilities,
Minimum age 10, Restricted smoking,
Open all year except Christmas, Map Ref G

Tarn, Long Bank, Bewdley, Worcestershire DY12 2QT **Nearest Road A456**

Attractive country house with library. Set in 17 acres of gardens and fields with spectacular views, in a tranquil area by an ancient coppice. All bedrooms have basins and there are 2 bathrooms and a shower room. Excellent breakfasts with home baked rolls, served in the elegant dining room. Conveniently situated for Worcestershire Way Walk (guests can be collected), Wyre Forest, River Severn (fishing), Midland Safari Park, Severn Valley Steam Railway, gardens, stately homes, golf. $2^1/2$ miles west of Georgian Bewdley on A456. Ample parking.

Mrs Topsy Beves
Tel: 01299 402243

B&B from £18pp, Rooms 2 single, 2 twin,
No smoking, Children welcome, No pets,
Open February - end November, Map Ref H

Hill Farm, Rocky Lane, Bournheath, Bromsgrove, Worcestershire B61 9HU Nearest Road B4091

Hill Farm has overlooked the peaceful countryside of Bournheath for 250 years. This Georgian listed building, with its medieval cruck barn, makes the ideal base for touring the heart of England. Four generations of the Rutter family have lived and worked on the farm and, during the summer months, guests can enjoy the delights of 'pick your own' fruits. There is a spacious lounge/dining room with colour TV overlooking south facing gardens. Birmingham Convention Centre, National Exhibition Centre and Birmingham Airport are 20 minutes drive away along the M42.

Mr Steve Rutter
Tel: 01527 872403

B&B from £18.50pp,
Rooms 2 twin, 3 single, Minimum age 3,
Open all year, Map Ref I

Caulin Court, Ladywood, near Droitwich, Worcestershire WR9 0AL Nearest Road A449, A38

Caulin Court is a beautiful country residence set in 20 acres. It has a tennis court and swimming pool which residents are welcome to use. There is a stable yard behind the house and all pets are welcome to use the spacious stables. All rooms are centrally heated with private bathroom, colour TV, and tea/coffee making facilities. Caulin Court is 10 minutes drive from both Droitwich and Worcester. It has easy access to junction 6 of the M5 which leads to M42/M40/M6 Birmingham, B'ham Airport, NEC, Stratford and Cotswolds. A warm welcome assured.

Mrs S Harfield
Tel: 01905 756382

B&B from £22.50, Rooms 1 single, 1 twin, 1 double, all en-suite,
Restricted smoking, Pets allowed in stables only,
Open all year, Map Ref K

Old Parsonage Farm, Hanley Castle, Worcester WR8 0BU Nearest Road M5, M50

Old Parsonage Farm is a fine mellow brick 18th century country residence. The location is superb enjoying beautiful views of the Malvern Hills and surrounding countryside. The house is beautifully decorated with attention to detail thanks to Ann Addison's natural flair for interior design. Besides this she is an accomplished cook producing imaginative dishes of a high standard. To complement this, husband Tony, is a wine expert. There are over 100 wines in stock. All in all a very impressive house.

Mrs Ann Addison
Tel: 01684 310124

B&B from £21, Dinner £15.50, Rooms 2 double/twin, 1 family,
Restricted smoking, Minimum age 12,
Open January to December, Map Ref L

see PHOTO on page 226

Please mention
THE GREAT BRITISH
BED & BREAKFAST
when booking your accommodation

Cowleigh Park Farm, Cowleigh Road, Malvern, Worcestershire WR13 5HJ   **Nearest Road A449, A4103**

Delightful 17th century timber framed farmhouse, Grade II listed. This beautifully restored home is peacefully situated at the foot of the Malvern Hills, creating a tranquil setting for a relaxing and friendly stay. Period furnishing throughout. 3 comfortable rooms, all with en-suite facilities, tea/coffee making facilities and colour TV. Guests are welcome to enjoy the 2.5 acres of landscaped gardens before exploring some of Britain's finest scenery and walks. Plenty of secure parking within the grounds. ETB 2 Crown Highly Commended. Also self catering cottages.

Mrs Sue Stringer
Tel/Fax: 01684 566750

B&B from £22pp, Dinner £15 week nights only, Rooms 2 twin, 1 double, all en-suite, No smoking, Children over 7, Pets welcome, Open all year except Christmas and New Year, Map Ref M

The Red Gate, 32 Avenue Road, Malvern, Worcestershire WR14 3BJ   **Nearest Road A449**

Situated in a tree-lined avenue within walking distance of the town centre and hills. This late Victorian house has retained much of its traditional charm, which is matched by the courtesy and hospitality you would expect from a friendly family-run hotel. Six bedrooms, each quite different, some high and spacious, some cottagey with stripped pine furniture. All are non-smoking, have en-suite bathrooms, TV, tea/coffee, and the small comforts one would like to find when away from home. The Red Gate is a very special place.

Tel/Fax: 01684 565013

B&B from £25pp, Rooms 1 single, 2 twin, 3 double, all en-suite, Restricted smoking, Children from 8, No pets, Open all year except Christmas and New Year, Map Ref N

Elm Bank Guest House, 52 Worcester Road, Great Malvern, Worcs WR14 4AB   **Nearest Road A449**

We aim to provide a friendly atmosphere in our home where guests can come and relax in comfort. Bedrooms are en-suite, have TV, tea/coffee making facilities, and most enjoy views over the Severn Valley. Whether you want a strenuous activity holiday or just a place to come and unwind and put your feet up ... Elm Bank could be just the place for you. Come and be spoilt. Full English breakfast or individual tastes catered for wherever possible. The sunny comfortable lounge is always available with a collection of books and local information. ETB 2 Crowns Commended, AA 3Q's.

Richard & Helen Mobbs
Tel: 01684 566051

B&B from £18pp, Rooms 2 twin, 3 double, 2 family, all en-suite, Restricted smoking, Children welcome, Pets by arrangement, Open all year, Map Ref O

Wyche Keep, 22 Wyche Road, Malvern, Worcestershire WR14 4EG   **Nearest Road B4218**

Wyche Keep is a unique arts and crafts castle style house, perched high on the Malvern Hills, built by the family of Sir Stanley Baldwin, Prime Minister to enjoy the spectacular 60 mile views, having a long history of elegant entertaining. Three large luxury double suites, including a 4 poster. Traditional English cooking is a speciality and guests can savour memorable four course candlelit dinners, served in a 'house party' atmosphere in front of a log fire. Fully licensed. Magical setting with private parking. AA/RAC/ETB Highly Acclaimed.

Mr & Mrs Williams
Tel: 01684 567018
Fax: 01684 892304

B&B from £25-£30pp, Dinner from £18pp, Rooms, 2 twin, 1 double, all en-suite, No smoking, Children over 13 years, No pets, Open all year, Map Ref P

see PHOTO on page 228

---

left, Old Parsonage Farm- see details on page 225

St Elisabeth's Cottage, Woodman Lane, Clent, Stourbridge DY9 9PX   **Nearest Road A491**

Beautiful country cottage in tranquil setting with 6 acres of landscaped garden plus outdoor heated swimming pool. Lovely country walks. Accommodation includes TV in all rooms plus coffee and tea making facilities. Residents' lounge available. Plenty of pubs and restaurants nearby. Easy access to M5, M6, M42 and M40. 25 minutes from NEC and Birmingham Airport. Destinations within easy reach: Symphony Hall and Convention Centre in Birmingham, Black Country Museum, Dudley, Stourbridge Crystal factories, Severn Valley Railway.

Mrs Sheila Blankstone
Tel: 01562 883883

B&B from £23, Rooms 1 twin, 2 double, all en-suite,
No smoking, Pets welcome,
Open all year, Map Ref Q

"He's slipping - you catch him, Billy!"

left, Wyche Keep, Malvern - see details on page 227

KENT

'Kent, sir - everybody knows Kent - apples, cherries, hops and women,' so declared Mr. Jingle in Dickens' Pickwick Papers and Dickens knew Kent well. G.K. Chesterton even described Dickens' life as 'moving like a Canterbury pilgrimage along the great roads of Kent'. And what a joy this lovely county is, with its rolling downs - the North Downs passing through the full length of Kent and ending in the magnificent white cliffs of Dover. Between the North and the South Downs lies the Weald, once a vast forest. The High Weald is a highly fertile area, the Low Weald much heavier and colder. Although the estates here are small, the great houses are impressive. Between The Weald and the sea lie the flat, windswept Romney Marshes. Left by the receding sea, this drained and fertile farmland is grazed by Romney sheep. At the foot of the escarpment marking the ancient Saxon shore line is the Royal Military Canal built as a defence during the Napoleonic Wars. The canal runs through the charming town of Hythe, one of the Cinque Ports. The Romney, Hythe and Dymchurch narrow gauge railway runs between Hythe and Dungeness, by the massive nuclear power station at the tip of Denge Marsh. There is good

bathing at Dymchurch, an old smuggling port. At Saltwood, just north of Hythe, are the ruins of the Norman castle in which the four knights stayed before the murder of Thomas Becket.

Kent has more than its fair share of magnificent houses. Penshurst Place is an outstanding example of fourteenth century domestic architecture owned by the Sidney family, descendants of Sir Philip Sidney, the Elizabethan poet. Close-by Hever Castle, the birthplace of Anne Boleyn, Henry VIII's second wife, has wonderful gardens including a yew maze and yew topiary. Imposing as this moated manor house beside the River Eden is, it owes much of its charm to twentieth century adaptations by William Waldorf Astor. Knowle can claim to be England's largest house, having no less than three hundred and sixty five rooms. Formerly an archbishop's palace, like so many great houses of the period it became the property of Henry VIII. Set like a jewel amongst these stately homes is Royal Tunbridge Wells, an elegant old spa town greatly favoured by Beau Nash who considered it a rival to Regency Bath. This is an ideal base for visiting the glories of The Weald. It was Lord North who discovered the medicinal springs here which brought the town its royal patronage. The Pantiles, bordered by a collonade of eighteenth and nineteenth century houses and shops with Italianate columns are a delight. Nearby is Ashdown Forest, the landscape of A.A. Milne's Winnie the Pooh stories. Here too is Chartwell, the country home of Sir Winston Churchill.

Maidstone, standing on the Rivers Medway and Len in the centre of the 'Garden of England' and at the foot of the North Downs is a perfect centre for exploring the lovely valley of the Medway which for centuries played a major role in the history of Kent. Of course, road and rail transport has reduced the commercial importance of the river, but today it is a glorious path through orchards and hop gardens and it offers excellent fishing and boating.

The countryside is charming, but no visitor should leave the area without seeing Leeds Castle to the east of Maidstone, and also Sissinghurst Gardens, the wonderful 1930s creation of Harold Nicholson and Vita Sackville-West.

Canterbury on the River Stour is of course the centre of the Anglican church and seat of the Archbishop of Canterbury. The city was an important settlement in Roman times and became the capital of Ethelbert, king of Kent. It was his conversion to Christianity by St. Augustine here that established the importance of Canterbury. With the murder of Archbishop Thomas Becket in 1174, the town became a place of pilgrimage prompting the building of a number of charitable hospitals for their accommodation. The Poor Priest's Hospital is now a fine city heritage museum. Canterbury suffered devastating bombing in a Baedeker raid in 1942 in which most of the medieval city centre was destroyed... fortunately the cathedral was spared. What remains from the bombing is well worth seeing. The cathedral, built in Caen limestone with Bell Harry, its central tower, is a gem. The cathedral houses a magnificent collection of twelfth and thirteenth century stained glass and the tomb of the Black Prince. A stone marking the spot upon which Becket was murdered is in the fifteenth century Great Cloister.

East from Canterbury is fascinating scenery, thatched cottages and lovely timbered houses leading to Sandwich, another of the Cinque Ports despite the sea now being a couple of miles away. There are many reminders in the medieval centre of this charming town of the Flemish weavers who in the sixteenth century flocked into Kent.

And pleasurable as the beautiful interior of Kent is, it also offers the holidaymaker a fine coast line. Margate is Kent's Blackpool with superb sands, while Whitstable, Ramsgate, Herne Bay and Broadstairs provide between them all the delights of the seaside. The Channel towns, Dover, Folkestone, Deal and Hythe have a charm of their own, superb walks, picturesque harbours and an endless and fascinating passing show of ships.

Places to Visit

Canterbury Cathedral, *Canterbury* ~ the spiritual home of the Church of England, it contains medieval stained glass and some 12th century wall paintings.

Chartwell, *near Hever* ~ the home of Winston Churchill from 1922 to 1964. It remains furnished as it was when he lived there. To relax he would rebuild parts of the house, and some of his paintings are on display.

Dover Castle, *Dover* ~ dates back to 1066, much of the castle seen today is 12th century. A second elaborate set of fortifications built as a defence against Napoleon, consists of a network of tunnels. The castle was used during World War II by Vice Admiral Bertram Ramsey to organise the evacuation of three hundred and thirty thousand troops from Dunkirk.

Hever Castle, *Edenbridge* ~ a small, moated castle, it was the home of Anne Boleyn, the wife of Henry VII, executed for adultery. In 1903 it was bought by William Waldorf Astor, who restored the castle and built a Neo-Tudor village alongside to accommodate guests and servants. The gatehouse and moat were built in 1270 and still remain.

Ightham Moat, *near Sevenoaks* ~ a moated manor house in a wooded valley with lovely gardens and walks. The house underwent a massive restoration by the National Trust and includes an exhibition explaining the work involved.

Knole, *near Sevenoaks* ~ built in the late 15th century, this immense Tudor mansion was built on the foundations of an older house. The house is set in a thousand acre park and gardens and contains valuable collections of paintings and of 17th century furniture including a state bed made for James II.

Leeds Castle, *Maidstone* ~ surrounded by a lake, it is often considered to be one of the most beautiful castles in England. It was begun in the 12th century and has been continuously inhabited. Henry VIII visited the castle often and it contains a life size bust of him from the 16th century. The gardens were designed by Capability Brown and have a maze.

Sissinghurst Castle Garden, *near Cranbrook* ~ created by Vita Sackville-West and her husband SIr Harold Nicholson, their gardens between the surviving parts of an Elizabethan mansion. The gardens include an orchard, spring garden, white garden and herb garden.

South Foreland Lighthouse, *St Margaret's at Cliffe* ~ built in 1843 it has views to France. It was used by Marconi for the first radio communications as an aid to navigation in 1898. You can climb the spiral stairs to the balcony around the light.

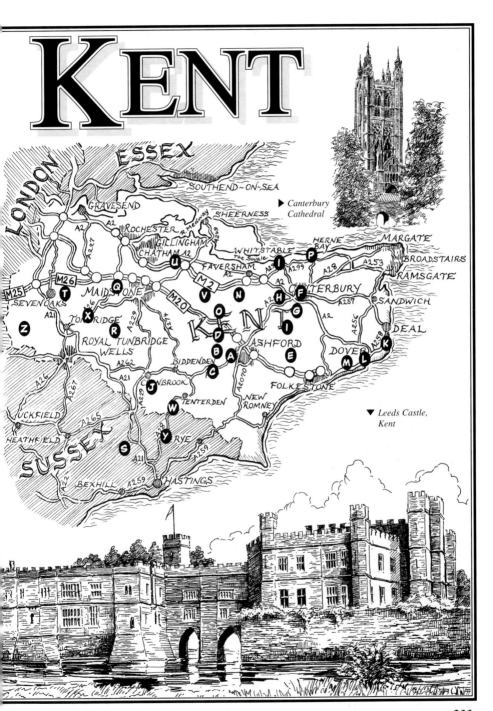

KENT

ESSEX

SOUTHEND-ON-SEA

LONDON

GRAVESEND

SHEERNESS

▶ Canterbury
Cathedral

ROCHESTER
A2
A2
A227
River Medway
A229

GILLINGHAM
CHATHAM A2

WHITSTABLE
The Swale

HERNE
BAY

MARGATE

BROADSTAIRS

RAMSGATE

FAVERSHAM
A2

M2

M26

M25

M20

SEVENOAKS

MAIDSTONE

A21

TONBRIDGE

A259

ROYAL TUNBRIDGE
WELLS

A262

A21

A20

CANTERBURY

SANDWICH

A257

DEAL

A256

A258

DOVER

FOLKESTONE

BIDDENDEN

CRANBROOK

TENTERDEN

NEW
ROMNEY

ASHFORD

UCKFIELD

A265

A267

HEATHFIELD

A26

A21

RYE

A259

SUSSEX

A22

BEXHILL

A259

HASTINGS

KENT

▼ Leeds Castle,
Kent

233

The Coach House, Oakmead Farm, Bethersden, near Ashford, Kent TN26 3DU

The Coach House with old world charm is set amidst "Darling Buds of May" country one mile from Bethersden Village, being well served with country pubs for evening meals and within reach of many tourists attractions. Guests are warmly welcomed with an informal atmosphere. Your host's speciality is breakfast of your choice cooked from fresh local produce. Secluded courtyard parking and garden. Dutch spoken. TV and tea/coffee making facilities. Easy reach Eurotunnel, Ferry ports, Leeds Castle and Canterbury.

Bernard & Else Broad
Tel: 01233 820583

B&B from £17.50pp, Rooms 1 twin, 1 double with private bathroom, 1 family, all en-suite, Restricted smoking, Children welcome, No pets, Open March - October, Map Ref A

Goldwell Manor, Great Chart, Ashford, Kent TN23 3BY   Nearest Road M20 (Junction 9)

A peaceful secluded historic 11th century manor mentioned in the Doomsday Book (1066) as 'Godesel'. Surrounded by farmland with 10 mile views over the Weald. Antiques, oak beams galore and 13 foot fireplaces provide a comfortable relaxed atmosphere. Easy for sea, gardens, castles, Canterbury, London, Paris and Brussels. Golf, walks, riding, shooting, flying and ballooning also nearby.

Mr & Mrs P Wynn Green
Tel/Fax: 01233 631495

B &B from £23-£28pp, Dinner arranged, Rooms 1 single, 1 double, 1 twin/family, Short & long stay reductions. Open all year except Christmas & New Year, Map Ref B

Lion House, Church Hill, High Halden, Ashford, Kent TN26 3LS   Nearest Road A28

Situated on the village green with pub, village shop, historic church; Lion House is a listed Queen Anne farmhouse set in a large mature garden. Caroline and Gerald offer a friendly welcome, comfortable centrally heated accommodation with en-suite bath and shower, TV, tea/coffee making facilities and trouser press, etc. Private dining room and patio garden. Within easy reach of Sissinghurst and Leeds castles, Canterbury, channel tunnel and ports. Early departures and late arrivals catered for. Supper or dinner by arrangement.

Gerald & Caroline Mullins
Tel: 01233 850446
Fax: 01233 850446

B&B from £20pp, Dinner incl wine from £5/£15 by arrangement, Rooms 1 single, 1 twin, 1 family, all en-suite, Restricted smoking, Children welcome, Open all year except Christmas, Map Ref C

Elvey Farm Country Hotel, Pluckley, Ashford, Kent TN27 0SU   Nearest Road M20/A20

Stay in the 15th century Yeoman Barn, Oast House, or Elvey Stables. All traditional oak beamed Kentish farm buildings converted to give comfortable, charming accommodation in the heart of "The Garden of England". Very secluded and peaceful with beautiful views, yet near the channel ports, tunnel, Canterbury, and the castles, country houses, and gardens of Kent and Sussex. Large car park and garden, licensed dining room, lounge. All rooms have colour TV and hospitality facilities.

Mr & Mrs Harris
Tel: 01233 840442
Fax: 01233 840726

B&B from £27.75pp, Dinner available, Rooms 2 twin, 2 double, 5 family, all en-suite, Children welcome, Pets restricted, Open all year, Map Ref D

Number One Dryden Close, Canterbury - see page 237 for details

Bulltown Farmhouse, Bulltown Lane, West Brabourne, Ashford, Kent TN25 5NB   Nearest Road M20

Bulltown Farmhouse is an attractively restored 15th century timber framed Kentish farmhouse on the south western side of the North's Downs and Pilgrims Way offering unspoilt countryside and superb walks. The cathedral city of Canterbury is 12 miles, and the Channel Ports, Folkestone and Dover are 10 and 18 miles. The M20 Junc 10 is 5 miles giving easy access to other motorways and airports. All the rooms have tea/coffee facilities. There is an excellent award winning country inn close by. Cycles available.

Lilly Wiiton
Tel: 01233 813505 or
01227 709818

B&B from £20pp, Rooms 1 twin, 1 double, 1 family, all en-suite,
No smoking, Children welcome, No pets,
Open all year, Map Ref E

Number One Dryden Close, Pilgrims Way, Canterbury, Kent CT1 1XW   Nearest Road A2

Delightfully furnished Georgian style family home offers non-smoking facilities throughout. TV, tea/coffee making, central heating, en suite. Grade 3 disability accommodation. Savour the taste of a full English Breakfast. Continental or any special diet catered for by prior arrangement. Situated ³/4 mile from Canterbury's Historic Centre on the 16 cycle route. Free street parking. Cycle lock up. Full use of lounge-diner and garden. Whether your interests are golf cycling, swimming, riding, fishing. walking, sightseeing, theatre or business book early to avoid disappointment. ETB Commended.

Elaine & Tony Oliver
Tel/Fax: 01227 764799

B&B from £18pp, Rooms 1 single, 2 double, all H&C, 1 shower,
No smoking, Children from 14, No pets,
Open from March - December, Map Ref F

see PHOTO's on page 235

Zan Stel Lodge, 140 Old Dover Road, Canterbury, Kent CT1 3NX   Nearest Road B2068, A2

Gracious Edwardian house offering high standards of cleanliness and service. The spacious bedrooms include colour TV with tea/coffee making facilities. Hair dryer and ironing facilities also available. The elegant dining room overlooks a pretty cottage garden and fishponds. Ten minute walk to the city centre, thirty minute drive to the Channel Tunnel and ferry ports. Private car park. Recommended by the Which? Good Bed & Breakfast Guide, ETB 2 Crown Highly Commended.

Zandra & Ron Stedman
Tel: 01227 453654

B&B from £20pp, Rooms 1 twin, 2 double, 1 family, 2 rooms en-suite,
No smoking, Children welcome,
Open all year, Map Ref F

see PHOTO opposite

Maynard Cottage, 106 Wincheap, Canterbury, Kent CT1 3RS   Nearest Road A28

Come and join us in our totally relaxed beautifully restored Grade II listed cottage with inglenook fireplace. Built in 1695, oozes with history and charm. Bedrooms are tastefully decorated with period style furniture, home comforts include colour TV, radio clock alarm, hair dryer and complimentary tea/coffee and goodie tray. Full English breakfast is provided and all diets catered for. Why not try our evening meals. Excellent value, all homemade and cooked with love and pride. Packed lunches also available. Ideally situated 6 minutes walk from city centre. 20 minutes Dover.

Fiona Ely
Tel: 01227 454991
Mobile: 0468 074177

B&B from £19pp, Dinner from £11.50,
Rooms 1 twin, 1 double, 1 family, Restricted smoking,
Open all year, Map Ref F

---

left, Zan Stel Lodge, Canterbury- see details above

see PHOTO opposite

Thanington Hotel, 140 Wincheap, Canterbury, Kent CT1 3RY   Nearest Road A28

Spacious Georgian bed and breakfast hotel, ideally situated 10 minutes stroll from the city centre. 15 en-suite bedrooms, beautifully decorated and furnished, all in immaculate condition with modern day extras. King size 4 poster beds, antique bedsteads and 2 large family rooms. Walled garden with patio, indoor swimming pool, intimate bar, guest lounge and snooker/games room. Delicious breakfast served in the elegant dining room. Secure private car park. An oasis in a busy tourist city, convenient for channel ports, tunnel and historic houses of Kent. Gatwick 60 minutes.

Jill & David Jenkins
Tel: 01227 453227
Fax: 01227 453225

B&B from £32pp,
Rooms 10 double, 2 family, 3 twin,
Open all year, Map Ref F

Oriel Lodge, 3 Queens Avenue, Canterbury, Kent CT2 8AY   Nearest Road A2

In a tree-lined residential avenue, five minutes' walk from the city centre and restaurants, Oriel Lodge is an attractive Edwardian detached house, retaining a warm and restful period character. The six well-furnished bedrooms have clean, up-to-date facilities. Afternoon tea is served in the garden or lounge, with a log fire in winter. There is private parking for six cars. ETB 2 Crowns Highly Commended, AA QQQ, RAC Acclaimed.

Keith & Anthea Rishworth
Tel/Fax: 01227 462845

B&B from £19pp, Rooms 1 single, 1 twin, 3 double, 1 family,
some en-suite, Restricted smoking, Children from 6, No pets,
Open all year, Map Ref F

---

see PHOTO on page240

Iffin Farmhouse, Iffin Lane, Canterbury, Kent CT4 7BE   Nearest Road A2, M2

A warm welcome awaits you in this old 18th century farmhouse, renovated to a high standard in the mid 50's. Offering luxury en-suite bedrooms with TV and tea/coffee trays and set in 10 acres of gardens, orchards and paddocks in a quiet rural setting only 6 minutes drive to the centre of historic Canterbury. In an ideal position for touring Kent and East Sussex, and the following are only a short drive away: Chilham, Dover, Leeds, and Hever castles; Chartwell, Penshurst Place, Sissinghurst Gardens, and many more. Also within easy reach of channel ports and tunnel.

Rosemary & Colin Stevens
Tel: 01227 462776
Fax: 01227 462776

B&B from £20pp, Dinner from £15 (by arrangement), Rooms 1 twin,
2 double, 2 family, all en-suite, No smoking, Minimum age 4, No pets,
Open all year except Christmas & New Year, Map Ref G

The Willows, Howfield Lane, Chartham Hatch, Canterbury, Kent CT4 7HG   Nearest Road A28, A2/M2

Dr & Mrs Gough welcome you to their home. We are situated in a quiet country lane just two miles from Canterbury Cathedral. Dover and the channel ports are 30 minutes by car, likewise Ashford International Station for easy access to the continent. Kent being correctly named the garden of England offers other features such as many castles with spectacular gardens. The Willows offers a full English breakfast taken in the garden room overlooking a garden for the enthusiast, we are also on the Northdown Way and Stour Valley Walk. Ample Parking. No smoking.

Dr & Mrs Gough
Tel/Fax: 01227 738442

B&B from £20-£22.50pp, Dinner from £15pp, Rooms 1 single, 1 twin,
1 double, most en-suite, No smoking, Children over 5 years, No pets,
Open all year, Map Ref H

Iffin Farmhouse, Canterbury
- see page 238 for details

Waltham Court Hotel, Kake Street, Petham, Canterbury, Kent CT4 5SB   **Nearest Road B2069**

Set in the valley of the Kent Weald in two acres on peaceful gardens we are only 12 minutes from Canterbury and 20 minutes from the tunnel. All of our rooms have colour TV and tea/coffee making facilities. Our restaurant Chives is renowned for quality food, you can relax in our bar/lounge before and after your meal. Waltham Court was built as a poorhouse in 1796 and retains much of its character. Ideally located for a relaxing or touring break.

Mr Weaver
Tel: 01227 700413
Fax: 01227 700127

B&B from £27.50pp, Dinner from £15.00, Rooms 2 twin, 1 double, 1 family, all en-suite, Restricted smoking, Children welcome, No pets, Open all year except Christmas, Map Ref I

Upper Ansdore, Duckpit Lane, Petham, Canterbury, Kent CT4 5QB   **Nearest Road B2068/A2**

Medieval farmhouse in a very quiet secluded valley, with beautiful views. Once the home of the Lord Mayor of London, it overlooks a Kent nature reserve. Take a short break or a longer stay, and sample over 600 years of history. Breakfast served in the oak beamed dining room with Tudor inglenook fireplace and furnished with antiques. Canterbury 15 minutes, Dover 30 minutes. AA QQQ Listed. SAE please for a colour brochure.

Roger & Susan Linch
Tel: 01227 700672

B&B from £19pp, Rooms 1 twin, 3 double, 1 family, all en-suite, No smoking, Open all year except Christmas, Map Ref I

Hancocks Farmhouse, Tilsden Lane, Cranbook, Kent TN17 3PH   **Nearest Road A229**

Hancock's Farmhouse is a well preserved 16th century timber framed listed building situated just outside the attractive Wealden town of Cranbook with its famous windmill and fine parish church. Surrounded by farmland, the house is comfortably furnished with fine fabrics and lovely antiques. Guests have the use of the spacious drawing room which has a large inglenook fireplace with log fires for cooler evenings. Superb home cooking. There is a lovely garden for guests to enjoy. Cranbook is an ideal centre for visiting picturesque villages and places of interest. Close to Sissinghurst Gardens.

see PHOTO on page 243

Bridget & Robin Oaten
Tel: 01580 714645

B&B from £27pp, Dinner from £20, Rooms 2 double, 1 twin, Minimum age 12, No smoking, Open all year, Map Ref J

Wallett's Court, West Cliffe, St Margaret's, Dover, Kent CT15 6EW   **Nearest Road A258, A2**

Wallett's Court is an old manor house set in lovely open countryside within easy reach of spectacular cliff scenery, the channel ports, championship golf courses and the cathedral city of Canterbury. The house has great character with beamed ceilings, red brick walls, inglenook fireplaces, and leaded lights. The en-suite bedrooms have tea/coffee making facilities, TV and telephone. All are furnished with flair and one room has a 4 poster bed. There is a guests' lounge. The renowned restaurant is open to non residents all week and offers a special 5 course menu on Saturdays.

Chris & Lea Oakley
Tel: 01304 852424
Fax: 01304 853430

B&B from £30pp, Dinner from £23, Rooms 2 twin, 8 double, all en-suite, Restricted smoking, AA 3 rosettes Open all year, Map Ref K

Castle House, 10 Castle Hill Road, Dover, Kent CT16 1QW — Nearest Road A2/M2 and A20/M20

Close to the town centre at the foot of Dover Castle, this small guest house dates from 1830 and provides comfortable accommodation, good food and a warm welcome from Rodney and Elizabeth. All rooms have private facilities and colour television. There is a small lounge for guests and a payphone. Ideally situated for the ferries, cruise liner terminal and hoverport and 10 minutes from the channel tunnel.

Rodney & Elizabeth Dimech
Tel: 01304 201656
Fax: 01304 210197

B&B from £18pp, Rooms 4 double, 1 twin, 1 single,
No smoking,
Open all year, Map Ref L

Rose Hill Farm, Mill Lane, West Hougham, Dover, Kent CT15 7BD — Nearest Road M20/A20

A sympathetically restored 17th century farmhouse in peaceful, unspoilt countryside, 10 minutes' drive from Dover and Channel Tunnel. 1.5 acres of beautiful gardens, croquet lawn, swimming pool - a joy for garden-lovers and an excellent centre for touring, walking, sailing, golf and visiting the numerous castles, historic houses and gardens in Kent. Comfortable en-suite bedrooms with colour TV, tea/coffee making facilities. Two fully equipped luxury cottages with wood-burning stoves for longer, self-catering stays.

Diana & Roger Brooks
Tel: 01304 240609

B&B from £21pp, Rooms, 1 twin, 1 double,
Restricted smoking, Children welcome, No pets,
Open all year except Christmas and Boxing Day, Map Ref M

The Granary, Plumford Lane, Ospringe, Faversham, Kent ME13 0DS — Nearest Road A2, M2

Set deep in apple orchard country, The Granary - recently part of a working farm - has been tastefully and beautifully converted to provide an interesting and spacious home. All rooms are delightfully furnished to a very high standard, whilst retaining a certain rustic charm. The guests' own lounge, with balcony, overlooks the surrounding countryside. Well situated for local pubs specialising in excellent food. Ideal location for touring historic Kent. Alan and Annette assure you of a warm welcome.
EMail: THEGRANARY@COMPUSERVE.COM

Alan & Annette Brightman
Tel/Fax: 01795 538416
Mobile: 0410 199177

B&B from £21pp, Rooms 1 twin, 1 double, 1 family, all en-suite,
No smoking, Children welcome, No pets
Open all year except Christmas & New Year, Map Ref N

Frith Farm House, Otterden, Faversham, Kent ME13 0DD — Nearest Road A20, A2

see PHOTO on page244

Frith Farm is situated on the North Downs in an area of outstanding natural beauty. The house, an elegant Georgian building, is reached by a sweeping drive and surrounded by well looked after lawns and gardens. The interior is decorated with flair and great individuality using fine fabrics and antiques. A delightful and relaxing place to stay. One bedroom has a 4 poster and all have en-suite shower, tea/coffee making facilities, and TV. Horse riding, golf, Pilgrims and North Downs Way are all nearby. A warm welcome is assured.

Markham & Susan Chesterfield
Tel: 01795 890701
Fax: 01795 890009

B&B from £24.50pp, Dinner £18.50, Rooms 1 twin, 2 double,
all en-suite, No smoking, Minimum age 10,
Open all year, Map Ref O

Foxden, 5 Landon Road, off Beltinge Road, Herne Bay, Kent CT6 6HP   Nearest Road M2/A299

This spacious house and garden offers 'a haven of peace and tranquillity', set in a quiet area of the attractive Victorian seaside town of Herne Bay. Elegantly furnished bedrooms with colour televisions, hospitality trays, a wide selection of books and fresh flowers. Enjoy a substantial breakfast with eggs from our hens - explore our delightful garden with lily and fish ponds and walk-through aviary. Perfectly situated for visiting Canterbury, touring Kent and en-route to Ports. Excellent restaurants/pubs within walking distance. Off street parking.

Michael Williams
Tel: 01227 363514/369820/794148

B&B from £17.50pp, Rooms 1 single, 2 double, most en-suite, No smoking, Children welcome, No pets, Open all year except New Year, Map Ref P

Woodgate, Birling Road, Leybourne, Kent ME19 5HT   Nearest Road M20/A20

17th century cottage surrounded by woods in large pretty garden with tropical birds and chickens. Easy access to London and Dover and close to Leeds castle, Knole, Sissinghurst, Ightam Mote and Chartwell amongst others. House has many interesting objects gathered during owner's many overseas and is tastefully furnished with antiques. Bedrooms are attractive and all have colour TV and coffee/tea making facilities. There is a large guest sitting room with open fire in cold weather. Breakfast is served in large lovely conservatory. EMail: ludlow@easynet.co.uk

Mr & Mrs Ludlow
Tel: 01732 843201

B&B from £20pp, Dinner from £15.00, Rooms 1 twin, 1 twin, 1 double, 1 family, all private/en-suite, No smoking, Children & pets welcome, Open December - February, Map Ref Q

Merzie Meadows, Hunton Road, Chainhurst, near Marden, Kent TN12 9SL

Merzie Meadows is a country home individually designed with water fowl and horse paddocks. Tranquil surroundings central to many historical interest and London. Traditional elegance with modern comforts the spacious rooms are decorated to a high standard and include a guest wing with small sitting room, study and terrace the rooms overlook landscaped gardens with swimming pool all designed for conservation. ETB Highly Commended, Recommended by Which? Good Bed & Breakfast.

Pamela & Rodney Mumford
Tel: 01622 820500

B&B from £20-£22pp, Rooms, 2 double, both en-suite, No smoking, Children over 5 years, No pets, Open mid January - mid December, Map Ref R

Swale Cottage, Poundsbridge Lane, Penshurst, Kent TN11 8AH   Nearest Road A26, B2176

Swale Cottage, listed Grade II*, is a large converted Kentish barn of architectural merit. In a unique and tranquil setting, it overlooks a mediaeval manor house, gardens and glorious countryside. Furnished with antiques and decorated throughout in English country style decor. There are three spacious and luxurious bedrooms including a romantic 4 poster. Colour TV. Memorable breakfasts. Nearby is 14th century Penshurst Place with its Tudor garden. Within 10 minutes drive of Hever, Chartwell, Chiddingstone NT and Tunbridge Wells. ETB Highly Commended. AA Premier Selected (5 Q's) and prestigious awards.

Mrs Cynthia Dakin
Tel: 01892 870738

B&B from £27-£32pp, Midweek winter breaks, Rooms 1 twin, 2 double en-suite, No smoking, Children over 10 years, Open all year, Map Ref S

---

*left, **Frith Farm House, Otterden** - see details on page 242*   **245**

Kent

Jordans, Sheet Hill, Plaxtol, Sevenoaks, Kent TN15 0PU   **Nearest Road A227**

An exquisite picture postcard 15th century Tudor house situated in the picturesque village of Plaxtol among orchards and parkland. Jordans, awarded a historic building of Kent plaque, has an enchanting English cottage garden with winding paths, rambler roses and espalier trees. Inside there are oak beams, inglenook fireplaces, leaded windows and beautifully furnished with antiques and paintings many by Mrs Lindsay, who is also a Blue Badge Guide and can help in planning your tour. Jordans is close to Ightham Mote, Hever Chartwell, Penshurst Knole and Leeds Castle.

Mrs Jo Lindsay N.N.D., A.T.D.
Tel: 01732 810379

B&B from £25pp, Rooms 2 double/single, 1 en-suite, 1 private facilities, No smoking, Open mid January - mid December, Map Ref T

Hartlip Place, Place Lane, Hartlip, Sittingbourne, Kent ME9 7TR   **Nearest Road M2, A2, M20**

A fine Georgian house in a peaceful setting on the edge of the village in 4 acres of grounds with a pond, wilderness and "secret" rose garden. Bedrooms all have en-suite or private bathroom, hot drinks tray and antique furniture. Your hosts entertain you in their beautiful drawing room and dining room where breakfast includes fresh eggs from their own hens. You may meet Peony the pot bellied pig! Very centrally placed; 5 minutes from M2 and under one hour from the Channel Tunnel, Gatwick and London (BR). Easy reach for Canterbury, Rochester & Leeds Castle.

Mrs Gillian Yerburgh
Tel: 01795 842583
Fax: 01795 842763

B&B from £35pp, Dinner £25 by arrangement, Rooms 1 twin, 2 double, 1 en-suite, 2 private facilities, No smoking, Minimum age 12, No pets, Open all year except Christmas and New Year, Map Ref U

The Cottage, Milstead, near Sittingbourne, Kent ME9 0SA   **Nearest Road M2/M20**

Set in two acres of garden on the north downs between Sittingbourne and Hollingbourne, The Cottage is a lovely period house mentioned in Jane Austen's novel 'Persuasion'. An ideal touring and walking centre for Rochester, Canterbury, Medway towns, Leeds Castle, Sissinghurst Gardens and the coastal towns of Kent. En Route to channel crossings. Bedrooms have private or en-suite facilities and also tea/coffee making facilities. Elegant Georgian sitting room available for guests use. Milstead is a peaceful village situated in Orchard country and local pubs serve excellent evening meals.

Hazel Shaw Cotterill
Tel: 01795 830367

B&B from £20pp, Rooms 2 twin, 1 double, all en-suite or private, Children over 12 years, No pets, Open all year except Christmas and New Year, Map Ref V

Brattle House, Watermill Bridges, Tenterden, Kent TN30 6UL   **Nearest Road A28**

This mellow tiled and weather boarded Georgian house, with 11 acres of meadow, woodland and garden, is surrounded by the rolling countryside. Once the home of Thomas Brattle who was on visiting terms with Horatia Ward, wife of the local vicar; and illegitimate daughter of Nelson and Lady Hamilton. The house now provides 3 en-suite bedrooms. Breakfast is served in the conservatory and dinner in the candlelit dining room. Caring and personal cosseting are the features of Brattle House. Many NT properties and gardens are on the 'doorstep' including Sissinghurst Castle.

Mo & Alan Rawlinson
Tel: 01580 763565

B&B from £28-£30pp, Dinner from £20 (guests bring own wine), Rooms 1 en-suite twin, 2 en-suite double, No smoking, Minimum age 12, No pets, Open all year except Christmas & New Year, Map Ref W

Kent

Leavers Oast, Stanford Lane, Hadlow, Tonbridge, Kent TN11 0JN **Nearest Road A26**

A warm welcome awaits you at Leavers Oast. An excellent base for touring the many historic buildings including Leeds and Hever Castles, Chartwell and Sissinghurst. Built circa 1880, Anne and Denis have modernised the accommodation and created a very attractive garden. They have many interests including antiques, art and travel. Two bedrooms are in roundels, the other in the barn. All are spacious and comfortably furnished with TV and coffee/tea making facilities. There are many good places to eat or by prior arrangement excellent evening meals are available.

Anne & Denis Turner
Tel/Fax: 01732 850924

B&B from £27pp, Dinner £17.50 (guests bring own wine), Rooms 1 twin, 2 double, 1 en-suite, No smoking, Children from 12, No pets, Open all year, Map Ref X

The Old Parsonage, Church Lane, Frant, Tunbridge Wells, Kent TN3 9DX **Nearest Road A267**

The Old Parsonage is a magnificent Georgian house in a quiet, pretty village providing superior accommodation: luxurious en-suite bedrooms including two 4-posters, antique-furnished reception rooms and a spacious sunny conservatory, where guests may relax in armchair comfort with afternoon tea, overlooking the ballustraded terrace and secluded walled garden. For evening meals the village pub restaurants are 2 mins walk away. Short drive to many historic houses and gardens. SEETB award winner 'Bed & Breakfast of the Year', AA Premier selected. ETB Deluxe.

Mrs Mary Dakin
Tel: 01892 750773
Fax: 01892 750773

B&B from £29pp, Rooms 1 twin, 2 double, all en-suite, Restricted smoking, Pets by arrangement, Open all year, Map Ref Y

Danehurst House, 41 Lower Green Road, Rusthall, Tunbridge Wells, Kent TN4 8TW **Nearest Road A264**

Danehurst is a charming gabled house standing in a lovely village setting in the heart of Kent. Our tastefully furnished bedrooms afford you excellent accommodation - breakfast is served in our delightful Victorian conservatory - you can also enjoy an intimate candlelit dinner in our elegant dining room from November - April. We would be delighted to welcome you to our home. We like to feel that once you are in our care you can relax and enjoy everything we and the area have to offer. Private parking is available.

Angela & Michael Godbold
Tel: 01892 527739
Fax: 01892 514804

B&B from £22.50pp, Dinner from £16.95, Rooms 2 twin, 3 double, all en-suite, No smoking, Children over 8 years, No pets, Open all year, Map Ref Z

Windyridge Guest House, Wraik Hill, Whitstable, Kent CT5 3BY **Nearest Road M2/A299**

Directions for Windyridge Guest House: on leaving M2 continue on A299 (signposted Whitstable and Ramsgate) to first roundabout. Complete roundabout thus coming back back on oneself for a further 100 yards and then turn left into Wraik Lane.

Elisabeth Dyke
Tel: 01227 263506
Fax: 01227 771191

B&B from £20pp, Rooms 3 single, 1 twin, 3 double, 1 family, all en-suite, Children & pets welcome, Open all year, Map Ref 1

*"I dreamed that, as I wandered by the way,
Bare Winter suddenly was changed to Spring."*
Percy Bysshe Shelley

LANCASHIRE

It was the soft water, moist climate and swiftly running streams together with an abundance of coal and iron-ore that laid in Lancashire the foundations of the Industrial Revolution, and unfortunately its reputation as a holiday venue has suffered ever since. This is a shame, as within a short distance of the great industrial cities of this area is scenery which can compare with some of the best in the country - the Trough of Bowland with its exhilarating views across the lovely Fylde and the Wyre valley, the Rivers Lune, Ribble and Hodder, their valleys scattered with lovely villages. There is no doubt that the great cities dominate this area, but because their populations have demanded local resorts, there is also a coastline blessed with some of the finest seaside resorts in Britain, their attractions honed through the years to international prominence. Blackpool, surely the Queen of seaside resorts offers over seven miles of sandy beaches, a massive amusement park and pleasure beach, and every conceivable form of entertainment plus the tower, a 518ft imitation of the Eiffel Tower, and the best known seaside landmark in Britain, as well as the spectacular Illuminations which considerably extend the resort's season.

Blackpool has its brash side, but behind its garish facade there is a resort of delightful parks, wooded gardens and also a Zoo. The town is ideally situated to explore the Fylde, Lytham St. Anne's with its bracing promenade and windmill, and of course the Royal Lytham St. Anne's championship golf course; Morecambe and Heysham, Blackpool's sister resort; and Lancaster at the head of the Lune estuary, the ancient county town with the imposing castle of John of Gaunt, father of Henry IV. The city with its fine Georgian houses was once a busy port handling a bigger tonnage than Liverpool. Lancaster possesses two impressive monuments - the imposing castle housing the Shire Hall of 1796 in which assizes are held; and the Ashton Memorial- sometimes known as the "Taj Mahal of the North', built by Lord Ashton in 1909 as a memorial to his wife.

Southport, a seaside resort renowned for its beautiful Lord Street, a shaded tree-lined boulevard of fine shops, is the annual venue of the international Southport Flower Show, as well as being the home of the famous Royal Birkdale golf course. Five miles east of the town is the Martin Mere Wildfowl Sanctuary.

Preston, at the head of the estuary of the River Ribble and of strategic importance since Roman times, became rich from the weaving of wool during the Middle Ages only to switch to cotton in 1786. It was Sir Richard Arkwright, a Preston man who in the middle of the eighteenth century invented the spinning frame that revolutionised the textile industry. Another Preston man to make his mark was a certain Joseph Livesay, who founded the Temperance Movement. The Preston Temperance Advocate' was England's first newspaper for abstainers. The town's prosperity during the Industrial Revolution is reflected in some fine architecture. The Harris Museum and Art Gallery, opened in 1893 is a magnificent Classical building containing an outstanding collection of paintings. Well sited to visit the Fylde, the Trough of Boland and the west coast seaside resorts, this pleasant town was in 1648 at the very centre of a battle which saw Cromwell's army rout twenty thousand Scottish supporters of Charles I.

Until the early eighteenth century Lake Martinmere covered a large area of land around Ormskirk. It was the Scarisbrick family who were largely responsible for draining this land, the produce from the resulting rich farming land established Ormskirk as an important market town. Scarisbrick Hall, rebuilt in the nineteenth century in the Neo Gothic style is three miles north-west of the town. Rufford Old Hall, a short distance away is a quite magnificent half-timbered medieval mansion not to be missed.

Nor indeed should one miss the wonderful views over the Lancashire Plain from Parbold Beacon. It is hard to believe today that the delightful country roads around the pretty village of Wrightington Bar were once the haunt of footpads and highwaymen.

There are some fascinating cotton towns in the east of the county - Clitheroe beneath its Norman keep is a pleasant market town close to Pendle Hill from which are superb views over the Forest of Bowland. The hill is forever associated with witches, ten of whom were hanged in Lancaster. However it was on Pendle Hill that George Fox had a vision which inspired him to form the Society of Friends (Quakers). It was at Hoghton Tower near Blackburn that James I jokingly dubbed a loin of Lancashire beef 'Sir Loin', and at Chorley, where the founder of the Tate Gallery was born is Astley Hall, a wonderful Elizabethan mansion. Healey Nab close by, at six hundred and eighty two feet gives wonderful views across the moors and valleys of Anglezarke and White Coppice. Turton Bottoms with its twelfth century Turton Tower is a grand centre for walking this area - the Hall i' th' Wood nearby is an impressive half-timbered manor house built in 1483 and one time home of Samuel Crompton. Between these towns immortalized by such painters as L.S. Lowry is much unspoilt countryside, expanses of moor and forest scattered with ancient manor houses, Tudor farmhouses and old stone churches.

Places to Visit

Blackpool Tower, *Blackpool* ~ it was built in 1894, and is a five hundred and nineteen feet tall replica of the Eiffel Tower in Paris. It rises out of a large building containing a world famous circus and the Tower Ballroom with its Wurlitzer organ. A lift can be taken to the top of the tower to enjoy the views of the town and along the coastline.

Gawthorpe Hall, *near Burnley* ~ built between 1600 and 1605, it was restored in the 1850's by Sir Charles Barry. Gawthorpe was the home of the Shuttleworth family, it now houses Rachel Kay-Shuttleworth textile collections and a collection of paintings on loan from the National Portrait Gallery.

Leighton Hall, *Carnforth* ~ the estate dates back to the 13th century but most of the present building is 19th century including its Neo-Gothic facade. There is a large collection of birds of prey and in the afternoon there is an air show by eagles and falcons.

Martin Mere Wildlife and Wetlands Trust Centre, *near Ormskirk* ~ established in 1976, it has birds from all over the world which can be observed from hides overlooking the floodwaters. Up to one tenth of the worlds population of pink footed geese arrive in here in winter, they can also be viewed from the hides or from the comfort of the heated Raines Observatory.

Lancaster Castle, *Lancaster* ~ a Norman castle which was expanded in the 14th and 16th centuries. Since the 18th century the castle has housed the county courts and prison. The famous Pendle witches, who were convicted and hanged in 1612, were held here while awaiting their trial. The Shire Hall is decorated with six hundred heraldic shields.

Morecambe Bay ~ the best way to explore Morecambe Bay is by train from Ulverston to Arnside. The train travels over a series of low viaducts across the tidal flats where many wading birds feed and breed. Hampsfield Fell and Humphrey Head Point give the best views of the bay. The bay can walked across but is very dangerous as there are strong currents, quicksands and the speed of the incoming tide. Walks are available with an official guide taking three hours and subject to the weather.

Rufford Old Hall, *near Ormskirk* ~ built in 1530, it became the Hesketh family home for the next two hundred and fifty years. It houses collections of 16th and 17th century oak furniture, arms, armour and tapestries.

◀ *The Ashton Memorial, Lancaster*

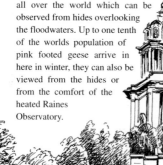

LANCASHIRE

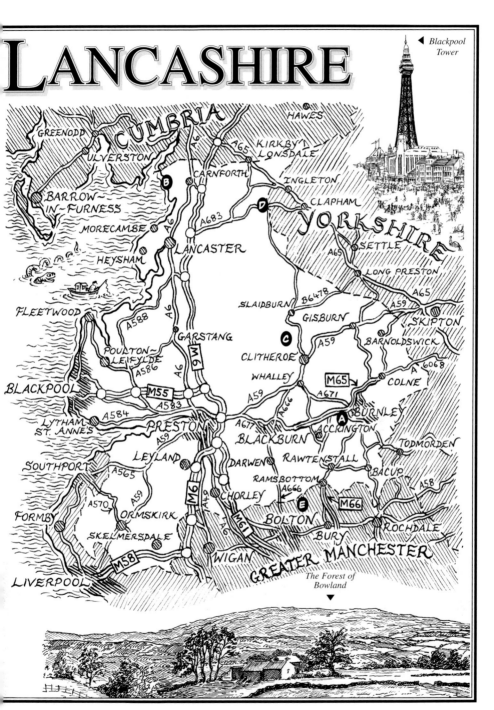

◄ Blackpool Tower

The Forest of Bowland ▼

253

Eaves Barn Farm, Hapton, Burnley, Lancashire BB12 7LP Nearest Road A679, M65

Eaves Barn is a working farm with a spacious cottage attached to the main house offering luxurious facilities. The elegant guests lounge has a log open fire and is traditionally furnished including antiques. Individually designed bedrooms with colour TV, private/en-suite facilities. A full English breakfast is served in the Victorian style conservatory. "Best Bed & Breakfast" in Lancashire 1992. Situated within easy reach of the Ribble Valley and Flyde Coast, Lake District, Yorkshire Dales and the Lancashire hills. Burnley, Blackburn, Preston and Manchester Airport can be reached using the motorway network.

Mrs M Butler
Tel: 01282 771591
Fax: 01282 771591

B&B from £20pp, Dinner from £10, Rooms 1 single, 2 double, all en-suite, Smoking allowed, Children welcome over 12, No pets, Open all year except Christmas, Map Ref A

The Limes Village Guest House, 23 Stankelt Road, Silverdale, near Carnforth, Lancs LA5 0TF A6, M6

The Limes, a charming Victorian house set in beautiful landscaped gardens, has been tastefully refurbished. The spacious bedrooms, decorated with flair, have private bathrooms, TV, easy chairs, and tea and coffee tray. The owners serve delicious food, with an incredibly wide breakfast choice and an optional five course candlelit dinner. Silverdale, an area of outstanding natural beauty, with a wealth of coastal and wooded footpaths, is in close proximity to the Lake District, and Yorkshire Dales and an ideal stopover between England and Scotland. Secure parking.

Noel & Andree Livesey
Tel: 01524 701454
Fax: 01524 701454

B&B from £17.50, Dinner £12.50, Rooms 1 twin, 1 double, 1 family, all with private bathrooms, No smoking, No pets, Open all year, Map Ref B

Peter Barn Country House, Cross Lane, Waddington, Clitheroe, Lancashire BB7 3JH Nearest Road A59

Peter Barn is situated 'far from the maddening crowd' (with apologies to Thomas Hardy), in the Forest of Bowland area of the Ribble Valley are in an area of outstanding natural beauty. The bedrooms are tastefully furnished with welcome trays, central heating, en-suite/private bathrooms and wonderful views of the garden and lane. There is a large comfortable sitting room with a pitched roof and log fire on chillier evenings. There are many good food pubs and restaurants in the area. A must is Jean's home made marmalade. Clitheroe 4 miles. Easy travelling distance to the Lake District.

Gordon & Jean Smith
Tel: 01200 428585

B&B from £19.50, Rooms 1 twin, 2 double, all en-suite/private bathrooms, No smoking, Minimum age 12, No pets, Open all year except Christmas and New Year, Map Ref C

Stonegate House, Main Street, Low Bentham, via Lancaster LA2 7DS Nearest Road A683

House dates from 1609 with Victorian Tower. En-suite rooms with romantic 4-poster beds and beverage tray, plus TV. Residents lounge. Large off road car park. Dovecot Room has kingsize 4-poster bed, private balcony, three piece suite, stereo TV with teletext. Large private bathroom with shower and hot air bubble bath. Stonegate House; the ideal base from which to explore the Yorkshire Dales, Lake District, the Forest and Trough of Bowland, plus the west coast seaside resorts.

Anne Wardlow
Tel: 015242 61362

B&B from £17.50pp, Dinner from £11.95, Rooms 1 twin, 2 double all en-suite, Restricted smoking, Children welcome from 5 years, Small dogs only, Open all year, Map Ref D

Knotts Cottage, Bury Road, Edgworth, Turton, Lancashire BL7 0BY　　　**Nearest Road A676**

Built in 1635 this picturesque former farmhouse is set in two acres of gardens overlooking rolling countryside. A rural location but centrally situated for easy access to the motorway network, and 10 minutes from Bury or Bolton and 30 minutes to Manchester Airport. The two double bedrooms, both en-suite are south facing, beautifully furnished and decorated, have colour TV's, tea/coffee making facilities. There is a guest sitting room and breakfast is served in the Imari dining room. Guests are invited to use the games room, with its full size snooker table and mini gym. There is also ample secure parking. ETB Deluxe.

Mrs Tolhurst
Tel: 01204 852062

B&B from £25pp, Dinner by arrangement, Rooms 2 double, all en-suite,
Restricted smoking, No Children, No pets,
Open all year except Christmas and New Year, Map Ref E

Please mention
THE GREAT BRITISH
BED & BREAKFAST
when booking your accommodation

LEICESTERSHIRE & NOTTINGHAMSHIRE

Leicestershire in the west part of the industrial East Midlands is endowed with large country estates and lovely rolling countryside. Leicester, on the River Soar was an important Roman settlement where the great Roman road, the Fosse Way crossed the river. Simon de Montfort, who led the revolt against his brother-in-law Henry III and set the pattern for future parliamentary government, was a great benefactor of the city. The fine fifteenth century Guildhall was the scene of a great banquet to celebrate the defeat of the Spanish Armada. A branch of the Grand Union Canal joins Leicester and Market Harborough, a delightful town rich in Georgian architecture and the centre of fox hunting country. The canal passes in a wide loop through Foxton, where a series of locks lifts the water level by seventy five feet. Built in the early nineteenth century for the busy canal-borne trade, the town is now a centre for pleasure craft. Lutterworth, once a busy coaching town was the parish of John Wycliffe the great reformer, who preached against the abuses of papal politics and promoted the first translation of the

Bible into the common tongue. The wolds around Melton Mowbray present magnificent walking country. Much of the land is planted with small coverts for the breeding of foxes with the Quorn, Cottesmore and Belvoir hunting this area. The kennels of the Belvoir, one of the oldest of the hunts are at Belvoir (pronounced 'Beever') Castle, the massive nineteenth century Gothic Revival mansion of the Dukes of Rutland, built on the site of a Norman castle which dated back to the eleventh century. Ashby Castle was chosen by Sir Walter Scott as the setting for Ivanhoe's tournament. The castle has had a turbulent history; in the seventeenth century Royalist forces were besieged there for more than a year by Cromwell's troops. Ashby-de-la-Zouch, its name taken from the La Zouch family from Brittany can boast a wide variety of interesting architecture. The houses in the Classical style date from the nineteenth century when the town developed as a Spa. This is an area of great appeal, from the open heath of Charnwood Forest with its glorious views from Bardon Hill and Beacon Hill, to the pleasures of Bradgate Park.

Nottinghamshire to many is simply the county of Robin Hood and Sherwood Forest, and indeed the county was once virtually covered with forest. Sherwood Forest, stretching for more than twenty miles north of Nottingham, is now considerably smaller and less wild than it once was. It is more a region of glades and open tracts, but nevertheless some fine great oaks still stand, most of the oak long since gone for the building of castles, abbeys and churches. One section however which survives more or less unaltered is the Sherwood Forest Country Park, which contains an old tree known as the Major Oak, now supported on crutches. Traditionsally said to be the oak under which Robin Hood held his camp, the tree must be at least five hundred years old. Nottingham, an ancient city on the River Trent is a fine centre for exploring the surrounding countryside, and is in itself of great interest. Occupied in the ninth century by the Danes, its Norman castle on a high outcrop of rock was dismantled during the Commonwealth, the mansion which replaced it was then burnt down during the riots of 1831 leading to the Reform Act. The ruins, restored in 1870 became the town Museum and Art Gallery. The rock on which the castle

stands is riddled with passages and caves. At the foot of the rock is the famous inn, 'Ye Olde Trip to Jerusalem' established in 1189, and said to be the oldest Inn in England. The old Market Square, the town centre since Norman times, was until 1928 the site of the Goose Fair held each October. The fair now held a mile away is no longer the traditional livestock market, but a huge fun-fair.

North of Nottingham is Southwell whose lovely Minster is well worth visiting. Its Chapter House boasts some of the finest medieval stone carving to be seen. The Leaves of Southwell are a celebration of the foliage of Sherwood Forest in stone. The Saracen's Head, the oldest inn in the town is where Charles I surrendered to the Scots in 1646. Newstead Abbey in the west was built by Henry II as an atonement for the murder of Archbishop Thomas Becket, and after the Dissolution the abbey became the home of the Byron family. Lord Byron's body was brought from Greece for burial at Hucknall. It was however D.H. Lawrence who was the true Nottinghamshire man; his early novels, poems and stories are set in the mining and farming area around Eastwood. He described the area as, 'an extremely beautiful countryside, just between the red sandstone and the oak trees of Nottingham, and the cold limestone, the ash trees, the stone fences of Derbyshire'.

LEICESTERSHIRE &

Places to Visit

Belvoir Castle, Leicestershire ~ although it looks more like a fairy tale medieval castle, Belvoir Castle is 19th century, but there has been a castle on the site since the 11th century. Inside are many lavishly decorated rooms with works by Poussin, Reynolds and Holbein.

Burrough Hill, *near Burrough on the Hill, Leicestershire* ~ an Iron Age hill fort, with high earthen ramparts making it an important fort in its time. It was in use from the Bronze Age until the last years of the Roman occupation.

Castle Donington, *Leicestershire* ~ the village is well known for its race track and the Donington Collection, the largest collection of single seater racing cars in the world including those driven by Ayrton Senna, Stirling Moss and Juan Fangio. There is also a reconstructed 1920's garage and the Speedway Hall of Fame.

Rutland Water, *Leicestershire* ~ created in the 1970's, it is one of the largest man made lakes in Europe. On the banks of the lake is 18th century Normanton Church which is now a museum.

Welland Viaduct, *Leicestershire* ~ built in 1876-8, its arches carry the Midlad Railway Line across the Welland Valley for three quarters of a mile.

Holme Pierrepont Hall, *Nottinghamshire* ~ a 16th century Hall containing period furnishings and the ceiling of one of the bedrooms has been taken down to show how the roof was constructed.

Nottingham Castle, *Nottingham* ~ stands on a roock with many underground passages. Today, only the 13th century gatehouse, sections of the medieval wall and moat remain. It houses a museum with information on the city's history and collections of ceramics, glass, silver and Alabaster carvings.

Sherwood Forest Visitor Centre, *near Edwinstone, Nottinghamshire* ~ set in four hundred and fifty acres of ancient oak woodland. The Visitor Centre has a exhibition on the forest and the story behind Robin Hood, who supposedly lived there.

An Ancient Oak, ▶
Sherwood Forset

NOTTINGHAMSHIRE

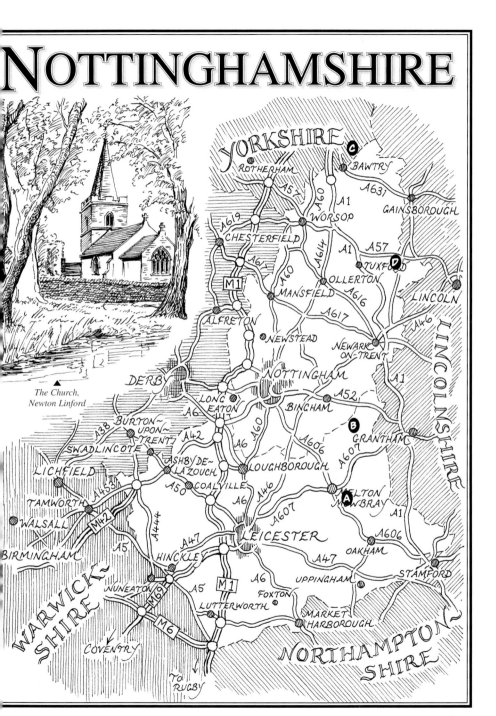

The Church,
Newton Linford

Hillside House, 27 Melton Road, Burton Lazars, Melton Mowbray, Leics LE14 2UR   Nearest Road A606

Charming converted comfortable old farm buildings with superb views over rolling countryside. Accommodation comprises 3 double rooms, 2 en-suite. 1 with private facilities. Centrally heated throughout. All rooms have colour TV, radio alarm, hair dryer and tea/coffee making facilities. Pleasant garden. Situated within easy reach of Burghley House, Belvoir Castle, Stamford and Rutland Water - or just enjoy the villages and countryside.

Mrs Sue Goodwin
Tel: 01664 566312
Fax: 01664 501819
Mobile: 0585 068956

B&B from £16.50pp, Rooms 1 twin en-suite, 1 twin private facilities, 1 double en-suite, Minimum age 10, Open all year except Christmas, Map Ref A

The Grange, New Road, Burton Lazars, Melton Mowbray, Leicestershire LE14 2UU   Nearest Road A606

This beautiful country house surrounds you with elegance, comfort and friendly care. Outstanding views and lovely formal garden of 2¹/₂ acres. Formerly a hunting lodge now provides attractive accommodation. Each bedroom is en-suite with telephone, TV and tea/coffee making facilities. The drawing room is furnished with antiques and has an open log burning fire. Dinner is served in a spacious dining room. Pam Holden presents a Cordon Bleu 3 course meal (by prior arrangement only). Only 1¹/₂ miles to Melton Mowbray and close to Rutland Water and Belvoir castle.

Pam and Ralph Holden
Tel: 01664 60775
Fax: 01664 60775

B&B from £22.25pp, Dinner from £15, Rooms 1 single, 1 twin, 1 double, 1 family, all en-suite, Children welcome, No pets, Restricted smoking, Open all year, Map Ref A

Peacock Farm Guest House & Feathers Restaurant, Redmile, Leicestershire NG13 0GQ   Nearest Road A52

Peacock Farm is a 280 year old farmhouse tastefully modernised and surrounded by open farmland. Most rooms have an unbroken view of the village and Belvoir Castle. All bedrooms are en-suite have TV, and tea/coffee making facilities. After 21 years in the pursuit of excellence we feel the service we offer is ideal for business people and holiday makers alike. Redmile is surrounded by stately homes, parks and market towns. Local attractions include swimming pool, croquet, riding, golf, fishing, cycling, walking country and much more. Antique Centre.

Miss Nicky Need
Tel: 01949 842475
Fax: 01949 843127

B&B double £49, single £35, terms for children and long stay, Dinner £14.50, 1 single, 2 twin, 4 double, 3 family, all en-suite, Restricted smoking, Children welcome, Pets by arrangement, Open all year, Map Ref B

The Old George Dragon, Scrooby, near Bawtry, Doncaster, Nottinghamshire DN10 6AU   A638, A1M

A warm welcome awaits you at this 18th century cottage. Situated in the picturesque and historic village of Scrooby. Internationally known for it's links with the Pilgrim Fathers and within easy reach of Robin Hood country. Accommodation is tastefully furnished retaining many original features and offers 2 double rooms and 1 twin room all with en-suite/private facilities, colour TV, tea/coffee making facilities. 2 miles from A1M.
The Old George Dragon is not a pub.

John & Georgina Smithers
Tel: 01302 711840

B&B from £19pp,
Rooms 1 twin, 2 double, all en-suite,
Open all year, Map Ref C

Wilmot House, Church Walk, Dunham-on-Trent, Newark, Nottinghamshire NG22 0TX   Nearest Road A1

Wilmot House is a Georgian listed building with original beams. Situated in the heart of the village, close to the Church, Antique Shop, Village store and only a short walk from the River Trent. There are extra individual heaters in the bedrooms together with hair driers, TV and refreshment trays. Pub food is within walking distance. Plenty of parking space with security lighting. An ideal base to visit Lincoln, Newark, Sherwood Forest or a stop over as we are only 6 miles from the A1.

Ruth & David East
Tel: 01777 228226

B&B from £17pp, Rooms, 1 twin, 2 double, most en-suite,
No smoking, Children over 14 years, No pets,
Open all year, Map Ref D

*"I'm so thankful **you** won the pig, Billy!"*

261

LINCOLNSHIRE

The glorious and ancient city of Lincoln, strategically situated at the junction of the two great Roman highways, Fosse Way and Ermine Street, was the headquarters of the Roman ninth Legion, and by the time of the Norman Conquest was one of the largest settlements in the country. The cathedral, mainly built during the thirteenth and fourteenth centuries was to replace a Norman structure destroyed by an earthquake of all things. The cathedral was begun just four years after the adjacent Norman castle, built in 1068 by William the Conqueror. The huge central tower contains the five and a half ton bell - Great Tom of Lincoln. The magnificent Angel Choir was built during the later thirteenth century to contain the shrine of St. Hugh. No visitor should miss seeing the cheeky Lincoln Imp, a stonemason's joke carved between the arches. The prosperity of early Lincoln was based upon wool and the city had a rich and influential Jewish community. The Jew's House in The Strait dates from around 1170 and is one of the oldest houses in Britain still in use. Lord Tennyson, Poet Laureate and lover of Lincolnshire, whose statue stands outside the cathedral, was born at Somersby rectory. His favourite poem 'Maud', of 'come into the garden' fame is traditionally linked to the gardens of Harrington Hall in the Lincolnshire Wolds. Lincoln Cathedral was described by Ruskin as being 'out and out the most precious piece of architecture in the British Isles'. Lincoln dominates the Plain of Lincolnshire renowned during World War II for its airfields... Scampton being the home base of six hundred and seventeen Squadron, the 'Dambusters'. Grantham, south of Lincoln is a fine old coaching town. The George Inn dating from the eighteenth century is described by Charles Dickens in Nicholas Nickleby. A statue of Sir Isaac Newton stands before the Guildhall. Newton, who formulated the Theory of Gravity lived at nearby Woolsthorpe and attended Grantham's fifteenth century King's School. The chalk uplands of the Lincolnshire Wolds is wonderful walking country. Louth is the ideal holiday centre and contains some fine Georgian houses. The church of St. James built in 1506 has an impressive spire built of Ancaster stone. Old Bolingbroke is a lovely Wold village, the birthplace of Henry IV, and just three and a half miles away near Winceby is the site of one of the major battles of the Civil War.

262

Boston, the capital of Lincolnshire's Fenland was a major port during the Middle Ages. The great tower of the fourteenth century church of St. Botolph, at two hundred and eighty eight feet is a landmark for miles around, in fact from the top, a third of the county can be seen. Known as the Boston Stump, the church has impressive misericordes dated 1390. It was from Boston that the main group of Pilgrim Fathers embarked in 1608 to eventually reach the New World. Boston in Massachusetts is so named because many of the leading settlers came from the area around Lincolnshire's Boston. Over the centuries the marsh has been drained section by section to provide rich agricultural land. The marshes, once the domain of Hereward the Wake, now supply tulips to the markets of London. Spalding is the main bulb-growing area. Every May it holds a Flower Parade which must be one of the most spectacular free shows in England. Over three million tulips are used to decorate the procession of floats. No visitor should leave this county without visiting Stamford with its glorious buildings. Its number of medieval churches includes St. Martin's, with its alabaster monument to Lord Burghley, and St. Mary's, with its gold-star-embellished fifteenth century chapel of the 'golden choir'. Burghley House, the palatial mansion with its Capability Brown landscaped park was built for William Cecil, chief minister to Elizabeth I, and is a veritable treasure house of Art and superb furniture.

Here in Lincolnshire is so much to attract the holidaymaker, wonderful architecture, fascinating history, bright and breezy seaside resorts, sailing, fishing, splendid expanses of sand dunes and salt marsh....and glorious open skies.

Places to Visit

Belton House, *Grantham* ~ Edward VIII often stayed here during his reign and two hundred and fifty years earlier William III also stayed here. The house contains many Old Masters and outside the gardens are formal with an orangery.

Boston Parish Church, *Boston* ~ a huge church with a distinctive octagonal tower, locally known as 'The Boston Stump'. It can be seen for miles from across the surrounding fens.

Burghley House, *near Stamford* ~ an impressive late Elizabethan mansion, built between 1565 and 1585 it is surrounded by parkland landscaped by Capability Brown. It houses a collection of 17th century Italian paintings, as well as furniture and porcelain.

Doddington Hall, *near Lincoln* ~ set in formal gardens, it was built for Thomas Taylor in the late 16th century by the architect of Longleat, Robert Smythson. The Hall has a Georgian interior but the outside has hardly changed at all.

Lincoln Cathedral, *Lincoln* ~ the third largest medieval cathedral in the country, after St. Paul's and York Minster. It was built in the 11th century but has had many additions and alterations since. The Library contains four copies of the Magna Carta.

Old Hall, *Gainsborough* ~ parts date back to 1484 when Richard III stayed here. In later years, the Hickmans built a new house and the Old Hall was put to a variety of uses including an inn, theatre and Congregational chapel. In 1952 it was saved for posterity and is now on of Britain's best preserved manor houses.

Stamford Museum, *Stamford* ~ covers the history of the town. The most popular exhibit is a waxwork of the country's fattest man, Daniel Lambert, he weighed fifty three stone and died at Stamford Races in 1809.

St Ediths, *Coates-by-Stow* ~ a small church whose interior has been barely touched since the Middle Ages. It also has a Norman font, Elizabethan brasses, early pews and 15th century rood screen.

Woolsthorpe Manor, *Woolsthorpe-by-Colsterworth* ~ Sir Isaac Newton grew up in this 17th century house. His study has prints of other famous scientists of his day, it also has an upright desk reflecting the 17th century fashion for writing while standing up.

Woolsthorpe
▼

LINCOLNSHIRE

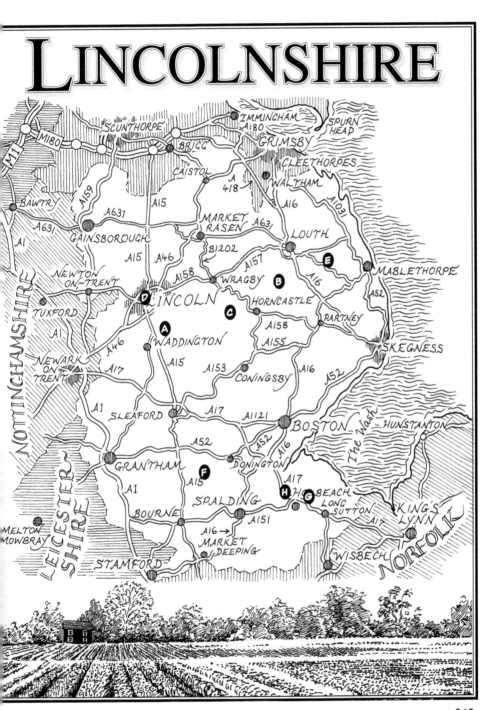

The Manor House, Bracebridge Heath, Lincoln LN4 2HW   **Nearest Road A15**

The Manor House is a charming late 18th century stone-built house set in an attractive walled garden. All rooms are spacious and comfortable with en-suite or private facilities and tea/coffee making facilities. Great care is paid to every detail in this beautiful home where the atmosphere is relaxed and you are assured of an individual welcome. ETB 2 Crown Highly Commended.

Jill & Michael Scoley
Tel: 01522 520825
Fax: 01522 542418

**B&B from £21pp, Rooms 2 twin, 1 double,
No smoking, Minimum age 10, No pets,
Open mid January - mid December, Map Ref A**

The Old Rectory, Fulletby, near Horncastle, Lincolnshire LN9 6JX   **Nearest Road A153**

Experience our lovely country house nestling in the beautiful Lincolnshire Wolds, an area of outstanding natural beauty. Undiscovered, rural tranquillity awaits you, yet we are near to historic Lincoln and the coast. Enjoy walks, cycling, fishing, golf, bird watching, antiques, gardens or just relaxing! We offer Aga home cooking, fresh flowers, 4 acres of gardens, wonderful views and a warm welcome - with superior B&B en-suite, lovingly furnished, accommodation. Our guests often return having discovered this 'real gem'. We look forward to meeting you for a truly relaxing, memorable stay.

Michael & Jill Swan
Tel: 01507 533533
Fax: 01507 533533

**B&B from £20pp, Dinner £12 (4 course) by prior booking, Rooms 1 twin
en-suite, 3 double, 2 en-suite, No smoking, Dogs by arrangement,
Open all year except Christmas & New Year, Map Ref B**

Greenfield Farm, Mill Lane/Cow Lane, Minting, near Horncastle, Lincs LN9 5RX   **Nearest Road A158**

Judy and Hugh welcome you to stay at their lovely farmhouse set in a quiet location yet centrally placed for all the major Lincolnshire attractions. Relax by the large pond or enjoy the forest walks that border the farm. Guests have their own sitting room with colour television and wood burning stove, modern en-suite shower rooms with heated towel rails, and tea/coffee making facilities. Excellent pub with traditional country cooking, 1 mile. ETB 2 Crowns Highly Commended, AA Selected QQQQ, All private facilities.

Judy & Hugh Bankes Price
Tel: 01507 578457

**B&B from £20pp, Rooms 2 double, 1 twin, all private facilities,
No smoking, Children over 10, No pets,
Open all year except Christmas & New Years, Map Ref C**

D'Isney Place Hotel, Eastgate, Lincoln LN2 4AA   **Nearest Road A15/A46**

The D'Isney Place is a very special hotel in the heart of the old city of Lincoln. Its atmosphere is one of elegant luxury and quiet discretion. The rooms are all individually designed and each has its own bathroom. Each honeymoon suite has a jacuzzi bath. English or continental breakfast served in your room, on Minton China. All rooms have TV, radio, direct dial telephone and tea/coffee making facilities. The cathedral close wall, built in 1285 forms the southern boundary of the house gardens.

Mr & Mrs D. C. Payne
Tel: 01522 538881
Fax: 01522 511321

**B&B from £36pp, Rooms 1 single, 3 twin, 13 double, 3 family, all en-suite,
Children welcome, Pets welcome,
Open all year, Map Ref D**

Gordon House, Legbourne, Louth, Lincolnshire LN11 8LH   Nearest Road A157

A warm welcome awaits you at Gordon House, an elegant country house on the fringe of the Lincolnshire Wolds. There are many lovely country walks from the doorstep which encompass the beauty of this unspoilt area of Lincolnshire. The comfort of our guests is our primary concern. Both guest rooms are individually decorated to a high standard, have tea/coffee making facilities, wasbasins and colour TV. The 'Gordon House Breakfast' which includes local sausage and Lincolnshire plum bread must be tried. The large rear garden is available for guests to relax in.

see PHOTO on page 267

Keith & Elizabeth Norman
Tel: 01507 607568

B&B from £17pp, Dinner from £8.50, Rooms 1 twin, 1 double, No smoking, Children welcome, Pets by arrangement, Open all year, Map Ref E

Greenoaks, Pointon, near Sleaford, Lincolnshire NG34 0NB   Nearest Road A15, A52

Set in a quiet Lincolnshire village, Greenoaks is a Georgian house standing in three acres of grounds. Centrally situated for cathedral cities of Lincoln, Peterborough, stately homes, Belvoir Castle, Burghley House and Belton House. It has large well furnished comfortable rooms with tea/coffee making facilities. Ann enjoys her cooking and welcomes her guests with tea and cakes and her evening meals use only fresh home or locally grown produce. Picnic hampers are available for events such as Burghley Horse Trials and Stamford Shakespeare season.

Mrs Ann Firth
Tel: 01529 240193
Fax: 01529 240612

B&B from £20pp, Dinner from £14, Rooms 1 single, 2 twin, one en-suite, No smoking, Minimum age 8, No pets, Open all year except Christmas and New Year, Map Ref F

Cackle Hill House, Cackle Hill Lane, Holbeach, Lincolnshire PE12 8BS   Nearest Road A17

A warm and friendly welcome awaits you at our comfortable home set in a rural position. All rooms are tastefully furnished, have en-suite/private facilities and hospitality trays. There is an attractive guests lounge with colour TV. We are ideally situated for many attractions in Lincolnshire, Norfolk and Cambridgeshire. ETB 2 Crowns, Highly Commended.

Mrs Maureen Biggadike
Tel: 01406 426721
Fax: 01406 424659

B&B from £18pp, Rooms 2 twin, 1 double, 2 en-suite, 1 private facilities, No smoking, Pets by arrangement, Open all year except Christmas & New Year, Map Ref G

Pipwell Manor, Saracens Head, Holbeach, Spalding, Lincolnshire PE12 8AL   Nearest Road A17

This Georgian house was built around 1740 and is a Grade II listed building. It has been tastefully restored and redecorated in the appropriate style and retains many of its original features. All 4 bedrooms are attractive and well furnished and have tea/coffee making facilities. Parking is available and guests are welcomed with home made cakes and tea. Pipwell Manor stands amid gardens and paddocks in a small village just off the A17 in the Lincolnshire Fens. A lovely place to stay. AA selected QQQQ, 'Which' Good B&B Guide, 'Country Living' Highly Recommended. ETB 2 Crowns Highly Commended.

see PHOTO opposite

Mrs Lesley Honnor
Tel: 01406 423119

B&B from £19pp, Rooms 2 double, 1 twin, 1 single, all with en-suite or private facilities, No smoking, Children welcome, No pets, Open all year except Christmas & New Year, Map Ref H

---

left, Pipwell Manor, Holbeach - see above for details

NORFOLK

Little wonder that in this county of deep blue skies, crystal clear visibility and singularly low rainfall, there was established probably the greatest School of English landscape painters...The Norwich School. Add to this, wonderful heathland and marsh, water meadows, ancient manor houses and picturesque thatched cottages, and you have in Norfolk an area of irresistible appeal to the holiday maker.

The Norfolk Broads National Park is a magnet which attracts birdwatchers and boat enthusiasts of every level of proficiency. The Broads, to the east of Norwich, contain the slow-moving rivers of Yare, Waveney and Bure which all meander languidly between the shallow expanses of water which are in fact the flooded sites of ancient peat workings, eventually converging on Breydon Water before joining the coast at Great Yarmouth. The Broads are best appreciated from a boat, and there are numerous boatyards where boats can be hired, particularly at Wroxham and Hoveton, but there is fine walking too around Horsey where the pumping mill is open to the public. Why the Norfolk Broads should be such an attraction to crime writers I simply can't tell, but for some reason the lakes, pools and rivers of the Broads have provided inspiration to dozens of crime writers, including Wilkie Collins, P.D. James, Dorothy L. Sayers and C.P. Snow.

The north Norfolk coast is a wide and wonderful holiday area with Europe's largest expanse of saltmarshes, fine sandy beaches and of course quite dramatic skyscapes. Cromer, famed for its crabs, is the centre of this area and with its neighbour Sheringham are fine holiday resorts retaining much of their old fishing-village character. Picturesque Cley, with its grand windmill boasts some fine flint houses, as does nearby Blakeney, a busy yachting centre, Wells-next-the-sea, now certainly not next-the-sea is famous for its sprats and whelks. Inland at Little Walsingham is the Shrine of Our Lady of Walsingham, a centre for pilgrimage for over nine hundred years for both Roman Catholics and Anglicans. Hunstanton, the largest of the north western resorts is unique amongst East Anglian seaside towns in that it faces west, its heavily eroded cliffs formed of multicoloured layers of rock.

The slightly Continental atmosphere of King's Lynn may well be due to its ancient membership of the fourteenth century Hanseatic League. The town's prosperity is revealed in the grand seventeenth and eighteenth century houses, chief among them being the fine Customs House. The two market places each contain a guildhall...the Saturday Market boasts the fifteenth century Guildhall of the Holy Trinity with a chequerboard facade of flint and stone, the largest medieval guildhall in England. It was a charter of 1537 that gave Lynn its regal prefix. Sandringham, the large estate and country home built for the Prince of Wales, later to become King Edward VII, is to the north of King's Lynn.

Norwich has been a regional centre of importance since Anglo-Saxon times and its fascinating medieval city centre is rich in fine old streets...Elm Hill, Bridewell Alley and Colegate - and outstanding churches, St. Peter Mancroft and St. Peter Hungate being two not to be missed. The cathedral is of course the jewel of the city, its glorious fifteenth century spire, at three hundred and fifteen feet being second in England only to Salisbury. The Norman cloister is the largest in the country. Norwich possesses some quite outstanding museums; the Castle Museum shows a magnificent collection of paintings by the Norwich School, also a remarkable collection of tea-pots; the Sainsbury Centre for Visual Arts, part of the University of East Anglia campus, houses a superb collection of modern sculpture and paintings, displayed in a gallery designed by Norman Foster.

Great Yarmouth, at the mouth of Breydon Water, Norfolk's east coast port and busy holiday resort, was badly bombed during the war, but much of the old town has been restored including the narrow streets of fisherman's houses known as the Rows. Five miles of promenade, golden beaches and a spectacular pleasure beach make it one of Britain's major seaside resorts. Scattered over this county are some extremely fine houses...Houghton Hall, an elegant Palladian mansion, once the seat of Sir Robert Walpole, the first English Prime Minister - Holkham Hall, another Palladian house built for Thomas Coke, the eighteenth century agricultural pioneer - Blickling Hall, a grand seventeenth century house with lavish Jacobean plasterwork belonging to the National Trust. - Felbrigg, another seventeenth century National Trust property with Georgian furniture. The list is long, but so too is the list of pleasures facing the holidaymaker in this glorious county.

Places to Visit

Blicking Hall, *Aylsham* ~ with symmetrical Jacobean front was where Anne Boleyn, Henry VIII's second wife spent her childhood. Very little of the original house survives and most the present building dates from 1628 when it was the home of James I's Chief Justice Sir Henry Hobart. The house features reliefs of Anne Boleyn and her daughter, Elizabeth I, a huge tapestry and paintings by Gainsborough.

Bure Valley Railway, *Aylsham to Wroxham* ~ a narrow gauge railway running diesel and steam trains across Broadland between Aylsham and Wroxham. with three stops at Coltishall, Brampton and Buxton.

Burgh Castle ~ a well preserved Roman fort that formed part of the so called Saxon Shore. It is in a secluded setting, close to the junction of the Rivers Waveney and Yare.

Cockley Clay, *near Swaffham* ~ set in the Breckland, close to the River Gadder is a reconstruction of a settlement of the Iceni tribe of the 1st century on what is thought to be the site of the original village. It dates from the days of Queen Boudicca, who led the Iceni revolt against the Romans.

Castle Rising, *Norfolk* ~ a 12th century keep of a ruined Norman motte and bailey castle. It has retained much of its orginal decoration including vaulted ceilings.

Norwich Cathedral, *Norwich* ~ founded in 1096 by Bishop Losinga who had the white stone shipped in from Normandy in France. The thin cathedral spire was added in the 15th century making it the second tallest in Britain. In the nave, Norman pillars support the 15th century vaulted roof with stone bosses.

Oxburgh Hall, *near Kings Lynn* ~ built in 1482 on an island in the Fens by Sir Edmund Bedingfeld, the surrounding land has been drained but the house is has a medieval moat. The rooms and their contents range from Tudor to Georgian and Victorian times and feature a Mary Queen of Scots embroidery and a tapestry map of Oxfordshire and Berkshire.

Sandringham ~ a large 18th century house, which has been in royal hands since 1862 when it was bought by the Prince of Wales, later Edward VII, who refurbished it. The stables are now a museum and there is also a collection of royal motor cars. The Royal Family spend every Christmas at Sandringham House.

The Gardens at
Blickling Hall
▼

NORFOLK

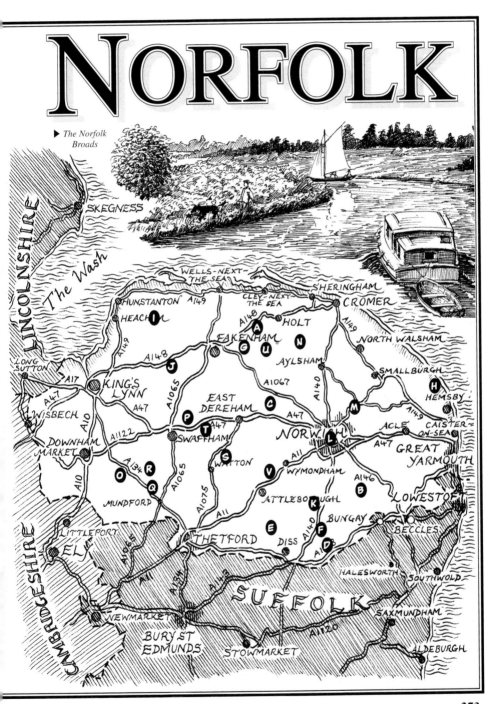

▶ The Norfolk Broads

LINCOLNSHIRE

The Wash

SKEGNESS

WELLS-NEXT-THE-SEA

HUNSTANTON A149 CLEY-NEXT-THE SEA SHERINGHAM CROMER

HEACHAM **I**

A149 A148 HOLT A149 NORTH WALSHAM

FAKENHAM **A** **G** **U** **N**

A148 AYLSHAM SMALLBURGH

LONG SUTTON A148 **J** A1067 A140 **H** HEMSBY

A17 A1065 EAST DEREHAM **C** A47 ACLE CAISTER-ON-SEA

KING'S LYNN A47 **P** A47 **M** NORWICH **L**

WISBECH A10 SWAFFHAM **T** A47 GREAT YARMOUTH

DOWNHAM MARKET A1122 **S** WATTON A11 A47 A1149

A10 A134 **R** A1065 **V** WYMONDHAM A146 **B** LOWESTOFT

O **Q** A1075 ATTLEBOROUGH **K** BUNGAY BECCLES

MUNDFORD A11 **E** DISS **F** **D**

LITTLEPORT THETFORD A140

ELY HALESWORTH SOUTHWOLD

CAMBRIDGESHIRE SUFFOLK SAXMUNDHAM

NEWMARKET A1120 ALDEBURGH

BURY ST EDMUNDS STOWMARKET

The Old Brick Kilns, Little Barney Lane, Barney, Fakenham, Norfolk NR21 0NL   Nearest Road A148

Pam & Alan wish to warmly welcome you to their home set in a quiet rural location, central to all north Norfolk's activities and attractions. All our rooms are non smoking with en-suite facilities and all the comforts of home, colour TV, tea/coffee, firm beds and direct dial phones. Meals are taken in our spacious dinning room overlooking the cottage garden, afterwards you can relax in our licensed guests lounge and chat, play games or watch TV. AA QQQQ. ETB 3 Crowns Highly Commended.

Pam & Alan Greenhalgh
Tel: 01328 878305
Fax: 01328 878948

B&B from £20pp, Dinner from £15.00, Rooms 1 single, 1 twin, 1 double, all en-suite, No smoking, Children welcome, No pets, Open all year except Christmas and New Year, Map Ref A

Waterfield Cottage, High Green, Brooke, Norwich NR15 1JE   Nearest Road B1332

Waterfield Cottage, is an attractive 400 year old thatched cottage, set in an acre of delightful gardens and surrounded by a moat. It is situated on the edge of a conservation village amongst fields and woodlands. The accommodation is very comfortable, bedrooms have tea/coffee making facilities, and TV. A delightful lounge is available for guests to relax in. The fine cathedral city of Norwich is only 15 minutes away by car, and the Norfolk Broads and coasts of Norfolk and Suffolk are within easy reach.

Mrs Rosemary Price
Tel: 01508 550312

B&B from £20pp, Dinner £12, Rooms 1 double, 1 twin, 1 bed/sitting room en-suite, Restricted smoking, Minimum age 5, Open all year except Christmas week, Map Ref B

Bartles Lodge, Church Street, Elsing, Dereham, Norfolk NR20 3EA   Nearest Road A47, A1067

If you would like a peaceful, tranquil stay in the heart of Norfolk's most beautiful countryside, yet only a short drive to some of England's finest beaches, then Bartles Lodge could be the place for you. All rooms are tastefully decorated in country style, and have full en-suite facilities, etc. Overlooking 12 acres of landscaped meadows with its own private fishing lakes. Although the lodge is fully licensed the local village inn is nearby. Why not telephone David or Annie so that we can tell you about our lovely home.

David & Annie Bartlett
Tel: 01362 637177

B&B from £22.50pp, Rooms 3 double, 1 family, 3 twin, Minimum age 10, Open all year, Map Ref C

Grove Thorpe, Grove Road, Brockdish, Diss, Norfolk IP21 4JE   Nearest Road A143

Grove Thorpe Country House is a grade II listed 17th Century farmhouse beautifully renovated to a very high standard with inglenook fireplaces and beamed rooms set in mature secluded gardens and grounds of 6 acres with private fishing and livery facilities for horses. Afternoon tea on arrival around log fires in winter or lazing in the gardens in summer. Excellent 3 course dinner. Conveniently situated for touring Norfolk and Suffolk, 5 miles from the town of Diss, Bressingham, Norwich and Norfolk Broads 30 minutes drive. Otter Trust 15 minutes. 2 Crown Highly Commended.

Angela & John Morrish
Tel/Fax: 01379 668305

B&B from £22pp, Dinner from £15.00, Rooms, 3 double/twin, all en-suite, No smoking, Children over 12 years, Pets by arrangement, Open all year except Christmas and New Year, Map Ref D

Strenneth, Airfield Road, Fersfield, Diss, Norfolk IP22 2BP　　　Nearest Road A1066

Strenneth is a family run business, situated in unspoiled countryside just 10 minutes drive from the market town of Diss and Bressingham Gardens. The 17th century building has exposed beams, and has been fully renovated with a single storey courtyard wing with off road parking and plenty of walks nearby. The seven bedrooms, including a Four Poster are tastefully arranged with period furniture. All have colour TV, hospitality trays, central heating and en-suite facilites. The main house is smoke free and the guest lounge has a log fire on cold winter evenings. There is an extensive breakfast menu using local produce.

Ken & Brenda Webb
Tel: 01379 688182
Fax: 01379 688260

B&B from £20pp, Rooms 1 single, 2 twin, 4 double, all en-suite, Restricted smoking, Children and pets welcome, Open all year, Map Ref E

The Old Bakery, Church Walk, Pulham Market, Diss, Norfolk IP21 4SJ　　　Nearest Road A140

Welcome to a superb combination of a licensed listed 16th century oak-beamed house with excellent cooking from your host, a Master Chef. We stand by the village green in an award winning conservation village. All rooms are spacious and en-suite and have hospitality tray and colour TV. Log fires in winter, sunny walled garden in summer. Visit Norfolk and Suffolk with their NT coasts, historic buildings, splendid gardens, windmills and thatched churches. Convenient for Bressingham, the Broads and Norwich yet only 1 1/2 hours from London. ETB Highly Commended.

Martin & Jean Croft
Tel: 01379 676492
Fax: 01379 676492

B&B from £20pp, Dinner from £14, Rooms 2 twin, 1 double, all en-suite, No smoking, Children welcome, No pets, Open all year except Christmas & New Year, Map Ref F

see PHOTO on page 276

Manor Farm House, Stibbard Road, Fulmodeston, near Fakenham NR21 0LX　　　Nearest Road A1067

Manor Farmhouse is a period farmhouse set in 500 acres of peaceful arable farmland. The 1 acre of garden has croquet set out in summer. All bedrooms have tea/coffee making facilities and colour TV. Sandringham House, Blickling Hall and Felbrigg Hall are within 1/2 hour drive; and the coast at Blakeney is 20 minutes; both Norwich and King's Lynn can be reached in 35 minutes. An evening meal is available by arrangement and special diets catered for. ETB 1 Crown Commended. Parking available. Visa & Mastercard accepted.

Mrs Anne Savage
Tel: 01328 829353
Fax: 01328 829741

B&B from £19pp, Dinner from £12.50 by arrangement, Rooms 1 twin, 2 double, Minimum age 7, No pets, No smoking, Open all year, Map Ref G

Tower Cottage, Black Street, Winterton-on-Sea, Gt Yarmouth NR29 4AP　　　Nearest Road Black Street

A charming, flint cottage, with many original features in a pretty village. Attractive bedrooms (2 on ground floor) have beverage trays, colour TV and wash hand basins, (one double is en-suite with its own sitting room, in a converted barn). Generous breakfasts including homemade preserves are served amongst the grapevines in the conservatory in summer. A beautiful, unspoilt sandy beach and traditional village pub are a few minutes walk away. Norfolk Broads 2 miles, Norwich 19 miles. 'Which' entry since 1994.

Alan & Muriel Webster
Tel: 01493 394053

B&B from £17pp, Rooms 1 twin, 2 double, 1 double is en-suite, Restricted smoking, Minimum age 8, Dogs in barn accom only, Open all year except Christmas & New Year, Map Ref H

The Old Bakery,
Pulham Market

- see page 275 for details

North Farmhouse, Station Road, Docking, Kings Lynn, Norfolk PE31 8LS   Nearest Road A149

North Farmhouse is an attractive typical Norfolk Flint and Brick building standing in an acre. It is at least 300 years old and has accommodation for four people. We have one twin bedroom and one double bedroom both with their own facilities. We are excellently situated for anyone wishing to visit the North Norfolk area or Sandringham. We are fairly central for Kings Lynn, Wells, Fakenham and Hunstanton. The area is superb for walking, bird watching, cycling, golf and beaches.

Helen & Roger Roberts
Tel: 01485 518493

**B&B from £18-£22pp, Rooms 1 twin, 1 double, all en-suite,
No smoking, Children welcome,
Open February - November, Map Ref I**

Lower Farm, Harpley, King's Lynn, Norfolk PE31 6TU   Nearest Road A148

Lower Farm is set in delightful countryside, off the beaten track. It is south east of Sandringham, 1½ miles from Peddars Way, and 20 minutes from the coast. There is an excellent pub in the village. Stabling available for horses. Lovely garden and trees. The comfortable and spacious bedrooms are well equipped and include TV, tea/coffee making facilities and fridge. Parking available.

Mrs Amanda Case
Tel: 01485 520240

B&B from £18pp, Rooms, 1 twin with private bathroom, 2 double with en-suite bathroom, Pets by arrangement, Children by arrangement, Restricted smoking, Open all year except Xmas week, Map Ref J

Wilderness House, Church Road, Wacton, near Long Stratton, Norfolk NR15 2UG   Nearest Road A140

The Wilderness, being an ancient title for this 16th century longhouse and surrounding farmland. A well timbered farmhouse standing peacefully at the end of a long drive in 2 ½ acres of leafy grounds abounding with roses. An ideal retreat only 12 miles south of historic Norwich city and near the Norfolk Broads and Bressingham Gardens. Guests have use of their own well equipped kitchen complete with washing machine and dryer and may relax in attractive beamed sitting rooms with inglenook fireplaces and television.

Juliet Pettitt
Tel: 01508 531006

B&B from £19pp, Rooms 1 single, 2 double, all with en-suite or private facilities, Restricted smoking, Children over 5, Pets by arrangement, Open March - November, Map Ref K

Kingsley Lodge, 3 Kingsley Road, Norwich, Norfolk NR1 3RB   Nearest Road A11, A140

Quiet, friendly, Edwardian house in Norwich city centre. Situated less than 10 minutes walk to the Market Place, castle, shops, restaurants and other places of interest in this historic city. All rooms have en-suite bathroom, colour TV and tea/coffee making facilities. Guests are issued with keys to enable easy access. A full English breakfast is cooked to order - in summer this can be taken in the conservatory. Permits are provided for parking in the street. Kingsley Lodge is graded to 2 crowns commended by the English Tourist Board. Self Catering also available.

Sally Clarke
Tel: 01603 615819
Fax: 01603 615819

**B&B from £19pp, Rooms 1 single, 1 twin, 1 double (all en-suite),
No smoking, No children, No pets,
Open February - December, Map Ref L**

Earlham Guest House, 147 Earlham Road, Norwich, Norfolk NR2 3RG   Nearest Road B1108

Susan and Derek Wright extend a warm welcome to their elegant late Victorian residence, ideally situated five minutes from the southern bypass on the B1108, close to historic Norwich and the university. 7 well appointed and beautifully decorated rooms (all non smoking), provide comfort with modern facilities including colour TV, hospitality tray and full central heating. English or vegetarian breakfasts, cooked to order are served in the pretty breakfast room. Residents Lounge. Patio garden. Local Parking. AA QQQ. 2 Crowns commended. Most cards accepted.

Susan & Derek Wright
Tel: 01603 454169
Fax: 01603 454169

B&B from £18pp-£22pp, Rooms 2 single, 3 twin, 2 double, 3 family, most en-suite, No smoking, Children welcome, No pets, Open all year except Christmas & New Year, Map Ref L

Brooksbank, 1 Lower Street, Salhouse, Norwich NR13 6RW   Nearest Road Salhouse Road

Brooksbank House is next door to a quiet public house, where meals are obtainable, centred in the broadland village of Salhouse. TV lounge for guests use only. Extensive breakfast menu. 2 double on first floor and 1 twin bedded ground floor en-suite rooms. Satellite colour TV, hospitality trays in all rooms. Ample car parking at rear. Outside heated swimming pool in summer only. Salhouse is situated 2 miles from Wroxham and 6 miles from Norwich. Also adjoining self catering cottage with TV. Please telephone for brochure.

Phil & Ray Coe
Tel: 01603 720420

B&B from £17pp, Rooms 1 twin, 2 double, all en-suite, No smoking, Children welcome, No pets, Open all year, Map Ref M

Westwood Barn, Crabgate Lane South, Wood Dalling, Norwich NR11 6SW   Nearest Road B1149

Outstanding accommodation all on ground floor level. All rooms have en-suite bathroom with TV and tea/coffee making facilities. Magnificent guest sitting room with original beams and an enormous inglenook fireplace. Beautiful four poster bedded room. ETB Highly Commended. Idyllic rural location for discovering the charms and tranquillity of north Norfolk. Two miles from the picturesque village of Heydon, the location of many films. National Trust properties, Norwich, the coast and Norfolk Broads within a twelve mile radius. Illustrated brochure on request.

Sylvia & Geoffrey Westwood
Tel: 01263 584108

B&B from £21, Dinner £16, Rooms 1 en-suite twin, 2 en-suite double, 1 4-poster, Restricted smoking, Children welcome, No pets, Open all year, B&B only at Christmas, Map Ref N

The Limes, Wretton Road, Stoke Ferry, Norfolk PE33 9QJ   Nearest Road A10, A134

The Limes is a charming 200 year old farmhouse set in beautiful secluded gardens. Oak beamed ceilings and inglenook fireplace give the dining room great 'olde worlde' charm. We offer traditional bed & breakfast at its best - attractive bedrooms have tea/coffee making facilities, TV and private bathrooms. We make every effort to ensure the comfort of our guests and provide excellent breakfasts, comfortable beds and a very warm welcome. Individual tastes are catered to when preparing meals. The heated swimming pool and bicycles are available for our guests' use.

Gordon & Margaret Burgin
Tel: 01366 500340

B&B from £16.50pp, Dinner from £7.50, Rooms 1 twin, 2 double, Restricted smoking, Children welcome, Pets only by arrangement, Open all year except Christmas, Map Ref O

Corfield House, Sporle, Swaffham, Norfolk PE32 2EA   Nearest Road A47

Corfield House is an attractive brick-built house standing in half an acre of lawned gardens in the peaceful village or Sporle near Swaffham, an ideal centre for touring Norfolk. The comfortable en-suite rooms (one ground floor) have fine views across open fields or the garden, and all have television, clock radio, tea tray and a fact file on places to visit. There is a separate guest living room. Good home cooking using excellent local produce. Licensed. ETB 3 Crowns High Commended. No smoking throughout.

Martin & Linda Hickey
Tel: 01760 723636

B&B £21.50pp, Dinner £12.50, Rooms 2 twin, 2 double, all en-suite,
No smoking, Children welcome, Pets by arrangement,
Open December - March, Map Ref P

Old Bottle House, Cranwich, Mundford, Thetford, Norfolk IP26 5JL   Nearest Road A134

A warm welcome is assured at The Old Bottle house. This is a 275 year old former coaching inn, which has a lovely garden and rural views set in a wonderful position on the edge of Thetford Forest. The spacious colour co-ordinated bedrooms have tea/coffee making facilities, and colour television. Delicious meals are served in the dining room which has an inglenook fireplace. There is a pleasant lounge where guests may relax after a busy day.

Mrs Marion Ford
Tel: 01842 878012

B&B from £17pp, Dinner from £12, Rooms 2 twin, 1 double/family,
No smoking, Minimum age 5,
Open all year, Map Ref Q

The Grange, Northwold, Thetford, Norfolk IP26 5NF   Nearest Road A134

This beautiful 18th century Regency house has easy access to Cambridge, Norwich, King's Lynn and Bury St Edmunds. It is also well situated for the North Norfolk coast, Sandringham and many National Trust properties. The comfortable bedrooms are all on the first floor and have central heating, tea/coffee making facilities. TV and clock radio. There are a drawing room and dining room with log fires both with views over the lawns with ducks strolling around. Guests are welcome to use the heated swimming pool in the summer.

Sue & Malcolm Whittley
Tel: 01366 728240
Fax: 01366 728005

B&B from £19pp, Dinner £13, Rooms 1 twin, 2 double,
both en-suite, 2 singles, Children welcome, Pets by arrangement,
Open all year except Christmas & New Year, Map Ref R

White Hall, Carbrooke, near Watton, Thetford, Norfolk IP25 6SG   Nearest Road B1108

White Hall is an elegant listed Georgian house standing in delightful grounds of 3 acres with large natural pond, surrounded by fields and providing a haven of peace and tranquillity. Spacious accommodation, full central heating, log fires on chilly evenings, early morning tea and evening drinks ensure your stay is enjoyable and relaxing. Situated on the edge of Carbrooke village and in the centre of the interesting and attractive area of Breckland, we are ideally situated for the many attractions in both Norfolk and north Suffolk. Good choice of local eating places. ETB 2 Crowns Highly Commended.

Mrs S Carr
Tel: 01953 885950
Fax: 01953 885950

B&B from £19pp, Rooms 1 double en-suite, 1 twin and 1 double,
Restricted smoking,
Open all year, Map Ref S

Greenbanks Country Hotel & Restaurant, Swaffham Road, Wendling, Norfolk NR19 2AB Nearest Road A47

A charming 18th century country hotel with delightful restaurant offering peace, comfort and relaxation. Greenbanks is situated in the heart of Norfolk with its own 8 acres of meadows with 2 private fishing lakes. We offer excellent short breaks in elegant en-suite rooms with superb cuisine, special diets catered for. An ideal touring base for the coast, Norwich and Norfolk Broads! Nearby golf, walking and Sandringham, plus National Trust properties. ETB 3 Crowns Highly Commended. Secure Parking.

see PHOTO opposite

Jennie Lock
Tel: 01362 687742

B&B from £23pp, Dinner from £17, Rooms 1 twin, 3 double, 1 family, all en-suite, Restricted smoking, Children welcome, Pets by arrangement, Open all year Christmas and New Year by arrangement, Map Ref T

The Old Rectory, Wood Norton, Norfolk NR20 5AZ   Nearest Road B1110

Set in secluded gardens and grounds of 5 acres, in rural north Norfolk. This fascinating house originated in the 17th century with later Victoria additions and is now a delightful family home. Large bedrooms, double with en-suite bathroom and huge canopied brass bedstead. Twin room with private bathroom is similarly attractive. Both rooms have easy chairs, colour TV, tea/coffee making facilities. Full English breakfast, optional evening meal in large elegant dining room. This is a strategic location for the coast, 10 miles, the Georgian market town of Holt and Cathedral city of Norwich, 20 miles.

Jo & Giles Winter
Tel: 01362 683785

B&B from £20pp, Dinner from £12.50, Rooms 1 twin, 1 double, Restricted smoking, Children welcome, Pets by arrangement, Open all year except Christmas and New Year, Map Ref U

Home Farm, Morley, Wymondham, Norfolk NR18 9SU   Nearest Road A11

A comfortable accommodation set in 4 acres. Quiet location, secluded garden, conveniently situated. 1/2 mile from A11 between Attleborough and Wymondham. Excellent location for Snetterton and Norwich. 45 minutes from Norfolk Broads. TV and tea/coffee in all rooms, also central heating. A warm welcome awaits you.

Mrs Joy Morter
Tel/Fax: 01953 602581

B&B from £17pp, Rooms 1 twin, 2 double, No smoking, Children from 5, No pets, Open all year except Christmas, Map Ref V

Please mention

THE GREAT BRITISH
BED & BREAKFAST

when booking your accommodation

NORTHUMBERLAND

This great and glorious region contains amongst a seemingly never-ending list of places to visit, four hundred square miles of National Park running from Hadrian's Wall in the south to the Cheviots and the Scottish border in the north. The Wall itself is a great attraction and to walk along its length is a wonderful experience, with spectacular views from the ridge of the Great Whin Sill across the Northumberland moors. Northumbria, in the seventh century the most powerful of the Anglo-Saxon kingdoms, now combines the four counties of Cleveland, Durham, Tyne and Wear and Northumberland. Each of the old counties has its own particular qualities...combined they form the ideal holiday venue.

The varied countryside is staggering. Kielder Forest, a vast open expanse of woods and lakes, offering many walking, cycling and riding trails, a host of picnic sites, fishing, lake cruises, water sports on Europe's largest man-made lake, exhibitions, shops and restaurants. For

the holiday maker who appreciates nature on a slightly smaller scale there are the glorious woodland gardens of Howick Hall, the Gertrude Jekyll gardens at Lindisfarne Castle, Kirkley Hall College gardens, the quarry gardens of Belsay Hall or the lovely rock-gardens at Cragside House, Wallington Hall and the National Thyme collection at Hexham Herbs...these are just a few from the long list of delights awaiting the visitor. Add to this list a host of garden centres and the choice is quite astonishing. For the visitor who favours the seaside, this north east coast without doubt offers the finest stretches of sand in the kingdom, not overcrowded resorts, but unspoiled beaches...Alnwick, Marsden with its spectacular cliffs and world famous seabird colony, Whitley Bay and Tynmouth with its award winning beaches, Seaburn and Roker, Saltburn-by-the-sea with its Victorian inclined tramway and its intriguing Smugglers Heritage Centre, Redcar with its fine sands and RNLI Zetland Lifeboat Museum. This remarkable coastline is also rich in magnificent castles - Bamburgh Castle superbly sited on a basalt crag overlooking its charming village, Alnwick, known as

'The Windsor of the North'. This great fortress is a treasure house of paintings, furniture and Meissen china. And could there be a more emotive castle than Lindisfarne perched on Holy Island. The castle was converted in 1903 into a private house by Edwin Lutyens. The ruined Benedictine Priory here was founded in 635AD by St. Aidan from Iona, and is regarded as the cradle of British Christianity. Close to Holy Island are the Farne Islands, a bird reserve containing no less than fifty five thousand breeding birds and also the breeding ground of grey seals. And then there are the cities. Durham, its cathedral 'Half Church of God, half castle 'gainst the Scots', magnificently situated on sandstone cliffs overlooking a loop of the River Wear and the city, a wonderful jumbled collection of ancient streets. The cathedral, the finest Norman church in Britain, is the resting place for the remains of St. Cuthbert and the Venerable Bede. Newcastle, the capital of Northumbria is the ideal base from which to explore this area, a major shopping centre and an elegant example of early nineteenth century townscaping. Its six great river bridges include the famous double-decker road and rail bridge built by Robert Stephenson in 1840. There are theatres and superb galleries and museums, including the remarkable 'interactive' Museum of Science and Engineering. Middlesbrough, the administrative centre of Cleveland developed rapidly from a tiny fishing village, with the extension of Stephenson's Stockton and Darlington railway. At the heart of the beautiful valley of the Tees, the town is an excellent centre from which to visit the picturesque fishing villages of Staithes, Robin Hood's Bay, Runswick Bay and Whitby. There is much to see in Middlesbrough itself - The Newport Bridge, the largest vertical lift bridge in the country if not the world, the unique Transporter bridge, the Captain Cook Birthplace Museum in Stewart Park and Fairy Dell Park. Between these larger centres are the little gems...Guisborough with its quaint streets and fascinating antique shops, Hartlepool with its remarkable reconstructed eighteenth century North East Seaport, together with two of the world's oldest floating warships, South Shields, the centre of Catherine Cookson country; Jarrow where the Venerable Bede wrote the first history of England....and Beamish, that quite remarkable North of England Open Air Museum with its recreation of colliers' cottages, its trams, buses and steam engines....and Barnard Castle with the wonderful Bowes Museum.

Through the year this region abounds with exhibitions, gatherings, marches, festivals and shows, ranging from the colourful Durham Miners' Gala to the prestigious Teesside International Eisteddfod. Truly this region is alive with interest for the holiday maker the whole year round.

Places to Visit

Beamish Open Air Museum, *County Durham* ~ set in three hundred acres, it recreates northeast life before World War I. It features a high street, a colliery village, a disused mine, a school, a chapel and a farm with guides dressed in period costume.

Bowes Museum, *Barnard Castle* ~ started in 1860 by local aristocrat John Bowes and his French wife Josephine. It was always intended as a museum and it finally opened in 1892, by which time the couple had died. The museum houses a collection of Spanish art, clocks, furniture, porcelain, toys and tapestries. It also features a mechanical silver swan.

Cragside House and Gardens, *near Morpeth* ~ the former home of William Armstrong, it was the first house in the world to be lit by hydro electric power with hydraulics powering both the new lift systems and telephones which amazed his guests. Today, hydro electric and hydraulic machinery are housed in the Ram and Power Houses. The Victorian Garden is a short walk from the house.

Farne Islands ~ it is home to over seventeen different species of seabird and large colony of seals. St Cuthbert died on Inner Farne in 687, where a chapel was built in his memory in the 14th century and was later restored in 1845.

Gibside, *near Burnopfield* ~ set in the Derwent Valley, it is supposed to be haunted by its previous owners, the Bowes-Lyons. The chapel contains a rare triple mahogany pulpit.

Kielder Water, *near Hexham* ~ surrounded by spectacular scenery, it is Europe's largest manmade lake. Sailing, windsurfing, canoeing, water skiing and fishing facilites are all available at the lake.

Lindisfarne Castle, *Holy Island* ~ built in the 1520's as a defence against the frequent border raids by the Scots. It fell into ruins and was bought by Edward Hudson, the founder of "Country Life' magazine who commissioned Edwin Lutyens to restore it as his summer retreat and Gertrude Jekyll designed the pretty walled garden.

St Nicholas Cathedral, *Newcastle* ~ one of Britain's tiniest cathedrals. Inside, there are remnants of the original Norman church on which the current 14th and 15th century building is founded. It has a rare 'lantern tower' which is half tower and half spire, of which there are only three in the country.

Wallington, *near Morpeth* ~ inherited by Sir Walter Calverley Blackett in 1728, he laid out the gardens and park and transformed the house. There is a collection of dolls houses, a 19th century gentleman's bathroom and a collection of coaches and carriages.

▼ *Bamburgh Castle*

Northumberland

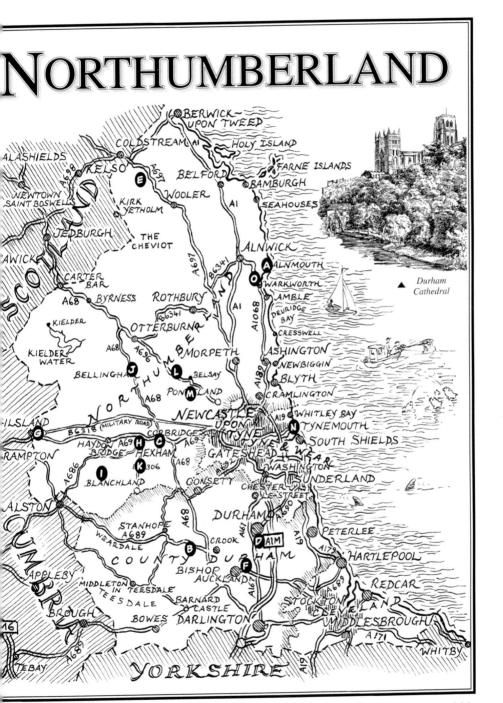

BERWICK-UPON TWEED
COLDSTREAM A1 HOLY ISLAND
ALASHIELDS
KELSO BELFORD FARNE ISLANDS
NEWTOWN SAINT BOSWELLS E A697 BAMBURGH
WOOLER A1 SEAHOUSES
KIRK YETHOLM
JEDBURGH THE CHEVIOT
ALNWICK
AWICK A CARTER BAR A ALNMOUTH
B6341 O WARKWORTH
BYRNESS ROTHBURY AMBLE
A68 B6341 A1 DRURIDGE BAY
KIELDER OTTERBURN CRESSWELL
A68 A696 MORPETH ASHINGTON
KIELDER WATER NEWBIGGIN
BELLINGHAM J BELSAY BLYTH
L CRAMLINGTON
PONTELAND M
ILSLAND A68 NEWCASTLE WHITLEY BAY
G B6318 (MILITARY ROAD) UPON TYNE A19 TYNEMOUTH
HAYDON A69 CORBRIDGE N SOUTH SHIELDS
RAMPTON BRIDGE H C A69 GATESHEAD
A686 HEXHAM A68 WASHINGTON
I K A306 CONSETT SUNDERLAND
BLANCHLAND CHESTER-LE-STREET
ALSTON DURHAM A690
STANHOPE A689 PETERLEE
WEARDALE CROOK A19 A178 HARTLEPOOL
APPLEBY B A1M D
COUNTY DURHAM F REDCAR
MIDDLETON IN TEESDALE BISHOP AUCKLAND A689 STOCKTON
BROUGH TEESDALE BARNARD CASTLE CLEVELAND MIDDLESBROUGH
BOWES DARLINGTON A171
TEBAY A689 A19 WHITBY
YORKSHIRE

▲ Durham Cathedral

Marine House Private Hotel, Alnmouth, Northumberland NE66 2RW   Nearest Road A1

Relax in the friendly atmosphere of this 200 year old listed building of considerable charm, on the edge of the Village golf links with panoramic sea views. 10 individually appointed bedrooms, some with tester/crown drapes. All en-suite with colour TV and teas-made. 4-course gourmet candlelit dinners by our resident chef. Cocktail bar, spacious seafront lounge. Children over 7 years and pets welcome. Visit the Farne Islands or Kielder Forest. Discover the Roman Wall. Impressive border fortresses, romantic ruins and elegant stately homes.

Sheila & Gordon Inkster
Tel: 01665 830349

B&B from £23pp, Dinner from £13.00, Rooms 2 twin, 6 double, 2 family, all en-suite, Restricted smoking, Children over 7 years, Pets welcome, Open all year, Map Ref A

Coves House Farm, Wolsingham, Bishop Auckland, County Durham DL13 3BG   Nearest Road A689

Coves House Farm is an historically important listed early 17th century farmhouse, which has been lovingly restored by the present owners. Secluded setting in 400 acres of hill farmland within designated area of outstanding natural beauty. Extremely comfortable twin bedded room with private bath room and sitting room in own wing. Extra twin bedded room available if required for a family or group of friends. Full central heating. Home cooked food using local produce by owner with professional catering qualifications.

Anthony & Marguerite Todd
Tel: 01388 527375
Fax: 01388 526157

B&B from £26pp, Dinner from £17.00, Rooms 2 twin, Restricted smoking, Children over 12 year, Pets by arrangement, Open all year except Christmas and New Year, Map Ref B

Clive House, Appletree Lane, Corbridge, Northumberland NE45 5DN   Nearest Road A68, A69

Originally built in 1840 as part of Corbridge village school, Clive House has been tastefully converted to provide 3 lovely bedrooms, one of which has a four-poster and its own sitting area. All are en-suite with tea/coffee making facilities, colour TV, hair dryer and telephone. The village centre with many speciality shops and eating places is a few minutes walk away. At the centre of Hadrian's Wall country, historic Corbridge is an ideal base for exploring Northumberland and a convenient break between York and Edinburgh. ETB 2 Crowns Highly Commended.

Mrs Ann Hodgson
Tel: 01434 632617

B&B from £22pp, Rooms: 2 double, 1 single, all en-suite, No smoking, Minimum age 16, Open all year, Map Ref C

Ash House, 24 The Green, Cornforth, Durham DL17 9JH   Nearest Road A1M/A167/A688

Ideally situated on lovely quiet conservation village green in the heart of "The Land of the Prince Bishops". Adjacent A1(m) motorway, 10 minutes Durham city. Ash House is a beautifully appointed victorian home, lovingly restored. The elegant rooms are spacious and include clock/radio and hairdryer. Traditional carved four poster available. Mature trees surround the property, all bedrooms have open views. Hearty breakfast provided. Private parking. Convenient for Hartlepool Napoleonic quay and marina, Metro Centre and Beamish Museum. Well placed between York and Edinburgh. Excellent value.

Delia Slack
Tel: 01740 654654

B&B from £18pp, Rooms 1 twin, 1 double, 1 family, Restricted smoking, Children from 8, Pets welcome, Open all year except Christmas & New Year, Map Ref D

*right, **The Coach House at Crookham, Cornhill on Tweed** - see page 288*

The Coach House at Crookham, Cornhill on Tweed, Northumberland TD12 4TD   Nearest Road A697

see PHOTO on page 287

Ideally situated for exploring Northumberland's National Trust coastline. The Coach House is one hour's drive on excellent roads from Edinburgh or Newcastle. Built about 1680 the brick and stone buildings around a courtyard have been converted into spacious bedrooms. They are accessible to wheelchair-bound guests. The food is fresh and varied reflecting modern ideas on healthy eating with some Mediterranean influence. Where possible, local produce is used. Breakfast satisfies all tastes with fruits, homemade cereals and porridge plus a cooked breakfast using top quality ingredients.

Lynne Anderson
Tel: 01890 820293
Fax: 01890 820284

B&B from £23pp, Dinner £16.50, Rooms 1 single, 5 en-suite twin, 2 en-suite double, Restricted smoking, Children & pets welcome, Open March - November, Map Ref E

Idsley House, 4 Green Lane, Spennymoor, Durham, Northumberland DL16 6HD   Nearest Road A167, A688

see PHOTO opposite

Idsley House is a long established guest house run by Joan and David Dartnall. A large detached house in a quiet area just off the A167/A688, 8 minutes from Durham City. All rooms are spacious and furnished to a high standard. Double, twin and triple rooms are en-suite and have TV and welcome trays. Breakfast is served in a pleasant conservatory overlooking a mature garden. A large quiet lounge for guests to relax in. Ample safe car parking. ETB 2 Crowns Highly Commended. Mastercard, Visa, Eurocard and Switch welcome.

Joan & David Dartnall
Tel: 01388 814237

B&B from £19pp, Rooms singles, doubles, twins & family, most en-suite, Children welcome, Pets by arrangement, Open all year except Christmas, Map Ref F

Holmhead Farm Guest House, Hadrians Wall, Greenhead, via Carlisle CA6 7HY

see PHOTO on page 290

Enjoy fine food and hospitality with a personal touch, in a smoke free atmosphere. This lovely old farmhouse is built with Hadrians wall stones, near the most spectacular remains. Four cosy bedrooms with shower/wc en-suite. Quality home cooking using fresh produce, guests dine together at candlelit table dinner party style. Speciality list of organically grown/produced wine featuring world award winners. Small cocktail bar and TV books, maps and guides in lounge. Your host was a former Northumbria Tour Guide and is expert on Hadrians Wall. Special breaks arranged.

Brian & Pauline Staff
Tel/Fax: 016977 47402

B&B from £24pp, Dinner from £16.95, Rooms 2 twin 1 double, 1 family, all en-suite, No smoking, Children welcome, No pets, Open all year except Christmas & New Year, Map Ref G

East Peterel Field Farm, Hexham, Northumberland NE46 2JT   Nearest Road A68, A69

East Peterel Field Farm is a charming home only 2 miles away from Hexham and yet hidden away in stunning countryside. It is primarily a stud farm with large stable block housing thoroughbred horses. The bedrooms, 2 of which are en-suite, have tea/coffee making facilities, and TV. There is a lovely snug, where guests may relax, with log fire in the winter. Mrs Carr is a Cordon Bleu cook and will be happy to prepare dinner. This is an excellent base to explore the area. Hadrians Wall, Beamish, Wallington, Kielder Water are among nearby attractions. EMail: ben@petfield.demon.co.uk

David & Susan Carr
Tel: 01434 607209
Fax: 01434 601753

B&B from £22.50pp, Dinner from £17.50, Rooms 2 double, 1 twin, 1 single, Open January - December, Map Ref H

right, Idsley House, Spennymoor - see above for details

Thornley House, Allendale, Northumberland NE47 9NH   **Nearest Road B6303**

Beautiful country house in spacious and peaceful grounds surrounded by field and woodland. 1 mile out of Allendale. Relaxed comfortable accommodation, 3 roomy light bedrooms, 2 en-suite, 1 with private bathroom next door. All have tea/coffee facilities. 2 lounges, 1 with TV, 1 with Steinway grand piano, ample books, games, maps, good food and home baking. Bring your own wine. Marvellous walks (guided sometimes available) and bird watching. Hadrian's Wall, Stately homes, Kielder Forest nearby. Vegetarian meals and packed lunches on request. Brochure available.

Mrs Finn
Tel: 01434 683255

B&B from £18.50pp, Dinner from £11.00, Rooms 1 twin, 2 double, all en-suite, No smoking, Children over 10 years, Pets by arrangement, Open all year, Map Ref I

see PHOTO on page 293

Planetrees, Keenley, Allendale, Hexham, Northumberland NE47 9NT   **Nearest Road A686**

Panoramic setting for Planetrees high in the Northern Pennines with views to Hadrians Wall and the Cheviot Hills. Ideal for visiting Beamish, English Lakes, Metro Centre, Hadrians Wall and an overnight stop for Scotland. All rooms have central heating, electric blankets, radios, tea making facilities and hair dryers. Visitors have their own lounge with TV, video and log fires. Local inns nearby for evening meals. This is a designated area of outstanding natural beauty with many interesting walks. Golf course and pony trekking nearby.

David & Isobel Lee
Tel: 01434 345236

B&B from £17pp, Rooms 1 single, 2 double, 1 en-suite, Restricted smoking, Children and pets welcome, Open all year except Christmas, Map Ref 1

Westfield House, Bellingham, Hexham, Northumbria NE48 2DP   **Nearest Road B6320**

Westfield is a truly hospitable home. Built as an elegant, but cosy Victorian gentleman's residence, with nearly an acre of gardens. The five bedrooms, including 3 en-suite and a 4-poster, are all totally comfortable, with more than a touch of luxury. Tea trays in all rooms. Breakfast and dinner are superb, with traditional cooking at its best. Lounge always available. Ideal touring spot with wonderful countryside, Roman wall, castles and NT properties. Safe car parking. Not licenced, but you are welcome to bring your own. Stay awhile and be spoilt!

David & June Minchin
Tel: 01434 220340
Fax: 01434 220340

B&B from £19-£26pp, Dinner from £14.50, Rooms 2 twin, 1 en-suite, 2 en-suite double, 1 en-suite family, No smoking, Children welcome, free for under 2 year olds, Pets by arrangement, Open all year, Map Ref J

Rye Hill Farm, Slaley, Hexham, Northumbria NE47 0AH   **Nearest Road A68, A69, B6306**

Rye Hill Farm offers you the freedom to enjoy the pleasures of Northumberland throughout the year whilst living comfortably in the pleasant family atmosphere of a cosy farmhouse adapted especially to receive holidaymakers. Bedrooms are all en-suite, centrally heated and have large bath towels. A full English breakfast and an optional 3 course evening meal are served in the dining room which has an open log fire and a table licence. Telephone and tourist information in the reception lounge. Guests are invited to use the games room and look around the farm. Credit cards accepted.

Mrs E A Courage
Tel: 01434 673259
Fax: 01434 673608

B&B from £20pp, Dinner from £12, Rooms 2 double, 2 family, 2 twin, Pets welcome by arrangement, Open all year, Map Ref K

see PHOTO on page 294

---

left, Holmhead Farm Guest House, Greenhead - see details on page 288

Shieldhall, Wallington, Morpeth, Northumbria NE61 4AQ　　　　　　**Nearest Road A696**

Shieldhall has been charmingly and elegantly restored from the original 18th century house, nestling in the rolling landscape and overlooking the National Trust estate of Wallington. The main buildings form a well ordered courtyard onto which each of the guests' suites have their own entrances. The bedroom suites are self contained with independent heating, and tea/coffee making facilities. The oak dining room has Inglenook fire-place and antique furniture. The lounge and library both have french doors which open into the large garden with croquet lawn and herbaceous borders.

Stephen & Celia Gay
Tel: 01830 540387
Fax: 01830 540387

B&B from £19pp, Dinner from £13.50, Rooms 2 twin, 2 double, 1 family, all en-suite, No smoking, Minimum age 10, Open March - November, Map Ref L

Dalton House, Dalton, near Ponteland, Newcastle-upon-Tyne, Northumberland NE18 0AA　　**A696**

Dalton is a small peaceful village near Hadrian's Wall yet an easy 30 minute drive from Newcastle, Morpeth and the airport. Ideal for exploring the beautiful county of Northumberland and very convenient for business people who prefer to stay out of town. A warm welcome and friendly atmosphere are assured. Bedrooms have tea/coffee making facilities, and guests have a large sitting room with TV and separate dining room. Evening meal by arrangement.

Mrs Trevelyan
Tel: 01661 886225

B&B from £18pp, Dinner, by arrangement, from £12, Rooms 2 single, 2 twin (with private bathroom), No smoking, Minimum age 12, Open April - October, Map Ref M

Hope House, 47 Percy Gardens, Tynemouth, Tyne & Wear NE30 4HH　　　　**Nearest Road A1058**

Hope House is a beautifully refurbished sea front town house overlooking the wild unspoiled stretch of long sandy beach just a short stroll from Tynemouth village. Anna and Pascal pride themselves on their personal attention to detail, friendliness and service. The period dining room, were the best of Northumberland and French fayre are served with excellent wines, has a unique ambience which is complimented by arts and antiques. All the main rooms offer splendid sea views and particularly from the large drawing rooms. All rooms have double glazing, central heating, colour TV and tea/coffee facilities.

Anna & Pascal Delin
Tel/Fax: 0191 2571989

B&B from £39.50pp, Dinner from £16.50, Rooms 1 twin, 2 double, all en-suite, Children welcome, No pets, Open all year, Map Ref N

North Cottage, Birling, Warkworth, Northumbria NE65 0XS　　　　　　**Nearest Road A1068**

Dating back to the 17th century, North Cottage has a cosy home from home atmosphere. Substantial full breakfasts are served in the dining room. Afternoon tea served free on arrival or when required. The bedrooms, which are all on the ground floor, are comfortable and well furnished with tea/coffee making facilities, electric blanket, clock radio, colour TV and the beds have either duvet or blankets. The double and twin rooms are en-suite and the single room has a wash hand basin.

John & Edith Howliston
Tel: 01665 711263

B&B from £18.50pp (weekly rate from £123), Rooms 2 double, 1 twin, 1 single, most en-suite, No smoking, Open all year except Christmas, Map Ref O

---

　　　　　　　　　right, Thornley House, Allendale - see page 291 for details

"I chatter over stony ways,
In little sharps and trebles,
I bubble into eddying bays,
I babble on the pebbles."
The Brook, Alfred, Lord Tennyson

left, Rye Hill Farm, Slaley, Hexham - see page 291 for details

OXFORDSHIRE

The holiday visitor could be excused for believing that the handsome city of Oxford is the sum total of the county's offerings, but they would be quite wrong. There is considerably more than the undoubted glories of this ancient city.

The region is made up of four areas quite different from each other, even to the extent of each area having architecture of its own. The great Oxfordshire plain extends over most of this county being the basin of the Thames which is fed by four tributaries, the Windrush, Thame, Cherwell and Evenlode, each bordered by charming and picturesque villages. Down the eastern side of the county is moorland ringed with villages of thatched cottages and bordered by the Oxfordshire Chilterns, an area of beechwoods and chalk. Here the ancient pre-Roman grass track, the Ridgeway runs to the Vale of the White Horse, named after the prehistoric horse cut into the escarpment of the Berkshire Downs on the Vale's southern border. There are superb views of this monument from Uffington, the village at the heart of the Vale. Uffington Castle, the Iron Age camp, stands on White Horse Hill straddling the old Ridge Way. The fine town of Wantage was the birthplace of Alfred the Great, whose statue stands in the market place. It is claimed that at nearby Faringdon Alfred had a great palace...certainly the town was mentioned in the Domesday Book. William Morris lived for twenty years at the impressive Elizabethan manor house at Kelmscot. In fact the whole of this lovely area has strong literary associations; Rossetti, Arnold and Pope all lived and worked here. Thomas Hughes, the author of 'Tom Brown's School Days' opens his book with chapters set in Uffington where he was born. Of course these delightful places pale against the Baroque splendours of Blenheim. This sumptuous palace at Woodstock is reckoned to be the finest truly Baroque house in Britain. Built to the design of John Vanbrugh for the 1st. Duke of Marlborough in recognition of his victory at Blenheim. It was also the birthplace of Winston Churchill. The gardens laid out by Henry Wise include the Triumphal Way, the Column of Victory and the superb Italian Gardens.

The Oxfordshire Cotswolds offer the visitor undulating wolds, excellent walking country and the rich honey-coloured stone buildings so typical of this region. Chipping Norton, with its superb nineteenth century Tweed Mill, is an ideal centre for touring. Nearby Burford has an impressive church, the second largest in the county, and a distinguished main street lined with shops and inns leading down to an old stone bridge. Witney with its strange gabled seventeenth century Butter Cross is close to Minster Lovell, one of the loveliest villages on the Windrush, with its fascinating fifteenth century manor house steeped in legend. Banbury to the north is an interesting town with a long history dating back to Saxon times. Best known for its cakes and its cross, the latter is in fact a Victorian replacement of the original cross of nursery rhyme fame. Bicester set in lovely countryside, is a well known hunting centre with some fine buildings.

But at the end of the day, no matter what the attractions of the countryside, all roads do lead to Oxford, the medieval town first mentioned in the tenth century and site of Britain's oldest university. The city grew up at the junction of two rivers, the Thames, known locally as the Isis, and the Cherwell.

The university began in the twelfth century and probably the most famous of its colleges is Christ Church, known as 'the House', which was founded by Cardinal Wolsey. Each college has its own intriguing history, treasures and charm. Alongside the colleges have developed some remarkable public buildings...the Sheldonian Theatre, based on the Theatre of Marcellus in Rome...the Radcliffe Camera and the Bodleian Library, the oldest section of which is Duke Humfrey's library completed in 1488. The seventeenth century Ashmolean Museum now houses the Museum of History and Science. The university church of St. Mary is the church in which Cranmer, Ridley and Latimer were tried for heresy, and later burnt at the stake.

But the university apart, Oxford offers other delights for the visitor. There is boating on the Thames and Cherwell, there is excellent fishing, there are festivals and happenings the year through, there are large swathes of greenery along the rivers with delightful walks....and of course all the other amenities of a modern city.

Places to Visit

Ashmolean Museum, *Oxford* ~ the first purpose-built museum in England, it opened in 1683 and is based on a collection curiosities collected by two John Tradescants, father and son. On their many visits to the Orient and and the Americas they collected stuffed animlas and tribal artefacts. There are also paintings on display by Bellini, Raphael, Turner, Rembrandt and Picasso.

Blenheim Palace, *Woodstock* ~ Quuen Anne gave the 1st Duke of Marlborough the Manor of Woodstock in 1704 after he defeated the French at the Battle of Blenheim and had this palace built for him. Winston Churchill was born here in 1874. The palace is set in two thousand acres of parkland with lakes and woodlands landscaped by Capability Brown.

Botanic Gardens, *Oxford* ~ founded in 1621, they are Britains oldest botanic gardens with one ancient yewtree surviving from that period. The Earl of Danby paid for the garden to be created and now his statue adorns the gate along with those of Charles I and Charles II. The gardens are well labelled and have a walled garden, herbaceous border and rock garden.

Kelmscott Manor ~ the designer and writer William Morris lived here from 1871 until his death in 1896. The house, a classic Elizabethan house is now home to works of art by members of the Arts and Crafts movement which William Morris was part of.

The Rollright Stones, *near Great Tew* ~ three Bronze Age monuments, they comprise a stone circle of stones, thirty metres in diameter, known as the Kings Men. There is also a burial chamber called the Whispering Knights and and the solitary King Stone.

The Sheldonian Theatre, *Oxford* ~ completed in 1669, this was the first building Christopher Wren designed. Its classical design is based on the Theatre of Marcellus in Rome, Italy. The spectacular painted ceilings in the theatre illustrate the triumphs of religion, art and science over envy, hatred and malice.

Vale of the White Horse, *Uffington* ~ a lonely valley dominated by a huge chalk horse, which it gets its name from. The horse measures one hundred metres from nose to tail. Some say it was created by Saxon leader Hengist, whose name means stallion in German, and others think it was to do with Alfred the Great, who is thought to have been born nearby.

Magdalen Tower and Bridge, Oxford ▼

OXFORDSHIRE

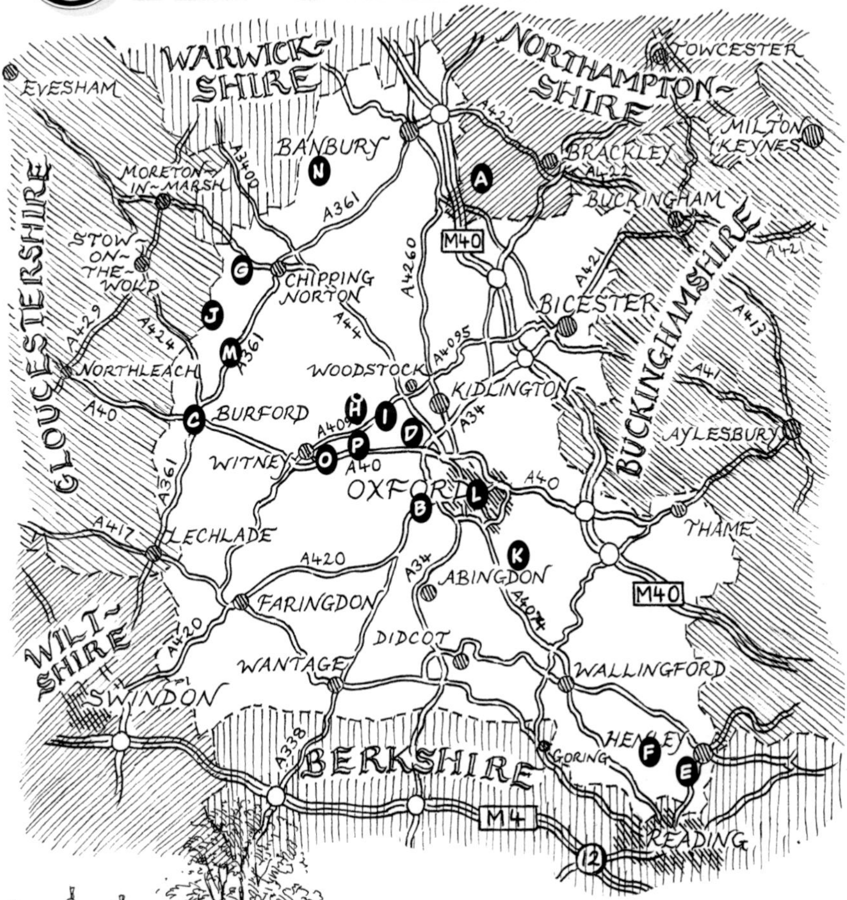

Bl;enheim Palace,
Oxfordshire
▼

College Farmhouse, Kings Sutton, Banbury, Oxfordshire OX 17 3PS   Nearest Road M40, B4100

Fine period farmhouse with lovely views, set in its own secluded grounds which include a lake and tennis court. Ideally located for visits to Oxford, Warwick, Stratford upon Avon and the Cotswolds. The house has been decorated to a high standard by the owners. Stephen and Sara have lived at College Farmhouse for 26 years and have considerable local knowledge. They enjoy racing, gardening, bridge and entertaining and you can be sure of a comfortable and peaceful stay.

Stephen & Sara
Tel: 01295 811473
Fax: 01295 812505

B&B from £24pp, Dinner by arrangement, Rooms 2 twin, 1 double,
all en-suite, Restricted smoking, Children welcome, Pets by arrangement,
Open all year except Christmas and New Year, Map Ref A

Tilbury Lodge, 5 Tilbury Lane, Eynsham Road, Botley, Oxford OX2 9NB   M40, A34, B4044

Tilbury Lodge Private Hotel, is situated in a quiet country lane just 2 miles west of the city centre, 1 mile from the railway and 2 miles from Farmoor Reservoir with trout fishing and sailing. All rooms are en-suite with telephone, hair dryer, TV, radio and tea/coffee making facilities,. The hotel benefits from central heating, double glazing and ground floor bedrooms. There is a guest lounge, jacuzzi, 4 poster and ample parking. An ideal base for touring the Cotswolds or visiting Blenheim and Stratford-upon-Avon. AA 'Selected', RAC High Acclaimed.

Eileen & Eddie Trafford
Tel: 01865 862138
Fax: 01865 863700

B&B from £28,
Rooms 2 family, 5 twin/double, 2 single, Non smoking,
Open all year except Christmas, Map Ref B

Providence Cottage, 26 Lower High Street, Burford, Oxon OX18 4RR   Nearest Road A424, A40

A delightful Cotswold stone cottage in the centre of Burford situated at the bottom of the High Street towards the bridge. Quiet bedrooms with own bathrooms. Furnished to a high standard with antiques, designer fabrics, fresh flowers and comfortable beds. Tea/coffee making facilities in bedrooms. There is a guests' lounge with colour TV. Within easy walking distance of excellent restaurants, pubs, etc. Good base for touring Cotswolds, Oxford, Stratford-on-Avon, Cheltenham and may other places of interest. Heathrow airport 75 mins. ETB 2 Crown Highly Commended.

Michael & Patricia Theodorou
Tel: 01993 823310

B&B from £24pp, Rooms 1 twin with private bathroom, 1 en-suite
double, No smoking, Minimum age 14,
Open all year except Christmas and New Year, Map Ref C

Burleigh Farm, Bladon Road, Cassington, Oxfordshire OX8 1EA   Nearest Road A40, A4095

A listed stone farmhouse in a quiet position. This is a working pedigree Holstein/Friesian dairy farm on the Blenheim Estate. The comfortable bedrooms, have private/en-suite facilities, all have TV, and tea and coffee making facilities. There is a pleasant lounge and garden for guests' use. Situated conveniently for Blenheim Palace, Oxford and the Cotswolds. ETB 2 Crowns Commended, Elizabeth Gundry Recommended.

Mrs Jane Cook
Tel: 01865 881352

B&B from £20pp, Rooms 1 twin, 1 family, both en-suite,
No smoking, Pets welcome,
Open all year, Map Ref D

Holmwood, Shiplake Row, Binfield Heath, Henley on Thames, Oxfordshire RG9 4DP   Nearest Road A4155

Holmwood is the home of Wendy and Brian Talfourd-Cook who welcome you to their large Georgian country house, set in three acres of secluded gardens, with extensive views over the Thames Valley. All bedrooms are large and furnished in period and antique furniture, and all are en-suite with bathrooms, colour TV and tea/coffee making facilities. Holmwood is 7 minutes from Henley. 10 minutes to Reading. Approx 35 minutes from Heathrow. Ideally situated for exploring Windsor, Oxford, The Chilterns and Thames Valley. No restaurant.

Wendy & Brian Talfourd-Cook
Tel: 0118 947 8747
Fax: 0118 947 8637

B&B from £22.50pp, Rooms 1 single, 2 twin, 2 double, all en-suite,
Restricted smoking, Children over 12, No pets,
Open all year except Christmas and New Year. Map Ref E

Shepherds, Shepherds Green, Rotherfield Greys, Henley on Thames, Oxon RG9 4QL   M4, M40

Comfortable, peaceful and welcoming, Shepherds is a delightful part 18th century house which stands in its own gardens on the quiet village green. All bedrooms have either en-suite or private facilities, clock radios and tea/coffee making facilities, some have TV. Guests have their own splendid drawing room furnished with antiques and have a cosy open fire. Conveniently situated for touring Windsor, Oxford and the Chilterns. Good access to Heathrow.

Mrs Susan Fulford-Dobson
Tel/Fax: 01491 628413

B&B from £20pp, Rooms 2 double, 1 twin, 1 single,
Minimum age 12, Restricted smoking,
Open all year except Christmas and New Year, Map Ref F

Kings Head Inn, The Green, Bledington, near Kingham, Oxfordshire OX7 6XQ   Nearest Road B4450

Quintessential Cotswold Inn which enjoys peaceful location beside village green with brook and resident ducks. Retains all olde worlde charm of bygone years, original old beams, inglenook fireplace, pews and settles. Delightful en-suite rooms complement with full facilities and thoughtful extras. Award winning restaurant offering 'personal' inventive cuisine, includes bar fayre, lunch, table d'ote and A la carte evenings. Excellent value and well situated for exploring prime attractions, Blenheim, Stratford on Avon, etc.

Annette & Michael Royce
Tel: 01608 658365
Fax: 01608 658902

B&B £60 per room,per night, Dinner from £9.95, Rooms 2 twin,
10 double, 2 family, all en-suite, Restricted smoking, Children welcome,
No pets, Open all year except Christmas Eve & Day, Map Ref G

Gorselands Farmhouse Auberge, Boddington Lane, Long Hanborough, near Woodstock OX8 6PU   A4095

Old Cotswold stone farmhouse with oak beams, flagstone floors and log fires in winter, situated in one acre of grounds and surrounded by idyllic countryside. Full sized billiards table and lawn tennis court for guests' use. En-suite facilities. French style evening meals by arrangement. Table licence. Ideal location for visiting Blenheim Palace, Woodstock, Oxford, Cotswold villages, North Leigh Roman Villa, etc. Lovely walks by the River Windrush. Tourist Board 2 crowns, RAC listed. Credit cards accepted.

Mrs B Newcombe-Jones
Tel: 01993 881895
Fax: 01993 882799

B&B from £20pp, Dinner from £10.95, Rooms 1 twin, 3 double,
1 family, all en-suite, No smoking, Pets by arrangement,
Open all year, Map Ref H

The Old Bakery, Nuneham Courtenay - see opposite page for details

Wynford House, 79 Main Road, Long Hanborough, Oxon OX8 8JX   Nearest Road A4095, A44

Wynford Guest House is situated in the village of Long Hanborough only 1 mile from Bladon, final resting place of Sir Winston Churchill and 3 miles from famous Woodstock and Blenheim Palace. There is a warm welcome, excellent food and comfortable accommodation. All bedrooms, one of which is en-suite, have colour TV and tea/coffee making facilities. Conveniently situated for the Cotswolds. The City of Oxford is 12 miles away. Evening meal is available by arrangement and there are several local pubs and restaurants within walking distance.

Mrs C Ellis
Tel: 01993 881402
Fax: 01993 883661

B&B from £19pp, Dinner £10 by arrangement, Rooms 1 family, 1 twin, 1 double, 1 en-suite, No smoking, Pets by arrangement, Open all year, Map Ref H

Old Farmhouse, Station Hill, Long Hanborough, near Woodstock, Oxfordshire OX8 8JZ   A4095, A44

We welcome you to our former farmhouse dating from 1670 with many original features and charming bedrooms. Delicious breakfasts with freshly baked bread, marmelade/jams and fresh orange juice which can be enjoyed in our delightful cottage garden on summer mornings. Lovely country walks and good pubs within walking distance. Woodstock & Blenheim Palace 3 miles and Oxford a ten minute train ride. ETB 2 Crowns Highly Commended.

Robert & Vanessa Maundrell
Tel: 01993 882097

B&B from £19.50pp, Rooms 2 double, 1 en-suite, No smoking, Minimum age 12, Open all year except Christmas, Map Ref I

Hillborough House, The Green, Milton-under-Wychwood, Oxfordshire OX7 6JH   Nearest Road A361/A424

Facing the village green in a delightful Cotswold village. All rooms are en-suite, spacious, warm and cheerful. All with colour TV, telephones and complimentary beverage trays. Cosy residential lounge and gardens to relax in. Parking. Willows Licensed Restaurant occupying ground floor is open 5 nights a week (Tuesday - Saturday). Other well known restaurants in next village just 1 mile away. Excellent location for touring famous university city of Oxford, Stratford upon Avon, Warwick and the Cotswolds. 90 minutes from London.

Wendy Jones
Tel: 01993 830501
Fax: 01993 832005

B&B from £26pp, Dinner from £12.50, Rooms 3 twin, 3 double, 3 family, all en-suite, Restrcited smoking, Children welcome, Pets by arrangement, Open February - December, Map Ref J

The Old Bakery, Nuneham Courtenay, Oxfordshire OX44 9NX   Nearest Road A4074

C18th Century large country cottage in conservation village. Inglenook fireplaces, oak beams, self contained rooms. Pretty gardens. Believed to be the oldest planted village in England, lots of pleasant walks around, 5 miles from centre of Oxford city. Good breakfast. Tea/coffee, TV in all rooms. Lots of parking. Next to famous Arboretum. Large well. Furnished rooms. Pleasant host and hostess. Easy reach M40.

Maggie Howard
Tel/Fax: 01865 343585

B&B from £22.50pp, Rooms 1 single, 1 twin, 2 double, 1 family, most en-suite, No smoking , Children & pets welcome, Open all year, Map Ref K

see PHOTO's opposite

Green Gables, 326 Abingdon Road, Oxford OX1 4TE

Green Gables is a characterful, detached Edwardian house, secluded from the road by trees and 1 mile from city centre on a frequent bus route. Bright, spacious rooms, many en-suite. Ample parking.

EMail: ellis.greengab@pop3.hiway.co.uk

Connie & Charles Ellis
Tel: 01865 725870
Fax: 01865 723115

B&B from £19pp, Rooms 1 single, 2 twin, 4 double, 2 family,
No pets,
Open all year except Christmas and New Year, Map Ref L

Shipton Grange House, Shipton-Under-Wychwood, Oxfordshire OX7 6DG   **Nearest Road A361**

A unique conversion of a Georgian Coach House and stabling situated in the former grounds of Shipton Court. Secluded in its own walled garden and approached by a gated archway. There are three elegantly furnished guest bedrooms each with an en-suite/private bathroom, colour TV and tea/coffee making facilities. Shipton Grange House is a delightful house and ideal for visiting Blenheim Palace, Oxford, Stratford, Warwick and many beautiful and well-known gardens. Excellent restaurants within walking distance.

see PHOTO opposite

Veronica Hill
Tel: 01993 831298
Fax: 01993 832082

B&B from £25pp, Rooms 1 twin, 2 double, all en-suite/private facilities,
No smoking, Children from 12, No pets,
Open all year except Christmas & New Year, Map Ref M

Gowers Close, Sibford Gower, Oxon OX15 5RW   **Nearest Road B4035**

Gowers Close is an intriguing 17th Century thatched village house. Two pretty bedrooms have private/en-suite bathrooms, and tea/coffee making trays. The sitting room has a huge inglenook fireplace for blazing log fires, and the cottage garden is enchanting, with views over distant hills. Sibford Gower is a sleepy Cotswold village close to Stratford-on-Avon, Oxford, Blenheim, Hidcote gardens and Warwick Castle. Judith is a gardener, writer, and award winning Gourmet cook and often cooks in the evenings for her guests, who may bring their own wine.

Judith Hitching
Tel: 01295 780348

B&B from £28pp, Dinner from £20.00, Rooms 1 twin, 1 double,
both en-suite, Restricted smoking, Children from 10, No pets,
Open all year except Christmas, Map Ref N

Field View, Wood Green, Witney, Oxfordshire OX8 6DE   **Nearest Road A40, A4095**

Attractive Cotswold stone house set in 2 acres, situated on picturesque Wood Green, Witney midway between Oxford University and the Cotswolds. It is an ideal centre for touring, yet only 8 minutes walk from the centre of this lively Oxfordshire market town. A peaceful setting and a warm, friendly atmosphere await you. Three comfortable, en-suite, rooms with colour TV and tea/coffee making facilities. ETB 2 Crowns Highly Commended.

Liz & John Simpson
Tel: 01993 705485
Mobile: 0468 614347

B&B from £20pp, Rooms 2 twin, 1 double, all en-suite,
No smoking, No children, No pets,
Open all year except Christmas and New Year, Map Ref O

---

left, Shipton Grange House, Shipton Under Wychwood - see details above   **305**

Wrestler's Mead, 35 Wroslyn Road, Freeland, Witney, Oxford OX8 8HJ **Nearest Road A4095**

Wrestler's Mead is a chalet bungalow with a spacious garden for guests to use if required. The name of the bungalow refers to the wrestling bouts held on our ground in the 1700's and not to the antics of your hosts Babs and David, who assure you of a warm welcome. Accommodation consists of a double and single room at ground floor level and a family room on the first floor. Tea/coffee making facilities, and colour TV are provided in the double and family rooms. The family room also has en-suite shower, washbasin and toilet.

Babs & David Taphouse
Tel: 01993 882003

B&B from £17pp, Rooms 1 single, 1 double, 1 family,
Pets by arrangement,
Open all year, Map Ref P

Forge Cottage, East End, near North Leigh, Witney, Oxon OX8 6PZ **Nearest Road A4095**

Knock yourself out in our old Cotswold cottage, recover with a delicious English breakfast including homegrown and homemade preserves. Our home is traditionally furnished with firm comfortable beds and there are hot drink facilities and TV in the rooms. There is off road parking. Home of conservation crazy and cat loving biologist. Take A4095 to Witney from A44 for 4 miles. Then twice right to East End following Roman Villa signs. Forge Cottage is 8 utility poles on the left beyond the pub. Non smoking home.

Jill French
Tel: 01993 881120

B&B from £18pp, Rooms 1 single, 2 double or twin, 1 en-suite,
No smoking, No children, Pets welcome,
Open February - November, Map Ref H

Please mention
THE GREAT BRITISH
BED & BREAKFAST
when booking your accommodation

"Season of mists and mellow fruitfulness!
Close bosom-friend of the maturing sun"
John Keats

SHROPSHIRE

Shropshire is a gem amongst holiday counties. A mere fifty miles long by forty wide, this county of so many faces is more or less cut in two by the River Severn, the longest river in England and Wales. At the centre of the county is a spectacular isolated mass of volcanic rock, the oldest in England, the Wrekin, from which are impressive views across the rich arable plains cut by the Severn. In the west of the county the hills rise gradually to the mountains of Wales, while to the south is the heather-covered plateau of the Long Mynd and the narrow spine of Wenlock Edge. In the north are the lovely Shropshire meres, seven glorious lakes, a magnet to anglers and boat enthusiasts, rich in bird life and a paradise for walkers.

Ellesmere is the obvious centre for exploring this district, a town of handsome Georgian houses and interesting half-timbered buildings. To the west is Oswestry, where remains of Offa's Dyke and Wat's Dyke built along the border of Anglo-Saxon Mercia to keep out the wild Welsh, tell of the constant friction between English and Welsh in this region. For centuries the two factions battled for Oswestry, until in 1535 by an Act of Union, Henry VIII made the town a part

of England. Market Drayton, in the east, well endowed with fine architecture, was the birthplace in 1725 of Robert Clive of India fame. If the wonderful black and white houses of this region excite your interest, then Hodnet is the place to visit. The grand fourteenth century church of St. Luke has a chained Nuremberg Bible dated 1479.

Telford, sited on the slopes of Wrekin and named after Thomas Telford the eighteenth to nineteenth century engineer who was County surveyor of Shropshire, is one of the 'new towns', a concept pioneered by the Labour Government after the Second World War. This town combines many sites responsible for the Industrial Revolution. Here, where the Severn rushes through the Iron Bridge Gorge, is the two hundred foot bridge built in 1779 by Abraham Darby - the first use of iron in industrial architecture. Here in 1709, Darby's grandfather discovered how to smelt iron using coke instead of charcoal. Here too in 1804 Richard Trevithick made the first steam engine to run on rails. Bridgnorth is a delight, perched above the River Severn, its high and low towns connected by a cliff railway, as well as by quaint winding lanes and steep paths. The mixture of Half-

timbered architecture and red brick is most attractive...as too is Castle Walk, the cliff top esplanade. It is claimed that Ethelward, the grandson of Alfred the Great, lived in a cave here at Bridgnorth, a recluse surrounded by his books. His four rock caves are still to be seen on Hermitage Hill. Not to be missed is the Severn Valley Railway which runs between Bridgnorth and Kidderminster through beautiful countryside.

Ludlow's 'Broad Street' is undoubtedly its most celebrated thoroughfare, lined with Tudor timber-framed buildings and seventeenth and eighteenth century red brick houses. The Feathers must be one of the country's finest examples of seventeenth century half-timbering. Ludlow claimed, and with good cause, to be England's finest country town, owing much to its glorious hilltop setting and spacious town planning. The poet A.E. Housman, who in 1896 wrote 'The Shropshire Lad' is buried in the churchyard of the cathedral-like church of St. Lawrence. Ludlow Castle is a spectacular sight, it was built in the eleventh century to repel Welsh raiders. John Milton saw the first production of his masque 'Comus' performed in the castle in 1634, a tradition continued today when during the Ludlow Festival in June and July, outdoor performances of Shakespeare plays are held in the inner bailey. No visitor to Ludlow should miss seeing Stokesay Castle, a wonderfully preserved thirteenth century fortified manor house. Another place of interest, Clun, in the valley of the River Clun, overlooked by its Norman keep, is one of the most ancient settlements in the country.

Shrewsbury, the administrative centre of Shropshire, has been a place of strategic importance between England and Wales from the fifth century. It holds a natural defensive position within the tight loop of the River Severn, its proud Norman castle having been adapted for modern living by Telford, it now provides the council chamber. The town owes much of its fine architecture to its prosperous wool trading period. Charles Darwin was born and educated here. Leading out of the town across the river in opposite directions are two wonderful eighteenth century bridges, the Welsh Bridge and the English Bridge. Edith Pargeter, creator of Brother Cadfael under the pen name Ellis Peters, centred her medieval whodunits on the city, in fact there are metal footprints let into Shrewsbury's pavements as clues to the crime sites!

Places to Visit

Acton Scott Working Farm and Museum, *near Little Stretton* ~ experience farming on Shropshire hills before the days of tractors and combine harvesters. Ploughing and pulling carts is done by Shire horses, and there is also a varied range of demonstrations from this era.

Attingham Park, *Atcham* ~ a Palladian mansion, built in 1782 by Lord Berwick to designs by John Nash. The grounds were landscaped by Humphrey Repton and have deer and views towards the Wrekin.

Dudmaston, *near Bridgnorth* ~ a late 17th century house with collections of modern art and sculpture. The house is surrounded by an extensive lakeside garden with rockery and woodland walks.

Ironbridge, *near Telford* ~ a lace-like iron bridge spanning the River Severn, it was the first iron bridge in the world. It was built in 1777 by the son of Abraham Darby, who first used coke to fire an iron furnace, which led to the start of the Industrial Revolution.

Coalport China Museum, *Ironbridge Gorge* ~ one of the largest porcelain producers in the 19th century. The company still makes porcelain but now at Stoke on Trent. The china shops have been converted into a museum, where visitors can watch demonstrations of the stages of making porcelain.

Jackfield Tile Museum, *Ironbridge Gorge* ~ there were two tile making factories here, they produced a large variety of tiles from the clay mined nearby. The museum has a collection of decorative wall and floor tiles produced from the 1850's to the 1960's.

Ludlow Castle, *Ludlow* ~ the castle, now in ruins is sited on cliffs high above the River Teme. Built in 1086, it was damaged in the Civil War and abandoned in 1689.

Stokesay Castle, *near Craven Arms* ~ a 13th century fortified manor house with a half timbered construction topping its North Tower, this was built around 1240. It also has a polygon South Tower and an Elizabethan gatehouse.

Ironbridge

SHROPSHIRE

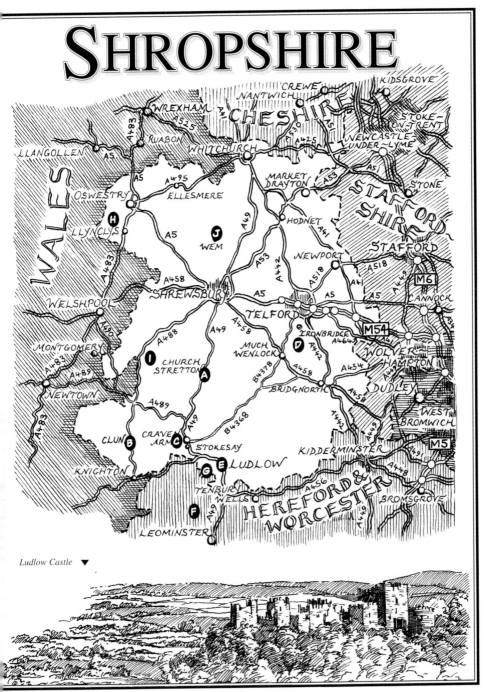

Ludlow Castle ▼

Belvedere Guest House, Burway Road, Church Stretton, Shropshire SY6 6DP   **Nearest Road A49**

Belvedere is a 12 bedroomed Edwardian house standing in its own gardens. All rooms are centrally heated and contain teas-made, clock/radios and hairdryers. We have a drinks licence for your benefit, and evening meals and packed lunches are available on request. There are two guest lounges - one with TV and one with books and games. There is adequate off road parking and Belvedere is ideally situated for both town and hills. Shrewsbury, Ironbridge and Ludlow are a short drive away.

Don & Rita Rogers
Tel/Fax: 01694 722232

B&B from £23pp, Dinner from £10, Rooms 3 single, 4 twin, 3 double, 2 family, most en-suite, Restricted smoking, Children welcome, Open all year except Christmas, Map Ref A

New House Farm, Clun, Shropshire SY7 8NJ   **Nearest Road A488, A489**

Peaceful 18th century farmhouse set high in Clun Hills near Welsh border - a hill farm which includes an Iron Age Hill Fort. Walks from the doorstep include 'Offa's Dyke', 'Shropshire Way' and 'Kerry Ridgeway'. Accom-modation is spacious with scenic views. Tea/coffee facilities, TV and furnished to a high standard. Books and more books to browse in a large country garden. Home cooked dinners and packed lunches available. "New House provides a family welcome and a standard of comfort which a grand hotel would find hard to match, "B'ham Evening Post". ETB 2 Crowns Highly Commended.

Luke & Miriam Ellison
Tel: 01588 638314

B&B from £20pp, Dinner from £10.50, Rooms 1 double, 1 family, 1 twin, all with private/en-suite facilities, Restricted smoking, Open February - November, Map Ref B

see PHOTO opposite

The Gables, Broome, Craven Arms, Shropshire SY7 0NX   **Nearest Road A49**

The Gables is a charming house with spacious gardens, amid the open countryside of the Clun Valley. Only 8 miles from Ludlow and well placed for exploring the Long Mynd, Wenlock Edge and Offa's Dyke. Excellent walking/cycling. The Heart of Wales Railway stops at Broome - ideal for day trips into mid Wales. All rooms are on the ground floor suitable for wheelchair users. Evening meals and packed lunches by arrangement. Private parking.

David & Penny Parry-Handford
Tel: 01588 660667
Fax: 01588 660799

B&B from £18pp, Dinner from £10.50, Rooms 2 twin, 1 double, Restricted smoking, Children & pets welcome, Open all year, Map Ref C

The Severn Trow, Church Road, Jackfield, Ironbridge, Shropshire TF8 7ND   **Nearest Rd M54, A442**

For centuries, travellers to the area have enjoyed the hospitality and comfort of The Severn Trow, a former ale house, lodgings and brothel, catering for boatmen of the river. Today, more discerning visitors are able to enjoy luxurious four-poster beds. Some rooms have TV, all have tea/coffee making facilities. Superb English breakfast served, vegetarian or special diets prepared on request. There is accommodation for guests of limited mobility. Lounge with TV. Ample car parking space.

Jim and Pauline Hannigan
Tel: 01952 883551

B&B from £20pp, Rooms 1 twin, 2 double, all en-suite, No smoking, Open January to October, Map Ref D

left, New House Farm, Clun - see details above   *313*

Number Twenty Eight. Lower Broad Street, Ludlow, Shropshire SY8 1PQ   Nearest Road A49

A warm welcome awaits you at this guest house which now comprises three period houses in this historic street. Snug sitting rooms, book lined walls, and open fires make for a relaxing atmosphere. Every bedroom is en-suite (most bath and shower) and each furnished individually with loving care. Ludlow now has a wealth of excellent eating houses; all within walking distance. Riverside and hill walks, castles and lots of antique and book shops to explore in this lovely Tudor and Georgian market town, near the Welsh border. AA QQQQQ Premier Selected. ETB 4 Crown Highly Commended.

Patricia & Philip Ross
Tel: 01584 876996
Fax: 01584 876860

Rooms 2 twin, 4 double, all en-suite,
No smoking, Pets welcome,
Open all year, Map Ref E

The Marcle, Brimfield, Ludlow, Shropshire SY8 4NE   Nearest Road A456/A49

Parts of this delightful house date back to the 16th century, in more recent times it has been extensively renovated and tastefully modernised. Separate tables are provided in the traditionally furnished dining room, which has exposed oak ceiling beams and wall timbers. Simular features can also be found in the spacious and comfortable lounge with an attractive original inglenook fireplace. The house set in large garden is situated in the centre of the village and both the A49 and A456 are a short distance away. Colour TV and tea/coffee facilities in all bedrooms. AA 4Q Selected. ETB 2 Crowns Highly Commended.

Mrs Patricia Jones
Tel/Fax: 01584 711459

B&B from £24pp, Dinner from £15.00, Rooms 1 twin, 2 double,
all en-suite, No smoking, Children from 5, No pets,
Open February - November, Map Ref F

The Brakes, Downton, near Ludlow, Shropshire SY8 2LF   Nearest Road A4113, A49

In the heart of beautiful rolling countryside only 5 miles from the historic town of Ludlow, The Brakes offers delightful accommodation with excellent cuisine. A period farmhouse tastefully furnished with central heating throughout, standing in 3 acres of grounds with a beautiful garden. Bedrooms are en-suite with TV and there is a charming lounge with log fire Excellent walking country including Offa's Dyke and the Long Mynd; also golf, riding, and fishing are available. Steeped in history with many places of interest nearby. ETB 2 Crowns Highly Commended.

Tim & Tricia Turner
Tel: 01584 856485
Fax: 01584 856485

B&B from £25pp, Dinner from £18.50, Rooms 2 twin, 1 double,
all en-suite, Restricted smoking, Minimum age 13, Licensed,
Open March - October inclusive, Map Ref G

Four Gables, Nantmawr, near Oswestry, Shropshire SY10 9HH   Nearest Road A5

June and Bill offer you a warm and friendly welcome and good home cooked food at their country home, set in a small hamlet on the borders of Wales. The guest lounge overlooks 5 acres of landscaped gardens, which are abundant with wildlife, birds and butterflys. Excellent for bird watchers. The garden and 2 large coarse fishing pools have been featured on BBC Midlands TV. The countryside is unspoilt and near to horse riding and Offas Dyke footpaths. ETB 1 Crown Commended. Licensed to sell alcohol to our guests.

June & Bill Braddick
Tel: 01691 828708

B&B from £18pp, Dinner from £8.50,
Rooms 1 twin, 1 double, 1 single, all en-suite, Children welcome,
Open all year, Map Ref H

Tankerville Lodge, Stiperstones, Minsterley, Shrewsbury SY5 0NB   **Nearest Road A488**

1100 feet up in the Shropshire hills and yet only 25 minutes from Shrewsbury, Tankerville Lodge nestles close to the Stiperstones nature reserve in a land of lore, legend and sheer natural beauty. The views from the hilltop, just a few minutes walk away, are breathtaking - a vast panorama stretching from the Brecon Beacons to Snowdonia and across Shropshire to the Peak District. Tankerville Lodge offers the ideal combination - a quiet rural haven and an ideal base for touring Ironbridge, Ludlow, Lake Vyrnwy and Cadfael country, too.

Sylvia and Roy Anderson
Tel: 01743 791401

B&B from £16.50pp, Dinner from £9.50, Rooms 3 twin, 1 double, all have tea/coffee making facilities, Restricted smoking, Minimum age 5, Pets by arrangement, Open all year, Map Ref I

Foxleigh House, Foxleigh Drive, Wem, near Shrewsbury, Shropshire SY4 5BP   **A49, B5476**

Foxleigh House a home of character in the heart of Wem. Relax in the spacious rooms, delightfully furnished in the style of a more leisured age with modern comforts. Foxleigh offers bed and breakfast in a large twin bedded room with private bathroom, and a family suite of three rooms (sleeps 5-6) with private bathroom. All rooms have colour TV and tea/coffee trays. Wem is a small market town and is an ideal touring centre for Shropshire, Cheshire and Wales. Wem is the home of the sweet pea but to see display gardens it is easy to travel to Hodnet and Powis. Brochure. ETB 2 Crown Commended, AA 4-Q.

Mrs Barbara Barnes
Tel: 01939 233528

B&B from £19, Dinner £11 by arrangement, Rooms 1 twin, 1 family suite (sleeps 5-6), both with private bathroom, Minimum age 8, Pets by arrangement, Open all year except Xmas, Map Ref J

Please mention
THE GREAT BRITISH BED & BREAKFAST
when booking your accommodation

SOMERSET

Where does the visitor to this holiday county start? Such is the variety of countryside and attractions offered, that I suppose the simple answer is...anywhere. Certainly it would be impossible to see and enjoy everything Somerset offers in one stay and little wonder that visitors return again and again. From between Taunton and Bridgwater stretching to the sea are the Quantock Hills, twelve miles of gloriously undulating uplands that so attracted Wordsworth and Coleridge. Not that all the Lakeland poets were equally impressed. Robert Southey was singularly disappointed with the weather when he stayed at Porlock. He must have been very much in the minority however, as this attractive seaside village, the choice of Saxon kings as their base for hunting the Exmoor Forest, is the haunt of artists, has a renowned riding centre and is a popular centre for touring the region. Porlock Weir, a haven for small pleasure craft, has a quaint shingle beach. But beware, Porlock Hill, despite the spectacular views from its summit, is one of the steepest in Britain. Minehead, an ancient harbour and popular resort situated within the wide bay of the Bristol Channel, offers all the attractions of a seaside town and is a perfect base for exploring the surrounding countryside. Dunster close by, was once the centre of a prosperous cloth industry, and with its quaint Yarn Market and its picturesque street of medieval houses leading up to its castle, is one of England's most perfect small towns.

The West Somerset Steam Railway, the largest privately run railway in the country, meanders its way from Minehead to Bishops Lydeard...the home of the fascinating National Museum of Fire and Firefighting. In this area the visitor must certainly visit Hestercombe House garden which is near Cheddon Fitzpaine. The garden, designed by Gertrude Jekyll and Sir Edwin Lutyens, is arguably the finest of its kind in the country.

Taunton, the county town of Somerset, lies in the valley of Taunton Deane on the River Tone. In fact the river flows through the centre of the town, providing the opportunity of leisurely narrow-boat trips on the river and on the Taunton and Bridgwater Canal. The town has a very long and interesting history. Founded in the seventh century, it was here that the infamous Judge Jeffreys held his 'Bloody Assizes' resulting in the hanging of hundreds of rebels following the Battle of Sedgemoor in 1685. The town has some noteworthy buildings and the towers of the churches of St. Mary and St. James are particularly splendid. From Taunton, the Blackdowns and Brendons are within easy reach, and are marvellous areas for walking, riding and cycling. The Blackdown Area of Outstanding Natural Beauty is rich in attractive villages, walks and picnic sites. The Neroche Forest is only a short distance from the Widcombe Wildlife Park. Outside Wellington, another tourist centre with some fine Georgian Buildings, stands the Wellington Memorial, commemorating the Duke's victory at Waterloo. Standing on the highest point of the Blackdown Hills, the monument gives magnificent views across some of the most beautiful landscape in Somerset. To the east, at the foot of the Mendip Hills is the lovely city of Wells. Its cathedral, noted for its wonderful west front, is part of England's largest medieval ecclesiastical precinct. At the moated Bishop's Palace, swans ring a bell near the drawbridge for food. Nearby are the intriguing Wookey Hole caves, a massive underground system hollowed out of the Mendips by the River Axe. Towering over the surrounding countryside is the five hundred and twenty feet pinnacle of Glastonbury Tor. Glastonbury, probably founded in Celtic times has a strange and fascinating mixture of history and legend. It is claimed that King Arthur is buried in Glastonbury Abbey. Bridgwater, where the ill-fated Duke of Monmouth proclaimed himself king in 1685, is close to Sedgemoor where the last battle fought on English soil took place. South at Burrow Bridge and Burrow Mump are glorious views across the Mendips. Somerton was in Saxon times the capital of Somerset, and is renowned for its fine market place surrounded by handsome old buildings which

include the seventeenth century Town Hall and Hext almshouses. At nearby Huish Episcopi there is a glorious church possessing probably the finest fifteenth century church tower in the country, as well as magnificent glass by Burne-Jones. Cadbury Castle to the east was once thought to be King Arthur's Camelot, certainly Ethelred the Unready established his mint here in Saxon times.

From Taunton the holidaymaker has a bewildering number of attractions within a remarkably small area, being a mere seventy five minutes by car from the glories of Bath or the delights of the Cheddar Gorge. In the same time you could visit Stourhead or Selworthy, while the pleasures of Exmoor are only an hour away...Incidentally, did you know that John Horner, the steward to the Abbot of Glastonbury, lived at the Elizabethan manor house in the pretty village of Mells. The good Abbot Selwood, hoping to save his abbey from the Dissolution sent the title deeds of the manor to Henry VIII hidden in a pie. John Horner it appears stole the pie...hence the nursery-rhyme 'Little Jack Horner'.

317

Places to Visit

Barrington Court, *near Ilminster* ~ a garden laid out in a series of 'rooms' with a kitchen garden. The Tudor manor house was restored in the 1920's by the Lyle family.

Cheddar Gorge, *Cheddar* ~ a spectacular ravine cut through the Mendip Hills by fast flowing streams in the Ice Age. The limestone rocks either side rise vertically to a height of four hundred feet. The Gorge has many caves which were once used for storing and maturing Cheddar cheese.

Dunster Castle, *Dunster* ~ for six hundred years, the Luttrell family have moulded the property from a coastal fortress to a secluded country house. The house and medieval ruins are surrounded by sub tropical plants including palm trees and kiwi fruit.

Montacute House, *Montacute* ~ an Elizabethan mansion, built by Sir Edward Phelips between 1558 and 1601. It has the longest Gallery in Britain, where there are portraits on loan from the National Portrait Gallery.

Glastonbury Abbey, *Glastonbury* ~ founded around 700AD, monks encouraged the association between Glastonbury and Avalon, the last resting page of King Arthur and the Holy Grail. The abbey was left in ruins after the Dissolution, yet some relics survive including parts of the Norman Abbey church, the Abbot's Kitchen with its octagonal roof and the abbey barn.

Lytes Cary Manor, *near Somerton* ~ a manor house with a 14th century chapel, 15th century hall and 16th century great chamber.

Tintinhull House Garden, *near Yeovil* ~ the inspiration of Mrs Phyllis Reiss who moved here in 1933. A delightful walled garden separated into sections by clipped hedges.

Wells Cathedral, *Wells* ~ building of the cathedral started in the 1100's, a massive 'scissor arch' was installed in 1338 to support the collapsing tower. The west front features three hundred and sixty five medieval statues of kings, knights and saints, many of which are life size.

Wookey Hole, *near Wells* ~ three underground chambers through which the River Axe flows into a lake from the Mandip Hills. Here there is evidence of Iron Age and possibly Stone Age occupation. There is a guided tour of the floodlit caves.

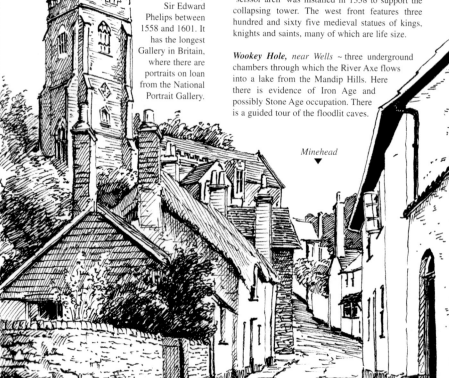

Minehead
▼

SOMERSET

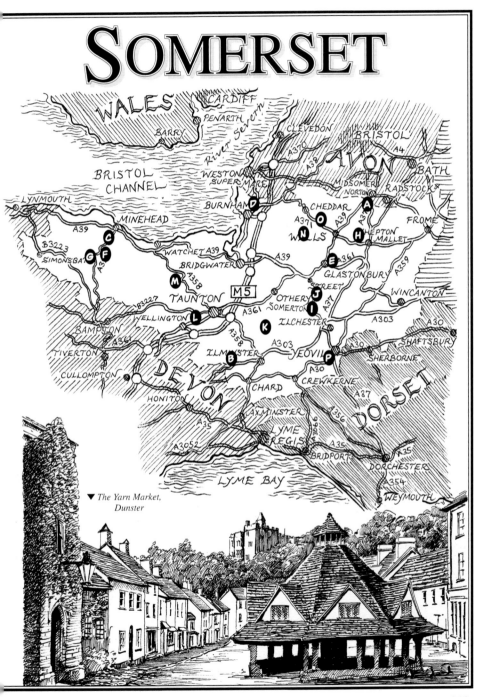

WALES · CARDIFF · PENARTH · BARRY · CLEVEDON · BRISTOL · AVON · BATH · RADSTOCK · A4

River Severn · A370 · A38 · WESTON SUPER MARE · MIDSOMER NORTON · BRISTOL CHANNEL · A370

BRISTOL CHANNEL · BURNHAM · CHEDDAR · A371 · A39 · SHEPTON MALLET · FROME · A359

LYNMOUTH · MINEHEAD · A39 · WATCHET · A39 · WELLS · A39 · A361 · GLASTONBURY

B3223 · SIMONSBATH · A358 · BRIDGWATER · STREET · WINCANTON

TAUNTON · M5 · OTHERY · SOMERTON · A37

B3227 · WELLINGTON · A361 · ILCHESTER · A303 · A30 · SHAFTSBURY

BAMPTON · A361 · A358 · A303 · YEOVIL · A30 · SHERBORNE

TIVERTON · ILMINSTER · CREWKERNE · A37 · DORSET

CULLOMPTON · DEVON · CHARD · A30 · B3066

HONITON · AXMINSTER · A356

A35 · LYME REGIS · A35 · BRIDPORT · DORCHESTER · A35

A3052 · LYME BAY · A354 · WEYMOUTH

▼ *The Yarn Market, Dunster*

319

see PHOTO opposite

Redhill Farm, Emborough, near Bath, Somerset BA3 4SH   **Nearest Road A37, B3139**

Our listed farmhouse, built in Cromwellian times is situated high on the Mendips between Bath and Wells. We are a working smallholding with sheep and poultry. Central Heating. Guests private bathroom. Fresh home produce. Tea making facilities and washbasins in bedrooms. TV in guests private sitting room. No dogs. Shepton Mallet Showground, 7 miles. ETB Commended. More details can be seen on the Internet - http:// www. webscape.co.uk/ farmaccom/england/bath+wells/redhill_farm/

Mrs Jane Rowe
Tel: 01761 241294

B&B from £18, Rooms 1 single, 1 twin, 1 family,
Restricted smoking, Children welcome, No pets,
Open all year except Christmas & New Year, Map Ref A

Keymer Cottage, Buckland St Mary, Chard, Somerset TA20 3JF

A warm welcome awaits you at this AA QQQQQ Premier Selected Victorian farmhouse. Keymer Cottage is attractively furnished, centrally heated, offering a very high standard of comfort and cuisine. Each bedroom has tea/coffee making facilities. The guests' sitting room has TV. Historic Dommett Woods provide a stunning view from the front of the property whilst from the breakfast room far reaching views of the Blackdown Hills (AONB) may be enjoyed. The gardens are within the National Gardens Scheme having been fully restored in 1996.

Mrs Hilary Cumming
Tel: 01460 234460
Fax: 01460 234226

B&B from £20pp, Dinner from £10, Rooms 1 single, 1 twin, 1 double, all
with en-suite or private facilities, No smoking,
Open all year except Christmas & New Year, Map Ref B

Conygar House, 2A The Ball, Dunster, Somerset TA24 6SD   **Nearest Road A39, A358**

Conygar House is situated off the main street of Dunster. The village of Dunster has many attractions including the castle, church, working mill and yarn market and the beach which is just 1 1/2 miles away. There is a good selection of restaurants, pubs and bars serving a wide range of meals. All bedrooms are well furnished and decorated to a high standard and have views towards the castle and moors. There is a pleasant guests' lounge which has colour television.

Mrs B Bale
Tel: 01643 821872

B&B from £18pp, Rooms 2 double, 1 twin,
No smoking,
Open March - October, Map Ref C

---

see PHOTO on page 322

Dollons House, 10 Church Street, Dunster, Somerset TA24 6SH   **Nearest Road A396**

A Grade II listed building, Dollons House, is an attractive house believed to be much older than its early 19th century facade. The house is situated in the heart of mediaeval Dunster, with its cobbled pavements and is probably the prettiest village in the Exmoor National Park. Ideally situated for exploring the beautiful coastline. The en-suite bedrooms are individually decorated, and have tea/coffee making facilities and TV. There is a sitting room for guests which leads onto a large verandah overlooking the pleasant garden.

Major & Mrs G H Bradshaw
Tel: 01643 821880
Fax: 01643 822016

B&B from £25pp, Rooms 1 twin, 2 double all en-suite,
No smoking, Minimum age 16,
Open all year except Christmas & Boxing Days, Map Ref C

right, ***Redhill Farm, Emborough - see details above***

Knoll Lodge, Church Road, East Brent, Somerset TA9 4HZ　　　　Nearest Road M5/A38/A370

Knoll Lodge is a 19th century Somerset house set in an acre of old orchard at the foot of Brent Knoll in the quiet Sedgemoor village of East Brent. 2.5 miles from the M5 and 3 miles from the coast, it is an ideal centre for visiting Axbridge, Cheddar, Wookey Hole, Wells and Bath. There is ample parking, a guest lounge and conservatory; and all rooms have colour TV, tea/coffee, hairdryer and American patchwork quilts. A non smoking house. Highly Recommended for good food.

Jaqui & Tony Collins
Tel: 01278 760294

B&B from £21pp, Dinner from £10, Rooms 1 twin with private bath, 2 double en-suite, No smoking, Children over 12 years, No pets, Open all year except Christmas, Map Ref D

Laverley House, West Pennard, near Glastonbury, Somerset BA6 8NE　　　　Nearest Road A361

Tony & Liz Ruddle look forward to welcoming you to their attractive and spacious listed Georgian farmhouse with superb views, paddocks and gardens, all set in a rural area. A good area for touring - Wells 6 miles, Bath 20 miles and there are many National Trust houses and gardens in the vicinity. There are 2 double bedrooms with en-suite bathrooms and a family room with private bathroom. Colour TV and hospitality trays in all bed-rooms. We have a comfortable guests' lounge and dining room and are happy to provide facilities for children.

Tony & Elizabeth Ruddle
Tel: 01749 890696

B&B from £19.50pp, Rooms 2 double, 1 family, all en-suite, Children welcome, Pets by arrangement Open all year February - December, Map Ref E

The Dell, Cowbridge, Timberscombe, Minehead, Somerset TA24 7TD　　　　Nearest Road A396

Situated in the Exmoor National Park affords visitors an ideal centre from which to enjoy many attractive and interesting places. Walking, riding and fishing particularly good. Stabling and grazing available. Double rooms have wash basins, television and tea/coffee making facilities, twin and single rooms have television and tea/coffee making facilities. Spacious garden and ample parking. Excellent local inn and restaurants, one within walking distance. Exmoor ponies, donkey and black welsh mountain sheep may be grazing from time to time in paddock adjacent to the house.

Harry & Sue Crawford
Tel: 01643 841564

B&B from £15pp, Rooms 1 single, 1 twin, 2 double, 1 with shower, Restricted smoking, Children and Pets welcome, Open all year except Christmas, Map Ref F

The Rest & Be Thankful Inn, Wheddon Cross, near Minehead, Somerset TA24 7DR　　　　Nearest Road B3224

Standing at the 'Gateway to Exmoor', The Rest & Be Thankful formerly a coaching inn offers en-suite bedrooms with tea/coffee facilities, direct dial telephone, refrigerated mini bar, radio alarm, colour TV, hair dryer. Double glazing and beautiful views of Dunkery Beacon and the moors. This is an excellent base for exploring Exmoor either by walking, horse riding or by car. Large menu offers selection of home cooking, complemented by a well stocked bar with traditional ales. Large car park, residents private lounge.

Michael Weaver & Joan Hockin
Tel/Fax: 01643 841222

B&B from £52pp, Dinner from £10, Rooms 1 single, 1 twin, 3 double, all en-suite, No smoking, Children from 11, No pets, Open all year except Christmas and Boxing Day, Map Ref G

---

left, Dollons House, Dunster - see page 320　　　　*323*

Park Farm House, Forum Lane, Bowlish, Shepton Mallet BA4 5JL   Nearest Road A371

Formerly a working farm, this gracious and comfortably converted 17th century house is situated in a conservation area. Accommodation comprises a twin bedded room (bathroom en-suite) and a suite of double and twin room with private bathroom. Situated close to the cathedral city of Wells, Cheddar Gorge and Wookey Hole, Clarke's Village at Street, Longleat Fleet Air Arm and Haynes motor museum, Bath, Bristol, Sherborne and Yeovil. Shepton Mallet has good restaurants, pubs and easy access to the Mendip Hills plus many National Trust houses and gardens.

Mr & Mrs J Grattan
Tel: 01749 343673
Fax: 01749 345279

B&B from £17.50pp, Rooms 1 en-suite twin, 1 double & twin with private bathroom, Children welcome, Open all year, Map Ref H

The Lynch Country House, 4 Behind Berry, Somerton, Somerset TA11 7PD   Nearest Road A303

see PHOTO opposite

The Lynch in a charming small hotel, standing in acres of carefully tended, wonderfully mature grounds. Beautifully refurbished and decorated to retain all its Georgian style and elegance, it now offers accommodation in a choice of five attractively presented rooms, some with 4-posters, other with Victorian bedsteads. Each room has en-suite facilities, phone, radio, TV and tea/coffee making facilities. The elegant dining room overlooks the lawns and lake. Single occupancy supplement.

Roy Copeland
Tel: 01458 272316
Fax: 01458 272590

B&B from £24.50pp, Rooms 1 twin, 4 double, 1 family, all en-suite, Restricted smoking, Children welcome, Pets by arrangement, Open all year except Christmas and New Year, Map Ref I

Church Farm Guest House, Compton Dundon, Somerton, Somerset TA11 6PE   Nearest Road B3151

Church Farm Guest House is a part thatched farm house reputed to be 400 years old. It enjoys a tranquil setting in a typically en village nestling below St Andrew's Church in the Dundon part of the village about 1 mile off the B3151 so is very peaceful. The Down's of Glastonbury, Wells, Street and Somerton are only a few minutes drive. The rooms are in converted farm building and are all en-suite with television, tea making facilities and central heating. Full fire reg's. Car park.

Brian & Jean Middle
Tel: 01458 272927

B&B from £19.50pp, single £25, Dinner by arrangement, Rooms, 1 single, 2 double, 2 family, all en-suite, Restricted smoking, Children over 5 years, No pets, Open January - November, Map Ref J

Langford Manor, Fivehead, Taunton, Somerset TA3 6PH   Nearest Road A378

see PHOTO on page 326

Peter and Fiona Willcox welcome you to their beautiful Grade II Manor House set in 9 acres on the edge of the Somerset levels offering peace tranquillity and seclusion. The house dating from the 13th Century affords every comfort whilst retaining the original character. All rooms are en-suite and the panelled drawing room and dining room are available for guests. Relax in the garden, play croquet or tennis followed by an excellent dinner. Soak up the country house atmosphere.

Peter & Fiona Willcox
Tel: 01460 281674
Fax: 01460 281585

B&B from £35pp, Dinner from £20, Rooms 3 double, all en-suite, No smoking, Children over 14 years, No pets, Open all year except Christmas, Map Ref K

Huntersmead, Hele, Taunton, Somerset TA4 1AJ **Nearest Road A38**

Huntersmead is an old farmhouse set in 15 acres of garden and grounds offering a warm welcome in a rural, peaceful and tranquil situation yet within 4 miles of the county town of Taunton and the M5 motorway. The rooms are attractively decorated and furnished with antiques. There are log fires and beautiful gardens. A hearty cooked breakfast is provided and a quality dinner available if booked in advance. An ideal centre for touring the west country including the Quantock and Blackdown Hills, Exmoor and north and south coasts.

Mrs Bimmy Amor
Tel: 01823 461315

B&B from £18pp, Dinner from £12, Rooms 1 twin, 1 double,
Restricted smoking, Children welcome, No pets,
Open all year except Christmas, Map Ref L

Higher Vexford House, Higher Vexford, Lydeard St. Lawrence, Taunton, Somerset TA4 3QF **B3224**

Tucked away in a stunning hidden valley, this beautiful large country house is between The Quantocks, Brendons and Exmoor. A spacious sitting room and dining room furnished with antiques, log fires and flagstones floors. 3 lovely bedrooms decorated in traditional country-house style all with their own bathrooms. Lots of books and magazines. Walled gardens. Use of swimming pool. A friendly welcome awaits you. A great place to come and relax, perfect for unwinding. Colour brochure available.
EMail: 101752.1124@compuserve.com

Nigel & Finny Muer-Raby
Tel: 01984 656267
Fax: 01984 656707

B&B from £28pp, Rooms 2 twin, 1 double,
No smoking, Children welcome, Pets by arrangement,
Open all year except Christmas & New Year, Map Ref M

see PHOTO on page 328

Nut Tree Farm, Stoughton Cross, Wedmore, Somerset BS28 4QP **Nearest Road M5/A38/B3139**

Nut Tree Farm is a 16th Century farmhouse set in 2 acres of peaceful semi-wild garden and orchard, 1.25 miles from the historic village of Wedmore. Traditional English or wholefood breakfast, probably the most extensive menu in the UK, and of the highest quality. Comfortable lounge with inglenook fire, elm beams. Also self-catering cottage, drying room for walkers. The work of Melvyn Firmager, internationally renowned Sculptural woodturner, maybe seen in the gallery. Woodturning courses. Golf course within walking distance. Convenient for Wells, Glastonbury, Cheddar, Mendip Hills. Excellent pubs and restaurants.

Anne Firmager
Tel/Fax: 01934 712404

B&B from £19.50pp, Rooms 1 single, 1 twin, 2 double, most en-suite,
No smoking, Children from 12, No pets,
Open all year except Christmas and Boxing Day, Map Ref N

see PHOTO on page 329

Box Tree House, Westbury-Sub-Mendip, Wells, Somerset BA5 1HA **Nearest Road A371**

A warm welcome is assured at this delightful converted 17th century farm house, located in the heart of the village next to a local inn where excellent food is served. Accommodation is in 3 comfortable rooms with en-suite and private facilities. There is a charming TV lounge. Generous breakfast with local preserves, croissants and home made muffins. Also work shops for stained glass and picture framing with many unique items for sale.

Mrs Carolyn White
Tel: 01749 870777

B&B from £19pp, Rooms 2 double, 1 twin, all en-suite,
Restricted smoking,
Open all year, Map Ref O

see PHOTO on page 330

---

left, Langford Manor, near Taunton - see page 324 for details

Higher Vexford House, Higher Vexford - see page 327

*right, **Nut Tree Farm, Wedmore** - see page 327*

Stoneleigh House, Westbury sub Mendip - see page 332

see PHOTO on page 331

Stoneleigh House, Westbury-sub-Mendip, near Wells, Somerset BA5 1HF Nearest Road A371

A delightful 18th century farmhouse with lovely garden and wonderful views across open countryside. Situated on the southern slopes of the Mendip Hills between Wells and Cheddar. Excellent accommodation is offered. En-suite rooms available with TV and tea/coffee making facilities. A guests' lounge for your relaxation. A generous breakfast is served with homemade preserves and free range eggs. Vegetarians catered for. Good pub nearby. Tourist information available. Ideal position for walking or touring holidays.

Mrs Wendy Thompson
Tel: 01749 870668
Fax: 01749 870668

B&B from £20pp, Rooms 2 double, 1 twin, 2 en-suite,
Minimum age 10, No smoking,
Open all year except Christmas, Map Ref O

Holywell House, Holywell, East Coker, Yeovil, Somerset BA22 9NQ Nearest Road A30

Delightful Hamstone house built in 1780. Lovingly restored, tastefully decorated and furnished with many fine antiques. Guests every need seems to have been anticipated. Even to the hot water bottles for chilly nights. Jackie enjoys cossetting her guests, which is why she wins top awards. The house stands in three acres of glorious NGS open gardens with a tennis court and croquet lawn. Holywell House has litery connections with Thomas Hardy and T.S. Eliot. Highly recommended for country holidays. Please phone for brochure.

Jackie Somerville
Tel: 01935 862612
Fax: 01935 863035

B&B from £30pp, Rooms 1 twin full suite, 2 double en-suite,
Restricted smoking, Children welcome, No pets,
Open all year except Christmas & New Year, Map Ref P

Please mention
THE GREAT BRITISH
BED & BREAKFAST
when booking your accommodation

The Kiss of the sun for pardon
The song of the birds for mirth,
One is nearer God's heart in a garden
Than anywhere else on earth.
Dorothy Frances Gurney

SUFFOLK

Breckland, in the north west of the county of Suffolk, is an area of some three hundred square miles which is shared between Suffolk and Norfolk, and in the early days was populated with settlers who found the low-lying land and plentiful supply of water ideal for their simple farming methods. Today, the stability of this Breckland soil is dependant on extensive afforestation. Between Breckland and the crumbling and constantly eroded coastline lies fertile high Suffolk, reliant upon a complicated system of drainage to carry off the winter rains. Suffolk is a perfect holiday venue because there are so many contrasts. From Great Yarmouth down to Felixstowe, the coastline is punctuated with delightful coves and bays offering excellent sailing. Southwold, Orford, Woodbridge and Aldeburgh, particularly so. Southwold, the former home town of George Orwell, is a wonderful centre for exploring coastal Suffolk. After a disastrous fire in 1659, the town was replanned around a series of green areas bordered by quaint flint, brick and

colour-washed cottages. Behind the Sole Bay Inn stands the white painted lighthouse, while the grand church in the Perpendicular style boasts an impressive interior. The region surrounding the town is excellent for walking and is a naturalist's paradise. To the south is Aldeburgh. It was here that the Rev. George Crabbe lived. His poem 'The Borough' was adapted by Benjamin Britten for his opera 'Peter Grimes'...an evocation of life on the Suffolk coast. Britten is buried in the churchyard of St. Peter and St. Paul. Visitors mustn't miss seeing his memorial window designed by John Piper. Benjamin Britten was co-founder of the Aldeburgh Music Festival held in June at The Maltings at Snape. The hall was burnt down just two years after its opening, but within a year was restored. At nearby Thorpeness, beside the village's artificial lake the Meare, is a former corn windmill. Woodbridge, set in the slopes above the River Deben, is an attractive town of small boats and pleasure craft...on the opposite bank is the site of the Sutton Hoo ship-burial where in 1939, a Saxon ship and its priceless treasure was unearthed.

The River Stour which separates Suffolk and Essex runs through delightful water-meadows and is crossed by picturesque bridges. This is Constable country. John Constable was born in this valley, and his father owned mills at Flatford and Dedham, which became the subject's of the artist's paintings. Probably England's greatest landscape artist, Constable has immortalised this beautiful region. Another great English artist Thomas Gainsborough, renowned for his elegant portraits, was born at Sudbury where his statue overlooks the market place. The town was to become 'Eatanswill' in Dickens' Pickwick Papers. Two towns dominate the county of Suffolk, Ipswich and Bury St. Edmunds. The latter an ancient town, was a Saxon settlement when the bones of St. Edmund the Martyr were brought to the monastery of Beodricsworth in 910AD. Edmund was the last king of East Anglia, and was killed by the Danes for refusing to deny Christianity. His shrine became a major centre of pilgrimage during the Middle Ages. Except for its two gateways the abbey is now a ruin, but two fine fifteenth century churches survive, St. James', being now the cathedral of the diocese of St. Edmundsbury and Ipswich. It was at the great altar of the abbey in 1214 that the Barons swore to force King John to honour the Magna Carta. There is a great deal of wonderful

seventeenth and eighteenth century architecture in the town. Cupola House and Angel Corner being excellent examples. The lovely rivers Lark and Linnet flow into the city from delightful countryside, at one time almost exclusively hunting land. At nearby Newmarket is the historic centre of English horseracing, and the home of the Jockey Club. It was Charles II who established the sport here, although horses had been raced here since the times of James I. The National Stud was formed at Newmarket in 1967.

Ipswich is the county town and administrative centre of Suffolk, and there has been a settlement here from the Stone Age. King John granted the town its first charter in 1200. Its position as a safe harbour at the head of the estuary of the River Orwell ensured its place as an important port trading Suffolk cloth with the Continent. Ipswich was the birthplace of Cardinal Wolsey, who established a college here in 1536, although it was abandoned when the Cardinal fell from power, and all that now remains is the Wolsey Gateway. The visitor should certainly not miss the Ancient House in Buttermarket built in 1560 and sometimes known as Sparrowe's House, Its exterior is covered in Pargeting, a peculiarly East Anglian form of plaster decoration.

Suffolk has attracted a remarkably large number of writers...E.M.Forster, who wrote 'Billy Budd', M.R. James, who wrote that vintage ghost story 'Oh, Whistle, and I'll Come To You', Susan Hill, who wrote 'The Woman in Black'....I wonder why it inspires so many ghost stories!

Places to Visit

Bridge Cottage, *Flatford* ~ a thatched cottage on the banks of the River Stour, upstream from Flatford Mill. It has been restored and contains a display of the actual places that John Constable composed his paintings.

Euston Hall, *Euston* ~ built in the 1660's by the Earl of Arlington, it overlooks a lake. The house contains a fine art collection including portraits of Charles I and Charles II as well as paintings by Stubbs and Van Dyck.

Framlingham Castle, *Framlingham* ~ built in 1190 by the Earl of Norfolk, today little of the castle survives except for the curtain wall and its turrets.

Ickworth House, *near Bury St Edmunds* ~ an unusual house started in 1795 and based around a large rotunda with two wings. It is set in parkland landscaped by Capability Brown, and in the house is a collection of paintings, includings works by Gainsborough and Tiziano.

Little Hall, *Lavenham* ~ a timber framed house built in the 15th century. Now the headquarters of the Suffolk Preservation Society, it is a good example of life in the 15th century.

Melford Hall, *Long Melford* ~ a turreted Tudor mansion, which has changed little since 1578. It still has its original 18th century drawing room, Regency library and Victorian bedroom.

National Horseracing Museum, *Newmarket* ~ tells the story of the sport and contains many unusual exhibits such as the skeleton of Eclipse, one of the greatest horses, it was unbeaten in eighteen races in 1769 and 1790. There is also a large collection of sporting art.

Theatre Royal, *Bury St Edmunds* ~ built in 1819 by William Wilkins, it is a rare example of a late Georgian playhouse with pit, boxes and gallery.Throughout the year it presents a programme of professional drama, comedy, dance, music, pantomime and amateur work.

West Stow Counrty Park ~ set in one hundred and twenty five acres of country park is a recreated Anglo Saxon village. The village was built on the site of excavations made between 1965 and 1972 of a settlement dated 420-650 AD. Six buildings have been reconstructed using the same techniques, tools and materials that would have been used in the original village. ▼ *Willy Lott's Cottage, Flatford Mill*

SUFFOLK

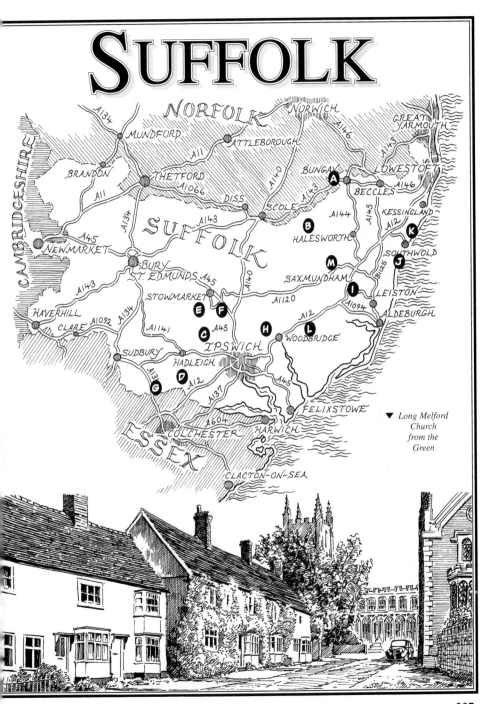

NORFOLK

NORWICH

GREAT YARMOUTH

MUNDFORD

ATTLEBOROUGH

CAMBRIDGESHIRE

BRANDON

THETFORD

A1066

DISS

SCOLE

BUNGAY

LOWESTOFT

A

BECCLES

KESSINGLAND

K

NEWMARKET

SUFFOLK

HALESWORTH

B

SOUTHWOLD

J

BURY ST. EDMUNDS

SAXMUNDHAM

M

LEISTON

I

HAVERHILL

STOWMARKET

E **F**

A1120

ALDEBURGH

CLARE

C

H

L

WOODBRIDGE

SUDBURY

IPSWICH

HADLEIGH

D

FELIXSTOWE

ESSEX

COLCHESTER

HARWICH

CLACTON-ON-SEA

▼ *Long Melford*
Church
from the
Green

Earsham Park Farm, Harleston Road, Earsham, Bungay, Suffolk NR35 2AQ   Nearest Road A143

Escape to the countryside. This family run delightful quiet and friendly farmhouse is set in a superb location overlooking the Waveney Valley. The rooms are spacious and elegantly furnished, but with comfort as a priority. They have extensive facilities from TV's, tea-trays, 4 poster available, easy chairs etc. to embroidered white linen and thick towels. Enjoy the lovely gardens and farm walks. Delicious local food. Many local places to visit Norwich, coast 1/2 hours drive away. AA 4Qs Selected. ETB 2 Crown Highly Commended.

Mrs Bobbie Watchorn
Tel/Fax: 01986 892180

B&B from £19pp, Dinner from £14.50, Rooms 1 twin, 2 double, all en-suite, No smoking, Children welcome, Pets by arrangement, Open all year, Map Ref A

Priory House, Priory Road, Fressingfield, Eye, Suffolk IP21 5PH   Nearest Road B1116

A warm welcome awaits visitors to this lovely 16th century farmhouse, set in an acre of secluded lawns and gardens. The comfortable bedrooms have tea/coffee facilities, and 2 rooms have private bathroom. Centrally heated. The house has a wealth of exposed beams, and is furnished with antique furniture. There is a guests lounge and pleasant dining room. Fressingfield is ideal for a peaceful relaxing holiday and as a touring base for Norwich, Bury St Edmunds, the Broads, coasts, historic buildings and gardens. Excellent food available in the village, 8 minutes walk. Colour brochure on request.

Mrs Rosemary Willis
Tel: 01379 586254

B&B from £23.50pp, Rooms 1 twin, 2 double, private bathrooms, Restricted smoking, Children from 10 years, Pets by arrangement, Open all year except Christmas & New Year, Map Ref B

Mulberry Hall, Burstall, Ipswich, Suffolk IP8 3DP   Nearest Road A1071

A lovely old farmhouse with log fires and good home cooking. The property, was once owned by Cardinal Wolsey during the 16th century. Henry VIII's coat of arms is over the large Inglenook fireplace in the attractive sitting room. Nicely situated in a small village 5 miles west of Ipswich and within easy access of the A12, A14, and A1071. The comfortable bedrooms are prettily furnished. Guests may also like to relax in the garden or play tennis.

Mrs Penny Debenham
Tel: 01473 652348

B&B from £18pp, Dinner £15, Rooms 1 single, 1 twin, 1 double, No smoking, Open all year except Christmas, Map Ref C

Sparrows, Shelley, Hadleigh, near Ipswich, Suffolk IP7 5RQ   Nearest Road A12, A14

Sparrows is a 15th century former farmhouse set in 2 acres of garden in unspoilt countryside. Grass tennis court, table tennis and bicycles for use by guests. Beach hut available in the summer by arrangement. Within easy reach of the Suffolk coast, Constable country and many other pretty Suffolk villages. Two golf courses within 3 miles and many first class pubs and restaurants in the immediate vicinity. Dinner provided by Inglenook fire-place in dining hall at 24 hours notice. Kingsize bed, private bathroom/ shower, colour TV, tea making facilities, central heating.

Mrs Rachel Thomas
Tel: 01206 337381

B&B from £20pp, Dinner from £12, Rooms 1 double in house, 1 double in annexe, Open all year except Christmas, Map Ref D

---

right, Pipps Ford, Needham Market - see page 341

Mill House, Water Run, Hitcham, Ipswich, Suffolk IP7 7LN   B1115 (Stowmarket to Hadleigh)

Mill House is a country house of the late Regency period. Set in 4 acres of beautiful grounds with peacocks, ducks, paddocks, stables tennis court and many nearby walks of natural beauty. Twin and double rooms include TV, central heating, vanity units and tea making facilities. Evening meals can be provided by arrangement. Self catering cottages are also available. Hitcham is ideally situated in the heart of Suffolk, surrounded by some of the most beautiful villages in the country and within easy reach of many market towns, and 'Constable' countryside.

Mrs Judith White
Tel: 01449 740315

B&B from £13pp, Dinner by arrangement from £6,
Rooms 1 twin, 2 double, 1 en-suite, Pets welcome,
Open all year, Map Ref E

Pipps Ford, Needham Market, near Ipswich, Suffolk IP6 8LJ   Nearest Road A14, A140

Fine and beautiful long, low, black and white timbered house parts of which date from 1540. A house with sloping floors, beams, inglenooks, with log fires, and historic associations. The cottagey sitting rooms are filled with antique furniture and china collections and have a wonderful atmosphere. Bedrooms are attractive with en-suite bathrooms and have tea/coffee making facilities, radio/clock alarms, and hair dryers. More bedrooms in the Stables.

Mrs Raewyn Hackett-Jones
Tel: 01449 760208
Fax: 01449 760561

B&B from £22.50pp, Dinner from £16, Rooms 4 double, 3 twin,
Restricted smoking, Pets by arrangement,
Open all year except Christmas & New Year, Map Ref F

see PHOTO on page 339

Hill House, Gravel Hill, Nayland, Suffolk CO6 4JB   Nearest Road A134

Comfortable 16th century timber framed "Hall House" set on edge of "Constable" village in a quiet location. Secluded garden with views over the valley. Good base for touring. Easy reach of Lavenham, Dedham and Flatford Mill. Golf course 1 mile. Excellent restaurants and good pub food locally. Easy access to A12. Convenient for Harwich and Felixstowe. Colchester 6 miles. 1 twin, 1 double, 1 family and 1 single room with private bathroom, tea/coffee making facilities, CTV, radio and central heating.

Mrs P Heigham
Tel: 01206 262782

B&B from £18pp, Rooms 1 single, 1 twin, 1 double, all with private bathrooms, No smoking, Children welcome over 10, No pets,
Open all year except Christmas & New Year, Map Ref G

Bowerfield House, Helmingham Road, Otley, Suffolk IP6 9NP   Nearest Road A14, A12, A140

Bowerfield House is a large, very handsome 17th century listed stable and barn conversion set in peaceful mature grounds with ponds, terraces and full size croquet lawn. The bedrooms with en-suite bathrooms are beautifully furnished with antiques, TV, radio and tea/coffee making facilities. There is a billiard room and drawing room with log fires and grand piano for guests to use. Lise, who is Danish, is the winner of several East Anglian B&B awards. Full English or Scandinavian breakfast. Otley is situated on the B1079.

Lise & Michael Hilton
Tel: 01473 890742
Fax: 01473 890059

B&B from £23pp, Dinner from £18 by request, Rooms 3 double with en-suite bathrooms, 1 four poster, No smoking, Minimum age 12,
Open mid March - end October, Map Ref H

see PHOTO opposite

---

left, Bowerfield House, Otley - see above for details

Sternfield House, Saxmundham, Suffolk IP17 1RS   Nearest Road A12

An exquisite Queen Anne country house set in delightful parkland and formal gardens of 25 acres. Former royal retreat. Swimming pool and tennis court. Luxurious en-suite facilities offer pampered accommodation to the discerning guest. Close to Aldeburgh (5 miles), Snape Maltings (1 mile), Minesmere and Southwold.

Mrs M Thornton
Tel: 0728 602252
Fax: 0728 604082

B&B from £35pp, Rooms 1 single, 1 twin, 6 double, all en-suite, Minimum age 12, No Pets, No smoking, Open all year except Christmas, Map Ref I

Ferry House, Walberswick, Southwold, Suffolk IP18 6TH   Nearest Road A12

Just 200m from the River Blyth estuary and seashore in this picturesque artists village. Ferry House was built to an unusual design for a playwright's summer residence. The fireplace surround in the dining room depicts scenes believed to be from one of his plays. Now this character home offers a warm welcome with stylish, well provided guest accommodation. Snape Maltings, Minsmere Bird Reserve and the Regency town of Southwold are within easy reach. Good pubs serving food are well within walking distance.

Mrs C Simpson
Tel/Fax: 01502 723384

B&B from £17.50pp-£20pp, Rooms 2 single, 1 double, No smoking, Children from 10, No pets, Open all year except Christmas & New Year, Map Ref J

Poplar Hall, Frostenden Corner, Frostenden, near Wangford, Suffolk NR34 7JA   Nearest Road A12

Peaceful and quiet yet only 3^1/2 miles from the lovely seaside town of Southwold. Poplar Hall is a 16th century thatched house in 1^1/2 acre garden. Walks abound in the area, either coastal or country. Walberswick, Dunwich, Aldburgh, Snape are just a short distance. Poplar Hall offers luxury accommodation with TV, tea/coffee making facilities and vanity units in all rooms. Guests library sitting dining rooms are a pleasure to be in whilst enjoying our famed breakfast of fresh fruit, local fish, sausages, bacon and home made preserves.

Anna & John Garwood
Tel: 01502 578549

B&B from £17pp, Rooms 1 single, 2 double, cot available, 1 en-suite, Restricted smoking, Children welcome, No pets, Open all year except Christmas, Map Ref K

The Old Rectory, Campsea Ashe, near Woodbridge, Suffolk IP13 0PU   Nearest Road A12

Peaceful Georgian rectory set in mature gardens. Relaxed and homely atmosphere. Log fires in drawing rooms and dining room. Spacious conservatory. Honesty bar. Fully licensed. All bedrooms en-suite with tea/coffee making facilities. Delicious home cooked food in restaurant. Outside diners welcome. Local home-made bread, variety of home-made marmalade, jam and local honey. Ideally situated for Snape, Woodbridge and coastal areas. Brochure available on request. Children welcome. Television and games in drawing room.

Stewart Bassett
Tel/Fax: 01728 746524

B&B from £27pp, Dinner from £18, Rooms, 1 single, 2 twin, 6 double, all en-suite, Restricted smoking, Children and pets welcome, Open all year except Christmas, Map Ref L

Grange Farm, Dennington, Woodbridge, Suffolk IP13 8BT

Nearest Road A1120

This is a charming house with a delightful hostess in a superb spot. The house dates from the 15th century but there has been a farmhouse on the site since the 13th century and the remains of an old moat now form a lake and ponds. There is a lovely garden with tennis court. The beamed guests' dining room and sitting room are very comfortable and beautifully furnished. The bread and marmalade are homemade. Situated on the Stowmarket - Yoxford Road.

Mrs E Hickson
Tel: 01986 798388
Mobile: 0374 182835

B&B from £20pp, Dinner from £10, Rooms 1 double, 3 twin, 1 single,
No smoking,
Open all year except Christmas, Map Ref M

"That's it, you won't see a better bit of butter anywhere!"

343

SURREY

Despite the massive development in commuterdom, this small county with the ever increasing population remains Britain's most wooded county. The glorious North Downs cut through the middle of Surrey, with the low-lying belt of the Thames valley in the north, the fresh heather covered moorlands of Bagshot Heath, Bisley, Chobham and Pirbright Commons in the west, and the fertile Surrey Weald in the south. Lacking a coastline, the county is certainly not without its wide stretches of water. Great Pond at Frensham covers over one hundred acres, and is popular for sailing and fishing. The Little Pond, something of a misnomer, is not much smaller than its neighbour. Both are renowned for birdwatching, as many rare species are to be seen here. Virginia Water, an artificial lake one and a half miles long in a lovely wooded setting, is a part of Windsor Great Park. Virginia Waters was laid out during the reign of George III by the landscape gardeners Paul and Thomas Sandby. No one should leave the vicinity of Virginia Water without visiting Runnymede, that meadow on the south bank of the River Thames just downstream from Windsor, where in 1215 King John signed

Magna Carta. The American Bar Association built the Magna Carta Memorial, a domed Classical temple at the foot of Cooper's Hill. Overlooking the memorial on the top of the hill is the Air Forces Memorial, commemorating the twenty thousand, four hundred and fifty six Allied airmen who died in World War II and have no known grave. The view from the monument is quite superb, covering seven counties and Windsor Castle. Following the assassination of John F. Kennedy in 1963, an acre of ground here was given to the people of America by the people of Britain as a memorial to their president. At the beautiful village of Shere under the North Downs, and with glorious views across the Weald is the Silent Pool. Legend tells that a country girl was startled by King John while she was bathing and drowned in its dark waters.

Guildford, the county town of Surrey though not the administrative centre, has held on to much of its Georgian character. Many of the Georgian facades cover even older buildings. The fine seventeenth century facade of the Guildhall actually conceals a Tudor building. The Guildhall is famous for amongst other things its clock, which projects

over the town's steep High Street. The cathedral, designed by Sir Edward Maufe in a simplified Gothic style has a red brick exterior, and stands on a hilltop north-west of the town. The University of Surrey occupies sites by the cathedral and north of the town. Guildford is a fine holiday centre and is within easy reach of Sutton Place, an Elizabethan mansion, and one of the first non-fortified manors in Britain. Losely House, another Elizabethan mansion has panelling from Henry VIII's Nonesuch Palace; Hatchlands has Robert Adams interior decoration and for plant lovers there is Wisley, the gardens of the Royal Horticultural Society, containing many specialist sections laid out for fruit, herbs, hedges and ground cover, and three gardens showing what can be achieved in small areas and one for the elderly or disabled. Nearby is Ripley, a fine old coaching village of quaint half-timbered houses. Godalming is another place with superb half-timbered Tudor buildings. The famous Charterhouse School is on the outskirts of the town, and Winkworth Arboretum is only three miles to the east, ninety-five acres of rare trees and shrubs, with a lake and spectacular views across the North Downs. North of Guildford is Bagshot Heath, once notorious for its highwaymen. To the North-west is the Royal Military Academy of Sandhurst, while to the south-east is Bisley Camp, which has been since 1890 the headquarters of the National Rifle Association. The most prestigious event at Bisley is the Queen's Prize.

Dorking is sited in some of the finest scenery in Surrey, standing where the Roman Stane

Street crosses the ancient Pilgrim's Way. The town is surrounded by hills. Leith Hill at nine hundred and sixty five is the highest point in south-east England. Twelve counties can be seen from its summit on a clear day. Leith Hill Place was the home of composer Ralph Vaughan Williams. The Burford Bridge Hotel on the River Mole, is where Lord Nelson and Lady Hamilton said their final farewell in 1800. Box Hill named after the ancient box trees which grew here, is one of the most popular viewpoints in southern England...a glorious area for walking and picnics. North is Epsom, well known as a health resort after the discovery in 1618 of mineral springs, which later led to the manufacture of Epsom Salts, but today Epsom is renowned for its racecourse, home to the Oaks and Derby. Racing has been a permanent feature here since 1730. A bridleway extends along the old Roman road to Box Hill. Esher, a pleasant Georgian town surrounded by lovely countryside, including the National Park Claremont Woods with its lake. Close by is Sandown Park Racecourse, opened in 1875. The Whitbread Gold Cup, a steeplechase established here in 1957 was one of the first examples in Britain of the commercial sponsorship of sport.

Surrey was a magnet to literary names from way back. To Jane Austen, Box Hill was familiar ground, Sheridan too; Keats immensely enjoyed his visits. E.M. Forster, Lord Tennyson and George Meredith revelled in the peace and tranquillity of this lovely region....little wonder holiday makers follow in their footsteps.

Places to Visit

Claremont Landscape Garden, *Esher* ~ one of the earliest surviving English landscape gardens, carefully restored to its former glory with lake, island with pavillion, grotto and avenues.

Hampton Court, *East Molesey* ~ it was not originally a royal palace, as it was built by Cardinal Wolsey, Henry VIII's most powerful minister, but the display of power and wealth was not to the king's liking, so the Cardinal gave the palace to the king. The palace was remodelled by Christopher Wren for William and Mary. Many of the state rooms are decorated with furniture, paintings and tapestries taken from the Royal Collection.

Hatchlands Park, *near Guildford* ~ built in 1758 for Admiral Boscawen with interors by Robert Adam. It has been extensively restored and now houses the Cobbe collection of keyboard instruments, paintings and furniture. The garden was designed by Gertrude Jekyll.

Kew Gardens, *Richmond* ~ three hundred acres of landscaped gardens devoted to the propagation, study and display of plants.

Polesden Lacey, *near Dorking* ~ a peaceful country estate surrounded by trees. The elegant Regency house was furnished in Edwardian times by the Hon. Mrs Greville. Lovely walled garden with walks through the North Downs.

Oakhurst Cottage, *near Godalming* ~ a small 16th century timber framed cottage. It has been restored and furnished as a simple cottager's dwelling with delightful cottage garden.

Runnymede, *Egham* ~ one hundred and eighty eight acres of historic meadows where King John sealed the Magna Carta in 1215. One hundred and ten acres of woodland on Cooper's Hill overlook the meadows. There are also memorials dedicated to the Magna Carta, John F. Kennedy and the Air Forces.

Winkworth Arboretum, *Godalming* ~ planned and planted as a woodland in the 1930's, it covers over one hundred acres and has two lakes and many trees, shrubs and plenty of wildlife including butterflies and moths.

Farnham Castle
▼

346

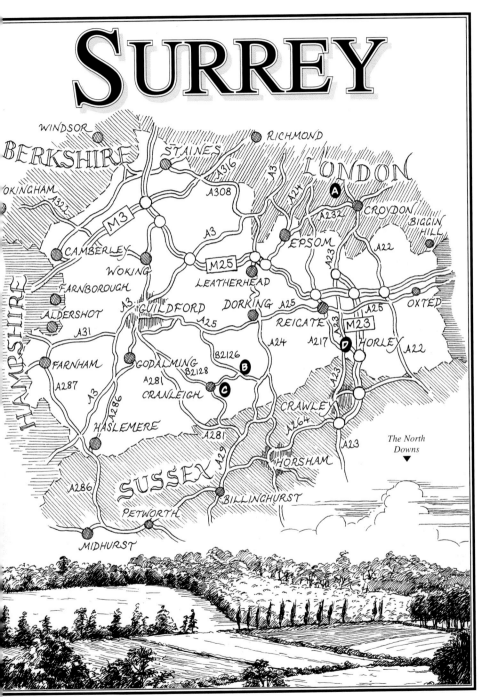

SURREY

WINDSOR
BERKSHIRE
RICHMOND
STAINES
OKINGHAM
A322
A316
A3
LONDON
A24
A308
A232
CROYDON
BIGGIN HILL
A3
M3
CAMBERLEY
EPSOM
A22
WOKING
M25
A23
FARNBOROUGH
LEATHERHEAD
A3
GUILDFORD
DORKING
A25
OXTED
ALDERSHOT
A25
A25
REIGATE
A31
A24
A217
M23
FARNHAM
A25
HORLEY
A22
GODALMING
B2126
A287
A281
B2128
A3
CRANLEIGH
A286
CRAWLEY
HASLEMERE
A281
A64
HORSHAM
A23

The North
Downs
▼

A286
SUSSEX
A29
A281
BILLINGHURST
PETWORTH
MIDHURST

Foxholm, Redhill Road, Cobham, Surrey KT11 1EF   **Nearest Road M25,J10/A245/A3**

Foxholm is a grade II listed Victorian Gothic country house furnished with antiques and set in 14 acres of woodland garden planted with azaleas, camelias and rhododendrons. Within 2 miles of M25 Junction 10, with the A3 giving easy access to London by road or rail. Close to Royal Horticultural Society Gardens at Wisley, Painshill Park, Hampton Court, Windsor and both Heathrow and Gatwick. Good food available at lakeside golf club opposite.

Mrs Lynn Legget
Tel: 01932 867961
Fax: 01932 866310

B&B from £25pp, Rooms, 1 twin with private bath, 1 single with private shower, No smoking, Children over 14 years No pets, Open all year except Christmas and New Year, Map Ref A

High Edser, Shere Road, Ewhurst, Cranleigh, Surrey GU6 7PQ   **Nearest Road A25**

High Edser is an early 16th century farmhouse set in an area of outstanding natural beauty surrounded by its own land. A tennis court is available for guests' use. There is a guests' lounge with television and all rooms have tea/coffee making facilities. Within easy reach of Guildford, Dorking and Horsham and many National Trust properties and other places of interest are close by. Gatwick and Heathrow are approximately 30 minutes drive. We welcome children and dogs by prior arrangement

Mrs C A Franklin-Adams
Tel: 01483 278214
Fax: 01483 278200

B&B from £20pp, Rooms 1 twin, 2 double, Restricted smoking, Children welcome, Pets by arrangement, Open all year except New Year, Map Ref B

North Breache Manor, Ewhurst, Surrey GU6 7SN   **Nearest Road A24, A39**

North Breache Manor surrounded by its estate has a warm and relaxed atmosphere with magnificent views over its park. The interior of the house has been totally modernised to a very high standard and each attractively furnished bedroom has its own en-suite bathroom. There are extensive gardens with about 2 acres of lawns, many shrubs and some fine specimen trees. There is a practice golf course, tennis court and heated outdoor swimming pool. We have horses and riding can be arranged for guests.

Mrs Peter Nutting
Tel: 01483 277328
Fax: 01483 276055

B&B from £40pp, Rooms 3 double, Restricted smoking, No pets, Open all year, Map Ref C

The Lawn Guest House, 30 Massetts Road, Horley, Surrey RH6 7DE   **Nearest Road A23**

The Lawn Guest House is an attractive Victorian house set in pretty gardens just 1 1/2 miles from Gatwick airport and 2 minutes walk from Horley town centre where there are pubs, restaurants, shops and a main line railway station to London and the south coast. The comfortable bedrooms have tea/coffee making facilities and colour TV, all are en-suite. A full English breakfast is served and/or a healthy alternative of fruit, yoghurt, muesli, etc. For the comfort of all guests this is a totally non smoking home, with plenty of car parking space.

Carole & Adrian Grinsted
Tel: 01293 775751
Fax: 01293 821803

B&B from £22.50pp, Rooms 4 twin, 1 double, 2 family, all en-suite, No smoking, Children welcome, Pets welcome, Open all year, Map Ref D

It was a summer evening,
Old Kaspar's work was done,
And he before his cottage door
Was sitting in the sun.
Robert Southey

SUSSEX

The South Downs form the backbone of Sussex, bsandwiched between the forest ridge composed of St. Leonards Forest, Ashdown Forest and the Sussex Weald, and the narrow coastal strip. Now almost entirely built up, this 'Sussex by the Sea' has long been a magnet to the holiday maker...and with very good reason the many amenities, historical associations and excellent weather records ensure a regular and loyal clientele. Eastbourne, arguably the Queen of the Sussex coast, has a remarkable natural beauty, and is truly a floral town. Motcombe Gardens, containing the pond which was the town's first reservoir, and through which flows the Bourne which gave the town its name, Hampden Park, Princes Park, and Manor Gardens are a blaze of colour in season. The famous Carpet Gardens on the sea front have charmed visitors for over a hundred years. Eastbourne has been a fashionable seaside resort since the late eighteenth century when the children of George III holidayed here. As you would expect the town offers all the amenities of a first class resort, excellent shops, theatres, restaurants, nightclubs, a magnificent pier and the Grand Parade Bandstand, featuring the traditional military and brass bands. Drusillas Zoo Park at Alfriston is a great attraction to adults as well as children.

The South Downs is a designated Area of Outstanding Beauty and part of the Heritage Coast, a region of glorious walks and breathtaking sights. At Beachy Head, a short distance south of Eastbourne, the spectacular chalk cliffs rise to over five hundred feet giving fine views to the distant Royal Sovereign light tower. Between Cuckmere Haven and Beachy Head the South Downs end in seven dramatic chalk cliffs known as the Seven Sisters. At the Seven Sisters Country Park, there are 700 acres of unspoiled countryside, through which flows the River Cuckmere. To the north is the intriguing Long Man of Wilmington, a striking two hundred and twenty six feet high Saxon figure, etched into the chalk hillside overlooking the picturesque village of Wilmington with its Benedictine monastery. To the east of Eastbourne is lovely Pevensey, an historic village of quaint houses dominated by the ruins of Pevensey Castle...the first castle to be built by William the Conqueror on English soil in 1066.

Hastings, like its sister Eastbourne, can boast a pleasant summer climate and a host of seaside attractions. Hastings is an ancient town and part of its particular attraction is its Old Town where, built between the East and West Hills, the Tudor houses are crushed cheek by jowl. A singular delight is charming Sinnock Square between Bourne Street and the High Street, the haunt of artists. Fine Georgian houses with wrought iron balconies border elegant Wellington Square, and another Georgian attraction is Pelham Crescent built by the Earl of Chichester in 1824. Here St. Mary-in-the-Castle is worth a visit - a natural spring which once fed the baptismal font flows through the building. The West Hill Cliff Railway, sliced through a natural cave in the rock leads to the castle at the very heart of Hastings.

This is certainly the area for castles. At nearby Battle, where in fact the Battle of Hastings actually took place, are the ruins of the abbey William the Conqueror vowed he would build here if he was victorious. The high altar marks the spot where Harold is said to have fallen. Only the gatehouse of 1338 and the east range of the abbey are intact, but there is an interesting battlefield trail and audiovisual display detailing the story of the battle. Twelve miles inland from Hastings is the fourteenth century Bodiam Castle, surrounded by a wide moat filled with water lilies...a wonderful medieval fortress in a perfect setting. At Herstmonceux Castle is a fascinating hands-on science centre, but the pride of the castle are the spectacular Elizabethan gardens. The visitor to this area should try not to miss Northiam, a pretty country village with a station on the Kent and East Sussex Railway line - a treat for steam train enthusiasts. Virtually a part of Hastings is St.Leonards-on-Sea, a relatively modern town by comparison...a town built in the early nineteenth century by James Burton in a charming mixture of styles, elegantly laid out in squares with beautiful gardens. Sir Henry Rider Haggard lived at the top of St. Leonards Gardens in North Lodge.

Of course no visitor to Sussex could miss that other seaside resort, Brighton, the oldest of British seaside resorts. Here the Prince Regent, later to become George IV, initiated the fashion for seaside holidays and bathing and here that he built his Royal Pavilion, an oriental extravaganza with one of the most extraordinary interiors in Europe. The Lanes survive from Brighton's humble fishing village days, now a very upmarket warren of antique shops, galleries and pavement cafes. Lewes, north-east of Brighton is an interesting town with some fine architecture, while Ditchling Beacon gives splendid views across open country.

Sussex's longest river the Arun rises in St. Leonards Forest, cutting through the South Downs by Arundel to the sea at Littlehampton. Arundel, a handsome town is an excellent centre for touring, its main street climbing up to the medieval-Victorian castle home of the Dukes of Norfolk. To the north of the town is a large Wildfowl Reserve.

Few counties can claim so much to see in so small an area....rich in history, blessed with glorious countryside and a pleasant climate, the visitor can only regret that in a limited stay, so much must be missed out.

Places to Visit

Arundel Castle, *Arundel* ~ a hilltop castle surrounded by castellated walls. The castle was originally built by the Normans, but only the keep remains. It was rebuilt in 1643 and restored in the 19th century.

Bodiam Castle, *Rye* ~ a late 14th century castle surround by a wide moat. It was built as a defence against an anticipated invasion by the French, which attack never came though the castle was damaged in the Civil war. It has been uninhabited ever since, the roof was restored in 1919 by Lord Curzon who gave the castle to the nation.

Brighton Pavillion, Brighton ~ a lavish Oriental palace by John Nash, built for George IV. It was completed in 1822, and the exterior has remained largely unchanged. Queen Victoria sold the Pavillion to the town of Brighton in 1850.

Nymans Garden, *Haywards Heath* ~ thirty acres of rare and beautiful tress, shrubs and plants collected from around the world. The garden features a walled garden with fountain and hidden sunken garden. The ruins of the house overlook the lawns and many woodland walks start from the garden.

Petworth House and Park, *Petworth* ~ set in seven hundred acres of park, landscaped by Capability Brown. There are over three hundred paintings on display including works by Turner, Van Dyck, Gainsborough, Reynolds and Blake. Also on display are collections of ancient and neo classical sculpture, furniture and wood carvings by Grinling Gibbons.

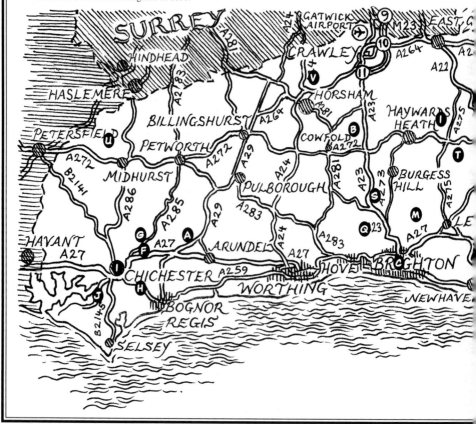

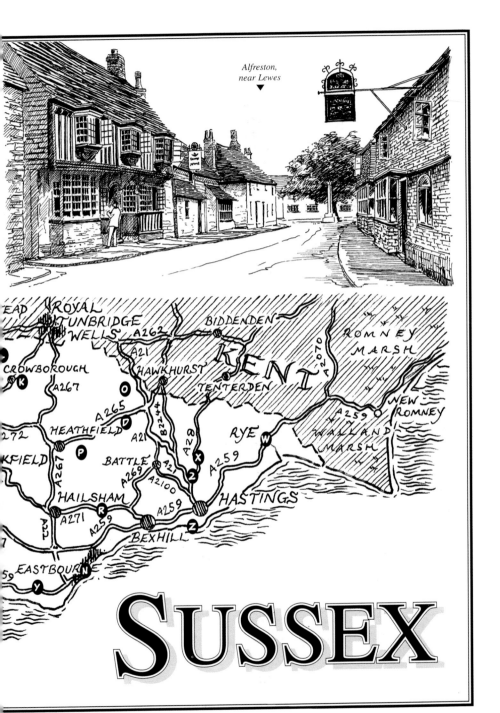

Alfreston,
near Lewes
▼

SUSSEX

Mill Lane House, Slindon, Arundel, Sussex BN18 0RP Nearest Road A27, A29

A mainly 17th Century house with coach house, a large garden and magnificent views to the coast; situated in a beautiful National Trust village on the South Downs. Direct access to walking on the Downs; superb bird watching locally and at nearby reserves. Within easy reach of Arundel Castle; Goodwood; Chichester with Roman Palace, cathedral and festival theatre. Good pubs within easy walking distance. Central heating, log fires. All rooms are en-suite and have television. 2 rooms have wheelchair access. Evening meals by arrangement.

Peter & Sarah Fuente
Tel: 01243 814440

B&B from £20pp, (weekly terms), Dinner by arrangement from £10.25, Rooms 1 single, 2 twin, 3 double, 1 family, all en-suite, Children welcome, Pets by arrangement, Open all year, Map Ref A

Timbers Edge, Longhouse Lane, off Spronketts Lane, Warninglid, Bolney, Sussex RH17 5TE Nearest Road A272, A23

Beautiful Sussex country house set in over two acres of formal gardens surrounded by woodlands. Breakfast is served in the spacious conservatory overlooking the pool. Timbers Edge is located within easy reach of Gatwick (15 mins), Brighton (20 mins) and Ardingly (South of England Showground) (20 mins). The beautiful gardens of Nymans and Leonardslee (10 mins), Hickstead Show Jumping Ground (10 mins). All rooms have TV and beverage making facilities.

Sally & Geoffrey Earlam
Tel: 01444 461456

B&B from £20pp, Rooms 2 twin, 2 single,
No smoking,
Open all year, Map Ref B

Adelaide Hotel, 51 Regency Square, Brighton, East Sussex BN1 2FF Nearest Road A259

A warm welcome, friendly service, comfort and delicious food are the hallmarks of this elegant Grade II listed Regency Town House Hotel, modernised but retaining the charm of yester year. Centrally situated in Brighton's Premier sea-front square with NCP underground car park. There are 12 peaceful en-suite bedrooms, individually designed and furnished with co-ordinating decor, and equipped with phone, colour TV etc. A beautiful 4-poster bedroom available. Easy access to A23, 30 minutes to Gatwick. Discounts available when staying 2 nights or more.

Ruth & Clive Buxton
Tel: 01273 205286
Fax: 01273 220904

B&B from £32.50pp, Rooms, 3 single, 1 twin,
7 double, 1 family, all en-suite, Restricted smoking, Children welcome,
No pets, Open all year, Map Ref C

Trouville Hotel, 11 New Steine, Marine Parade, Brighton, Sussex BN2 1PB Nearest Road A23/A259

The Trouville is a grade II listed regency townhouse tastefully restored to a high standard, and situated in a delightful seafront square. The Marina Pavilion Lanes Conference Centre and many restaurants are all within walking distance. Accommodation is in nine attractive rooms each with colour TV and tea/coffee making facilities, en-suite and 4 poster rooms available. There are many places of interest in this area including National Trust Properties and gardens, beautiful Downland villages and countryside and historic towns and castle.

John & Daphne Hansell
Tel: 01273 697384

B&B from £19pp, Rooms 2 single, 1 twin, 5 double, 1 family,
most en-suite, Restricted smoking, Children welcome, No pets,
Open all year except Christmas, Map Ref C

Abelands Barn, Main House - see page 358

Abelands Barn - The Cow Shed

Glydwish Place, Fontridge Lane, Burwash, East Sussex TN19 7DG Nearest Road A265

Glydwish Place is a charming mock Tudor home. It is set on a lovely wooded site with far reaching views. There are four attractively furnished rooms which have been created for your comfort and relaxation, two of which include executive 7ft sq beds. Also available is a beautiful self-contained wing for self catering (sleeps four). The surrounding countryside is a delight with numerous interesting places to visit including many National Trust Houses/Gardens. Lovely walks and excellent pubs in surrounding villages. Facilities available sauna, solarium, gamesroom, gymnasium.

Mr & Mrs Collins
Tel: 01435 882869
Fax: 01435 882749

B&B single room from £20, double rooms from £45, Rooms 1 single, 4 double, 2 en-suite, 2 private, No smoking, Children over 15 years, No pets, Open all year, Map Ref D

Ashlands Cottage, Burwash, Sussex TN19 7HS Nearest Road A265

Pretty period cottage in quiet Wealden farmland within designated area of outstanding natural beauty. Glorious views, gardens and picnic spots. Kipling's 'Batemans' only 5 minutes walk across the fields and many more places of interest nearby. Ideal for walking, touring, etc. The bedrooms are comfortable and welcoming and there is a sitting room where guests may relax.

Mrs Nesta Harmer
Tel: 01435 882207

B&B from £17pp, Rooms 2 twin, Restricted smoking, Minimum age 12, Open all year, Map Ref D

The Brufords, 66 The Street, Boxgrove, near Chichester, West Sussex PO18 0EE Nearest Road A27

This turn of the century village house with quiet rear annex accommodation, offers one twin and one four poster en-suite bedrooms, each with remote control colour TV's, radio/alarm clocks, trouser press plus tea/coffee making facilities. Approached through the quiet garden with its own private breakfast room with pay-phone. This accommodation is renowned for it's sumpitous English breakfast. Both rooms feature beamed and flint walls, and there is off road parking from 4 cars. Excellent pubs and restaurants within walking distance.

Allan & Silma Bruford
Tel: 01243 774085

B&B from £20pp, Rooms 1 twin, 1 double, both en-suite, No smoking, children or pets, Open all year, Map Ref F

The Old Store Guest House, Stane Street, Halnaker, Chichester, PO18 0QL Nearest Road A285, A27

An impressive 18th century Grade II listed house adjoining the Goodwood Estate. All bedrooms at The Old Store Guest House have en-suite shower rooms, colour tv, tea/coffee making facilities, hair dryer and trouser press. A full English breakfast is served in a charming breakfast room. Guests lounge and car park. Excellent pub/restaurant within walking distance. Well situated for Goodwood House, Goodwood racecourse and Chichester Festival Theatre. Also close by are Petworth House, Arundel Castle, Fishbourne Roman Palace and, at Portsmouth, Nelson's Flag ship The Victory.

Robert Grocott
Tel/Fax: 01243 531977

B&B from £27.50pp, Rooms 1 single, 3 twin, 2 double, 1 family, all en-suite, Restricted smoking, Pets by prior arrangement, Open all year except Christmas & New Year, Map Ref G

Hatpins, Old Bosham - see page 358 for details

Sussex

see PHOTO on page 355

Abelands Barn, Merston, Chichester, West Sussex PO20 6DY   Nearest Road A259

A traditional 1850 Sussex Barn converted into a beautiful, interesting, family home. It provides spacious and flexible accommodation, with all facilities. A period, flint, outbuilding contains a large, en-suite bedroom, and the imposing main Barn offers a ground floor 'family' suite of two bedrooms, bathroom and 'snug'. Attractive gardens overlook the lovely South Downs, and a courtyard offers secure, overnight, parking. Abelands Barn is situated two miles from Chichester, with many local attractions including Goodwood, Arundel, the coast and prestigious Festival Theatre. ETB 2 Crowns Highly Commended.

Mike & Gaile Richardson	B&B from £22.50pp, Rooms 1 twin, 2 double, 1 family, en-suite,
Tel: 01243 533826	Children welcome, No pets,
Fax: 01243 555533	Open all year except Christmas and New Year, Map Ref H

Chichester Lodge, Oakwood, Chichester, Sussex PO18 9AL   Nearest Road A27, B2178

Chichester Lodge is a charming 1840 Gothic Lodge with wonderful interior design and antique furnishings. Lots of flag stone floors, polished wood, beautiful Gothic windows, every attention to detail. Wood burning stove in hall way. There are two acres of very pretty garden with hedges and honeysuckle and hidden corners. The en-suite bedrooms are comfortable with nice decorations and furnishings and all rooms have TV. There is also a garden room with wood burning stove for winter evening. Nearby activities include fishing, golf, theatre and Goodwood.

	B&B from £20 pp, Rooms 3 double, 1 single, all en-suite,
Jeanette Dridge	No smoking, Minimum age 14,
Tel: 01243 786560	Open all year, Map Ref I

---

see PHOTO on page 357

Hatpins, Bosham Lane, Old Bosham, Chichester, Sussex PO18 8HG   Nearest Road A259

Mary Waller, a former designer of hats and wedding dresses, has combined her talents with a natural flair for decorating to transform her home into delightful bed and breakfast accommodation. Enhancing the decor is the warmth of Mary's hospitality. Bosham is an appealing coastal town and Old Bosham brims with charm and it is fun to wander down to the waterfront and explore the tiny lanes. Also nearby are Portsmouth and the cathedral city of Chichester with its lovely harbour. A few miles inland is Downland Museum a collection of very old cottages and buildings. Honeymoon couples welcome. ETB Listed.

Mrs Mary Waller	B&B from £25pp, Rooms 4 with en-suite,
Tel: 01243 572644	No smoking, Children welcome, No pets,
Fax: 01243 572644	Open all year, Map Ref J

Laurel Tree Farmhouse, Boars Head, Crowborough, East Sussex TN6 3HD   Nearest Road A26

see PHOTO opposite

Grade II listed farmhouse with beams and inglenooks. 16th century charm, situated in its own grounds, adjacent to a fruit farm. Off street parking. An area of outstanding natural beauty. Tea/coffee making facilities in both bedrooms. Private guest lounge with TV. Close by are Great Dixter, Sheffield Park, Sissinghurst Garden, Hever Castle, Leeds Castle, Scotney Castle and many more attractions. Ideal for National Trust properties. Local pub for evening meals is within easy walking distance. ETB 2 Crown Highly Commended. A home from home.

	B&B from £20pp, Rooms 2 twin, 1 en-suite, 1 private facilities,
Carol Carlile	No smoking, Children over 10, No pets,
Tel/Fax: 01892 652061	Open all year except Christmas & New Year, Map Ref K

---

       right, Laurel Tree Farmhouse, Crowborough - see above for details

Lye Green House, Lye Green, Crowborough, East Sussex TN6 1UU Nearest Road B2188

Lye Green House is an elegant Sussex country house offering spacious, tastefully decorated accommodation. The en-suite bedrooms are large and luxurious with king size beds for comfort. The beautiful six acre garden was laid out in Edwardian times. Clipped yew hedges divide the nine gardens, each with their own style including a potage/kitchen garden and some huge herbaceous borders. A lime walk leads to the natural water gardens set in woodland and a rowing boat and fishing rods are available. ETB De-Luxe.

Ann Hynes
Tel: 01892 652018

**B&B £27.50pp, Rooms 1 twin en-suite, 1 double en-suite,
1 double with private bathroom, No smoking, No children, No pets,
Open all year except Christmas & New Year, Map Ref L**

Longcroft House, Beacon Road, Ditchling, Sussex BN6 8UZ Nearest Road A23, A27, B2112

Longcroft House is situated near the foot of Ditchling Beacon in 2 acres of garden and paddock, between the vineyard and the centre of the village, in easy walking distance of all amenities, and easy access to reach the main roads with Gatwick. Longcroft is a beautiful house built in traditional style and offers a relaxing and comfortable stay in one of three rooms all with private or en-suite facilities & TV. Guests may chose a 4-poster bed. Beautifully decorated throughout, and there is a lounge where guests may relax. Ditchling with its ancient buildings and charm has much to offer visitors.

Robert & Helen Scull
Tel: 01273 842740

**B&B from £22.50pp, Dinner from £18, Supper £10, Rooms 1 twin,
2 double, all en-suite, No smoking, Children by arrangement,
Open all year, Map Ref M**

Brayscroft Private Hotel, 13 South Cliff Avenue, Eastbourne, Sussex BN20 7AH Nearest Road A259

Brayscroft is an Edwardian family house typical of the fine architecture which makes Eastbourne one of Englands's most attractive towns. All rooms have their own facilities and there is a lounge with TV. The seafront is minutes away and provides views towards Beachy Head. A seaside holiday wouldn't be complete without a pier, Carpet Gardens, bandstand, deckchairs and ice cream - Eastbourne has them all. For those who enjoy the outdoors, the walks around Beachy Head and the Seven Sisters can be accessed from the hotel or a short car journey will take you to some pretty Sussex villages. ETB Highly Commended.

The Manager
Tel: 01323 647005

**B&B from £21pp, Rooms 1 single, 2 twin, 2 double, all en-suite,
Children and pets by arrangement, No smoking,
Open all year, Map Ref N**

King John's Lodge, Sheepstreet Lane, Etchingham, East Sussex TN19 7AZ Nearest Road A21

Historic listed house on Kent/Sussex border in over 4 acres of beautiful gardens. Second sitting room for guests with TV, easy parking and tea/coffee facilities in bedrooms. Very attractive bedrooms with furniture of the various periods of the house, mainly Jacobean, Elizabethan and Victorian. Legend has it that King John of France was held hostage in this house. Between Tunbridge Wells and Rye with Batemans, Dixter, Sissinghurst, Pashley, nearby. Also Leeds, Bodiam, Hever castles. Glynde-bourne, Battle, Chartwell and trains to London. Beautiful place.

Jill & Richard Cunningham
Tel: 01580 819232
Fax: 01580 819562

**B&B from £30pp-£35pp, Dinner by arrangement, Rooms 1 twin, 2 double,
1 family, all en-suite or private, Restricted smoking, Children from 7,
No pets, Open all year, Map Ref O**

---

right, ***Great Crouch's, near Heathfield - see page 363 for details***

Great Crouch's, Rushlake Green, near Heathfield, East Sussex TN21 9QD   Nearest Road B2096

This Grade II country house is set in the conservation village of Rushlake Green, an area of outstanding natural beauty, in the heart of rural East Sussex. Oak beams, original doors and antiques furnish the house, whilst the bedrooms, both with en-suite or private bathroom, have TV, magazines, fruit, etc. One bedroom in adjacent Sussex barn is a small suite. 15 acres of garden and pasture, an indoor heated swimming pool, plus a warm and friendly welcome, make this a great place to relax and unwind.

see PHOTO on page 361

Richard & Ruth Thomas
Tel: 01435 830145

**B&B from £27.50pp, Rooms 1 twin, 1 double, both en-suite,
No smoking, children or pets,
Open all year except Christmas & New Year, Map Ref P**

Frylands, Wineham, Henfield, Sussex SN5 9BP   Nearest Road A272, A23

Frylands is a half timbered farmhouse dating from the 16th century which has been carefully restored. It is set in 250 acres of farm and woodlands with good coarse fishing in ponds and a stretch of the River Adur. There is a large garden with outdoor swimming pool (heated in summer) and available to guests. All bedrooms have central heating, 1 with private facilities, wash basins and facilities for making hot drinks. There is a separate guests' bathroom. Transport to and from Gatwick airport can be provided at a reasonable price. EMail: fowler@pavilion.co.uk

Mrs Sylvia Fowler
Tel: 01403 710214
Fax: 01403 711449

**B&B from £18pp
Rooms 1 twin, 1 double en-suite, 1 family,
Open all year, Map Ref Q**

Cleavers Lyng Country Hotel, Church Road, Herstmonceux, Hailsham, Sussex BN27 1QJ   A271

Photogenic Cleavers Lyng is a small family run hotel adjacent to the west gate of Herstmonceux Castle dating from 1577 with oak beams and inglenook fireplace. Panoramic views. Good home cooking in traditional English style and full English breakfast and lunches served daily. Fully licensed with lounge bar serving fine wines and draught beers. TV lounge. All bedrooms are fully en-suite, centrally heated and have tea/coffee making facilities. Special attraction - badger watch!

see PHOTO opposite

Sally & Douglas Simpson
Tel: 01323 833131
Fax: 01323 833617

**B&B from £22.50pp, Dinner from £12.50,
Rooms 4 double, 3 twin,
Open all year, Map Ref R**

Clayton Wickham Farmhouse, Belmont Lane, Hurstpierpoint, Sussex BN6 9EP   Nearest Road A23

A warm welcome awaits you in this beautifully restored 16th century farmhouse with masses of beams and huge inglenook in the drawing room. Set in 3 acres of splendid gardens with tennis court and lovely views. Enviably quiet and secluded, yet conveniently situated for all transport facilities and places of interest. Rooms, including 1 4-poster en-suite, have all usual amenities and more, plus room service for early morning tea, etc. The genial hosts serve truly delicious food with a wide breakfast choice. An excellent candlelit dinner, or simpler meal, available on request.

Mike & Susie Skinner
Tel: 01273 845698
Fax: 01273 846546

**B&B from £21pp, Rooms 3 twin/double, 1 double en-suite, 1 single,
1 family, Restricted smoking, Children welcome, Pets by arrangement,
Open all year, Map Ref S**

---

left, Cleavers Lyng Country Hotel, Herstmonceux - see above for details   **363**

Fairseat House, Newick, near Lewes, East Sussex BN8 4PJ

Nearest Road A272

Fairseat House is an Edwardian period house on the edge of the picturesque village of Newick. Set in 4 acres of gardens and paddocks it enjoys rural aspects yet is easily accessible to main routes and Gatwick. Covered heated swimming pool. Open fires, chesterfields, ancestral portraits and antique books are just part of the charm Fairseat has to offer. A candlelit dinner with wine, or a relaxing light supper are available. Enjoy the luxury of a romantic night in the Edwardian room with its 4 poster bed and champagne breakfast. Close to Bluebell Railway and Glyndebourne. EMail: bnbuk@pavilion.co.uk

see PHOTO opposite

Carol & Roy Pontifex
Tel: 01825 722263
Fax: 01825 722263

B&B from £21pp, Dinner from £22.50, Rooms 3 double, 1 twin,
No smoking,
Open January - December, Map Ref T

Redford Cottage, Redford, Midhurst, West Sussex GU29 0QF

Nearest Road A272,A3,A286

A warm welcome in attractive country house dating back to the 16th century in a area of outstanding natural beauty. Comfortable rooms include a self-contained garden suite with own beamed sitting room and en-suite facilities. Rates include full English breakfast and tea/coffee making facilities, television provided in bedrooms and drawing room. Convenient to Midhurst, Petworth, Goodwood, Chichester and South Downs. Excellent walks and National Trust Properties within easy reach. An ideal retreat for a peaceful stay.

Caroline Angela
Tel/Fax: 01428 741242

B&B from £24pp, Rooms 1 twin, 1 double, 1 en-suite,
Restricted smoking, Children & pets welcome,
Open all year except Christmas & New Year, Map Ref U

Blackfriars, Friday Street, Rusper, Sussex RH12 4QA

Nearest Road A24, A264

Blackfriars is a charming country house, set in its own 4 acres of grounds. Although dating back to Jacobean days, Blackfriars offers every modern amenity including outdoor swimming pool during the summer months, games room and tennis court which guests may use. The comfortable bedrooms are equipped with tea/coffee making facilities. The guest cottage offers en-suite/private facilities and a sitting/TV area plus fridge for cold drinks. Convenient for Gatwick (15 mins), and Central London (40 mins). A warm welcome from Peggy & John awaits all guests.

Mrs Peggy Cooper
Tel/Fax: 01293 871263

B&B from £24.50pp,
Rooms 1 twin, 2 double, Children welcome, No pets,
Restricted smoking, Open all year except New Year, Map Ref V

Old Borough Arms, The Strand, Rye, East Sussex TN31 7DB

Nearest Road M20

A three hundred year old former sailors Inn now a family run licensed hotel situated adjacent to the cobbled streets and riverside walks of Rye. A flower decked patio overlooks the bustling Strand full of interesting antique centres. Breakfasts are served in our beamed dining room where a log fire is alight during the winter months. Via the M20 we are 40 minutes away from the Channel Tunnel and ferry ports of Dover and Folkestone and 11/2 hours from central London.

Mrs Cox
Tel/Fax: 01797 222128

B&B from £25pp, Dinner from £8.50, Rooms 2 single, 1 twin, 5 double,
1 family, all en-suite, Restricted smoking, Children welcome,
Pets by arrangement, Open all year except Christmas, Map Ref W

---

left, Fairseat House, near Lewes - see above for details

Little Orchard House, West Street, Rye, Sussex TN31 7ES

Nearest Road A259, A268

Little Orchard House is centrally situated in peaceful surroundings. Rebuilt in 1745, the house has been lovingly renovated over the years and retains it original fascinating character. All bedrooms are en-suite two with a 4 poster. There are personal antiques, paintings, books and bears throughout the house. There is a peaceful bookroom and a sitting room with an open fire. The generous breakfast provides as much as can be eaten at a time to suit you. Large walled garden available for guests' use. ETB Highly Commended.

Sara Brinkhurst
Tel: 01797 223831

B&B from £30pp, Rooms 2 double, 1 twin,
Minimum age 12,
Open all year, Map Ref W

Playden Cottage Guesthouse, Military Road, Rye, East Sussex TN31 7NY

Nearest Road A259

On the old Saxon Shore, less than a mile from Rye Town and on what was once a busy fishing harbour, there is now only a pretty cottage with lovely gardens, a pond and an ancient right of way. The sea has long receded and, sheltered by its own informal gardens, Playden Cottage looks over the River across sheep-studded Romney Marsh. ETB Highly Commended, AA Premier Selected and Recommended by "Which". It offers comfort, peace, a care for detail - and a very warm welcome.

Sheelagh Fox
Tel: 01797 222234

B&B from £25pp, Dinner from £12.00, Rooms, 2 twin, 1 double,
all en-suite, Restricted smoking, Children over 12 years, No pets,
Open all year, Map Ref W

Springetts Bed & Breakfast Goatham Lane, Broad Oak, Rye, East Sussex TN31 6EY

Nearest Road B2089

Springetts can be found in a quiet country lane off the B2089 between Rye and Battle. The accommodation offers comfortable en-suite rooms and a lounge, with colour TV, for guests; use. Tea/coffee making facilities are always available and breakfast is accompanied by a choice of homemade preserves. Visit the many National Trust houses and gardens in the are and explore the ancient Cinque Port town of Rye with its cobbled streets and historic buildings.

Mrs Angela Morris
Tel: 01424 882242

B&B from £17.50pp, Rooms 1 twin, 1 double, both en-suite,
No smoking, Children from 12, No pets,
Open March - October, Map Ref X

The Old Parsonage, West Dean, Alfriston, near Seaford, East Sussex BN25 4AL

Nearest Road A259

The Old Parsonage, built in 1280 and reputed to be the oldest continually inhabited small house in England, is situated in a hamlet in the Friston Forest, 1 mile from the Seven Sisters coastline. With chalk and flint walls 2¹/2 feet thick, massive oak beams, stone spiral staircases, log fires in guests' sitting room and extensive gardens, the house beautifully combines an antique setting with modern comforts. All bedrooms have private bathrooms and tea/coffee making facilities. Eastbourne, Brighton, Newhaven and Glyndebourne nearby.

Raymond & Angela Woodhams
Tel: 01323 870432

B&B from £25pp, Rooms 1 twin, 2 double, all private facilities,
No smoking, No pets, Minimum age 12,
Open all year except Christmas & New Year, Map Ref Y

*right, **Sliders Farm, Furners Green** - see page 368 for details*

Filsham Farm House, 111 Harley Shute Road, St Leonards on Sea, East Sussex TN38 8BY   A21/A27

An historic 17th Century listed Sussex farm house, with old beams and a large inglenook fireplace. Where a log fire burns at breakfast time in the winter months. The house is within easy reach of the town centre, sea and surroundings countryside and is furnished with an interesting collection of antiques to provide a high standard of accommodation. All rooms have TV sets and tea/coffee making facilities and there is ample private parking space at the rear of the house.

Barbara Yorke
Tel: 01424 433109
Fax: 01424 461061

B&B from £17.50pp, Rooms 1 twin, 2 double, 1 family, most en-suite, Restricted smoking, Pets restricted, Open all year except Christmas & New Year, Map Ref Z

Sliders Farm, Furners Green, near Uckfield TN22 3RT   Nearest Road A275

see PHOTO on page 367

Sliders Farm is quietly situated, surrounded by fields and woodland within walking distance of Sheffield Park Gardens, The Bluebell Railway and Ashdown Forest. Gatwick, Ardingly Showground, Glyndeboure and Brighton are easily accessible. London, 45 minutes by train. The 30 acres of grounds and gardens contain swimming pool, tennis court and fishing lakes. All bedrooms have TV and tea/coffee making facilities. The guests' lounge and oak panelled dining room both have large inglenook fireplaces. A 400 year old barn contains two self-catering units. Plenty of parking.

Jean & David Salmon
Tel: 01825 790258
Fax: 01825 790125

B&B from £19pp, Dinner from £14.00, Rooms 1 twin, 2 double, all en-suite, Restricted smoking, Children welcome, No pets, Open all year except Christmas, Map Ref 1

Little Lankhurst, Stonestile Lane, Westfield, East Sussex TN35 4PH   Nearest Road A21

Lovely views. Detached country house in an acre of garden. Set back from pretty lane. Very comfortable accommodation. Rural but a mile from village of Westfield and 2 miles from coast and historic Hastings, with delightful old town. Battle Abbey 6 miles. National Trust properties nearby include Bodiam and Batemans. Fascinating Rye 11 miles. Accommodation double bedroom with patio door onto balcony, en-suite shower room/wc, 5 foot bed and own entrance. Twin bedded room with vanity unit and private use of bathroom. Both rooms enjoy lovely views, colour TV and tea/coffe making facilities.

Mrs Bunny Chittenden
Tel: 01424 751138

B&B from £21pp, Rooms 2 double, 1 en-suite, 1 private bathroom, No smoking, children or pets, Open all year, Map Ref 2

Please mention
THE GREAT BRITISH
BED & BREAKFAST
when booking your accommodation

"Here tulips bloom as they are told"
Rupert Brooke

369

WARWICKSHIRE & WEST MIDLANDS

The great forest of Arden once covered a large proportion of the county northwest of the River Avon, which is now the highly industrialised and densely populated Metropolitan county of West Midlands, consisting of seven districts, Birmingham, Coventry, Dudley, Sandwell, Solihull, Walsall and Wolverhampton. South of Coventry, itself a fascinating and ancient city, with its war-ruined medieval cathedral blending with Basil Spence's innovative modern replacement, the visitor is faced with a wonderful selection of stately homes, palaces and manor houses. This is the very heart of England, and the holidaymaker could do worse than to select Warwick, the administrative centre as the base for touring the delights of the county...and there are many.

It is believed that Ethelfleda, a daughter of Alfred the Great, built the first fortress here in wood in 915AD, as a defence against the Danes. The great castle of Warwick the Kingmaker, with its two splendid towers, Caesar's Tower and Guy's Tower, dates from the early fourteenth century, and is best seen from Castle Bridge. The sumptuous and opulent interior is of the seventeenth and eighteenth centuries and is filled with treasures collected on the Grand Tour. The gardens are splendid, and include a re-created Victorian rose garden, the formal Peacock Gardens and a wonderful expanse of parkland. Warwick itself, although largely destroyed by a fire in 1694 contains some excellent buildings, particularly around High Street and Northgate Street. The Leycester Hospital, a

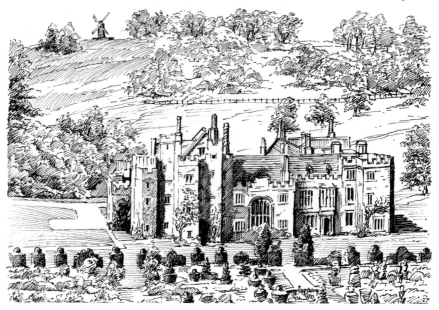

spectacular half-timbered building of the fourteenth to fifteenth century was built originally for religious guilds, but since 1571 has been an almshouse. Whatever the attractions of glorious Warwick, only a short distance south-west is Stratford-upon-Avon, the birthplace of William Shakespeare. The town is dedicated to the Bard, and monuments to him and to his family are all around, and conveniently close. Within a small radius is Shakespeare's birthplace; Hall's Croft, the home of his daughter and her husband Dr. John Hall; Anne Hathaway's Cottage...though hardly most people's idea of a cottage..., home of William's wife before her marriage; and Mary Arden's House, the home of Shakespeare's mother. The grand Memorial Theatre, the Stratford home of the Royal Shakespeare Company stands very attractively by the Avon. To the south of Stratford-upon-Avon is Compton Wynyates, a quite remarkable Tudor house, claimed by many to be the most beautiful house in England, and scarcely changed since it was built in 1520. It is said that it was in Charlecote Park, with its fine lime avenue approach, that the young William Shakespeare was caught poaching deer, and that it was his banishment to London which established his career and fortune. Only the gatehouse of the 1550 mansion remains unaltered, the rest being reconstructed in the nineteenth century. Upton House, a delightful William and Mary mansion surrounded by lovely grounds, is in the valley south-west of Edge Hill, at the foot of which the first major battle of the Civil War took place in 1642.

To the east of Warwick is Royal Leamington Spa on the River Leam, whose chalybeate and saline springs made it a fashionable place to take the waters from the late eighteenth century. Queen Victoria designated the town a Royal spa following her visit in 1838. The Royal Pump Room was opened in 1814. The Parade, a magnificent example of Georgian architecture dates from around 1820. Kenilworth Castle, situated on the western edge of the town, built in Norman times, but much altered by Queen Elizabeth I's favourite, the Earl of Leicester, is the venue for events featuring medieval pageantry, music and drama. Now mostly an impressive ruin, the sixteenth century northern gatehouse survives, as well as John of Gaunt's banqueting hall. Rugby, an important engineering centre since the arrival of the railway in the nineteenth century, is of course renowned for its public school founded in 1567. The school's most famous headmaster was Dr. Thomas Arnold, whose son the poet Matthew Arnold was a scholar at Rugby. Another well known scholar Thomas Hughes, described Dr. Arnold in his novel 'Tom Brown's Schooldays'.

Despite being known as the Black Country, there is a great deal to see and enjoy around the big cities, themselves no cultural backwater. There is Arbury Hall, the Gothic-style mansion with a large landscaped garden; Henley-in-Arden, a fine centre for walking by the River Alne; and Packwood House which has a quite remarkable seventeenth century garden of clipped yew trees depicting the Sermon on the Mount...the list is seemingly endless. Certainly the visitor would be well advised to plan their itinerary most carefully, as there are so many fascinating diversions.

WARWICKSHIRE &

Places to Visit

Charlecote Park, *Charlecote* ~ an Elizabethan mansion by Sir Thomas Lucy, set in parkland filled with deer and Jacob sheep. The grounds were landscaped by Capability Brown and the house built in 1558 was altered and enlarged in the 19th century with some building remaining unchanged. On display is a collection of ceramics, lacquerware and furniture, much of which was collected by 18th century eccentric William Beckford.

Shakespeare's Birthplace, *Stratford upon Avon* ~ bought for the nation in 1847 when it was a public house, it was converted back to Elizabethan style. The room is which Shakespeare was supposed to have been born has a window etched with visitors autographs including Sir Walter Scott.

Warwick Castle, *Warwick* ~ the original Norman castle was rebuiltin the 14th century when huge outer walls and towers were added. In the 17th and 18th century, the Greville family transformed it into a country house. In 1978, the owners of Madame Tussaud's bought the castle and set up a selection of wax figures to illustrate the castles history.

Shakespeares School, Stratford upon Avon
▼

Coventry Cathedral, *Coventry* ~ in 1940 the medieval cathedral was hit by German bombing raids. After the war the first totally modern cathedral, designed by Sir Basil Spence was built alongside the ruins of the bombed building. Sir Jacob Epstein added sculptures of 'St Michael subduing the Devil, and Graham Sutherland did the tapestry 'Christ in Majesty'.

Packwood House, *near Solihull* ~ a timber framed house dating from the 16th century which has been extended and altered over the years. Inside are a wealth of tapestries and furniture and outside, are yew topiary, Carolean garden and herbaceous borders.

Wightwick Manor, *Wolverhampton* ~ begun in 1887, the house was influenced by William Morris, with many original Morris wallpapers and fabrics. There are also Pre-Raphaelite pictures, Kempe glass and de Morgan ware. The Victorian/ Edwardian garden has yew hedges and topiary, terraces and two pools.

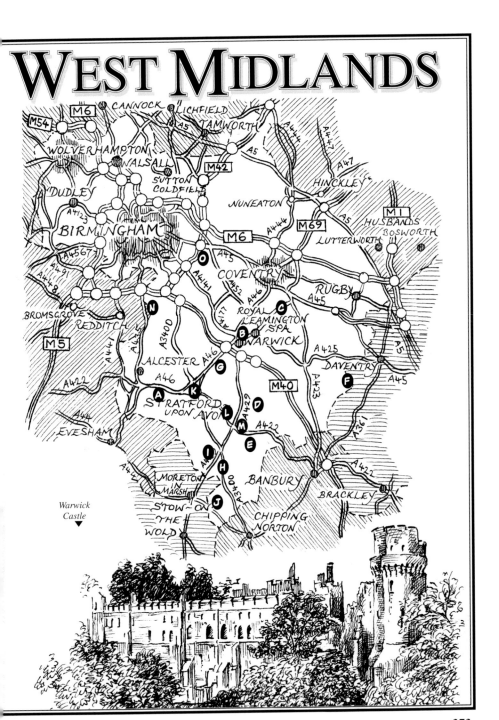

WEST MIDLANDS

M54 · M6 · CANNOCK · LICHFIELD · TAMWORTH
WOLVERHAMPTON · WALSALL · M42 · A5
DUDLEY · SUTTON COLDFIELD · NUNEATON · HINCKLEY · M1
A4123 · BIRMINGHAM · M6 · M69 · HUSBANDS BOSWORTH
A4567 · O · A45 · COVENTRY · LUTTERWORTH · RUGBY
A491 · A448 · N · A3400 · ROYAL LEAMINGTON SPA · C · A45
BROMSGROVE · REDDITCH · B · WARWICK · A425 · DAVENTRY
M5 · ALCESTER · A46 · G · A425 · M40 · F · A45
A422 · K · STRATFORD UPON AVON · L · D · A422 · A423
EVESHAM · A44 · M · E · A361
I · H · MORETON IN MARSH · A3400 · BANBURY · A422 · BRACKLEY
STOW-ON-THE-WOLD · J · CHIPPING NORTON

Warwick
Castle
▼

373

The Old Vicarage, Temple Grafton, Alcester, Warwickshire B49 6NX   Nearest Road A46/A439

The Old Vicarage is a large comfortable Victorian House, in a quiet village, close to Stratford upon Avon. There is a private sitting room for guests, ample off-road parking and mature gardens of 1.5 acres. The village has several good pubs nearby serving hearty evening meals. Separate cottage with double bedroom, bathroom, its own sitting room and tea/coffee making facilities, breakfast in the main house. Ideal for Theatre weekends, touring the Cotswolds or conferences at the NEC.

Mrs Hilary Leather
Tel: 01789 773348

B&B from £30pp, Rooms, 1 twin, 2 double, most en-suite,
No smoking, Children over 12 years, No pets,
Open all year except Christmas and New Year, Map Ref A

Woodside, Langley Road, Claverdon, Warwick CV35 8PJ   Nearest Road A4189

Set in 22 acres of conservation woodland and garden. All bedrooms are spacious, furnished cottage style with antiques and period furniture, and have tea/coffee making facilities, TV and radio. Lovely outlook over woodland and garden. Full central heating, large log fire with TV and video in comfortable lounge makes for a relaxed evening after a busy day and after a home cooked dinner served to order. Or visit one of the interesting eating places locally. Doreen and her Burmese mountain dog will give you a warm welcome.

Mrs Doreen Bromilow
Tel: 01926 842446

B&B from £18pp, Dinner from £12.50, Rooms 1 double, 1 single with
shower, 2 twin with bathroom, 1 family en-suite, Restricted smoking,
Pets by arrangement, Open all year except Christmas, Map Ref B

Crandon House, Avon Dassett, Leamington Spa, Warks CV33 0AA   Nearest Road B4100, A423, M40 J12

Crandon House is set in 20 acres with beautiful views over unspoilt countryside. The attractive bedrooms all have private or en-suite facilities, colour TV, tea/coffeee facilities and central heating. Guests dining room and 2 comfortable sitting rooms 1 with colour TV and woodburning stove. Excellent breakfast menu offers traditional farmhouse or a selection of other dishes. There are excellent pubs and restaurants nearby. Situated in a peaceful part of Warwickshire within easy reach of Stratford upon Avon, Warwick, and Heritage Motor Centre. ETB 2 Crowns Highly Commended. Winter breaks.

David Lea & Deborah Lea
Tel: 01295 770652
Fax: 01295 770652

B&B from £19pp, Rooms 3 double, 2 en-suite, 2 twin en-suite,
Minimum age 12 Restricted smoking,
Open all year except Christmas, Map Ref C

Stonehouse Farm, Leicester Lane, Cubbington Heath, Leamington Spa, Warks CV32 6QZ   A445

A delightful, Grade II Queen Anne farmhouse set within Warwickshire's unspoilt countryside, enjoying extensive views from all of its large and comfortable rooms. Only 2 miles from the Regency town of Royal Leamington Spa, 5 miles from Warwick, and 1 ½ miles from the Royal Showground at Stoneleigh. The bedrooms are comfortable with tea/coffee making facilities and there is a guests' sitting room with television. Meals are served in the traditional dining room which overlooks mature gardens and orchard.

Mrs Kate Liggins
Tel: 01926 336370

B&B from £18.50pp, Evening meal from £8.50, Rooms 3 twin, 1 en-suite,
Restricted smoking, Minimum age 2,
Open all year except Christmas & New Year, Map Ref C

---

*right, **Nolands Farm, Oxhill** - see page 376 for details*

Docker's Barn Farm, Oxhill Bridle Road, Pillerton Hersey, Warwick CV35 0QB

Docker's Barn is an idylically situated old barn conversion surrounded by its own land. Handy for Warwick, Stratford, NEC, NAC, Cotswolds and Heritage Motor Centre. M40 J12 is six miles. The attractive, beamed en-suite bedrooms have hospitality trays and CTV, and the 4 poster suite has its own front door. Wildlife abounds and lovely walks lead from the Barn. We keep a few sheep, horses and hens. Service is friendly and attentive. French and Spanish are spoken.

Carolyn Howard
Tel: 01926 640475
Fax: 01926 641747

B&B from £18.50pp, Rooms 1 twin, 2 double, all en-suite,
No smoking, Children over 8, Pets by arrangement,
Open all year except Christmas & New Year, Map Ref D

Nolands Farm, Oxhill, Warwickshire CV35 0RJ

Nearest Road A422

see PHOTO on page 375

The farm is situated in a tranquil valley with fields, woods and wildlife. It is a working arable farm and offers the country lover a ahappy relaxing stay. The bedrooms, all en-suite with TV and hostess trays are mostly on the ground floor in tastefully restored annexed converted stables. There are romantic 4 poster bedrooms with bathroom. There is a licensed bar adjoining the garden conservatory. For the energenic, fly and coarse fishing is available, claypigeon shooting, cycles for hire and riding nearby. Ample parking. Stratford 8 miles, Warwick 12 miles. Dinner by arrangement.

Sue & Robin Hutsby
Tel: 01926 640309
Fax: 01926 641662

B&B from £18pp, Dinner from £16.95, Rooms 6 double, 1 family, 2 twin,
all en-suite, Minimum age 7,
Open all year, Map Ref E

Marston House, Priors Marston, near Rugby, Warwickshire CV23 8RP

Nearest Road A361

Marston House is a stylish turn of the century family home furnished with antiques, situated in a conservation village of charm. Excellent base to explore Warwick, Stratford, Blenheim and the Cotswolds. Silverstone and Gaydon Motor Museum are also handy. TV in drawing room (guests lounge). Tea/coffee making facilities on request. Large car park. Tennis court and croquet lawn. One good pub in the village within walking distance. Our postal address is misleading, our location is between Banbury and Leamington Spa. £5 supplement for singles (adults).

Mrs K S Mahon
Tel: 01327 260297
Fax: 01327 262846

B&B from £22pp, Dinner from £18, Rooms 1 single for children, 1 twin
with private bathroom, 1 double with private bathroom, No smoking,
Children welcome, Pets by arrangement, Open all year, Map Ref F

The Old Rectory, Vicarage Lane, Sherbourne, Warwick CV35 8AB

Nearest Road A46, M40 (J 15)

A licenced Georgian country house rich in beams, flagstones and inglenooks, perfectly situated between those two tourist honeypots of Warwick and Stratford-upon-Avon. 14 elegantly appointed en-suite rooms, antique brass beds; a romantic French bed and Victorian style bathrooms. The coachhouse is ideal for families, Spa bath and 4 posters available. Hearty English breakfasts and a la carte licensed restaurant and bar. Walled garden and safe parking in a courtyard, pretty with flower baskets. Telephones in bedrooms. Recommended by all major guides. AA QQQQ. ETB 3 Crowns. Which magazine Selected.

Ian & Dawn Kitchen
Tel: 01926 624562
Fax: 01926 624995

B&B from £26pp, Dinner a la carte,
Rooms 4 single, 5 double, 5 twin, all en-suite, Pets by arrangement,
Open all year except Christmas, Map Ref G

Wolford Fields, Shipston on Stour, Warwickshire CV36 5LT   Nearest Road A44, A3400

A large Cotswold farmhouse and gardens built by Lord Campendown in 1857 and farmed by the Mawle family since 1901. The 3 comfortable bedrooms share 2 warmly decorated bathrooms which are fitted with power showers. Guests may relax in the pleasant TV lounge where tea, coffee and chocolate making facilities are available. Guests may also stroll in the large garden. Space available for car parking. Conveniently situated for Stratford-upon-Avon and the Cotswolds.

Richard Mawle
Tel: 01608 661301
Mobile: 0958 649306

**B&B from £14, Rooms 2 double, 1 twin,
Restricted smoking,
Open all year, Map Ref H**

Blackwell Grange, Blackwell, Shipston-on-Stour, Warwickshire CV36 4PF   Nearest Road A3400/A429

Blackwell Grange is a Grade II listed farmhouse, part of which dates from 1603. It is situated on the edge of a peaceful village with an attractive garden and views of the Ilmigton Hills. The spacious bedrooms are all en-suite and have tea/coffee making facilities (one ground floor bedroom suitable for disabled). A stone flagged dining room with inglenook fireplace and guests drawing room with a log fire in winter and deep sofas to sink into, make it a very relaxing place to stay.

Mrs L Vernon Miller
Tel/Fax: 01608 682 357

**B&B from £26pp, Dinner by arrangement, Rooms 1 single, 1 twin,
2 double, all en-suite, Restricted smoking, Children from 12, No pets,
Open mid February - December, Map Ref I**

See PHOTO on page 378

Lower Farm Barn, Great Wolford, Shipston on Stour, Warks CV36 5NQ   Nearest Road A44, A3400

This lovely 100 year old converted barn stands in the small, peaceful Warwickshire village of Great Wolford. The property retains much of its original form including exposed beams and ancient stonework. Now modernised and very comfortable. The beautifully furnished bedrooms have tea/coffee making facilities. A warm and welcoming sitting room with TV is for guests' use. Great Wolford has a lovely old pub, only 5 minutes walk from Lower Farm Barn, where traditional home made food is served. Convenient for Warwick and Stratford upon Avon.

Mrs Rebecca Mawle
Tel: 01608 674435

**B&B from £16pp, Rooms 1 double, 1 en-suite family,
Restricted smoking, Pets by arrangement,
Open all year, Map Ref J**

Oxstalls Farm Stud, Warwick Road, Stratford-upon-Avon CV37 0NS   Nearest Road A439

Built in 1840 and a listed building Oxstalls Farm Stud offers comfortable bed and breakfast accommodation in "The Barn" and "The Old Cow Shed". All rooms are pleasantly furnished and have TV and tea/coffee making facilities; and many with en-suite facilities. Conveniently situated for touring the Cotswolds, Royal Shakespeare Theatre, Shakespeare properties, NEC etc. Nearby golf is available. 1 mile to Stratford-upon-Avon. ETB Commended 2 crowns.

S A Evans
Tel: 01789 205277

**B&B from £16pp, Rooms 2 single, 5 twin, 14 double, 6 family,
many en-suite, Also four poster rooms, Children welcome, No pets,
Restricted smoking, Open all year, Map Ref K**

Ravenhurst, 2 Broad Walk, Stratford-upon-Avon, Warks CV37 6HS   Junction of B439 and A4390

Victorian town house ideally situated in a quiet part of town, centrally located for places of interest. Five minutes walk to theatre and town centre and ten minutes walk to railway station. Very popular with theatre goers. Short drive to Cotswolds and Warwick Castle. Pleasant bedrooms are all en-suite with tea/coffee making facilities, and colour TV. Four poster bed available. Enjoy a 'Ravenhurst' substantial traditional English breakfast. The Workman family, born and bred Stratfordians, offer a warm welcome and plenty of local knowledge. All major credit cards accepted.

The Workman Family
Tel: 01789 292515

**B&B from £19, Rooms 1 twin, 4 double, all en-suite,
No smoking,
Open all year, Map Ref K**

Parkfield Guest House, 3 Broad Walk, Stratford-Upon-Avon CV37 6HS   Nearest Road B439

Parkfield is an elegant Victorian house in a quiet road, yet only a few minutes walk to the theatres and town centre. Most rooms are en-suite with TV, clock-radio, hot drinks and central heating. Breakfast is ample with a wide choice including vegetarian, and are served on fine china. Warwick Castle is 7 miles drive away and the Cotswolds are only a short drive. The rail station is 10 minutes walk with connections to London, Warwick and Birmingham. Brochure with pleasure on request. AA QQQ, ETB Commended.

Roger and Joanna Pettitt
Tel/Fax: 01789 293313

**B&B from £18pp, Rooms 1 single, 1 twin, 4 double, 1 family,
most en-suite, No smoking, Children from 5, No pets,
Open all year, Map Ref K**

Nando's, 18-20 Evesham Place, Stratford-upon-Avon, Warks CV37 6HT   Nearest Road A439

A Victorian town house where Pat and Peter Short extend a warm welcome to all their guests. We pride ourselves on our quality of food and high standard of hygiene. Nando's is conveniently located only minutes away from the Royal Shakespeare Theatre. 20 rooms, 17 with en-suite facilities and all with colour TV and tea/coffee making facilities. A residents TV lounge is also available. Nando's makes the perfect base for visiting the many places of interest in the town and surrounding area.

Pat & Peter Short
Tel: 01789 204907
Fax: 01789 204907

**B&B from £14pp, Dinner from £7.50 by request, Rooms 6 single, 4 twin,
6 double, 4 family, mostly en-suite, Restricted smoking, Children
welcome, Pets by arrangement, Open all year, Map Ref K**

Penshurst Guest House, 34 Evesham Place, Stratford upon Avon CV37 6HT   Nearest Road A439

You'll get an exceptionally warm welcome from Karen and Yannick at this prettily refurbished, totally non-smoking, Victorian townhouse, situated just 5 minutes walk from the town centre. The bedrooms have been individually decorated and are well equipped with many little extras apart from the usual TV and beverages. Perhaps you'd like a lie-in while on holiday? No problem!! Delicious English or Continental breakfasts are served from 7.00am right up until 10.30am. Home-cooked evening meals by arrangement. Facilities for disabled. Brochure available. ETB Listed COMMENDED.

Mrs Karen Cauvin
Tel: 01789 205259
Fax: 01789 295322

**B&B from £15pp, Dinner from £7.50,
Rooms 2 single, 2 twin, 2 double, 2 family, some en-suite, No smoking,
Open all year, Map Ref K**

---

left, Blackwell Grange, near Shipston on Stour - see page 377   **379**

Victoria Spa Lodge, Bishopton Lane, Stratford-upon-Avon CV37 9QY   Nearest Road A3400, A46

An attractive Victorian building, originally, a Spa opened in 1837. Queen Victoria graciously gave it her name and her coat of arms is built into the gables. Situated in a country setting overlooking Stratford canal. Pleasant walks along the canal tow path to Stratford and other villages. Bruce Bairnsfather (creator of "Old Bill" during the Great War) lived here as also did Sir Barry Jackson founder of the Birmingham Repertory Theatre. Comfortable bedrooms are equipped with hostess tray, TV, hair dryer and radio/alarm. Ample parking, full fire certificate. Completely non smoking.

Paul & Dreen Tozer
Tel: 01789 267985
Fax: 01789 204728

B&B from £22.50pp, Rooms 1 twin, 3 double, 3 family, all en-suite,
No smoking, Children welcome, No pets,
Open all year, Map Ref K

Grove Farm, Ettington, near Stratford upon Avon, Warwickshire CV37 7NX   Nearest Road A422, A429

Lovely, comfortable old farmhouse dating from the 1790's with a friendly and warm welcome assured. Rooms are furnished with antiques. Log fires and excellent views are some of the delights awaiting you at Grove Farm. This is a 500 acre working farm complete with 2 labrador's and a spaniel. Guests are welcome to meander through the fields and woods. The bedrooms are delightful and have private bathroom facilities. The Cotswolds and Stratford upon Avon are within easy travelling distance and the local inns serve delicious food.

Bob & Meg Morton
Tel: 01789 740228

B&B from £19pp, Rooms 1 twin, 2 double, all en-suite,
Restricted smoking, Minimum age 12, Pets by arrangement,
Open all year except Christmas, Map Ref L

Thornton Manor, Ettington, Stratford-upon-Avon, Warwickshire CV37 7PN   Nearest Road A429

16th century stone manor house overlooking peaceful fields and woodland including historical sites, on a working farm. Garden, tennis court, fishing and an ideal centre for touring. The bedrooms have either a private bathroom or shower room en-suite. There is a kitchen which guests may use and a log fire in the hall to relax by with a television and a piano for musically minded guests. Conveniently situated for Stratford-upon-Avon, Banbury, Cotswolds and Warwick.

Mrs G Hutsby
Tel: 01789 740210

B&B from £18pp, Rooms 1 twin, 2 double en-suite or private facilities,
Restricted smoking, Minimum age 5,
Open March - December except Christmas & New Year, Map Ref M

Ardendane Manor, Outhill, Studley, Warwickshire B80 7DT   Nearest Road A4189

Ardendane Manor is a non smoking house set in 25 acres. Luxury double and twin accommodation with private facilities, central heating, tea/coffee making trays, and TV. Situated on the A4189 halfway between Redditch and Henley-in-Arden. Close to the NAC, NEC, ICC. Access to motorway network (M42 junction 3).

see PHOTO opposite

Michael & Sue Neale
Tel: 01527 852808

B&B from £40 single, £50 double, Rooms 1 twin, 1 double, both en-suite,
No smoking, No children, No pets,
Open 1 January - 23 December, Map Ref N

---

left, Ardendane Manor, Outhill, Studley - see above for details

The Hollies Guest House, Kenilworth Road, Hampton-in-Arden, Solihull B92 0LW   Nearest Road A452

The Hollies Guest House is excellent accommodation offering en-suite bedrooms, colour TV, tea/coffee facilities in all rooms. Sky TV. Private car parking. Birmingham Airport 3 miles, National Exhibition Centre and National Motorcycle Museum 2.5 miles, Birmingham Business Park 3 miles. Royal Agriculture Centre 6 miles. International Convention Centre and Birmingham City Centre 9 miles. Golf courses at easy reach.

Tina & Jim Fitzpatrick
Tel: 01675 442681
Fax: 01675 442941

B&B from £20pp, Rooms 1 single, 3 twin, 4 double, 1 family, most en-suite, Restricted smoking, Children welcome, Pets by arrangement, Open all year, Map Ref O

"So this is your butter in our sandwiches, eh?"

"Come into the garden, Maud, I am here at the gate alone;"
Alfred Lord Tennyson 1890-92

WILTSHIRE

The inland county of Wiltshire has been described as a lonely county, dominated by the vast chalk-lands of Salisbury Plain, a region of strange monuments and scattered villages. Salisbury is certainly the jewel in the county's crown, with a cathedral which is the pinnacle of the early English style. It is sited below the Plain where three chalk streams, the Nadder, the upper Avon and the Bourne join. Salisbury is quite unlike many medieval cities, which are usually an unplanned jumble of quaint streets clustering under their cathedral. Old Sarum - medieval Latin for Salisbury - was built on the site of an old Iron Age hill fort, but the thirteenth century builders of its cathedral found the position too windy and waterless, so they transferred to the watermeadows a couple of miles away and planned Salisbury on a grid system around it. Regarded as one of the most beautiful cities in England, the city as well as the surrounding countryside is dominated by its magnificent cathedral, its slender spire rising higher than any other in England. The body of the building was finished in 1258, the spire was added some fifty years later. The octagonal chapter house has a remarkable medieval carved frieze depicting scenes from the books of Genesis and Exodus, and contains the finest of four manuscripts of the Magna Carta. Britain's earliest clock....faceless, as its sole purpose is to strike a bell in the tower....dates from 1386 and is in the north aisle of the nave. The cathedral boasts the largest and finest close in the country, including Malmesbury House built in 1327 and Mompesson House, a fine Queen Anne house with a walled garden and a rare collection of English drinking glasses.

Wilton, a small town close to Salisbury, has long been associated with the manufacture of high quality carpets...the Royal Wilton Carpet Museum opened in 1983 explains the history of carpet making. Nearby is Wilton House, originally a Tudor house built on the site of Wilton Abbey. The house is famous for its elegant 'double cube' room, built to hold a magnificent collection of paintings by Van Dyck. The priceless Wilton Dyptich was here for two centuries before going to the National Gallery. Strangely enough, much of the D Day planning during World War II took place here.

If the visitors can drag themselves away from the fascination of Salisbury and its surrounding district, a little way to the north is Stonehenge, Britain's most famous prehistoric stone circle standing on Salisbury Plain. Established around 2,800 BC, with local Sarsen stones and stones from the Preseli Hills of Wales, which were added later, the whole being eventually remodelled during the Bronze Age. Its purpose still remains a mystery to this day....its central axis aligns with the sun on Midsummer's Day, so the arrangement may perform a calendar function. Whatever its true function theories abound, even to suggesting that it was built by beings from outer space, from Atlantis, or by King Arthur! The monument attracts vast numbers of visitors at the time of the summer solstice.

To the north of Stonehenge is one of the largest and most important Stone Age monuments in Europe. Constructed before 2,000 BC at Avebury, is a ring of over a hundred standing stones of sandstone from the North West Downs, each weighing up to fifty tons. The West Kennet Avenue of stones, now partly restored, stretches two and a half miles south, and ends in a double circle of stones known as the Sanctuary.

Within a short distance of this is Silbury Hill, the largest prehistoric mound in Europe. It has been calculated that it would have taken seven hundred men over ten years to build.

Stourhead one of England's first Palladian mansions, built by the successful banker Henry Hoare and completed in 1785, it is most famous for its quite remarkable gardens, probably the finest landscape design of the eighteenth century. Inspired by the Grand Tour, in 1741 Henry Hoare's son, with the architect Henry Flitcroft set about creating an exotic landscape scattered with classical follies...the temple of Apollo and Flora, a grotto, a pantheon - he dammed the River Stour and constructed the famous picturesque curving stone bridge across the newly formed lake. The mansion is filled with many treasures, including carvings by Grinling Gibbons, paintings by Angelica Kauffman and furniture by Chippendale.

Warminster at the head of the lovely Wylye Valley, is a

handsome town of eighteenth century houses and an excellent centre for touring the area. There are fine views from Cley Hill on the ancient Ridge Way. Below is Longleat House built for John Thynne in 1580, the earliest and one of the most attractive Elizabethan mansions, greatly embellished by the fourth Marquess of Bath after his Grand Tour. The mansion looks out over a park made hugely popular by its safari park and many other modern attractions. The grounds, landscaped by Capability Brown include the world's largest maze.

With such attractions the holidaymaker should not lose sight of the pleasures of Georgian Marlborough, the Savernake Forest and the delightful Marlborough Downs; Chippenham, and Malmesbury high above the rivers Avon and Inglebourne; and Castle Combe, one of the most picturesque villages in England.

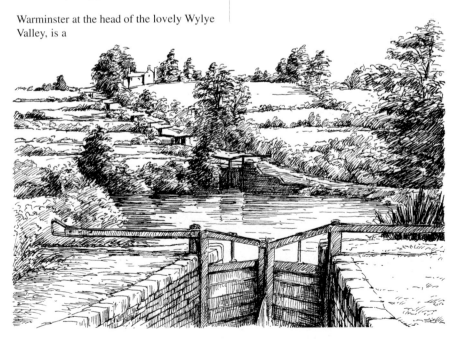

WILTSHIRE

Places to Visit

Avebury Stone Circle, *Avebury* ~ built around 2500 BC, the stone circle surrounds the village of Avebury and was probably a religious centre. Superstitious villagers smashed many of the stones in the 18th century believing the circle to have been a place of pagan sacrifice.

Dyrham Park, *Chippenham* ~ there has been a deer park here from Saxon times, but the present house dates from the time of William and Mary and much of its contents reflect this period. There is a collection of Delft, and painting by Dutch masters.

Great Chalford Manor, *near Melksham* ~ dating from 1480, the manor house is set across a moat between the parish church and stables. Restored by Major R. Fuller, whose family still lives there. Guided tours only.

Lacock Abbey, *near Chippenham* ~ founded in 1232, it was converted to a country house in the 16th century. At the gates is the Fox Talbot Museum of Photography about early photography.

Longleat House, *Warminster* ~ the house was started in 1540 when John Thynn bought the ruins of a priory on the site. Over the years, its owners have each added their own eccentric touches. The grounds were landscaped by Capability Brown and were turned into a safari park in 1966 where lions, tigers and other wild animals may roam freely.

Silbury Hill, *near Beckingham* ~ the largest manmade mound in Europe. It was constructed in three stages around 2800 BC. Its purpose is not known as no remains have ever been found in this one hundred and thirty feet high mound.

Stourhead, *near Warminster* ~ the gardens were started in the 1740's by Henry Hoare who inherited the estate and turned it into a work of art. He created a lake surrounded by rare trees and plants, Neo-Classical temples, grottos and bridges. The house dates from 1724 and was reconstructed in 1902 after a fire. It contains Chippendale furniture and an art collection.

Salisbury
Cathedral
▼

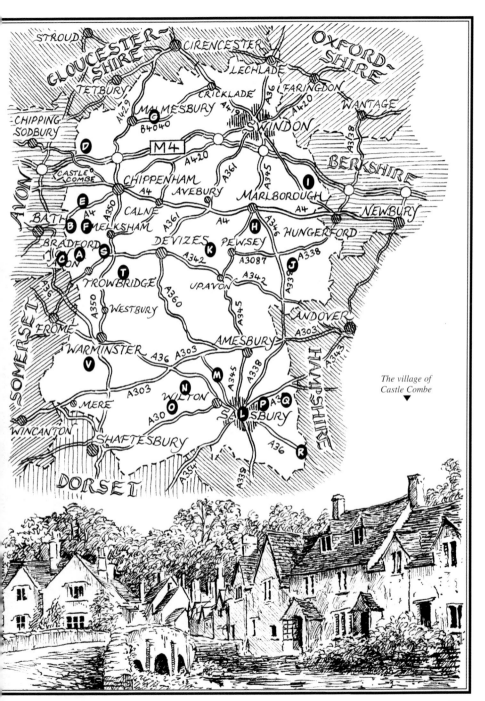

The village of
Castle Combe
▼

Bradford Old Windmill, Masons Lane, Bradford on Avon, Wilts BA15 1QN Nearest Road A363

The circular tower of this former windmill dominates Bradford on Avon and provides spectacular views. Three unusual bedrooms furnished with mellow old pine, masses of books and are decorated with interesting finds from around the world. Friendly, laid-back, smoke free atmosphere and vegetarian ethnic meals from around the world, (Caribbean, Mexican, Thai, Nepali). There are a variety of vegetarian breakfasts including Passionate Pancakes, American and Horribly Healthy. Also an English for carnivores. A DISTINCTLY DIFFERENT place to stay. AA Premier Selected QQQQQ.

Priscilla & Peter Roberts
01225 866842
Fax: 01225 866648

B&B from £29.50pp, Dinner from £18, Rooms 2 double, 1 family, Tel: all en-suite, No smoking, Minimum age 6, No pets, Open February - December, not Christmas & New Year, Map Ref A

Fern Cottage, Monkton Farleigh, Bradford-on-Avon, Wiltshire BA15 2QJ Nearest Road A363

Delightful stone cottage dating from 1680, in quiet conservation Village. Oakbeams, open fire, antiques and family heirlooms. Three beautifully appointed bedrooms with private bath/shower, colour TV, tea/coffee facilities. Traditional English breakfast is served at a large attractively arranged table and there is a lovely Conservatory where guests may relax and look out over a well maintained garden. No smoking. Ample parking. Local Inn, 100 yards away, serves excellent fare. Many places of interest within a few minutes drive.

Christopher & Jenny Valentine
Tel: 01225 859412
Fax: 01225 859018

B&B from £25pp, Rooms 3 double, all en-suite, No smoking, Children welcome, No pets, Open all year, Map Ref B

Burghope Manor, Winsley, Bradford-on-Avon, Wiltshire BA15 2LA Nearest Road A36

This historic 13th century family home is set in beautiful countryside on the edge of the village of Winsley, 5 miles from Bath and 1 1/2 miles from Bradford on Avon. Although steeped in history, it is first and foremost a living family home, which has been carefully modernised so that the wealth of historical features may compliment the present day comforts which include full central heating and en-suite bathrooms with bath and shower. Colour TV and tea/coffee making facilities.

see PHOTO opposite

Elizabeth & John Denning
Tel: 01225 723557
Fax: 01225 723113

B&B from £32.50pp, Rooms 3 twin, 2 double, 2 family, all en-suite, No smoking, Children over 10 years, No pets, Open all year except Christmas and New Year, Map Ref C

Manor Farm, Alderton, Chippenham, Wiltshire SN14 6NL Nearest Road B4040

Manor Farm is a beautiful 17th century farmhouse. It may be found nestling near the church in picturesque Alderton. Home to the Lippiatt family the house offers warmth and comfort coupled with high standard in a relaxed setting. The lovely bedrooms are spacious and well equipped, with delightful views. The farm is only 4 miles from junction 17 and 18 of the M4. Bath, Malmesbury, Badminton and Castle Combe are all a short drive away. We have a selection of super English country pubs nearby.

Jeffrey & Victoria Lippiatt
Tel/Fax: 01666 840271

B&B from £30pp, Rooms 1 twin, 2 double, all en-suite, Restricted smoking, Children from 6, Pets restricted, Open all year except Christmas & New Year, Map Ref D

---

left, Burghope Manor, Winsley - see above for details   **389**

Pickwick Lodge Farm, Corsham, Wiltshire SN13 0PS

Nearest Road M4,J17/A4

Enjoy a stay at our beautiful home set in wonderful countryside where you can take a short stroll or longer walk and see rabbits, pheasant and occasional deer, or relax in our garden, yet only 15 minutes drive from Bath. Ideally situated to visit Lacock, Castle Combe, Avebury, Stonehenge, many National Trust properties or explore some of the idyllic villages and have lunch or supper at a quaint pub. 2 well appointed and tastefully furnished bedrooms, refreshment trays with home-made biscuits. Start the day with a hearty delicious breakfast using local produce.

Mrs Gill Stafford
Tel: 01249 712207
Fax: 01249 701904

B&B from £18pp, Rooms 1 twin, 2 double, en-suite or private bathroom,
No smoking, Children welcome, No pets,
Open all year except Christmas and New Year, Map Ref E

Hatt Farm, Old Jockey, Box, Corsham, Wiltshire SN13 8DJ

Nearest Road A365, B3109

Extremely comfortable Georgian farmhouse in peaceful surroundings, far from the madding crowd. A scrumptious breakfast is served overlooking beautiful views of the rolling Wiltshire countryside. What can be nicer than sitting by a log fire in winter or enjoying the spacious garden in summer? Lovely walks and good golfing nearby. Ideally situated for touring the Cotswolds or visiting the endless delights of the relatively undiscovered county of Wiltshire. All this yet only a short distance away is the city of Bath. West Country Tourist Board 2 Crowns Commended. AA QQQ.

Carol & Michael Pope
Tel: 01225 742989
Fax: 01225 742989

B&B from £18pp, Rooms 1 en-suite twin, 1 double/family with
private bathroom, Restricted smoking, Children welcome, No pets,
Open all year except Christmas & New Year, Map Ref F

Heatherly Cottage, Ladbrook Lane, Gastard, near Corsham, Wiltshire SN13 9PE

Nearest Road A4, A350

Delightful 17th century cottage in a quiet country lane with 1 1/2 acres and ample parking, overlooking open countryside. The accommodation, with separate entrance, has three well appointed and tastefully furnished bedrooms with colour TV and tea/coffee making facilities. The cottage is located eight miles from the M4 and nine miles from Bath. Ideal for visiting Avebury, Stonehenge, the National Trust village of Lacock and Lacock Abbey, Castle Combe, Bowood House, Corsham and Corsham Court and other historic places of interest. Excellent pubs nearby for evening meals.

Peter & Jenny Daniel
Tel: 01249 701402
Fax: 01249 701412

B&B from £18pp, Rooms 1 twin en-suite, 2 double en-suite,
No smoking, Children welcome from 8 years, No pets,
Open all year except Christmas and New Year, Map Ref F

Stonehill Farm, Charlton, Malmesbury, Wiltshire SN16 9DY

Nearest Road B4040

STOP! you've found us!!! 15th century Cotswold stone farmhouse on family run dairy farm in lush rolling countryside on the Wiltshire/Gloucestershire border. Three pretty rooms, 1 en-suite all with new mattresses. Wonderful breakfasts, friendly welcome and pets can come too. Ideal for 1 night or several days. Oxford, Bath, Stratford upon Avon, Stonehenge and the delightful Cotswold hills and villages are all within easy reach by car. Hope to see you soon.

Mrs Edwards
Tel/Fax: 01666 823310

B&B from £17.50pp,
Rooms 2 double, 1 twin,
Open all year, Map Ref G

Clench Farmhouse, Clench, Marlborough, Wiltshire SN8 4NT   Nearest Roads A345, A346

Attractive 18th century farmhouse set in its own grounds with lovely views and surrounded by farmland. There are 2 double bedrooms, one with its own bathroom and the other with a shower en-suite. The 2 single rooms share a shower and all rooms have tea/coffee makers, The house has a happy and relaxed atmosphere and a warm welcome awaits guests. There is a tennis court, heated pool and croquet lawn for guests use. Delicious dinners are offered by prior arrangement. Lovely walks and within easy reach of Saverake Forest, Stonehenge, Oxford, Salisbury, and Bath.

Mrs Clarissa Roe
Tel: 01672 810264

**B&B from £22pp, Dinner from £16, Rooms 1 twin, 2 double, some en-suite,
Children welcome, Pets by arrangement,
Open all year, Map Ref H**

Marridge Hill, Ramsbury, Marlborough, Wiltshire SN8 2HG   Nearest Road B4192, M4

A mainly Victorian family home set in glorious countryside, yet only one hour's drive from Heathrow Airport. You will be warmly welcomed into a relaxed, informal atmosphere. There are three comfortable, attractive bedrooms (one with spacious en-suite facilities) and both bathrooms have power showers. Pleasant sitting room and dining room, books galore, and an acre of well kept garden. Ideal base for touring this historic area, including Neolithic Avebury, Salisbury, Bath, Oxford and the Cotswolds. Good pubs and restaurants nearby. Car parking. ETB 2 Crowns Highly Commended. EMail: dando@impedaci.demon.co.uk

Mrs Judy Davies
Tel: 01672 520237
Fax: 01672 520053

**B&B from £18pp, Rooms 3 twin, 1 en-suite,
No smoking, Minimum age 5, Pets by arrangement,
Open all year except Christmas & New Year, Map Ref I**

Mayfield, West Grafton, Marlborough, Wiltshire SN8 3BY   Nearest Road A338

A delightful thatched house, partly dating back to the 15th century, surrounded by well kept and peaceful gardens. The 3 attractive bedrooms are all en-suite. There is a friendly family atmosphere in the rest of the house which is decorated with beautiful furnishings and fine antiques. Guests can sometimes use the tennis court and heated swimming pool. Very centrally located for visiting Stonehenge, Avebury, Salisbury, Bath and Oxford. ETC highly commended, AA 5Q premier selected.

Mrs Angela Orssich
Tel: 01672 810339
Fax: 01672 811158

**B&B from £22pp,
Rooms 2 double, 1 twin,
Open all year except Christmas & New Year, Map Ref J**

St Cross, Woodborough, Pewsey, Wiltshire SN9 5PL

Seperate sitting room with TV. Samll car park. Tea/coffee making facilities in bedrooms. Kennet and Avon canal 8 minutes walk on Pewsey Downs. Avebury 7 miles away, Salisbury 20 minutes. Very quiet village with good pub, French cooking, riding on the Downs. Woodborough 3 miles from Pewsey. The house is 17th century with beams and open fireplaces. Pretty colourful garden but small. Very friendly and cosy.

Mrs Serena Gore
Tel: 01672 851346

**B&B from £18pp, Rooms 1 twin, 1 double,
Restrcited smoking, Children over 5, Pets by arrangement,
Open all year except Christmas, Map Ref K**

Wiltshire

Farthings, 9 Swaynes Close, Salisbury, Wiltshire SP1 3AE   **Nearest Road A30**

Central but very quiet, Farthings is the charming home of Mrs Gill Rodwell. Parking is no problem in this peaceful Close. The comfortable, nicely furnished, bedrooms all have tea/coffee making facilities, and there is a good choice of breakfast. The breakfast room, with its interesting collection of old family photos, opens onto a delightful garden. This is an ideal base for visiting this old Cathedral/market town and the surrounding area.

Mrs Gill Rodwell
Tel: 01722 330749

B&B from £18pp, Rooms 2 single, 1 twin, 1 double, twin and double rooms are en-suite, No smoking,
Open all year except Christmas, Map Ref L

The Mill House, Berwick St James, near Salisbury, Wiltshire SP3 4TS   **Nearest Road A303, A36**

see PHOTO opposite

Stonehenge 3 miles, Diana welcomes you to the Mill House set in acres of nature reserve abounding in wild flowers and infinite peace. An island paradise with the River Till running through the working mill and beautiful garden. Diana's old fashioned roses long to see you as do the lovely walks; Antiquities and Houses. Built by the miller in 1785, the bedrooms all with tea/coffee making facilities, and TV, command magnificent views. Fishing or swimming in the mill pool and close to golf courses and riding. Attention to healthy and organic food. Sample superb cuisine at Boot Inn, Berwick St James.

Diana Gifford Mead
Tel: 01722 790331

B&B from £20, Rooms 2 single, 2 twin, 4 en-suite double,
Minimum age 5,
Open all year, Map Ref M

Wyndham Cottage, St Mary's Road, Dinton, Salisbury, Wiltshire SP3 5HH   **Nearest Road A303, A36, B3089**

see PHOTO on page 394

Stonehenge lies two beautiful valleys north, an evenings drive of 15 minutes from the idyllic thatched 300 year old Wyndham Cottage, an English dream set in a National Trust area. Most sensitively renovated for extreme comfort. The views and walks are exceptional, as are the bluebells, lambs and calves in spring. Ian, a horticulturalist, has created a delightful cottage garden. Rosie is a nurse and will attend to all medical needs! Excellent pubs nearby. Close to Salisbury, Wilton House, Longleat, Stourhead, Bath and many other historical sites. Tea/coffee making facilities and TV.

Rosie & Ian Robertson
Tel: 01722 716343

B&B from £20pp, Rooms 2 en-suite double or 1 double, 1 twin,
No smoking, Children welcome over 12 years old, No pets,
Open all year, Map Ref N

Morris' Farmhouse, Baverstock, near Dinton, Salisbury, Wiltshire SP3 5EL   **Nearest Road Hindon Road**

100 year old farmhouse with attractive garden set in open countryside. Very peaceful with a homely and friendly atmosphere. Plenty of car parking. Small guest sitting room with TV. Breakfast served in south facing conservatory. Tea,coffee and hot chocolate making facilities in each room. Excellent pub 2 minutes walk for evening meals. Local attractions include Wilton House and Wilton carpet factory 4 miles; Salisbury with Cathedral and Museum 7 miles; Old Sarum 9 miles; Stonehenge 12 miles; Stourhead 15 miles; Longleat Safari Park 15 miles.

Martin & Judith Marriott
Tel/Fax: 01722 716874

B&B from £17pp, Rooms 1 twin, 1 double, shared bathroom,
No smoking, Children & pets welcome,
Open all year except Christmas, Map Ref O

---

     right, The Mill House, Berwick St James - see above for details

The Mill House - see opposite for details

Wiltshire

1 Riverside Close, Laverstock, Salisbury, Wiltshire SP1 1QW Nearest Road A30

Charming, well appointed home, in a quiet area 1 1/2 miles from Salisbury Cathedral. Tastefully furnished suites enjoying their own en-suite bath or shower room, TV and drink making facilities. Salisbury is the centre of an area steeped in antiquity, rich in natural beauty, with many places of outstanding historical interest. Your hosts take endless care to ensure the well being of their guests and are happy to plan itineraries for them.

Mrs Mary Tucker
Tel: 01722 320287
Fax: 01722 320287

B&B from £22.50pp, Dinner from £12 with 48 hours notice,
Rooms 1 double, 1 family, No smoking,
Open all year, Map Ref P

The Beadles, Middleton, Middle Winterslow, Salisbury SP5 1QS Nearest Road A30

Delightful Georgian-style residence in quiet village, 7 miles east of Salisbury. Tastefully decorated. Beautiful drawing room and well equipped en-suite bedrooms. Breakfast and evening meals served in elegant dining room or conservatory. Special diets catered for. Non smoking household. Collection from airports. Briefing on routes to take and what to see. Tours of gardens in Wessex. TV and tea/coffee making facilities in rooms. Car parking on property. Warmth and tranquillity abound in this welcoming home. AA Premier Selected 5Q's. ETB Highly Commended 3 Crowns.

David & Anne Yuille-Baddeley
Tel/Fax: 01980 862922

B&B from £25pp, Dinner from £17.50, Rooms 2 twin, 1 double,
all en-suite, No smoking, Children welcome, No pets,
Open all year, Map Ref Q

Brickworth Farmhouse, Whiteparish, Salisbury, Wiltshire SP5 2QE Nearest Road A36

A perfectly situated 18th century listed farmhouse, renovated and furnished to maintain its period charm. Salisbury, Stonehenge, Romsey, the New Forest, Winchester and Bath are all within easy reach and Sue Barry is a registered tourist guide and will assist you to plan ideal excursions. There are excellent local pubs which provide good meals at realistic prices. Home baked bread and fresh farm eggs for your breakfast. A warm welcome awaits you at this family home.

Mrs Sue Barry
Tel: 01794 884663
Fax: 01794 884581

B&B from £20pp,
Rooms 1 single, 2 double, 1 family, all en-suite,
Open all year except Christmas, Map Ref R

Newton Farmhouse, Southampton Road, Whiteparish, Salisbury, Wiltshire SP5 2QL Nearest Road A36

Historic listed 16th Century farmhouse bordering the New-Forest and originally part of the Trafalgar Estate. Convenient for Salisbury, Stonehenge, Romsey, Winchester, Portsmouth and Bournemouth. Delightful bedrooms, all with pretty en-suite facilities, three with genuine period four poster beds. Beamed dining room with flagstone floor and fireplace with bread oven and collection of Nelson Memorabilia and antiques. Superb breakfast complimented by fresh fruits, home made breads, preserves and free range eggs. Swimming pool idyllicly set in extensive grounds. Dinner by arrangement using kitchen garden produce.

see PHOTO on page 396

Suzi Lanham
Tel: 01794 884416

B&B from £17.50pp, Dinner from £15, Rooms 3 twin, 4 double,
1 family, all en-suite, No smoking, Children welcome,
Open all year, Map Ref R

left, Wyndham Cottage, Dinton - see page 392 for details **395**

Brook House, Semington, Trowbridge, Wiltshire BA14 6JR   **Nearest Road A350**

This Georgian bath stone house has been in the family for several generations. Its extensive gardens include tennis and croquet lawns and a swimming pool. The property is bordered by a brook and Kennet and Avon canal with cycling towpath to Devizes and Bradford-on-Avon. Bath, Avebury, Longleat, Stonehenge, Glastonbury, Castle Combe and Lacock are all within easy reach. The village has an excellent restaurant and pub for evening meals. The bedrooms are equipped with facilities to make guests feel at home.

Mr & Mrs M Bruges
Tel: 01380 870232

B&B from £19pp, Rooms 1 twin, 1 en-suite double, 1 family, Restricted smoking, Children & pets welcome, Open January - November, Map Ref S

Spiers Piece Farm, Steeple Ashton, Trowbridge, Wiltshire BA14 6HG   **Nearest Road A361**

Try our 'home away from home' farmhouse bed and breakfast in the heart of the Wiltshire countryside. Spacious Georgian farmhouse, large garden, great views, peace and tranquillity. Adjacent to an historical, picturesque village. Many tourist attractions including Bath and Stonehenge within easy reach. All rooms have tea/coffee making facilities and washbasins. Guests own luxury bathroom, sitting room/colour TV and dining room. Great breakfasts to last you all day.

Mrs Jill Awdry
Tel: 01380 870266
Fax: 01380 870266

B&B from £16pp, Rooms 2 double, 1 twin, Open February - November, Map Ref T

Springfield House, Crockerton, near Warminster, Wiltshire BA12 8AU   **Nearest Road A36, A350**

Situated in the beautiful Wylye Valley and on the edge of the famous Longleat Estate, this is a charming and welcoming village house dating from the 17th century. Guests enjoy tastefully furnished rooms with lovely garden and woodland views. Grass tennis court. The cities of Salisbury, Wells and Bath are easily reached, with Stonehenge, Stourhead Gardens, Stately homes and Castles nearby. There are endless walks through woodland or over Salisbury Plain, 2 golf courses nearby. Excellent village pub and lakeside restaurant just a few minutes walk. ETB 2 Crowns Commended.

Rachel & Colin Singer
Tel: 01985 213696

B&B from £23pp, Dinner from £14, Rooms 2 double, 1 twin, all with private/en-suite facilities, No smoking, Open all year, Map Ref U

Please mention
THE GREAT BRITISH
BED & BREAKFAST
when booking your accommodation

---

left, Newton Farmhouse, Whiteparish - see page 395 for details   **397**

YORKSHIRE

In so small a space it is impossible to give more than the briefest impression of the pleasures to be experienced in this the largest of the English counties. This is a region of great national parks, of picturesque dales and vast tracts of open moorland. The Pennine Chain of hills forms the backbone of the county, along which stretches the Pennine Way, a two hundred and fifty mile footpath...though prospective walkers should realise that in places this is an extremely rugged route. Historically split into North, East and West Ridings, in 1971 it was divided into North Yorkshire and Humberside, and includes the two metropolitan counties of West and South Yorkshire. The industrial parts of West Yorkshire however should certainly not be overlooked by the holiday visitor. There is some spectacular scenery between these towns....the 'Bronte country' around Haworth being only one example.

The Vale of York is a magnet to the holiday maker, dominated by York, itself under the Romans the ancient capital of the region.

The city is a treasure house of delights. The city walls complete a three mile circuit of the city, and are the finest of their type in Europe. The magnificent Minster, the largest Gothic cathedral in Britain, is the city's crowning glory, and contains more than half of all the medieval glass surviving in England. There is so much to see in York...the castle, museums, great houses, churches and quaint medieval streets, that a single days visit could not do it justice. Within easy reach of the city is Castle Howard, one of the most spectacular houses in Britain, and accepted as Vanbrugh's greatest achievement. The great domed mansion overlooks grounds of over a thousand acres, containing Hawksmoor's circular mausoleum and the lovely Temple of the Four Winds. At Hovingham the stone cottages cluster round the village green under the Saxon tower of All Saints' Church, by the yellow limestone eighteenth century Hovingham Hall, while at nearby Slingsby is the romantic ruin of an eleventh century castle. Kirkham Priory to the south between the

Yorkshire Wolds and the Howardian Hills is the ruin of an ancient Augustinian house.From the seventeenth century visitors came to Harrogate to take the waters from 88 separate mineral springs, and the Royal Baths, opened in 1897 grew to be one of the largest hydrotherapy establishments in the world. As the demand for 'the cure' declined, Harrogate developed into a major conference centre. The Northern Horticultural Society have here at Harlow Car Gardens, sixty acres of ornamental, woodland and rock gardens.

Malton, an important market town above the River Derwent is the gateway to the North York Moors and the Vale of Pickering. Two important houses the visitor must not miss in this area are Sledmere House and Elizabethan Burton Agnes Hall. The North York Moors form the barrier between the North-east coastal region and the Vale of York. The Lyke Wake Walk, a very popular track named after an ancient Cleveland Dirge, crosses the Cleveland Hills from Osmotherly, over the moors to Ravenscar, a distance of forty miles. Helmsley on the southern rim of the moor is a perfect centre for touring. Nearby is Kilburn, renowned for the fine woodcarving of the Thompson family, whose trademark is a carved mouse. The White Horse was cut into the turf above the village in 1857 by the local schoolmaster and his pupils. At Coxwold there is the home of Laurence Sterne, the author of 'Tristram Shandy', and only a short walk away are the lovely ruins of Byland Abbey. A little way further to the north are the majestic ruins of Rievaulx Abbey founded in 1131.

The north-east coast can justly claim superb stretches of sandy beach. Robin Hood's Bay, Runswick Bay and Staithes are picturesque little fishing villages clinging precariously to the cliffs, their narrow cobbled streets a great attraction to artists and holiday makers. Whitby, a once famous whaling centre is overlooked by the ruins of the abbey of St. Hilda. It was here that Captain Cook's vessel 'Endeavour' was built. The great man was born at Marton, now a part of Middlesbrough, lived at Great Ayton and was apprenticed at Staithes. The ruins of twelfth century Scarborough Castle stand on the headland above the regions most popular seaside resort, a Regency spa and a Victorian favourite. The church of St. Martin-on-the-Hill contains a wealth of pre-Raphaelite work. Anne Bronte died in the town, and is buried in the graveyard of St. Mary's church. South along the coast at Filey, Bridlington and Hornsea are excellent sandy beaches, while at Burton Constable is a grand eighteenth century Hall with two hundred acres of parkland. Beverley is dominated by its Minster with its twin western towers. It contains the impressive Percy Tomb, shrine to the Percy family who owned land in the area.

The Yorkshire Dales, each with its own particular character, provide the holiday visitor with a bewildering choice of activities. The National Park is of course a perfect venue for walking, climbing, riding or simply getting away from the stress of life into the wide open spaces. There is quite spectacular scenery...Hardraw Force, the tallest waterfall in England; glorious Aysgarth Falls; the White Scar caverns at Ingleborough and Gaping Gill, a cavern big enough to swallow St. Paul's cathedral; Pen-Y-Ghent, where potholers come to sample the joys of Hell Pot and Hunt Pot. From the top of Pen-Y-Ghent one of the famous Three Peaks, are superb views across to the Lake District. At Malham Cove is some of the finest scenery in the National Park...a huge natural amphitheatre surrounded by a sheer two hundred and forty feet cliff, while at Gordale Scar is a winding gorge of crashing waterfalls and cascades. Skipton is a fine old market town, dominated by its handsome castle of the Cliffords, and a perfect centre for exploring the Dales, Bolton Abbey; The Strid and Barden Tower, Grassington and Kilnsey Crag.

From quiet Swaledale down to the busy industry of the north-west, across to the fresh and blustery Hornsea Mere then up to the Cleveland Hills....within these boundaries lies a vast incomparable holiday area, that once sampled leaves a lasting impression.

Places to Visit

Beverley Minster, *Beverley* ~ co-founded in 937 by Athelstan, King of Wessex in place of the church John of Beverley had chosen as his resting place in 721. The nave is the earliest surviving building work dating from the 1300's. On the north side of the altar is the Fridstol or Peace Chair said to date from 924-39. Anyone who sat on it would then be granted thirty days sanctuary.

Buttertubs, *near Thwaite* ~ a series of potholes that streams fall into, these became known as Buttertubs when farmers going to market lowered their butter into the holes to keep it cool.

Castle Howard, *near Malton* ~ Charles, 3rd Earl of Carlisle commissioned Sir John Vanbrugh to design a palace in 1699, the grand designs were put into practice by architect Nicholas Hawksmoor and the main body of the house was completed in 1712. The West Wing was built in 1753-1759. Today, the Howard family still lives here. The Long Gallery has a large number of portraits of the Howard family, including works by Lely, Holbein and Van Dyck. The Great Hall, rising twenty metres to the dome from its floor has columns by Samuel Carpenter and wall paintings by Pellegrini.

National Railway Museum, *York* ~ set in a steam engine maintenance shed, it is the world's largest railway museum. It covers two hundred years of history and visitors can try wheel tapping and shunting in the interactive gallery. On display are uniforms, rolling stock from 1797 onwards and Queen Victoria's carriage from the Royal Train.

Nunnington Hall, *near Helmsley* ~ a 17th century manor house on the banks of the River Rye. It has a panelled hall with a fine carved chinmey piece, fine tapestries, china and the Carlisle Collection of Miniature Rooms. Parliamentarian troops left their sword marks in the window frames.

Rievaulx Abbey, *near Helmsley* ~ founded in 1132, it was the first major monastery in Britain. It is set in the steep wooded valley of the River Rye. The remains of the Norman nave show how the abbey would have looked all those centuries ago.

Yorkshire Sculpture Park, *Wakefield* ~ an open air gallery, set in one hundred and ten acres of parkland.The park includes work by Barbara Hepworth, Sol LeWitt and Mimmo Paladino. Henry Moore, the parks first patron, believed that to appreciate sculpture, sun and daylight were necessary.

Beverley Minster
▼

YORKSHIRE

The 'Cow and Calf' Rocks,
on Ilkley Moor
▼

Hyperion House, 88 South End, Bedale, North Yorkshire DL8 2DS Nearest Road A684

Hyperion House is large with spacious accommodation and every comfort. Attractively furnished rooms with excellent beds, TV and tea and coffee. The two doubles have en-suite bathrooms. Guests have a lounge with TV and video, giving the opportunity to view a video on this lovely area and its attractions. Bedale is well situated within five minutes walking distance for bar meals, etc. Sheila and Ron your friendly hosts have advice and literature for you on the Dales, Yorkshire Moors walks,etc. Private car parking and guests entrance with your own key. Bargain breaks, please enquire. ETB 2 Crowns Highly Commended.

Sheila & Ron Dean
Tel: 01677 422334

B&B from £17-£20, Rooms 1 twin, 2 double en-suite,
No smoking, Children from 8 years, No pets,
Open all year except Christmas, New Year & February, Map Ref A

The Old Vicarage, Crakehall, near Bedale, Yorkshire DL8 1HE Nearest Road A684 (off A1)

The Old Vicarage is the delightful home of Jane and Peter Young in the pretty village of Crakehall. Situated one mile from Bedale; a wonderful situation for country walks and for exploring The Dales. Guest rooms are spacious with colour TV, tea/coffee makers, and some en-suite. Guests may relax with tea in their sitting room in front of the fire. Good Yorkshire breakfast of ham and free range eggs and home made preserves. Dinner is not normally available, but can be arranged during winter months if required. Excellent pubs and restaurants close by.

Mrs J C Young
Tel: 01677 422967

B&B from £22pp, Winter breaks available,
Rooms 2 double, 1 twin, 2 en-suite, No smoking,
Open all year except Christmas, Map Ref A

---

1 Woodlands, Beverley, Yorkshire HU17 8BT Nearest Road A164

A warm welcome awaits you in this interesting Victorian family house in a quiet conservation area within 2 minutes walk of this charming, historic, market town. Delicious home cooking, guests are welcome to bring their own wine. Enjoy breakfast and dinner in library/dining room and relax and watch TV in our comfortable sitting room. The house is full of character, interesting decor, many pictures, books, log fires, and a lovely garden. Bedrooms have tea/coffee making facilities. Car parking. A good centre from which to explore York, Lincoln, the coast, the Wolds and the Moors.

Neil & Sarah King
Tel: 01482 862752

B&B from £17.50pp, Dinner from £12, Rooms 1 twin, 2 double, some en-suite,
Restricted smoking, Children welcome, Pets by arrangement,
Open all year except Christmas & New Year, Map Ref B

March Cote Farm, Cottingley, Bingley, Yorkshire BD16 1NB Nearest Road A650

see PHOTO opposite

Friendly atmosphere awaits you in our 17th century farmhouse, fully modernised with central heating and a high standard of furnishings and decor. Character still maintained with original oak beams and mullion windows. Top quality farmhouse cooking, served in guests dining room. Colour TV and tea/coffee making facilities in all rooms. Many places of interest within comfortable travelling distance - Moors, Dales, Museums and National Trust properties. Pretty garden. Many repeat bookings. Professional, business, tourist guests all welcome. Plenty of car parking.

George & Jean Warin
Tel: 01274 487433 Fax: 01274 488153
Mobile: 0589 162257

B&B from £18pp, Dinner from £8 by arrangement, Rooms 1 twin,
1 en-suite double, 1 family, Restricted smoking, Children welcome,
No pets, Open all year except Christmas, Map Ref C

---

right, March Cote Farm, Cottingley - see details above

The Old Vicarage, Market Place, Easingwold, York YO6 3AL   Nearest Road A19

A charming Grade II house standing in pleasant gardens adjacent to the Georgian market square, having the benefit of good and varied places to dine. Equi-distant from York, the Yorkshire Moors and Dales which are all within $^{1}/_{2}$ hour drive. Bedrooms are en-suite and equipped with remote colour TV, radio alarm and beverage tray. Guests may enjoy relaxing in their own sitting room, or perhaps a game of croquet, or just sitting in the secluded gardens surrounding the house. Ample private parking.

Christine & John Kirman
Tel: 01347 821015

B&B from £22.50pp, Rooms 1 single, 2 twin, 2 double, all en-suite, No smoking, Children welcome, No pets, Open February to November, Map Ref D

Alderside, Thirsk Road, Easingwold, York YO6 3HJ   Nearest Road A19

Alderside is a comfortable Edwardian family home quietly situated in its own large gardens, secluded, yet only 10 minutes walk from Easingwold Market Place and within easy reach of York, the moors and coast. The 2 double bedrooms each have a private or en-suite bathroom, colour TV, clock radios, and tea/coffee making facilities. There is an additional room for accompanying relatives or friends. Traditional English breakfast is served using local produce and home-made preserves. Excellent eating places nearby. Private parking.

see PHOTO opposite

Daphne Tanner-Smith
Tel: 01347 822132

B&B from £19pp, Rooms 2 double with private bathroom or en-suite, No pets, Minimum age 10, No smoking, Open April - November, Map Ref D

Town Head Guest House, 1 Low Lane, Grassington, Yorkshire BD23 5AU   Nearest Road B6265

Our friendly guest house stands at the head of the village between the cobbled streets and the moors. The ideal location for unspoilt walks and for touring the Dales. The comfortable bedrooms are all equipped with H&C, TV and tea/coffee making facilities. ETB 2 Crowns Commended.

Marian Lister
Tel: 01756 752811

B&B from £22, Rooms 1 twin, 3 double, all en-suite, No smoking, Open all year except Christmas, Map Ref E

Manor House Farm, Ingleby Greenhow, Great Ayton, North Yorkshire TS9 6RB   Nearest Road A172

Delightful farmhouse (part 1760) built of Yorkshire stone, set in 164 acres of park and woodlands at the foot of the Cleveland hills in the North York Moors National Park. Environment is tranquil and secluded. Ideal for nature lovers, relaxing, touring and walking. Accommodation is attractive with exposed beams and interior stonework. Atmosphere is warm and welcoming. Guests have separate entrance, lounge and dining room. Fine evening dinners, special diets if required, excellent wines. ETB 2 crown Highly Commended, AA 4-Q Selected. Brochure. Credit & Debit cards accepted.

Dr & Mrs M Bloom
Tel: 01642 722384

Dinner, Bed & Breakfast from £38.00pp, Rooms 2 twin, 1 double, all have en-suite/private facilities, No smoking, Minimum age 12, Open all year except Christmas, Map Ref F

---

left, Alderside, Easingwold - see above for details   **405**

Acacia Lodge, 21 Ripon Road, Harrogate, North Yorkshire HG1 2JL   Nearest Road A61

"Highly Commended", warm, lovingly restored family run Victorian hotel with pretty gardens in select central conservation area. Short stroll from Harrogate's fashionable shops, many restaurants and conference/exhibition facilities. Retaining original character with fine furnishings, antiques and paintings. All bedrooms luxuriously en-suite with every comfort and facility. Award winning breakfasts served in oak furnished dining room. Beautiful lounge with open fire and library of books. Private floodlit parking for all guests. Entirely "No Smoking". "Somewhere special". AA 4Q Selected. Brochure on request.

Dee & Peter Bateson
Tel: 01423 560752
Fax: 01423 503725

B&B from £24pp, Rooms 3 twin, 3 double, all en-suite,
No smoking, Children from 7, No pets,
Open all year, Map Ref G

Crescent Lodge, 20 Swan Road, Harrogate, North Yorkshire HG1 2SA   Nearest Road A61/A1

Charming Grade II listed family home over-looking Crescent Gardens and close to Valley Gardens and Pump Room. Four well appointed rooms 2 en-suite, with tea/coffee trays, clock/radios and complimentary toiletries. A hairdryer and laundry facilities on request. An elegant and comfortable guests' drawing room with colour TV. Ideally placed for Harrogate town centre as well as for Yorkshire's finest scenery. Limited off street parking.

Julia Humphris
Tel/Fax: 01423 503688

B&B from £23pp, Rooms 1 single, 3 twin, most en-suite,
No children,
Open all year except Christmas & New Year, Map Ref G

Ruskin Hotel & Restaurant, 1 Swan Road, Harrogate, Yorkshire HG1 2SS   Nearest Road A61

The Ruskin is an outstanding "Highly Commended" Victorian hotel, set in lovely grounds with car park. In a quiet conservation area yet only a few minutes stroll from town, theatres and magnificent gardens. Beautiful antique furnished bedrooms, including a four poster and ground floor room, offering every comfort and facility. Relax in our delightful bar/lounge with open fire or sample our superb English/French cuisine in our award winning candlelit restaurant with Victorian balcony. Maria and John look forward to welcoming you to this "rather special Hotel".

John & Maria Simmons
Tel: 01423 502045
Fax: 01423 506131

B&B from £35pp, Dinner from £16.95, Rooms 3 double, 2 twin/family,
2 single, all en-suite, Restricted smoking, Bargain Breaks.
Open January -December, Map Ref G

Daryl House Hotel, 42 Dragon Parade, Harrogate, Yorkshire HG1 5DA   Nearest Road A59

Friendly run home with excellent accommodation. Tea/coffee making facilities and colour TV in all rooms. An attractive lounge and garden for guest enjoyment. Home cooked food and personal attention are the hallmark of Daryl House. Close to Conference Centre and Railway Station. Ideal for visiting Harrogates famous gardens. Also gateway for visiting the Dales. A very warm welcome awaits all visitors.

Mick & Liz Young
Tel: 01423 502775

B&B from £16pp, Dinner on request £6, Rooms 2 single, 2 twin,
2 family/double, Restricted smoking, Children & pets welcome,
Open all year, B&B only at Christmas, Map Ref G

Ashley House Hotel, 36-40 Franklin Road, Harrogate, North Yorkshire HG1 5EE   Nearest Road A1

Ron & Linda Thomas offer you a cheery welcome and value for money in quality bedrooms, all en-suite with colour TV and hospitality tray. Sample our generous breakfast before walking into the town centre or Valley Gardens. Drive through the Yorkshire Dales or Moors, visit Fountains Abbey or Harewood House or take the train to Knaresborough, York or Leeds. Try one of over 100 superb whiskies in our cosy bar before enjoying a four-course dinner (home-cooked from fresh ingredients).

Ron & Linda Thomas
Tel: 01423 507474
Fax: 01423 560858

B&B from £25pp, Dinner from £15, Rooms 5 single, 5 twin, 5 double, 2 family, all en-suite, Children & Pets welcome, Open all year, Map Ref G

The Duchy Hotel, 51 Valley Drive, Harrogate, Yorkshire HG2 0JH   Nearest Road A61, A1

This warm and welcoming small hotel offers 10 comfortable en-suite bedrooms each with TV, direct dial telephone and courtesy trays. The hotel is located on Valley Drive overlooking the "Valley Gardens", yet only a 5 minutes walk from the town centre with its fashionable shops, restaurants and conference facilities. An ideal base for touring the Yorkshire Moors and Dales. Licensed for residents and their guests with an attractive bar and lounge. Noreen and Brian assure their guests of a very pleasant stay in Harrogate.

Noreen Vilarrubi & Brian Ellis
Tel: 01423 565818
Fax: 01423 504518

B&B from £25pp, Dinner from £12.50, Rooms 2 single, 2 twin, 4 double, 2 family, all en-suite, Children welcome, No pets, Open all year except Christmas, Map Ref G

High Winsley Cottage, Burnt-Yates, near Harrogate, Yorkshire HG3 3EP   Nearest Road A61

A traditional Yorkshire Dales stone cottage situated well off the road in peaceful countryside with lovely views all around and ideally placed for both town and country. A warm welcome, good food, and comfortable accommodation are assured. All bedrooms are en-suite, and have tea/coffee making facilities. There are 2 guests' sitting rooms with television, books, magazines, local guides and maps. Great care is taken to provide first class fare and includes home bred beef, fresh fruit and vegetables from the garden, free range eggs and home baked bread.

Clive & Gill King
Tel: 01423 770662

B&B from £23.50pp, Dinner is £12.50, Rooms 3 twin, 2 double, all en-suite, Residential licence, Restricted smoking, Minimum age 11, Open March - December, Map Ref H

Grassfields Country House Hotel, Low Wath Road, Pateley Bridge, Harrogate, N. Yorks HG3 5HL   B6265

Set in private grounds, Grassfields is a listed Georgian building, quietly reflecting the elegance of the period. Grassfields has been recommended since 1986 as a 'hidden jewel' in 'Staying Off The Beaten Track' with wholesome Yorkshire food prepared from local produce and an excellent wine cellar. Only a few miles from Harrogate, Grassfields is situated in beautiful walking country with many walks from the hotel door and an ideal centre for touring the Yorkshire Dales, 'Heartbeat' and 'Herriot' country. AA ✳✳, ETB 3 Crown Commended.

Barbara Garforth
Tel: 01423 711412

B&B from £20pp, Dinner from £13, Rooms 1 single, 2 twin, 3 double, 1 family, all en-suite, Children and pets welcome, Open all year, Map Ref I

Woodlands, Bewerley, Pateley Bridge North Yorkshire HG3 5HS
Nearest Road B6265

Beautifully situated late Victorian house with magnificent views over parkland from residents' sitting room. In quiet area with interesting garden but only five minutes walk from small country town of Pateley Bridge, where excellent restaurant and pub meals can be found. Woodlands is warm and welcoming and a very good centre for walking in Nidderdale and touring the other Dales. Private car park, coffee/tea making facilities. TV in residents' lounge. Many outstanding beauty spots nearby including Fountains Abbey, Newby Hall, Harewood and Ripley Castle.

John & Pauline Shaw
Tel: 01423 711175

B&B from £20pp, Rooms 1 twin, 1 double, all en-suite,
No smoking, No Children, Pets welcome,
Open all year except Christmas and New Year, Map Ref I

Laskill Farm, Hawnby, near Helmsley, York YO6 5NB
Nearest Road B1257

Charming, warm country farmhouse on 600 acre farm in the north Yorkshire National Park in the heart of James Herriot and Heartbeat country. All rooms are lovingly cared for and well equipped. Lovely garden with own lake, peace and tranquillity. Lots of places of historical interest and stately houses nearby. York only 45 minutes away. Generous cuisine of high standard using fresh produce whenever possible. Natural spring water. A walker's paradise.

Mrs S Smith
Tel: 01439 798268

B&B from £21.50pp, Dinner from £11.00,
Rooms 4 en-suite double, 3 en-suite twin, 1 single,
Open all year, Map Ref J

Laurel Manor Farm, Brafferton, Helperby, York YO6 2NZ
Nearest Road A1/A19

A gracious Georgian residence amid orchards, gardens and 28 acres of pastures which run down to the river Swale. Antiques and family portraits abound, and Sam and Annie Key, from an old Yorkshire family, will take a personal interest in your needs. Within 5 minutes walk are 4 delightful village pubs, all serve excellent meals. York and Harrogate are under 20 minutes, and Sam has mapped 200 places of tourist interest within easy reach. They keep black sheep, ducks and horses, and boast complete tranquillity!

Sam & Annie Key
Tel/Fax: 01423 360436

B&B from £25pp, Dinner from £16, Rooms 1 twin, 2 double en-suite,
Restricted smoking, Children welcome, Pets welcome,
Open from March - November, Map Ref K

Treble Sykes Farm, Brafferton, Helperby, York YO6 2SB
Nearest Road A1, A19

Treble Sykes is a large farmhouse peacefully situated on a 500 acre working farm. Set in a large garden with unspoilt panoramic views over the Vale of York. All bedrooms are spacious and airy with tea/coffee making facilities. A 10 minute walk beside the River Swale will take you to the village of Brafferton/Helperby where village inns provide a choice of evening meals. Within easy reach of both historic York and Ripon also the North Yorkshire Moors and Dales with their spectacular scenery and many attractions.

Mrs Ruth Sowray
Tel: 01423 360667
Fax: 01423 360785

B&B £18pp, Rooms 2 twin, 1 family,
Children welcome, Pets by arrangement,
Open March - October, Map Ref K

---

*right, **Laskill Farm, Hawnby** - see above for details*

Porch House, High Street, Northallerton, Yorkshire DL7 8EG   Nearest Road A684

Porch House was built in 1584 and took its name from the porch that still frames the entrance. Throughout its history Porch House has offered comfort and shelter to travellers including royalty - James (VI of Scotland/I of England) and Charles I. All rooms are en-suite, have tea/coffee facilities and TV. Traditional English breakfast/vegetarian. There is a residents lounge; original fireplaces and beams; walled garden; private parking; central position (opposite church). ETB 2 Crowns Highly Commended. 2nd in 1996 Best B&B White Rose Award. 1997 Best B&B White Rose Award.

Jackie Smith
Tel: 01609 779831

B&B from £21pp, Dinner by arrangement, Rooms 1 single, 1 twin, 2 double, 1 family, all en-suite, No smoking, No pets, Open all year, Map Ref L

Nursery Cottage, Leeming Bar, Northallerton, North Yorkshire DL7 9BG   Nearest Road A1/B647

Charming modernised cottage conveniently situated with routes provided whilst you tour this area that has everything! You are assured of comfort and a warm welcome whether your stay is long or short, with tea and home-made scones or arrival. Pretty ground floor bedrooms with wash basins. Visitors own bath/shower room, lounge and dining room, tea making facilities, TV, car park. Beautiful gardens and adjacent Nursery Garden Centre. York, Harrogate 40 minutes. Dales, Moors, Castles, Historic Abbeys and Houses nearby. Come and be pampered! Excellent pubs. Restaurants nearby.

David & Edna Braithwaite
Tel: 01677 422861

B&B from £18pp, Rooms 1 double, 1 twin/triple, private facilities available, Children over 12, No pets, Open March - October, Map Ref M

Millgate House, Richmond, North Yorkshire DL10 4JN   Nearest Road A1/A66

Georgian town house, ideally placed for touring with secluded national award-winning garden (RHS/Daily Mail 1995). Town centre location yet blissfully peaceful with views beyond the garden over the River Swale and its waterfalls. A very special house with its own enchanting character and atmosphere. Bedrooms overlook the garden. French and Italian spoken. All rooms full facilities including tea/coffee, colour TV. EMail: oztim@millgate.demon.co.uk

Austin Lynch & Tim Culkin
Tel: 01748 823571
Fax: 01748 850701

B&B from £25pp, Rooms 1 twin, 1 double, all en-suite, Children over 10 years, No pets, Open all year, Map Ref N

St George's Court, Old Home Farm, Grantley, Ripon, North Yorkshire HG4 3EU   Nearest Road B6265

Enjoy the friendly welcome and warm hospitality of St George's Court, situated in the beautiful Yorkshire Dales, near Fountains Abbey in 20 acres of peaceful farmland. Our en-suite rooms in renovated farm building, offer comfort and all modern facilities - TV and tea/coffee making facilities whilst retaining character and charm. Delicious breakfasts served in our lovely listed farmhouse in winter in front of a log fire and in summer breakfast with a view in a charming conservatory dining room. Lots of parking. Peace and tranquility is our password.

see PHOTO opposite

Mrs Sandra Gordon
Tel: 01765 620618

B&B from £20pp, Rooms 1 twin, 3 double, 1 family, all en-suite, Restricted smoking, Children and pets welcome, Open all year except Christmas, Map Ref H

---

left, **St Georges Court, Grantley** *- see details above*

Aldermans Head Manor, Hartcliffe Hill Road, Langsett, Stocksbridge, Sheffield S30 5GY   **A616**

Set in 50 acres of dramatic countryside, the Manor enjoys panoramic views across the Langsett and Midhopestones reservoirs with the Peak District Moorland beyond. 7 centuries ago the monks of Kirkstead Abbey owned the farm. Today the welcoming atmosphere of peace and tranquillity still prevails. Four poster bed, log fires, beamed ceilings, home cooking with local produce. An ideal centre for walking and exploring Derbyshire and the summer wine countryside of Yorkshire. ETB 3 Crowns Highly Commended. White Rose Award for Tourism (YHTB).

Mrs Ann Unitt
Tel: 01226 766209
Fax: 01226 766209

B&B from £22.50pp, Meals from £12.50, Rooms 2 twin, 2 double, some en-suite, No smoking, Minimum age 12, Open all year except Christmas & New Year, Map Ref O

High Fold, Kettlewell, Skipton, North Yorkshire BD23 5RJ   **Nearest Road A59/B6160**

High Fold is a Dales Barn converted to a high standard of accommodation offering elegant yet relaxing surroundings in a quiet and picturesque location, enhanced by beamed ceilings, stone features and antiques. Four beautifully furnished and well equipped en-suite bedrooms, three on the ground floor carefully designed for disabled/elderly guests. A large drawing room with log fire, books, games etc. Imaginative cuisine using quality produce. Residents Licence. Ideal base for exploring the National Park. ETB Three Crown De Luxe.

Tim Earnshaw & Robin Martin
Tel: 01756 760390

B&B from £27pp, Dinner from £16.00, Rooms 1 single, 1 twin, 1 double, 1 family, all en-suite Restricted smoking, Children & pets welcome, Open February - December, Map Ref P

Langcliffe Country House, Kettlewell, Skipton, North Yorkshire BD23 5RJ   **Nearest Road B6160**

Yorkshire Dales. 6 pretty en-suite bedroom,s all individually furnished. Conservatory restaurant with panoramic views. Emphasis on freshly prepared imaginative food using local produce . Lounge with log fire in winter. Personally run by resident owners. Ground floor adapted room. Open all year. Places of interest included Malham Cove and Tarn Bolton Abbey, Skipton, Aysgarth Falls. Which Hotel Guide 1997. AA Selected 4Q's. RAC Highly Acclaimed. ETB 4 Crowns Commended. Private car park and fully licensed. Special rates November to Easter. Telephone for brochure and tariff. Ideal walking country.

Mr & Mrs Elliott
Tel: 01756 760243

B&B from £30pp, Dinner from £16, Rooms 2 twin, 2 double, 1 family, all en-suite, Restricted smoking, Children welcome, Pets restricted, Open all year, Map Ref P

The Country House Hotel, Long Preston, Skipton, North Yorkshire BD23 4NJ   **Nearest Road A65**

An elegant Victorian country house situated in its own grounds in the Yorkshire Dales, in the village of Long Preston, 3 miles from Settle. 7 double en-suite rooms with colour TV, tea/coffee facilities. Drawing Room with log fire. Extensive Library. Piano. Fine food. Please bring your own wine. Sauna and spa bath provided for relaxation. Delightful house offering a personal service in homely, informal and restful surroundings. Secure car parking. ETB 3 Crowns Commended. Ideal for touring the beautiful countryside and walking, there are many places of interest to visit.

Don & Dorothy Hutton
Tel: 01729 840246

B&B £27.00pp, Dinner by advance booking £14, Rooms 2 twin, 4 double, 1 family, all rooms en-suite, No smoking, Children from 4, No pets, Open February - mid December, New Year Party, Map Ref Q

     right, Aldermans Head Manor, Langsett - see details above

Busby House, Stokesley, North Yorkshire TS9 5LB　　　　　　　　　**Nearest Road A172**

This is a lovely old farmhouse with pretty cobbled courtyard to the rear. Delightfully furnished, the principle rooms look south over the large garden and fields to the hills beyond. The atmosphere is peaceful and relaxed and exudes warmth and friendliness. Renowned for comfort and excellent candlelit dinners. Busby House is very well located for exploring the moors, dales and coast and within easy reach of York, Durham and many places of historic interest. The house is only 25 minutes from the A1 and so makes a good stop between the south and Edinburgh.

Mrs Anne Gloag
Tel: 01642 710425
Fax: 01642 713838

B&B £30pp, Dinner from £17, Rooms 2 twin with private bathrooms,
No smoking,
Closed December & January, Map Ref R

Spital Hill, York Road, Thirsk, North Yorkshire YO7 3AE　　　　　　　**Nearest Road A19/A1**

Set in 1½ acres of garden surrounded by parkland, this peaceful and secluded home offers beautiful bedrooms with warm bathrooms and a drawing room with open fire. The delightful home prepared food (all our own bread) is complemented with a short but interesting wine list. Whether on business or pleasure you will fell 'at home' and relaxed at Spital Hill. Just ten minutes from the A1, the North Yorkshire Moors, Yorkshire Dales, Harrogate and York are all easily accessed. There is ample car parking.

Robin & Ann Clough
Tel: 01845 522273
Fax: 01845 524970

B&B from £28.50pp-£32pp, Rooms 1 twin, 2 double, all en-suite,
No smoking, Children from 12, No pets,
Open all year, Map Ref S

Thornborough House Farm, South Kilvington, Thirsk, North Yorkshire YO7 2NP　　　**Nearest Road A19**

Thornborough House Farm is a 200 year old farmhouse which provides first class accommodation and a warm welcome. Guests can enjoy their own sitting and dining room which has an open fire and colour TV. Two of the bedrooms are en-suite and the third has private facilities. All rooms are warm and comfortable and have tea/coffee making facilities, and colour TV. Families are very welcome and a cot and high chair are available. The houses lies 1½ miles north of Thirsk, the town made famous by James Herriot. 2 Crown commended.

Mrs Tess Williamson
Tel: 01845 522103
Fax: 01845 522103

B&B from £14.50pp, Dinner from £9.50,
Rooms 1 double, 1 twin/single, 1 family,
Open all year, Map Ref T

Red Hall, Great Broughton, Stokesley, North Yorkshire TS9 7ET　　　　　**Nearest Road A172, B1257**

Red Hall, our elegant country house offers personal service in a friendly caring atmosphere. The spacious, centrally heated bedrooms have hairdriers, colour TV's and hospitality trays; the guests' private dining room, with full drinks license, opens onto the secluded gardens. Our lovely 17th century Grade II listed country house is set in tranquil meadowlands at the foot of the rugged North York Moors National Park comprising some of England's most dramatic and beautiful scenery with attractions ranging from ruined abbeys and castles to a spectacular, renowned coastline.

Mrs Carol Richmond
Tel: 01642 712300
Fax: 01642 712300

B&B from £30pp Dinner from £18.50, Rooms 1 single, 1 double, 1 family,
all en-suite, Restricted smoking, Children welcome,
Pets by prior arrangement, Open all year, Map Ref R

Whitfield House Hotel, Darnholm, Goathland, Whitby, North Yorkshire YO22 5LA   Nearest Road A169

Quietly situated in the heart of the North York Moors National Park. Once a 17th century farmhouse, Whitfield House has been carefully modernised to provide every comfort whilst retaining its old world charm. We have nine en-suite bedrooms, (non smoking), each having colour television, telephone, tea-makers, radio and hairdryer. Superb country cooking using fresh produce. Personal attention and a warm friendly atmosphere. Licensed. The ideal base for walking or touring the North York Moors, steam railway and the coast. Goathland is "Aidensfield" in Yorkshire TV's "Heartbeat".

Adrian & Sue Caulder
Tel: 01947 896215

B&B from £26pp, Dinner from £11.50, Rooms 1 single, 2 twin, 6 double, all en-suite, Restricted smoking, Children over 5, Pets by arrangement, Open all year, Map Ref V

Barbican Hotel, 20 Barbican Road, York YO1 5AA   Nearest Road A19

Friendly northern welcome in this delightful Victorian residence with lots of charm and character. Carefully restored to retain many of its original features. All bedrooms are en-suite and have TV and tea/coffee making facilities. One room is at ground floor level. There is a comfortable guests' lounge and the dining room retains a classic 19th century cooking range where a substantial traditional English breakfast, or a vegetarian breakfast is served. Central York is only a 5 minute walk and the Barbican Leisure Centre a 100 yards. A private car park is situated at the rear of the hotel.

Elsie & Len Osterman
Tel: 01904 627617
Fax: 01904 647140

B&B from £20pp, Rooms 1 twin, 5 double, 1 family, all en-suite, No smoking, E Mail: barbican@thenet.co.uk Open all year, Map Ref W

Eastons, 90 Bishopthorpe Road, York YO2 1JS   Nearest Road A19, A64

see PHOTO on page 415

Centrally situated 300 yards from city walls. William Morris style and decor, period furniture and original paintings. Fully equipped en-suite bedrooms. Eastons provides a standard of style and comfort not normally associated with Bed and Breakfast, but which is entirely in accord with the standard of excellence that the owners strive for. "Victorian Sideboard" breakfast menu. White Rose B&B of the Year Winner 1996. Private car park. RAC Highly Acclaimed. ETB Highly Commended.

Mr M D Easton & Ms L M Keir
Tel: 01904 626646

B&B from £22pp, Rooms 2 twin, 7 double, 2 family, all en-suite, No smoking, Children over 5, No pets, Open all year, Map Ref W

St George's Hotel, 6 St George's Place, York YO2 2DR   Nearest Road A1036, A64

A 10 bedroomed Victorian house in a quiet cul-de-sac by York's beautiful racecourse. All the comfortably furnished bedrooms are en-suite and have TV and tea/coffee trays. St George's has quality awards from the Tourist Board, AA and RAC. There is excellent access from the A64 from the south and A19 from the north so it is well placed for Castle Howard, Scarborough, Herriot country, the North Yorkshire Moors and many historic places in York. Just a short walk into the centre of York. All pets very welcome. Private enclosed car parking.

Brian & Kristine Livingstone
Tel: 01904 625056
Fax: 01904 625009

B&B £21.50pp, Dinner £5.00, Rooms 5 double (2 4-posters), 5 family, all en-suite, Pets welcome, Open all year, Map Ref W

---

right, Arndale Hotel, York - see page 419 for details

Arndale Hotel, 290 Tadcaster Road, York YO2 2ET   **Nearest Road A64/A1036**

A delightful Victorian house, directly overlooking York Race course with beautiful enclosed walled gardens giving a country-house atmosphere within the city. Warm, cosy lounge, complete with many antiques, fresh flowers, paintings and a small bar. Ten outstanding thoughtfully equipped bedrooms, all en-suite many with Victorian style bathrooms and whirlpool baths. Antique half tester four poster beds, generous hospitality tray, colour television, hair dryer, trouser press, books, magazines. Superb breakfast to suit all tastes. AA QQQQQ Premier Selected. ETB Highly Commended. Large enclosed gated car park.

see PHOTO on page 417

David & Gillian Reynard
Tel: 01904 702424

**B&B from £24.50pp, Rooms 1 single, 2 twin, 6 double, 1 family,
all en-suite, Restricted smoking, Children over 7 years, No pets,
Open all year except Christmas and New Year, Map Ref W**

Holmwood House Hotel, 114 Holgate Road, York YO2 4BB   **Nearest Road A59**

Holmwood House Hotel was built as two private houses in the 19th century, backing onto one of the prettiest squares in York. The 2 listed buildings have been lovingly restored to retain the ambience of a private home and provide peaceful elegant rooms where the pressures of the day disappear. Bedrooms have their own en-suite facilities with shower, bath or even spa-bath, plus the usual TV, coffee & tea making facilities, direct dial telephone, etc. There is a car park to the rear and we are only 5 minutes walk from the City Walls with the railway station and city centre 5-10 minutes walk away.

Bill Pitts & Rosie Blanksby
Tel: 01904 626183
Fax: 01904 670899

**B&B from £27.50pp, Rooms 3 twin, 8 double, all en-suite,
No smoking, Minimum age 8, No pets, Open all year, Map Ref W
E-Mail: holmwood.house@dial.pipex.com**

Four Seasons Hotel, 7 St Peters Grove, Bootham, York YO3 6AQ   **Nearest Road A19**

A delightful Victorian residence, ideally situated in peaceful tree lined grove, yet only five minutes walk from Minster and York's historical attractions. Awarded Highly Commended by the English Tourist Board and offering beautifully appointed en-suite bedrooms, all fully equipped. A cosy residents lounge and bar. Ample private car parking. Delicious four course breakfast. This is an ideal base from which to explore York and surrounding countryside.

see PHOTO opposite

Adrian & Julie Brown
Tel: 01904 622621
Fax: 01904 620976

**B&B from £26pp, Rooms 1 twin en-suite, 2 double en-suite,
2 family en-suite, Restricted smoking, Children welcome,
Open February - December, Map Ref W**

Hobbits Hotel, 9 St Peter's Grove, Clifton, York YO3 6AQ   **Nearest Road A19**

Hobbits is a comfortable, Edwardian house, situated in a quiet cul-de-sac only 10 minutes walk from the city centre. Bed and breakfast in a home-from-home style, in beautifully decorated bedrooms, all with private facilities. Each room has central heating, colour TV, mini bars, and tea/coffee making facilities. There is a licence for alcohol and a comfortable guests' lounge. The city centre offers a wide variety of attractions including York Minster and museums. Within a short drive it is possible to get to the coast, moors, dales and wolds. Parking available.

Mrs Rosemary Miller
Tel: 01904 624538/642926
Fax: 01904 651765

**B&B from £27pp, Rooms 2 single, 2 twin, 3 double/family,
all en-suite, Restricted smoking, Pets by arrangement,
Open all year except Christmas, Map Ref W**

---

left, **Four Seasons Hotel, York -** *see above for details*

Arnot House, 17 Grosvenor Terrace, York YO3 7AG   Nearest Road A19

Built in the 1860's, Arnot House stands over looking Bootham Park, five minutes walk from York Minster. The four guest bedrooms are furnished with antiques and paintings, brass or wooden beds, colour TV, alarm clock radio, hairdryer and hospitality tray. There is a guest lounge and car parking. Breakfast includes cereals, fruit juices, fresh fruit salad, English or vegetarian breakfast or even scrambled eggs with smoked salmon! Arnot House is totally non smoking.

Kim & Ann Sluter-Robbins
Tel/Fax: 01904 641966

B&B from £22.50pp, Rooms 1 twin, 3 double, all en-suite,
No smoking, Children over 10 years, No pets,
Open all year, Map Ref W

see PHOTO opposite

Grange Lodge, 52 Bootham Crescent, Bootham, York YO3 7AH   Nearest Road A19

The Grange Lodge offers a warm and friendly welcome. Accommodation is in a choice of 7 comfortable and attractively furnished bedrooms, many with en-suite facilities and all have TV and tea/coffee making facilities. Conveniently located for all of York's attractions and only 10 minutes away from York Minster. An ideal place for touring this most beautiful region.

Jenny Robinson
Tel: 01904 621137

B&B from £16, Dinner from £8,
Rooms 3 double, 2 family, 1 twin, 1 single, many en-suite, No pets,
Open all year, Map Ref W

The Hazelwood, 24-25 Portland Street, Gillygate, York YO3 7EH   Nearest Road Gillygate

Situated in the centre of York only 400 yards from York Minster yet with a private car park and in an extremely quiet location, the Hazelwood comprises of two elegant Victorian houses with many original features. In our tastefully decorated dining room, we offer a wide choice of quality breakfasts which cater for all tastes including vegetarian. All our comfortable en-suite bedrooms have colour TV, radio alarm, hair dryer and tea/coffee facilities. Relax in our secluded garden or in our peaceful residents' lounge with its original kitchen range and selection of books and local information and where tea and coffee are available.

Ian & Carolyn McNabb
Tel: 01904 626548
Fax: 01904 628032

B&B from £19.50pp, Rooms 1 single, 3 twin, 7 double, 2 family,
all en-suite, No smoking,
Open all year, Map Ref W

see PHOTO on page 422

Spa House, Hovingham, York YO6 4LP   Nearest Road A170/B1257

Built in 1840 as a health resort Spa House still retains the original sulphur spring and plunge bath. Now a comfortable country home, centrally heated, with a log fire in guests' sitting room and set in a secluded and tranquil area of outstanding natural beauty. One mile from Hovingham, one of the prettiest villages in North Yorkshire. Excellent choice of inns for evening meals. Easy access to York, Castle Howard and North Yorkshire Moors.

Lynne & Jim Allen
Tel: 01653 628824

B&B from £20pp, Rooms 1 twin, 1 double, all en-suite,
No smoking, Children welcome, No pets,
Open all year except Christmas and New Year, Map Ref X

---

left, Arnot House - see above for details

The Counties of
ENGLAND,
SCOTLAND
&
WALES

Thurso
Wick
Ullapool
Portree
Inverness
HIGHLAND
REGION
GRAMPIAN
Aberdeen
Fort William
Oban
TAYSIDE
Dundee
Perth
FIFE
Stirling
LOTHIAN
Edinburgh
Glasgow
Berwick
CENTRAL
Ayr
BORDERS
STRATHCLYDE
Dumfries
NORTHUMBERLAND
TYNE AND WEAR
Newcastle upon Tyne
COUNTY DURHAM
Stranraer
Carlisle
Durham
CLEVELAND
DUMFRIES AND GALLOWAY
CUMBRIA
Middlesbrough
DERBYSHIRE
Kendal
YORKSHIRE
Scarborough
NOTTINGHAMSHIRE
LANCASHIRE
LEICESTERSHIRE
GREATER MANCHESTER
Lancaster
York
NORTHAMPTON~SHIRE
Blackpool
Leeds
Hull
CHESHIRE
Manchester
Sheffield
Grimsby
LINCOLNSHIRE
CLWYD
Liverpool
Lincoln
GWYNEDD
Caernarfon
Chester
CAMBRIDGESHIRE
STAFFORDSHIRE
Stoke
Derby
Nottingham
NORFOLK
SHROPSHIRE
Shrewsbury
Leicester
King's Lynn
Great Yarmouth
WEST MIDLANDS
Aberystwyth
Birmingham
Peterborough
Norwich
POWYS
Coventry
Northampton
Ely
Cambridge
SUFFOLK
Fishguard
Worcester
Bedford
DYFED
Pembroke
Hereford
Buckingham
Felixstowe
HEREFORD & WORCESTER
Gloucester
Oxford
St. Albans
Chelmsford
BEDFORD~SHIRE
WARWICKSHIRE
Swansea
Bristol
Swindon
ESSEX
GLAMORGAN
Cardiff
Bath
Reading
London
Canterbury
GWENT
Salisbury
KENT
GLOUCESTERSHIRE
Taunton
Guildford
Dover
HERTFORD~SHIRE
BATH, BRISTOL & NORTH EAST SOMERSET
Exeter
Southampton
Brighton
GREATER LONDON
Weymouth
Bournemouth
SUSSEX
BUCKINGHAMSHIRE
Truro
Plymouth
DORSET
HAMPSHIRE
SURREY
CORNWALL
DEVON
SOMERSET
WILTSHIRE
BERKSHIRE
OXFORDSHIRE

left, **The Hazelwood, York**-see page 421 for details

423

SCOTLAND

The history of Scotland is rich and complicated, the nation always being divided between the Highlands and the Lowlands. Despite inter-trading, the two factions always kept their distance...even their language was different, the Highlanders largely Gaelic speaking, the Lowlanders English speaking.

The Highlanders were mobile cattle farmers, while the Lowlanders were static arable farmers, who firmly established themselves in burghs. The division still remains obvious today...the Lowlands, the land of Sir Walter Scott and Robert Burns, a land of impressive castles, palaces, medieval burghs and the great cities of Glasgow and Edinburgh....The Highlands a region of magnificent mountain scenery, an awesome and majestic coastline, lonely glens and haunting open moors. Scottish history is written deep in every region. The Jacobite rebellions of the 'fifteens' and forty-fives' ending in the tragedy of Culloden, was followed by the systematic destruction of the Highland way of life and the loss of the power of the Clan Chiefs, followed later by the Clearances - the eviction of the traditional highland crofters to make way for lowland sheep farmers.

Against such a background each region has jealously preserved its own particular and very distinctive character, making Scotland the perfect holiday venue. Of course, add to this some of the most spectacular and stimulating scenery in Great Britain and you have attractions that the holiday visitor will find hard to resist.

SCOTLAND

Places to Visit

Castle Fraser, *Inverurie* ~ begun in 1575, it incorporates an earlier building and the work was completed in 1636. The interior was remodelled in 1838 and some of the decoration and furnishings of that period survive.

Drumlanrig Castle, *Thornhill* ~ built from pink sandstone between 1679 and 1691 on the site of a 15th century Douglas stronghold. It contains a collection of treasures and Jacobite relics including Bonnie Prince Charlie's camp kettle, sash and money box. There are paintings by Leonardo da Vinci, Holbein and Rembrandt.

Glencoe & Dalness ~ a historic glen with visitor centre, set in some of the finest climbing and walking country in the Highlands. The Glencoe hills are an important geological site as they demonstrate the phenomenon of a volcano collapsing in on itself during eruptions.

Glamis Castle, *Forfar* ~ it was a royal hunting lodge in the 11th century but underwent extensive reconstruction in the 17th century. It was the childhood home of Queen Elizabeth the Queen Mother, and her former bedroom can be seen.

Loch Ness Monster Exhibition Centre, *Inverness* ~ first sighted in the 6th century by St Columba, the Loch Ness monster as attracted increasing attention. The exhibition centre provides audio visual information on the loch's most famous resident.

Stirling Castle, *Stirling* ~ the present castle dates from the 15th and 16th centuries, but legend says that King Arthur took the original castle from the Saxons. From 1881 until 1964 the castle was a depot for recruits into the Argyll and Sutherland Highlanders.

Willow Tea Room, *Glasgow* ~ created by Charles Rennie Mackintosh at the turn of the century. Everything was his own design, including the cutlery and chairs.

Loch Sunart ▼

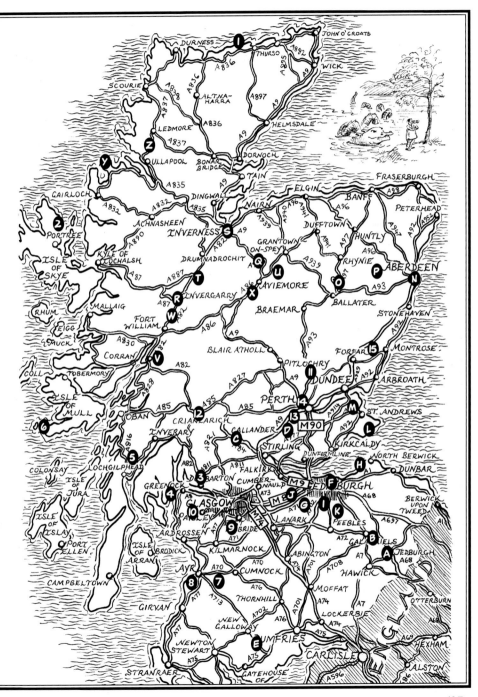

BORDERS

Once the scene of bloody battle, witnessed by the numerous castles and ruined abbeys, this area so steeped in Scottish history, proudly boasts a fine array of stately homes, including Traquair, claimed to be the oldest inhabited house in Scotland; Abbotsford, the impressive home of Sir Walter Scott; glorious Georgian, Mellerstain; Manderston House at Duns; and Thirlstone Castle. There is a wealth of beautiful gardens here too, including the National Trust for Scotland's Priorwood Gardens. The greater part of the Berwickshire coastline and the full length of that wonderful fishing river the Tweed, are designated as Sites of Special Scientific Interest.

Willow Court, Friars, Jedburgh, Roxburghshire TD8 6BN   **Nearest Road A68**

Willow Court is a modern professional run guest house with superb views over Jedburgh yet only 3 minutes walk from town centre. All accommodation is all en-suite expect for one with private facilities, all have colour TV and tea/coffee making facilities and most accommodation is on ground floor. Edinburgh and New Castle is only one hours drive making Jedburgh an ideal base for walking the Scottish borders and touring central Scotland. Car park. Guest lounge and two acres of gardens. Restaurants are all less than 3 minutes walk away. AA QQQQ. STB 2 Crown Highly Commended.

Mike McGovern
Tel: 01835 863702
Fax: 01835 864601

B&B from £18pp, Rooms 1 twin, 2 double, 1 family, all en-suite,
Restricted smoking, Children & pets welcome,
Open all year, Map Ref A

Dunfermline House, Buccleuch Street, Melrose, Scottish Borders TD6 9LB   **Nearest Road A7, A68**

Dunfermline House is obviously very much a family home run in a smooth professional manner. It is centrally situated in the small historic town of Melrose which nestles comfortably between the Eildon Hills and the silvery River Tweed in the beautiful rolling countryside of the Scottish Borders. The house is tastefully furnished and decorated. each room has individual character as well as private facilities, colour TV, tea/coffee makers. Dinners are not available but Melrose boasts some of the best eating establishments in the area. STB Highly Commended, AA 4 Q Selected.

Susan & Ian Graham
Tel: 01896 822148
Fax: 01896 822148

B&B from £22pp, Rooms 1 single, 2 twin, 2 double, all en-suite,
No smoking, Children welcome, Pets by arrangement,
Open all year, Map Ref B

CENTRAL

Standing at the geographical and historical centre of the country, Stirling is perfect for exploring this glorious region. The town guards the gateway to the Highlands beyond its magnificent castle standing on a two hundred and fifty foot crag. At nearby Bannockburn owned by the National Trust for Scotland, was fought the country's most famous battle. Callander, where the rivers Teith and Leny meet, is ideal for touring the Trossachs. Known as the Highlands in miniature, and popularised by Sir Walter Scott, this is Rob Roy country and one of the most visited areas in Scotland. From Callander Crags are superb views over the mountains.

Arran Lodge, Leny Road, Callander, Perthshire FK17 8AJ   Nearest Road A84/M9

Arran Lodge is an enchanting and luxuriously appointed period bungalow on the banks of the River Leny by Callander's western outskirts. Delight in romantic 4-poster bedrooms, all with private/en-suite bathrooms and colour TV. Enjoy Robert's cooking in the ideal ambience of the Victorian dining room, or sit and relax in the tranquillity of the "river-view lounge", or river-gardens. Robert and Pasqua Margarita bid you welcome into their utterly delightful non-smoking home. Every comfort is provided. Children over 12 welcome, Private parking. 'Which? Hotel Guide".

Pasqua Margarita
& Robert Moore
Tel: 01877 330976

B&B from £29pp, Dinner from £27.50, Rooms 4 double, all en-suite/private bathrooms,No smoking, Children from 12, No pets, Open March - November, Map Ref C

see PHOTO's on page 430

Westbourne, 10 Dollar Road, Tillicoultry, Clackmannanshire FK13 6PA   Nearest Road A91

A fascinating Victorian mill-owner's mansion set within wooded grounds, beneath the Ochil Hills. The atmosphere at Westbourne is warm and friendly with log fires on cool evenings and a croquet lawn. Off-the-road parking is available. Located amid glorious country-side in central Scotland, with The Trossachs, Loch Lomond, Edinburgh and Glasgow just 1 hour away. Motorway connections are within 15 miles. A wide range of activities are available nearby: sight-seeing in historic Stirling, numerous golf courses, fishing, hill walking in Braveheart country! EMail: odellwestbourne@compuserve.com

Jane & Adrian O'Dell
Tel: 01259 750314
Fax: 01259 750314

B&B from £20pp, Rooms 1 twin, 2 double en-suite, 1 family, No smoking, Children welcome, Pets by arrangement, Open all year except Xmas & New Year, Map Ref D

Please mention
THE GREAT BRITISH
BED & BREAKFAST
when booking your accommodation

Arran Lodge, Callander - see page 429 for details

DUMFRIESSHIRE & GALLOWAY

This is the country of Robert Burns, and where the poet wrote most of his works. He is buried in Dumfries, where there are many memories of the great man. Like much of this part of Scotland the scenery is spectacular. The 'Devil's Beef Tubs' and 'Grey Mare's Tail'...a two hundred feet waterfall, are but two of the many glorious sights. Dramatic Caerlaverock Castle, the romantic Sweetheart Abbey, and of course Maxwelton House, the birthplace of Annie Laurie should not be missed by the holiday visitor. Warmed by the Gulf Stream this is a region of fine gardens, superb walking, wonderful fishing, and in the Galloway Forest Park, all the outdoor pursuits one could wish for.

Culgruff Farm, Crossmichael, Castle Douglas, Kirkcudbrightshire DG7 3BB   **Nearest Road A713**

Culguff Farm is situated in glorious Galloway countryside between Gretna Green and Stranraer. This renovated farmhouse with all en-suite bedrooms offers relaxed comfort for the discerning traveller. For the more energetic there is walking, bird-watching, golf, fishing, sailing and spectacular gardens to visit. A warm welcome awaits you.

Mrs Helen Sledge
Tel/Fax: 01556 670285

B&B from £25pp, Rooms 1 single, 2 double, all en-suite,
No smoking, children or pets,
Open all year except Christmas and New Year, Map Ref E

"Come on - its grand once you're in!"

EDINBURGH & LOTHIAN

Edinburgh, the capital of Scotland is a very elegant city of gracious squares and Georgian crescents...and also of quaint medieval streets clustering around its castle. The Royal Mile, the city's original main street; the Palace of Holyroodhouse, the official Scottish residence of the Queen; St. Giles Cathedral, Princes Street, The Forth Bridge; the volcanic hill, Arthur's Seat, in Holyrood Park, these are all permanent attractions. The Edinburgh International Festival, the largest of its kind in the world, attracts vast numbers of tourists. To the east of the city is spectacular countryside, regarded by many as one of the most picturesque parts of Scotland. There are over forty miles of lovely coastline where North Berwick offers two fine beaches, while Dunbar has been recorded for over thirty years, as the sunniest town in Scotland.

Two Saxe Coburg Place, Edinburgh EH3 5BR   **Nearest Road Henderson Row**

In the late 18th century, within the period of Georgian architectural excellence, an elegant 'New Town' was built in Edinburgh. It is here that we live in a quiet square within easy walking distance of the city centre and botanical gardens. In a discreetly arranged, spacious townhouse, we offer accommodation in 3 well appointed bedrooms, each with private bathroom and shower, direct dial telephone, tea/coffee making facilities and TV. There is a comfortable sitting room for the use of guests. STB DeLuxe 2 Crowns.

George & Alicia Ogilvy   **B&B from £40pp, Rooms 1 en-suite single, 1 en-suite twin, 1 en-suite**
Tel: 0131 315 4752   **double, No smoking, Children over 10 years, No pets,**
Fax: 0131 332 4934   **Open all year, Map Ref F**

---

27 Heriot Row, Edinburgh EH3 6EN   **Nearest Road Heriot Row**

Built in 1804, 27 Heriot Row is in Edinburgh's premier residential street and although only 4 streets away from Princes Street and the world famous Edinburgh castle, your stay here will not only be luxurious but will also be quiet and relaxing. Each room is furnished to the highest deluxe standard with en-suite bath and shower facilities, direct dial telephone, hair dryer, TV and tea/coffee making facilities. Your hosts will be delighted to help plan your sightseeing. French, German, Italian and Spanish are spoken. Scottish Tourist Board 3 Crowns Deluxe. EMail: t.a@cableinet.co.uk

Andrea & Gene Targett-Adams   **B&B from £40pp, Rooms 1 single, 1 twin, 1 double, all en-suite,**
Tel: 0131 225 9474   **No smoking, Children welcome, No pets,**
Fax: 0131 220 1699   **Open all year, Map Ref F**

---

17 Abercromby Place, Edinburgh 17 Abercromby Place, Edinburgh EH3 6LB

The former home of William Playfair, Edinburgh's famous architect of Georgian times. Set amidst the historic 'New Town' and overlooking large private gardens it is furnished with antiques and offers a friendly, relaxing and comfortable location in the heart of Edinburgh. Within minutes of Princes Street its central position enables guests to take advantage of Edinburgh's many attractions. There is ample private car parking.

Mrs Lloyd   **B&B from £35pp, Dinner available, Rooms 2 single, 2 double, all en-suite,**
Tel: 0131 557 8036   **No smoking, Children welcome, No pets,**
Fax: 0131 558 3453   **Open all year except Christmas & New Year, Map Ref F**

Gloria's Place, Edinburgh - see page 434 for details

Gloria's Place, 20 London Street, Edinburgh EH3 6NA   Nearest Road A1

Gloria welcomes you to her luxurious Georgian home, minutes on foot from the city centre. An atmosphere of elegance and warmth will be your first impression. A hall vibrant with colour, a magnificent drawing room - yours to enjoy - where breakfast is served. All three bedrooms sleep two people, have en-suite (private)bath/shower room and every other extra, both practical and pampering. The house is totally no smoking. Nether a one night reservation. No triple occupancy of one room is available.
E-Mail: gloriasplace@cableinet.co.uk

Gloria Stuart
Tel: 0131 5570216
Fax: 0131 5566445

B&B from £60-£80pp, Rooms 1 twin, 2 double, all en-suite,
No smoking, children or pets,
Open all year except Christmas, Map Ref F

Ellesmere House, 11 Glengyle Terrace, Edinburgh EH3 9LN   Nearest Road A702

Attractive and comfortable house centrally located in a residential area and facing south over a park. The castle, Royal Mile (Edinburgh old historic town), and Princes Street (one of Britain's best shopping venues) are all within very easy reach. Close to International Conference Centre. Rooms are spacious, individually decorated and well equipped with TV, heating and tea/coffee making facilities. All rooms are en-suite and a 4-poster bed is available. There are many varied restaurants and pubs locally. Scottish Tourist Board Award 2 crowns Highly Recommended, AA 4 Q Selected.

Celia & Tommy Leishman
Tel: 0131 229 4823
Fax: 0131 229 5285

B&B from £23pp, Rooms 1 single, 2 twin, 2 double, 1 family
all en-suite, Minimum age 10,
Open all year, Map Ref F

The Town House, 65 Gilmore Place, Edinburgh EH3 9NU   Nearest Road A702,A1

Attractive privately owned Victorian town house, located in the city centre. Theatres and restaurants are only minutes walk away. The Town House has been fully restored and tastefully decorated, retaining many original architectural features. Our bedrooms are tastefully furnished and individually decorated, all have en-suite bath or shower and w.c., central heating, radio alarm, colour television, hair dryer and tea/coffee tray. Our parking is situated at the rear of the house. Scottish Tourist Board 2 Crowns Highly Commended, AA 4Q's Selected, Les Routiers. Totally non smoking.

Susan Virtue
Tel: 0131 229 1985

B&B from £25-£33pp, Rooms 1 single, 1 twin, 3 double, all en-suite,
No smoking, Children from 10, No pets,
Open all year except Christmas, Map Ref F

Barony House, 4 Queen's Crescent, Edinburgh EH9 2AZ   Nearest Road Dalkeith Road, Craigmiller Park

Comfortable Victorian house, just 15 minutes from the city centre. En-suite rooms with colour TV, central heating and tea/coffee making facilities. Ironing boards and hair dryers available on request. Barony House is famous for its full Scottish buffet style breakfast and the friendly helpful staff managed by Susie Berkengoff. Scottish evenings and dinner at local restaurants can be arranged. Susie will also cater for special dietary requirements. Car parking. A memorable stay.

Susie Berkengoff
Tel: 0131 667 5806

B&B from £18pp, Evening meals available, Rooms 2 single,
2 en-suite twin, 2 en-suite double, 2 family, 1 en-suite, No smoking,
Children welcome, No pets, Open all year except Christmas, Map Ref F

International Guest House, 37 Mayfield Gardens, Edinburgh EH9 2BX　　　Nearest Road A701

Attractive stone built Victorian House situated 1¹/₂ miles south of Princes Streets on the main A701. Private parking. Luxury bedrooms with en-suite facilities, colour televisions and tea/coffee makers. Magnificent views across the extinct volcano of Arthur's Seat. Full Scottish breakfast served on the finest bone china. International has received many accolades for its quality and level of hospitality. 19th Century setting with 21st Century facilities "In Britain" magazine has rated The International as their "find" in all Edinburgh.

Mrs Nivin
Tel: 0131 6672511
Fax: 0131 6671112

B&B from £19.35pp, Rooms, 3 single, 1 twin, 2 double, 3 family, all en-suite, Restricted smoking, Children welcome, No pets, Open all year, Map Ref F

Hopetoun Guest House, 15 Mayfield Road, Edinburgh EH9 2NG　　　Nearest Road City Bypass

Hopetoun is a small, friendly, family-run guest house close to Edinburgh University. 1 ¹/₂ miles south of Princes Street, with an excellent bus service into the city. Very comfortable accommodation is offered in a completely smoke free environment. Having only three guest bedrooms, and now offering private facilities, the owner prides herself in ensuring personal attention to all guests in a friendly, informal atmosphere. All rooms have central heating, wash-basins, colour TV, tea/coffee facilities. Parking is also available. Which? Books - Good B&B Guide. AA QQ. STB 2 Crowns Commended. Access/Visa.

Rhoda Mitchell
Tel: 0131 667 7691

B&B from £17-£30pp, Rooms 1 double, 2 en-suite family, No smoking, Children welcome, No pets, Open all year except Christmas, Map Ref F

Kildonan Lodge Hotel, 27 Craigmillar Park, Edinburgh EH16 5PE　　　Nearest Road A701

Ideally situated in central Edinburgh. Kildonan Lodge is an outstanding example of Victorian elegance providing the perfect setting for your visit to Scotland's capital. Relax and enjoy a dram at our "Honesty" Bar. All well appointed non-smoking en-suite bedrooms have colour TV, telephone, radio/alarm and welcome tea/coffee tray. With a private car park, easy access to city centre and city by-pass. Kildonan Lodge is an ideal retreat for guests and businessman in search of a home away from home.

Maggie Urquhart
Tel: 0131 667 2793
Fax: 0131 667 9777

B&B from £28-£45pp, Dinner from £10.95, Rooms 4 single, 2 twin, 4 double, 2 family, all en-suite, Restricted smoking, Children welcome, No pets, Open all year, Map Ref F

Newmills House, 1 Newmills Road, Balerno, Edinburgh EH14 5AG　　　Nearest Road A70

Newmills House is a charming Georgian house set in one acre of garden with tennis court. Lois May and David welcome you to their relaxed and informal family home. Breakfast is served in the conservatory, where dried flowers hang from the ceiling. Original drawing room is available for guests. City centre is 20 minutes by frequent bus, the airport 15 minutes away. Glasgow 45 minutes. Good local eating places. 1 twin, 1 double, 1 single, 1 bed and bunk room. Private facilities available.

David & Lois May Donaldson
Tel: 0131 449 4279
Fax: 0131 449 2919

B&B from £25pp, 1 single, 1 twin, 1 double, 1 bunk, private facilities, Restricted smoking, Children from 5, Pets restricted, Open all year except Christmas & New Year, Map Ref G

Faussetthill House, 20 Main Street, Gullane, East Lothian EH31 2DR   Nearest Road A198/A1

Very comfortable private Edwardian House providing a high standard of Bed & Breakfast with TV in guest lounge, tea/coffee making facilities in bedrooms also car parking. Situated in a delightful quiet coastal village on A198 road where there is a wide choice of local restaurants, many golf courses within easy reach, 4 in village including Muirfield, nearby is Aberlady Nature Reserve. Edinburgh 30 minutes by car. Highly Commended by Scottish Tourist Board. Also 4Q's selected by AA. Non-smoking.

George & Dorothy Nisbet
Tel/Fax: 01620 842396

B&B from £22pp, Rooms 2 twin, 1 en-suite, 2 double, 1 en-suite,
No smoking, Children over 12 years, No pets,
Open March - December, Map Ref H

Craig Cottage, 5 New Pentland, By Loanhead, Midlothian EH20 9NT   Nearest Road A701

A warm welcome awaits you from the hosts and their assorted pets. We are 100 yards off the A701 and within ¹/₂ mile of Edinburgh by-pass which facilitates travel to all parts of Scotland. For golf, riding and sightseeing. There is a good bus service to city centre. Hot drinks are served on request and bedrooms have TV, there is ample off street parking. A variety of breakfasts will suit all tastes. There are several good restaurants nearby.

Mrs Ciupik
Tel: 0131 4400405

B&B £15pp, Rooms 1 twin, 1 double,
No smoking, Children over 6 years, Pets by arrangement,
Open February - October, Map Ref I

Whitecroft, East Calder, Livingston, West Lothian EH53 0ET   Nearest Road A71

Douglas and Lorna extend a warm Scottish welcome with all bedrooms on ground level. The bedrooms are all en-suite and furnished to the highest standard. Each bedroom has a remote colour TV and tea/coffee making facilities. Whitecroft is surrounded by farmland yet only 10 miles from Edinburgh city centre. Safe private parking. A full hearty Scottish Breakfast is served using local produce, even whisky marmalade. There are restaurants in the area providing evening meals. STB Commended, 2 Crowns, AA Selected, 4 QQQQ.

Douglas & Lorna Scott
Tel: 01506 882494
Fax: 01506 884327

B&B from £22pp, Rooms 1 twin, 2 double, all en-suite,
No smoking, Children over 12 years, No pets,
Open all year, Map Ref J

The Mill House, Temple, Midlothian EH23 4SH   Nearest Road A7

The Mill House is set in charming river-side garden, open on set days for Scottish garden charities. A taste of Scotland member and Highly Commended 1 Crown by Scottish Tourist Board. Cordon Bleu cooking in a relaxed atmosphere. Within easy reach of Edinburgh and River Tweed for fishing.

Mrs Caroline Yannaghas
Tel/Fax: 01875 830253

B&B from £35pp, Dinner from £35, Rooms 2 twin, 1 en-suite,
No smoking, Children from 14, No pets,
Open April - September, Map Ref K

KINGDOM *of* FIFE

Dunfermline, for six hundred years the capital of Scotland...the burial place of Scottish kings, including Robert the Bruce, and the birth place of both James I and Charles I, ensured for this regian its title, The Kingdom of Fife. This area of quite remarkable beauty and quaint fishing villages, seemingly unchanged by the passage of time, is of course famous for its golf, which was played here as far back as 1547. The Royal and Ancient Golf Club was founded here in 1750. The lovely city of St. Andrews, the site of the oldest university in Scotland is an ideal centre for touring. The Royal Palace of Falkland, Kellie Castle, St. Monans Windmill, Cambo Gardens, Kinburn Park, are all within easy reach.

The Hermitage Guest House, Ladywalk, Anstruther, Fife KY10 3EX   Nearest Road A917

Part of The Hermitage existed in 1588 when exhausted sailors from the ill fated Spanish Armada were helped ashore and shown mercy and kindness by 'Anster folk'. Today, The Hermitage carries on that tradition, offering the stranger friendship and relaxation in a beautifully restored 'home from home'. The house faces south with superb views across the River Forth. Our 'secret garden' is a joy. The area is a golfer's mecca, with St Andrews only 10 miles away. STB Highly Commended, AA 5-Q Premier Selected. STB Welcome Host.

Margaret McDonald
& Eric Hammond
Tel: 01333 310909

B&B from £20pp, Dinner from £13.50, Rooms 2 suites each comprising 2 dble bedrooms, bathroom & lounge, Non smoking, Licensed, Children welcome, No pets, Open all year except Xmas, Map Ref L

Todhall House, Dairsie, By Cupar, Fife KY15 4RQ   Nearest Road A91

Todhall is a Georgian style country house set in attractive gardens overlooking the superb vistas of the Eden Valley, 7 miles from St Andrews. You will experience quality accomodation in this warm friendly home. The Kingdom of Fife - rich in history, offers a wide variety of pursuits. Golf on some of Scotland's finest courses. Explore the university town of St Andrews, East Neuk, fishing villages and National Trust properties. There are quality restaurants and good pub food nearby. STB Highly Commended. AA 5Q's Premier Selected. STB - Scotland's best. Come!

John & Gill Donald
Tel: 01334 656344
Fax: 01334 656344

B&B from £23-£30pp, Dinner from £16, Rooms 1 twin, 2 double, all en-suite, No smoking, Children over 12, No pets, Open mid March - October, Map Ref M

Please mention
THE GREAT BRITISH BED & BREAKFAST
when booking your accommodation

GRAMPIAN

This corner of Scotland is blessed with outstanding scenery, spectacular seascapes and celebrated fishing rivers. The holiday location for the Royal Family, and particularly loved by Queen Victoria, this area is world famous as castle country, in fact there are over seventy castles in this region. Aberdeen, the granite city known as 'The Flower of Scotland', is the undoubted capital of Grampian Highlands, but if visitors can drag themselves away, they can enjoy the delights of Ballater; Braemar, the eastern gateway to the Cairngorm Mountains and home to the famous Braemar Gathering; Crathie; Cruden Bay; Elgin; Forres; Fraserburgh; Tomintoul.....the list of pleasures seems almost endless.

Craiglynn Hotel, 36 Fonthill Road, Aberdeen AB1 2UJ　　　　　　　　　Nearest Road A90

Built in 1901 of local granite Craiglynn offers modern comforts with Victorian elegance. Situated in a residential area mid-way between Union Street and the award winning Duthie Park. Craiglynn is ideally positioned for business or leisure. All bedrooms and the dining room are strictly non smoking. However, there are two lounges where smoking is permitted. The bedrooms have colour TV, telephone, welcome tray, central heating and most have en-suite facilities. STB 3 Crowns Highly Commended, and a member of 'Taste of Scotland' good food scheme. E Mail: 106053.1542@COMPUSERVE.COM

Chris & Hazel Mann
Tel: 01224 584050
Fax: 01224 212225

B&B from £25pp, Dinner from £15.50, Rooms 5 single, 1 twin, 2 double, 1 family, most en-suite, Restricted smoking, Children welcome, No pets, Open all year except Christmas, Map Ref N

Migvie House, By Logie Coldstone, Aboyne, Aberdeenshire AB34 4XL　　　　Nearest Road A97

Migvie House nestle in the secluded upper reaches of Royal Deeside. We provide a delightful base from which to explore the serenity and grandeur of the Grampian Highlands, with their romantic castles, famous distilleries and numerous outdoor pursuits. Lovingly restored to create an atmosphere of warmth and comfort. Charming fully equipped en-suite bedrooms. Antiques and country furnishings, wood fires in the guest sitting room, outside mountain views and track walks. Combine all this with good farmhouse cookingand you may decide to move no further.

Carole & Bruce Luffman
Tel/Fax: 013398 81313

B&B from £20pp, Dinner by arrangement, Rooms 2 twin, 1 double, all en-suite, No smoking, Children over 14 years, Pets by arrangement, Open by arrangement from November - March, Map Ref O

Backhill Country Homestay, Backhill of Burnhervie, By Kemnay, Inverurie, Aberdeenshire AB51 5JT

Backhill is a mid 19th century farmhouse set in six acres of gardens and woodland in a peaceful riverside location. Traditional country food is served with home baked breads, homemade preserves and honey. Castles and distilleries galore, walking on the Bennachie range, bird watching, golf and fishing - all are within easy reach. Visit Aberdeen - thirty minutes or journey back 6000 years via Archaeolink to prehistoric Aberdeenshire. STB 2 Crowns Highly Commended. Experience the best in comfort and hospitality and discover the magic of this unique retreat.

Julie Dainty
Tel: 01467 642139
Fax: 01467 642139

B&B from £25pp, Rooms 1 twin en-suite, 1 double with private bathroom, No smoking, Children over 12 years, No pets, Open April - October, Map Ref P

HIGHLANDS

In its strategic position at the head of the Great Glen, Inverness is the capital of the Highlands. It was here that King David built his castle in 1141, and close by in 1746 was fought the last battle on British mainland soil - the battle of Culloden. The National Trust for Scotland tends the site on Culloden Moor. Fort William, the tourist centre for the Western Highlands is a base for climbers of Ben Nevis, Britain's highest mountain, and is also the 'Road to the Isles'. The Glen More Forest Park together with the mountain mass of the Cairngorms, offer the climber and skier the ultimate in their sport. For the less energetic, the whole region is a delight of rugged coves, lovely fishing villages, nature trails and beautiful Lochs.

Feith Mhor Country House, Station Road, Carr-bridge, Inverness-shire PH23 3AP   **B9153**

The peaceful secluded setting of Feith Mhor, 1 1/2 miles from the village, enables you to relax and enjoy the beauty of the Highlands. This lovely late 19th century house, set in 1 1/2 acres of attractive garden, offers a warm welcome and traditional comfort. The pleasantly furnished bedrooms are all en-suite with colour TV, radio and tea/coffee making facilities. We offer good home cooking and like to use local and garden produce whenever possible. This is a wonderful area for birdwatchers, tourists, walkers, fishing and golf. STB 3 crowns commended, AA 3Q's. Recommended by 'Which'.

Penny & Peter Rawson
Tel: 01479 841621

B&B from £25pp, Dinner £12, Rooms 3 twin, 3 double, all en-suite,
Restricted smoking, Minimum age 10, Pets by arrangement,
Open all year, Map Ref Q

Craigard House, Invergarry, Inverness-shire PH35 4HG   **Nearest Road A82**

Set in the breathtaking splendour of the highlands, Craigard, a large country house on the western outskirts of the village of Invergarry is the perfect base for a relaxing and varied holiday. Each of the well furnished bedrooms has a washbasin and tea/coffee making facilities. Guests can enjoy a quiet drink in the relaxed atmosphere of the residents' lounge and on cooler evenings pull up to a roaring log fire. TV in all bedrooms. The magnificent scenery surrounding Craigard makes it an ideal point for touring.

Mr R L Withers
Tel: 0180 9501 258

B&B from £18pp, Dinner £15, Rooms 2 double en-suite, 1 single en-suite,
3 double, 1 twin with wash handbasins, No children, No pets,
Open Easter - end October, Map Ref R

Talisker, 25 Ness Bank, Inverness IV2 4SF   **Nearest Road A9, A82**

Situated on the east bank of the River Ness just minutes from the town centre and Eden Court Theatre. Single, family, double and twin rooms available all having tea/coffee facilities, colour TV and some rooms with en-suite. Private parking.

Mrs Sheila Hall
Tel: 01463 236221

B&B from £20-£40, Rooms 1 single, 2 twin, 1 double, 2 family,
No smoking, Children welcome, No pets,
Open all year, Map Ref S

Foyers Bay House, Lower Foyers, Loch Ness, Inverness-shire   **Nearest Road A82, A9**

In its own magnificent grounds of wooded pine slopes abundant rhododendrons and apple orchard with fabulous view of Loch Ness, nestles the splendid Victorian villa of Foyers Bay House. The grounds are set amid beautiful forest, nature trails and adjoin the famous Falls of Foyers. The villa is tastefully and luxuriously refurbished. Rooms have telephone, TV and en-suite bath or shower room, tea/coffee making facilities, fresh fruit and bath/shower gel, compliments of your hosts Otto & Carol Panciroli. The guest house is not licensed but guests are welcome to bring their own wine.

Mr & Mrs OE Panciroli
Tel: 01456 486624
Fax: 01456 486337

B&B from £18pp, Dinner from £10.50,
Rooms 1 double, 2 twin,
Open all year, Map Ref T

Aultmore House, Nethybridge, Inverness-shire PH25 3ED   **Nearest Road B970**

Arthur and Marjorie are friendly informal hosts who, during the last seven years, have returned this Edwardian home to forgotten former glory by sympathetic restoration of its guest bedrooms, 3 lounges, conservatory, billiards room and gardens. Enjoy a drink in this secluded and peaceful retreat set in 25 acres of woodland gardens that nestle in extensive forests high in the hills above Nethybridge and complimented by a panoramic Cairngorm mountain backdrop. You are warmly invited to linger awhile.
"As guests who leave as our friends".

Arthur & Marjorie Edwards
Tel: 01479 821473

B&B from £19.50pp, Dinner from £10.00, Rooms 1 single, 2 twin,
2 double, most en-suite, Restricted smoking, Children from 12,
Pets restricted, Open April - October, Map Ref U

Ceol-na-Mara, North Ballachulish, Inverness-shire PH33 6RZ   **Nearest Road A82**

Set in beautiful location, surrounded by breathtaking views of Loch Linnhe, Ardgour and Glencoe. After your day of touring, walking or ski-ing, simply relax. Free use of swimming and leisure club at local hotel includes steam room, sauna, jacuzzi and mini gym. Breakfast menu caters for traditional or individual preferences. Homely facilities in each room. From A82 take Kinlochleven Road (B863) north of Ballachulish Bridge. Turn immediately right-adjacent to St Bride's school - into private drive. Secure off road parking.

Norman & Annette Laing
Tel: 01855 821338

B&B from £17pp, Dinner £10, Rooms 1 twin, 2 double, private/en-suite,
No smoking, Children from 12, Pets by arrangement,
Open March - October, Map Ref V

Invergloy House, Spean Bridge, Inverness-shire PH34 4DY   **Nearest Road A82**

Invergloy House welcomes non-smokers. This is a converted coach house and stables set in 50 acres of attractive wooded grounds. Guests have their own large sitting room with magnificent views over Loch Lochy and mountains. All rooms are tastefully and traditionally furnished. Bedrooms have en-suite facilities. The house lies 5^1/2 miles north of Spean Bridge on the main road to Inverness overlooking Loch Lochy where free fishing is available from a private shingle beach, reached by footpath. Rowing boats for hire. Hard tennis court. SAE for details.

Mrs M H Cairns
Tel: 01397 712681

B&B from £20pp, Rooms 3 twin, en-suite facilities,
Minimum age 8, No smoking,
Open all year, Map Ref W

Riverside, Invergloy, Spean Bridge, Inverness-shire PH34 4DY   Nearest Road A82

This bungalow sits in lovely wooded gardens fronting Loch Lochy, totally hidden from passing traffic.It is conveniently situated midway between Fort William and Fort Augustus. You will find a warm welcome, a log fire in the lounge on chilly evenings, and traditional comfortable furnishings. There are several excellent restaurants within a 5 mile radius. Most credit cards accepted. STB 2 Crowns Highly Commended.

Mr & Mrs D E Bennet
Tel/Fax: 01397 712684

B&B from £19pp, Rooms 1 double with private bathroom,
1 family with en-suite shower,
Open all year, Map Ref W

Balcraggan House, Feshiebridge, by Kincraig PH21 1NG   Nearest Road A9, B970

Balcraggan House situated at Inshriach Forest where pine marten, buzzard, osprey, roe deer and red squirrel abound, with a badger sett nearby. Miles of cycle routes and walks straight from the front door or use your car to explore the magnificent Highlands. All rooms are tastefully and traditionally furnished with log, peat fires in drawing room and dining room.

Helen Gillies
Tel: 01540 651488

B&B from £25pp, Dinner from £15, Rooms 1 twin, 1 double,
both en-suite with baths, No smoking, No pets, Minimum age 10,
Open all year, Map Ref X

The Sheiling, Achgarve, Laide, Rosshire IV22 2NS   Nearest Road A832

The Sheiling is a modern Bungalow situated on the Gruinard Peninsula near Gruinard Bay on the West Coast of Scotland. Set amongst beautiful hills with distant views of the high mountains of An Teallach you can explore the outstanding scenery walk the fine shell beaches whilst watching seals possibly otters and a myriad of seabirds. Rooms are furnished to a high standard offering typical Scottish hospitality. TV and tea/coffee facilities. Within easy reach of Gairloch Ullapool, An Teallach mountains, Invereue Gardens and Beinn Eighe Nature Reserve.

Annabell MacIver
Tel: 01445 731487

B&B from £20pp, Rooms 1 twin, 1 double, all en-suite,
No smoking, Children over 14 years, No pets,
Open March - October, Map Ref Y

Birchbank Holiday Lodge, Knockan, Elphin, Sutherland IV27 4HH   Nearest Road A835

Conveniently located on the boundary of Inverpolly National Nature Reserve,14 miles south of Ullapool, Birchbank Holiday Lodge offers comfortable licensed accommodation with purpose built modern facilities, including sauna suite and drying room, and afriendly family atmosphere - the ideal base for exploring the unspoiled lochs, glens and mountains of Northwest Sutherland. Organised hillwalking and glen rambling excursions by arrangement; boat and bank fishing for wild brown trout also available on wellknown local lochs. All with professional guidance and expert local knowledge.

Tom & Ray Strang
Tel/Fax: 01854 666 215

B&B from £20pp, Dinner from £16, Rooms 1 single, 4 twin/double,
most en-suite, Restricted smoking, Children & pets welcome,
Open May - October, Map Ref Z

Catalina Guest House, Aultivullin, Strathy Point, Sutherland KW14 7RY Nearest Road A836

Out on a headland along the remote Far North coastline with only two people per square kilometre! The Atlantic Ocean on three sides. Totally non-smoking. We take only two guests with their own private suite complete with its own lounge, dining room and shower room. Treat it as your own home, stay in all day if you wish, books, television, tea/coffee, delicious home-cooked meals served at any time. Excellent walking area. Which? Books Good Bed & Breakfast Guide, AA 4Q Selected, STB 3 Crowns Highly Commended.

Peter & Jane Salisbury
Tel: 01641 541279
Fax: 01641 541314

B&B £17pp, Dinner £10.00, Rooms 1 en-suite twin,
No smoking, children or pets,
Open all year except Christmas, Map Ref 1

Glenview Inn & Restaurant, Culnacnoc, Staffin, Isle of Skye IV51 9JH Nearest Road A855

A charming inn nestling between mountains and sea and ideally situated for exploring the magnificent scenery of North Skye. We have pretty country style bedrooms with private facilities and tea/coffee making trays and our cosy lounge has television and open peat fire. Our restaurant, fully licensed, is much acclaimed and offers the best of fresh Skye seafood, as well as traditional, ethnic, and vegetarian specialities. Members of Taste of Scotland and Scottish Tourist Board (3-Crown Commended).

Paul & Cathie Booth
Tel: 01470 562248
Fax: 01470 562211

B&B from £25pp, Dinner from £12.00, Rooms, 1 twin, 3 double, 1 family,
all en-suite, Restricted smoking, Children welcome, Pets welcome,
Open March - October, Map Ref 2

Please mention
THE GREAT BRITISH BED & BREAKFAST
when booking your accommodation

STRATHCLYDE

The northern area of this region has been described as Scotland in miniature. Warmed by the Gulf Stream, this lovely area is rich in fine gardens. Oban is a grand holiday resort, a busy fishing harbour and the centre of ferry traffic to the islands of Mull, Coll, Tiree, Colonsay and the outer Hebrides. To the north is the thirteenth century Dunstaffnage fortress of the MacDougalls. At Ayr, overlooking the Forth of Clyde are excellent beaches. Alloway on the southern outskirts of the town is the birthplace of Robert Burns, Scotland's national poet. The Land o' Burns Centre explains by audiovisual displays the popularity of Burns. Culzean Castle built in the late eighteenth century, and seat of the Kennedys, contains a wonderful classical interior by Robert Adams, and with its lovely Country Park is one of the National Trust for Scotland's most popular properties.

Kirkton House, Darleith Road, Cardross, Argyll & Bute G82 5EZ   **Nearest Road A814**

An 18/19th Century converted farmstead, in a tranquil country setting, commanding panoramic views of the Clyde. Loch Lomond, Glasgow City or Airport, and the main West Highland routes are easily accessible. Guest lounge and dining areas have original stone walls. Rooms have full hotel amenities - bath/shower, TV, telephone, tea/coffee tray, desk and hair dryer. Wines, draught beer, and spirits are available. Dine by oil lamplight! Extensive daily menu for home cooked dinners. Guest comment: One of the finest places we have stayed. E-Mail: Kirktonhouse@compuserve.com

see PHOTO on page 445

Stewart & Gillian Macdonald
Tel: 01389 841 951
Fax: 01389 841868

B&B from £28.50pp, Dinner from £14.50, Rooms 2 twin, 4 family, all en-suite, Restricted smoking, Children welcome, Pets welcome, Open all year except Christmas and New Year, Map Ref 3

Abbot's Brae Hotel, West Bay, Dunoon, Argyllshire PA23 7QJ   **Nearest Road A815**

Welcoming and friendly country house hotel in secluded 2 acre woodland glen with breathtaking views of the sea and hills. Spacious and tastefully furnished bedrooms all en-suite with colour TV, radio, direct dial telephone, tea/coffee making facilities, and full central heating. Unwind with a drink by the fire in the well appointed lounge and dine in the cosy dining room with delicious a la carte menu and select wine list. Residential licence. The perfect base to explore Argyll and the Western Highlands. Only one hour from Glasgow airport.

see PHOTO on page 446

Helen & Gavin Dick
Tel: 01369 705021
Fax: 01369 705021

B&B from £24.50pp, Dinner £14.50,
Rooms 4 double, 3 family, all en-suite,
Open all year, Map Ref 4

Tigh an Lodan, Ford by Lochgilphead, Argyll PA31 8RH   **Nearest Road A816**

In scenic and tranquil surroundings at the southern end of Loch Awe yet within easy reach of the main west coast road. Ford is ideally situated for enjoying the unspoilt attractions of mid Argyll, as well as for fishing and walking. We offer imaginative cuisine, using local produce, especially game and seafood, fruits from our own garden and homemade bread. The elegant sitting room, with a fine outlook, has plentiful books and an open fire for chilly evenings. There are three comfortable well equipped bedrooms.

Dr & Mrs Bannister
Tel/Fax: 01546 810287

B&B from £21pp, Dinner by request £13, Rooms 2 en-suite twin,
1 en-suite double, No smoking, Children from 13 years, Pets welcome,
Open May - October, Map Ref 5

Knock Cottage, Lochgair, Lochgilphead, Argyll PA31 8RZ Nearest Road A83

Knock Cottage has a beautiful wild garden and glorious views over lochs and hills. The cottage, an ancient croft with modern additions, offers warm, comfortable rooms with private facilities, tea/coffee making equipment and a cheerful drawing-room with an open fire, delicious meals and a friendly, relaxed style. There is plenty of room for car parking. Nearby are mountains, castles, museums, superb gardens and beaches; all the ingredients for a special holiday.

Mark & Nisa Reynolds
Tel: 01546 886 331

B&B £30pp, Dinner £19, Rooms 1 twin, 1 double, both en-suite, Restricted smoking, Children welcome, Pets by arrangement, Open all year except Christmas & New Year, Map Ref 5

Red Bay Cottage, Deargphort, Fionnphort, Isle-of-Mull, Argyll PA66 6BP Nearest Road A849

Red Bay Cottage is a modern house built on the shoreline of the south west coast of Mull. John and Eleanor have built up a very good reputation for the quality of food in their adjoining restaurant and guests can eat in the pleasant dining room, overlooking Iona Sound and the white sands of Iona. An ideal base for touring Mull, Iona and the Treshnish Isles. Eleanor is a qualified practising silversmith so why not enjoy a winter break. Send for details of residential silversmithing courses.

John & Eleanor Wagstaff
Tel: 01681 700396

B&B from £16pp, Dinner from £7.50, Rooms 2 twin, 1 double, Pets by arrangement, Open all year, Map Ref 6

Low Coylton House, Manse Road, Coylton, South Ayrshire KA6 6LE Nearest Road A70

Spacious, very comfortable and quiet country house (Old Manse 1820) set in attractive garden. TV and tea/coffee making facilities in bedrooms all with private bathroom. Golfers paradise, courses nearby including Ayr, Troon and Turnberry. Ayr 6 miles. Safe, sandy beaches 7 miles. Hill walking 15 miles. Culzean Castle (National Trust). Galsgow 35 miles. Edinburgh 70 miles. Dinner by arrangement.

Anne & George Hay
Tel: 01292 570615

B&B from £23pp, Dinner £15 on request, Rooms 2 twin, 1 double, all with private/en-suite facilities, Children welcome, Open all year except Christmas & New Year, Map Ref 7

Dunduff Farm, Dunure, Ayrshire KA7 4LH Nearest Road A719

Dunduff Farm, perfect for relaxing and unwinding, situated just south of Ayr at the coastal village of Dunure. It's location is ideal for walks, Culzean Castle, Burns Cottage, Turnberry, Galloway Forest, and many more. Accommodation is of a high standard. Our bedrooms have panoramic coastal views and all facilities. Breakfast has something for all appetites, try our "Dunduff Grand" to set you up right for the day and our home baked soda bread and locally smoked kippers.

John & Agnes Gemmell
Tel: 01292 500 225
Fax: 01292 500 222

B&B from £20pp, Rooms 1 twin, 2 double, 1 family, all en-suite, No smoking, Children from 10, No pets, Open February - November, Map Ref 8

---

*right, **Kirkton House, Cardross** - see details on page 443*

Annecy, 60 Montgomery Street, Eaglesham, Glasgow G76 0AU   Nearest Road M74,B764

Attractive cottage with lovely garden in centre of 18th century conservation village, 10 miles south of central Glasgow. Convenient for Burrell Collection and Glasgow airport. Four restaurants nearby. Large lounge/dining room. TV's and tea/coffee facilities for guests. Warm comfortable bedrooms with view of garden. Owners happy to help with advice on travelling in Scotland and places of interest in Glasgow. Off street parking behind house. Loch Lomond 1¹/₂ hours away via Erskine Bridge.

Anne & David Margetts
Tel: 01355 302413

B&B from £20pp, Rooms 1 single, 1 twin, 1 family, 2 private facilities,
No smoking, Children welcome, No pets,
Open all year except October, Christmas & New Year, Map Ref 9

East Lochhead, Largs Road, Lochwinnoch, Renfrewshire PA12 4DX   Nearest Road A760

Janet Anderson guarantees you a warm welcome at East Lochhead where you will find every home comfort. The one hundred year old farm house has spectacular views over Barr Loch and the Renfrewshire hills. You can wander around the landscaped gardens or explore the Paisley/Irvine cycle track which passes close to the house. Janet is an enthusiastic cook and would be delighted to prepare you an evening meal with prior notice. Both rooms are beautifully furnished and have colour TV and tea/coffee making facilities. STB Highly Commended. EMail: winnoch@aol.com

Janet Anderson
Tel/Fax: 01505 842610

B&B from £25pp, Dinner from £15, Rooms 1 twin, 1 double, both en-suite,
Restricted smoking, Children welcome, Pets by arrangement,
Open all year, Map Ref 10

Please mention
THE GREAT BRITISH
BED & BREAKFAST
when booking your accommodation

left, Abbot's Brae Hotel, Dunoon - see details on page 443   **447**

TAYSIDE

Sir Walter Scott greatly admired this glorious area centred on Perth, the 'Fair City' made a Royal Burgh in 1210. And a fair city it certainly is, and within a fair region. Within easy reach is Scone, the coronation place of Scottish kings, and the origin of the 'Stone of Destiny'. The city is delightfully situated on Scotland's longest river, the silver Tay. To the north-west is Blair Atholl the meeting place of several glens, and surrounded by magnificent mountain scenery. Glamis, the picturesque village in the lovely Vale of Strathmore, is the castle and ancestral home of the Earls of Strathmore, and childhood home of the Queen Mother.

Craigbank Guest House, Crianlarich, Perthshire FK20 8QS   Nearest Road A85

Craigbank is an attractive stone built house situated in the very heart of the central Highlands, surrounded by some of the finest scenery in Scotland. Ideal for hill walking and fishing and within one hours drive you can visit the Trossachs, Loch Lomond or Glencoe. The attractive bedrooms and comfortable lounge with open fire offer a peaceful sanctuary after a busy day sightseeing and the full Scottish breakfast provided by Peter and Carole will set you up well for the day.

Peter & Carole Flockhart
Tel: 01838 300279

B&B from £16pp, Rooms 3 twin, 1 en-suite, 1 double, 1 family,
Restricted smoking, Children welcome, Pets by arrangement,
Open all year except Christmas & New Year, Map Ref 12

Allt-Chaorain House, Crianlarich, Perthshire, Central Highlands FK20 8RU   Nearest Road A82

Allt-Chaorain House is a small residential hotel affording guests the amenities, comfort and atmosphere of your own home. The lounge has a log fire burning throughout the year, a trust bar and adjoining sunroom which offers one of the most picturesque views of the Highlands, with Ben More dominating the landscape. We are a 'Taste of Scotland' member and proud of our reputation for home cooked food which is made from fresh local produce. An honesty bar and a comprehensive wine list is available for those guests who enjoy a relaxing drink.

Roger McDonald
Tel: 01838 300283
Fax: 01838 300238

B&B from £33-£39pp, Dinner from £15, Rooms 4 en-suite twin,
4 en-suite double, Restricted smoking, Children from 7-12 years,
Pets welcome, Open 20th March - 30th April, Map Ref 12

Dupplin Castle, By Perth, Perthshire PH2 0PY   Nearest Road A9

Dupplin was rebuilt on the site of the original castle in 1969 and stands in private parkland of some antiquity. The old balustraded terrace and rose garden remain with stunning views south over the grounds and lovely Earn valley. The gracious reception rooms and the bedrooms are furnished to a high standard creating an atmosphere of tranquility and elegance. Dupplin is an ideal base for Central Scotland. Golf (St Andrews, Carnoustie, Rosemount), castles and beautiful old gardens (Scone Palace, Falkland Palace & Drummond Castle to name a few) abound nearby. EMail: DUPPLIN@netcomuk.co.uk

Derek & Angela Straker
Tel: 01738 623224
Fax: 01738 444140

B&B from £45pp/£55pp, Dinner from £30, Rooms 2 twin, 2 double,
all en-suite, Restricted smoking, Minimum age 12,
Pets by arrangement, Open all year, Map Ref 13

see PHOTO opposite

right, Dupplin Castle, By Perth - see above for details

Kinnaird Guest House, 5 Marshall Place, Perth, Perthshire PH2 8AH   Nearest Road M90/A85

Would you like to relax in comfort? Then the warm friendly atmosphere at Kinnairo is just the place. We aim for high standards and traditional home comforts and cater for individual needs. Beautifully situated overlooking a leafy park to the south and our charming town centre is within easy walking distance. Buses and trains also within easy reach. An ideal base from which to explore this beautiful region and its many historical attractions.

John & Tricia Stiell
Tel: 01738 628021
Fax: 01738 444056

B&B from £22pp, Dinner from £10, Rooms 3 twin, 4 double, all en-suite, No smoking, Children from 12, No pets, Open all year except Christmas & New Year, Map Ref 14

Wood of Auldbar, Aberlemno, By Brechin, Angus, Tayside DD9 6SZ   Nearest Road A90

A warm welcome awaits you at our lovely farmhouse. We are a working farm. Excellent food and tea facilities in all bedrooms. Smoke alarms throughout. Hygiene Certificate held. Ideal for touring Glens of Angus, Royal Deeside. Many castles nearby. Fishing, golf, all leisure activities nearby. Birdwatching, standing stones can be viewed. Aberdeen, Dundee, St Andrews, Edinburgh within easy reach. Breakfast and dinner is served in lovely conservatory, overlooking garden. TV in lounge. Plenty of room for parking. Children welcome. STB Commended.

Mrs Stewart
Tel: 01307 830218

B&B from £15pp, Dinner from £9.50, Rooms 1 single, 1 twin, 1 family, No smoking, Children welcome, Pets by arrangement, Open all year, Map Ref 15

Please mention
THE GREAT BRITISH BED & BREAKFAST
when booking your accommodation

"This darksome burn, horseback brown,
His rollrock highroad roaring down"
Gerard Manley Hopkins

WALES

Tourism is now Wales' largest industry, and little wonder, Wales has such a lot to offer, and so much that is peculierly Welsh. The wonderful lilting Welsh language is the first language of many in the north and west of the country, in fact roughly one in five of its inhabitants are Welsh speaking. The Welsh are famously musical, and this is expressed in festivals and events all over the country, culminating in the colourful Llangollen International Musical Eisteddfod, where singers and dancers from all over the world gather; and Wales' most important cultural festival, the Royal National Eisteddfod which dates back to 1176. Needless to say Wales possesses some superb theatres and concert halls including the very fine St. David's Hall, Cardiff. Wales is very much an 'outdoor' country, and has a fine reputation as a sporting nation. The three National Parks offer all the walking and climbing visitors could wish for. The Snowdon National Park, rugged and rocky, the Brecon Beacons National Park, presenting the walker with a much more open and rolling landscape, and one of Europe's classic coastal walks which follows the Pembrokeshire Coast National Park coast path a distance of one hundred and ninety miles around the western shore of Wales. For the slightly less energetic and for families, there

are the delights of forest walks in the Coed y Brenin Forest and around lovely Betws-y-Coed.

But surely the glory of Wales must be in its magnificent medieval castles, well over a hundred in number, and varying considerably in style and size. The superb fortress of Caernarfon, reputed to be the birthplace of the Emperor Constantine, with its Eagle Tower, one of the largest built in the Middle Ages. Here in 1284 Edward I presented his son to the Welsh people as Prince of Wales. HRH Prince Charles was similarly invested in 1969....The grand Beaumaris Castle, which was never attacked....Harlech Castle built by Edward I, and where Owen Glendower's wife and family were captured by Henry V....and glorious Conwy Castle, guarding the Conwy estuary.

As well as the spectacular mountains and waterfalls, historic castles and houses, the rugged coasts, the music and song, the wide spaces and open skies, there are also some grand traditional seaside resorts...Llandudno, Colwyn Bay, Prestatyn and Rhyl, Aberystwyth, Aberdovey and Porthcawl ....and then there are the delights of Clough Williams-Ellis's Portmeirion.

WALES

Places to Visit

Cardiff Castle, *Cardiff* ~ it began as a Roman fort whose remains are separated from later work by red stone. The keep was built in the 12th century and in 1867 William Burges created an ornate mansion. The Banqueting Hall shows the castle's history with murals and a castellated fireplace.

Llechwedd Slate Mines, *Blaenau Ffestiniog* ~ opened to visitors in the early 1970's, a tramway takes passengers into the caverns. On the Deep Mine tour, visitors go down Britain's steepest passenger incline railway to the underground chambers. Also, there are demonstrations of slate splitting and reconstructed quarrymen's cottages, showing the cramped living conditions of workers.

Pentre Ifan, *between Fishguard and Cardigan* ~ a Neolithic chambered long barrow on the northern slopes of the Preseli Hills. The capstone is thought to weigh over seventeen tons and is balanced on three pointed uprights.

Pen y Fan, *Brecon Beacons* ~ at over two thousand and nine hundred feet high this is the highest point in South Wales. Its flat summit was once a Bronze Age burial ground and can be reached by footpaths from Storey Arms.

Powis Castle, *Welshpool* ~ it began life in the 13th century as a fortress, to control the border with England. The dining room is decorated with 17th century panelling and family portraits. The gardens were created between 1688 and 1722 and are the only gardens of this period in Britain to keep their original form.

St David's Cathedral, *St Davids* ~ set in Britain's smallest city, St David, the patron saint of Wales founded a monastic settlement here in 550, but the cathedral was built in the 12th century and the nearby Bishops Palace was added in the 13th century. Inside is St David's Shrine; the original was stolen in 1089 and the present shrine of 1275 was stripped of jewels in the Dissolution.

Strata Florida Abbey, *near Pontrhydfendigiad* ~ Prince Rhys ap Gruffydd founded a community of Cistercian monks here in 1184 and they looked after large sheep ranches over the surrounding Cambrian Mountains. All that remains of their abbey is a western doorway, some foundations laid out in the grass and some medieval floor tiles.

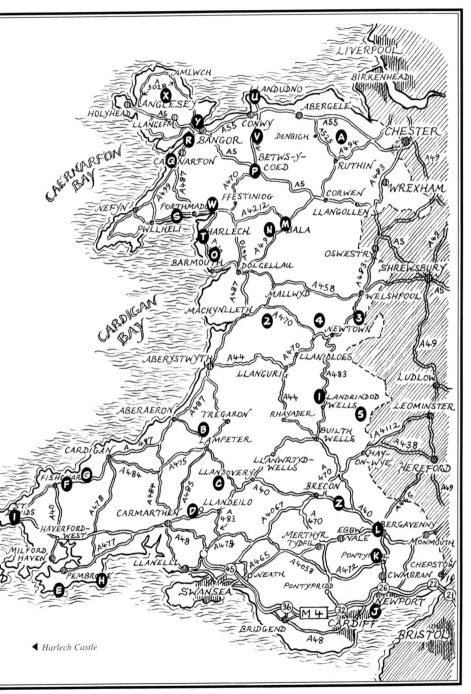

◀ Harlech Castle

CLWYD

Clwyd offers a quite amazing variation of scenery, from the mountains and valleys around Llangollen to the popular seaside resorts of Colwyn Bay, Rhyl and Prestatyn with their long sandy beaches. Ruthin, the old market town ringed by wooded hills, is a fine centre for touring the area. Corwen on the River Dee is renowned for its trout and salmon fishing, and is a wonderful centre for walking the Berwyn Mountains. This is the country of Owen Glendower the fifteenth century Welsh hero, who in 1404 declared himself Prince of Wales. From Moel Fammau are quite spectacular views eastward to the Peak District, and westward to the mountains of Snowdonia.

The Old Mill Private Hotel, Melin-y-Wern, Denbigh Road, Nannerch, Mold CH7 5RH   **A541**

A small and friendly private hotel, created by the conversion of 19th century stone built stables. Now forming part of a garden setting water mill conservation area together with adjacent wine bar, restaurant and gallery. Our fully equipped en-suite rooms are complemented by a residents' lounge, with over 100 local attraction brochures on display. Enjoy a first class breakfast in our pine furnished dining room. WTB Highly Commended and RAC Highly Acclaimed. All year special value short break tariff. Brochure available. Phone free 0800 454233 (UK) for information and reservations. EMail: guest-services@old-mill.u-net.com

Susan & Neil Evans
Tel: 01352 741542
Fax: 01352 740254

B&B from £28pp, Dinner from £13.75, Rooms 1 twin, 3 double, 2 family, all en-suite, No smoking, Pets by arrangement, Children at special rates, Open all year except Christmas, Map Ref A

"Mmm, the smell of newly baked bread - oh Bertie, our last cooked breakfast tomorrow..."

DYFED & PEMBROKESHIRE

Cardigan Bay is ringed by delightful resorts, with comfortable Victorian Aberystwyth at its centre. From Constitution Hill are magnificent views to the Preseli Hills and the Snowdon Range. The visitor must not miss the Devil's Bridge, in fact three bridges, over the River Mynach, the oldest built in the twelfth century by the monks from Strata Florida. In the wild Cambrian mountains are the picturesque Elan Valley reservoirs, and the glorious Teifi Valley is a magnet to trout and salmon fishermen. The Pembrokeshire Coast National Park, a vast area of fine walking country is a paradise for the naturalist and bird lover. Dinas Island, really a peninsular, affords spectacular views from its cliff-top path.

Dremddu Fawr Farm, Creuddyn Bridge, Lampeter, Ceredigion SA48 8BL   **Nearest Road A482**

Ann, Dilwyn and their family extend a warm welcome (croeso cynnes) to their Edwardian farmhouse on 163 acre working farm. Bedrooms have en-suite facilties, central heating through out, equipped with hair dryer, hospitality tray and colour TV. Guests' lounge and dining room. Candle light dinners and open fires. Former winner of "All-Wales Top Cook" Award. Conveniently located off A482 between Lampeter and Aberaeron - Georgian coastal town. WTB 3 Crowns Highly Commended. WTB Farmhouse award. Welcome Host. Credit and debit cards accepted. Attractive scenery and Cambrian mountains.

Dilwyn & Ann Jones
Tel: 01570 470394

B&B from £21pp, Dinner from £12.50, Rooms 1 twin, 1 double, both en-suite, No smoking, Children welcome, Pets by arrangement, Open all year, Map Ref B

Glanrannell Park, Crugybar, Llanwrda, Carmarthenshire SA19 8SA   **Nearest Road A40/A482**

Near historic towns of Llandovery, Llandeilo and Lampeter this country house is a haven of peace and tranquillity. With the Brecon Beacons, castles, abbeys, gold mines and much more nearby, it's a wonderful centre for West Wales. All rooms have private bathrooms, colour TV, radio and tea/coffee making facilities. There is a licensed bar, extensive wine cellar with dining room overlooking lawns and lake. Run by the Davies Family for 29 years, here you will find a real Welsh welcome, Wales Tourist Board Highly Commended 3 Crown, AA 2 Star 72%. EMail: GLANPARKHOTEL@BTINTERNET.COM

David & Bronwen Davies
Tel: 01558 685230
Fax: 01558 685784

B&B from £30-£36pp, Dinner from £16.00, Rooms 2 single, 3 twin, 2 double, 1 family, all en-suite, Restricted smoking, Children and pets welcome, Open April - October, Map Ref C

see PHOTO on page 458

Plas Alltyferin, Pontargothi, Nantgaredig, Carmarthenshire SA32 7PF   **Nearest Road A40**

A classic Georgian Country House lying in the hills above the beautiful Towy Valley, overlooking a Norman hillfort, the River Cothi -famous for salmon and sea trout, and its own private cricket pitch. There are two spacious twin bedrooms, each with private bathroom and stunning views, for guests who are welcomed as friends of the family. Antique furniture. Log fires. Excellent local pubs and restaurants. Marvellous touring country for castles, beaches and Welsh-speaking Wales. Total peace but under 4 hours from London.

Charlotte & Gerard Dent
Tel/Fax: 01267 290662

B&B from £20pp, Rooms 2 twin, all en-suite, Children over 12 years, Pets welcome, Open all year except Christmas and New Year, Map Ref D

The Old Vicarage, Manorbier, Pembrokeshire SA70 7TN   Nearest Road A4139

Situated in the village of Manorbier with its castle and beaches, the Old Vicarage offers gracious accommodation with glimpses of Barafundle Bay. Guests are free to enjoy the gardens or log fire in the drawing room. Both spacious bedrooms are furnished with antiques and have tea/coffee making facilities. For the more energetic the Pembrokeshire Coastal Path passes through the village. The old servants' quarters are available as a 2 bedroomed self-catering unit for longer stays. Irish ferries from Pembroke and Fishguard. Beaches a 5 minute walk. Absolutely no smoking.

Mrs Jill McHugh
Tel/Fax: 01834 871452

B&B from £19pp, Rooms 1 en-suite twin, 1 double with private facilities, No smoking, Children welcome, No pets, Open all year except Christmas, Map Ref E

Fernley Lodge, Manorbier, near Tenby, Pembrokeshire   Nearest Road B4585

Fernley Lodge is in the centre of the beautiful coastal village of Manorbier. The Pembrokeshire coastal path and superb beach, overlooked by church and Norman castle, are just 1/4 mile away. The house is a wonderfully restored property, classically decorated with antique furnishings. All rooms have TV and tea making facilities. The guests' drawing room overlooking a croquet/tennis lawn, is warmed by an open log fire on cooler evenings.

Mrs Jane Cowper
Tel: 01834 871226

B&B from £19pp, Rooms 2 double, 1 en-suite family, No smoking, Children welcome, Pets by arrangement, Open all year, Map Ref E

Grove Park Guest House, Pen-y-Bont, Newport, Pembrokeshire SA42 0LT   Nearest Road A487

Small friendly guest house situated on the edge of a coastal town at the foot of the Preseli Hills, which are steeped in magic and mystery. 100 yards from Pembrokeshire coast path and protected bird sanctuary. Excellent country, hill and coast walking nearby. Built in 1879 for a sea captain and his family, the house has been completely refurbished but still retains its original character. Most bedrooms are en-suite, all have colour TV and tea/coffee making facilities. Imaginative three course dinner menu. Vegetarians welcome. WTB Three Crowns Highly Commended. Licenced.

Ann King & Malcolm Powell
Tel: 01239 820122

B&B from £19pp, Dinner from £13.50, Rooms 2 en-suite double, 1 twin, 1 double, No smoking, Children welcome, Open all year except Christmas & New Year, Map Ref F

Parc Glas Bach, Newport, Pembrokeshire SA42 0QU   Nearest Road A487

We offer a double room, with spectacular views across the bay, in a secluded old stone cottage just 800 yards from the Pembrokeshire National Park Coast Path. Guests have TV lounge, dining room and conservatory overlooking landscaped gardens and the estuary. We have an extensive breakfast menu and facilities for making snacks at all times. Access is directly onto the Preseli Hills with good drying facilities for walking and sailing gear. We are central for touring the counties beauty spots and ancient monuments.

Ann Jones
Tel: 01239 820451

B&B from £20pp, Rooms 1 en-suite double, No smoking, children or pets, Open March - October, Map Ref G

Wychwood House, Penally, near Tenby, Pembrokeshire SA70 7PE   Nearest Road A4139

Large country house offering sea views from some of its elegant and spacious bedrooms, some with large sun balcony and all with tea/coffee facilities, and TV. Dine by candlelight and relax and enjoy Lee's interesting and freshly cooked 4-course menu of the day. Open fires in lounge and dining room. 2 miles south of Tenby, Penally lies 1/4 mile off the A4139 and is situated between two full size golf courses. Nearby is an excellent beach, which you can walk along to the ancient walled town of Tenby. Boat trips are also available to visit the monastic Island of Caldey. WTB Highly Commended.

Lee & Mherly Ravenscroft
Tel: 01834 844387

B&B from £19pp, Dinner from £13, Rooms 3 double (1 with four poster and private bathroom), 1 en-suite family, Restricted smoking, Pets by arrangement, Open all year, Map Ref H

Ramsey House, Lower Moor, St David's, Pembrokeshire SA62 6RP   Nearest Road A487

Catering exclusively for discerning couples (non-smoking) who appreciate fine food and wines to complement fully-appointed en-suite bedrooms. Award-winning dinners with Welsh emphasis and affordable wines make Ramsey House the place to stay in West Wales. Ideally situated for St. David's Cathedral, Coast Path, beaches and attractions. All rooms have remote-control colour TV, hospitality trays, hairdryers and powerful electric showers. Private parking. Dogs welcome. Bookings for dinner, B&B only please during high season (£41-£44pppn). Stay 7 nights for the price of 6. WTB 3 Crown Highly Commended.

Mac & Sandra Thompson
Tel: 01437 720321
Fax: 01437 720025

B&B from £25-£29pp, Dinner from £13.00, Rooms 3 twin, 4 double, all en-suite, No smoking or children, Pets welcome, Open all year, Map Ref I

Please mention
THE GREAT BRITISH
BED & BREAKFAST
when booking your accommodation

GWENT

The market town of Abergavenny is beautifully situated on the River Usk, a fine trout river. Overlooked by the majestic Ysgyryd Fawr, Blorenge and Sugar Loaf mountains, the town is the gateway to the Brecon Beacons National Park. Monmouth, on the River Wye is traditionally said to be the birthplace of Henry V, and is a touring centre for the Wye Valley. From nearby Kymin Hill are glorious views across the Wye and the valley of Monnow. Newport on the Usk, has been an important town since Roman times, its Cathedral of St. Woolos on Stow Hill is believed to stand on the site of a sixth century church. There is sailing on the Llandegfedd reservoir, coarse fishing and trout in the Wye, Monnow and Usk, and numerous castles and places of historic interest in this lovely region.

The West Usk Lighthouse, St Brides, Wentloog, near Newport, Gwent NP1 9SF　　　B4239, M4 (J28)

Grade II listed, The West Usk is a real lighthouse built in 1821 to a unique design. Rooms are wedge-shaped within a circular structure. The entrance hall is slate-bedded and leads to a central stone spiral staircase and the internal collecting well! The views are panoramic from the roof patio. All the bedrooms are en-suite and have been individually furnished to include a king size waterbed and 4-poster bed. Guests can try the flotation tank for deep and immediate relaxation. Most amenities are close by and there are many interesting places to visit in the area. Distinctly different.

Frank & Danielle Sheahan
Tel: 01633 810126/815860
Fax: 01633 815582

B&B from £35pp, Dinner by arrangement only,
Rooms 3 double with en-suite facilities, No smoking,
Pets by arrangement, Open all year, Map Ref J

Ty'r Ywen Farm, Lasgarn Lane, Mamhilad, via Trevethin, Pontypool, Gwent NP4 8TT　　　Nrst Rd A472

A 16th century Welsh longhouse on a mountainside, with breathtaking views down the Usk Valley and across the Bristol Channel. Retaining many original features every modern comfort has been embodied including 1 room with its own jacuzzi. From Pontypool town centre follow the sign for Blaenavon, at the roundabout turn right over river (sign Trevethin), take 2nd right at Yew Tree Inn, carry on for 1/4 mile to top of hill, turn right into Lasgarn Lane (sign Pontypool Golf Club), carry on for 1 mile to end of lane, through gate, turn right up a concrete ramp. Proceed with care.

Mrs Susan Armitage
Tel: 01495 785200
Fax: 01495 785200

B&B from £20pp, Light supper from £2.50, Rooms 3 double (4 poster beds), 1 twin, all rooms en-suite, Minimum age 14, No smoking, Open all year except Christmas & New Year, Map Ref K

The Wenallt, Abergavenny, Monmouthshire　　　Nearest Road A465

This historic 15th century longhouse, Wenallt Hotel nestles in the rolling hills of the Brecon Beacons described by some guests as the perfect peace and tranquillity. The small quiet hotel offers comfort personal service and excellent home cooking. This ideal location for enjoying country walks, breathtaking views or just relax on the spacious lawns, if you happen to be a budding artist or photographer then this is the ideal base with it's panoramic views. En-suite rooms. Inglenook log fires. Restaurant licensed. AA, RAC 3 Crowns Commended.

Mr Harris
Tel: 01873 830694

B&B from £16.50pp, Dinner from £11.50, Rooms 4 single, 1 twin, 5 double, 1 family, all en-suite, Children & pets welcome, Open all year, Map Ref L

See PHOTO on page 462

GWYNEDD

Wherever you are in this very special region you are surrounded by spectacular scenery. The glorious Snowdonia National Park covers most of the area. The great ranges, Snowdon, Tryfan, the Glyders, the Carneddau, the Moelwyns, Aran and Arennigs and Cader Idris...which is Welsh for 'chair of Idris'. Idris the Welsh hero, the tale is told, had a chair in which whoever slept awoke either a bard or a lunatic! The nature trail around Llyn Idwal gives access to wonderful scenery, including the crags of the Devil's Kitchen beneath Glyder Fawr. Here too is the attractive coast of the Llyn Peninsula and of course the lovely Isle of Anglesey, its fine coast designated an area of Outstanding Natural Beauty.

Melin Meloch, Bala, Gwynedd LL23 7DP   On the B4401

This picturesque former water mill close Bala stands in 2 acres of beautiful water scaped gardens, a delight for garden lovers. Pretty en-suite rooms some with own front doors in Granary and Millers Cottage, TV, hot drinks trays. The spectacular galleried interior of the mill is furnished with antiques and paintings. Here home cooked meals with fresh produce are served in a friendly relaxed atmosphere. 2 minutes drive Bala Lake and town, excellent for touring. Ample easy parking. Peaceful location. Highly Commended, Wales Tourist Board 2 Crown.

see PHOTO on page 465

Richard Fullard & Beryl Gunn
Tel: 01678 520101

B&B from £20pp, Dinner from £12.50, Rooms 2 single, 2 twin, 2 double, 1 family, most en-suite, No smoking, Children welcome, Pets by arrangement, Open March - November, Map Ref M

Frondderw Private Hotel, Stryd-y-Fron, Bala, Gwynedd LL23 7YD   Nearest Road A494

Frondderw is a 17th century period mansion quietly situated in its own grounds overlooking Bala town and Lake Tegid. There is a lounge, dining room and separate television lounge for guests use. Accommodation comprises many en-suite bedrooms. All bedrooms have hot/cold water, central heating and tea/coffee making facilities. Good home cooking with vegetarian and special diets catered for given advance notice. Ample free car parking. Ideal centre for sightseeing in North/Mid Wales, walking, cycling and watersports. WTB 3 crowns commended, AA 2Q.

Glynn & Wenda Jones
Tel: 01678 520301

B&B from £16, Dinner £10, Rooms 2 single (1 en-suite), 2 twin (1 shower), 2 double (1 shower, 1 en-suite), 3 family (2 en-suite), Restricted smoking, Children welcome, No pets, Open March - End November, Map Ref N

Llwyndu Farmhouse Hotel, Llanaber, Barmouth, Gwynedd LL42 1RR   Nearest Road A496

Llwyndu Farmhouse is a delightful 16th Century house which nestles in a spectacular location with panoramic views over Cardigan Bay, just north of Barmouth. Here Peter & Paula Thompson have created a very special place for you to stop and relax for a few days. A real historic farmhouse with inglenooks, oak beams, nooks and crannies. Seven very comfortable en-suite bedrooms, a fully licensed restaurant and imaginative cuisine make a stay here one to remember. A very beautiful area to explore for more details ring Peter or Paula. WTB 3 CRowns Highly Commended. All leading guides.

see PHOTO on page 466

Peter & Paula Thompson
Tel: 01341 280144
Fax: 01341 281236

B&B from £25.50pp, Dinner from £13.50, Rooms 1 twin, 4 double, 2 family, all en-suite, No smoking, Children welcome, Pets by arrangement, Open all year, Map Ref O

Royal Oak Farm Cottage, Betws-y-Coed, Gwynedd LL24 0AH   **Nearest Road A5**

An attractive old stone farm cottage and buildings set in a sunny courtyard on the banks of the beautiful river Llugwy. The cottage is quiet and secluded but only three minutes walk from the village centre and railway station. Betws-y-Coed is a walkers paradise with its rivers, lakes and tumbling streams amid forested hills and rugged mountains. Salmon and trout fishing, golf, walking, climbing, riding, shops, motor and railway museums are all available locally.

Mrs Kathleen Houghton
Tel: 01690 710760

B&B from £15pp, Rooms 1 twin with private facilities, 2 double en-suite, No smoking, Open all year except Christmas, Map Ref P

Bryn Afon, Pentre Felin, Betws-y-Coed LL24 0BB   **Nearest Road A5**

Old Welsh stone house on side of river. Own car park. All rooms have TV, beverage tray, central heating, some en-suite. Central for visiting mills, castles, National Trust. Beautiful scenery lakes, hills and forest walks on the door step. Golf, beaches, horse riding close by. A warm welcome awaits.

Marion & Bill Betteney
Tel: 01690 710403

B&B from £16pp. Rooms 2 twin, 4 double, most en-suite, No smoking, Children welcome, No pets, Open all year, Map Ref P

Fron Heulog Country House, Betws-y-Coed LL24 0BL   **Nearest Roads A5, A470**

"The Country House in The Village", Fron Heulog offers the welcome for which Wales is famous. This is a stone built house of Victorian charm with an excellent standard of comfort and modern amenities. The atmosphere is friendly and the home cooking delicious. Turn off the busy A5 road over picturesque Pont-y-Pair Bridge (B5106), immediately turn left between shop and river. Fron Heulog is up ahead 150 metres from bridge in quiet peaceful wooded riverside scenery with private parking. Short holidays; special prices. WTB 3 Crowns Highly Commended. Guest House award.

Jean & Peter Whittingham
Tel: 01690 710736
Fax: 01690 710736

B&B £20-£26pp, Dinner £15 all inclusive by arrangement, Rooms 2 double, 1 twin, all en-suite, Children minimum age 12, No smoking, No pets, Open all year, Map Ref P

The White House, Llanfaglan, Caernarfon, Gwynedd LL54 5RA   **Nearest Road A487**

A comfortably appointed modern country house enjoying splendid views of the Menai Straits and Snowdonia. A haven for bird watchers and sea anglers. A swimming pool is available for guests. Caernarfon Golf Club is only 2 miles away. Access to The White House is via the A487 Caernarfon/Porthmadog, on leaving Caernarfon, acrooss roundabout then turn right for Saron/Llanfaglan. Set mileometer to zero and proceed for 1.6 miles and turn right. The White House is on the left in half a mile, last house before the sea.

Beverley & Richard Bayles
Tel: 01286 673003

B&B from £17.50pp, Rooms 2 double, 2 twin, all with en-suite/private facilities, Pets by arrangement, Open March - November, Map Ref Q

---

      right, Melin Meloch, Bala - see page 463 for details

Gwern, Saron, Caernarfon, Gwynedd LL54 5UH Nearest Road A487

A warm Welsh welcome awaits you at Gwern, providing excellent accommodation on a family run beef and sheep farm. The farmland runs down to the Foryd Nature Reserve where guests are welcome to wander. Situated in open, peaceful countryside with beautiful views of the Snowdonia mountains, the Menai Straits and Anglesey. The spacious rooms have central heating, coffee/tea making facilities and colour television. Children welcome. Ample parking. No smoking. Choice of breakfasts using local produce and home made preserves. Perfect centre for touring or relaxing.

Ellen Pierce Jones **B&B from £19pp, Rooms 1 double, 1 family, all en-suite,**
Tel: 01286 831337 **No smoking, Children welcome, No pets,**
Open October - April, Map Ref R

Min-Y-Gaer, Porthmadog Road, Criccieth, Gwynedd LL52 0HP

A pleasant Victorian house, conveniently situated overlooking the sea and close to the beach. The hotel has delightful views of Criccieth Castle and the Cardigan Bay coastline. Ten comfortable, centrally heated rooms, all with colour TV and tea/coffee making facilities, some of which are non smoking. A lounge and licensed bar are available for guests and there is a private car park on the premises. An ideal base for touring Snowdonia and the Llyn Peninsula. WTB 3 Crowns and Highly Commended, AA Recommeded and RAC Acclaimed. EMail: minygaer.hotel@virgin.net

Mrs Rita Murray **B&B from £19.50 - £22.50pp, Dinner from £10, Rooms 1 single, 2 twin, 4**
Tel: 01766 522151 **double, 3 family, most en-suite, Restricted smoking, Children welcome,**
Fax: 01766 523540 **Pets by arrangement, Open March - October, Map Ref S**

Noddfa Hotel, Lower Road, Harlech, Gwynedd LL46 2UB Nearest Road A496

Noddfa (place of safety) was protected by Harlech Castle in earlier times but was extensively rebuilt in 1850. The comfortable bedrooms are equipped with TV and tea/coffee making facilities. Noddfa is situated close to the castle within the Snowdonia National Park having splendid views of Snowdon and Tremadoc Bay near swimming pool, beach and theatre. Gillian and Eric are keen historians and will be pleased to explain the displayed medieval weapons or use the bows to give you a traditional archery lesson. A guided tour of Harlech Castle is a speciality.

Gillian & Eric Newton Davies **B&B from £18pp, Dinner from £12, Rooms 4 double, some en-suite,**
Tel: 01766 780043 **Restricted smoking, Minimum age 4, No pets,**
Fax: 01766 781105 **Open all year, Map Ref T**

White Lodge Hotel, Central Promenade, Llandudno LL30 1AT Nearest Road A470, B5115

White Lodge Hotel is in an excellent position on the promenade and has retained the character of the Victorian period. A well kept hotel with a friendly and relaxing atmosphere. The en-suite bedrooms are all spacious and individually decorated, with tea/coffee making facilities, and colour TV. Breakfast and dinner are served in the pleasant dining room. Guests may relax in the lounge, enjoy a drink in the licensed bar and have use of the nearby swimming pool. There is a private car park. Well situated for Llandudno's many attractions.

Eileen & Peter Rigby **B&B from £24pp, Dinner from £9, Rooms 4 twin, 6 double,**
Tel: 01492 877713 **2 family, all en-suite, Minimum age 5,**
Open March - November, Map Ref U

---

left, Llwyndu Farmhouse Hotel, Llanaber - see page 463 for details

---

Albany House, Promenade, Llandudno, North Wales LL30 1BG   Nearest Road A55

A warm welcome and friendly atmosphere are assured at Alton House, situated on Llandudno's beautiful Victorian promenade. All bedrooms are en-suite and have colour TV, tea/coffee making facilities, hair driers, radio alarms. Convenient for theatre, shops and leisure centre, (several golf courses). Alton House is the ideal centre for touring the breathtaking Snowdonia National Park and North Wales coastline, Conway, Anglesey and Chester. Excellent food guaranteed, as well as cleanliness and comfort. Car park. WTB 3 Crown. Linda and Mike look forward to welcoming you.

Mike & Linda Bentley
Tel/Fax: 01492 878908

B&B from £18pp, Rooms 1 single, 4 twin, 4 double, 1 family, all en-suite, Restricted smoking, Children welcome, Pets by arrangement, Open March - October, Map Ref U

Firs Cottage, Maenan, near Llanrwst LL26 0YR   Nearest Road A470

Our 17th century Welsh cottage is a comfortable family home on the A470 with a beautiful garden and patio where guests may relax and plan visits to all the many local attractions. Bodnant Garden, Conwy Castle, Llandudno and Snowdon are all within easy reach - as are many excellent places for a pleasant evening meal. We offer 3 well furnished cottage bedrooms and a full cooked Welsh breakfast with home-made bread, jams and marmalades.

Mary & Jack Marrow
Tel: 01492 660244

B&B from £15.50 per person per night, Rooms 2 twin or double, 1 double, Restricted smoking, Well behaved pets by arrangement, Open all year except Christmas, Map Ref V

Y Wern, Llanfrothen, Penrhyndeudraeth, Gwynedd LL48 6LX   Nearest Road A4085/B4410

'Y Wern' is a 17th Century stone-built farmhouse situated in beautiful countryside within the Snowdonia National Park. 'Wern' abounds with oak beams and inglenook fire places, and the large comfortable bedrooms have delightful views, and are equipped with beverage making facilities. An excellent centre for walking, riding; well-placed for beaches and attractions such as Portmeirion, castles and the Ffestiniog Railway. Imaginative home cooked meals are served in the large oak-beamed kitchen, truly the heart of a warm welcoming home.

Paddy & Tony Bayley
Tel/Fax: 01766 770556

B&B from £19pp, Dinner from £11.50, Rooms 3 twin, 2 double, all en-suite, No smoking, Children welcome, No pets, Open all year, Map Ref W

Drws y Coed Farm, Llannerch y Medd, Isle of Anglesey LL71 8AD   Nearest Road A5/A5025

With wonderful panoramic views of Snowdonia and unspoilt countryside, enjoy peace and tranquility at this beautifully appointed farmhouse on a 550 acre working beef, sheep and arable farm. It's centrally situated to explore Anglesey. Tastefully decorated and furnished en-suite bedrooms with all facilities. Excellent meals served in cosy dining room. Inviting spacious lounge with log fire. Full central heating. Games room. Historic farmstead. Lovely private walks. Warm welcome assured from Tom and Jane. Wales Tourist Board 2 Crowns De luxe Graded. 25 minutes to Holyhead for Irish Sea crossings.

Mrs Jane Bown
Tel: 01248 470473

B&B from £20-£22.50pp, Rooms 1 twin, 1 double, 1 family, all en-suite, No smoking, Children welcome, No pets, Open all year except Christmas, Map Ref X

Bwthyn, Brynafon, Menai Bridge, Isle of Anglesey LL59 5HA   Nearest Road A545

Warm, welcoming, non smoking B&B, 1 minute from beautiful Menai Strait and bowling green. Bwthyn ('dear little house' in Welsh), a former Victorian quarryman's cottage, offers comfort, character and genuine hospitality. 2 pretty en-suite double rooms, with power shower   (1 also with bath), colour TV, tea/coffee, complemented by scrumptious real home cooking. 1 1/2 miles A5/A55, 2 miles rail/coaches, 40 mins Holyhead Ferry. Limited private parking. Special over 45's break - 3 nights dinner, bed & breakfast £79pp. WTB 2 Crown Highly Commended. Farm and Guesthouse Award. Come as guests - leave as friends.

Rosemary Abas   **B&B from £15pp, 4 course Dinner £12.50 by arrangement,**
Tel: 01248 713119   **Rooms 2 double en-suite, No smoking, No children or pets,**
Fax: 01248 713119   **Open all year except Christmas, Map Ref Y**

"Goodbye, Mr Beezon! Thank you for having us!"

POWYS

Powys is the heart of rural Wales. The Brecon Beacons, designated a National Park in 1957 includes the Black Mountains with Fan Brycheiniog, its highest peak, the twin peaks of Corn Ddu and Pen-y-fan forming the Beacons, and confusingly another range called the Black Mountains. Not that this region is all spectacular mountain scenery...far from it - there is the splendour of Powis Castle in its lovely gardens, cruises along the Montgomery Canal, the Welshpool and Llanfair Light Railway, and the impressive Dan-yr-ogof Caves - Western Europe's largest cave complex, and Brecon Cathedral Heritage Centre. And throughout the year there are festivals of all descriptions including the colourful Llandrindod Wells Victorian Festival.

The Old Rectory, Llansantffraed, Brecon, Powys LD3 7YF   Nearest Road A40

See PHOTO opposite

The Old Rectory dating from the 18th century, has been extended to form a home of character and charm. The back of the house faces south west with views of the mountains; the grounds run down to the River Usk. Conveniently situated for walking, horse riding or motoring in the Beacons and Black Mountains. The house is centrally heated with log fires in the winter and colour TV for guests use. Also self contained 1 bedroomed cottage, delightfully renovated - details available.

Mrs Margaret Howard
Tel: 01874 676240

B&B from £18pp, Dinner/Light suppers by arrangement, (Wine can be brought in), Rooms 2 double, 1 twin, all en-suite, Restricted smoking, Open all year, Map Ref Z

Dolycoed, Talyllyn, near Brecon, Powys LD3 7SY   Nearest Road A40

An attractive Edwardian house in mature gardens offering home comforts in a beautiful part of Wales at the foot of the Brecon Beacons, 5 miles from Brecon. Directions to Dolycoed are: from Brecon A40/A470 take the A40 for Abergavenny, left onto the B4558 to Llangorse, turn right at the post office and next right, the house is on the right before the next 'T' junction.

Brian & Mary Cole
Tel: 01874 658666

B&B from £17pp, Rooms 1 twin, 1 double, disabled guests welcome, Open all year, Map Ref Z

Guidfa House, Crossgates, Llandrindod Wells, Powys LD1 6RF   Nearest Road A44/A483

See PHOTO on page 472

This stylish Georgian Guest House has earned an enviable reputation for it's comfort, good food and service. It offers superior en-suite accommodation including a ground floor room. Relax in the elegant sitting room with it's open log fireplace and discreet corner bar. Enjoy the imaginative meals prepared by "Cordon Bleu" trained Anne accompanied by an excellent wine list. Set in the very heart of Wales, 3 miles North of Llandrindod Wells, Guidfa House is an excellent base for touring the wonderful local countryside.

Tony & Anne Millan
Tel: 01597 851241
Fax: 01597 851875

B&B from £24pp, Dinner from £15.50, Rooms 2 single, 3 twin, 2 double, most en-suite, Restricted smoking, Children from 10, No pets, Open all year, Map Ref 1

---

*right, **The Old Rectory, Llansantffraed** - see this page for details*

Yr Hen Felin, (The Old Mill), Abercegir, Machynlleth, Powys SY20 8NR   Nearest Road A489

Relax at our stone watermill, built in 1820 on the peaceful banks of the River Gwydol, where you can listen to the sound of the river from your bedroom window. The walking and scenery are some of the finest in Wales and the coast with its fine sandy beaches can be reached in 20 minutes. Heavily beamed throughout with original pine floors and antique furniture. All our bedrooms are en-suite and there is a large guests sitting room with TV. Private parking. Brochure available. AA QQQQSelected. WTB Highly Commended.

Jill & Barry Stevens
Tel: 01650 511868

**B&B from £19pp, Rooms 2 twin, 1 double,
No smoking, Children from 12, No pets,
Open all year except Christmas and New Year, Map Ref 2**

Little Brompton Farm, Montgomery, Powys SY15 6HY   Nearest Road B4385

Robert and Gaynor welcome you to this charming 17th century farmhouse situated on this working farm. The house has much original character with beautiful old oak beams. Furnished with traditional antiques. Pretty bedrooms with en-suite or private bathroom enhanced by quality furnishings. TV. Home cooking is a speciality (meals by arrangement). Offa's Dyke runs through the farm. Powys Castle and Llanfair Light Railway nearby. On the B4385, 2 miles east of the beautiful Georgian town of Montgomery. Come and relax in peaceful, stress free countryside. A warm welcome.

Mrs G Bright
Tel: 01686 668371

**B&B from £19pp, Dinner £10 by prior arrangement, Rooms 1 twin,
1 double, 1 family, all en-suite, No smoking, Children welcome,
Pets by arrangement, Open all year, Map Ref 3**

Dyffryn Farmhouse, Aberhafesp, Newtown, Powys SY16 3JD   Nearest Road B4568

Come and stay with us in lovingly restored 17th Century farmhouse. Set in the heart of a 200 acre working sheep and beef farm. There is an abundance of wildlife and flowers along the stream outside the door, with woodland and lakes nearby. Golf, fishing and glorious walks nearby. Luxury en-suite rooms with full central heating. Traditional farmhouse fare including vegetarian specialities totally non smoking. Garden and banks of stream for guests to sit by. Come and enjoy life on a Welsh hill farm. You might want to say! AA Premier Selected 5Q's. WTB De Luxe Grade 3 Crowns.

Dave & Sue Jones
Tel: 01686 688817
Fax: 01686 688324

**B&B from £22pp, Dinner from £12, Rooms 1 twin, 2 double, 1 family,
all en-suite, No smoking, Children welcome, No pets,
Open all year except Christmas & New Year, Map Ref 4**

The Old Vicarage, Evancoyd, Evenjobb, Presteigne, Powys LD8 2PA   Nearest Road B4357

Superb Victorian former Vicarage set in extensive grounds in the glorious countryside of Mid Wales. Recently restored to provide elegant and spacious living. Each of the three large bedrooms has its own private bathroom. Meals are taken in the beautiful dining room. Guests have exclusive use of a large, comfortable drawing room. Use The Old Vicarage as a base to explore the local historic Border towns and countryside or as a gateway to Mid Wales and the Welsh Coast - or simply to relax and unwind!
E-Mail: richmar@oldvic.kc3ltd.co.uk

Richard & Mary Hill
Tel: 01547 560308
Fax: 01547 560265

**B&B from £21pp, Dinner by arrangement, Rooms 3 double,
all private bathroom, No smoking, Children from 10, Pets restricted,
Open all year except Christmas & New Year, Map Ref 5**

---

left, Guidfa House, Llandrindod Wells - see page 470 for details

THE
GREAT
BRITISH
BED
AND
BREAKFAST

KGP Publishing
Penrith, Cumbria, England

the Great British
Self Catering
Cottage GUIDE

including

BUNGALOWS

CABINS

CASTLES

CHALETS

CONVERTED BARNS

COTTAGES

FARMHOUSES

& TOWN HOUSES

How often I wonder, have you wished that you could spend just a little bit longer at that special place you've just discovered...maybe while staying at one of our recommended bed and breakfast venues...to further explore its fascination. But time didn't allow and you had to move on, to groans and grumbles from the rest of the family.

Now 'The Great British Bed & Breakfast' are offering self-catering cottages to fulfill that wish...your own base to return to each evening to your 'own fireside'. Specially selected is some of the most attractive places that can be imagined - out of the way places that offer perfect peace and relaxation - or if you prefer, in regions packed with interests and activities to suit the most energetic family. Unrestricted by regular mealtimes...dress as you like...come and go as you please...what could be more convenient.

These are all cottages of the same high standards that you have come to expect from our bed and breakfast guide, but tailored to suit the holidaymaker who wants to stay that little bit longer.

CONTENTS

"Calm down Jack! We've got all the journey to go yet!"

❖❖❖

The Cream of Cottages

At the Cream of Cottages we are dedicated to ensuring that each and everyone of our customers enjoys a truly, satisfying and carefree holiday. Whether its a remote peaceful hideway for two or a base for the family holiday, you can select a Scottish Coach House to a converted Somerset Cheese Loft or a 15th century Cumbrian Tower to a Stately Manor....the choice is yours!

350 cottages, sleeps 2-21, Price per week £99-£798,
Available all year.

Contact: Mr A C Harding, The Cream of Cottages, 1 West Walks, Dorchester DT1 1RE
Tel: 01305 266877 Fax: 01305 267001

Cream of Cottages

❖❖❖

❖❖

Cottage: Hideaways, Chapel House, Luke Street, Berwick St. John. Shaftesbury, Dorset

A wide range of high quality cottages, farmhouses, country homes and apartments, many of period character, in rural and coastal settings and in historic towns throughout the heart of England, South, South East and South West. Short breaks available September to May. Phone or fax for our full free colour brochure giving detailed descriptions.

110-120 cottages, sleeps 1-12, Price per week £146 low season, £1421 high season, Children welcome, Pets welcome, Available all year.

Contact: Mr Pash, Hideaways, Chapel House Luke Street, Berwick St. John, Shaftesbury, Dorset SP7 0HQ
Tel: 01747 82800 (Brochure request) Tel: 01747 828170 (Reservations) Fax: 01747 829090

Hideaways

❖❖

Bath, Bristol
& North East
Somerset

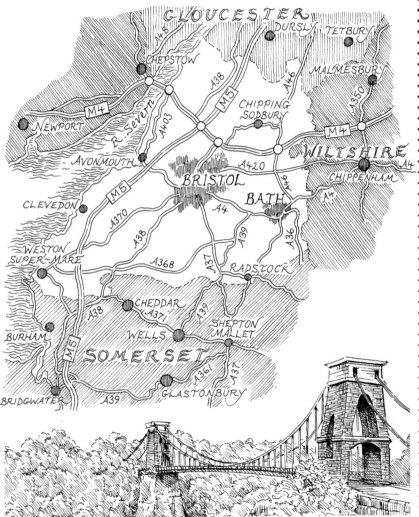

❖❖

Cottage: Conygre Mew, Farmborough, Bath

Set in two acres of beautiful gardens, 7 miles from Bath and near Cotswolds, Stonehenge, Wells and Cheddar. 3 bedroom, 2 bathrooms, former stables from 1710. Extremely comfortable, well equipped and tastefully decorated Rose and Wisteria clad facade with french windows opening onto patio, white plaster walls exposed stonework, beams, parquet flooring, persian rugs, country antiques and open fireplace. Barbecue, garden furniture. Ample parking.

1 cottage, sleeps 5/6, Price per week £300 low season, £450 high season, Children welcome, No pets, Available April - November.

Contact: Jamie Blair Gould, Conygre House, Farmborough, Bath BA3 1AZ
Tel: 01761 470363 Fax: 01761 472995

above, Congyre Mews, Farmborough, near Bath

❖❖

Cambridgeshire & Northamptonshire

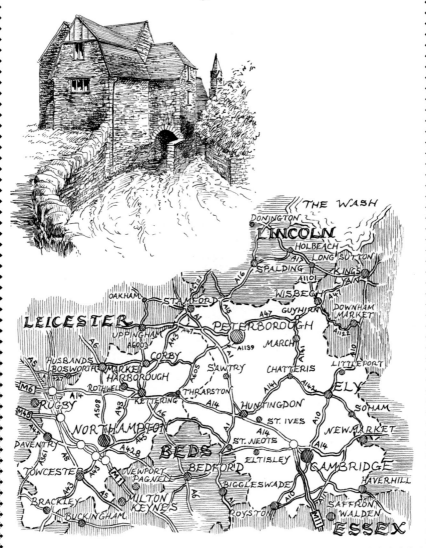

❖❖

Cottage: Hill House Farm Cottage, 9 Main Street, Coveney, Ely

A tasteful barn conversion in a farmyard. Furnished and decorated to a high quality in a quiet peaceful village location with open views of Ely Cathedral and the surrounding countryside. Situated three miles west of Ely, with easy access to Cambridge, Huntingdon and Newmarket.

1 cottage, sleeps 6, Price per week £180.00 low season, £300.00 high season, No smoking, Children from 8, No pets, Available all year.

Contact: Mrs Hilary Nix, Hill House Farm, 9 Main St, Coveney, Ely, Cambridgeshire CB6 2DJ
Tel: 01353 778 369

above, Hill House Cottage, Coveney, Ely

❖❖

Cornwall

CORNWALL
The Great British Self Catering Cottage Guide

❖❖❖

Cottage: Penrose Burden Holiday Cottages, St Breward, Bodmin, Cornwall

See PHOTO on opposite page

Situated in North Cornwall within easy reach of both coasts. Over looking a beautiful wooded valley and private salmon and trout fishing, river. Birds can be watched from the cottage windows. The stone cottages with exposed beams and quarry tiled floors, wood burning stoves have been featured on TV and are award winners. Home made meals can be delivered daily. All are suitable for disabled.

**8 cottages, sleeps 2 - 6 and extra bed or cots,
Price per week £155 low season, £535 high season,
Children welcome, Dogs welcome, Available all year.**

Contact: Nancy & Rodney Hall, Penrose Burden, St Breward, Bodmin, Cornwall PL30 4LZ
Tel: 01208 850277 & 01208 850617 Fax: 01208 850915

❖❖❖

Cottage: Frogapits, Old Road, Boscastle, North Cornwall

See PHOTO on opposite page

An idyllic 18th century detached cottage with a stream running through the pretty "cottage garden". Just two minutes from Boscastle's Old Harbour, village and wonderful cliff walks with spectacular coastal views. Old beams, huge open fire and TV. Stripped pine kitchen with wood burner. Microwave/freezer. Large utility room for muddy boots and fishing nets! Tintagel Castle, sandy beaches, rocky coves and Bodmin Moor all close by.

**1 cottage, sleeps 4, Price per week £200 low season, £495 high season,
Children welcome, No pets, Available March to October.**

Contact: Richard & Beth Soar, The Manor House, Culworth, Banbury, Oxon OX17 2BB
Tel: 01295 760099 Fax: 01295 760098

❖❖❖

Cottages: Coverack Sea Front Cottages, Helston, Cornwall

See PHOTO on page 486

Coverack is one of Cornwall's most unspoilt, picturesque and romantic villages. We offer you three very different cottages; Tervarrow with its thatched roof, low shipwrecked beams and charm of bygone smuggling days. Puffin offers a special tranquillity, with its garden extending to the cliff-edge. Sandpiper conveys a more modern beach-top atmosphere. All are fully equipped, have luxury fitted kitchens and enjoy magnificent sea views.

**3 cottages, sleeps 6,5,6, Price per week £185 low season, £600 high season,
Children welcome, Pets by arrangement, Available all year.**

Contact: Raymond & Iris White, Little Pengwedna Farm, Helston, Cornwall TR13 0AY
Tel/Fax: 01736 850 649

❖❖❖

Penrose Burden Holiday Cottages, Bodmin - see page 484

Frogapits, Boscastle - see page 484

Coverack Sea Front Cottages, Helston - see page 484

Barnham Farm Cottages, Launceston - see page 487

❖❖❖

Cottage: Godopolphin Cross, Helston, Cornwall

Delightful cottage in peaceful sheltered valley, 200 yards attractive village between Helston/Penzance, 3 miles beaches. Lovely countryside. Lounge open fire, colour TV/video. Kitchen - dishwasher, microwave, electric cooker, utility room, washing machine, tumble drier, fridge/freezer, cloakroom, one double bedded room, two twin bedded rooms, bathroom, bath, washbasin, toilet, electric shower, central heating, garage, patio, garden.

1 cottage, sleeps 6, Price per week £265.00 low season, £415.00 high season, Children welcome, No pets, Available May - September.

Contact: Mr & Mrs Broughton, Orchard House, Wall, Gwinear, Hayle, Cornwall TR27 5HA Tel: 01736 850201 Fax: 01736 850046

❖❖❖

Cottage: Bamham Farm Cottages, Launceston, Cornwall

Superb farm cottage in beautiful countryside, ETB 4 Keys Commended and Highly Commended. ³/₄ mile from ancient market town of Launceston with its Norman Castle (restaurant, golf, riding etc.) Magnificent heated indoor pool, sauna, satellite television, some cottages have open fires, dishwasher, microwave, children's outdoor and indoor play area, games room, laundry room, ample parking, easy reach beaches, moors and many places of interest.

See PHOTO on opposite page

8 cottages, sleeps 2-8, Price per week from £175 - £230 low season, £425 - £680 high season, Children welcome, No pets, Available all year.

Contact: Jackie Chapman, Higher Bamham Farm, Launceston, Cornwall PL15 9LD Tel: 01566 772141 Fax: 01566 775266

❖❖❖

Cornish Collection, Looe, Cornwall

Luxury waterfront apartments (4 Keys Highly Commended by the Tourist Board), and delightful cottages all within walking distance of the beach. Microwaves, dishwashers, washing machines, colour TV, sea views, whirlpool baths, four poster beds and log fires, all available in different properties. Super pubs and restaurants nearby. Also golf, watersports, riding, fishing, tennis, National Trust homes and gardens.

20 properties, sleeping 2-8, Price per week from £130 low season, from £400 high season, Children welcome, No pets, Available all year.

Contact: Mr Dixon, Cornish Collection, 73 Bodrigan Rd, Barbican, East Looe, Cornwall PL13 1EH Tel/Fax: 01503 262736Tel: 01736 850201 Fax: 01736 850046

❖❖❖

CORNWALL
The Great British Self Catering Cottage Guide

❖❖

Cottage: Classy Cottages, Blanches Windsor, Lansallos

See PHOTO on opposite page

Classy cottages, 3 superlative coastal cottages. 2 cottages in Polperro; along the coast isolated residence with sea views and 3 acres of gardens; small group of 10 farm cottages. All visitors welcome to use our private indoor pool with spa, sauna, solarium. We offer high quality accommodation with dishwashers, washing machines, telephones, maid and cleaning service etc. To complete our welcome a cornish cream tea awaits your arrival.

14 cottages, sleeps 2-10, Price per week £95 low season, £1,500 high season, Children & Pets welcome, Available all year.

Contact: Mrs Fiona Nicolle, Classy Cottages, Blanches Windsor, Lansallos, Looe, PL13 2PT
Tel: 01720 423000

❖❖

Cottage: Cant Cove, Rock, Cornwall

Cant Cove cottages are in a superb location in seventy acres of private grounds overlooking the Camel estuary. The houses are extremely well equipped with dishwashers, microwaves, washing machines and driers. Each house has a log fire, TV, video, whirlpool bath and shower. Cant Cove has a tennis court, golf practice and beautiful gardens. The cottages are situated close to safe sandy beaches.

6 cottages, sleeps 5-8, Price per week £265 low season, £1565 high season, Children welcome, No pets, Available all year.

Contact: Mrs G M Barlow, Cant Cove, Rock, Cornwall PL27 6RL
Tel: 01208 862841 Fax: 01208 862142

❖❖

Cottage: Tregeath Cottage, Tregeath Lane, Tintagel, North Cornwall

Charming character cottage, situated in a peaceful, rural surrounding, about 1 mile from historic village of Tintagel. Modernised detached stone and slate farm cottage with 3 bedrooms, night storage heaters, coal grate, colour TV, microwave, small secluded garden. Car parking. Stunning cliff walks. King Arthur's castle and hall, Trebarwith strand beach, $1^1/2$ miles by road. An area of outstanding natural beauty. Tregeath is the ideal cottage for a relaxed and private retreat all year round.

1 cottage, sleeps 5 + cot, Price per week £100 low season, £360 high season, Children welcome, Dogs welcome, Available all year.

Contact: Mrs Broad, Davina, Trevillett, Tintagel, North Cornwall PL34 0DZ
Tel: 01840 770217

❖❖

Classy Cottages, Lansallos - see page 488

"Ta guv, 'ave a good holiday!"

Cumbria

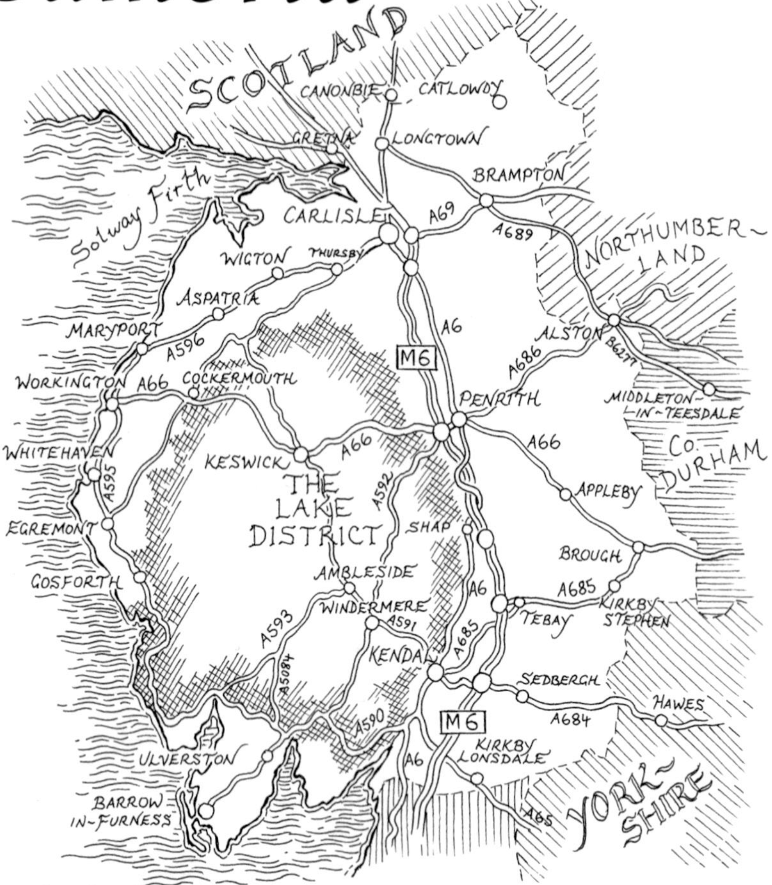
SCOTLAND
CANONBIE
CATLOWDY
GRETNA
LONGTOWN
BRAMPTON
Solway Firth
CARLISLE
A69
A689
NORTHUMBER-LAND
WIGTON
THURSBY
ASPATRIA
MARYPORT
A596
A6
ALSTON
B6277
A686
M6
WORKINGTON
A66
COCKERMOUTH
PENRITH
MIDDLETON-IN-TEESDALE
WHITEHAVEN
KESWICK
A66
A66
Co. DURHAM
A595
THE LAKE DISTRICT
A592
APPLEBY
EGREMONT
SHAP
BROUGH
GOSFORTH
AMBLESIDE
A6
A685
KIRKBY STEPHEN
WINDERMERE
A591
TEBAY
A593
A5084
KENDAL
A685
SEDBERGH
HAWES
A590
M6
A684
ULVERSTON
A6
KIRKBY LONSDALE
BARROW-IN-FURNESS
A65
YORKSHIRE

❖❖❖

Various Cottages in the North Lakes & Eden Valley area

Excellent and varied selection of Apartments, Cottages and Houses, fully equipped to suit all tastes and requirements. We cater for non-smoking/smoking, children, disabled persons and pets. Offering a wide variety of settings from town properties to secluded locations.

60 cottages, Price per week £140-£150 low season, £1450-£1500 high season, Children & Pets welcome, Available all year.

Contact: Mrs Thompson, Clark Scott-Harden, St Andrews Churchyard, Penrith, Cumbria
CA11 7YE
Tel: 01768 868989 Fax: 01768 865578

❖❖❖

Greycroft, The Raise, Alston, Cumbria

Luxury bungalow with open views south toward Crossfell on the fringe of the raise hamlet. One mile from the historical market town of Alston. Fully equipped and furnished to a very high standard. Two bedrooms with double and single beds. Linen provided, fitted kitchen, dishwasher, microwave, washer/dryer, gas central heating, open fire, TV and telephone. Ideal for Lakes, Northumberland, Durham and Hadrians Wall. Open all year. ETB 5 Keys Highly Commended.

See PHOTO on page 492

1 cottage, sleeps 6, Price per week £170 low season, £340 high season, No smoking, Children welcome, Pets welcome, Available all year.

Contact: Pat Dent, Crossgill Farm, Garrigill, Alston, Cumbria CA9 3HE
Tel: 01434 381383

❖❖❖

Cottage: Heart Of The Lakes & Cottage Life, Fisherbeck Mill, Old Lake Road, Ambleside

For the very best selection of quality self catering holiday homes in the very heart of England's beautiful central Lakeland. Many in rural locations, Ambleside, Grasmere, Langdale. Mostly ETB Commended to Highly Commended, many with gardens and views. Some accept a pet. Fully illustrated brochure offers something for everyone.

See PHOTO on page 492

180 cottages, sleeps 2-10, Price per week £149 low season, £1077 high season, Children & Pets welcome, Available all year.

Contact: Mr & Mrs Jackson, Heart Of The Lakes & Cottage Life, Fisherbeck Mill, Old Lake Road, Ambleside, Cumbria LA22 0DH
Tel: 015394 32321 Fax: 015394 33251

❖❖❖

Greycroft, Alston - see page 491

Heart of The Lakes & Cottage Life - see page 491

Old Farm Cottage & Barn Cottage, Bewcastle - see page 494

Bessietown Farm, Longtown - see page 494

❖❖❖

Cottage: Milburn Grange Cottages, Knock, Appleby, Cumbria

Cosy quality cottages nestling in pretty hamlet at foot of Pennines with superb views. Some beamed, 4 poster beds, all are centrally heated, all have microwaves, colour TV and washing/drying facilities. Larger cottages have dishwasher. Enclosed garden, barbecue area, plenty of off road safe parking. Short breaks. Special couple rates. Excellent for walking, visiting Lakes (Ullswater 25 mins away), Yorkshire and Scotland. ETB 3-4 Key Commended.

8 cottages, sleeps 2-7 + cot, Price per week £130.00 low season, £360.00 high season, Children & pets welcome, Available all year.

Contact: Robert & Margaret Burke, Milburn Grange, Knock, Appleby, Cumbria CA16 6DR
Tel/Fax: 017683 61867 or: 08365 47130

❖❖❖

Cottage: Old Farm Cottage & Barn Cottage, Bewcastle, Carlisle

See PHOTO on page 493

All the privacy of a commended cottage - but home cooking too! Meals and home baking from the farmhouse if you wish. Central heating, electric blankets, dishwasher, fridge/freezer, microwave, video, open fire, utility room and much more. Pretty garden. Attractive quiet countryside close to Scots Border; good walking by our river or in the forest, plenty of wildlife on our small hill sheep farm. Brochure/photo available.

2 cottages, sleeps 2-6 and cot, Price per week £140 - £330, Children welcome, Pets welcome, Available all year.

Contact: Dorothy & Boy Downer, Bank End Farm, Roadhead, Bewcastle, Carlisle, Cumbria CA6 6NU
Tel/Fax: 016977 48644

❖❖❖

Cottage: Bessietown Farm, Catlowdy, Longtown, Carlisle, Cumbria

See PHOTO on page 493

Three tastefully converted two bedroom courtyard cottages enjoying extensive views over border country. Well furnished, spacious, warm and welcoming. Waken to birds singing, swim in the pool, Meander through the meadows, picnic by the stream. Dine in the farm restaurant - simply unwind - open all year. Indoor heated pool open mid May - mid September. Special winter breaks. Phone for colour brochure.

3 cottages, sleeps 4 - 5, Price per week £160 low season, £340 high season, Children welcome, No pets, Available all year.

Contact: Jack & Margaret Sisson, Bessietown Farm, Catlowdy, Longtown, Carlisle, Cumbria
CA6 5QP
Tel/Fax: 01228 577219

❖❖❖

❖❖

Cottage: High Swinside Farm Holiday Cottages, Lorton, Cockermouth, Cumbria

High Swinside Farm lies above the Vale of Lorton on the northern slopes of Hopegill Head. Panoramic views range from the local fells and valley to the distant Scottish hills. Our peaceful location offers a quiet retreat yet only 6 miles from the busy towns of Keswick and Cockermouth. Please call for our full brochure and details about our comfortable well equipped cottages.

See PHOTO on page 496

**3 cottages, sleeps 2,5,6, Price per week £180 low season, £450 high season,
Children welcome, Pets welcome, Available all year.**

Contact: Tony & Veronica Cresswell, High Swinside Farm, Lorton, Cockermouth, Cumbria
CA13 9UA
Tel: 01900 85206 Fax: 01900 85076 EMail: tony.cresswell@btinternet.com

❖❖

Cottage: Fisherground Farm Holidays, Eskdale, Cumbria

Get away from it all on our lovely Lakeland farm. Inside your lodge are all the comforts of home - colour TV, microwave, dishwasher, etc. Outside is paradise. Children love the adventure playground and raft pools, or taking Dad on at table tennis or badminton. Or a ride on the miniature railway to Muncaster Castle. (We have our own station!). Pets welcome, Colour brochure on request.

**2 cottages, 3 pine lodges, sleeps 2-6,
Price per week £170-£220 low season, £280-£459 high season,
Children & Pets welcome, Available all year.**

Contact: Mr Hall, Fisherground Farm Holidays, Eskdale, Cumbria CA19 1TF
Tel: 01946 723319

❖❖

Cottage: Melbreak Cottage, High Park, Loweswater

Absolutely no traffic - just breathtaking mountain and lake views, luxury and seclusion. Sympathetically renovated 3 bedroomed oak beamed 17th century cottage. Four poster bed, whirlpool bath, open fire, full heating plus dishwasher, microwave, freezer, CD, TV, and telephone. Large garden with barbecue. Just 5 minutes from the lake and a 15 minute stroll to the pub. Ideal base for exploring the Lake District. ETB 5 Keys Deluxe.

See PHOTO on page 496

**1 cottage, sleeps 2-6, Price per week £370 low season, £680 high season,
No smoking, Children welcome, Pets welcome, Available all year.**

Contact: Dani Edwards, Pickett Howe, Buttermere Valley, Cumbria CA13 9UY
Tel: 01900 85444 Fax: 01900 85209

❖❖

CUMBRIA
The Great British Self Catering Cottage Guide

High Swinside Farm Holiday Cottages, Lorton - see page 495

Melbreak Cottage, High Park, Loweswater - see page 495

High Swinside Farm Holiday Cottages, Lorton - see page 495

Preston Patrick Hall Cottage, Crooklands - see page 498

❖❖❖

Cottage: Preston Patrick Hall Cottage, Crooklands, Milnthorpe, Cumbria

See PHOTO on page 497

Green fields with sheep and cows will be your first sight as you open your bedroom curtains. Our cottage is a self-contained, fully equipped wing of a magnificent medieval manor house. You may spend your time walking the quiet lanes, swimming in our pool or perhaps take advantage of the easy access to the Lakes, Dales and Morecambe Bay. Brochure available. Open all year.

1 cottage, sleeps 6, Price per week £105 low season, £305 high season, Children welcome, No pets, Available all year.

Contact: Stephen & Jennifer Armitage, Preston Patrick Hall, Milnthorpe, Cumbria LA7 7NY
Tel/Fax: 015395 67200

❖❖❖

Eden Grove Holiday Cottages, Lazonby, Penrith, Cumbria

Peaceful character cottages ideally situated in Lazonby, one of Cumbria's best kept villages. Built in local stone by the prestigious Midland Railway Company on the famous Carlisle-Settle Line. Completely modernised offering spacious well equipped accommodation with coal fire and central heating. Large play area for children, ample parking. Colour brochure. Colour TV, video, microwave washing machine, tumble drier, dishwasher etc.

5 cottages, sleeps up to 6, Price per week £135 low season, £300 high season, Children welcome, No pets, Available all year.

Contact: Mrs Bell, The Old Rectory, Lazonby, Penrith, Cumbria CA10 1BX
Tel: 01768 898242 or 01768 898437 Fax: 01768 898720

❖❖❖

Cottage: Manor Cottage, Caldbeck, Wigton, Cumbria

Relax in this unspoilt corner of Lakeland. The 17th Century converted barn gives well equipped spacious accommodation. The picturesque village of Caldbeck (2 miles) has a pond, church, public house and sports facilities. Keswick is 30 minutes away with south lakes, Scottish Borders and Hadrian's wall within easy reach. Storage heaters, electric cooker, microwave, fridge, TV, small garden, patio, ample parking. Lovely walks from door. ETB 3 Keys Highly Commended.

1 cottage, sleeps 2-3, Price per week £110 low season, £250 high season, No smoking, Children welcome, No pets, Available March - November.

Contact: Mrs Ann Wade, Manor Cottage, Caldbeck, Wigton, Cumbria CA7 8HA
Tel: 016974 78214

❖❖❖

❖❖❖

Cottage: Ghyll Bank Fell & Hillside, Staveley, Windermere

On a hillside with a stunning views of the lakeland hills and coastline. Many walks from the door. Quiet but close to Windermere. Lounge, dining room, kitchen, bathroom, shower room, garden, barbecue, good parking, TV, video, microwave, fridge/freezer. Large rooms with open fires or wood burning stove. Relax in a lovely home in a quiet valley on your own or with a large family group.

See PHOTO on page 500

2 cottages, sleeps 2-16, Price per week £140 low season, £400 high season, Children welcome, Pets welcome, Available all year.

Contact: Mr J D Beaty, Garnett House Farm, Burneside, Kendal, Cumbria LA9 5SF Tel: 01539 724542

❖❖❖

Please mention
THE GREAT BRITISH SELF CATERING COTTAGE GUIDE
when booking your accommodation

❖❖❖

Ghyll Bank Fell & Hillside, Staveley - see page 499

"Boys! You can take turns in the bed by the window!"

Derbyshire & Staffordshire

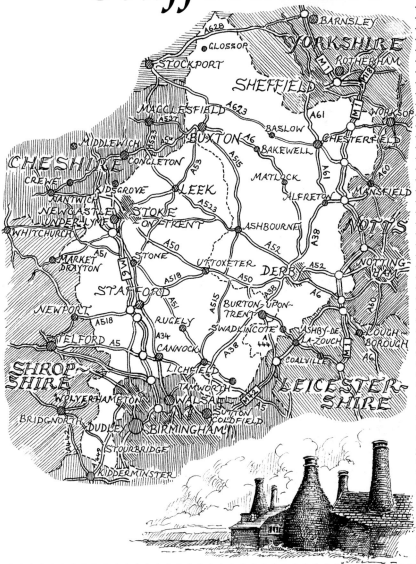

❖❖

Cottages: Honeysuckle & Brook Cottage, Weston Underwood, Ashbourne, Derbyshire

Honeysuckle is a truly delightful peaceful country cottage with secluded garden set amidst lovely countryside. Beamed sitting room, antique furnishings, three pretty bedrooms one with romantic four poster bed. Brook is an attractive village cottage situated in the centre of Weston Underwood. Ideally situated for Alton Towers and the Peak District. Access to the working farm. See the cows milked and collect the eggs. ETB 4 Keys Commended.

2 cottages, sleeps 4-6, Price per week £150 low season, £390 high season, Children welcome, No pets, Available all year.

Contact: Linda Adams, Park View Farm, Weston Underwood, Ashbourne, Derbyshire DE6 4PA
Tel: 01335 360352

❖❖

Cottage: Stable Cottage, Elkstone, near Buxton, Derbyshire

See PHOTO on opposite page

3 Keys Commended. Character country cottage, sympathetically modernised to retain original oak beams and galleried landing. In quiet Peak District village near Manifold Valley with Dovedale six miles away. Comfortable and very well equipped including bed linen and towels. Patio garden with sunny aspect. Parking. Convenient for National Trust Properties in Derbyshire, Staffordshire, Cheshire, Alton Towers and RSPB Reserve. Pub/Restaurant nearby. Short Winter breaks.

1 cottage, sleeps 2-3 and baby, Price per week £125 low season, £205 high season, Children welcome, Pets by arrangement, Available all year.

Contact: Mrs Lawrenson, Grove House, Elkstones, near Buxton, Derbyshire SK17 0LU
Tel: 01538 300487

❖❖

Please mention
THE GREAT BRITISH
SELF CATERING
COTTAGE GUIDE
when booking your accommodation

❖❖❖❖❖❖❖❖❖❖❖❖❖❖❖❖❖❖❖❖❖❖❖❖❖❖❖❖❖❖❖❖❖ — ❖❖❖❖❖❖❖❖❖❖❖❖❖❖❖❖❖❖❖❖❖❖❖❖❖❖❖❖❖❖❖❖❖

Stable Cottage, Elkstone, near Buxton - see page 502

"Come on Rosie, its only cold at first"

503

Devonshire

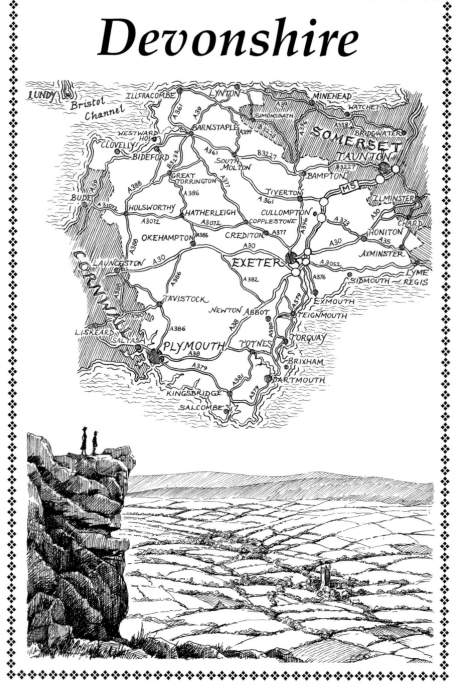

❖❖

Helpful Holidays

Helpful Holidays has cottages and houses all across some of England's most beautiful countryside. They range from snugs for two grand hotels for great gatherings and simple cottages with a roaring log fire. To see cottages close to beaches, on farm, on the moors and in the countryside all over the West Country, call 01647 433 535 (24hrs) for a free colour brochure.

See PHOTO on page 507

450+ cottages, sleeps 2-30, Price per week £65 low season, £750 high season, Children & pets welcome, Available all year.

**Contact: Mr Bowater, Helpful Holidays, Coombe, Chagford, Devon TQ13 8QF
Tel: 01647 433 593 Fax: 01647 433 694 E-Mail bowater@btinternet.com**

❖❖

Cottage: Mariners Cottage, Irsha Street, Appledore, Devon

Sea edge fishermans cottage: high tide comes up to back garden wall. Extensive open sea and estuary views of ships, lighthouses, sandy island. Spacious cottages sleeps 6 in 3 bedrooms, second wc downstairs, modern kitchen, dining room, lounge, garden with garden furniture. Dog welcome. Colour TV, washing machine. Fishing trips from quay, beach, waterside restaurants and pubs, cliff and coastal walks, stately homes, golf nearby. SAE please to K M Barnes, Boat Hyde, Northam, Bideford, Devon EX39 1NX

See PHOTO on page 507

3 cottages, sleeps 6, Price per week, £90 low season, £530 high season, Children & pets welcome, Available all year.

**Contact: Mr & Mrs Barnes, Boat Hyde, Northam, Bideford, Devon EX39 1NX
Tel: 01237 473801**

❖❖

Cottage: Cider Room Cottage, Membury, Axminster, Devon

Attractively converted thatched cider barn adjoining main 16th century farmhouse overlooking old orchard and ponds, surrounded by delightful countryside. Comfortable lounge, colour TV, many beams, exposed stonework. Well equipped galley kitchen, all electric including microwave. Open plan staircase leading to double bedroom, twin bedroom and shower room. Night store heating. Parking in old cobbled yard. Many interesting places to visit. Linen, evening meals available.

See PHOTO on page 508

1 cottage, sleeps 4 and cot, Price per week £130 low season, £250 high season, Children welcome, Pets by arrangement, Available all year.

**Contact: Pat & David Steele, Hasland Farm, Membury, Axminster, Devon EX13 7JF
Tel: 01404 881558 Fax: 01404 881834**

❖❖

◆◆

Cottage: Braddon Cottages, Ashwater, Devon

Six detached country cottages on 150 acre estate with access, 500 acres woodland. Surrounded by gardens, meadow and forest. Lake. Fishing. Boat. Summer house. All weather tennis court. Children's games room. Adult's snooker room. Barbecues. Gas central heating. Woodfires. Payphones. Bed linin, towels, fishing, fire wood included. Gas, electric extra. Colour brochure. Owner managed. ETB 4 Key Commended. Ten miles North Cornish Coast. For country lovers.

6 cottages, sleeps 12+cot, Price per week £90-£140 low season, £150-£595 high season, Restricted smoking, Children welcome, Dogs welcome, Available all year.

Contact: George & Anne Ridge, Braddon Cottages, Ashwater, Beaworthy, Devon EX21 5EP
Tel/Fax: 01409 211350

◆◆

Cottage: Lake House Holiday Cottages, Lake Villa, Bradworthy, Devon

There are two cottages here surrounded by peaceful countryside with the spectacular North Devon/Cornwall coastline 8 miles away. Both have central heating, plenty of parking, and one acre of gardens. Lake House is Victorian. It sleeps up to 6 in 3 bedrooms, has 2 bathrooms, an open fire and a fully fitted kitchen. Gardeners cottage is older and sleeps 3 in two cosy bedrooms.

2 cottages, sleep 2-6, Price per week £150 low season, £415 high season, Children & Pets welcome, Available all year.

Contact: Lesley & Peter Lewin, Lake Villa, Bradworthy, Devon EX22 7SQ
Tel: 01409 241962

◆◆

Cottage: Barn Cottage & Stable Cottage, Lufflands, Yettington, Budleigh Salterton, Devon

Country views from Barn Cottage sleeping six. Beamed, open plan living area. Three bedrooms above. Stable Cottage sleeps five. Open plan living area overlooking courtyard and two bedrooms on one level. Suitable for wheelchairs. Both cottages comfortably furnished. Fully equipped with auto. washing machine, microwave, TV, fridge. Large garden, ample parking. Children welcome. Excellent walking. Short drive to beaches. B&B accommodation in old farmhouse.

2 cottages, sleeps 5,6, Price per week £160 low season, £350 high season, Children welcome, No pets, Available Easter - September.

Contact: Stuart & Janet Lovett, Lufflands, Yettington, Budleigh Salterton, Devon EX9 7BP
Tel: 01395 568422

◆◆

A Cornish Fort to be married in - see Helpful Holidays on page 505

Mariner's Cottage, Appledore - see page 505

Cider Room Cottage, Membury, Axminster - see page 505

Dairy Cottage, The Granary, Cider Barrel & The Hayloft, Northleigh - see page 509

❖❖

Cottage: Dairy Cottage, The Granary, Cider Barrel, The Hay Loft, Northleigh, Colyton, Devon

Travel back in time leaving the 'fast lane' behind. Discover a rural scene, little changed since chronicled as a Domesday Manor . You are welcome to explore the farm and meet our prize winning pigs and other friendly farm animals. Self catering accommodation in converted stone barns and B&B in farmhouse. 'England for Excellence Award' 1995 'Best Self Catering Accommodation 1996'. Some suitable for wheelchair users.

See PHOTO on opposite page

4 cottage, sleeps 2,4,6,8, Price per week £95 - £625
Children welcome, No pets, Available all year.

Contact: Mrs Maggie Todd, Smallicombe Farm, Northleigh, Colyton, Devon EX13 6BU
Tel: 01404 831310 Fax: 01404 831431

❖❖

Cottage: Wheel Farm Country Cottages, Berrydown, Combe Martin, Devon

Enjoy the freedom of self catering with friendly 5 star service. A little bit of heaven, Gold Award gardens surround watermill and pretty cottages, nestling in a valley, a wildlife haven, lovely Exmoor views, superb beaches. Spoil yourself, inclusive indoor pool, fitness room, maid service, flowers, four poster beds, log fires. Plus home baking, sauna, tennis with tuition. Families welcome, walking, riding and cycling nearby.

10 cottages, sleeps 2-6+cot, Price per week £190 low season, £920 high season,
Children & pets welcome, Available March - October.

Contact: Mr & Mrs Massey, Wheel Farm Country Cottages, Berrydown 10, Combe Martin,
North Devon EX34 0NT
Tel: 01271 882100

❖❖

Cottage: Bodmiscombe Farm, Blackborough, Cullompton

A Devonshire cream tea and a welcoming smile greet new and returning guests to our tiny peaceful hamlet set in the Blackdown Hills. Our English Tourist Board 3 Keys commended standard guarantees cleanliness and comfort. The choice of activity is yours private coarse fishing, wonderful walks including a private woodland trail, tour Devon's moors and shores or sit and watch us at work. Contact us for details.

See PHOTO on page 511

1 cottage, sleeps 4 and cot, Price per week £115 low season, £285 high season,
No smoking, Children welcome, Pets by arrangement, Available all year.

Contact: Ray & Brenda Northam, Bodmiscombe Farm, Blackborough, Cullompton, Devon EX15 2HR
Tel/Fax: 01884 266315

❖❖

❖❖❖

Cottage: Glebe House Cottages, Bridgerule, Holsworthy, Devon

See PHOTO on opposite page

Grade II listed Georgian Estate with original Coach House, Stables and Barns beautifully converted into 7 well equipped, warm and comfortable cottages sleeping 2/6, with exposed beams, some 4-poster beds and double spa baths. Set in 5 acres of tranquil countryside, but only 10 minutes drive from beaches. Games room, children's play area, cellar bar and restaurant with log fire. Superb home-cooked food. ETB 4 Keys Highly Commended.

7 cottages, sleep 2-6, Price per week £195-£375 low season, £270-£695 high season, Children welcome, No pets, Available all year.

Contact: James & Margaret Varley, Glebe House, Bridgerule, Holsworthy, Devon EX22 7EW
Tel: 01288 381272

❖❖❖

Cottage: Oldaport Farm Cottages, Modbury, Ivybridge, Devon

See PHOTO on page 512

Four comfortable fully equipped cottages carefully converted from stone barns. Peaceful setting in beautiful South Hams Valley on historic 70 acre working sheep farm and miniature Shetland pony stud. There is an abundance of wildlife and many fascinating walks - The South coastal footpath and a sandy beach is nearby - Dartmoor just 8 miles away. Short breaks in low season. ETB 3 & 4 Keys Highly Commended.

4 cottages, sleeps 2 - 6, Price per week £142 - £220 low season, £275 - £420 high season, Children welcome, Dogs welcome in low season, Available all year.

Contact: Miss C M Evans, Oldaport Farm Cottages, Modbury, Ivybridge, Devon PL21 0TG
Tel: 01548 830842 Fax: 01548 830998

❖❖❖

Cottage: Dairymans Corner & Shepherds Rest, Galmpton, Kingsbridge, Devon

Cob and slate cottages situated in a pretty hamlet, 3 miles from the famous sailing town of Salcombe. Many other tourist attractions within a short drive. Many original features, open fireplace, garden. Takeaway meal available. Guests welcome to enjoy farm activities including summer barbecues. Cottages are 5 minutes walk from the farm. They are well equipped with washing facilities, microwave, dishwasher, cot and highchair.

2 cottages, sleeps 5-6,4-5, Price per week £100 low season, £450 high season, Children welcome, Pets welcome, Available all year.

Contact: Mrs Rossiter, Burton Farm, Galmpton, Kingsbridge, Devon TQ7 3EY
Tel/Fax: 01548 561210

❖❖❖

Bodmiscombe Farm, Blackborough - see page 509

Glebe House Cottages, Bridgerule, Holsworthy - see page 510

Oldaport Farm Cottages, Modbury, Ivybridge - see page 510

Budleigh Farm, Moretonhampstead - see page 513

❖❖❖

Cottage: Budleigh Farm, Moretonhampstead, Devon

All properties are equipped to make your stay comfortable and carefree: warm and cosy in winter, ready for outdoor eating and leisure, including outdoor heated swimming pool, in summer. Moreton, 1/2 mile away, is a little town with a big heart. We are in the National Park - pretty valleys and gushing rivers - and the open moor is only 3 miles away. Easy parking.

See PHOTO on opposite page

7 cottages, sleeps 2-6, Price per week £95 - £150 low season, £198 - £350 high season, Children welcome, Pets welcome, Available all year.

Contact: Judith Harvey, Budleigh Farm, Moretonhampstead, Devon TQ13 8SB
Tel: 01647 440835 Fax: 01647 440436

❖❖❖

Cottage: Netton Holiday Cottages, Netton Farm, Noss Mayo, near Plymouth, Devon

Attractive coastal complex, 10 miles Plymouth. 3/4 mile to picturesque villages, River Yealm estuary and the fabulous walks and beaches as seen in Sense & Sensibility. Indoor pool, games room, tennis court and private gardens. All cottages comfortably furnished and well equipped to high standard. Brochure and inquiries Sandy Cherrington 01752 872235. Also B&B.

5 cottages, sleeps 2-12, Price per week £260 low season, £1300 high season, Children welcome, Pets by arrangement, Available all year.

Contact: Sandy Cherrington, Slade Barn, Netton Farm, Noss Mayo, near Plymouth, Devon
PL8 1HA
Tel: 01752 872235

❖❖❖

Cottages: Stowford Lodge and 1 & 2 South Hill Cottages,Torrington, North Devon

Stowford Lodge - four attractive cottages converted from Victorian stone farm buildings. Heated indoor pool. Acres of play space. South Hill - Two spacious period farm cottages. Glorious views. Open log fires. Private patio. All cottages have colour TV, microwave, plenty of off-road parking, under-cover cycle storage. Tarka Trail and Rosemoor Gardens nearby. Lovely beaches and coastal walks. Moorlands within easy reach.

See PHOTO on page 514

6 cottages, sleep 6,4,4,4,4,4, Price per week £180 low season, £410 high season, Children welcome, Pets welcome, Available all year.

Contact: David & Sally Milsom, Stowford Lodge, Langtree, Torrington, North Devon EX38 8NU
Tel: 01805 601540 Fax: 01805 601487

❖❖❖

❖❖❖

Cottage: Venn Farm Cottages, Venn Farm, Kingsnympton, Umberleigh, North Devon

Comfortable well equipped cottages converted from stone barn on small working farm set in beautiful countryside near Exmoor within reach of sandy beaches. The children are encouraged to help feed the animals:- sheep, goats, chickens and ducks. Patios with picnic tables and barbecues. Laundry room. Adventure playground. Bed linen provided. Clay pigeon shooting. Pets welcome.

5 cottages, sleeps 2-7, Price per week £120.00 low season, £470.00 high season, Children & pets welcome, Available March - December.

Contact: Isla Martin, Venn Farm, Kingsnympton, Umberleigh, North Devon EX37 9TR
Tel: 01769 572448

❖❖❖

Stowford Lodge and 1 & 2 South Hill Cottages, Torrington - see page 513

❖❖❖

Dorset

❖❖

Cottage: Lyme Bay Holidays, Stanley House, The Street, Charmouth, Bridport, Dorset

Quality West Country cottages, houses, flats etc. Many in and around Lyme Regis and Charmouth. Close to the sea, stunning countryside and famous for fossils. Free colour brochure.

100 cottages, sleeps 2-12, Prices vary according to season & size, see our free colour brochure, Children & pets welcome, Available all year.

Contact: Lyme Bay Holidays (Dept K), Stanley House, The Street, Charmouth, Bridport, Dorset
DT6 6PN
Tel: 01297 560755 Fax: 01297 560415

❖❖

Cottage: Mallard Lodge, Whistley Waters, Milton on Stour, Gillingham, Dorset

Mallard Lodge overlooks lakes in beautiful quiet location. Living room with kitchenette, double bedroom and bathroom downstairs. One twin bedroom and two single upstairs, and WC. Double glazed, electric heating, microwave, 2 colour TV's, BBQ, garden chairs. Use washing machine. 6 hectares gardens, woods, lakes, good trout and carp fishing. Excellent centre for National Trust visiting. One hour cities Bath, Salisbury and coast. ETB 4 Keys Commended.

1 cottage, sleep up to 6, Price per week £170 low season, £420 high season, Children welcome, Dogs welcome, Available March - January.

Contact: Mrs Cleo Campbell, Whistley Waters, Milton on Stour, Gillingham, Dorset SP8 5PT
Tel/Fax: 01747 840666

❖❖

Cottage: Hartgrove Farm, Hartgrove, Shaftesbury, Dorset

Far from the madding crowd! Discover this glorious unspoilt corner of Dorset. Our family farm has breathtaking views. 4 superbly equipped cottages (ETB 4 Keys Highly Commended) and lovely farmhouse flat. Old beams, log fires, laundry room, tennis, games barn, free swimming at leisure centre. Coast 30 minutes. Pretty villages. Good pubs. Children will enjoy cows, calves, sheep, pony, chickens. One cottage suitable disabled, ETB Cat. 1.

5 cottages, sleeps 2-5, Price per week £155-£220 low season, £265-£490 high season, No smoking, Children & Pets welcome, Available all year.

Contact: Mrs Smart, Hartgrove Farm, Hartgrove, Shaftesbury, Dorset SP7 0JY
Tel/Fax: 01747 811 830

❖❖

❖❖❖

Cottage: Yew House Cottage, Yew House Farm, Husseys, Marnhull, Dorset

Secluded quiet off road location. Super view westwards from Verandahs. Individual privacy and space. Excellent centre for exploring this unspolit area. Good village pubs for food. Parking close to each cottage. One cottage suitable for less able visitors.

3 cottages, sleeps 4-5, Price per week £95 low season, £300 high season
Children welcome, No smoking, Available all year.

Contact: Gill Espley, Yew House Cottage, Yew House Farm, Husseys, Marnhull, Dorset
DT10 1PD
Tel: 01258 820412 Fax: 01258 821044

above, Yew House Cottage, Husseys, Marnhull

❖❖❖

Essex

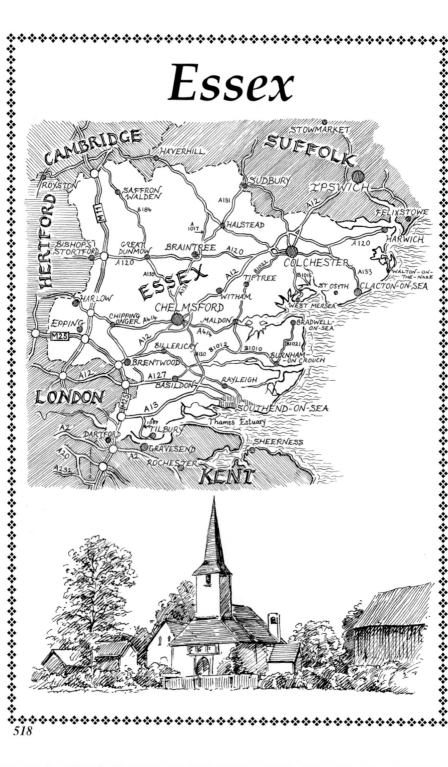

❖❖

Cottage: Whitensmere Farm Cottages, Ashdon, Saffron Walden

Converted 17th century barns still retaining many original features. All cottages are extremely well equipped, with TV, videos, microwaves, dishwashers etc. 'The Brues' sleeps 8/10,"Woodmore' sleeps 6/7 and 'Ladywell' 4/5. There is a games rooms and drying facilities, children play area and pets corner. Close to Cambridge and London only 1 hour. Heating by storage radiators and wordburners. Fresh flowers and welcome pack on arrival. 4-5 Keys Highly Commended.

3 cottages, sleeps 2-10, Price per week £160 low season, £680 high season, Children & dogs welcome, Available all year.

Contact: Mrs Ford, Whitensmere Farm, Ashdon, Saffron Walden, CB10 2JQ
Tel/Fax: 01799 584244

above, Whitensmere Farm Cottages, Ashdon, Saffron Walden

❖❖

Gloucestershire

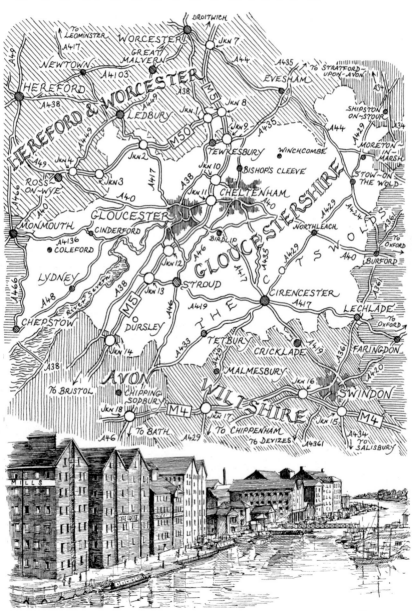

❖❖

Cottage: The Old Coach House, Draycott, near Moreton in Marsh, Gloucestershire

Sitting/dining room, kitchen, 1 double, 1 single bedroom - power shower - beautiful 2¹/₂ acre garden, original oak beams in first floor apartments of 1622, Grade II listed Coach House, well kept and very comfortable. Excellent centre for touring the Cotswolds. Near Oxford Stratford on Avon, Cheltenham, Moreton in Marsh, Broadway and Warwick. Excellent pubs and restaurants nearby. Electric heating included. Colour TV. 3 Key Highly Commended Tourist Board.

1 cottage, sleeps 3, Price per week £250 low season, £300 high season, No smoking, Children from 12, No pets, Available all year.

Contact: Mrs Kelly, The Old Coach House, Draycott, near Moreton in Marsh, Gloucestershire
GL56 9LF
Tel/Fax: 01386 700597

❖❖

Cottage: The 3 Cottages at Cinderhall House, Cider Cottages, Bigbarn, Cinder Hill Cottage

3 separate stone built cottages in the grounds of 14th century house. All equipped and furnished to a high standard; one has 2 en-suite bedrooms, one a 4-poster bed, and one is for the disabled. Very peaceful and beautiful location yet ideal for walking and touring. It is also possible to book in for dinner at the house which is open for very comfortable bed and breakfast.

3 cottages, sleeps 2-6, Price per week £203 low season, £410 high season, No smoking, Children & Pets welcome, Available all year.

Contact: Mrs Peacock, Cinderhill House, St Briavels, Gloucestershire GL15 6RH
Tel: 01594 530393 Fax: 01594 530098

❖❖

Cottage: Postlip House Cottage, Postlip House, Winchcombe, Gloucestershire

Beautifully appointed cottages set in seven acres of wooded grounds providing superb accommodation. Individual gas central heating, modern fitted kitchens, wedgewood china, silver infact everything for a relaxing country holiday and the ideal centre for touring the Cotswolds, Stratford and Oxford. Dinner if required prepared by proprietors and delivered to the cottages. ETB 4 Keys Highly Commended.

5 cottages, sleeps 2-6, Price per week £220-£270 low season, £350-£480 high season, Children welcome, Pets welcome, Available all year.

Contact: Mary & Paul Sparks, Postlip House, Winchcombe, Gloucestershire GL54 5AH
Tel/Fax: 01242 602390

❖❖

Herefordshire &
Worcestershire

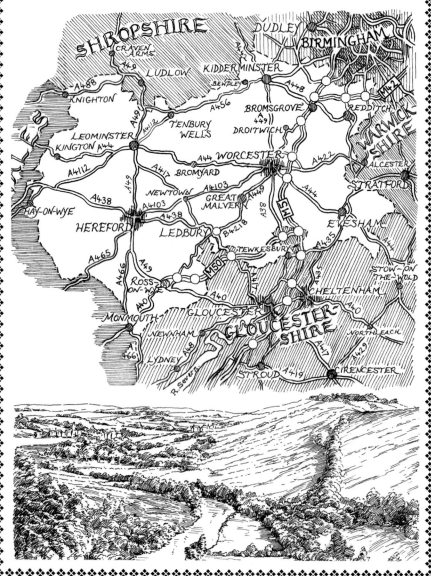

The Swiss Cottage & Lime Cottage, Canon Frome, Ledbury - see page 524

Anvil Cottage, Grafton - see page 524

❖❖

Cottage: The Swiss Cottage & Lime Cottage, Mill Cottage, Canon Frome, Ledbury

See PHOTO on page 523

The cottages are situated in beautiful 5-acre wooded grounds in peaceful spot amid lovely countryside. The Swiss Cottage is on the banks of the River Frome overlooking waterfall. Both are well equipped for two people. Excellent for wildlife including resident kingfishers. Well situated for the Malverns, Wye Valley and the Black Mountains. Bed & Breakfast also available in Mill Cottage - two en-suite rooms.

2 cottages, sleeps 2, Price per week £103-£148 low season, £212-£305 high season, No smoking, Children & Pets by arrangement, Available all year.

Contact: Julian & Lorna Rutherford, Mill Cottage, Canon Frome, Ledbury HR8 2TD Tel: 01531 670506 or: 0378 591899

❖❖

Cottage: Anvil Cottage, Grafton Villa, Grafton, Hereford

See PHOTO on page 523

Beams, natural wood and redbrick together with beautiful fabrics and antiques, makes our recently converted main house into a very delightful holiday base. Comfortable spacious bedrooms. A twin/triple and double, both en-suite shower and bathrooms. Lovely open plan lounge, leading to large enclosed patio. Kitchen with microwaves, wash/dryer, etc. Super maple wood units. Suitable for disabled. Surrounded by lawns and rolling Herefordshire countryside. Linen and electric included.

1 cottage, sleeps 4/5, Price per week from £180 low season, £320 high season, No smoking, Children welcome, No pets, Available all year.

Contact: Jennie Layton, Grafton Villa, Grafton, Hereford HR2 8ED Tel/Fax: 01432 268689

❖❖

Cottage: Somers Arms House, Cottage Wing, Eastnor, Ledbury, Herefordshire

The cottage is part of a former Georgian coaching inn, situated in Eastnor village at the foot of the Malvern Hills. Overlooking a cider orchard, near to Eastnor Castle and surrounding estate. Featured in 'Country Living', the cottages rusticity with its beamed ceilings and white walls is complemented by furnishings designed by it's owners. Heating and linen included in rental price. ETB 4 Keys Commended.

1 cottages, sleeps 3, Price per week £180 low season, £260 high season, No smoking, Children welcome, Pets welcome, Available all year.

Contact: Mrs Morgan-Oates, Somers Arms House, Eastnor, Ledbury, Herefordshire HR8 1EL Tel: 01531 631622 Fax: 01531 631361 E-Mail: roger@oates.demon.co.uk

❖❖

Mill House Flat, Leysters - see page 526

Mill Cottage, Ross-on-Wye - see page 526

HEREFORDSHIRE & WORCESTERSHIRE
The Great British Self Catering Cottage Guide

❖❖

Cottage: Mill House Flat, Woonton Court, Leysters, Leominster

See PHOTO on page 525

A former cider house converted to a high standard of comfort. 4 Keys Commended. Sleeps 3/4. Central heated accommodation, large double room, small bedroom single or two children, kitchen, electric cooker, microwave, fridge, colour TV, linen provided. Electricity included, payphone, washing machine/dryer. Patio garden parking. Freedom to walk on farm. Nature trail farm produce. Short breaks. **Extra accommodation in farmhouse nearby.**

1 flat, sleeps 3-4, Price per week £140 low season, £250 high season, Short breaks from £95, Children welcome, No pets, Available all year.

Contact: Mrs Thomas, Woonton Court Farm, Leysters, Leominster, Herefordshire HR6 0HL
Tel/Fax: 01568 750232

❖❖

Cottage: Mill Cottage, Rudhall, Ross-on-Wye, Herefordshire

See PHOTO on page 525

Picturesque 17th century cottage in attractive garden nestling beside millstream. Renovated and furnished to a high standard retaining its character. Panoramic views across rolling Herefordshire countryside. Cosy base from which to explore the beautiful Wye Valley and beyond. Garage. Entrance to oak all-electric kitchen. Dining room leading to sunroom/garden. Sitting room with colour TV. Pretty double and twin rooms, double glazing, NSH/electric. Heaters (by meter) throughout.

1 cottage, sleeps 4, Price per week from £200 low season, £400 high season, out of season 3 night breaks, No smoking, Children welcome, No pets, Available all year.

Contact: Michael & Heather Gammond, Rudhall Farm, Ross-on-Wye, Herefordshire HR9 7TL
Tel: 01989 780240 Mobile: 0585 871379

❖❖

Cottage: Hopeway Cottage, The Village, Clifton-upon-Teme, Worcestershire

See PHOTO on page 527

Hopeway Cottage, ETB 5 Key 'Highly Commended', is welcoming, comfortable and very well appointed. It has full central heating, double glazing, comprehensively fitted kitchen and bathroom, antique furnishings, security system, telephone, TV, video and radio. Situated in the picturesque village of Clifton-upon-Teme in the beautiful unspoilt Teme Valley, it offers a peaceful retreat within easy reach of interesting visits and activities.

1 cottage, sleeps 4, Price per week £205-£235 low season, £275-£350 high season, No smoking, Children welcome, No pets, Available all year.

Contact: Elizabeth & Colin White, Hope Wynd, The Village, Clifton-upon-Teme, Worcestershire
WR6 6EN
Tel: 01886 812496 Fax: 01886 812429

❖❖

Hopeway Cottage, The Village, Clifton-upon-Teme - see page 526

The cottages at Westwood House, West Malvern - see page 528

❖❖

Cottage: The Mill House, Broad Meadows Farmhouse, Bayton, near Kidderminster, Worcestershire

16th century timbered mill house wing on village edge, with stunning views. Traditional style, comfy beds, power showers. Large gardens, patio, ample parking. Rural location ideal for peaceful relaxation; walking, painting, wildlife. Ludlow, Worcester, Hereford, Ironbridge 20-45 minutes away. Numerous attractions for children within 20 miles. Wyre Forest 5 miles, Good Pub & Craft Centre 1 mile. Welcoming owners and animals, glad to help you enjoy your stay. Free brochure.

1 cottage, sleeps6-8 + cot, Price per week £200-£325 low season, £300-£450 high season, Children & pets welcome, Available all year.

Contact: Mrs J Chance, Broad Meadows Farmhouse, Bayton, near Kidderminster,
Worcestershire DY14 9LP
Tel: 01299 832608 Fax: 01299 832137

❖❖

Cottage: The Cottages at Westwood House, Park Road, West Malvern

See PHOTO on page 527

Three individual cottages and spacious garden flat sleeping between 2 and 6, high on Elgar's Malvern Hills and providing the standards of a private home. National award-winners whose aim is to offer the most elegant and best equipped holiday accommodation for people who prefer to cater for themselves in private home comfort. Cleanliness, presentation and attention to detail are paramount. Owners resident.

3 cottages, 1 flat, sleeps 2-6, Lowest price per week £205 low season, £305 high season, Children welcome, No pets, Available all year.

Contact: Mrs Jill Wright, The Cottages at Westwood House, Park Road, West Malvern,
Worcestershire WR14 4DS
Tel: 01684 892308 Fax: 01684 892882

❖❖

Please mention
THE GREAT BRITISH
SELF CATERING
COTTAGE GUIDE
when booking your accommodation

Kent

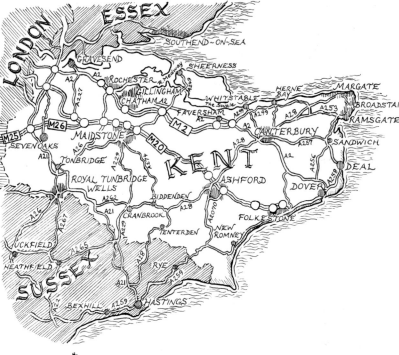

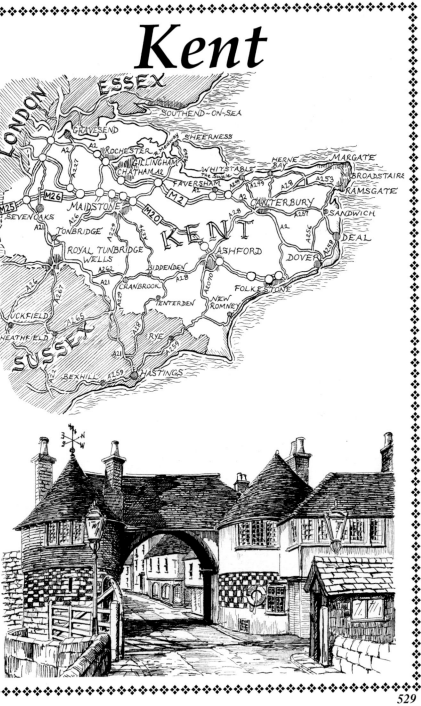

Haybarn, Upper Hardes, Canterbury - see page 531

Birdwatchers Cottage, Leysdown on Sea - see page 531

❖❖❖

Cottage: Haybarn, Lynsore Bottom, Upper Hardres, Canterbury, Kent

Barn conversions to very high standard. Situated in 6 acres of sheep grazing pasture. The perfect escape for country lovers. 6 miles to Canterbury, 12 miles to coast. Horse riding, John Aspinals Zoo close by. All electric with wood burning stoves, microwave, washing machine, TV, steep stairs, use of family pool, garden, pretty villages, good pubs locally, safe parking.

See PHOTO on opposite page

2 cottages, sleeps 2-4, Price per week £200 low season, £320 high season, No smoking, Children over 5, No pets, Available November - March.

Contact: Sheila Wilton, Walnut Tree Farm, Lynsore Bottom, Upper Hardres, Canterbury, Kent CT4 6EG
Tel: 01227 709375

❖❖❖

Cottage: Risebridge Farm Holiday Cottages, Goudhurst, Kent

Comfortable spacious cottages converted from traditional farm buildings and Oasthouse. Situated on a small 40 hectare farm amidst beautiful countryside in the "Garden of England". Leisure facilities, include indoor heated pool, sauna, jacuzzi, solarium, tennis, squash and badminton courts, superbly equipped gymnasium, games room and playground. Easy access to London and the coast. Fully illustrated brochure available on request.

10 cottages, sleeps 2-8, Price per week £180-£410 low season, £370-£760 high season, Children & pets welcome, Available April - December.

Richard Hillier, Risebridge Farm, Goudhurst, near Cranbrook, Kent TN17 1HN
Tel: 01580 211775 Fax: 01580 211984

❖❖❖

Cottage: Birdwatcher's Cottage, Newhouse Farm, Leysdown-on-Sea, near Sheernes, Kent

Come and relax in this peaceful, tucked away, quality country cottage on a sheep and arable farm. It has beamed ceilings, four bedrooms, warmth from central heating and panoramic views. A large garden to sit in and daydream. Visit the Nature Reserves or wander along to the beach. Ideal touring base and a quiet hideaway. Send a stamped address envelope for many more details!

See PHOTO on opposite page

1 cottage, sleeps up to 8, Price per week from £170-£300 low season, £200 - £375 high season, No smoking, Children welcome, No pets, Available all year.

Contact: Mrs Sally Marsh, Newhouse Farm, Leysdown-on-Sea, near Sheerness, Kent ME12 4BA
Tel: 01795 510201 Fax: 01795 880379

❖❖❖

❖❖❖

Cottage: Walnut Tree Cottage & Ciderpress Cottage, Goldengreen, Tonbridge, Kent

Idyllic award winning period cottages, peacefully situated by the mill stream, within the 20 acre grounds of an ancient millhouse, beautifully decorated, comfortably furnished and comprehensively equipped with ETB 5 Key Deluxe rating. Dishwasher, microwave, washing and drying machine, all linen, TV/VCR, direct dial telephone, ample parking, garden, use of all weather tennis court. Excellent base for touring the gardens, stately homes and castles of Kent and Sussex.

2 cottages, sleeps 4-6, Price per week from £325 low season, £500 high season, No smoking, Children welcome, No pets, Available all year.

Contact: Vernon & Shirley Cole, Goldhill Mill, Goldengreen, Tonbridge, Kent TN11 0BA
Tel: 01732 851626 Fax: 01732 851881

above, Walnut Tree Cottage & Ciderpress Cottage, Tonbridge

❖❖❖

Lancashire

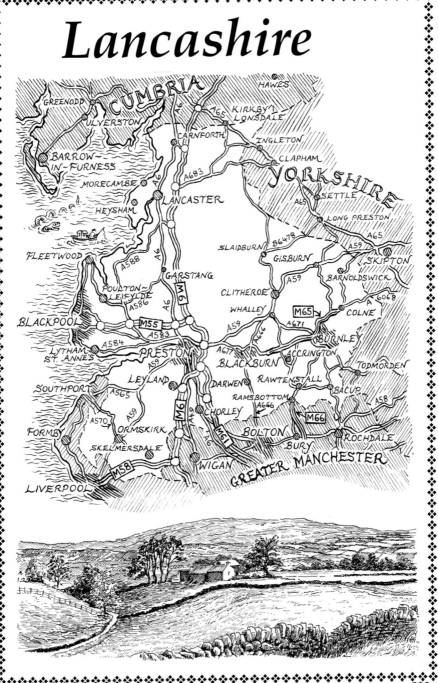

GREENODD
CUMBRIA
HAWES
ULVERSTON
A65
KIRKBY
LONSDALE
CARNFORTH
INGLETON
BARROW~
IN~FURNESS
CLAPHAM
A683
MORECAMBE
A6
YORKSHIRE
HEYSHAM
LANCASTER
A65
SETTLE
LONG PRESTON
FLEETWOOD
A588
A6
SLAIDBURN
B6478
A59
A65
GISBURN
SKIPTON
GARSTANG
A59
BARNOLDSWICK
POULTON~
LE~FYLDE
A586
A6
M6
CLITHEROE
A·6068
WHALLEY
M65
COLNE
BLACKPOOL
M55
A59
A666
A671
BURNLEY
LYTHAM
ST. ANNES
A584
A583
PRESTON
A677
ACCRINGTON
TODMORDEN
SOUTHPORT
A565
LEYLAND
A59
DARWEN
RAWTENSTALL
BACUP
A58
RAMSBOTTOM
A666
A570
A59
CHORLEY
FORMBY
ORMSKIRK
M6
A49
M66
SKELMERSDALE
A6
BOLTON
ROCHDALE
M58
M61
BURY
LIVERPOOL
WIGAN
GREATER MANCHESTER
BLACKBURN

❖❖❖

Studio Apartment, The Old Hayloft, Harcles Hill Farm, Holcombe, Bury, Lancashire

Working hill farm, ¹/₂ mile from village up farm road, 1,100 ft. Spacious open plan, living and bedroom with kitchen area. Separate shower room. Double bed, bed settee, TV, radio, electric fire, electric cooker, microwave, fridge, central heating, price includes all linen, towels and basics, i.e. toilet paper, soap, tea, coffee, etc. Superb views, mullion window, car parking, garden. Extra folding bed/cot available. Brochure available.

1 apartment, sleeps 2-5, Price per night from £25, Children & pets welcome, Available all year.

**Contact: Mrs Hilditch, Harcles Hill Farm, Holcombe, Bury, Lancashire BL8 4NT
Tel: 01706 823467**

❖❖❖

Cottage: Mansergh Farmhouse Cottages, Borwick, Carnforth, Lancashire

Unique cottages of quality and charm with lovely views across open country-side, sleeps 4/6, heated indoor swimming pool Easter/September, play area, games room. Each cottage has colour TV, gas central heating, microwave, washing machine, shared tumble dryer, patio, walled garden, barbecue, parking. Excellent for touring Lakes, Dales, Forest of Bowland, coastal regions of Morecombe, Silverdale, Fylde Coast. Superb location for touring. 4 Keys Commended ETB.

5 cottages, sleeps 4-6, Price per week £185 low season, £480 high season, Children & Pets welcome, Available all year.

**Contact: Mrs Morphy, Mansergh Farmhouse, Borwick, Carnforth, Lancashire LA6 1JS
Tel: 01524 732586**

❖❖❖

Cottage: Garden Cottage, High Snab, Gressingham, Lancaster

See PHOTO on opposite page

Adjoining our farmhouse on a working dairy and beef farm in a quiet location with open views and its own private drive and garden. Ideal for touring Lakes, Dales and Coast. Lancashire farm landscape trophy and NWTB Award Winner. Well equipped kitchen, oak-beamed lounge with colour TV, 1 double 1 twin, snooker table, bathroom with shower, central heating from farmhouse electric and linen included, cot/high chair. Brochure available.

1 cottage, sleeps 4 and cot, Price per week £180 low season, £260 high season, Children welcome, No pets, Available November - March.

**Contact: Mrs Margaret Burrow, High Snab, Gressingham, Lancaster LA2 8LS
Tel: 015242 21347**

❖❖❖

Garden Cottage, Gressingham - see page 534

"There they are, Rosie, building castles"

535

Leicestershire & Nottinghamshire

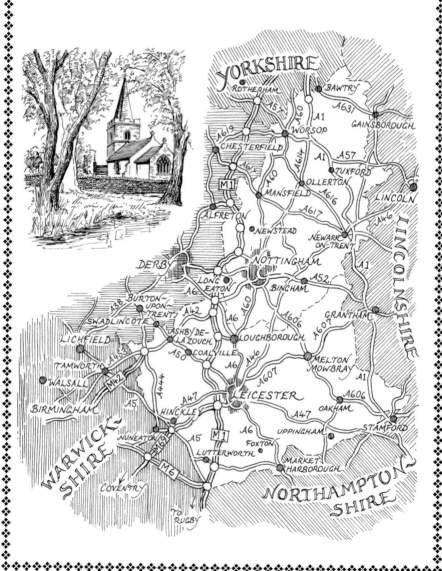

❖❖❖

Cottage: The Loft House, Criftin Farm, Epperstone, Nottinghamshire

17th century granary on a working farm in the heart of Robin Hood country close to the historic towns of Southwell, Nottingham and all the stately homes around. Woodland walks behind farm. 4 golf courses and water sports centre close by. Central heating, colour TV, washer/dryer. Two twin bedded rooms with own bathrooms. Heated swimming pool May - September. Snooker room. Barbecue all in a walled garden.

1 cottage, sleeps 4, Price per week £260.00 low season, £285.00 high season, Children welcome, Pets by arrangement, Available all year.

Contact: Jenny Esam, Criftin Farm, Epperstone, Nottinghamshire NG14 6AT
Tel: 0115 9652039 Fax: 0115 9655490

above, The Loft House, Epperstone

❖❖❖

Lincolnshire

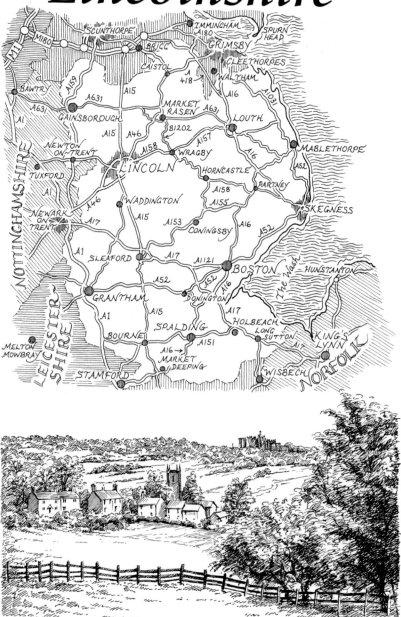

❖❖

Cottage: The Old Farmhouse, Bramble and Hawthorn Cottages, Waingrove Farm Country Cottages, Fulstow, Louth, Lincolnshire

"Country Cottage Recipe" Mature a farmhouse and old barns for 150 years. Carefully blend in excellent facilities and pretty furnishings with country flavours. Sprinkle with fresh flowers, magazines and welcome tea tray. Result: Charming Farmhouse and pair of single storey 'Courtyard Cottages'. Served with chilled wine! Come and be spoiled at Waingrove Farm. English Tourist Board 4 Keys, Highly Commended. 1997 'Runners Up' England for Excellence - East of England Tourist Board Self Catering Holiday Cottage of the Year.

3 cottages, sleeps 6,4,4, Price per week £180 minimum, £450 maximum, No children, No pets, Available all year.
Contact: Mac & Stephanie Smith, Waingrove Farm, Fulstow, Louth, Lincolnshire LN11 0XQ
Tel/Fax: 01507 363704 EMail: MESJSmith@msn.com

above, Waingrove Farm, Louth, Lincolnshire

❖❖

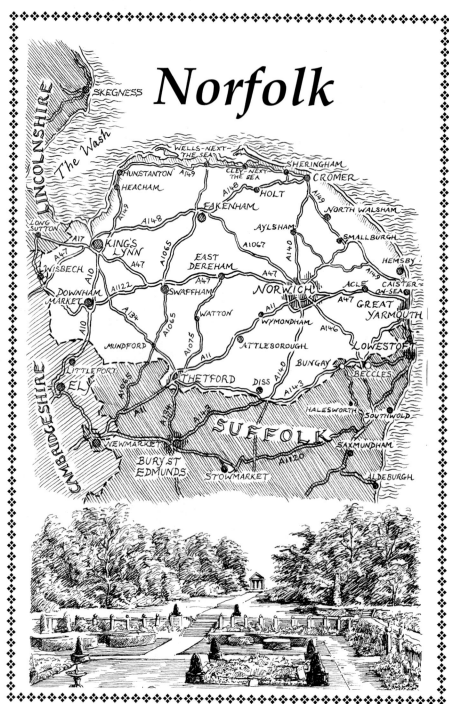

Norfolk

❖❖❖

Cottage: Clippesby Holidays, Clippesby, near Great Yarmouth, Norfolk

Broadland is famous for its natural beauty and tourist attractions. The pine lodge and cottages at family run Clippesby Holidays are in courtyard and woodland settings in the grounds of Clippesby Hall, 5 miles from the sea. Nature Reserves, Broads and rivers nearby. Pine lodge sleeps 6, 3 bedrooms, central heating, double glazing, woodburner, bbq, sunbathing deck, microwave, dishwasher, tv/video, parking, wheelchair ramp, country view, birds.

22 cottages, sleeps 2-10, Price per week £140-£350 low season, £199-£495 high season
Children & Pets welcome, Available all year.

Contact: Jean Lindsay, Clippesby Holidays, Clippesby, near Great Yarmouth, Norfolk NR29 3BJ
Tel: 01493 369367 Fax: 01493 368181

❖❖❖

Cottage: Sid's Cottage, West Rudham, King's Lynn, Norfolk

Sid's Cottage is a traditional Norfolk cottage, built in mellow red brick and flint. It adjoins another cottage and has views across lawns and an orchard with hens and peacocks. There is a patio and lawns but no enclosed garden. Set well away from public roads pleasant walks can be taken from the cottage and there is a carp fishing pond. An indoor heated swimming pool close to the cottage is available for use by holiday tenants.

See PHOTO on page 542

1 cottage, sleep 4, Price per week £120 low season, £240 high season,
Children welcome, Regret no pets, Available all year.

Contact: Mrs Angela Ringer, The Grange, West Rudham, King's Lynn, Norfolk PE31 8SY
Tel: 01485 528229

❖❖❖

Cottage: Wood Farm Cottages, Plumstead Road, Edgefield, Melton Constable

Wood Farm is located outside the village down a long lane surrounded by trees and fields. The accommodation consists of 19 century barns around a courtyard, delightfully converted to provide seven well equipped cottages. Features include exposed flint, beams, a wood burner, a four poster bed, stereos and video players. Outside there is a superb play area for children which include a 1959 David Brown tractor. Colour brochure.

See PHOTO on page 542

7 cottages, sleep 2-6, Price per week £155 low season, £445 high season,
Children welcome, Dogs welcome, Available all year.

Contact: Mrs Diana Elsby, Wood Farm, Plumstead Road, Edgefield, Melton Constable, Norfolk
NR24 2AQ
Tel/Fax: 01263 587347

❖❖❖

Sid's Cottage, West Rudham - see page 541

Wood Farm Cottages, Melton Constable - see page 541

❖❖

Cottage: Norfolk Holiday Homes, 62 Westgate, Hunstanton, Norfolk

We offer an excellent choice of holiday homes along the North West Norfolk coast and unspoilt countryside. Traditional, modern, large or small. Something to suit all budgets. All have various facilities and are close to holiday amenities and interests. Golf, sailing, safe beaches, leisure centre, sea life centre, theatre, unlimited walks. Superb choice of traditional pubs, local food and real ales. Discounts available. Free brochure.

45 cottages, sleeps 2-9, Price per week between £180 low season and £650 high season, Children & Pets welcome, Available all year.

Contact: Mrs Hohol, Norfolk Holiday Homes, 62 Westgate, Hunstanton, Norfolk PE36 5EL Tel: 01485 534267 Fax: 01485 535230

❖❖

"Dad's shouting for you to break the dam, Jack!"

❖❖

Northumberland

❖❖

Cottage: 1, 2 & 3 Cottages, Titlington Hall Farm, Alnwick, Northumberland

Our lovely cottages are situated in a quiet and beautiful area. They are spacious and well equipped with TV, fridge, microwave and washing machine, also tumble drier and pay phone. Each cottage has parking at the front and an enclosed back garden. All linen, electricity and gas for central heating included in the rent. Can sleep families of ten, children welcome, Pets by arrangement.

See PHOTO on page 547

3 cottages, sleeps 14, Price per week £165 - £195 low season, £265 - £295 high season, Children welcome, Pets by arrangement, Available all year.

Contact: John & Vera Purvis, Titlington Hall Farm, Alnwick, Northumberland NE66 2EB
Tel/Fax: 01665 578253

❖❖

Cottage: Clove Lodge Cottage, Baldersdale, Barnard Castle, County Durham

For those seeking peace and solitude, a listed stone built cottage in the Northern Pennines. Idyllic location adjoining the fells near a wooded gorge. Accommodation includes converted coach house breakfast room/kitchen with microwave. Lounge with Victorian open fireplace. Two twin bedded rooms. All modern facilities. Exclusive use of small gym and sauna. Private garden and barbecue area. Ample parking. ETB 3 Keys Commended.

1 cottage, sleeps 4, Price per week £180 low season, £250 high season, No smoking, Children & Pets by arrangement, Available all year.

Contact: Mrs Heys, Clove Lodge, Baldersdale, Barnard Castle, County Durham DL12 9UP
Tel: 01833 650030

❖❖

Cottage: The Teesdale Hotel, Middleton-in-Teesdale, near Barnard Castle, County Durham

Three self-catering cottages set in hotel courtyard, all comfortably furnished, TV, washing machine, microwave, bed-linen, towels and self dial telephone. Breakfast, barmeals and dinner served in the cottages at your request. Pets very welcome, free of charge. Middleton is situated in the heart of the beautiful Pennines very central for travelling to Lake District, Yorks Moors, Beamish Museum and of course England highest Waterfall High Force and Couldren Stout.

3 cottages, sleeps 2,4,6, Price per week £110-£260 low season, £260-£300 high season, Children & pets welcome, Available all year.

Contact: Mr & Mrs Streit, The Teesdale Hotel, Middleton-in-Teesdale, near Barnard Castle,
County Durham DL12 0QG
Tel: 01833 640264 Fax: 01833 640651 Internet: http://www.free pages.co.uk/teesdale/

❖❖

❖❖❖

Cottage: No2 & No3 Cottage, West Kyloe, Berwick upon Tweed

Situated in a 600 acre family run farm these warm, comfortable terraced cottages have magnificent views of the coast. Both have open fires in the sitting rooms and electrical heaters in each room. Each cottage is furnished and decorated to a high standard. There is a large lawn at the front of the cottages with picnic benches and space to park cars. Lovely scenic walks on the farm.

2 cottages, sleeps 4,6, Price per week £125 low season, £300 high season, Children welcome, Available all year.

Contact: Mrs Teresa Smalley, Garden Cottage, 1 West Kyloe, Berwick Upon Tweed, Northumberland TD15 2PG
Tel/Fax: 01289 381 279

❖❖❖

Cottage: The Old Smithy, Brackenside, Bowden, Berwick on Tweed, Northumberland

See PHOTO on opposite page

Splendid three bedroom conversion of the Old Smithy on our friendly working farm with stunning views of the Cheviots and Holy Island. Close to gentle woodland walks meandering by ponds and conservation areas. The Smithy provides superb accommodation with colour TV, central heating, washer/dryer and a wood burning stove in the original blacksmiths fireplace (all fuel free!) The Smithy has its own private walled garden.

1 cottage, sleeps 6, Price per week £180 low season, £420 high season, Children welcome, Pets welcome, Available all year.

Contact: John & Mary Barber, Brackenside, Bowsden, Berwick on Tweed, Northumberland TD15 2TQ
Tel: 01289 388293

❖❖❖

Cottage: The Old Barn, High Kitty Crag, Westgate in Weardale, Bishop Auckland, County Durham

This converted barn full of charm and character lies in a hillside position in the Northern Pennines of Upper Weardale former hunting grounds of the Prince Bishops of Durham set in a 6 acre holding with glorious views over the valley only a short drive to many major attractions in Northumberland, Cumbria and Durham. Sitting room, dining room, kitchen, two double bedrooms, bathroom, electric heating, log fires, gas fire, TV/video, microwave, auto washer, fridge. ETB 3 Keys Highly Commended.

1 cottage, sleeps 4-6, Price per week £200 low season, £295 high season, No smoking, Children welcome, No pets, Available May - October.

Contact: Mrs Heselton, High Kitty Crag, Westgate in Weardale, Bishop Auckland, County Durham DL13 1LF
Tel: 01388 517562

❖❖❖

1,2 & 3 Cottages, Titlington Hall Farm - see page 545

The Old Smithy, Bowden, Berwick on Tweed - see page 546

Bank Cottage, Lyndale Guest House, Bellingham - see page 550

The Old Byre, Slaley, near Hexham - see page 550

❖❖❖

Cottage: Bradley Burn Holiday Cottages, Bradley Burn Farm, Wolsingham, Bishop Auckland

Small group of cottages, comfortably furnished, thoughtfully equipped microwave, TV, all linen, set around a courtyard on working farm at eastern end of Weardale, gateway to North Pennines Englands last wilderness. Good location for sightseeing, explore small market towns, remote villages, cathedrals, castles, cities, countryside, museums, coast all within an hour's drive or less. Open all year, phone for our brochure.

3 cottages, sleeps 5,2,2 Price per week £135-£200 low season, £175, £320 high season, Children & pets welcome, Available all year.

Contact: Mrs Stephenson, Bradley Burn Farm, Wolsingham, Bishop Auckland, County Durham DL13 3JH Tel/Fax: 01388 527285

❖❖❖

Cottage: Holmhead Farm, Hadrian's Wall, Greenhead, via Carlisle, Northumberland

The cottage is an annex of the farmhouse which is run as a guest house. There is a ruined castle and a stream in the back garden. The property stands amid field and footpaths in a sheltered valley on the route of Hadrian's Wall near the most spectacular remains and the Roman Army Museum. Open plan french windows onto patio south facing. Games room/garden. ETB 4 Keys Commended.

See PHOTO on page 288

1 cottage, sleeps 4, Price per week £150 low season, £325 high season, No smoking, Children welcome, No pets, Available all year.

Contact: Mr & Mrs Staff, Holmhead Farm, Hadrian's Wall, Greenhead, via Carlisle CA6 7HY Tel/Fax: 016977 47402

❖❖❖

Cottage: Ald White Craig Farm, near Hadrian's Wall, Haltwhistle, Northumberland

Unusually comfortable award-winning country cottages. Peaceful surroundings just 2 minutes drive from A69, Hadrian's Wall, Inn-food and shops. We provide everything you could expect at 4 Keys Highly Commended and more! Tyndeddle will enchant you with it miles of way reached footpaths, superb scenery, villages, Inn, fairs, quiet roads. Peace and space to relax and solitude, visit the varied attractions or enjoy the many activities.

4 cottages, sleeps 3-6+cot, Price per week £145-£190 low season, £190-£415 high season, Children & pets welcome, Available all year.

Contact: Mrs Laidlow, Ald White Craig Farm, nr Hadrian Wall, Haltwhistle, Northumberland NE49 9NW Tel/Fax: 01434 320565

❖❖❖

NORTHUMBERLAND
The Great British Self Catering Cottage Guide

❖❖

Cottage: Bank Cottage, Lyndale Guest House, Off The Square, Bellingham, Hexham

See PHOTO on page 548

Delightful 18th century cottage. A conservatory has been added, especially for the splendid views of Dunterlyfell beyond the River North Tyne and the Old Market Square. "Your Welcome Pack" including flowers and wines awaits you, in this superbly furnished cottage: kitchen, cooker, fridge, microwave, washer/dryer. Living/dining room, colour TV, radio/tape, includes phone, electric 50p meter, storage-heating free. Garden furniture. 2 comfortable bedrooms, teasmade, hairdryer, full bathroom. Private parking. Hadrians Wall, Kielder Lake. Good walks, golf, pubs, restaurants and shops.

1 cottage, sleeps 4, Price per week from £169-£295 low season, £218-£328 high season,
No smoking, Children welcome, No pets, Available April - October

Contact: Joyce Gaskin, Lyndale Guest House, off The Square, Bellingham, Hexham, Northumberland
NE48 2AW
Tel/Fax: 01434 220361

❖❖

Cottage: The Old Byre, Slaley, near Hexham, Northumberland

See PHOTO on page 548

A spacious barn conversion on a small family run livestock farm. Deep in the countryside, yet easily accessiible to Hadrians Wall, Durham etc. The cottage has 4 bedrooms (2 en-suite) and 1 general bathroom. Open plan lounge, kitchen, dining room with woodburning stove and colour TV. Games rooms, laundry facility. Home bakery and evening meals to order. Full wheel chair facilities in ground floor bedroom. B&B next door.

1 cottage, sleeps 9, Price per week £350 low season, £650 high season,
Children welcome, Pets welcome, Available all year.

Contact: Elizabeth Courage, Rye Hill Farm, Slaley, near Hexham, Northumberland NE47 0AH
Tel: 01434 673259 Fax: 01434 673608

❖❖

Cottage: Gallowhill Farm, Whalton, Morpeth, Northumberland

Early 19th century semi detached cottages situated on a family farm. Orchard sleeps 6, Paddock sleeps 4. Both cottages have fully fitted kitchens, including dishwasher. Spacious rooms with gas central heating. Colour TV in sitting rooms. Safe private garden with furniture and barbecue. Sorry no pets. Gallowhill is a ideal base to visit lots of attractions such as Hadrian's Wall. Farne Islands and Metro Centre.

2 cottages, sleep 4,6, Price per week £200-£260 low season, £270-£395 high season,
Children welcome, No pets, Available all year.

Contact: Mrs Coatsworth, Gallowhill Farm, Whalton, Morpeth, Northumberland NE61 3TX
Tel: 01661 881241

❖❖

The Pele Tower, Whitton, Rothbury - see page 552

The Stables and Byre, near Wolsingham - see page 552

❖❖

Cottage: The Herdsman Cottage, Cornhills, Kirkwhelpington, Newcastle

This traditional cottage with large enclosed garden was built in 1998. The beamed lounge has open fire, night storage heater. Three bedrooms, double, twin, single and cot. The kitchen contains electric cooker, fridge microwave, washing machine, tumble dryer. The farm is all grass with two small streams, ideal for walking and wild life observation. All linen, towels provided. All fuel included in the price.

1 cottage, sleeps 5, Price per week £160 low season, £320 high season, No smoking, Children welcome, No pets, Available all year.

Contact: Lorna Thornton, Cornhills, Kirkwhelpington, Newcastle NE19 2RE Tel: 01830 540232

❖❖

Cottage: The Pele Tower, Whitton, Rothbury, Northumberland

See PHOTO on page 551

19th century wing of tower (origins 13th century). Grade II* Listed. ETB 5 Keys Deluxe. Many home comforts including 4 TV's, satellite, video, music centre, nintendo, telephone, mountain bikes, golf clubs, whirlpool bath, dishwasher, washing machine, tumble dryer, barbeque, wood burning stove and much more. Close to the delightful small town of Rothbury with excellent pubs, restaurants and shops. We are ideally situated for visiting the many spendours of this spectacular county.

1 cottage, sleeps 4, Price per week £220 low season, £520 high season, No smoking, Children welcome, No pets, Available all year.

Contact: Mr D. Malia, The Pele Tower, Whitton, Rothbury, Northumberland NE65 7RL Tel: 01669 620410 Fax: 01669 621006 EMail: 106055.1325@compuserve.co.uk

❖❖

Cottage: The Stables and Brye, near Wolsingham, Tow Law, County Durham

See PHOTO on page 551

Enjoy a relaxing stay in comfortable well-equipped cottages. A traditional farm in peaceful countryside. Marvellous views, pleasant walks and nature trails. The larger cottage has a four poster bed, dishwasher and en-suite bedrooms. Gas central heating, double glazing, natural beams, pine furniture, fitted carpets, comfy chintzy suites and wood burning stoves. Evening meals available.

2 cottages, sleeps 4-6, Price per week £165 - £195 low season, £200 - £365 high season, Children welcome, Pets by arrangement, Available all year.

Contact: Mike & Linda Vickers, Greenwell Farm, Wolsingham, Tow Law, County Durham DL13 4PH Tel: 01388 527248 Fax: 01388 526735

❖❖

❖❖❖

Cottage: Firwood Bungalow, Humphreys House, Middleton Hall, Wooler, Northumberland

Unique holiday homes standing in 1¹/₂ acres of well maintained gardens in the hamlet of Middleton Hall, within the National Park. Ideal for waling, fishing and golf. Ideal family homes equipped to a high standard with period furniture, log & coal fires, central heating, and washbasins in most rooms. Kitchen with every appliance. Unique opportunity to explore the Border Country and North Northumberland. ETB 4 Keys Highly Commended.

2 cottages, sleeps 6,10, Price per week £200 low season, £550 high season, Restricted smoking, Children welcome, Pets by arrangement, Available all year.

Contact: Mr & Mrs Armstrong, Earle Hill Head Farm, Wooler, Northumberland NE71 6RH
Tel/Fax: 01668 281243

Firwood Bungalow, Wooler

❖❖❖

Oxfordshire

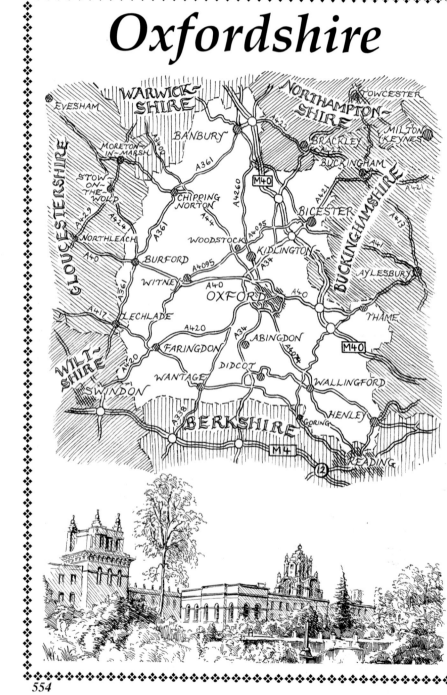

❖❖❖

Cottage: Pimlico Farm, Tusmore, Bicester, Oxon

Cotswold stone barn conversions into six top quality Tourist Board inspected cottages. Situated in Oxfordshire, Cotswolds on two working farms. Tastefully furnished and decorated to reflect warmth and natural charm. Fully equipped kitchens with dishwasher, microwave, laundry facilities. Modern bathrooms, showers. Delightful gardens, fishing barbecues, country walks. Pets by arrangement. Resident owners will make guests welcome. 5 Keys Highly Commended. Ideal touring base for Cotswolds, London, Stratford Upon Avon, Oxford.

6 cottages, sleeps 2-6, Price per week £169-£236 low season, £276-£448 high season, Children welcome, Pets by arrangement, Available all year.

Contact: Mr & Mrs Harper, Pimlico Farm, Tusmore, Bicester, Oxon OX6 9SL
Tel/Fax: 01869 810306

❖❖❖

Cottage: Summer Haze & Wenrisc Apartment, Swinbrook, Burford, Oxon

Cotswold Cottage (sleeps four) and apartment (sleeps two/three). Full of character in peaceful scenic Swinbrook near Burford, well equipped with all modern conveniences including television, microwave, spindryers, central heating, as well as wood burning fires. Both are like hides from which to view the surrounding wild life. Terraced garden to rear of cottage. Patio and private lawn adjacent to apartment. Lovely walks all around.

Prices per week Cottage for 4 £150 low season, £235 high season,
Apartment for 2 £125 low season £210 high season,
Children & dogs accommodated, Available all year.

Contact: Mr Picken, Upper Wenrisc, Swinbrook, Burford, Oxon OX18 4EE
Tel: 01993 823272

❖❖❖

Cottage: Cavaliers Cottage & The Old Dairy, Culworth, Banbury, Oxon

Next to the owners historic 17th century Manor House on Culworth's peaceful Village Green, these two cottages offer wonderful rural retreats. Four poster bed, open fires, old oak beams, both superbly equipped with dishwashers, washing machines, microwaves. ETB 5 Keys Highly Commended. Pretty cottage gardens and charming old Herb garden with far reaching views. Oxford, the Cotswolds, Stratford upon Avon and Warwick Castle are all close by.

2 cottages, sleeps 4 & 5, Prices per week £195 low season £475 high season, Children welcome, No pets, Available all year.

Contact Richard & Beth Soar, The Manor House, Culworth, Banbury, Oxfordshire OX17 2BB
Tel: 01295 760099 Fax: 01295 760098

❖❖❖

Somerset

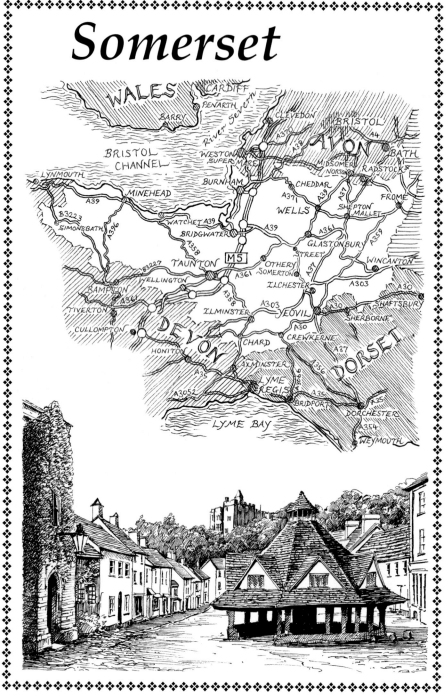

✧✧

Cottage: Little Quarme Cottages, Wheddon Cross, Exmoor National Park

Six stone cottages offering top quality, comfort and cleanliness in a idyllic peaceful location with outstanding panoramic rural views. Quality furnishings. Nicam TV, microwaves etc. Lovely gardens. Many animals, pony rides. Non smoking. Ideally situated in the heart of Exmoor National Park. Farmhouse bed and breakfast also available. ETB 4 Keys Deluxe.

6 cottages, sleeps 2-6, Price per week £120 low season, £475 high season, Non smoking, Children & Pets welcome, Available all year.

Contact: Tammy Cody-Boutcher, Little Quarme Cottages, Wheddon Cross, near Minehead, Somerset TA24 7EA
Tel/Fax: 01643 841249

✧✧

"Jack, lend a hand with the peas!"

Suffolk

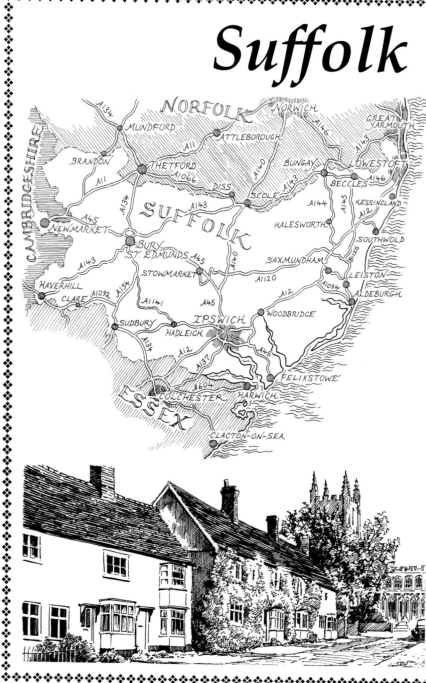

❖❖

Cottage: The Court, Melford Road, Lawshall, near Bury St Edmunds, Suffolk

Tastefully converted Queen Anne Farmhouse, composing double en-suite, 1 twin with washbasin, 1 singe bedroom separate bathroom, well equipped kitchen diner, fridge, washing machine, w/c, hall with telephone, lounge woodburning stove, TV, full central heating, linen provided. Set in glorious countryside. Ideal for farm walks exploring Constable Country, Lavenham, historic Bury St Edmunds Garden and ample car parking.

1 cottage, sleeps 5, Price per week £250 low season, £375 high season,
No smoking, Children welcome, No pets, Available all year.

Contact: John & Roberta Truin, Brighthouse Farm, Lawshall, near Bury St Edmunds, Suffolk
IP29 4PX
Tel: 01284 830385

above, The Court, Lawshall

❖❖

❖❖❖

Cottage: St Peter's View, Monk Soham, Woodbridge, Suffolk

ETB 3 Keys Highly Commended. These owner managed properties are peaceful, spacious, equipped to a high standard and enjoy uninterrupted delightful views. Close to Suffolk Heritage Coast, Minsmere Bird Reserve, Snape Maltings and Numerous Golf courses, Monk Soham is ideally situated for a splendid long or short breaks. Extensive grounds, adjacent to 13th century church. Every comfort to ensure a happy and relaxed time. Central heating, electricity included. Wheelchair accessible.

4 cottages, sleeps 2-4, Prices per week £130 low season, £310 high season, No smoking, Available all year.

Contact: Gay & Geoffrey Clarke, Monk Soham Lodge, Monk Soham, Woodbridge, Suffolk IP13 7EN
Tel/Fax: 01728 685358

above, St Peter's View, Monk Soham

❖❖❖

Surrey

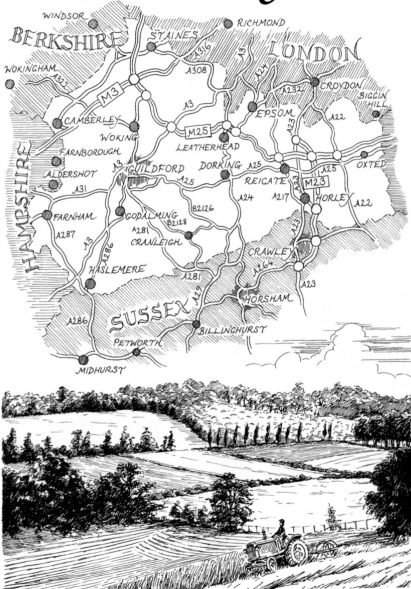

❖❖❖

Cottage: Badgerholt or Foxholme, Holmbury St. Mary, Dorking, Surrey

Two delightfully cosy single storey cottages, sympathetically converted from a Surrey barn forming a courtyard with the farmhouse. Fully carpeted, electric central heating, colour TV and linen (beds made up), communal laundry room. Use of 2 acre farmhouse garden. Situated in picturesque quiet valley, ideal walking country, bird watching, woodland walk to conservation lake, convenient Wisley National Trust Properties in South East. Frequent trains to London from Dorking.

2 cottages, sleeps 2,4, Price per week from £150 - £230 low season, £200 - £300 high season, Children welcome, Pets welcome, Available all year.

Contact: Gill Hill, Bulmer Farm, Holmbury St. Mary, Dorking, Surrey RH5 6LG
Tel: 01306 730210

above, Badgerholt & Foxholme, Holmbury St Mary

❖❖❖

Sussex

BODIAM CASTLE, EAST SUSSEX

❖❖❖

Cottage: Black Cottage, Newells Farm, Newells Lane, Lower Beeding, Horsham

Charming, secluded period cottage with lovely views on 650 acre arable and woodland farm. Own fenced garden, car parking, open fire, TV. Comfortably furnished. Surrounded by fields and woodland. Many famous Sussex, Kent and Surrey gardens within reach. Walk in our beautiful ancient woodlands, relax or visit Brighton and the seaside or pretty local villages. May bluebell time especially recommended.

1 cottage, sleeps 4, Price per week £140 - £160 low season, £190 - £250 high season, Children welcome, Pets welcome, Available all year.

Contact: Vicky Storey, Newells Farm, Newells Lane, Lower Beeding, Horsham, Sussex RH13 6LN
Tel: 01403 891326 Fax: 01403 891530

above, Black Cottage, Lower Beeding

❖❖❖

❖❖❖

Best of Sussex Cottages

We are a small family run agency based in the beautiful ancient seaside village of Rottingdean. All of our properties have been personally inspected by the proprietor Richard Harris who also own two of the cottages available for holiday letting. Many have been inspected by the English Tourist Board and range between 3 Keys Commended and 5 Keys De-Luxe.

70 cottages, sleeps 2-12, Price per week £170.00 low season, £1,600 high season, Children & Pets welcome, Available all year.

Contact: Mr Richard Harris, Best of Sussex Cottages, Horseshoe Cottage, 2 Whipping Post Lane, Rottindean, Sussex BN2 7HZ
Tel: 01273 308779 Fax: 01273 300266

❖❖❖

"Here comes a big one!"

Warwickshire
& West Midlands

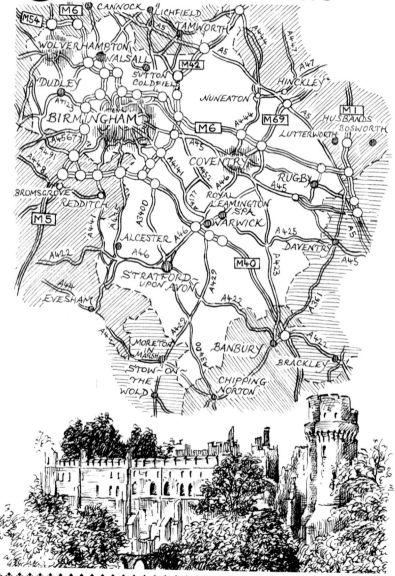

❖❖

Cottage: Winton House Cottage, The Green, Upper Quinton, Stratford, Warwickshire

Winton House Cottage is situated in a peaceful rural area 6 miles from Stratford. This studiostable conversion features a four poster bed with colour TV, video, chairs, pine wardrobe and dresser. Fully equipped kitchen cooker, microwave and antique pine sideboard, coal fire Parkray. Bathroom, bathtub, sink separate shower. South facing garden. Barbecue, picnic table, car parking. Ideal for touring, walking, cycling. Cycles for hire.

1 cottage, sleeps 2, Price per week £145 low season, £250 high season, Special winter rates from £35, No smoking, No pets, Available all year.

Contact: Mrs Lyon, Winton House, The Green, Upper Quinton, Stratford, Warwickshire CV37 8SX
Tel: 01789 720500 E-Mail: 1yong@ibm.net

above, Winton House Cottage, Upper Quinton,

❖❖

❖❖

Cottage: Glebe Farm Cottages, Exhall, near Alcester, Warwickshire

Located in one of Shakespeares most inspoiled villages, these cottages have been skillfully converted from redundant farm buildings into comfortable 1, 2 and 3 bedroomed accommodation, some single storey, some thatched, one suitable for a wheelchair. All are furnished in pine, with fitted carpets and garden furniture. Prices include electricity, heating, bed-linen and towels. There is a shared laundry, pay-phone, ample parking and small shop.

8 cottages, sleeps 2-7, Price per week £125 low season, £440 high season, Children welcome, Pets by arrangement, Available all year.

Contact: Mr & Mrs Canning, Glebe Farm Cottages, Exhall, near Alcester, Warwickshire B49 6EA
Tel/Fax: 01789 772202

❖❖

"You're shivering like two jellies!"

Yorkshire

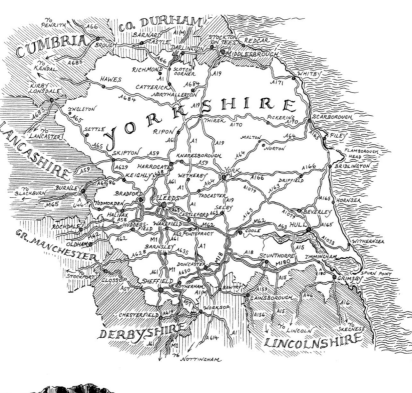

❖❖❖

Cottage: The Cottages, Muston Grange Farm, Muston Road, Filey North Yorkshire

Each cottage comprises lounge, dining area, fitted kitchen, two bedrooms, and bathrooms. Facilities include colour television, microwave, gas fires in all rooms, ample parking and patio seating. Cot and high chair available. Welcome pack provided on arrival. Filey shops, stations, and facilities half mile away. Scarborough, Bridlington, Whitby, The Wolds, and North York Moors nearby. Prices include gas, electricity, bedding and towels. Pets welcome.

5 cottages, sleeps up to 5, Price per week £199 low season, £375 high season, Children & pets welcome, Available all year.

Contact: David Teet, Muston Grange Farm, Muston Road, Filey North Yorkshire YO14 0HU
Tel: 01723 516620

❖❖❖

Cottage: Laskill Farm, Hawnby, near Helmsley, Yorkshire

See PHOTO on page 572

Situated in idyllic setting in North York Moors. Stone cottages of great charm. Well equipped from dishwasher to microwave. BBQ areas. All with gardens. Free private fishing. Lots of interesting places nearby. A walkers paradise. Cleanliness assured. Personally supervised. Lots of excellent eating places locally. York only 40 minutes. Come and relax in peace and comfort, a real rural retreat. Linen included.

5 cottages, sleeps 4-6, Price per week £215 low season, £260 high season, Children & pets welcome, Available all year.

Contact: Mrs Sue Smith, Laskill Farm, Hawnby, near Helmsley, Yorkshire YO6 5NB
Tel: 01439 798 268

❖❖❖

Cottage: Rains Farm, Allerson, Pickering, North Yorkshire

See PHOTO on page 572

Five warm and comfortable newly converted barns. Very peaceful magnificent views relax, unwind, and ease away the pressures of life in this idyllic rural retreat. Gaze on the ponies grazing in the paddocks. Furnished, decorated, and equipped for luxury living. We are centrally situated for York, Pickering and Steam Railway, North York Moors, coast, stately homes, castles and quaint villages. ETB Four Keys Highly Commended.

5 cottages, sleeps 2-6, Price per week £140 low season, £395 high season, No smoking, Children welcome, No pets, Available all year.

Contact: Jean & Lorriane Allanson, Rains Farm, Allerston, Pickering, North Yorks YO18 7PQ
Tel/Fax: 01723 859333

❖❖❖

❖❖

Cottage: Keld Head Farm Cottages, Keld Head, Pickering, North Yorkshire

The gateway to the North Yorkshire Moors. Within 15 minutes walk of town centre, seven single and two storey character stone cottages around secluded courtyard. Each with open beamed ceilings, stone fireplaces and fitted with mellow pine and Laura Ashley fabrics. All have television, microwave, coffee machine, fridge/freezer and central heating. Extensive grounds with large garden, barbecue area, play equipment, and private parking. ETB 4 Keys Highly Commended.

7 cottages, sleeps 2-7, Price per week £180 low season, £442 high season, Children welcome, No pets, Available all year.

Contact: Penny & Julian Fearn, Keld Head Farm Cottages, Keld Head, Pickering, North Yorkshire YO18 8LL
Tel: 01751 473974

❖❖

Cottage: Green Loaning, 6 Castle Road, Thornton-Le-Dale, near Pickering, North Yorkshire

Probably one of the nicest detached holiday bungalow's in pretty village. Sleeps 1 to 8 plus cot and high chair. Magnificent views from 25ft conservatory. Colour TV's/video. Microwave, fridge/freeze, washer/dryer. Central heating. Lovely gardens and ample parking. No pets, No linen, No silly meters. Close to 3 village pubs and direct bus to Whitby, Scarborough and York. Not your normal holiday let!

1 cottage, sleeps 1-8+cot, Price per week £235-£300 low season, £325-£435 high season, Children welcome, No pets, Available all year.

Contact: Frances Boardman, 10 Green Gables Close, Heald Green, Cheadle, Cheshire SK8 3QT
Tel: 0161 498 8605

❖❖

Cottage: Cliff House, Ebberston, near Scarborough, North Yorkshire

Heated indoor pool, Jacuzzi, games rooms, tennis court and warm comfortable cottages in the beautiful grounds of a "listed" manor house. Situated on the edge of the North York Moors, the North Riding Forest Park and Vale of Pickering; yet only 40 minutes by car from York and 10 miles from Yorkshire's Heritage coast; Cliff House provides the base for truly memorable holidays. Colour brochure available.

See PHOTO on page 574

7 cottages, 1 apartment, sleeps 2-6 and cot,
Price per week £80 - £200 low season, £280 - £680 high season, Children welcome, No pets, Available all year.

Contact: Angela & David Wilcock, Cliff House, Ebberston, Scarborough, North Yorks YO13 9PA
Tel: 01723 859440 Fax: 01723 850005

❖❖

Ceadda Cottage, Keldholme - see page 570

Rains Farm, Allerson, Pickering - see page 570

Cottage: Dalegarth & The Ghyll Holiday Cottages, Buckden, near Skipton

Situated in the Heart of the Yorkshire Dales National Park, in Upper Wharfedale, surrounded by National Trust Lands. Character cottages, three designed with disabled guests in mind, set in beautiful walking/touring countryside and all furnished/equipped and decorated to high standards. Saunas, spa baths, videos, dishwashers, microwaves, barbeques, solarium, gym, laundry, indoor swimming pool combine to ensure carefree holidays. Inspections welcomed on changeover days. Colour brochure available. Dalegarth - ETB 4 Keys Commended. The Ghyll - ETB 5 Keys Highly Commended.

See PHOTO on page 574

13 cottages, sleeps 2-6, Price per week from £261 low season, £475 high season, Non smoking cottages available, Pets by arrangement, Available all year

Contact: Mr & Mrs Lusted, 11 Dalegarth, Buckden, nr Skipton, North Yorkshire BD23 5JU
Tel/Fax: 01756 760877 http://www.yorkshirenet.co.uk/accgde/dalegarth/index.html

Cottage: Blackmires Farm Cottage, Danby Head, Danby, Whitby, North Yorkshire

Stone cottage on small working farm adjacent to moors in North York Moors National Park. Information centre 3 miles away. Three bedrooms (one and mini lounge upstairs), ground floor one double bedroom, one twin, bathroom, kitchen with microwave and fridge/freezer, lounge, dining room with television, garden with swing, sandpit and barbecue. Visit Whitby, Flamingo Park, Castle Howard, Eden Camp, Folk Museums, Steam Railway and Aidensfield.

See PHOTO on page 575

1 cottage, sleeps 6, Price per week £200 low season, £350 high season, Children welcome, Available all year.

Contact: Mrs G M Rhys, Blackmires Farm, Danby Head, Whitby, North Yorkshire YO21 2NN
Tel: 01287 660352

Please mention
THE GREAT BRITISH
SELF CATERING
COTTAGE GUIDE
when booking your accommodation

Cliff House, Ebberston, near Scarborough - see page 571

9 Dalegarth, Buckden, near Skipton - see page 573

Blackmires Farm Cottage, Danby, Whitby - see page 573

"Well, would you believe it? Its raining!"

Scotland

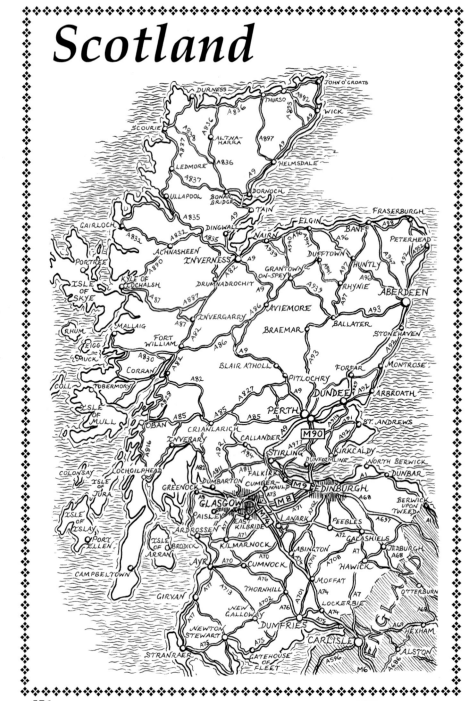

❖❖

Cottage: Barncrosh, Castle Douglas

All linen towels supplied, electric blankets, heating, cooking, fridge/freezer in all properties. Microwave and open fire in some. Ample garden and car parking space. On working farm in glorious varied countryside. Near coast, hills, forestry walks. Fishing, golfing, sailing, riding within easy reach. Also National Trust properties including Threave Gardens and castle. Abundant wild life and bird watching. We aim to give you freedom and peace.

13 cottages, sleeps 2-8, Price per week £90 low season, £400 high season, Children welcome, Pets welcome, Available all year.

Contact: Micky & Tessa Ball, Barncrosh, Castle Douglas, Scotland DG7 1TX
Tel: 01556 680216 Fax: 01556 680442

❖❖

Please mention
THE GREAT BRITISH SELF CATERING COTTAGE GUIDE
when booking your accommodation

❖❖

❖❖❖

Cottage: Ardtulloch, Church Road, Laurieston, near Castle Douglas

This beautifully restored Galloway Cottage, facing South, has stunning views overlooking peaceful rolling country. Tastefully furnished but geared to comfort. It has two tiled bathrooms (one en-suite) with extra shower/toilet downstairs, well equipped kitchen with dishwasher and microwave, large bedrooms, wood-burning stove and open fire. Large well-kept lawns and gardens. Private trout fishing by arrangement. Solway beaches, golf, fishing and walking trails all nearby.

1 cottage, sleeps 6, Price per week £400 low/high season,
Older children welcome, Pets by arrangement, Available April - November.

Contact: Mr B Dowling, 32 Lancaster Road, Wimbledon, London SW19 5DD
Tel: 0181 946 5871 or 0181 788 7941

above, Ardtulloch, Laurieston, near Castle Douglas

❖❖❖

❖❖❖

Cottage: Conifers Leisure Park, Kirroughtree, Newton Strewart, Dumfriesshire

Twenty-nine Scandinavian lodges, colour TV, heated swimming pool, sauna, jacuzzi, sunbeds, solarium and tennis court. Discounted golf and salmon fishing. Spend an active or relaxing time at Conifers at any time of the year and you are sure to enjoy yourselves. Lots of places to wine and dine within one mile.

**29 cottages, Price per week from £180-£500
Children welcome, Available all year.**

Contact: Conifers Leisure Park, Kirroughtree, Newton Stewart, Dumfriesshire DG8 6AN
Tel: 01671 402107 Fax: 01671 403576

❖❖❖

Visit our award winning
THE GREAT BRITISH
BED & BREAKFAST WEBSITE
http://www.cumbria.com/gbbb/

❖❖❖

❖❖

Cottage: Greenhill Farmhouse, Mid-Clyth, Lybster, Caithness

See PHOTO on opposite page

Relax in the romantic Highlands amidst tranquil surrounding and enjoy magnificent coastal scenery from your bedroom windows. Beautifully renovated farmhouse with every home comfort including colour TV, dishwater, fridge freezer, microwave etc. Day trip to Orkney Islands. Visit John O Groats, view seals, puffins, explore castles, ancient cairns and attend Highland Catherine. Perfect centre for exploring northern Scotland and discovering its attractions. STB 5 Crown Highly Commended.

1 cottage, sleeps 6, Price per week £150 low season, £375 high season, Children welcome, No smoking, Pets by arrangement, Available all year.

**Contact: Mrs Camilla Sinclair, Upper Latheron Farm, Latheron, Caithness KW5 6DT
Tel: 01593 741224**

❖❖

Cottage: High Range Holiday Chalets, Grampian Road, Aviemore, Inverness-shire

See PHOTO on opposite page

Small private complex 500 yards from Aviemore centre. Under the personal supervision of the Vastano family for the past 21 years, where standards and style have been influenced by continuity and continental flair. One - Three bedrooms providing all that is necessary for your comfort and well being. Magnificent view of the Cairngorm Mountains. Informal Ristornate and Cafe-Bar, on site highly renowned for it's excellent cuisine.

9 cottages, sleeps 2-6, Price per week from £170 low season, £495 high season, Children welcome, Pets by arrangement, Available all year.

**Contact: Mr & Mrs Vastano, High Range, Grampian Rd, Aviemore, Inverness-shire PH22 1PT
Tel: 01479 810636 Fax: 01479 811322**

❖❖

Cottage: Pine Bank Chalets, Dalfaber Road, Aviemore, Inverness-shire

For that special vacation enjoy the stunning beauty of the Highlands & Cairngorm Mountains from our choice of cosy log cabins & quality chalets - superbly appointed. Loch & Spey River fishing. 7 golf courses within 20 minutes drive. Great location - close to Spey River. Peaceful and relaxing setting. Friendly service staff. Sky TV, video, BBQ and mountains bikes. Leisure pool and restaurant nearby. Free colour brochure.

14 cottages, sleeps 2-6, Price per week from £196 low season to £595 high season, Children & pets welcome, Available all year.

**Contact: Pine Bank Chalets, Dalfaber Road, Aviemore, Inverness-shire PH22 1PX
Tel: 01479 810000 Fax: 01479 811469 E-Mail: pinebank@enterprise.net**

❖❖

Greenhill Farmhouse, Lybster, Caithness - see page 580

High Range Holiday Chalets, Aviemore - see page 580

Riverside Lodges, Invergloy - see page 583

Wildside Highland Lodges, Whitebridge - see page 583

❖❖

Cottage: Easter Duiar Cottage, Advie, Near Grantown-on-Spey

Set amidst the scenic beauty of the Spey Valley this former gamekeeper cottage has been tastefully refurbished to provide all of the comforts of home, modern farmhouse kitchen leads to an attractive lounge with open fire. All modern provided including satellite TV, dishwasher, washing machine, fridge/freezer and telephone. Newly fitted bathroom and shower room, large natural garden with excellent parking. Ideal for cycling, fishing and golf etc. STB 5 Crowns.

1 cottage, sleeps 8, Price per week £250 low season, £550 high season, Children & pets welcome, Available all year.

Contact: Mrs Wright, Dunveban, 34 Findhorn Place, Grange, Edinburgh EH9 2JP
Tel: 0131 668 4173 E-Mail: cwright@eyco.demon.co.uk

❖❖

Riverside Lodges, Invergloy, Spean Bridge, Inverness-shire

These three unique chalets are set in mature woodland gardens with private frontage on Loch Lochy. There is free Loch fishing and a stocked Trout pond. The location is ideal for walking and for touring, with Skye, Inverness, Aviemore, Oban, Mallaig all within easy reach. The chalets have "Highly Commended" status, TV, and central heating. Linen, cots, boat, fishing tackle, barbecues, all available for hire.

See PHOTO on opposite page

3 chalets, sleeps 6, Price per week £280 low season, £570 high season, Pets welcome, Children welcome, Available March - November.

Contact: Mr & Mrs Bennet, Riverside Lodges, Invergloy, Spean Bridge, Inverness-shire PH34 4DY
Tel/Fax: 01397 712684

❖❖

Cottage: Wildside Highland Lodges, Whitebridge, Inverness-shire

Set amongst a spectacular vista of rugged granite mountains and steep wooded glens this small group of luxury lodges are beautifully situated along the river bank. Warm and well-equipped, enjoying magnificent views. Located on the quiet south side of Loch Ness in the 'Heart of the Highlands'. Rich in wildlife. Weeks/short breaks welcomed. Colour brochure.

See PHOTO on opposite page

14 cottages, sleeps 1-5, Price per week £155 - £520 dependent upon choice of lodge, Children & pets welcome, Available all year.

Contact: Patricia Allen, Wildside-Highland Lodges, Whitebridge, Inverness-shire IV1 2UN
Tel: 01456 486373 Fax: 01456 486371

❖❖

❖❖

Cottages: Strathan House, Strathan Cottage, West and East Bothies, Attadale, Strathcarron

See PHOTO on opposite page

Comfortable farmhouse and three cottages on the beautiful highland estate seen in "Hamish Macbeth". Open fires or wood burning stoves. Free wood. Garden. A mile from A890 and sea. No television but 32000 acres of rugged country for walking, and watching wild-life. Boats for hire on stocked Hill Loch. Laundrette. Good restaurant. Perfect base for exploring Wester Ross and Skye. STB Four Crown Highly Commended.

4 cottages, sleeps 4-8, Price per week £220 low season, £390 high seaosn, Children welcome, Dogs welcome, Available March - November.

Contact: Ray Bright, Attadale, Strathcarron, Ross-shire IV54 8YX
Tel: 01520 722396 Fax: 01520 722546

❖❖

Cottage: Culkein BayChalets, Culkein, By Stoer, Sutherland

In a beautiful and remote location on the sandy shore of Culkein Bay. These 3 timber chalets have wonderful views of the bay and mountains and stand in a safely enclosed grassed area where children can play. The sandy beach is 30 metres away. Each chalet fully carpeted, all electric. Each has colour TV, microwave, fridge/freezer, spindryer.

3 cottages, sleeps 6, Price per week £150 low season, £295 high season, Children & pets welcome, Available March - October.

Contact: Mrs Vicki MacLeod, 7 Mount Stuart Road, Largs, Ayrshire KA30 9ES
Tel: 01475 672 931 Fax: 01475 674655

❖❖

Cottage: Lochinver Holiday Lodges, Lochinver, Sutherland

See PHOTO on opposite page

Seals, otter, deer and seabirds share the peace and tranquillity of this private bay. All seven lodges equipped with all home comforts. Sea shore cottage now available. Marvel at the coastal views. Enjoy sea and loch fishing, hill walking, mountains and white beaches. Gourmet meals. Village 1.5 miles. Open March-October. Fridge/freezer, washing machine and microwaves. Refurbished lodges.

7 cottages, sleeps 4/6, Price per week £375 low season, £780 high season, Children welcome, No pets, Available March-October.

Contact: Mrs Sheila Stewart, 33 Strathan, Lochinver, Sutherland IV27 4LR
Tel: 01571 844282 Fax: 01571 844418

❖❖

Strathan House, Attadale - see page 584

Lochinver Holiday Lodges, Lochinver - see page 584

Loudoun Mains Country Holidays, Newmilns - seep age587

Carmichael Country Cottage, Carmichael, Biggar - see page 588

❖❖❖

Kilchrist Castle, Campbeltown, Argyll

Six small, cosy, comfortably furnished, fully equipped cottages in Kilchrist Castle grounds, near Campbeltown and the famous Mull of Kintyre. Colour television, microwave, bed linen (duvets). Towels for hire, but free for overseas visitors. All electric. Electricity by meter reading. Children welcome. Meet our Shetland Ponies. Close to golf and sandy beaches. Featured in Good Holiday Cottage Guide. STB 2 and 3 Crown Commended. Brochure on request.

6 cottages, sleeps 2-6, Price per week £130-£183 low season, £267-£294 high season, Children & pets welcome, Available April - October.

**Contact: Col. W.T.C. Angus, Kilchrist Castle, Campbeltown, Argyll, Scotland PA28 6PH
Tel/Fax: 01586 553210**

❖❖❖

Cottage: Killean Estate, Tayinloan, via Tarbert (Loch Fyne), Kintyre, Argyll

Killean Estate offers a choice of well-equipped period accommodation from a Georgian villa through romantic "Arts & Crafts" cottages to Coach house apartments. Always dominated by the magnificent westerly views to the isles of Gigha, Islay and Jura, our mile of sheltered coastline soars from meadow, burn and woodland to heathery hills. Wild life abounds, good walks are everywhere and historic Kintyre is on your doorstep.

10 cottages, sleep 2-10, Price per week £195 low season, £800 high season, Children welcome, Pets by arrangement, Available Easter - December.

**Contact: The Estate Office, Killean Estate, Tayinloan, via Tarbert (Loch Fyne), Kintyre, Argyll
PA29 6XF
Tel: 01583 441 238 Tel/Fax: 01583 441 307**

❖❖❖

Cottage: Loudoun Mains Country Holidays, Newmilns, Ayrshire

Relax in our superb cottages located centrally in the Scottish Lowlands. Rich with wildlife and panoramic views of Burns Country Firth of Clyde and Isle of Arran. Only a short drive from seaside resorts, Prestwick or Glasgow airport, Turnberry or Loch Lomond Intervention Golf Course. All the cottages have TV, microwave, telephone, car parking, garden furniture with linen supplied and indoor heated swimming pool.

See PHOTO on opposite page

14 cottages, sleeps 2-6 per cottage, Price per week from £145 low season, £585 high season, Children welcome, Pets welcome, Available all year.

**Contact: Robert & Minnie Hodge, Loudoun Mains Country Holidays, Newmilns, Ayrshire
KA16 9LG
Tel: 01560 321246 Fax: 01560 320657**

❖❖❖

❖❖

Cottage: Carmichael Country Cottages, Westmains, Carmichael, Biggar, Lanarkshire

See PHOTO on page 586

Unique stone heritage cottages on 100 year old family owned and operated country "clan lands" estate. TV, telephone, VCR, dishwasher, microwave and open fires. STB 3-5 Crowns Commended to Highly Commended. Leisure facilities include fishing, walking, tennis, spa pool, orienteering, riding, trekking etc. Golf, squash and swimming available. Edinburgh, Glasgow and Carlisle all within one hour's drive. Visitors centre, farm shop and restaurant on site.

15 cottages, sleeps 2-7, Price per week £160.00 low season, £450.00 high season, Children welcome, Pets welcome, Available all year.

Contact: Richard & Patricia Carmichael, Carmichael Estate Office, Westmains, Carmichael, Biggar, Lanarkshire ML12 6PG
Tel: 01899 308336 Fax: 01899 308481 EMail: chiefcarm@aol.com

❖❖

Cottage: Kames Castle, Port Bannatyne, Isle of Bute

See PHOTO on opposite page

Small private estate on Kames Bay. Four courtyard cottages surrounding a 14th century keep. Two cottages by walled garden. Cosily furnished with colour TV. Prices include central heating and all linen. Beautiful parkland and gardens. Golf, riding, fishing, sailing, sandy bays and places of historical interest nearby. Good touring centre for Bute and the Cowal Peninsula. Boat cruises around the Kyles of Bute. Colour Brochure.

6 cottages, sleeps 4-9, Price per week £195 - £395 low season, £320 - £550 high season, Children welcome, Pets welcome, Available all year.

Contact: Peter & Jennifer Hardy, Kames Castle Port Bannatyne, Isle of Bute PA20 0QP
Tel: 01700 504500

❖❖

Glengorm Castle & Cottages, near Tobermory, Isle of Mull

See PHOTO on opposite page

Three comfortable flats in Victorian castle with spectacular setting, overlooking ocean and outer Hebrides. The views at sunset are especially stunning. There are also five cottages on the estate. Glengorm is a working hill farm with a flock of Blackface sheep and fold of pedigree cattle. The estate offers free fishing, with boat, on local Lochs. Beautiful walks, wildlife, golf and boat trips.

5 cottage 3 flats, sleeps 4-7,Price per week from £115 low season, £450 high season, Pets welcome, Children welcome, Available March - November.

Contact: Janet Nelson, Glengorm Castle, near Tobermory, Isle of Mull PA5 6QE
Tel/Fax: 01688 302321

❖❖

Kames Castle, Port Bannatyne - see page 588

Glengorm, near Tobermory - see page 588

589

❖❖

Cottage: Hunter's Cabins, Restenneth, Forfar, Angus

See PHOTO on opposite page

Family run luxurious cedarwood cabins, fully equipped, situated in a tranquil meadow overlooking the Southesk with glorious panoramic views of the Angus Glens. Ideal centre for touring, golf, fishing, rambling, birdwatching and castle haunting. 2/3 bedrooms all linen provided, heaters in all rooms, TV, microwave, cots available, pets welcome, ample play area with BBQ for added enjoyment. The prefect venue for your holiday at any time of year.

3 cottages, sleeps 6-8, Price per week £110 low season, £390 high season, Children welcome, Pets welcome, Available all year.

**Contact: Bruce & Jewdi Hunter, Hunter's Cabin, Restenneth, Forfar, Angus DD8 2SZ
Tel/Fax: 01307 463101**

❖❖

Cottage: Purgavie Farm, Lintrathen, By Kirriemuir, Angus

Forget the stress and relax in our chalet or bungalow on our farm. Both have dishwasher, microwave, telephone, TV, linen supplied, washer/dryer. Garden and car park. 10 miles from Glamis Castle and 7 miles from Barries birth place in Kirriemuir. Ideal for touring, birdwatching and hill walking. Lots of wildlife to be seen. STB 5 Crowns Commended & Highly Commended.

2 cottages, sleeps 4,6, Price per week £150 low season, £400 high season, Children & Pets welcome, Available all year.

**Contact: Mrs Moira Clark, Purgavie Farm, Lintrathen, By Kirriemuir, Angus DO8 5HZ
Tel/Fax: 01575 560213**

❖❖

Please mention
THE GREAT BRITISH SELF CATERING COTTAGE GUIDE
when booking your accommodation

Hunter's Cabins, Restenneth, Forfa - see page 590

It'll soon be teatime, Rosie"

Wales

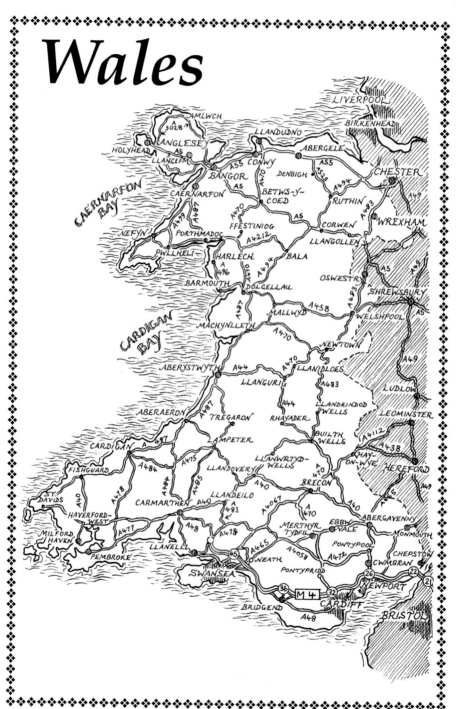

❖❖

Cottage: Maerdy Cottages, Taliaris, near Llandeilo, Carmarthenshire

Set beside a stream within mature gardens, these five lovely old cottages offer peace and tranquillity. Furnished with many antiques and traditional rugs they are a warm and welcoming retreat all year round. Accommodating from 2 - 10, each cottage features original beams and open fires as well as all modern creature comforts. Ideally situated for coast and countryside. B&B/Catering option. For a colour brochure call 01550 777448. WTB Grade 4. Disability Access Grade 2.

See PHOTO on page595

6 cottages, sleeps 4 - 10, Price per week £175 low season, £700 high season, Mini breaks on request, Children and pets welcome, Available March - January.

**Contact: Mrs Jones, The Annex, Dan Y Cefn, Manordeilo, Llandeilo, Carmarthenshire SA19 7BD
Tel: 01550 777448 Fax: 01550 777067**

❖❖

Penffynnon Properties, Penffynnon, Aberporth, Cardigan, Dyfed

Approached by a private road, our properties are adjacent to Aberporth's two safe sandy beaches. They are comfortable, fully equipped (including colour TV and microwave) and most have sea views. There is ample parking and dogs are welcome by arrangement. The village has several pubs and a range of shops. Local attractions include Cardigan Bay dolpins, water sports, golf, riding, and walking the Preseli Hills.

2 bunaglows, 5 apartments, sleeps 4-6, Price per week £100 low season, £350 high season, Children welcome, Dogs by arrangement, Available all year.

**Contact: Mrs Tucker, Penffynnon, Aberporth, Cardigan, Dyfed SA43 2DA
Tel/Fax: 01239 810387**

❖❖

Hotel Penrallt & Holiday Cottages, Abertporth, Cardigan

Penrallt Cottages are located in the grounds of Hotel Penrallt overlooking Cardigant Bay. Meticulously built to blend with the Edwardian architecture of the Hotel and furnished accordingly. The cottages are fully equipped for up to six people and bed linen is provided. Central heating is also available early and late season. There is a heated outdoor swimming pool, games room, sauna, solarium, gymisaum, tennis court and Pitch 'n' Putt.

26 cottages, sleeps 2-6, Price per week £120 low season, £450 high season, Children welcome, No Pets, Available all year.

**Contact: Hotel Penrallt & Holiday Cottages, Abertporth, Cardigan SA43 2BS
Tel: 01239 810227 Fax: 01239 811375**

❖❖

❖❖❖

Cottage: Croft Farm, Croft, near Cardigan

See PHOTO on opposite page

A warm welcome awaits at Croft Farm, situated in beautiful North Pembrokeshire countryside, nearby sandy beaches, coastal path and National Park. Enjoy the indoor heated pool, and sauna; also meeting room. The slate cottages offer home-from-home accommodatoin. Each is lovingly furnished and fully equipped. Croft has very attractive gardens, patio, BBQ and playarea. Help feed Tabitha (Pig), Pearl and Hazel (Goats) and others.

6 cottages, sleeps 2-7, Price per week £145 low season, £599 high season,
Children welcome, Pets by arrangement, Available all year.

Contact: Andrew & Sylvie Gow, Croft Farm, Croft, near Cardigan, Pembrokeshire SA43 3NT
Tel/Fax: 01239 615179

❖❖❖

Cottage: Shepherd's Cottage, Treforgan Farm, Llangoedmor, Cardigan

Shepherd's Cottage is situated on a traditional farm 3 miles from sandy beaches and Pembrokeshire Coastal Path. The 200 years old cottage offers total comfort whilst retaining original beams and stonework. Luxurious accommodation (Welsh Tourist Board "5 Dragons" top award) includes TV, log fire, heating all rooms, fully equipped modern kitchen. Private sun terrace/herb garden overlook conservation pond and Preseli Hills. Welsh tea, fresh flowers on arrival.

1 cottage, sleeps 5, Price per week £120 low season, £450 high season,
No smoking, Children welcome, Pets by arrangement, Available all year.

Contact: Colin Lewis, Treforgan Farm, Llangoedmor, Cardigan SA43 2LB
Tel: 01239 614973

❖❖❖

Cottage: Penwern Fach Holiday Cottages, Pont Hirwaun, Cardigan

We have something for everyone - fishing on the Teifi, golf, walking or just lying on the beach. The original stone farm buildings have been converted into award winning cottages, combining a blend of old world charm and modern convenience. There is a play area and sand pit for our younger guests and a games room with table tennis and a pool table for the older ones.

5 cottages, sleeps 2-6, Price per week £125 low season, £435 high season,
Children & pets welcome, Available all year.

Contact: Mrs Adamson, Penwern Fach, Pont Hirwaun, Cardigan Ceredigion SA43 2RL
Tel/Fax: 01239 710697

❖❖❖

Maerdy Cottages, Taliaris, near Llandeilo - see page 593

Croft Farm, Croft, near Cardigan - see page 594

Quality Cottages, Cerbid, Solva, Haverfordwest - see page 597

Gwarmacwydd Farm Cottages, Llanfallteg, Whitland - see page 598

❖❖

Cottage: Ffosffald Isaf/Hen Dy Pair, Ffosffald Uchaf, Drefach, Llanybydder, Ceredigion

Tranquillity, seclusion, somewhere to unwind? Our cottages provide the answer. Panoramic views of Cambrian Hills and Teify Valley. Fully equipped for the discerning guest. Oil/gas central heating, barbecues, garden with swing and croquet. 186 acres to roam in. Visit our listed longhouse being renovated. 20 minute drive to coast and hills. Bed and Breakfast. Traditional meals by arrangement. Regret no pets. Brochure available.

2 cottages, sleeps 4,6, Price per week £160 low season, £320 high season, Children welcome, No pets, Available March - December.

Contact: Mrs Mary Thomas, Ffosffald Uchaf, Drefach, Llanybydder, Ceredigion, North Wales
SA40 9TA
Tel: 01570 434 200

❖❖

Coastal Cottages of Pembrokeshire

Voted "Best in Wales" and offer a stunning selection of over 450 cottages, castles and lighthouses! All our properties are quality graded and set in the National Park in smugglers coves, on safe sandy beaches or dominating cliff tops with pubs and shops nearby. Children and pets especially welcome with free booking for bikes, horseriding an watersports.

450 cottages, sleeps 1-18, Price per week £99 low season, £1250 high season, Children & pets welcome, Available all year.

Contact: Coastal Cottages of Pembrokeshire, 2 Riverside Quay, Haverfordwest, Pembrokeshire
SA61 2LJ
Tel: 01437 765765 Fax: 01437 769900 E-Mail: info-desk@coastalcottages.co.uk

❖❖

Cottage: Quality Cottages, Cerbid, Solva, Haverfordwest

WTB Tourist Award Winners with over thirty years experience in quality self catering. We offer a selection of quality cottages with exceptionally high residential standard, log fires etc. All situated around the magnificent Welsh coastline, with its numerous unspoilt sandy beaches, and superb scenic walks. A naturalist's paradise, wild flowers galore, badgers and foxes, kites, puffins and guilimets. Free colour brochure.

See PHOTO on opposite page

150 cottages, sleeps 2-15, Price per week £99 low season, £995 high season, Children & pets welcome, Available all year.

Contact: Moyra Slenfield, Quality Cottages, Cerbid, Solva, Haverfordwest SA62 6YE
Tel: 01348 837871 Fax: 01348 837876

❖❖

❖❖❖

Cottage: Gwarmacwydd Farm Cottages, Llanfallteg, Whitland, Pembrokeshire

See PHOTO on page 596

Gwarmacwydd is a working dairy and sheep farm of 400 acres idyllically situated in the wooded vale of the River Taf. 2 miles of river bank. The sandy beaches of Saundersfoot and Tenby are within 25 minutes drive. The stone cottages are furnished and equipped to a high standard. Welsh Tourist Board Grade4. All electicity and bed linen is included. Clour brochure available.

5 cottages, sleeps 2-8, Price per week £150 low season, £410 high season,
No smoking, Children welcome, Pets by arrangement, Available all year.

Contact: Mrs Angela Colledge, Gwarmacwydd Farm Cottages, Llanfallteg, Whitland, Pembrokeshire SA34 0XH
Tel: 01437 563260 Fax: 01437 563839 EMail: Farm.holidays@btinternet.com

❖❖❖

"Can we have another go after this, Mum?"

❖❖

Cottage: Llanerch Vineyard, Hensol, Pendoylan, Vale of Glamorgan

Converted from 19th Century farm buildings, Llanerch Cottages offer superb accommodation in an idyllic setting with six acres of vines and a further ten acres of conservation woodlands and lakes. 15 minutes from Cardiff and convenient for touring all South Wales. Rated 5 Dragons by the WTB, the highest accolade for quality, ambience and facilities which include washing machine, dishwasher, microwave, central heating, TV and telephone. Ample car parking.

4 cottages, sleeps 2,4,4,4, Price per week from £195 low season, £450 high season, No smoking, Children welcome, No pets Available all year.

Contact: Peter & Diana Andrews, Llanerch Vineyard, Hensol, Pendoylan, Vale of Glamorgan
CF72 8JU
Tel: 01443 225877 Fax: 01443 225546

above, Cottage: Llanerch Vineyard, Hensol, Pendoylan, Vale of Glamorgan

❖❖

❖❖

Cottage: Castle View, The Narth, Monmouth NP5 4QG

Three bedroomed bungalow in one third acre grounds. Comfortably furnished and carefully maintained by owners. Realistically priced for two to four persons. Colour TV, video recorder, microwave, washing machine and all essential equipment. Village environment with easy access M4, M5, M50, A40. Attractive towns nearby, as well as Wye Valley beauty spots. Scenic area for walking or touring; Rich in castles, churches and history.

1 cottage, sleeps 2-6, Price per week £165 low season, £298 high season, No smoking, Children from 3, No pets, Available all year.

Contact: Arthur & Grace Arnold, Molen, Bucklesham Road, Foxhall, Ipswich IP10 0AA
Tel/Fax: 01473 659361

❖❖

"Now you can paddle your own canoe, boys!"

❖❖

Apartments: Bryn Bras Castle, Llanrug, near Caernarfon,

Welcome to beautiful Bryn Bras Castle - romantic apartments, elegant tower house, mini-cottage within distinctive Romanesque castle, enjoying breathtaking scenery amid gentle Snowdonia foothills. Easy reach mountains, beaches, heritage, local restaurant/inns. Each fully self-contained, individual character, spacious, peaceful. Generously equipped from dishwasher to flowers. Central heating, hot water, linen - free. All highest grade (ex.one). 32 acre gardens, woodlands, panoramic walks. Warmth, convenience, comfort in serene surroundings.

7 apartments, sleeps 2-4, Price per week £300 - £600, Short breaks from £120, No young children or pets, Available all year.

Contact: Mrs Marita Gray-Parry, Bryn Bras Castle, Llanrug, Caernarfon, North Wales LL55 4RE Tel/Fax: 01286 870210

❖❖

Cottage: Y Bwthyn & Ty Cerbyd, Maentwrog, Gwynedd

Gloriously situated on a hillside in 28 acres of private grounds, overlooking the river Dwyryd and the Vale of Ffestiniog. Comfortable cottage and coach house. Equally suitable for summer or winter. Only 5 miles from sandy beaches and surrounded by the mountains of Snowdonia. Ideal centre for touring, walking or just relaxing. Laundry room. TV and video. Tennis court. Rowing Boat. Ample Parking. Payphone. Every comfort.

See PHOTO on page 602

2 cottages, sleeps 7-8, Price per week £150 low season, £350 high season, Children welcome, Pets welcome, Available all year.

Contact: Mrs Audrey Lea, Bryn Mawr, Maentwrog, Gwynedd LL41 3YY Tel/Fax: 01766 590285

❖❖

Cottage: Felin Parc Cottages, Tan Lan, Llanfrothen, Penrhyndeudraeth, Gwynedd

Discover this idyllic stone and beamed 17th Century Mill House on River Croesor with own falls, private waterfall valley near Snowdon, Portmeirion, Ffestininog Miniature Railway. Charming manager's cottage 100 yards distant overlooking ancient fording bridge and Cynicht mountain. Both delightfully furnished, open fires, central heating, colour TV, fully modernised kitchens, bathrooms, microwaves, washing machines, etc. with secluded terraces and ample parking. Beaches, golf, fishing, good pub all available locally.

See PHOTO on page 602

2 cottages, sleeps 8+2,4+2, Price per week £150-£400 low season, £250-£550 high season, Children & pets welcome, Available all year.

Contact: Mr Williams-Ellis, San Giovanni, 4A Sylvan Road, London SE19 2RX Tel: 0181 653 3118

❖❖

Y Bwthyn & Ty Cerbyd, Maentwrog, Gwynedd - see page 601

Felin Parc Cottages, Tan Lan, Llanfrothen, Penrhyndeudraeth - see page 601

❖❖❖

Cottage: Yoke House Farm, Pwllheli, Gwynedd

We are a group of farm wives marketing our own serviced and self-catering holidays on working farms. All 40 properties are 200yds to 5 miles from sandy beaches. Maximum 1 hour's drive from Snowdonia National Park. Book direct with owner, send for free colour brochure. Reductions arranged at attractions and restaurants. A bonus for visitors.

See PHOTO on page 604

40 cottages, sleeps 2-8, Price per week from £86, Children & pets welcome, Available all year.

**Contact: Mrs Hughes, Yoke House Farm, Pwllheli, Gwynedd LL53 5TY
Tel: 01758 612621 Fax: 01758 712570**

❖❖❖

Cottage: Shaw's Holidays, Y Maes, Pwllheli, Gwynedd

An excellent choice of holiday accommodation in beautiful North Wales. Shaw's Holidays (est 1971), are highly regarded self catering letting agents handling all sorts of property. Cottages, farms, bungalows, flats etc. in Snowdonia, Anglesey and especially on the scenic Lleyn Peninsula, contact Ref GBSC on 01758 612854 for a free colour brochure. From a cottage on a beach to a former working windmill contact Shaw's.

150+ cottages, sleeps 2-15, Price per week from £60 low season, £700 high season, Children & pets welcome, Available all year.

Contact: Mr Shaw, Shaw's Holidays, Y Maes, Pwllheli, Gwynedd LL53 5HA

❖❖❖

Cottage: Gwynfryn Farm, Pwllheli, Gwynedd

Organic dairy farm, 2 miles coast, 10-20 Snowdonia, castles, trains, mines, etc. Wales Tourist Board top grade 5, cleanliness and comfort assured. TV/video, fridge/freezer, dishwasher, all units. Washeteria on site. Playroom/area helping farmer keeps kiddies happy (wellies advised). Explore 50 miles Lleyn's heritage coast area, outstanding natural beauty. Relax, unwind, enjoy a warm Welsh welcome. Send for colour brochure.

See PHOTO on page 604

8 cottages, sleeps 2-8, Price per week from £120.00, Children & Pets welcome, Available all year.

**Contact: K P Ellis, Gwynfryn Farm, Pwllheli, Gwynedd LL53 5UF
Tel: 01758 612536 Fax: 01758 614324**

❖❖❖

Gwynfryn Farm, Pwllheli - see page 603

Yoke House Farm, Pwllheli - see page603

❖❖❖

Cottage: Rhydolio, Llangian, Abersoch, Pwllheli, Gwynedd

Surrounded by a peaceful countryside setting and farm interest, but only ³/₄ mile from sandy beach. The charming 16th Century farmhouse wing and groundfloor cottage - 'Olde Worlde Charm' and modern comfort, beams, inglenook fireplace, attractive four poster bed. Farmhouse - microwave, dishwasher etc laundry room. Ideal sailing, surfing, cycling, and good walks area. Out of season short breaks. Open March to November. Colour brochure. WTB Grade 5.

2 cottages, sleeps 6,7, Price per week £105 low season, £380 high season, Children welcome, Pets by arrangement, Available March - January.

Contact: Mrs Morris, Rhydolio, Llangian, Abersoch, Pwllheli, Gwynedd LL53 7LR
Tel/Fax: 01758 712342

❖❖❖

Please mention
THE GREAT BRITISH SELF CATERING COTTAGE GUIDE
when booking your accommodation

❖❖❖

❖❖

Cottage: The Old Vicarage Cottage, Llangorse, Brecon, Powys

See PHOTO on opposite page

Fully self contained semi detached cottage in lovely quiet garden. A short walk from shops and pubs. Facilities include colour TV, full central heating, fully equipped kitchen. Children and well behaved dogs welcome. Within easy walk of lake, sailing, fishing, pony trekking, rope climbing can be enjoyed, nearby the cottage is pretty decorated and close carpeted throughout. It is in within the Brecon Beacons National Park.

1 cottage, sleep 4, Price per week £125 low season, £260 high season, Children & well behaved dogs welcome, Available all year, Map Ref

Contact: Mrs Anderson, The Old Vicarage, Llangorse, Brecon, Powys LD3 7UB
Tel: 01874 658639

❖❖

Cottage: Brecon Beacon Holiday Cottages, Brynoyre Aber, Talybont-on-Usk, Brecon, Powys

Wide selection of properties throughout the Brecon Beacons and Black Mountains National Park, Hay-on-Wye and Wye Valley. Medieval Tower with fishing, Chapel, Castle and Riverside Cottages, isolated mountain farmhouses and cottages on working farms. Ideal location for walking, climbing, trekking, fishing, mountain biking, bird watching, touring and golf. Red Kite Country, superb mountains, rivers, valleys and waterfalls. Excellent pubs with Real Ales & open fires. WTB inspected.

150 cottages, sleeps 2-35, Price per week £85 low season, £1500 high season
Children & Pets welcome, Available all year.

Contact: Mrs Elizabeth Daniel, Brecon Beacon Holiday Cottages, Brynoyre Aber,
Talybont-on-Usk, Brecon, Powys LD3 7YS
Tel: 01874 676446 Fax: 01874 676416

❖❖

Cottage: Trallwm Forest Cottages, Abergwesyn, Llanwrtyd Wells, Powys

See PHOTO on opposite page

Tallwm Forest Cottages are reached via a twisting road to a hidden valley deep in the beautiful Cambrian Mountains. On our 625 acre working woodland/farm estate, 7 old stone farm buildings have been superbly converted into comfortable self-catering cottages. They provide a warm - most have wood burning stoves - relaxing base for which to explore mid Wales - the green heart of Wales.

9 cottages, Sleeps 2,4,6/7.9/10, Price per week from £170 low season, from £230 high season, Children & pets welcome, Available all year.

Contact: George & Christine Johnson, Trallwn Forest Lodge, Abergwesyn, Llanwrtyd Wells,
Powys LD5 4TS
Tel: 01591 610229

❖❖

The Old Vicarage Cottage, Llangorse, Brecon - see page 606

Cottage: Trallwm Forest Cottages, Abergwesyn, Llanwrtyd Wells - see page 606

"Hope we come back next year, Jack""

KGP Publishing
Penrith, Cumbria, England